The Puritan Lectureships

PAUL S. SEAVER

The Puritan Lectureships

The Politics of Religious Dissent
1560–1662

Stanford University Press
Stanford, California
1970

Stanford University Press
Stanford, California
© 1970 by the Board of Trustees of the
Leland Stanford Junior University
Printed in the United States of America
SBN 8047-0711-1
LC 71-93497

To my wife

Preface

Surely those approaching still another study of an aspect of English Puritanism deserve some note of explanation, if not justification. Though the subject seemed virgin territory to me when I first came to it a decade ago, the sense of discovery was due more to my ignorance than to any lack of maps, guides, or fellow explorers. Puritanism, long an object of Anglo-American interest, has in recent years become a minor scholarly industry. However, if English Puritanism is scarcely terra incognita any longer, it is nevertheless possible even now to come upon a vantage point that provides a fresh perspective.

My purpose in making this study was to examine an institution, not an "ism." Hence the study is primarily about the impact of the lectureships on English society during the century after 1560, and only indirectly about the impact of the content of the lectures on those who heard them. I have learned much from the works of William Haller and Perry Miller, and from Irvonwy Morgan's recent study of the Elizabethan preachers, but I have not attempted to retrace their steps. The significance of the lectureships has already been adumbrated in Christopher Hill's very suggestive chapters on preaching and the lectureships in his *Society and Puritanism in Pre-Revolutionary England*, a book familiar to all students of the period. I have attempted, particularly in my chapters on the lectureships in London, to add an empirical dimension to his more impressionistic analysis— to discover, for example, when and where lectureships were initiated, how they were financed, and who was recruited to preach them. What several generations of Englishmen made of the outpouring of sermons produced by the lecturers, and how many Englishmen espoused the various Puritan causes championed by the preachers, are questions that will probably never be answered with any precision. But the institutions men create do provide a crude index, albeit an imperfect and incomplete one, to their motives, convictions, and commitments, and it is in the light of such considerations that this study is offered as one way to assess the impact of the rather amorphous Puritan movement on English society.

King James's famous dictum "No bishop, no king" may have been a commonplace in the early seventeenth century, but why then did the behavior of some members of the governing elite violate this precept so profoundly? If monarchy, aristocracy, and episcopacy stood or fell together, why then did Puritan peers, gentry, and merchants risk revolution by working at cross purposes to a royal supremacy exercised through the episcopal bench? W. K. Jordan first suggested to me, when I was about to embark on my doctoral research, that the history of the lectureships might shed some light on the attitudes and behavior of lay Puritans; I hope this study witnesses to some degree the immense impact his teaching and scholarship have had on my understanding of the period.

My understanding of the organization and politics of the Puritan movement, like that of all recent students of Puritanism, has been profoundly influenced by Patrick Collinson's many studies. My conception of Puritan politics has also been colored by Michael Walzer's provocative and illuminating study, *The Revolution of the Saints*. The present work is about politics in two senses. In the stricter sense it is an account of a rather narrow corner of ecclesiastical politics, of the conflict generated by the ecclesiastical hierarchy's attempt to bring lecturing ministers within the ambit of ecclesiastical discipline and in some instances ultimately to suppress an institution that threatened Church and State. In the broader sense it is a study of one aspect of the attempt by communities of Protestant Englishmen to recast the priorities and structures of the Church in order to provide a preaching ministry answerable to their initiatives and responsive to their needs.

Over the years in which this study was in the making I have received more help of one kind or another than I can easily remember or note here. Certain debts, however, cannot be forgotten. My year of research in London archives was financed by a grant from Harvard University. Like many American students before and since, I found a ready welcome at the Institute of Historical Research, and I owe much to the stimulation and assistance generously provided in Joel Hurstfield's and R. C. Latham's seminars. As a tyro at the beginning of my archival work, I turned gratefully to the late H. Gareth Owen's doctoral dissertation, "The London Parish Clergy in the Reign of Elizabeth I," which provided an invaluable introduction to the clerical scene in London during the early part of the period I wished to study and an indispensable guide to many of the archival sources I subsequently used. On the one occasion we met he responded to my stumbling attempt to thank him for permission to use his dissertation much as though I had conferred a favor on him. I am grateful for the assistance I received from the archivists at the Public Record Office and at the London County Council Record Office, and in particular from Dr. A. E. J. Hollaender and his assistants at the Guildhall Library. I am also particularly grateful to the Honorable Secretary of the Haberdashers' Company for permission to consult the company's archives.

I want to thank the Department of History of Stanford University, which paid for typing the final draft, and Miss Cynthia A. Denenholz, who devoted some weeks of tedium to giving a measure of accuracy to my notes. I want to thank my wife for her fortitude and forbearance. Quite apart from the typing, proofreading, indexing, and so on that are the thankless lot of wives of harried and penurious academics, she saw the book through its various incarnations and its author through the repeated agonies of composition and revision with a solicitude and patience that the former scarcely warranted and the latter rarely deserved.

Spelling and punctuation have been modernized in all quotations. In dates the days of the month remain in the old style (Julian calendar), but the year is taken to begin on January 1. Hence to avoid confusion both years are given for dates between January 1 and March 25, the first day of the new year according to the old style, as follows: e.g., March 24, 1624/5.

P.S.S.

Contents

The Puritan Lectureships

Introduction

WRITING early in the seventeenth century, John Donne saw in the "New Philosophy" only a loss of coherence, further evidence that his age was "iron, and rusty, too."[1] Modern historians, less concerned with cosmological decadence than with temporal change, have seen the Englishman of the sixteenth and seventeenth centuries as buffeted by a variety of revolutions, ranging from the scientific revolution, Donne's "New Philosophy," with its revolutionary implications for thought and perception (to say nothing of a poet's sensibility), to the more mundane but no less profound price revolution. G. R. Elton has discovered a revolution in Tudor government during the 1530's, and Lawrence Stone a revolution in education between 1560 and 1640. More recently Michael Walzer has seen in Puritanism a movement bent on the radical transformation of English life: the revolution of the saints.[2]

Certainly for three or four generations of Englishmen—from those who witnessed the accession of the young Queen Elizabeth in 1558 to those who saw the triumphal restoration of the Stuart monarchy a century later—the impact of Puritanism was, if not revolutionary, at least pervasive and inescapable. Although perhaps no more than a minority of literate and politically conscious Englishmen, who were themselves a minority among their countrymen, ever espoused the various beliefs, practices, and policies associated with Puritanism, they were a minority that could not be ignored. Arising initially from dissatisfaction with what some saw as the incomplete reformation represented by the Elizabethan Settlement, Puritanism soon developed a dynamic of its own. Its ideologues not only pointed to shortcomings in established institutions and the majority position, but offered challenging alternatives. If Puritanism as a Protestant reform movement naturally found its ideological leadership in the ranks of the clergy, the potency of its challenge to orthodoxy came from the fact that increasing numbers of lay Englishmen looked to Puritan divines for spiritual guidance and in a larger sense for a new way of life.

Essentially Puritanism offered a new view of man's relationship to God (or of God's relationship to man), and hence of man's relationship to the world and to his fellow men. Not that this fundamental challenge is readily apparent to the student of the period. Rather than a great ideological confrontation, what he sees is a series of minor skirmishes fought by irritable divines over comparatively trivial issues. In the 1560's a small number of clergy objected to such apparently innocuous practices as using the sign of the cross in baptisms and the ring in marriage ceremonies, and wearing the surplice during performances of the service. Both the Puritans and their orthodox brethren admitted that the Vestiarian controversy, as it came to be called, was concerned not with fundamentals of faith and practice but with indifferent matters. Nevertheless, Archbishop Parker's attempts to enforce uniform practice led a number of Puritan clergymen to withdraw from their clerical posts, and their lay supporters angrily protested on their behalf. Ten years later one discovers Puritan clerical leaders admonishing Parliament to abolish the episcopal government of the Church and to replace it with a structure and discipline out of the Word, by which they meant a Presbyterian polity they believed they had found adumbrated in the New Testament. As Matthew Hutton, the Anglican Dean of York, wrote to Lord Burghley in 1573, "At the beginning, it was but a cap and a surplice, and a tippet; but now it is grown to bishops, archbishops and cathedral churches, and the overthrow of order established."[3] To be sure, the attack on episcopacy raised more significant questions than that of vestments, but it hardly involved a total way of life.

Indeed, as the issues continue to change with the years—Sabbatarianism replaces Presbyterianism as the focus of the conflict, only to be replaced later by Puritan attacks on the doctrinal and ceremonial proclivities of the "Arminians"—the impression that they are scarcely fundamental remains. But this is not to say that there were no basic differences dividing Englishmen. If one looks beneath the surface of public conflict, one can discern the essentials of the Puritan platform. What the Puritans were demanding was sacraments rightly administered, discipline out of the Word, and liberty to preach. The last of these comprehended the other two, for to the Puritans, who claimed the Bible as their authority, preaching meant preaching the Word. The Bible was believed to reveal not only how the sacraments were to be administered and under what kind of discipline man was to live, but far more important, God's promise of a life-giving faith to those destined by grace to be among the elect. The activity of the Holy Spirit was admittedly not bound by human conventions or expectations, but virtually to a man the Puritans were certain that the effectual preaching of the Word and the diligent hearing of it were the ordinary means of salvation. Hence, it is not in the admonitions to Parliament or in the academic debates but in the sermons preached from hundreds of Puritan pulpits that the Puritan ideology was set forth in its totality.

Quite apart from the unique position occupied by the sermon in the Puritan economy of salvation, preaching played a more important role in the life of the times than ever before or since. Not only did the pulpit outdraw bearbaiting and morris dancing, but even in sophisticated London the popular preachers attracted larger audiences week after week than Shakespeare and Jonson in their prime. Whether or not the sermon was the ordinary means of salvation, it was undoubtedly the ordinary means of mass communication. The government used the pulpit to create a favorable climate of opinion for potentially unpopular measures, and even in a time of rapidly expanding literacy the ordinary subject looked to the pulpit for knowledge of the greater world beyond his parish. Who controlled the pulpit was, therefore, a matter of moment.

For the Puritans control of the pulpit was a matter of survival. In the years before 1642 the Puritan drive to reform the ecclesiastical structure, the prayer book, and the discipline of the Established Church proved a resounding failure. However, though efforts aimed at revolution from above might fail, these efforts had never been more than a means to an end, a shortcut by which ordinary Englishmen could be brought to a different mode of thought and behavior. So long as the Puritan clergy had access to the pulpit, there was always hope that this more profound revolution from below might be brought about, if more slowly, with no less certainty.

In their efforts to control a sizable number of pulpits the Puritans faced three problems. The first was patronage. All parish livings, all benefices with cure of souls, were in someone's gift and presentation. In those parts of England where Puritan gentry and nobility possessed advowsons (the right to present to the local parish churches), patronage presented no problem. Elsewhere the Established Church provided no mechanism by which Puritans could satisfy their demands, even if the influential laity of the parish were Puritan. The second problem was economic. In a period that was heir to both the scholastic and the humanist educational tradition, preaching the Word did not imply the enthusiastic raptures of a Bible-thumping demagogue but rather the reasoned exegesis of a text. Preaching accordingly required long years of training, and the educated clergy, whether Puritan or orthodox Anglican, expected an income commensurate with their accomplishments. Hence, even if patronage presented no problem, it might still be impossible to attract a competent preacher if the income of the benefice were small. The final problem was the matter of discipline. The hierarchy of the Church could exercise little control over patronage by the laity and even less over the incomes of individual livings, but they could control the official acts of the parish priest. The Puritan clergyman, committed at least in theory to changes in the Church's procedures for worship, was constantly tempted to introduce the changes in his own parish. When he was caught committing breaches of uniformity, he became subject to the censures of the ecclesiastical courts, which had as their ultimate sanction excommunication and deprivation.

In the final analysis the disciplinary problem defied any single solution, for success in avoiding the censures of the church courts depended on the actions and conscience of the individual Puritan clergyman and on the rigor with which ecclesiastical law was enforced. The problems presented by lack of patronage and inadequate income proved more tractable; they could often be solved by an institutional arrangement known as the lectureship. If an incumbent minister could not or would not preach the number and kind of sermons demanded, the laity could hire another minister, the lecturer, to preach at times when the church was not being used for regular services. If the regular parochial income was too small to attract a preaching incumbent, the laity could supplement it by adding a lectureship. The success of this institutional device was due in part to its very simplicity, for it was infinitely adaptable to local circumstances.

Between the lectureship and the advowson the Puritan laity solved the problem of access to the pulpit for their clerical brethren. Although both the lectureship and the advowson offered opportunities for lay patronage, the lectureship also offered a large measure of lay control, for the supporters of a lectureship not only chose the lecturer but paid his stipend. The relationship between the Puritan laity and the Puritan lecturer was at once less formal, less structured, and less permanent than the relationship between the patron and the incumbent of a parochial living, but by the same token the relationship between laity and lecturer had the advantage of being more immediate, intimate, and flexible. The role of the ecclesiastical hierarchy was minimized by the lectureship and in fact was limited to the decision whether or not to license the lecturer to preach, but what the hierarchy lost in authority, the laity gained.

During the century in which Puritanism was a dynamic element in English life, it was always more than the ideology of a faction, and there is accordingly little point in characterizing Puritans as discontented clerics—narrow and intolerant in their enthusiasms and hypocritical in grasping after power—as their enemies sometimes did. Puritanism was more, too, than simply the name given to the Calvinist wing of the Established Church, for there were Calvinist Anglicans who were not Puritans, and Puritans, at least at the end of the period, who were no longer orthodox Calvinists. In fact Puritanism was never a movement of clerics alone, nor can it be defined easily in theological terms, even though its ideological leaders came largely from the ranks of the clergy and many were theologians of considerable influence. Doctrinal differences between Anglican and Puritan were by no means negligible.[4] But the point to be emphasized is that Puritanism, as a historical phenomenon, was from its very inception a movement that encompassed laity as well as clergy, and thus a movement that was unlikely to adhere rigorously and uniformly to a set of doctrinal propositions. Moreover, as a protest movement within the Anglican communion, it lacked central, institutionalized leadership capable of imposing an authoritative view.[5] Finally, it drew its support from many ranks in society, representing many interests and degrees of commitment.

Admittedly, most Puritans shared certain attitudes and ideas despite their differences. Most would surely have agreed, for example, with Oliver Cromwell that the "root of the matter" was the personal experience of conversion and regeneration, although they might not have agreed with the conclusions he drew from this proposition.* Most would surely have agreed, too, with the Puritan lecturer Richard Sibbes that "the sense of the love of Christ in pardoning of sins will constrain one to a *holy violence* in the performing of all duties."[6] But the activism, the "holy violence," was a matter of the energetic way goals were pursued; it does not define the goals or specify how to pursue them. Nor could such matters be left in theory to the workings of the individual conscience informed by the Holy Spirit, for the substance of the reformation needed in Church and State, in society and the individual, was given by the Word and made manifest in the Scriptures. Hence the importance of the exegetical sermon, and hence, too, the possibility of variety in interpretation.

Puritans of all varieties recognized a common bond of like-mindedness, but as an organized movement they present to the historian anything but the appearance of a monolithic party.† Unlike the French Huguenots in the 1550's and 1560's, they lacked both a common authority and discipline, such as emanated from Calvin's Geneva, and a centralized organization with a coherent political purpose.[7] Yet English Puritanism demonstrated the same capacity as its French counterpart to surmount the barriers of local interest and to cut through the lines separating rank and degree in a highly stratified, hierarchical society.[8] If English Puritanism, like French Protestantism, failed to become a real mass movement, it succeeded better than any other organization or institution in English society short of the

---

* Speaking of the qualities his ecclesiastical Triers looked for in those seeking admission to a living, Cromwell said, "Though a man be of any of those three judgments [Presbyterian, Independent, or Baptist], if he have the root of the matter in him, he may be admitted." Sir Charles Firth, *Oliver Cromwell* (World's Classics ed.; London, 1953), p. 352. Few conservative Puritans, Presbyterians in particular, would have followed Cromwell in seeing this quality as grounds for tolerating separatists and the sects.

† For the purposes of this study I have not included the separatists among the Puritans for three reasons. First, Puritans at the time drew the line at separation and in most cases disavowed those who crossed it. Second, though Professor Woodhouse and others have convincingly shown that there was continuity in the thought of the Puritans and the sectaries, as an organized movement Puritanism had little connection with separatism, since the one developed within the state church and the other outside it. Finally, the subject of this study, the lectureship, was an institution exploited by the Puritans and virtually ignored by the separatists, at least in the years before 1640.

monarchy itself, with which it was not directly in competition, in commanding the loyalty and directing the energy of its constituents. H. G. Koenigsberger has argued that the religious organizations of sixteenth-century France formed the basis or prototype for the later organization of political parties.[9] Much the same can be said of English Puritanism.

In the course of its relatively brief history the Puritan movement developed a wide variety of ad hoc institutions to serve its adherents' many needs and interests. At one extreme were small, tight conspiratorial groups operating in secret, such as the group that produced the scandalous but amusing Martin Marprelate tracts published in 1588 and 1589. Another group, more respectable and less conspiratorial than the Marprelate publishers, was the Feoffees for Impropriations of the later 1620's, a Puritan organization centered in London. This was a highly formalized group of ministers, lawyers, and merchants —Attorney General Noy denounced them as a corporation without a royal charter—established for the single purpose of collecting funds to purchase impropriated livings.[10] At the other extreme individual Puritans worked within existing institutions, ranging from parish vestries to town corporations, to secure a preaching ministry. They found in the Puritan connection both a means of mobilizing powerful interests to afford patronage and protection, and a means of recruiting Puritan ministers. They found in the lectureships the institutional structure appropriate to their end.

This study attempts to assess the impact of the lectureships to the extent that this can be measured by their growth and by the episcopal reaction to the threat they posed to ecclesiastical discipline and control. Although the development of lectureships in rural parishes and in town and borough corporations is sketched so far as printed sources permit, the principal focus of the study is on London, both because of its importance as an administrative, mercantile, and political center and because of the accessibility of its records. London presents a further characteristic of prime interest: the distribution of patronage within the City was such that approximately 70 per cent of the parochial benefices were in the gift of the Crown and Church (compared to a national average, so an observer claimed in 1604, of five livings out of six in the gift of the laity). Thus there was notably little opportunity in the City for the Puritan laity to exercise patronage.

It is the contention of this study that if in large measure the battle for the soul of the capital had been won by the Puritans by 1640, the victory was due at least in part to the success with which the laity shifted the balance of ecclesiastical patronage in their favor by means of the lectureship.

Recent studies, particularly those of Christopher Hill and Irvonwy Morgan, have referred at some length to the lectureships.[11] However, in the absence of information on the number of parishes having lectureships, for example, and on the quantity of resources—human and financial—that the Puritans were able to mobilize and willing to devote to securing a preaching ministry, it has been difficult to assess how important a role and how significant an impact the lectureships had. That the bishops feared lecturing preachers and sought to control or suppress them has long been known. Whether the need to discipline the preachers was seen as a major problem and whether the bishops were successful in meeting it has been less clear. Obviously a detailed study of lectureships in a limited geographic area will not provide the basis for conclusive answers to these questions, but it may help to suggest the form a definitive judgment might take.

This study is based primarily on two classes of manuscript material. One is the extant parish records—the vestry minutes and churchwarden's accounts found in the archives at the Guildhall Library, at the Westminster Public Library, and at the London County Council Record Office. The other is the records of the ecclesiastical authorities—the bishops' registers, visitation call books, and Consistory Court correction books found in the London County Council Record Office; Bishop Laud's surveys of the London lecturers, located among the manuscripts at the Lambeth Palace Library; and the surviving fragments of the High Commission Act Books, which remain among the state papers at the Public Record Office.

On the basis of these records I have tried to answer the following questions. How many parishes had lectureships? What were the professed motives of the laity in instituting them? How were lecturers recruited? How was the institution financed? By what means were the laity able to exercise continued control over the lecturer and to deal with the occasional hostility of the incumbent? In addition I have sought to discover where the lecturers came from, what kind of training they had, what brought them to London, how significant a role the lectureship played in their clerical careers, and how many of the London lecturers were actually Puritans. Finally, no estimate of the importance of this institution could be made without surveying the efforts of the ecclesiastical authorities to reduce the lecturers to conformity and to control the lectureship, if not to destroy it outright as an independent institution.

PART I

Puritanism and Lectureships

The judgment of God ... pierces deeply
into the hearts of true believers, and the
word that they hear, it worketh mightily
in them, more sharp than a two-edged
sword.

—EDWARD DERING

I

The Importance of Preaching

FROM its very inception Elizabethan Protestantism was committed to a preaching ministry. In opposition to the authority of popes and councils the reformers in England, as on the Continent, advanced the claims of Scripture; and for the primary emphasis on the sacraments as vehicles of grace they substituted the efficacious preaching of the Word. This shift led in turn to a redefinition of the sacraments but not, of course, to their abandonment. As the nineteenth of the Thirty-Nine Articles states so succinctly, "The visible Church of Christ is a congregation of faithful men, in which the pure Word of God is preached, and the Sacraments be duly ministered according to Christ's ordinance."[1] Hence a new balance was struck by the Protestants between the two functions of a true Church. In the earliest authoritative apologia for Anglicanism, Bishop Jewel sets forth the respective functions of preaching and the sacraments. On the one hand, he says, the power of the keys is the knowledge of the Scriptures, and Christ's ministers received this authority, as had Christ's disciples, "to the end they should go, they should teach, they should publish abroad the Gospel," for the key "whereby the way and entry to the kingdom of God is opened unto us, is the word of the Gospel and the expounding of the law and the Scriptures."[2] On the other hand, the sacraments retain a substantial significance. If they are "holy signs and ceremonies," they are also "tokens of grace"; and Jewel expressly asserts that "in the Lord's Supper there is truly given unto the believing the body and blood of our Lord ..., which quickeneth our souls."[3]

Theologically such a balance might be admirable; historically it proved unstable. As the acrimonious dialogue between the Puritans and the orthodox Anglicans progressed, the two sides tended to move away from the original common ground and to weigh the relative importance of preaching and the sacraments differently. This divergence was due in part to different expectations of the efficacy of the two functions in the larger scheme of salvation, in part to different responses to the practical problems facing the Elizabethan establishment.

Doctrinally the area of agreement on fundamentals remained large. In the later years of Elizabeth's reign, the Anglican Hooker stated with his accustomed measure that "as many therefore as are apparently to our judgment born of God, they have the seed of their regeneration by the ministry of the Church, which useth to that end and purpose not only the Word, but the Sacraments, both having generative force and virtue."[4] With all allowances made for the obvious dissimilarity in theological rhetoric, the Westminster Confession, issued half a century later by the Puritan Assembly of Divines, appears to differ little in substance: "Under the gospel, when Christ the substance was exhibited, the ordinances in which this covenant [of grace] is dispensed are the preaching of the word and the administration of the sacraments of Baptism and the Lord's Supper."[5]

However, given on the one hand the Puritans' stress on prevenient grace, which tended to reduce the sacraments to a ratification of God's activity, and on the other hand what Professor New has called the Anglicans' dynamic concept of the sacraments as vehicles of grace, a clash was possible despite large areas of agreement.[6] Had no more been at stake than the niceties of doctrinal definition, it is conceivable that the issue might have been confined to the polemics of the Anglican and Puritan theoreticians—to a Hooker and a Cartwright. But the issue of the proper balance between the preaching and sacramental functions of the Church had wider implications. On its resolution depended not only the proper allocation of the Church's scarce resources, but the very life of the Church—its relations with the faithful and the form their piety assumed.

The architects of the Elizabethan Settlement immediately faced two problems that had a bearing on this issue. First, they faced the task of evangelizing a generation of Englishmen who had witnessed the sudden collapse of the old order, followed by the rapid Edwardian Protestant advance and the equally rapid Marian retreat to the *status quo ante*. If such change produced fierce commitment among the few, it must have led to a self-regarding quietism among the unheroic many. The obvious solution to this problem was an educated Protestant clergy, committed to active proselytizing and sufficient in number to staff the thousands of parish churches across the length and breadth of England. However, the Protestant divines who came out of hiding or trooped back from exile on the Continent during the first years of Elizabeth's reign numbered in the hundreds, not the thousands. Given time the newly purged universities would train a new generation to the task, but in the short run there was no easy answer. This was the second problem confronting the new Elizabethan establishment.

How intractable this problem was is openly confessed in the first sentence of the Preface to the first Elizabethan Book of Homilies. While admitting "how necessary it is that the word of God, which is the only food of the soul, and that most excellent light that we must walk by in this our most dangerous pilgrimage, should at all convenient times be preached unto the people," it nevertheless points out that "all they which are appointed ministers have not the gift of preaching sufficiently to instruct the people committed unto them." Hence, to provide an "honest remedy" the Queen "caused [the Edwardian] Book of Homilies ... to be printed anew."[7]

Although the more uncompromising reformers, soon to be known as Precisians or Puritans by their opponents, could not escape the dilemma posed in the Preface, they did doubt whether a homily read by a minister too ignorant to be licensed to preach was an adequate substitute for the Scriptures zealously expounded and applied by an educated clergyman. As the Puritan authors of *An Admonition to the Parliament* (1572) complained, "Then [i.e., in the time of the primitive Church], as God gave utterance they preached the word only: now they read homilies, articles, injunctions, etc. Then it was painful: now gainful."[8] When such temporary expedients became accepted practices, and not only accepted but defended as good, when in addition Puritan ministers were sequestered from their pulpits and deprived of their livings for nonconformity, thus silencing some of the Church's most vigorous Protestant preachers, opposition inevitably followed. The argument used to defend the cardinal position of preaching was simple, and evidently no need was felt to change or modify it substantially during the period under consideration.

Queen Elizabeth is reported to have remarked to Archbishop Grindal, perhaps the prelate closest in his sympathies to the Puritans, "that it was good for the Church to have few preachers, and that three or four might suffice for a county; and that the reading of homilies to the people was enough."[9] Shortly before he was sequestered from his archiepiscopal functions for his opposition to the Queen's suppression of prophesyings,* Grindal indirectly replied with a defense of preaching couched in virtually the same terms used by the Puritans:

Public and continual preaching of God's word is the ordinary mean and instrument of the salvation of mankind. St. Paul calleth it the *ministry of reconciliation* of man unto God. By preaching of God's word, the glory of God is enlarged, faith is nourished, and charity is increased. By it the ignorant is instructed, the negligent exhorted and incited, the stubborn rebuked, the weak conscience comforted.[10]

However novel Grindal's sentiments were for an Elizabethan prelate, they were the veriest commonplace among Puritans. In 1571, for example, the Puritan authors of a supplication warned that "an infinite number of your Majesty's subjects, for want of preaching of the word (the only ordinary mean of salvation of souls ... without which the Lord God hath pronounced that the people must needs perish), have already run headlong into destruction."[11] In 1583 the puritanical Philip Stubbes wrote, "As the soul is the life of the body, ... so the word of God preached is the life ..., as well to the body, as to the soul. ... Now certain it is, these things cannot be applied without the presence of the preacher ... ; and therefore is his absence from his flock a dangerous and perilous thing."[12]

Obviously to the Puritan way of thinking the consequences of a non-preaching ministry were dire indeed. "Away with dumb dogs and blind guides," said the preacher Anthony Lapthorne to a large crowd assembled at Muggleswick parish early in 1638, "for they did lead the people into destruction and into the ditch of hell." As two of his auditors later deposed, they understood Lapthorne to mean "such ministers as were not preachers," for Lapthorne had "told them that preaching was the only means to salvation."[13] However, the Puritans did not greet all preaching with equal expressions of joy and thanksgiving. Sermons must be not only frequent, but sound and "profit-

---

* Prophesyings were conferences of the clergy held for the purpose of mutual edification and criticism. Frequently initiated by Puritan preachers and sometimes sanctioned by sympathetic members of the hierarchy, their principal purpose was to provide training in the exposition of the Bible and in preaching exegetical sermons. The best discussion of the prophesyings is in Patrick Collinson's *Elizabethan Puritan Movement* (London, 1967), esp. pp. 168–76.

able" in substance. The parishioners of Peniston, Yorkshire, complained in 1647 that their minister preached "sometimes twice a day, yet either altogether, or for the most part, other men's works; and one thing four or five times, or oftener repeated ... without any progress at all, only tiring the time with tautologies and vain iterations, to the wearying of the hearers and dishonor of the Great God."[14] Another class of irritating sermons were those that defended Anglican ceremonialism. John Rous, a Puritan divine from Suffolk, recorded in his diary having heard a minister declare that among those "liable to God's fearful judgment" were "adulterers, oppressors, atheists, [and] those that bowed not at the name of Jesus." Bowing at the name of Jesus seemed little short of idolatrous to most Puritans, and Rous concluded the entry with an exasperated "O tempora, quo pastores."[15]

As the controversy over preaching mounted, the Anglicans counterattacked on two fronts. First, although the orthodox Anglican could concede the importance of preaching, he could never grant it exclusive primacy at the expense of prayer or the mediation of grace through the sacraments. Second, when the pulpit was employed for polemical purposes, as it increasingly was, the orthodox Anglican came to oppose the emphasis on preaching as dangerous to the peace of both Church and State. From this point of view the issue was not doctrinal correctness but political expediency. Both lines of attack emerged in Elizabeth's reign and were used increasingly in the subsequent reigns to differentiate Anglican from Puritan.

On the whole, the Anglican attack appears to lack the unity and simplicity of the Puritan defense. However, there is little to indicate that contemporary Anglicans viewed the diversity of their approach as a sign of weakness. Certainly Archbishop Whitgift, who was not one to doubt the rightness of his cause, at least where the Puritans were concerned, made quick work of the opposition view. In the course of a hearing before the Court of High Commission, the Puritan John Penry had argued that nonresident ministers were "odious in the sight of God and man, because ... they bereave the people over whom they thrust themselves, of the ordinary means of salvation, which was the word preached." "What, sir (quoth the Archbishop), I tell thee it is an heresy, and thou shalt recant it as an heresy."[16] Lancelot Andrewes, more irenic in his approach, tried to end controversy on the point by suggesting that it was "a folly to fall to comparisons.

... Prayer or Preaching; the *Word*, or the *Sacraments*. What needs this? Seeing we have both, both are ready for us. ... It may be (who knows) if the one will not work, the other may."[17]

Evidently such a compromise appealed neither to the Puritan opposition nor to Andrewes's own side. In 1626 Henry Valentine, the lecturer in John Donne's parish, St. Dunstan's in the West, expressed the hope that clergymen would not "shrink up all religion into preaching" and appealed to the efficacy of public prayer, which he likened to a "concert of music ... more sweet and melodious than any one instrument."[18] Archbishop Laud, whose words carried greater weight, was more radical. Never one to equivocate, he simply reversed the Puritan position. Reverence is properly accorded to the altar, in his view, because it is "the greatest place of God's residence upon earth. I say the greatest, yea greater than the pulpit, for there it is 'Hoc est Corpus meum,' This is my body; but in the pulpit, it is at most but 'Hoc est Verbum meum,' This is my word. And a greater reverence, no doubt, is due to the Body than to the Word of our Lord."[19]

Between the Puritans and the Laudians the balanced position of Bishop Jewel was destroyed. During the palmy days of Anglican supremacy the Puritans could only expostulate and suffer when they did so too publicly and persistently. With the arrival of the Long Parliament, they came into the promised land. By then the time had passed when pleas for balance and moderation found many willing hearers; Archbishop Laud's policies, even more than his putative Arminianism, had seen to that. The Restoration in 1660 prevented the Puritans from having more than the penultimate word on the subject, but they made the most of their opportunity. A gloss setting out the reasons for the House of Commons' order "for the Establishing of Preaching Lecturers" makes claims for the efficacy of preaching that could not have been wider or more inclusive:

[Preaching] is even the very way to bring People into a state of Salvation; it is the way to save their souls, Rom. 10:13–14. Preaching is the declaring of the will of the Lord God, what His pleasure is, to have done by Others; as also what Himself will do, and that by the voice of the Minister, who comes to the People of God, as an ambassador, to publish and spread abroad the mind and message of God touching Man's duty, and salvation, and to instruct the Church of God.[20]

For those in authority and their loyal supporters, the inexpediency of overmuch preaching was self-evident. Unless all preachers sang the same tune, and that a tune composed by the Crown and its bishops, it was perhaps better to have no singing at all. Further, if the king or a bishop wished to regulate or limit preaching, it was far easier to base such action on practical exigencies than on doctrine. Regulation could be and was justified on the ground that the pulpit was abused; a frontal attack on preaching would have required more than the argument that its function was secondary to prayer and the sacraments in the life of the Church. Thus, the original Edwardian Book of Homilies had been issued in part, according to its Preface, "to put away all contention which hath heretofore risen through diversity of preaching" and to teach all faithful subjects "to honor God and to serve their King with all humility and subjection."[21] Ironically, the "political" case against preaching was perhaps never made more colorfully than in a sermon preached from that most famous of pulpits, Paul's Cross in London, by Henry King, the son of a bishop and a future bishop himself, in 1621. Having castigated the "papists," he turned to an attack on London's Puritan preachers:

No wonder then, if Preaching may breed surfeits, that so many Crudities lie in the stomachs of this City; that so many Fumes and giddy vapors fly up into the head, to the no small disturbance of the Church's quiet; that so many hot spirits, like Cannons overcharged, recoil against all Discipline, break into divers factions, and with the splints of those cracked opinions do more mischief than deliberation or Justice can suddenly solve.[22]

Factionalism and diversity of opinion were by no means of recent origin. Queen Elizabeth is said to have remarked "Nay, I have heard there be six preachers in one diocese the which do preach six sundry ways." It is perhaps no wonder, then, that she should have added, "There is more learning in one of those [homilies] than in twenty of some of their sermons."[23] For if the homilies did not actually offer more learning, what they offered was safer and more attuned to the needs of authority. The needs of the Puritans were different.

From the early years of Elizabeth's reign the more resolute religious reformers faced two acute problems. One was to evangelize an indifferent, if not hostile, population;[24] the other was to obtain protection from their "godly prince." Although a very Deborah in her willingness to oppose the scheming Jesuit and the invading Spaniard, Elizabeth remained content with—indeed defended with considerable ingenuity and pertinacity—her half-finished reformation. Puritanism was born out of this dilemma; yet at least a partial solution was inherent in the situation itself. For the Puritan clergy the duty to preach God's word was self-evident. Further, the sermon proved not only a means of conveying saving knowledge to the masses, but also a way to influence the lesser magistracy; and a sympathetic magistracy, whether of country magnates or town merchants, university colleges or borough corporations, could provide the Puritan clergymen both with local support and patronage and with a buffer between themselves and an unsympathetic prince and episcopate. "What they wanted in strength," wrote Thomas Fuller of the Puritans, "they supplied in activity; but what won them most repute was their ministers' painful preaching in populous places; it being observed in England, that those who hold the helm of the pulpit always steer people's hearts as they please."[25]

These were the circumstances in which the Puritan lectureships were created. For in the lectureship was found both a means of providing for regular preaching in addition to the legally required quarterly and monthly sermons and a nexus between the various components of the Puritan connection.[26] The universities provided the training ground and recruiting place for lecturers; the town corporation, gentry patron, or city parish provided not only the pulpit and frequently the financial basis for lectures, but also powerful friends to protect and intercede on the lecturer's behalf. It is probably safe to say that no other institution (not even the companies for colonial plantation) brought together lay and clerical Puritans in so many ways over so long a period at so many places.

THE LECTURESHIP AS A PURITAN INSTITUTION

Not all lecturers were Puritans nor all Puritans lecturers, but there can be no question that the lectureship was essentially a Puritan institution, that the impetus behind it was Puritan in motivation, and that it was staffed predominantly by Puritan preachers. To be sure, the lectureship at Windsor was briefly held by as unlikely a figure as the extremely royalist and Anglican Richard Montagu, who referred to Puritans as "riff-raff rascals" and "Allobrogical dormice," and who complained hysterically, "It will never be well till we have our Inquisition."[27] His motives, however, as expressed in a letter to his clerical friend John Cosin, only serve to confirm the Puritan character of the institution. "I am resolved," he wrote, "to take this Lectureship myself, because I know of no pretenders but Puritans in part or whole."[28] According to John Hacket, the chaplain and biographer of Bishop Williams of Lincoln, even that wily, luxury-loving prelate preached his turn at the market town of Kettering, "in a Lecture supplied by the learnedest Divines of the Vicinage." "But," Hacket continues, "who hath not heard him say that knew him, it was so often in his mouth, that the way to get Credit from the Non-Conformitants was to out-preach them?"[29] As for Miles Smith, Bishop of Gloucester, "a man that spared not to show himself upon all occasions in favor of the Calvinian party," he confirmed his Puritan sympathies in the eyes of one of Laud's followers, Peter Heylyn, "more particularly in countenancing the Lectures within his Diocese against the lawful Minister of the Parish whenever any complaint of their proceedings was made unto him."[30]

Even the wits of the age were at one with their more sober colleagues in linking lectures with the peculiarities of Puritan piety, and the union of lecture and Puritan apparently became a literary commonplace. Sir John Harrington's "Precise Tayler," for example, "bought a Bible of the new translation,/ And in his life, he shew'd great reformation"; what is more to the point, "He walked mannerly, and talked meekly;/ He heard three Lectures, and two Sermons weekly."[31] A generation later John Earle's "Shee Precise Hypocrite" displays the same propensities: "She loves preaching better than praying, and of Preachers, Lecturers, and thinks the Weekdays' Exercise far more edifying than the Sundays'."[32]

All Puritans agreed on the necessity of a preaching ministry, and the lectureship was clearly a means to that end. Whether it was regarded as more than a temporary expedient, an institution to be employed only until a truly reformed church placed a preaching minister in every parish, is another matter. The question as such does not appear to have been raised, and conflicting answers to it are implied by Puritan writings on the ministry. For the Elizabethan Presbyterian the proper discipline of the Church, ordained by God and prescribed in the Scriptures, required four offices: pastor, doctor, elder, and deacon. The offices of pastor and doctor were distinct and their functions different. The pastor or minister preached, administered the sacraments, and prayed; the doctor or teacher interpreted Scripture in order to expound sound doctrine. Although both preached, their preaching served different ends: "The pastor is to take one course, and the Doctor another, for the one is to direct himself principally to exhort, and the other to attend upon doctrine."[33] Hence, according to the disciplinarian model, the lecturer had a permanent place in the true Church, for the function of the lecturer was the same as that of the doctor or teacher. John Udall, a supporter of Cartwright and Travers, made this point obliquely in arguing that "Cathedral Churches have yet some show thereof [i.e., of the true discipline] left in them, who (besides the bishop) have also one that readeth a Lecture in divinity."[34]

However, by no means all Puritans were Presbyterians, even in the middle years of Elizabeth's reign, and the many whose major concern was to secure an evangelical ministry rather than a Presbyterian disciplinary order saw the lectureship simply as a convenience. For the Puritan divine who espoused this position, preaching rather than discipline was the most important attribute of the true Church. If he could preach as an incumbent of a parish, so much the better. However, if no living were available, or if he scrupled at the required ceremonies, or if he were deprived of his parochial living, a lectureship at least provided him with a pulpit, for preach he must in any event. The Puritan Edward Dering went so far as to define the Church itself as "a company called together by the voice of a preacher." Dering's last years were spent lecturing from the prestigious pulpit at St. Paul's Cathedral in London, to which he had been appointed by Bishop Sandys in 1572. However, the theme he hammered at incessantly was not the need for more lectureships, but the need for a preaching ministry of the sort that could be found in "scarce one parish of an hundred." "Without this preaching of the word," he wrote, "we can never have faith."[35] For Puritan divines of Dering's persuasion preaching was the essence of the ministerial function; they saw no significant difference between exhorting and expounding. To such Puritans the concerns of the Presbyterians were not so much wrong as untimely and ill-judged.

As might be expected, the views of the Puritan laity on this question are hard to ascertain. Testimony to the efficacy of the preached word abounds, and lay Puritans were not slow to complain when godly preachers were silenced. Typically, Lady Anne Bacon, the widow of the Lord Keeper, wrote in 1585 to Lord Burghley in defense of some deprived ministers:

For my own part, my good Lord, ... I confess as one that has found mercy, that I have profited more in the inward feeling knowledge of God his holy will, though but in a small measure, by such sincere and sound opening of the Scriptures by an ordinary preaching within these seven or eight years, than I did by hearing odd sermons at Paul's wellnigh twenty years together.[36]

The precise office or offices by which the Word was dispensed were of little importance compared to the overriding necessity of obtaining an evangelical ministry. The Londoner Philip Stubbes probably expressed the opinion of most of his fellow Puritan laymen when he defended lecturers in terms of the needs of the times rather than on grounds of scriptural authority:

But if it were so, that every church and congregation had his preacher (as every one ought to preach, else he is not sent by the Lord) then were [lecturers] not so necessary; but considering that most churches are planted ... with single reading ministers, they are very behoveful to help supply the defect of the others, that through the good industry as well of the one, as of the other, the churches of God may be instructed and nourished with the word of God to eternal life.[37]

Ideally, as Stubbes continued, "It were much better for [lecturers] to have particular flocks of their own," but while waiting for a magistracy willing to devote the Church's resources to placing a preaching minister in every parish, some compromise was called for. Although the moderate Puritans, by their very insistence on remaining within the Established Church, were committed to compromise on matters of ecclesiastical order, there could be no compromise on the need to provide "painful" preaching, for any such move would be "a taking away of their life and light from them."[38]

For the Anglican, satisfied with the status quo, the lectureship fulfilled no real purpose. Even for the devout and educated Anglican, who might find the homilies less all-sufficient than Elizabeth claimed, the lecturer did nothing that a preaching incumbent could not do better. To the Puritan charge that too many parochial ministers were ignorant and non-preaching "dumb dogs," the Anglican replied that an educated, preaching clergy required financial rewards appropriate to its talents. The Anglican solution was to be found in increasing tithes and parish endowments, in restoring impropriate and appropriate rectories, rather than in creating further competition for limited financial resources by introducing lecturers.[39] Finally, the tendency of Anglican piety, at least by the generation after Richard Hooker and Lancelot Andrewes, was almost wholly inimical to such a development. There were, of course, old-fashioned Anglican divines, such as Thomas Fuller, who ignored the "Arminian" and ceremonial practices of their generation and remained essentially Elizabethan in their outlook—Erastian in politics and Calvinist in theology—right through the Caroline period. But the dominant trend was not toward more preaching, but toward a more comely and decent service and a more elaborate liturgy. Little Gidding and Cosin's *Collection of Private Devotions* were logical, if rather extreme, manifestations of this temper. Preaching was perhaps useful and attendance at sermons was one of a Christian's duties, but it was no more his chief duty than preaching was the central function of the Church. In 1641, after lamenting the propensity of Londoners to abandon divine service for the sake of attending lectures—"so much, that [at morning prayers] ...there is a great assembly, if there be one person to forty pews"— an anonymous "Gentleman of Worth" pleaded that equal reverence, "if no more," be given to divine service, "the House of God being termed by his Son the House of Prayer."[40]

At the other end of the religious spectrum, among the true Separatists, there seems to have been even less interest in the lectureships. As a compromise solution to the problem of securing a preaching ministry, the lectureship necessarily had little appeal for those who had already decided not to wait for a godly prince willing to adopt and legitimize their form of church polity. Both Separatists and Puritans could agree in general on the attributes that distinguished the true, visible Church—"namely, preaching the word, ministration of the sacraments, and reformation of life." However, "reformation of life" did not mean quite the same thing as the Presbyterian "godly discipline": the former implied a gathered church of the saints, of those who had already made a "godly profession" to observe and obey

Christ in all things; the latter implied an order imposed by an elder-ship on saints, hypocrites, and sinners alike. Further, for the Separatist it was "amendment of life," not preaching, that Christ commanded as "the chiefest thing of all to set forth his Church and kingdom."[41] Finally, the willingness of the orthodox Puritans to settle for half a loaf, for a preaching ministry without a godly discipline, was to the Separatist as incomprehensible as it was reprehensible. "How shame-fully do they tarry for the magistrates," wrote Robert Browne, the Elizabethan Separatist. "How do they sever preaching from govern-ing, doctrine from discipline?"[42] To compromise, the Separatists argued, was futile. Even though the lecturer's office was equivalent to that of the "doctor," as the office was called in the Apostolic Church, the lecturer alone could not make an anti-Christian order Christian: "In some few places where he is, he cometh in much after the same manner [i.e., by the "evil calling" of a bishop], joining with some idle shepherd, or some time server, and withdraweth not the people from abominations."[43]

John Canne, a Separatist of a later generation, would not grant even this much legitimacy to the office of lecturer. He voiced his skepticism about the contemporary claim that lecturers were the "best ministers" not because he wished to pass judgment on their "life and doctrine" but because "their name, manner of entrance, and administration is unknown wholly to the scriptures, and I think never before heard of till these later broken and confused times." The lack of a scriptural basis for the lectureships was in itself sufficient ground for condemna-tion, but Canne also had other objections to the institution. Lecture-ships, he pointed out, were not permanent positions; lecturers con-tracted with parishes to serve them by the year, and both parties were free to make new arrangements when the year was up. "But," Canne objects, "a true pastor may not do so, for if he should he were worse than an hireling, which leaves not the sheep till he see the wolf com-ing; but many of these [leave their sheep] when they see a richer lectureship coming toward them."[44]

Most of the Separatists' diatribe against preachers and lecturers in particular was addressed not to their own followers but to their cau-tious Puritan brethren, for in reality the Separatists had little reason to concern themselves with parochial institutions. The Separatist laity looked on the conventicle rather than the local parish as the center of religious life.[45] For the radical clergyman, hounded as he was by both lay and ecclesiastical authorities, a public lectureship was much too exposed a position to preach from, even had there been no theoretical objections to such a post. In any event, what little evidence there is suggests that the Separatist clergy took regular lectureships on only a handful of occasions in the years before 1640.

One such occasion, the only well-authenticated one in London, occurred in 1569 at Holy Trinity Minories. Holy Trinity was scarcely a typical London parish, for the Minories, as a royal peculiar, was immune from episcopal visitation. In addition the parish presented its own minister, who entered the living without the need of the bishop's admission and institution. In short, the Minories was to all intents and purposes a self-governing, independent congregation. It was also a center of religious radicalism. Although it was heavily populated with Dutch and French refugees, its chief parishioner was native English and an old champion of Protestantism. Katherine Brandon, the Dowager Duchess of Suffolk, took up residence in the Minories after her return from continental exile during Queen Mary's reign, and in her wake came various of her chaplains and protégés: John Browne, who had been in exile at Frankfurt and who lectured at Holy Trinity in 1567; a Mr. Pattenson, who also preached at Holy Trinity and who along with Browne had Separatist affiliations; and old "Father" Coverdale, the former Edwardian bishop, who preached at the Minories in 1567 while deprived and suspended for nonconformity.

Indeed, the parish made a practice of hiring suspended and deprived ministers as lecturers in the years from 1567 to 1570. Nevertheless, when a Separatist congregation was associated with the lectureship in 1569, it was under the aegis not of the dowager duchess but of a much more unlikely figure—the Bishop of London, Edmund Grindal. A Separatist conventicle, tracing its origins to the years of Marian persecution and exile, was arrested while conducting services at Plumbers' Hall in 1567; in April 1569 Grindal interceded with the Privy Council and secured the Separatists' release without condition but with the understanding that renewed "factious and disorderly" behavior would lead to renewed imprisonment. Grindal did more; he released William Bonham and Nicholas Crane, two ministers in prison for preaching to various Separatist groups in London, and licensed them as preachers with the stipulation that they refrain from preaching to private assemblies and from practices contrary to those established by public authority. Bonham and Crane promptly secured appointments to the lectureship at Holy Trinity and brought their Separatist congregation with them. Within a year, "perceiving that these disordered persons, and their preachers, did keep no promise," Grindal returned the lecturers to prison and set about rounding up the leaders of the congregation.[46]

The extraordinary combination of factors that made possible the association of Separatism and the lectureship at Holy Trinity was unlikely to occur elsewhere and in fact could not have occurred again even at the Minories, for in 1574 Bishop Sandys successfully breached its immunity and brought the discipline of episcopal visitation to the parish. Several London lecturers were at various times accused of having Separatist affiliations, but in no instance is the evidence firm.

Dr. John Everard, whose frequent imprisonment for preaching against the negotiations for Prince Charles's Spanish marriage in the early 1620's led King James to pun, "What is this Dr. Ever-out? His name shall be Dr. Never-out," was accused before the High Commission, late in his career, of familism, antinomianism, and anabaptism. He seems in fact to have been guilty of little more than a rather unorthodox neoplatonism, and during the Interregnum his sermons were published with the imprimatur of Joseph Caryl, a London lecturer and moderate Independent.[47] At any rate, the charge of heresy was first leveled against him years after the end of his lecturing career, which had taken him from the aristocratic parish of St. Martin in the Fields to the equally aristocratic Kensington, with intermittent sojourns at the Gatehouse and the Marshalsea for "glancing ... at the Spanish match."[48] Earlier a John Trundle, who had been one of the lecturers at Christ Church Newgate, was apprehended, according to John Chamberlain, for preaching before "a nest or assembly of Brownists" in Finsbury, just beyond the walls of London.[49] Trundle had been in and out of the London Consistory Court repeatedly from February 1606 until his inhibition and suspension were finally confirmed late in 1607, but during that time only the usual charges of nonconformity—failure to read "public prayer and [administer] the sacraments in the surplice twice a year"—were leveled against him.[50] If Trundle did in fact become a Separatist, it was evidently after (and perhaps as a consequence of) his expulsion from the Church for non-conformity.

There may have been one or two others, but in all the number of true Separatists among the London lecturers was infinitesimal.[51] The ecclesiastical courts, normally vigilant where Separatism was concerned, record no Separatist lecturers in London. Separatist leaders were recruited from among the Puritan clergy, but ideologically they were committed to withdrawal, and theory may have been reinforced in practice by their tendency to recruit followers with little power in parish politics.[52] One way or the other, the parochial lectureship had little to offer them. It was far otherwise for the legions of their orthodox, if compromising, Puritan brethren.

THE LECTURESHIP IN THE LIFE OF THE PURITAN CLERGY

Within the mainstream of Puritanism, a movement clear enough in its central dissatisfaction with the Elizabethan establishment and its commitment to a "Calvinian" or "Reformed" economy of grace, the holding of a lectureship became a customary part of a clerical career.* Few, it is safe to say, preached on so heroic a scale as John Cotton of Boston, who "besides his ordinary lecture every Thursday ... preached thrice more every week; on the week-days, namely on Wednesdays and Thursdays, early in the morning, and on Saturdays at three in the afternoon," and who "kept a daily lecture in his house ... [to which] many pious people in the town would constantly resort."[53] Nevertheless, one would be hard put to recall any well-known Puritan cleric active between 1560 and 1640 who did not lecture at one time or another. Among the first generation, Thomas Cartwright lectured at Warwick, and Travers and Chaderton in London; Anthony Gilby at Ashby-de-la-Zouch, where he was succeeded by Arthur Hildersham; and John Field and Robert Crowley both in London.[54] In later years,

---

* A definition of my "mainstream" in ecclesiastical terms would include at the one extreme the proponents of a modified episcopacy, such as Richard Baxter, and at the other the "nonseparating congregationalists." For a definition of the latter, see Perry Miller, *Orthodoxy in Massachusetts, 1630–1650* (Cambridge, Mass., 1933), pp. 73–147, and for a brief discussion of the problems of definition, see Alan Simpson, *Puritanism in Old and New England* (Chicago, 1955), pp. 1–11. Heylyn's caveat is worth repeating: "Nor am I of the opinion, that Puritan and Calvinian are terms convertible. For though all Puritans are Calvinians both in doctrine and practice, yet all Calvinians are not to be counted as Puritans also; whose practices many of them abhor, and whose inconformities they detest." *Cyprianus Anglicus* (London, 1671), p. 119.

William Ames lectured at Dedham, and William Perkins and Paul Baynes at Great St. Andrew's in Cambridge; "Decalogue" Dodd at Banbury; various members of the clerical cousinhood of Essex Rogerses at Wethersfield, Dedham, and Haverhill; Greenham, Egerton, Preston, Sibbes, and Gouge in London.[55] The point is, of course, that one recalls these Puritans largely because they were famous in their own day, and that their fame rested largely on their preaching and on their subsequently collected and printed sermons. Perkins was perhaps known as much for his theological and casuistic writings and Preston for his abilities as an organizer and coordinator of the Puritan movement;[56] but the reputation of others, such as Chaderton, seems to have rested essentially on their "plain but effectual way of preaching."[57]

The young John Donne, before he himself became one of the most famous preachers of the day, mockingly suggested that the Puritans preached long sermons out of their "zealous Imagination that it is their duty to preach till their Auditory wake."[58] Paradoxically, a Puritan might have flung back the rejoinder that Donne was closer to the truth than he imagined in his wit, for quite literally the Puritan cleric saw himself as called to preach till not only his auditory but all England awoke to its true condition. To permit their congregations to slumber on was to leave them to the devil; the sermon was a call to a life of wakefulness and watchfulness, of wayfaring and warfaring, to an "adventuring of one's life upon the Lord."

Few among the preaching brotherhood had any illusions about the difficulty of their task. Even so powerful a preacher as Richard Baxter, who said that he "stirred up [his] sluggish heart to speak to sinners with some compassion as a dying man to dying men," testified early in his career to the limits of this form of suasion:

But the people [of Bridgnorth] proved a very ignorant, dead-hearted people. ... Though I was in the fervor of my affections and never anywhere preached with more vehement desires of men's conversions ... yet with the generality applause of the preacher was the most of the success of the sermon which I could hear of, and their tippling and ill company and dead-heartedness quickly drowned all.[59]

Yet, though many godly preachers experienced at one time or another the frustrations of an indifferent congregation, and though many must have shared Richard Rogers's periodic "unsettledness" and "unprofitableness," which led to a "want of providing for my lecture," few had reason to question the efficacy of the sermon itself, for their diaries and biographies testify again and again to their great debt to the preached word.[60] Adam Martindale, the Lancashire Puritan cleric, recalled in his old age that he owed his conversion while still a school-boy at his books to a sermon preached by a Mr. Smith, a man of "no great account for his abilities, but pious and serious." Mr. Smith's ser-mon, however, produced unsuspected results, for "he did so lay forth the desperateness and damnableness of a natural estate ... that I was roused to purpose, and this proved like a sharp needle, drawing after a silken thread of comfort in due season." Martindale ever after hon-ored the obscure Mr. Smith as his "spiritual father," not because the sermon led to a close relationship between the two, but because Smith had been the "chief instrument under God" in his conversion.[61] Mar-tindale's story is typical. When Laurence Chaderton was about to retire after half a century of lecturing at St. Clement's, Cambridge, forty clergymen petitioned him to continue, declaring that they owed their conversions to his painful preaching.[62]

As changed men themselves, the Puritan preachers set about pro-ducing a similar change in others from as many pulpits as they could gain access to. They constantly worried about their "liberty," by which they meant "liberty to work," and as Martindale laconically noted, there was "work enough to do." What looms largest in Martindale's catalogue of duties is preaching: two sermons on Sundays to his own congregation plus sermons at funerals and baptisms, at chapel ser-vices in his parish, at the "exercises" in Staffordshire, Lancashire, and Cheshire, and at the lecture in Chester.[63] To lose one's liberty was less a personal disaster than a disaster to one's congregation. News of his suspension from his lectureship produced in Richard Rogers "a deep heaviness," a state to which, it must be admitted, that rather finicky divine was frequently reduced. Nevertheless, though he feared the consequences of this loss of his livelihood, he also lamented that to be "void of a preaching ministry" would lead to the scattering of his people, an end "to all our sweet company and communion"; even for those not among the company of saints, the loss of a preacher would permit the "bad sort" to be "fleshed and hardened in evil."[64]

This very emphasis on preaching, which made holding a lectureship a logical activity, if not an inescapable duty, was at once a source of strength and a source of difficulty for the Puritan minister. As an evangelist he preached a new life, but a new life that implied and in fact required a new social setting—the godly commonwealth. At a time of unprecedented change, when old verities had lost their virtue and old habits of obedience were losing their hold on men's minds— in short, at a time when men were anxiously searching for a new source of stability and certainty—the Puritan economy of grace and salvation offered a compelling answer to their needs.[65] The sermon produced conversion, but conversion was the beginning, not the end, of personal and social transformation. The Puritans were prepared to defend to the last ditch the proposition that "a true, living, and justifying faith, and the Spirit of God justifying, is not extinguished, falleth not away ... in the elect, either finally or totally."[66] But this "comfortable" doc- trine was not intended simply to assuage the anxiety that had created the salvation panic; it was also expected to prepare the godly man to concentrate all his energies on the task of doing God's will on earth.

It was this need for reformation that required a preaching minister. Periodic revival meetings might have sufficed if conversion had been the only goal, but the zealous pursuit of reformation required a pro- gram for living in the world. The attempt to outline such a program produced, on the one hand, such Puritan tracts as Richard Rogers's *Seven Treatises*, "containing such direction as is gathered out of holy scripture, leading and guiding to true happiness, ... in the which, more particularly, true Christians may learn how to lead a godly and comfortable life everyday"; and on the other hand, such works as Robert Bolton's *Instructions for a Right Comforting Afflicted Con- sciences*, which aimed at solving the innumerable problems afflicting the saint in his uneasy attempt to live in a fallen world. The sermon served both to describe the goal and to reinforce the conviction of the godly that it was attainable. Had the godly felt less threatened by the confusion of the times, or had their new patterns of behavior been so familiar as to be habitual, they might have felt less keenly the need for constant preaching. As it was, their experience of "unsettledness" and their fear of backsliding led them to seek, as Rogers put it, a "sweet company and communion" held together by the preached Word.

The consequences for the Puritan divines were twofold: they were at the same time ideological leaders of the Puritan community and leaders of a minority that was barely tolerated by the more or less hostile Established Church. On the one hand, Anglican hostility reinforced their tendency to emphasize preaching, for their role as preachers was the sole basis of their hold on their congregations. On the other hand, they had no alternative but to seek support, patronage, and protection from their lay followers. And this was the source of their dilemma. Their high conception of their function—for were they not true shepherds of their flocks?—implied an office to which they were called by God, hence an office untrammeled by lay interference. Yet their support came exclusively from the laity. In the circumstances, their attitude toward the laity was necessarily ambiguous. In commenting on the activities of the Cromwellian Triers, Ralph Josselin, an Essex Puritan minister, noted in his diary: "Mr. Sparrow preached, he commended and encouraged the Commissioners; for my part I saw no beauty in the day, neither do I joy to see ministers put under the lay power, and thus on their own head."[67]

Having finally been granted the godly magistrate they had prayed for, the Puritans found Cromwell's interference as unwelcome as the bishops' had been and condemned his intrusion into ecclesiastical affairs in terms that echoed the clericalism of their archenemies, the divine-right followers of Archbishop Laud. This ambiguity of attitude and feeling had long been present. In 1573 Edward Dering, the lecturer at St. Paul's, had denounced to the Privy Council those London preachers who in hopes of preferment had courted the bishops by exalting their office: "For while they flatter to get [a] living, they make the pulpit to be contemned."[68] It was an appeal that Dering knew would find sympathetic hearers among the antiprelatical members of the council. Yet three weeks before this attempt to pander to lay prejudice, Dering had written to Lord Burghley: "They [the prince and the lay magistracy] may hinder the minister and make him forget his duty, they cannot profit him in his office and function. He must frame the heart, upon which you cannot set a crown; and edify the soul, which flesh and blood cannot hurt."[69]

The Puritan divines also faced a second and related predicament. Although they were committed to compromise by their decision to remain within the Established Church, compromise was never a Puritan virtue, and they sought in their ministry to dispense as much as possible with those aspects of the prescribed ceremonies and liturgy that seemed to them to lack Biblical precedent. A lectureship, which required only minimal participation in the compromising ministerial functions, should therefore have been a desirable post. More than desirable, indeed, for preaching was the prime duty and function of the godly minister. It was from the pulpit that he appeared in his heroic guise as a prophet speaking the Word of God; it was there that he performed as a divine instrument.

Yet when Ralph Josselin, the Essex Puritan, was offered the lectureship at Hornchurch "to preach twice on the Lord's day, without meddling with other duties," he hesitated until the vicarage at Earls Colne was offered to him, an offer he eagerly accepted.[70] The vicarage was not preferable financially, for both vicarage and lectureship carried stipends of £80 a year. Although a later offer by the corporation of Colchester of a lectureship wrung from Josselin the unhappy supplication "Lord, I am willing to do thee any service, though always afraid of that town as not fit to deal with their wrangling spirits," he certainly had no objection to lecturing and had done so at Earls Colne and later at Wakes Colne and Castle Hedingham.[71] What Earls Colne had to offer besides the salubrious air and the friendship of the Harlakenden family, the principal gentry in the area, was the prestige and security of tenure that a regular benefice provided. The lectureship carried lighter duties, but lecturers were normally appointed on annual contracts, and the minister entering such an arrangement always had to gamble on his ability to retain the support of the laity who appointed and paid him. Although many Puritans lectured at one time or another, the evidence suggests that few resisted the call to a benefice.[72]

This is not simply to say that considerations of personal profit and the desire for professional advancement always triumphed over the dictates of idealism. The issue was more complex. Quite apart from the tension between the role of professional clergyman and the role of a divine instrument immune to worldly interests, and quite apart, too, from the difficulties raised by the question of lay dependency, the Puritan ministers were apparently unable to arrive at a clear and authoritative position on the relative merits of ministering and lecturing. Part of the difficulty arose because they recognized quite correctly that the issue was not solely a theoretical one. In the course of the lengthy deliberations of the Dedham Conference in the 1580's, an association of Puritan ministers from the northern Essex–southern Suffolk region that met approximately once a month, the "godly brethren" considered various aspects of the issue but never came to a definitive judgment. They faced the problem most squarely in 1585, when one of their number, Bartholomew Andrewes, asked whether he should abandon his living at Wenham in order to accept a lectureship at Yarmouth. After lengthy debate the meeting deadlocked. One group maintained, as Mr. Stocton argued, that Andrewes "might not go from being a pastor, which was the higher calling, to be a Teacher [lecturer], which was the inferior"; but "some of the brethren answered, that in these disordered times they thought … it might be, wherein every teacher doth for the peoples' good exhort." An argument premised on what ought to be and another based on what actually pertained clearly had no common ground. As the conference broke up, one of the ministers remarked to Mr. Mayham, the Yarmouth representative, " 'I had as lief they shouldest pluck out mine eye as take from me my pastor,' to whom Mr. Mayham answered, 'But Sir, if you cast out your eye you will give me leave to take it up': and so the brethren ended debating about this matter and Mr. Mayham departed unsatisfied."[73]

In any event, whether the lectureship had a permanent place in a reformed church, or whether a minister should leave a living for a lectureship or a lectureship for a living, were questions that could wait until times were less "disordered." In the meantime, the Puritans' primary concern was their liberty to preach, for given that liberty they could expound the saving Word and stir up the godly to be zealous for reformation.

THE LECTURESHIP IN THE LIFE OF THE PURITAN LAITY

Precisely how many of the laity were ever zealous for the reformation preached by the Puritan ideologues has long been in dispute. M. M. Knappen claimed for the Puritan clergy the support of "the great majority of serious-minded Protestants"—perhaps 15 per cent of the population during the middle years of Elizabeth's reign. R. G. Usher, on the other hand, numbered the Puritan adherents at "perhaps fifty thousand able-bodied men," or at most a mere 2 per cent of the population.[74] Both estimates are highly conjectural. A study of the lectureships offers another, if only approximate, means by which the pervasiveness of Puritanism among the laity may be measured, for the very existence of a lectureship is in most instances an indication of lay demand for a preaching ministry.

In any attempt to estimate lay commitment to Puritanism it is necessary to specify which aspects of the clerical program the laity willingly subscribed to and promoted. Usher is undoubtedly correct in asserting that the full disciplinarian program of the Elizabethan Presbyterians commanded very little support among the laity. The failure of the Presbyterian majority in the Westminster Assembly to commit the Long Parliament to instituting a full-blown Presbyterian system, even at the urging of the Scottish commissioners, suggests that lay Puritans never did have much stomach for such a scheme. However, a layman who might have little desire to exchange a "pope" in Lambeth for a pope in his own parish might nevertheless object strenuously to the deprivation or suspension of his minister or lecturer for nonconformity. When John Field, a leading strategist of the Elizabethan Presbyterian movement, was suspended from his lectureship at St. Mary Aldermary in London, his parishioners petitioned for his return not because they favored Field's disciplinarian notions but because of Field's "faithful pains taken amongst us, ... preaching purely the word of God, and catechizing our youth, teaching obedience to God and our prince, and keeping us in great good order." In fact, they maintained, he was not even guilty of nonconformity, for "the things urged by law, whatsoever his opinions be, were never hindered, impugned, or any ways resisted by him, but were duly kept and observed in our Church."[75] Many parishioners who supported their Puritan minister for the sake of his preaching must have had little knowledge of and less interest in the niceties of ecclesiastical government that troubled so many clerical consciences. One gentleman is said to have remarked to Richard Rogers, the lecturer at Wethersfield, Essex, "Mr. Rogers, I like you and your company very well, but you are so precise."*

Among the many reforms requested by the Puritans a preaching ministry usually came first, for almost all Puritan schemes for the reformation of the Church considered such a ministry essential.[76] Moreover, the laity need not wait for enabling legislation or for a

---

* Rogers is said to have replied: "O Sir, I serve a precise God." *Two Elizabethan Puritan Diaries,* ed. M. M. Knappen (Chicago, 1933), p. 34, n. 31.

change in heart by their prince or bishop. John More, the city lecturer at Norwich, begged the assembled Norfolk justices of the peace not only to use their influence in Parliament on behalf of a preaching ministry, but to act on their own: "If you will be saved, get you preachers into your parishes, ... bestow your labor, cost and travel to get them. Ride for them, run for them, stretch your purses to maintain them."[77] Many Englishmen were receptive to such pleas. Sir Francis Hastings, one of the Earl of Huntingdon's younger brothers, wrote in 1602: "To further a good people to a good minister, ... a laboring speaking minister to teach them, is a bond of duty I may never forget, and a work of duty I must ever be ready to perform."[78] Urban elites in some instances apparently did not wait for the promptings of preachers but seized the initiative as soon as Elizabeth came to the throne. Thomas Lever, the old Edwardian reformer, had no sooner returned to England in 1559 from his exile at Zurich than he was invited "to proclaim the gospel to them at Coventry."[79] By 1562, if not earlier, the corporation at Leicester had not only provided Wednesday and Friday lectures but also ordered that at least one person from every household attend them.[80]

Such compulsory measures were seldom called for. By the early seventeenth century, if not before, Englishmen had developed an astonishing appetite for sermons, and this appetite was not confined to Puritans alone. In 1625, when the plague raged in London, Parliament responded by holding a solemn fast. Walter Yonge, the Devonshire Puritan squire, noted that the exercise of the King and Lords lasted six hours. As for the House of Commons, Yonge recorded with what must have been a mixture of pride and awe that the members were subjected to seven hours of preaching in the course of an exercise that "continued full nine hours, during all which time it was observed that not any one man of their company fainted."[81] If such a collection of the godly and the indifferent as the House of Commons contained found seven hours of sermons an appropriate measure in time of plague, it is easy to imagine the role the sermon played in the life of the Puritan laity, for whom diseases of the body were secondary to the many threats to the soul.

The Puritan layman, like his clerical counterpart, frequently ascribed his conversion to an efficacious sermon. Henry Newcome, a Puritan divine of Lancashire, claimed that several persons dated their "first awakening" from a lecture series he preached on Deuteronomy 32:29, and that the Roundhead Major Smethwick, who first "began at that time to be serious, . . . used to call it his birth day."[82] The orthodox Anglican charge that Puritan practice threatened "to shrink up all religion into preaching" was a fair one. While the Anglican Lady Katherine Paston urged her son William, a student at Corpus Christi College, Cambridge, to "meditate of all those things which may enlighten thine understanding in the knowledge of the right receiving of that blessed sacrament," the Puritan Brilliana Harley lamented to her brother Edward, a student at Magdalen Hall, Oxford, that in those declining times (1639), when one had to learn to lay down one's life for Christ, her brother did not have the Word of God preached to him in the right manner.[83] In Puritan circles sermons were called for not only at baptisms and funerals, where they were traditional, but even at festivities where they quite clearly were not customary fare. When Lady Russell arranged the wedding of her son, Thomas Posthumous Hoby, to Margaret Sidney, she dispensed with the usual music and dancing. As Posthumous rather primly wrote to his cousin, Anthony Bacon, he sought "only to please the Beholders with a Sermon and a Dinner, and myself with beholding my Mistress." That dancing should be eliminated was perhaps natural in view of the bridegroom's embarrassingly short stature, but that a sermon inflicted on an aristocratic wedding party should be regarded as a source of pleasure demonstrates the power of Puritanism to modify traditional modes of behavior.[84]

Puritanism drew its converts from many ranks in a highly stratified society, recruiting its numbers from as far down the social scale as the rural copyholder and the urban artisan, as well as from the upper ranges of status—merchants, gentry, and peers. When the convert became a Puritan, he entered a society that was insecure in its newness and uncomfortable in its coexistence with the old society. Unlike the French Huguenots, the English lay Puritans produced no theoreticians from their own ranks until the generation of John Milton and Lord Brooke. Before the 1640's they depended for ideological guidance on their preachers. They needed constant exposure to the pulpit, one suspects, for much the same reason that the mid–twentieth-century Chinese peasant requires constant exposure to posters, parades, speeches, and radio: without repeated reinforcement they were in danger of slipping back into traditional ways of thinking and acting. The range of media available for mass communication is infinitely greater in the twentieth century than it was three or four hundred years ago, but a new society's need for some means of continuous communication between the authorities and their constituency has not changed. The analogy should not be pressed too far. Unlike the Chinese Communist Party, the Puritan clergy never seized the reins of power; instead they depended on generating a conscious need for their message that would be translated into an active demand for their services. In this part of their program, more than any other, the preachers were eminently successful.

Hence, though the transforming power of a single sermon was universally recognized, the mark of the lay Puritan was his demand for constant preaching. Even the sophisticated and worldly Robert Greene, "being new come from Italy," testified that he had once felt "the terror of God's judgments ... in Saint Andrews Church in the City of Norwich, at a Lecture or Sermon then preached by a godly learned man." By the end of the lecture Greene had undergone the experience described so often in the Puritan diaries and biographies of the time and found himself calling on God to "have mercy upon me, and send me grace to amend and become a new man." Yet Greene, the dramatist and connoisseur of "the most horrible cosenages of the common Cony-catchers," was not a Puritan. Whereas the Puritan Ralph Josselin, as a young man, was accustomed after a sermon "to walk home alone, not with other boys or company ... and meditate upon the sermon and example myself by the same," Greene returned to his "copsemates,"

to whom when I had discovered that I sorrowed for my wickedness of life, and that the preacher's words had taken a deep impression on my conscience, they fell upon me in jesting manner, calling me Puritan and Precisian ... with such other scoffing terms, that ... the good and wholesome lesson I had learned went quite out of my remembrance: so that I fell again with the dog to my old vomit.[85]

The lay Puritan was as familiar as Greene with the temptation to return like the dog to his vomit, for the Puritan neither lacked self-awareness nor lived a cloistered life. The situation described by the Lancashire squire Nicholas Assheton in his journal must have had its counterpart in most Puritan communities. Assheton, born about 1590, was apparently the son of a Puritan, for he tells how his father defended a local curate who administered the sacraments without a surplice. Nicholas married the daughter of a neighboring Puritan squire, Richard Greenacres, and one of his sons was later an elder in the Lancashire Presbyterian classis. Yet Nicholas himself, despite his apparent good standing in the Puritan community and unflagging attendance at sermons and lectures—there was a Tuesday "exercise" of two sermons kept at Downham, the Asshetons' parish—could not have numbered himself among the local saints, for the traditional life of the rural squire was too obviously to his liking. His journal is little more than a record of fox hunting, horse racing, dicing, drinking, and feasting.[86] Serious matters occasionally intruded, but in the main Nicholas subscribed to Viscount Conway's dictum: "We eat, and drink and rise up to play and this is to live like a gentleman, for what is a gentleman but his pleasure?"[87] Many a Puritan community must have had its Nicholas Assheton, a man completely happy in his place and time, a man for whom the Puritan's self-discipline was unnecessary because conformity to the traditional life was so natural and easy.

To the true Puritan such a life seemed chaotic and directionless. The morbid introspection detectable in so many Puritan diaries suggests the strain and effort that went into the attempt to live as a pilgrim in an alien world. But consciousness of alienation does not necessarily confer knowledge of a life in which peace may be found. Like Bunyan's Christian, with the burden on his back and the insinuations of Pliable and Worldly Wiseman in his ear, the Puritan found it all too easy to turn out of the way; and he had as great a need as Christian for the directions of Evangelist. Lady Margaret Hoby's response to the fear of backsliding was a continual round of spiritual exercises, which began in the morning with prayer and ended at night with a "lecture," apparently an exercise for the family conducted by the Hobys' chaplain, Richard Rhodes. Even in the midst of such rigors Lady Margaret was constantly watchful, for after hearing two sermons on a Sunday she could still record in her diary, "The devil laboreth to hinder my profitable hearing of the word." Yet, when self-examination led her to detect a "coldness to all spiritual exercises," she attributed the absence of "spiritual Comfort" to the lack of "continual preaching" and promptly set about remedying the deficiency by attending five sermons in the next five days.[88]

The piety of a Lady Margaret required a lecturing clergy, for the traditional institutions of the Church were incapable of providing sermons in the quantity deemed necessary. And if lecturing came to be one of the distinguishing marks of the Puritan clergyman, diligent attendance at sermons came to be habitual among the Puritan laity. One of the ways in which Sir Simonds D'Ewes thought he differed from the "brute creatures" who attended church with him was that he had learned as a schoolboy "to take notes in writing at sermons, and so to become a rational hearer." His youthful training only whetted his appetite, for by the time he went up to Cambridge, Sunday was devoted almost entirely to the feast of "rational hearing," which, however, seems to have allowed no time for attendance at the ordinary Prayer Book service:

[It] being Sunday, having heard one sermon in our College chapel and afterwards another in St. Mary's in the forenoon, I went in the afternoon to another church in Cambridge, where my kind friend, Mr. Jeffray,... preached, being chosen by the town ... for their lecturer there.... Every sermon was orthodox and useful, and therefore after supper I busied myself in enlarging and correcting such notes as I had taken at the afternoon sermon.[89]

As a public action that revealed the inward character of the saint, lecture-going became a commonplace, and accounts of it abound in Puritan biography. Lucy Hutchinson, for example, notes that her mother "was a constant frequenter of weekday lectures, and a great lover and encourager of good ministers"—proof, if any were needed, that the "care of the worship and service of God" was "her principal care."[90] So, too, in the course of a funeral sermon for the godly London merchant Sir John Parker, Thomas Gataker observed that on "week days, once or twice at least, ordinarily he frequented the ministry of some of those of best note about the City."[91]

The primacy attached to sermons and lectures by the Puritans was entirely logical, given their special requirements; it may even be argued that the peculiar balance (or imbalance) struck by the Puritans in their religious practices was inevitable, given the Reformation emphasis on the authority and efficacy of Scripture. Be that as it may, the impact of such practices on the Established Church was profoundly disturbing. First of all, the ecclesiastical hierarchy's effort to maintain the parish as the focus of lay religious activity was continually compromised by the Puritan determination to attend sermons where they could be found. "When she was but young," wrote John Shaw in commendation of his wife, "she was much unsatisfied with (one called) a reading minister in Brampton parish, and therefore she went usually every Lord's day to Chesterfield (which was two long miles) to hear a faithful preacher."[92] The result was to move the center of religious loyalty from the permanent structure of the Church—that is, the parish—to the personality and capacity of the preacher.

A second consequence followed. To the degree that the Established Church made the liturgy its central activity, the intelligence and morals of the parish priest were of little importance in any ultimate sense. The sermon, however, appealed to the will and the intellect, and required an educated clergy capable of speaking with moral authority. Further, a lifetime spent listening to sermons—and not only listening as a passive audience, but writing down the heads of the sermon in notebooks and later rehearsing the sermon as part of the family's religious exercises—inevitably produced a knowledgeable and critical laity with definite ideas about preaching and preachers.[93] John Blakiston, a Newcastle Mercer, was haled before the Court of High Commission at Durham by his parson, to whom he is alleged to have said: "I will maintain that in your last sermon at Allhallows, you delivered seven errors." Yeldard Alvey, the parson, was an Arminian and evidently had no intention of taking lessons in divinity from a Puritan layman, but although Alvey won his case and Blakiston was sentenced in 1639 to excommunication and to pay a fine of £100, there is no evidence that the sentence was carried out, for the court ceased to sit a few months later. In 1641 Blakiston, as a Member of Parliament for Newcastle, was able to swear to the truth of a petition to Parliament against Alvey, and the latter was shortly after sequestered from his living as a delinquent. Apparently others had formed unfavorable opinions of Alvey and only needed the opportunity to express them. As for Blakiston, the destruction of Alvey's career was only the beginning, for he had strong political convictions as well and lived long enough to sign King Charles's death warrant.[94]

The Long Parliament's willingness to entertain petitions against the so-called "malignant" Anglican clergy led to a veritable flood of complaint and condemnation. Although it would be a mistake to accept the petitions as solid evidence of the facts to which they attest (for the presence of counter-petitions is sufficient to raise the question of their veracity), they do point both to the critical spirit Puritan practice had bred and to the importance the laity attached to plentiful and profitable preaching. One of the most frequent charges leveled against the malignant clergyman was that "he neither preached nor catechized on the Lord's day in the afternoon, nor suffered his parishioners to have any to perform the same, though they have desired it at their own charge." Since in this case the accused was also charged with being "a common haunter of taverns and ale-houses" and a practitioner of "superstitious bowing and cringing at the Communion Table," it is to be assumed that the parishioners were less concerned with his failure to preach than with his refusal to permit them to hire a lecturer.[95] No less reprehensible to their Puritan parishioners were parsons like William Fairfax, rector of St. Peter Cornhill in London, who is said to have charged his vestry £50 for giving them leave to have a Sunday afternoon lecture. It was only to be expected, or at least easily believed, that such a man should "prophane the Sabbath-day by playing cards" and should haunt "the company of women, notoriously suspected of incontinency."[96] Sermons or lectures on Sabbath afternoons were of vital importance, the parishioners of Maidstone, Kent, informed the House of Commons, "necessary occasions hindering servants and others in the forenoons . . . by reason whereof much ignorance, lewdness, and disobedience doth reign amongst us."[97] Indeed, at a time when the head of a household was responsible for the manners and morals of his servants, as well as of his children, there were quite practical reasons for condemning the clergyman who would neither preach himself nor permit a lecture on Sunday afternoons. In 1636 a Puritan observer noted that owing to the suppression of Sunday lectures and the permissiveness of the Book of Sports, "Masters of families complain exceedingly they cannot contain their servants from excursions into all prophane sports and pastimes on the Lord's day."[98]

The godly preachers aimed always at producing a laity zealous for reformation; had their sermons done no more than create laymen who could judge and criticize the preached Word, there would have been no Puritan movement. The summons to a reformation was a call to action, first to transform the individual into an instrument fit to serve the divine will, and then to employ that instrument to transform all of society. The opportunity to experiment with the politics of a godly commonwealth did not come until the 1640's, by which time the Puritan movement was old in years and rich in experience—not, unfortunately, in building a new Jerusalem, but rather in the art of surviving in Babylon. Doubtless it can be argued that Puritanism survived because neither prince nor bishop sought to extirpate it with any consistency or efficiency. But this is at best a negative explanation and fails to account for either the existence or the nature of the movement itself. What made Puritanism more than an attitude or a peculiar religious style, and what necessitated the development of at least the rudiments of organization, was the need to recruit, finance, and protect a preaching ministry. During the years before the Long Parliament was summoned, this was the prerequisite of survival and the minimal definition of zeal. As William Camden wrote of Henry Hastings, the Elizabethan Earl of Huntingdon, "Being a zealous puritan, [he] much wasted his estate by a lavish support of those hot-headed preachers."[99]

On the other hand, it need not be supposed that the Puritan laity acted only from high-minded motives. Episcopal interference invariably aroused the anticlerical and antiprelatical feelings that seem to have been latent at most among the laity during the generations immediately after the Reformation. In 1584 Sir Francis Knollys castigated Archbishop Whitgift for persecuting and silencing "the zealous preachers of the gospel," for although the Queen's protection had been given as an excuse for the archbishop's actions, Sir Francis saw only an attempt by the bishops to arrogate for themselves an absolute authority "without controlment of Prince or Council."[100]

A second mundane motive that appears to have led many of the laity to support the godly preachers was a desire to substitute control by the lay magistrates for episcopal discipline. Whereas many of the laity feared every move of the bishops to discipline the parochial clergy as presaging a return to pre-Reformation prelacy, lay magistrates on occasion were not averse to interfering in parochial affairs and interjecting themselves into clerical disputes. Just as the Crown had established its supremacy over the national Church at the time of the Reformation, so local magistrates sometimes pretended to an analogous power over the clergy of their neighborhoods. After a Suffolk minister, in a sermon at Bury St. Edmunds, had disparaged "the godly preachers of the town and country," calling them "vipers, serpents, stingers, and unsatiable beasts" and rather colorfully comparing them to "unbridled colts rushing through the whole hedge," a local justice of the peace summoned the minister to a conference, convinced that "he sought by all the terms he could devise to sever the hearts of the people from their faithful ministers." The minister, apparently anticipating trouble, appeared before the justice with his brother, the Bishop of Norwich's commissary; but the justice failed to be intimidated by this show of ecclesiastical power and bound over the minister to appear before the justices of assize the following day. When the Bishop of Norwich finally intervened in order to save some shreds of ecclesiastical independence, the impenitent justices attributed his intervention to "too great malice," rather than to any desire to reform "any amisses in us."[101]

A third mundane consideration was also doubtless in the minds of many of the Puritan laity who supported the godly preachers. The long-standing reluctance of the laity, whether Puritan or not, to pay tithes was notorious, and in all probability much of this reluctance can be attributed simply to niggardliness. However, in the 1580's Philip Stubbes argued that whoever supported a benefice financially was entitled to name its incumbent, and many laymen may have favored lectureships in part because those who paid the lecturer's stipend also controlled his tenure at that post.[102] Certainly some contemporaries believed so, for in a pamphlet published in 1648 a disgruntled Anglican minister charged that "purse-proud Londoners, accounting tithes but as a gift, ... would rather spend at law, or give to a lecturer of their own choice twice as much, as their full tithe come to."[103]

Lay intervention of various kinds in ecclesiastical affairs was a necessary consequence of the English Reformation, but whereas much of the anticlericalism of the time demanded no more than a circumscribing of clerical pretensions, Puritanism, with its demand for a preaching clergy, led to a far-reaching modification of a variety of traditional rights and relationships. If salvation depended on preaching, all laymen had a legitimate interest in the minister's ability to preach. Episcopal ordination was not a sufficient warranty, for priests were no longer interchangeable: what counted was preaching ability, not simply priesthood. Nor was presentation by a patron a sufficient warranty, for the patron, particularly if he was not a resident of the parish, might be led to his choice by a number of motives, among which the spiritual welfare of the parishioners might scarcely figure. The ultimate tendency of Puritanism was to reduce the complex ecclesiastical structure

to the single and simple relationship of preacher and congregation—
to produce, in fact, a congregational system. But this happened in the
long run, and it was a tendency, not necessarily a conscious policy. In
the short run the consequence of the Puritans' determined search for
a preaching ministry was a piecemeal invasion of traditional rights
and a gradual erosion of customary relationships.

One of the least dramatic but most significant changes occurred in
the relationship between patrons of livings and parishioners of those
livings. Theoretically the inhabitants of a parish had no say in the
choice of their minister, and the patron's right to present was limited
only by the need to obtain episcopal institution and induction of his
candidate. Theory, however, was not necessarily practice. When the
inhabitants of the manor and town of Hemsby, Norfolk, found that
their minister "by reason of his age, his gifts failing him," was no
longer able to preach, they canvassed the local talent and discovered
in Ludham some eight or ten miles away "a grave discreet and learned
preacher ... of whose sufficiency of learning and doctrine we have had
good trial amongst us." Then as "humble farmers and dutifull tenants
of Hemsby" they addressed Sir Nathaniel Bacon, the lord of the
manor and patron of the living, on behalf of their candidate, stating
that they aimed only "at the glory of God, the comfort of our own
souls, and the good of our Christian brethren," and requesting that
Bacon designate their choice as successor to their aging minister. With
all due allowance for the deferential style of the "humble suppliants"
of Hemsby, the petitioners' request was a presumptuous one. Nevertheless, Sir Nathaniel, nearing seventy himself, had grown old in the
service of the godly cause as well as in the service of the Crown, and
his reply to his "loving friends and tenants" expressed a willingness
to satisfy their desires.[104]

Puritan patrons and parishioners seem to have usually been able to
reach amicable agreements, for their interests were not fundamentally
in conflict. It was less easy for the episcopal hierarchy to accommodate
itself to what appeared to be thinly disguised attempts to circumvent
episcopal control, if not outright invasions of ecclesiastical jurisdiction.
Caught as the bishop was between the insistent demands of the laity
and the internal requirements of ecclesiastical government, his lot was
not a happy one. In November 1615, for example, the mayor and
chamber of Exeter wrote to Bishop William Cotton nominating John

Hazard as preacher of the recently endowed Bodley lectureship and asking for episcopal approval. The conditions of the lectureship were to all appearances unexceptionable. Lawrence Bodley, the donor, was a scion of a prominent Exeter family and had been a canon of the Cathedral of Exeter and a popular preacher in the city. His will had provided that the lecturer chosen by the city be "allowed for his sufficiency and conformity according to the law of the realm by the Bishop of the diocese or the Archbishop of Canterbury." Nevertheless, Bishop Cotton, whose relations with the city had been punctuated by occasional clashes, not only refused to give his permission, but, in the eyes of the chamber, did so "without any just cause." The mayor and chamber promptly wrote to Archbishop Abbot "shewing the refusal of the Bishop [and] requesting his grace's allowance," and in addition authorized a payment of £10 to Hazard for his expenses in pursuing the matter. By April 1616, Hazard was back with the archbishop's license. Subsequently, in an interview in which his mounting irritation is evident, Bishop Cotton sought to reassert his authority and control. Checked by the archbishop's license, the bishop floundered from one objection to another. First he said that the Bodley lecture would interfere with the city lectures already established. Next he complained that the lecture, because it was open to all the citizens of Exeter, would infringe on the pew rights of the parishioners of St. Peter's, where the Bodley lecture was to be preached. Then, having at first denied that he was obliged to show cause for refusing his approval, the bishop charged Hazard with preaching "false doctrine." Finally, he objected that Hazard was unable to produce letters "demissory" from the Bishop of Bristol or of Bath and Wells.

Some or all of these may have been real objections that the bishop had to the terms of the lectureship and to Hazard as a preacher, but underlying them all one senses the bishop's frustration with an institution he could not control and with a city whose will he could at best temporarily obstruct but never overcome.[105] As Bishop Laud later wrote in a letter to the Earl of Mulgrave concerning a chapel that the inhabitants of Hammersmith wished to erect, "I shall be very unwilling to give way to any popular nomination, [for] I have been beaten and forced to understand that some men under these titles bring in notorious disturbers of the peace of the Church." Instead Laud asked to be entrusted with the patronage of the chapel himself. "If they plead that they allow the maintenance, and therefore should have the nomination, I must answer that they give that allowance for their ease, not that they should dispose of the Bishop's office."[106]

By constantly preaching the need for reformation the Puritan ministers undoubtedly encouraged the laity to assert themselves in ecclesiastical affairs. Ultimately some laymen accepted the logic of such encouragement and emancipated themselves from the clerical order completely: the Quakers, a lay religious society that emerged at the end of the 1640's, conducted the most conspicuous experiment of this sort. The Puritans, however, had no intention of dispensing with their ideological guides, and turned instead to patronizing and protecting those ministers within the Church who answered their needs. It was, in fact, the endeavor to obtain their own ministry that brought together lay Puritans from almost every rank and order in English society, and that led them not only to exploit the traditional channels of patronage based on office, kinship, and personal loyalty but to develop new forms of association based on their common ideological commitment. Indeed, it was the attempt to overcome the difficulties in the way of obtaining a preaching ministry that gave the Puritan movement what unity and coherence it had.

Long before the Puritans appeared the laity had possessed rights of patronage over a variety of ecclesiastical benefices, and laymen had used their influence to protect unorthodox preachers: John of Gaunt's patronage of Wycliffe is a famous early example. What was new was the Puritans' organized and systematic effort to exploit influence and patronage on behalf of a growing number of clergy who had in common with each other and with their patrons only their commitment to Puritanism. The Puritan connection could transcend the limits of the older personal following because of its very impersonality; the Puritans gave their loyalty to certain principles, not to a commanding ego, and therefore viewed themselves as the impersonal agents of a divine will. "We bless God for you in particular," wrote Stanley Gower, the minister of Brampton Brian, to Sir Robert Harley, "whose zeal is not reckoned in the country amongst the thirty, but amongst the first three; yet do we behold you all but as several tools in God's hands to make up the watch of his church, now almost spoiled."[107]

Sir Robert Harley's correspondence illustrates the variety of services the zealous patron performed. In 1613 Thomas Pierson, an Emmanuel graduate whom Harley had presented to the family living at Brampton Brian the year before, was summoned before Francis Godwin, the Bishop of Hereford, and reproached for his nonconformity. Negotiations dragged on for the next three years, at the end of which the exasperated bishop, declaring that he would not jeopardize his bishopric for the sake of a nonconformist, gave Pierson two months to conform. Harley tactfully wrote a letter commending the bishop for his patience, and accompanied a later letter with a present of a pet doe. Within a few weeks Pierson was able to report that he had dined with the bishop, who used him "very kindly," and the Harley family continued to enjoy the preacher's ministrations until his death in 1633.[108]

Many Puritan patrons shielded their parish ministers from the full effects of episcopal displeasure, but Harley was strategically placed to do much more, since he was influential both in Brampton, his family seat, and in London, where he served for extended periods as Master of the Mint. It is worth noting that Harley's first London residence was in the parish of St. Anne Blackfriars during the period when two famous Puritan preachers, Stephen Egerton and William Gouge, occupied that pulpit; when he moved in the later 1620's to a house in St. Mary Aldermanbury, he entered into close and friendly relationships with two curates and lecturers there—Thomas Taylor and Taylor's successor after his death in 1632, John Stoughton. Surrounded by some of the most eminent preachers of the day, Harley functioned as a kind of clearinghouse for Puritans seeking livings and patrons seeking preachers. In 1627 his brother-in-law, Sir Edward Conway, who had earlier helped the Puritan John Davenport to the living of St. Lawrence Jewry, wrote to Harley requesting "a good preacher."[109] Some years later a friend from the west of England wrote recommending five ministers. One of them was described in the letter as "not conformable"; another, Thomas Porter, later lectured briefly at St. Lawrence Jewry, the parish immediately south of St. Mary Aldermanbury, where Harley then lived.[110]

Harley's correspondence was not limited to his friends and relations in London or along the Welsh border. The Puritan Thomas Hill, Fellow of Emmanuel and lecturer at St. Andrew, Cambridge, wrote in favor of David Ensing, also a Fellow of Emmanuel, who had the additional recommendation that he was well known to John Stoughton, the preacher at Aldermanbury.[111] Later, in reply to a letter from Peter

Thatcher, the rector of St. Edmund, Salisbury, who wrote requesting help to a new living, Stoughton stated that Harley had secured an offer of a benefice and urged Thatcher to accept it.[112]

One appointment that Harley suggested was evidently intended not so much to secure a happy match between a zealous patron and a godly preacher as to save a friend from what Harley clearly regarded as an unfortunate enthusiasm for error. In 1631 a benefice in the gift of the Crown fell vacant, the appointment to which depended on Lord Herbert of Cherbury's recommendation. Harley wrote to Lord Herbert, a friend of long standing, urging the candidacy of John Brinsley, the son of a famous nonconformist who had been curate to Arthur Hildersham, the Puritan parson of Ashby-de-la-Zouch. John Brinsley the younger, an Emmanuel graduate, followed in his father's footsteps and became a popular Puritan preacher. He was elected town lecturer at Great Yarmouth in 1625, but by 1631 he had been dismissed from that post, following a successful effort by the dean and chapter of Norwich Cathedral to reassert their right to appoint the Yarmouth preacher, and was leading a precarious existence as a preacher at the Dutch Church, where he had the support of a group of Yarmouth citizens who were unreconciled to his dismissal. Harley's motive in settling on such an odd choice for his philosophical friend is clearly stated in his letter to Brinsley: "His Lordship says he loves a puritan but not a predestinator, wherein I doubt not but God will give you wisdom to let his Lordship know that the mystery of Godliness is not to give liberty to presume to Him, but a restraint from Him."[113] During the 1640's Harley continued his active patronage of Puritan divines and was instrumental in establishing the joint lectureship at Hereford Cathedral. When the churches of Leominster were reformed at the end of the first civil war, the Committee for Plundered Ministers ordered Harley to nominate the requisite number of "orthodox and godly divines" to fill the vacancies.[114]

Although the wide circle of Sir Robert Harley's clerical correspondents demonstrates the pervasiveness of the Puritan connection, Sir Robert himself dispensed his patronage along traditional lines, depending heavily on his friends and neighbors in London and Hereford. Doubtless the Puritan gentry and merchants, exercising patronage in customary ways, were the main props of the Puritan movement, but the piecemeal efforts of godly individuals and town corporations were obviously unequal to the task of supplying a preaching ministry. The ultimate answer was institutional and political: Harley's parson, Stanley Gower, was neither the first nor the last to suggest that "the fault is not personal but official, and to [have] redress the government must be set upon a new base."[115] Being an impatient people, the Puritans experimented with whatever devices came to hand until their ultimate answer could be found.

In 1567 the Earl of Leicester secured letters patent incorporating a group of Puritan grandees in the Midlands as governors of the possessions and revenues of the "Preachers of the Gospel" in Warwickshire.[116] What the governors actually governed, if anything, is unknown, but the terms of the patent suggest a scheme to help the Puritan preachers, perhaps along the lines of the later Feoffees for Impropriations. John Shaw, the Yorkshire Puritan divine, described a later and somewhat less obscure effort by the laity to plant preachers in "dark corners." After earning his M.A. at Cambridge in 1630, Shaw accepted a lectureship at Brampton, Derbyshire.

During my stay at Brampton, I went up to London, and at the entreaty of some friends, I preached there, when some of the Devonshire merchants heard, and resolved (as they afterwards told me) that if it was possible they would prevail with me to send me (as the man whom they pitched on) to preach at a barren plaze, viz. Chimleigh [Chulmleigh], a market town in Devonshire.[117]

The group of west country merchants, according to Shaw's report, customarily established a lecture in some town that lacked a preaching minister and maintained the lecturer for three years at their own cost. If by that time the lecturer had gained local support, the merchants recruited a new preacher and chose a new place to send him. Otherwise the old lecturer was simply moved to the new location for another trial of three years. Shaw was impressed by their pious intentions and lectured at Chulmleigh for three years, but in 1636 the lectureship came to an end, owing, Shaw asserted, to complaints made by some bishops, "especially by Dr. Laud." Apparently the organization of Devonshire merchants shared the authorities' suspicions of organized attempts by the laity to control patronage—suspicions that led in 1632 to the prosecution of the Feoffees for Impropriations. Shaw rather disingenuously questioned the basis of the authorities' complaint against the merchants' activities, "as if they planted in the several counties puritanical and nonconforming preachers."[118]

Had the Englishmen of the time been given to coining slogans, that of the Puritan laity would undoubtedly have been "a preacher in every parish"; whether the preacher was a minister or a lecturer was a matter of relative indifference. That they failed in this, their cardinal aim, was due to insufficient resources and to official opposition, not to any want of trying. Indeed, their patronage had a powerful impact on Church and society precisely because they worked earnestly to further a cause, not simply to advance individual protégés. Lucy Hutchinson, who was one of the shrewder observers of the time, if no more objective than most of her contemporaries, noted that "many of wit and parts, discontented when they could not obtain the preferments their ambition gaped at, would declare themselves of the puritan party ... [and] would put on a form of godliness, finding devout people that way so liberal to them."[119] Such opportunism was possible only where social relationships, such as that of patron and client, depended on shared principles rather than personal favoritism.

Lucy Hutchinson's observation also suggests that despite its embattled status the Puritan connection was a powerful one; otherwise it would not have been attractive to the merely ambitious. Of the many kinds of patronage relied on by the Puritan movement, the lectureships were the most conspicuous, designed as they were to serve the Puritans' immediate spiritual needs. In all probability Stanley Gower exaggerated when he reported to Sir Robert Harley that of the 225 churches and chapels in Herefordshire, of which he claimed the bishop and dean and chapter presented to 100, only twenty had "constant preachers," and not one of the twenty owed his benefice to clerical patronage.[120] Whether Gower's estimates were true or not, the Puritans perceived the Crown, the Church, and most of the laity as using their ecclesiastical patronage to no real purpose. The lectureship provided an immediate short-term remedy. Only later, after the hierarchy and the Crown had rebuffed a generation of Puritans bent on continuing the reform begun in 1559, did the lectureship come to be viewed as a long-term solution to the ills of the Church, a change in attitude manifested in a rising number of permanently endowed lectureships.

In London there was notably little opportunity for developing the type of Puritan connection that predominated elsewhere. Here, in the only major city in the realm, the unfavorable balance of patronage imputed by Gower to Herefordshire actually existed. Whereas Bancroft claimed in 1604 that five out of every six benefices in England were in the gift of lay patrons, in London in the same period the hierarchy (the Archbishop of Canterbury, the Bishop of London, the dean and chapter of St. Paul's, etc.) presented to 62 out of the 111 city parishes.[121] Furthermore, of the remaining 49 some 18 belonged to the Crown, many of whose nominations (perhaps one-third) were made at the behest of the Bishop of London.[122] In short, between 60 and 70 per cent of the patronage of the city was permanently beyond the grasp of the laity, barring purchase or expropriation, and therefore beyond the power of the Puritans to manipulate in their own interest. Because the lay Puritans in London, according to the author of *Mercurius Civicus*, "found very few of the settled clergy here in the city (except Dr. Gough, M. Jackson, Votier, Simons, Walker, and a very few more) compliant with their endeavors, they labored by all means possible to introduce that gibbus, or excrescency of the clergy, called lecturers."[123] By the late 1630's, after three generations of Puritan activity, only about 10 per cent of the London incumbents were Puritan preachers, yet the city was notoriously hostile to Laudian Anglicanism. Richard Montagu, who was later to become a bishop, sought in 1625 to dissuade his friend John Cosin from preaching at Paul's Cross with a dire warning: "For cui bono fini? You cannot hold against the faction: strong, fierce, potent, especially there. . . . I never came at the Cross. I never will. It should do no good but my body harm, my reputation hazard, my cause hurt. For the City, you know, furioso more calvinisat."[124] The hysterical tone of Montagu's warning was not due entirely to his perfervid imaginings; had he wanted evidence, he could have pointed to some seventy parishes in that year with active lectureships.

The lectureship was not the only manifestation of the Puritan laity's zeal for reformation. Certainly in the long run the impact of Puritanism on England was felt most strongly in the realm of the spirit, not in particular institutional arrangements. But in the period from 1560 to 1662 the lectureship was undoubtedly the most conspicuous evidence of the Puritan laity's driving determination to obtain a godly, "painful," preaching ministry.

2

Preaching and Politics

IN an age when printing was still the only means of mass communication, and a means often obstructed by censorship and illiter-
acy, preaching understandably had a potency that it has largely lost
since. In an age, moreover, when theology still provided the basis
not only for cosmology but also for politics, when, as Sir John Eliot
observed in 1625, "Religion it is that keeps the subject in obedience,"[1]
preaching necessarily had political implications. Despite the radical
and disruptive uses to which Christianity had been put during the
Reformation, it remained inconceivable to most men that a truly secular society could survive; the fate of a society of atheists, as the preachers never tired of saying, was the destruction justly visited by God on
Sodom.[2] That Christianity was fundamentally conservative in its social
and political implications was a commonplace; that preaching was the
means of inculcating its lessons for the good of king and commonwealth seemed beyond question. Thus it was that Queen Elizabeth's
order for the suppression of prophesyings brought from her archbishop the pained and uncomprehending reply: "But surely I cannot
marvel enough how this strange opinion should once enter into your
mind, that it should be good for the church to have few preachers.
Alas, Madam! is the scripture more plain in any one thing, than that
the gospel of Christ should be plentifully preached?" If it was not
plain to the Queen, it seemed obvious to Archbishop Grindal that by
preaching "due obedience to Christian princes and magistrates is
planted in the hearts of subjects: for obedience proceedeth of conscience; conscience is grounded upon the word of God; the word of
God worketh his effect by preaching. So as generally, where preaching wanteth, obedience faileth."[3]

Elizabeth, of course, was neither an atheist nor, at least in her public
utterances, a Machiavellian. As she informed Parliament in 1585,
"One matter toucheth me so near, as I may not overskip, Religion, the
ground on which all other matters ought to take root, and being cor-
rupted, may mar all the tree." Having laid the groundwork with this

pious platitude, she then expressed her firm intention to guide her people "by God's holy true rule," the contents of which were, she asserted, no mystery to so experienced a student of "God's Book" as herself. The problem as she saw it was not preaching *per se*, but who preached and what was preached; her objection was to the "many over-bold with God Almighty, making too many subtle scannings of his blessed will, as lawyers do with human testaments." The unmitigated presumption of those who indulged in such scannings was an insult to God, and no less an insult to herself as God's lieutenant on earth.[4]

The nub of the issue, of course, was not the presumption of certain preachers, but rather the implied threat to the state. Church and state, though distinguishable, were inseparable; they stood or fell together. Since the Puritans were as aware of this as their opponents, the professions of loyalty that accompanied their attacks on the Established Church were regarded as merely hypocritical. It was dangerous "to a Kingly Rule," the Queen told Parliament, "to have every man make a doom of the validity and privity of his Prince's Government with a common veil and cover of God's Word, whose followers must not be judged but by private men's exposition."[5] Aspersions cast on the Church inevitably reflected on the prince's government. A generation later, in explanation of the "Directions Concerning Preachers" promulgated by King James in 1622, Archbishop Abbot told Bishop Mountaigne of London that "divers Preachers have cast out words in the pulpit, as if there were some danger that Religion should be changed among us, which cannot be esteemed less than a seditious speech, and very scandalous unto the King."[6]

Seditious and scandalous many of the sermons preached in the early 1620's doubtless were. Some clearly reflected the widespread Protestant fear that the projected marriage of the King's son to the Infanta of Spain would lead to the much dreaded toleration of Catholicism in England. Others gave offense quite inadvertently, for it was all too easy for the unwary preacher to trespass on forbidden fields. A month after King James's Directions were issued, Richard Sheldon, "a convert from out of Babylon," as he styled himself, used his invitation to preach from Paul's Cross in London to identify the Pope as the Beast of the Apocalypse and to denounce all those who believed that some modus vivendi could be reached with the Romanists. It was an unfortunate moment to return to this ever popular Protestant theme, and the hapless Sheldon was severely reprimanded for his lack of tact.[7] Even the more perceptive found the government's sensitivities hard to predict. Many preachers must have sympathized with John Donne's prayer: "God bless me from myself ... that I cast not aspersions or imputations upon the church, or the state, by my mistakings."[8]

How the government might or ought to respond to the political problem posed by the pulpit was by no means clear. The outright suppression of preaching, the response feared by Archbishop Grindal, was simply not a tenable solution. In the fifteenth century the Church in England had countered the threat of heretical sermons by rigidly restricting the issuance of preaching licenses; thus in one diocese only fourteen licenses were granted in twenty years.[9] But in the fifteenth century the Church could assert, although the argument did not go unchallenged, that it was not "lawful [for] lewd men to know the blessed law of the gospel of our Lord Jesus Christ, but only priests and clerks."[10] After the Reformation such a position would have seemed like dangerous obscurantism at best to layman and cleric alike. Further, much that was preached even by Puritan "hot-gospellers" was not only innocent of the taint of treason but positively beneficial to the stability of society and the state. In 1622 the Puritan Robert Harris, whom Archbishop Bancroft had instituted to the vicarage of Hanwell only with the greatest reluctance, preached from the pulpit at Paul's Cross a perfectly orthodox sermon on order: "Happy that State, wherein the Cobbler meddles with his Last, the Tradesman with his shop, the student with his book, the Councillor with State, the Prince with the Scepter, and each Creature lives in his own Element. . . . Woe to that body that will be all head; members misplaced are neither for use nor ease."[11] Even that princely student of political theory King James would have found such sentiments unexceptionable.

Finally, any response of the government to the dangers of political preaching was complicated by the obvious advantage to be reaped by the Crown from such a ready vehicle of propaganda as the pulpit. Parliamentary sessions, though rare and usually short in duration, gave the king a chance to address his leading subjects, and proclamations could be issued and instructions could be conveyed to the shire elites by the judges on their circuits; but only the pulpit could be depended on to reach the common man. Peter Heylyn, the ecclesiastical historian and controversialist, once observed that when Queen Elizabeth "had any business to bring about amongst the people, she used to *tune the Pulpits*, as her saying was; that is to say, to have some preachers in and about London, and other great auditories in the kingdom, ready at her command to cry up her design."[12] It occurred neither to Heylyn nor to anyone else that such a blatant exploitation of a religious institution for political ends required extenuation or justification. In fact, so doughty a champion of preaching as Edmund Grindal wrote to Secretary Cecil in 1562 to ask for information on the fate of Antoine de Bourbon, the King of Navarre, for he intended "to preach at the cross the next Sunday, and upon occasion offered would peradventure make some mention of God's judgments over him." More significantly, he requested that "if there be any other matter which you wish to be uttered there for the present state, I would be pleased to know it in time, if your leisure will serve."[13]

The open-air pulpit at Paul's Cross, advantageously located in central London, was an apt instrument of governmental suasion. In 1586, for example, the assembled Londoners heard Archbishop Sandys compare the Babington conspiracy with the rebellion of Absalom, and in 1591, they were spurred to renewed efforts against Spain by a sermon on Saul's successful summons of the Israelites against the invading Ammonites.[14] But the task of the preacher as a spokesman for the government was not always easy. In 1596 William Barlow, one of Whitgift's chaplains, preached at Paul's Cross on the greatness of the Earl of Essex's victory at Cadiz, only to return in 1601 to explain to a hostile city the government's version of the Essex rebellion—a thankless task, but a chaplain aspiring to be bishop was in no position to ignore the needs of the Crown.[15] It was Bishop Mountaigne's even less enviable lot to have to deliver a sermon in 1622 in favor of the benevolence (an unpopular, extra-Parliamentary form of taxation), "wherein he would prove that what we have is not our own, and what we gave was but rendering and restoring." Having begun on this unpromising note, the bishop then turned to a plea for money to repair St. Paul's Cathedral and finally to a refutation of Paraeus's theory that the people might restrain and limit a tyrannical prince—surely a deplorable subject to raise in conjunction with comments on the benevolence. The bishop apparently did not expect applause for his efforts; according to John Chamberlain, who heard the sermon, "His voice was so low that I think scarce the third part [of the assembly] was within hearing."[16]

The real difficulty the government faced in "tuning the pulpits" for political purposes was due not to the reluctance of an occasional preacher who mumbled through his apologia for some unpopular Crown policy, but to the impossibility of ensuring that all sermons sounded the same note. The danger came not from any difficulty in recruiting spokesmen willing to espouse the Crown's position, but from the fact that opponents of the status quo could easily exploit the same medium for their own ends. Even Paul's Cross was not immune, although appointment to that pulpit was made by the Bishop of London. In a sermon from the Cross in 1576 a minister was so indiscreet as to touch on the succession problem; a year later John Foxe, the martyrologist, was alleged to have preached that "the protestants of France had great cause to take arms against their king, for that he admitted their public enemy the Pope." In 1617 the assemblage at the Cross heard impositions condemned, and two years later they heard a preacher inveigh "somewhat scandalously" at Lord Chancellor Bacon "and his Catamites."[17]

Not all the indiscretions that troubled the government were calculated, nor were they all motivated by commitment to high principles; the attack on Bacon issued apparently from a disappointed litigant who vented his spleen before the largest audience he was ever likely to command. But one way or another, questionable sermons were far from rare, and not all Puritan divines who found their way to the Cross preached on such safe subjects as the terrors of Tophet or the furies of the Amalekites. The difficulty of regulating preaching is eloquently set forth in a letter from Bishop Sandys to Lords Burghley and Leicester after two supposedly "safe" ministers had used their opportunity at the Cross to defend Cartwright and the Presbyterian position:

I do what I can to procure fit men to preach at the Cross; but I cannot know their hearts, and these times have altered opinions. Such as preached discreetly the last year now labor by railing to feed the fancies of the people. ...Such men must be restrained if the state shall stand safe. Truly, my Lords, I have dealt so carefully as I can to keep such fanatical spirits from the Cross; but the deceitful devil enemy to religion hath so poured out the poison of sedition and so suddenly changed these wavering minds, that it is hard to tell whom a man may trust.[18]

The sermon was a problematic tool of government and a potent weapon for "fanatical spirits" precisely because of its unpredictability; there was no way of assessing a sermon's ill effects until the words had been spoken and the damage done, by which time, as Sandys discovered, the preacher might well have "gone out of the Town."

It was easier to state the problem than to solve it. Bishop Sandys's own answer was hopelessly naïve. Following the suspension of Edward Dering from his lecture at St. Paul's for preaching a seditious sermon in 1573, Sandys had suggested to Secretary Cecil that Dering might be permitted to return if he were required to "teach sound doctrine, exhort to virtue, and dehort from vice; and touching matters of order and policy, meddle not with them, but leave them to the magistrate to whom reformation pertaineth."[19] Such a formula implies that faith and morals can be not only distinguished from politics but entirely separated from it. Probably not even Sandys would have defended this position; certainly it was anathema to the Puritans, who believed that zeal for reformation was a positive virtue. A few years later, in 1579, the Council in effect acted on Sandys's advice and ordered the archbishop to admonish all preachers not to "meddle with any such matter of estate, being in very deed not ... appertaining to their profession," and in 1622 King James repeated this futile gesture by promulgating his Directions Concerning Preachers, which forbade the ordinary clergy not only to meddle with matters of state but also to preach on controversial "deep points" of doctrine.[20] As the Venetian ambassador commented, "The idea of bridling the tongues of preachers in matters considered to pertain to their faith is like damming torrents, which only rage the more furiously and easily break into sedition."[21] One can only surmise that the administrative mind found some satisfaction in taking action of some kind, no matter how absurdly inadequate.

Sermons, of course, were only the top of the iceberg; a more profound danger to the state lay in the organization and ideology of the Puritan movement.[22] When the Puritan message of wayfaring and warfaring, or righteousness and reformation, caught the lay imagination, it channeled lay interests and energies in new directions. In some it produced a heightened self-awareness—witness the diary of Lady Margaret Hoby. In others it led to a searching and discriminating concern with politics, a concern more like that of the modern newspaper-reading citizen than that of their contemporaries, whose political awareness rarely reached beyond neighborhood or shire and whose usual response to politics was passive.

The diary of Walter Yonge, a Devonshire squire of good family and a justice of the peace, suggests the political interests and watchful concern of the Puritan gentry. Although Yonge's diary was written at his manors of Colyton and Axminster, 150 miles from London, the news he so meticulously collected and recorded was mainly of national significance. Secular and ecclesiastical affairs received equal attention. The entries for 1606 mention not only the execution of the Gunpowder Plot conspirators, but also the news that "the silenced ministers of Lincolnshire exhibited a petition to the Parliament, now sitting." He notes both the attempted assassination of King Henry IV of France by a Jesuit and the death of Theodore Beza, "preacher of Geneva." The grant of two subsidies is duly recorded, and so is the fate of a bill for conformity, "so cunningly penned, that the drift thereof could not long be seen, which would very much have galled the ministry, and like to pass had not Mr. Snape descried the intents of it."[23]

Many items record the changing fortunes of the Catholic recusants; many more record Parliament's various attempts to accommodate nonconformist preachers and the ecclesiastical authorities' attempts to discourage them. The entry of 19 August 1622 is typical: "There is a report that Papists shall have a toleration here in England, and that the Protestant ministers shall preach but once a Sabbath." Six days later Yonge was able to confirm the report, and the entry concludes, "*quod Deus avertat.*" With what feelings he recorded the following it is easy to imagine: "There is a speech that all puritan justices of peace shall be put off the commission." Items on foreign affairs appear on almost every page; Yonge, like many other Puritans, followed the declining fortunes of Continental Protestantism with the closest attention, and the last entries in the diary, which stops in 1628, record the impending fall of La Rochelle.[24]

Yonge's diary tells us what he considered significant, rarely why. But a comparison of Yonge's terse entries with the gossipy letters of John Chamberlain, ambassador Carleton's London correspondent, does suggest how far the Puritan squire's conception of politics deviated from traditional views. Chamberlain, with his sensitive ear attuned to catch the first whisper of court intrigue, was not simply indulging an understandable love of political trivia; rather the rise and fall of favorites and the endless struggle for place and patronage were the very stuff and substance of traditional politics. For Yonge, how-

ever, issues and policies, not personalities, were the stuff of politics, and
the King and his courtiers, who made up Chamberlain's world, were
for Yonge little more than symbols of corruption, men whose "pompous vanities ... waste away and consume money, the country being
in poverty, and more necessary occasions calling for it."[25] As a court
preacher noted, "By their news you may know their religion, and by
their religion foreknow their news."[26]

Yonge was no mere idle observer of politics; he served as sheriff in
1628, was an investor in the Dorchester Company, and sat for Honiton
in the Long Parliament, with which he sided against the King. For
Yonge, as for other Puritans, political sophistication was a means, not
an end; it was the necessary background to action and reform. And
the action above all others that lay Puritans were called on to perform
in the years before the summoning of the Long Parliament was the
promotion and protection of an evangelical ministry. "I can not
preach to the whole land," John More, the Norwich lecturer, told the
assembled Norfolk justices, "but for the discharge of my conscience
I desire you, good brethren, so many of you as have any voices in place
and Parliament where these things may be reformed, consecrate your
tongues to the Lord in behalf of your poor brethren."[27] Such preaching had its effect. To advance their cause the Puritans used every political device and technique available to them: they prepared bills "for
the further reformation of the Church," collected petitions on behalf
of their bills, and compiled statistics to back up the claims made in
their petitions; they reached some Members of Parliament through
their Fast Day sermons and lobbied others at the very doors of the
House of Commons.[28] Puritan measures, it is true, met with little success; even the most sophisticated tactics were no match for the veto
of the Crown. Nevertheless, the Puritans' interests normally received
a sympathetic hearing in the House of Commons and their measures
had more support than the weight of their numbers would justify.

Outside Parliament the Puritans were more successful. For example, at some time during the 1580's, "the persecution growing hot
against the Nonconforming Ministers," Hugh Clarke, vicar of Wol-
ston, Warwickshire, "in his prayer, requested God to forgive the Queen
her sins." Bishop Overton, "being informed of it, and supposing that
he had gotten that advantage which he had long looked for, accused Master Clarke of Treason, and caused him to be committed to

the common jail." However, "it pleased God to stir up some worthy justices of the county to take his part, so that upon trial, he was acquitted."[29] Here, as elsewhere, God's stirring up was done through his chosen instruments, the preachers. When the ministers of the Puritan conference at Dedham wanted to have their suspended brethren freed to return to preaching, they sent a delegation "to my Lord Rich and to Sir Robert Jermyn with letters from the brethren to that end."[30] As a result of the Earl of Leicester's machinations, Laurence Humphrey and Thomas Sampson were invited to preach at Paul's Cross in London despite the fact that they were under deprivation for nonconformity; needless to say, their sermons were not printed.[31] Whatever reservations lay Puritans may have had about some of the Puritan clergy's reforming impulses and theocratic pretensions, the desirability of protecting individual ministers as preachers was rarely questioned.

From the Anglican point of view, Puritan preaching alone was sufficiently dangerous, even when it was not coupled with demands for a godly discipline or for the overthrow of the "canary-sucking" prelates. Thomas Cooper, Bishop of Winchester, may have been "an unskillful and deceitful tubtrimmer," and undoubtedly he paints too rosy a picture of the Edwardian reformation when he observes "there were fewer preachers and less teaching in the days of ... *Edward* the sixth, and yet did not the people then revolt, as now, although the reformation of the Church was then but greenly settled." Yet he was surely correct in suggesting that the quantity of preaching and the peace of Church and State were related in inverse proportion.[32] Further, the Puritan preachers and lecturers deliberately cultivated a popular preaching style. While the witty Anglican preachers aimed for the approbation of the courtly coterie in London, the Puritans aimed for the ear, if not for the applause, of the people. "Preaching," wrote the Puritan Richard Bernard, "is ... a sound and plainly laying open of holy Scriptures, by a public minister before the people, to their understanding and capacity, ... with words of exhortation applied to the conscience, both to inform and reform, and where they be well, to confirm."[33]

Such documents as John Manningham's commonplace book suggest how pervasive an effect Puritan preaching had even on those who were hostile to Puritanism. Manningham, who in the early 1600's was among the number of gentlemen law students at the Temple, seems to have fancied himself something of a connoisseur of Elizabethan wit and wordplay. Yet interspersed in his notes among the latest puns of City attorneys are page after page of sermon summaries. In October 1602, for example, he records a Paul's Cross sermon at which "the excessive pride and vanity of women in apparel" was castigated and the Puritan lecturer Stephen Egerton reprehended because his audience, "being most of women, abounded in that superfluous vanity." Six weeks later Manningham visited Blackfriars church to see for himself. Although he noted that Egerton had "a great congregation, specially of women," Manningham forgot that he came out of curiosity and remained to take notes on the sermon. It is characteristic of the man, and perhaps of many others, that he could make fun of a country cousin for praising "a good honest poor silly puritan" on the same page that he records, apparently with approval, the following puritanical aphorism: "The spending of the afternoons on Sundays either idly or about temporal affairs, is like clipping the Queen's coin; this treason to the Prince, that profanation, and robbing God of his own."[34] In short, however superior Manningham may have felt to Puritans, he was prepared to give God his due by attending their Sunday afternoon sermons. Manningham's Sabbatarianism was harmless enough at the time, but how would he and countless others like him react in 1618 to the King's promulgation of the Book of Sports, which permitted "lawful recreations" on Sunday afternoons?

As dangerous as the most innocuous sermon might prove to be in the long run, even more menacing was the way the Puritans set about securing a preaching ministry. Archbishop Bancroft, that scourge of the Puritans, saw lecturing as a "policy they have which in time may grow to be dangerous, if it be not prevented," and indeed as a deliberate policy "for the attaining of their Presbyteries." Bancroft had a predilection for seeing all Puritan activity as a consequence of a Presbyterian conspiracy, but the evidence supports the general accuracy of his observations. What he saw was an attempt to insinuate preachers not "where there is greatest need, but in the most populous places: as in the market towns, shire towns and cities":

[They] not only creep into noble and gentlemen's bosoms in the Country, ... but also thrust themselves forward by all the power of their friends, to be as they term it Readers [lecturers], but I fear Seducers in the Inns of Court.

For it is very probable (as they well know) that ... the flower of the Gentility of England being by that means trained up in a disobedient misliking of the present estate of the Church, if occasion serve to show themselves good scholars, they will bring forth corrupt fruit of so contentious an education.[35]

In general this was an accurate description and a perceptive prophecy. But what Bancroft overlooked, or perhaps wished to ignore, was that in most instances the preachers had no need to "creep" or "thrust," for they were welcomed, indeed actively recruited by the laity.

How great a political threat Puritanism became cannot be measured with any precision, but the changing definition of Puritanism is indicative of the growing awareness that Puritanism had come to imply certain political attitudes, or at least that its opposition to the Church had come to be associated with opposition to the Stuart state. In 1641 Henry Parker observed:

Puritans ... were at the first ecclesiastical only, so called because they did not like a pompous or ceremonious kind of discipline in the Church like unto the Romish; but now it is come about, that by an enlargement of the name, the world is full of nothing else but Puritans, for besides the Puritan in Church policy, there are now added Puritans in religion, Puritans in State, and Puritans in morality.[36]

Lucy Hutchinson's observations testify to much the same expansion of Puritanism's meaning: "If any were grieved at the dishonor of the kingdom, or the griping of the poor, or the unjust oppressions of the subject, ... he was a Puritan."[37]

This phenomenon can doubtless be explained partly by the general imprecision of popular usage, and partly by the tendency to regard Puritanism as the religion of those who held "country party" attitudes. Whatever the reason, the new identification of Puritanism with undesirable political opinions presented Puritan preachers with a ticklish problem. In 1624, when the Puritan John Davenport required Secretary Conway's support in order to secure the bishop's institution and admission to the curacy and lectureship at St. Lawrence Jewry, he assured Conway that "if by puritanically affected, be meant one, that secretly encourageth men in opposition to the present government, I profess an hearty detestation of such hypocrisy."[38] There is no reason to doubt that Davenport meant what he wrote in 1624, but his radicalism increased with age and within a decade he had resigned his living and was preparing to flee to the American wilderness. In 1642 George Lawrence, the Puritan lecturer at St. George Botolph Lane, made the following rather disingenuous distinction: "For whereas the *Bishop's Faction* and *Carnal Gospellers* do say that I and others are seditious, and seduce the people, let such first know that the nature of sedition is the drawing of a people out of the right path into a wrong, from good to evil, and not from evil to good."[39] In the eyes of the Puritan, of course, it was the royalist Anglican who preached a wrong and dangerous politics, but what is of real significance is Lawrence's open admission that sermons had political content and purpose.[40]

Long before 1640, Laudian churchmen had come to the conclusion that the sermon itself was the source of the trouble, for it inculcated attitudes inimical to the peace and security of the realm. At Paul's Cross in 1630 Edward Boughen suggested that the only remedy for the ill effects of sermons was to elevate the divine service above preaching. "At common prayers... humility, and fear, and reverence are showed.... But at sermons, where no humility is required, or at least not decried, there we are like gnats in the air."[41] There is no evidence that Boughen's London audience took his message to heart, but by then Londoners had heard several generations of preachers urge humility before God and zeal in the affairs of men. William Laud had come to much the same conclusion as Boughen years before. In a sermon preached before King James in 1621 on the text "Pray for the peace of Jerusalem," Laud had claimed that there was "nothing more needful for 'Jerusalem,' for State and Church, than 'prayer.' " The peace that Laud prayed and worked for when he subsequently came to power was the peace of silent pulpits.[42]

Laud came to the task too late. The situation Bancroft feared had come about: a generation had appeared for whom the word of the preacher or lecturer carried more weight than the threats and commands of the archbishop. When John Aston, who accompanied the Court to the north in the summer of 1639, reached Berwick, he found that the town had two preachers—Gilbert Dury, the vicar, and John Jemmet, a Puritan lecturer. The local populace during those critical months must have been outspoken, for within a day of his arrival Aston noted in his journal that "Mr. Dury, by preaching obedience to the higher powers since the beginning of the troubles, had so irritated his friends and countrymen [Dury was a Scot], that he durst not go amongst them; and he was generally hated in town, and rebuked as one that sought after a bishopric, which they abhorred." A few months later Jemmet, who had been lecturer since 1637, was accused of preaching sedition and removed. Yet Jemmet had apparently accomplished more in three years of preaching than Dury, who had been vicar since 1613, had accomplished in nearly thirty. Early in the spring of 1640 an Anglican divine of Durham ruefully observed, "If we, who are in the right way of church obedience, were as zealous in our course as Puritans are, I believe by this day a Puritan had not been a weed in our garden."[43]

The state of affairs that Aston observed was a portent, a straw in the wind, for in its essentials the situation he found at Berwick was duplicated at Newcastle, Hull, and other towns of strategic importance. By the spring of 1640 the Puritan lecturers and preachers had become the straw that broke the back of Church and State. In Gloucestershire the election for knights of the shire, which had been comfortably arranged ahead of time by the principal gentry, came unstuck at the last moment amid bitter accusations of treachery and foul dealing when Nicholas Stephens of Eastington unexpectedly entered the lists. Stephens, who had been removed from the commission of the peace for his opposition to the collection of Ship Money, claimed that he had been forced to stand for election, and a clerical observer reported that "those who first rolled this unwilling stone were principally men of our own coat, a pack of either deprived, silenced, or puritanically affected [clergy]men." The writer went on to name ten preachers, one with two sons named Help-on-High and Sion-Build, another a lecturer at Rodborough, a third a lecturer at Gloucester, a fourth chaplain to a Puritan knight who stood for the election with Stephens, and so on; he also noted that the rector of Eastington, Stephens's parish, was William Mew, a Puritan who had been lecturer at St. Giles in the Fields in London from 1628 to 1635, and who "stands affected as most lecturers do."[44] During the spring elections in Essex it was observed that the Puritan ministers and lecturers of the county frequently preached away from their own pulpits, and when the election took place gave their voices to the candidates of the faction led by the Earl of Warwick, Sir Thomas Barrington, and Sir Harbottle Grimston. Leading the election campaign was Stephen Marshall, an Emmanuel graduate who had succeeded Richard Rogers as lecturer at Wethersfield in 1618, and of whom it had been said in 1637 that "he governeth the consciences of all the rich puritans in those parts."[45] In March 1640, Secretary Nicholas learned from a friend at Sandwich, Kent, that his candidacy was opposed by the "factious Nonconformists," who "bruited a great scandal of your inclination to Popery." Nicholas was warned that they had "so crossed the business" as to put his chance of election in serious jeopardy.[46]

The Puritan connection, which for decades had been concerned above all with a preaching ministry, was now mobilized to return a godly Parliament. For the first time ideology entered electoral politics on a large scale, and if the events in Gloucestershire were in any way typical, it made a shambles of customary electoral behavior. The old rhetoric of reformation and warfare ceased to be metaphor and became instead a summons to revolution. In 1610 King James had told Parliament that "kings are not only God's lieutenants on earth, and sit upon God's throne, but even by God himself they are called gods."[47] In 1640, so wrote an embittered Anglican, "the lecturing house-creeping ministers," having got the Parliament they had prayed for, referred in their sermons to the House of Commons as *"the House of Gods, and the House of Mortal Gods,"* thus conferring the divinity that hedged the king on his rebellious legislature.[48] When the Long Parliament finally met, the Puritan pulpits became its mouthpiece, and it was said of the Londoners of the time that "by the Sunday's sermon, or a lecture, they could learn, not only what was done the week before, but also what was to be done in Parliament the week following; besides the information which the pulpits gave the people for coming in tumults to the House for justice."[49]

For the first time some of the London preachers did not limit themselves to prayers and exhortations addressed to the traditional authorities, to the King and Parliament. Instead a few turned their popularity to account and carried their cause directly to the people. The London mobs that cried "no bishops" before the walls of Westminster Hall in the winter of 1640–41 were apparently not simply a spontaneous expression of popular outrage. Cornelius Burgess, the parson and lecturer of St. Magnus and erstwhile chaplain-in-ordinary to King Charles, is reported to have boasted when he led the "City rabble" to the very doors of Parliament: "These are my Band-Dogs; I can set them on, and I can take them off again."[50] Although this story may be apocryphal (it is told by a royalist clergyman), we may note that the House of Commons thought well enough of Burgess's pulpit oratory to appoint him one of the St. Paul's lecturers in 1643 at the extraordinary salary of £400 a year.[51] And Burgess was not the only practitioner of Puritan demagoguery, nor was the fickle mob the only instrument on which the preachers played. Calybute Downing affirmed in a sermon before the brotherhood of the Artillery Garden that "for defense of religion and reformation of the church, it was lawful to take up arms against the king"—surely an inflammatory message to preach before an urban militia.[52]

Actions as radical and unprecedented as those of the 1640's cannot be explained solely in terms of a natural reaction to grievances and oppression. As Christopher Hill has pointed out, "Men...do not break lightly with the past: if they are to challenge conventionally accepted standards they must have an alternative body of ideas to support them."[53] Not only had Puritanism supplied an alternative body of ideas; it had legitimized an active interest in politics that made it possible to put those ideas into practice. Not that more than a handful of Puritan preachers were self-conscious revolutionaries; on the contrary, most preachers were the more effective for clothing their political ideas in the familiar garb of traditional religious rhetoric. Samuel Fawcett, the rector and lecturer of St. Mary Staining in London, warned the assembled Company of Haberdashers in 1641 to beware of the "troublers of *Israel*" who "profess a strict way of Religion, yet walk not according to the rules of Religion," but rather "disturb common order, run out of rank...[and] usurp the *Office of the Magistrate*." Yet earlier in the same sermon Fawcett had pronounced as an undeniable principle

> *that it is the duty of everyone to stand well affected to the common good, both of the Church and State wherein he lives.* Religion admits not distinction, between a good man, and a good Citizen: it is impossible that he should be a good Commonwealthsman, who is not a true friend unto the Church, nor can he be a good Church man, who is not a true friend to the Commonwealth.[54]

That an appeal to observe due order and rank, to leave politics to the duly constituted magistrate, was incompatible with an exhortation calling on all good men to be good citizens, active in the affairs of

Church and State, appears to have occurred neither to Samuel Fawcett nor to the worthy Haberdashers.

Yet what was obscure to the Puritan preachers was clear enough to their opponents. Thomas Hobbes was later to ask with a certain Swiftian maliciousness, "Had it not been much better that those seditious ministers, which were not perhaps 1,000, had been all killed before they had preached? It had been, I confess, a great massacre, but the killing of 100,000 [in the civil wars] is a greater."[55] Contemporaries pointed to the lecturers as the most conspicuous fomenters of rebellion. According to John Hacket, Bishop Williams's chaplain, the perfidious act of the citizens of Hull in denying entrance to the King's forces was attributable to "their lecturers..., the corrupters of that corporation, who had previously preached the people ... from subjects to rebels."[56] And the author of *Mercurius Civicus* argued that London would not have given its indispensable support to the "incendiaries of this present rebellion" but for the lecturers, who "preach such doctrine as may foment disloyalty, and instill such principles...as may...after engage [their auditors] in rebellion."[57]

As J. H. Hexter has observed, "individual cases can *illustrate* but cannot *demonstrate*" a thesis. In any event charges of conspiracy brought by the losing side in a revolutionary struggle as part of an explanation for their enemy's success should undoubtedly be heavily discounted. No attempt will be made here to substantiate contemporary assertions that the London lectureships were an integral part of a vast Puritan conspiracy, functioning as the propaganda department of militant Protestantism and as part of a fifth column in the mercantile and governmental center of England. The first lectureships were founded in the year following Elizabeth's coronation; it is hard to believe that they were part of a plot eighty years in the hatching. Puritanism was both too big and too diffuse a movement to justify giving much credence to conspiracy theories; it encompassed too many people, too many different theological and ecclesiastical positions (to say nothing of social and political theories), and too long a period to be described in monolithic terms. An institutional study of the lectureships cannot prove that the lecturers were the vanguard of revolution. What it can do is suggest why contemporaries thought they were, and hence attached such political importance to the lectureships.

An institutional study will have little to say about what doctrines, political or otherwise, were preached, but, if some questions must be neglected, others can be answered or at least possible answers may be suggested. What, for example, are the implications of the institution's sheer size? Can it be argued that at some point simple quantitative increase became qualitative change, that what began as an effort to secure an increase in preaching ended by virtually duplicating the parochial system? Such a notion is not entirely farfetched. Archbishop Laud seems to have felt on occasion that there were two churches in England, only one of which he controlled.[58] What, for instance, are the implications of the kind of support the institution required? Since the lectureships existed only so long as there was active interest and voluntary support from a large number of influential laymen, can it be argued that the lectureships demanded a much higher level of commitment from the Puritan laity than the parish church ordinarily commanded from the whole community? If so, does this help to explain why so many corporate towns, including London itself, were reputedly Puritan and Parliamentarian, although the leading magistrates of London apparently were royalist until the purge of 1641?[59]

Finally, there is the question of the relationship of the history of the lectureships to the history of the Puritan movement as a whole. Because the lectureship was never completely a part of the Established Church in the years before 1662 but pursued a precarious existence as at best a tolerated accretion, it remained an unstable and impermanent feature of the ecclesiastical landscape. Because of its very instability, however, it was capable of expanding quickly in response to the needs of the faithful and of contracting under pressure from the ecclesiastical and political establishments. Thus where there were a large number of lectureships, as in London, it should be possible to use the waxing and waning of the institution as a barometer for measuring the changing fortunes of organized Puritanism.

3

The Origins and Varieties of Lectureships

IN the last of his 1622 Directions Concerning Preachers, James I
defined lecturers as "a new body severed from the ancient clergy
of England, as being neither parsons, vicars, or curates."[1] The Directions express perfectly the suspicion with which King James had come
to regard what he plainly felt was a dangerous innovation. They are
less adequate as a historical account, however, since the office of reader
or "lector" was ancient and even the institution as King James knew it
was of long standing by the 1620's.[2] Peter Heylyn also saw the lecturers
as "a new invention," a "generation of men neither lay, nor clergy,
having no place at all in the prayers of the Church, where we find
mention only of bishops, pastors, and curates, . . . [being] to speak
them in the vulgar proverb, neither flesh, nor fish, nor good red
herring." But Heylyn was more precise, if still erroneous, about the
institution's past. According to him, lecturers were not the product of
the early years of the Reformation,

> but were in afterwards, borrowed by Travers and the rest, towards the latter
> end of Queen Elizabeth's reign, from the new fashions of Geneva; the lec-
> turer being super-added to the parson, or vicar, as the doctor was unto the
> pastor in some foreign churches. Nor were they raised so much out of care or
> conscience, for training up the people in the ways of faith and piety, as to
> advance a faction, and to alienate the people's minds from the government
> and forms of worship here by law established.[3]

The modern historian of Tudor Puritanism Marshall Knappen,
though he does not share Heylyn's view of the lectureship as an aspect
of an Elizabethan Presbyterian conspiracy, does see it as developing
from the needs of the Puritans specifically, and more generally as a
natural creation of an age that "took its preaching seriously" and therefore "saw nothing incongruous in having an extra clergyman attached
to a parish for preaching duties alone."[4] Such a view is, of course,
essentially the one that I have tried to adumbrate in earlier chapters.
There is more to be said, however, about the institutional antecedents

of the lectureships. Inventive as the Elizabethans were, it must be admitted that they had a rich heritage to draw on.

According to his *Table Talk*, the seventeenth-century lawyer John Selden is supposed to have made the sour but illuminating remark, "Lecturers do in a parish what the friars did heretofore; get away not only the affections, but the bounty that should be bestowed on the minister."[5] G. R. Owst's monumental study of medieval preaching establishes grounds for comparison beyond the threat presented by both preaching orders to the popularity and economic security of the secular priests. Some friars had anticipated the Puritans in assigning the sermon a more important role in divine service than the mass, and certain of the late medieval homily series could almost be considered as "foreshadowing" the Puritan lecture-course. Furthermore, Owst points out, the friars, like the lecturers, saw the ecclesiastical hierarchy as fair game for criticism from the pulpit; the secular government, too, was prey to their criticisms and proposals for reform. Even the practice of delivering sermons on Sunday afternoons and weekdays was anticipated by the friars. "If some churchmen in authority were continually complaining that there was not enough preaching by the seculars," Owst concludes, "others indeed might well complain that from some other quarters there was a great deal too much."[6]

The friars clearly anticipated in some respects both the function and the style of the later Puritan lecturers. Recognition of the kinship between the two is attested by the playful reprimand that John Foxe, the martyrologist, addressed in 1561 to his old friend and former fellow exile, Laurence Humphrey, shortly after Humphrey accepted the presidency of Magdalen College: "I change not my degree nor order, which is that of the mendicant brothers, or if you will, the preaching brothers."[7] Yet, however obvious the spiritual affinity between the two, it is equally clear that there were institutional differences. The friar belonged to a religious order; the lecturer was usually an ordained secular priest hired specifically to preach.* The friar was frequently itinerant; the lecturer was usually attached to a particular parish and pulpit. The friar, though he belonged to a mendicant order, did not depend on preaching for his livelihood; the lecturer, particularly if he held no cure, frequently did. There are many differ-

---

* Occasionally the lecturer had only deacon's orders, which enabled him to preach but not to administer the sacraments.

ences, and few grounds for positing any direct institutional continuity.

Even so, it is not necessary to conclude that the Tudor lectureships were simply a spontaneous response to a widespread need, although this is doubtless true of the institution's elaboration and proliferation under Puritan aegis during the early years of Elizabeth's reign. When the preaching friars vanished from England along with the other religious orders, they left a substantial vacuum in the religious life of the laity, particularly in the towns. At Yarmouth, for example, the Franciscans had provided a daily lecture in their abbey church of St. Nicholas prior to 1538. After the dissolution the priory and appropriate parsonage passed into the hands of the dean and chapter of Norwich Cathedral, and the chapter appointed a curate to officiate. By 1563 the corporation of Yarmouth had begun to supplement the impoverished curate's wages; seven years later the merchant guild purchased the living and set about raising a benevolence with which to hire a "town preacher." Subsequently the town secured a series of Puritan lecturers until 1635, when the lecturer, George Burdett, was suspended by the High Commission, and the lectureship lapsed in the face of Laudian opposition.[8]

There was not, nor could there have been at Yarmouth, any institutional continuity. However, during the early years of Elizabeth's reign, municipal authorities revived a number of institutions, formerly under the care of the Church, that had been temporarily submerged in the confiscations of the Henrician and Edwardian reformations.[9] The Grey Friars' lecture at Yarmouth had presumably once been popular, and in the new Protestant England lectures were fast becoming popular again. After purchasing the parsonage and advowson of St. Nicholas, it must have seemed natural and reasonable for the town's leading citizens to go one step further and revive the lectureship.

Quite apart from the lectures preached by the friars, a number of institutions prefiguring in one way or another the later lectureships were already in existence before the Reformation gave a new impetus to preaching. John Wodderspoon, the nineteenth-century historian of Ipswich, suggests that the town lecturer of the Elizabethan period was "of ancient origin" and "arose out of [the office] of Guild Priest."[10] Although I have been unable to trace the office of town lecturer at Ipswich back before the 1540's in the printed records, Wodderspoon's suggestion does deserve serious consideration. Town guilds, particularly the religious confraternities, did hire chantry chaplains.[11] It is also true that townsmen sometimes endowed commemorative sermons as well as prayers for the dead: the recorder of Coventry "left land to pay for 3 sermons to be preached yearly in this city for ever" in his will of 1490.[12]

If one turns to London, a similar predecessor of the lecture can be cited that was founded in the first half of the fifteenth century and that survived even the Edwardian Chantry Act more or less intact. When Richard Whittington, Mercer and thrice Lord Mayor, founded the college of St. Spiritus and St. Mary, converting and rebuilding the parish church of St. Michael Paternoster in the Royal for that purpose, he provided not only for prayers for the good estate of himself and his wife Alice, their parents, King Richard II, the Duke of Gloucester, and others of his patrons, but also for a divinity lecture in perpetuity.[13] The lecture was evidently still in existence in the reign of Henry VII, for in 1508 James Finch, Master of the Fraternity of Sheremen, who had already conveyed property to the value of some £250 in trust to Whittington College and almshouse, bequeathed additional property in the amount of about £400 to the Clothworkers and the Skinners for the support of the divinity lecture.[14] The chantry was suppressed by statute under Edward VI, but the almshouse survived under the care of the Mercers, and the Clothworkers continued to appoint lecturers to the reestablished parish of St. Michael Paternoster.

How quickly this medieval foundation came under the influence of religious radicalism is demonstrated by the nomination of Thomas Sampson to the lectureship in about 1570. Sampson, who had been among the Marian exiles at Strasbourg, returned a more uncompromising radical than his friends Sandys and Jewel, for unlike them he refused a bishopric in 1560. He did secure a number of preferments, which he enjoyed briefly until he was deprived of them all in 1564 for opposing Archbishop Parker on the issue of vestments. When he retired from his lectureship at St. Michael's in 1573, he recommended as his replacement Edward Dering, the recently suspended lecturer at St. Paul's, and apparently Dering's appointment would have been assured but for the refusal of Sandys and Parker to restore his license to preach.[15] Despite this setback, the lectureship continued to attract the support of influential Londoners. In 1579 John Heydon, Mercer, alderman, and sheriff when he died in 1583, left £400 to the Mercers' Company, which was directed to lend it at 3⅓ per cent; the interest thus earned was to supplement the £10 a year paid by the Clothworkers to the Wednesday evening lecturer at St. Michael's.[16]

This brief genealogy of the lectureships would not be complete without mention of the cathedral lectureships, although they were less a direct predecessor than a collateral family and a parallel development. Since the cathedral lectureships could not readily be controlled or manipulated by the laity, they could not readily be used as vehicles for Puritan preachers. Some were of ancient origin; the lecture at St. Paul's in London dates back to the episcopacy of William de Gravesend, who founded it about 1280. Its existence was not continuous, however, for when Dean Colet persuaded the chancellor to recover the endowment and revive the lectureship in the early years of the sixteenth century, it had been in abeyance for at least twenty years.[17] A lectureship that owed its revival to Colet and that numbered among its early preachers men like John Cardmaker, John Rogers, and John Major was undoubtedly influential and exemplary, but the significance of the cathedral lectureships as a precedent was limited by the fact that many of them, although not the St. Paul's lecture, were addressed to the clergy. Nevertheless, the cathedral lectureship had a considerable future ahead of it in Colet's day, for the reformers saw an educated clergy as the sine qua non of their success. Thus the Royal Injunctions of 1547 for the short-lived diocese of Westminster contained the following order:

Item, That whereas by the ignorance of the clergy not only God's glory is greatly obscured, but also the same clergy much disdained and evil spoken of by some of the laity, you [the bishop] shall cause that every parson, vicar, chantry-priest and other stipendiary within this [city] of Westminster be present at every lecture of divinity to be made within the college of St. Stephen, except they or any of them have some reasonable let.[18]

Similarly, in 1550 all members of the collegiate community at Windsor were ordered to attend "with all diligence" a twice-weekly "lecture of Holy Scripture" given in the chapel, and in 1552 a divinity lecture at York was begun by order of Archbishop Holgate.[19]

Under Queen Elizabeth cathedral lectures were founded or revived at Canterbury, York, Exeter, Winchester, St. Paul's, Carlisle, and Norwich, "according to the good meaning of the Queen's Majesty's Injunctions" of 1559. For Salisbury alone do the Injunctions specify that the lecture is to be given "in English . . . openly so that all people may come to it"; the others mention only that attendance is required of all clergy attached to the cathedral and resident at the time.[20] The effort to secure divinity lectures in collegiate churches did not cease with the 1559 Injunctions. Such preaching, confined ordinarily to a clerical audience and under the constant supervision of dean or chancellor, must have commended itself to a conservative Queen and an increasingly wary episcopal bench; as other lectureships proved to be platforms for critics of the establishment, cathedral lectures alone must have seemed immune from radical taint. At any rate, Bishop Bonner continued the St. Paul's lectureship during Mary's reign, though insisting that it be delivered in the scholastic style, and as canny an opponent of the unregulated lectureship as John Whitgift assisted in the founding of divinity lectures at the cathedrals of Lichfield and Hereford in 1582.[21]

The cathedrals of Bristol and Rochester still lacked lectures when Archbishop Laud conducted his metropolitical visitation in 1634, but other cathedral churches had preaching in plenty. St. Paul's had two lecturers who alternated in preaching on Sunday afternoons and a third lecturer who preached three times weekly during term time. Wells had a Friday lecture under the care of its chancellor, and Salisbury Cathedral a lecture in divinity preached on holidays, which the dean and chapter reported "might better be spared, and returned to divinity lectures again."[22] Many, but not all, of these lectures were preached to the laity, and there is no evidence that Puritans were put off by the fact that the lectures were given in cathedral precincts. However, the lectures were not always to the Puritans' taste. Walter Yonge, the Devonshire Puritan squire, noted in his diary (with what measure of incredulity and exasperation one is left to imagine) that the Friday lecturer at Exeter Cathedral "seemed to maintain in his sermon . . . non-residency out of Gal. 2:1, by the example of Titus, who had a pastoral charge, and yet Paul took him thence."[23] Doubtless most cathedral lecturers were, as the 1634 report to Laud from Exeter stated, "conformable men," for they were normally appointed by the bishop's chancellor or by the dean and chapter, a system of patronage that left little room for Puritan influence.[24]

Yet even so apparently safe an institution could be turned to advantage by a determined Puritan, if he was given the opportunity. When Edward Dering was appointed lecturer at St. Paul's, he had already acquired a considerable reputation as a scholar; he had held the Lady Margaret Professorship of Divinity in 1567, and Archbishop Parker had employed him as a controversialist against the Jesuit Harding.[25] He was also recognized as a leader by the Puritans, though as an evangelical preacher rather than as a Presbyterian theoretician. He had opposed Cartwright's expulsion from Cambridge and had been observed visiting the imprisoned authors of the *Admonition*, Field and Wilcox. Despite his puritanical connections, he had retained the friendship of Bishop Sandys, who appointed him to the lectureship in 1572, only to suspend him in 1573, apparently on the charge of preaching against the civil magistrate. In the course of defending himself in the Star Chamber and in a letter to Burghley, Dering not only denied the main charge but boldly went on to attack as unscriptural the jurisdictional competence of the episcopate.[26] Nevertheless, Burghley, the Earl of Leicester, and others intervened to secure his restoration until late in 1574, when Bishop Sandys finally succeeded in silencing him.[27] The whole incident seems to have been an aberration permitted by unusual circumstances—the friendship of Sandys, which Dering soon lost, and the support of Burghley, Leicester, and others of the Council. At any rate the authorities were more vigilant in the future; evidently no Puritan held that post again until after 1642.[28]

The brief reign of the young King Edward VI had a decisive effect on the development of the lectureship and its association with religious reform. It was during those hectic years that the close connection between religious radicalism and lectureships was first made, a connection nowhere stronger than at the pulpit of St. Paul's Cathedral, where the fiery reformer John Hooper held forth in 1549. As he wrote in an exultant letter to his old mentor, Henry Bullinger:

Great, great, I say, my beloved master and gossip, is the harvest, but the laborers are few.... Such is the maliciousness and wickedness of the bishops* that the godly and learned men who would willingly labor in the Lord's harvest are hindered by them; and they neither preach themselves, nor allow the liberty of preaching to others. For this reason there are some persons

---

* Hooper did not become Bishop of Gloucester until some months later, in the spring of 1550.

here who read and expound the holy scriptures at a public lecture, two of whom read in St. Paul's cathedral four times a week. I myself too, as my slender abilities will allow me, having compassion upon the ignorance of my brethren, read a public lecture twice in the day to so numerous an audience, that the church cannot contain them."[29]

What he preached can be learned from a letter he wrote to Bullinger several months later in which he refers to the bishops'

fraud and artifices, by which they promote the kingdom of antichrist, especially in the form of the oath; against which form I brought forward many objections in my public lecture before the king and the nobility . . . on which account I have incurred no small hostility. On the fourth day after the lecture an accusation was brought against me before the council by the archbishop of Canterbury.

"At length the end and issue was for the glory of God," is his bland comment on the successful outcome of his hearing.[30]

Hooper saw lecturers and preachers, supported by a godly king and council, as the spearhead of an attack on the unconverted masses, "that many-headed monster" who yet remained a prey to "ignorance" and to "the malice and impiety of mass-priests."[31] Others on the council did not. In June 1550 the council sent a letter to the Bishop of London concerning the weekday lectures, "being advertised from the lord chancellor, that diverse preachers within your diocese in the county of Essex do preach, as well the work days as the holy days, whereat some inconveniences may grow."[32] Ostensibly Lord Chancellor Rich objected to the practice of preaching on working days on the grounds that it might "increase the people's idleness." However, the lord chancellor was reputedly "no favorer of the Gospel," which, if true, would permit another interpretation of his objection.[33] But for the hiatus created by Mary's reign the Edwardian lectureships would probably have had a continuous existence into Elizabeth's reign, the radical reformers like Hooper gradually being replaced as times and terminology changed by the militant Puritans. Instead, Hooper's godly labor was transmuted by King Edward's death and Queen Mary's succession into "privy lectures . . . or other devices not expressly in this realm by laws allowable."[34]

If the Edwardian lectureships did not manage to survive the Marian reaction intact, a number of them were nevertheless the direct ancestors of Elizabethan lectureships. In London the parishes of St. Benet Gracechurch and St. Michael Cornhill employed lecturers by 1549, the parish of Allhallows Staining by 1551, and the parish of St. Antholin Budge Row in all probability at some time before Mary's accession.[35] None of the first three appears to be among the earliest of the Elizabethan parishes to hire lecturers. St. Benet's resumed the employment of a lecturer by 1571 at the latest, when it appears from the Churchwardens' Accounts that the vestry was paying the rector, William Wager, £8 a year for his lectures.[36] The lectureship at St. Michael's was not revived until 1575 when, according to a vestry minute, "This present vestry was moved to have a preacher to read a lecture twice a week."[37] Allhallows Staining may have resumed its lecture about the same time, but not until about 1580 did it have a lecturer who can be identified with certainty.[38] St. Antholin's alone resumed its lectureship at the first opportunity. The diarist Henry Machyn records that in September 1559 "began the new morning prayer at Saint Antholin's in Budge Row, after Geneva fashion." The bells "begin to ring at five in the morning; men and women all do sing, and boys." After the psalm singing the lecture began at the ungodly hour of six.[39]

Other lectureships besides those in London originated during Edward's reign. Among the records of the borough of Ipswich is a minute from 1551 mentioning the "common preacher of this town." The office evidently lapsed during Mary's reign, but in Lent of 1560 the town ordered that a lecturer be procured "who shall have for his salary £20 yearly."[40] The town lecture at Leicester also antedates Elizabeth's reign. In the Chamberlain's Accounts for 1547–48 appears an item for gifts of wine for "Master Turner the Preacher."[41] It is probable that the lecture was given at St. Martin's parish church from the beginning; in any event, the Churchwardens' Accounts for 1551–52 mention payments to the sexton "for knolling the bell to the lecture."[42] Again, there is no evidence of it during Mary's reign, but the borough authorities must have revived it soon after Elizabeth's accession, for among the Borough Ordinances for 1562 the following order occurs: "Item, that there be of every house one at every sermon upon Wednesday and Friday, upon pain of every householder making default to forfeit three pence."[43] Like Ipswich and Yarmouth later, the borough of Warwick possessed the advowsons to a number of town benefices, including the collegiate church of St. Mary's, where Hugh Latimer, the greatest preacher among the Edwardian reformers, introduced a lecture. Warwick later had in the Earl of Leicester a patron of commanding position, and it was under the earl's patronage and with his financial support that the lecture was resurrected at the accession of Queen Elizabeth.[44]

Thus by 1554 the two types of lectureship that would later be the most prominent—those endowed by the parish and those endowed by the town corporation—had already come into existence. Lectureships had not yet been established outside the towns, but far more important for the future was the connection already made between the lectureship and both lay control and militant Protestantism. The lectureship may have been in its infancy in the years of the Edwardian reformation, but at the onset of the Marian reaction it was a lusty baby, and the features of its maturity were already discernible.

From such meager beginnings and scattered precedents developed the institution that in three generations Laud and his followers would regard as a serious challenge, if not actually as a rival, to the ecclesiastical organization they led. Whatever its medieval antecedents, the continuous existence of the lectureship dates from these very years when the returned exiles and radical Protestants refused to accept as final the makeshift arrangements of the Elizabethan Settlement—Cecil cannily anticipated that they would find it at best "a cloaked papistry or a mingle mangle"[45]—and set out to adumbrate the form and content of a church truly reformed out of the Word. The lectureship was, then, coeval both with Puritanism and with the Established Church itself.

Yet it would be wrong to attribute to the lectureship a more central position in the Puritan movement than is warranted; it was, after all, only one of a number of institutions exploited by the godly. It would be a mistake, too, to assume that because the lectureship emerged fully developed at the beginning of Elizabeth's reign it remained unchanged. In fact, the term "lectureship" subsumes a variety of particular arrangements that can be described accurately and in detail only in their particular context. This should come as no surprise, given antecedents as diverse as the guild priest and the cathedral divinity lecture, or even more important, given the lack of unity and the decentralization of the Puritan movement. Although a few lectureships, such as those at St. Antholin's and Whittington College in London and at Dedham in Essex, had an institutional life lasting

several centuries, the majority had something of a temporary and improvised air about them.[46] The lectureships were, after all, born out
of an impatience with a church that would not or could not produce
sermons and a learned, preaching clergy fast enough either to satisfy
the needs of the godly or to meet the threat of the Counter-
Reformation as the Puritans perceived it. Only gradually, as various
Puritan groups despaired of easy victories or quick solutions, were attempts made to put some of the lectureships on a permanent footing.
In what must have been the vast majority of cases the lectureships
remained dependent for their continued existence on the enthusiasm
of the faithful. Thus their number changed with the temper of the
time.

Nor did any one center of Puritanism determine the manner in
which the lectureships developed. London, wrote Peter Heylyn,
"having a strong influence on all parts of the Kingdom, was generally looked on as the compass by which the lesser towns and corporations were to steer their course, the practice of it being pleaded upon
all occasions, for vestries, lectures, and some other innovations in the
state of the Church."[47] Heylyn was by no means the least acute observer of his times,[48] and no assumption could seem more natural
than his in an age that saw London move from strength to strength,
its population more than fifteen times that of Norwich, its nearest
rival, and its economic hegemony symbolized by its rising customs,
some twenty times as high as those of Bristol, the wealthiest of the
out ports.[49] Nevertheless, in this instance Heylyn seems to have gone
astray. London was an important center of Puritan strength, but even
in Heylyn's time it is hard to avoid the conclusion that though
London was probably the most exposed center of influence, other
centers—the Puritan colleges at Cambridge and the various provincial strongholds of the Puritan gentry and nobility—were of equal
importance.*

---

* Heylyn was not alone in his view. "Mercurius Civicus" wrote in a similar vein:
"To reflect a little, and look back on those times when this rebellion was but an
embryo..., though it were conceived (some say) near Banbury, and shaped in Gray's
Inn Lane, where the undertakers for the Isle of Providence did meet and plot it, yet
you know it was put out to nurse to London." *Somers' Tracts*, 2d ed., ed. Sir Walter
Scott (London, 1810), IV, 582. The prevalence of this notion may be due to the belief
that the rebellion was based on a conspiracy; if everything is to be accounted for in
terms of a Puritan plot, then centralized control is implied.

In any event, what evidence there is seems to point to rather diversified centers of innovation. The lectureships at Leicester and Ipswich, Heylyn's "lesser towns and corporations," were at least as old as the first parish lectures in London and were of a fundamentally different type. When Mathias Nichols covenanted in 1620 "to lecture and preach the word of God in the parish church [St. Andrew's] of Plymouth aforesaid twice every week, the one upon the Wednesday and the other upon the Friday in every week," he signed an agreement with the mayor and commonalty of the town.[50] In 1565, when John Bullingham was "rewarded with the sum of 53s. 4d. for his labor and pains taken in reading a lecture twice every week" in the church of St. Lawrence Jewry, London, it was by action of "the vicar, churchwardens and parishioners of this parish at this vestry." The vestry minute goes on to order that if Bullingham continued to preach the lecture, the masters of the parish were to "compound and take order with him as they shall see cause after their wisdoms and sad discretions."[51]

The lectureships in London from their Edwardian beginnings until the ebb of the period under consideration were all fundamentally similar to the one at St. Lawrence's: they were all *parish* lectureships. Although outsiders frequently attended, the lectureship existed to provide sermons primarily for the local congregation. Not all were initiated or financed by the parish vestry, as at St. Lawrence's, but in all cases the vestry exercised a decisive measure of control.

The record of a court case illustrates this central characteristic. In the spring of 1613 the churchwardens of St. Leonard, Bromley, issued a presentment against William Holbrooke, bringing him before the Consistory Court of London "for maintaining a lecture there against the churchwardens' minds."[52] That Holbrooke should have been hauled before the ecclesiastical authorities was only to be expected. On 3 December 1609 he had preached a notable sermon at Paul's Cross attacking those who delighted "in vexing the godly," and further, presenting a bitter analysis of the simoniac arrangements necessary to obtain a benefice.[53] Later, in November 1617, he was to be put on probation, as it were, for nonconformity while lecturing at West Ham.[54] However, in 1613 the charge of nonconformity was never mentioned, and the churchwardens went on to present a far more important personage than Holbrooke—Arthur Ingram,

the unpopular Jacobean financier—on the same charge. If Holbrooke's subsequent testimony can be accepted at face value, Ingram
as the patron of the living at Bromley had "taken upon him to place
...divers strange preachers to keep the lectures there against the
churchwardens' minds when they have taken order to have the doors
shut," although Holbrooke, who had "long since departed thence,"
could never remember their "gainsaying him." Charged as a result
of the churchwardens' presentment with placing ministers "without
license or approbation of the Lord Bishop of the Diocese or his Chancellor," Ingram nevertheless did not trouble to appear in court—he
was perhaps too important a City man to be handled in such a way—
and the case was dropped after the Easter session in 1613.[55] Yet the
case does illustrate the ultimate control that a vestry could exercise
over a parish lecture, even when the parish neither initiated nor financed it.

As in so many other ways, London was an anomaly, for most other
corporate towns and boroughs seem to have had lecturers who were
hired for the edification of the whole urban population, even though
they might preach from a particular parish pulpit. The parish lecture, the only type to take hold in London, was elsewhere in England
generally limited to small towns and rural areas. As always, there
were exceptions. For example, at Colchester, which had begun to
hire a "Common Preacher" as early as 1564, the Puritan John Nor-
thye held this office in the 1580's and preached twice weekly from the
pulpit at St. James parish church;[56] according to the Visitation Call
Book of 1589, another lecturer, Theodore Hill, was also preaching in
Colchester, presumably only to the parishioners of St. Michael's.[57]

Despite the similarity between the London and the provincial parish lectureships, the provincial lectureships had two peculiarities of
their own: the weekday lecture was frequently held early in the
morning on the market day, and it was sometimes preached not by a
single lecturer but alternately by a group of local clergymen. Simonds D'Ewes, the Puritan lawyer and antiquary, describes two provincial lectures in his diary. Once on a journey to Stow Hall, his father's principal manor, he broke his journey because his friend Mr.
Gibson, who was pastor of Kedington, Nathaniel Barnardiston's parish, "was this forenoon to preach at Bury St. Edmunds in the same
county (it being his course in a weekly exercise held there by divers

country ministers on the Monday, or market day), ... and therefore
I endeavored to be there in time to hear him preach, as, to my great
content and satisfaction, I did." At a later date D'Ewes writes:

I went early in the morning to Lavenham, being a fair market-town, and a
goodly manor (now devolved to me upon my father's decease), in the county of Suffolk, some eleven miles from Stow Hall, where I was partaker of a
good sermon, there being at this time a constant lecture of neighboring ministers upon each market day weekly, which was each Tuesday, the season of
harvest only excepted.[58]

The advantage of holding a rural lecture on market days is obvious; the advantages of having the lecture preached by several of the
local beneficed clergy were mainly two. First, this arrangement was
cheap because the local clergy, unlike an independent lecturer, had
their own livings from which to draw an income, and because the
preaching was less onerous, since it was shared among a group. Thus
neither D'Ewes nor the local parishioners of Lavenham paid for the
Lavenham lecture.[59] Second, the arrangement was generally regarded with approval by the ecclesiastical authorities, for a beneficed
minister was presumably orthodox, or at least more easily and
quickly exposed if he drifted away from conformity in the course of
his performance of the regular prayer book services at his parish
church. Further, a beneficed clergyman had more to lose by deprivation than an independent, salaried lecturer had by suspension.

Just when this type of arrangement commended itself to the bishops as an answer to the problem of the lectureship is not clear, but as
early as the first decade of the seventeenth century the Bishop of London tried unsuccessfully to persuade the town of Colchester to adopt
it.[60] Later William Laud evidently came to see it as part of the final
answer to the difficulties presented by the independent lecturer, for
the 1629 Instructions, sent out under the royal signature but promulgated by Bishops Laud and Harsnet, contain the following order:
"That where a lecture is set up in a market town, it may be read by
a company of grave and orthodox divines near adjoining, and in the
same diocese; and that they preach in gowns, and not in cloaks, as too
many do use."[61] Two entries in Laud's annual accounts of his Province to Charles I suggest that this formula seemed at least to the
Laudian bishops a real answer to a baffling problem. In 1663 he re-

ported that William Pierce, Bishop of Bath and Wells, "particularly
hath put down divers lecturers in market towns, which were beneficed men in other bishops' dioceses. Because he found, that when
they had preached factious and disorderly sermons, they retired into
other countries, where his jurisdiction would not reach to punish
them." A year later Laud was able to report concerning Bath and
Wells: "I must needs return to your majesty that which I would to
God I could do of all the rest, namely, that all your instructions are
punctually observed, and the lectures (as many as are in that diocese)
read, not by any particular factious persons, but by a company of
learned neighboring ministers, which are every way conformable to
the Church."[62] In this instance Laud, who can scarcely be accused of
having an overly sanguine temperament, was much too optimistic.
It may be that the "company" of lecturers in the diocese of Bath and
Wells were all conformable men, but a year later Laud learned that
four of the local ministers who preached the lectures at Guildford
and Dorking in Surrey utterly refused to read the Book of Sports.[63]

Altogether there is something rather mysterious about Laud's
adoption of the lecture preached by a combination of local ministers
as a solution to the problem of irregular preaching in market towns.
To be sure, he insisted that the divines be grave and learned, orthodox and conformable. From the early years of Elizabeth's reign, however, many of the group lectures in market towns had been closely
associated with, and in fact had had their origin in, the exercises or
prophesyings that were the Puritan answer to a sluggish, ignorant,
and non-preaching clergy and a hierarchy unable or unwilling to
provide a remedy. The exercise at Bury St. Edmunds, which D'Ewes
mentioned, had been in existence at least from the early 1570's. Over
the years it had admittedly been recognized and authorized to various degrees by the successive bishops of the diocese, Parkhurst,
Freake, and Jegon, but it was from the beginning dominated by the
local Puritan clergy and protected by the Puritan gentry, men of the
stamp of Sir Robert Jermyn and Sir John Higham.[64] In 1632, when
John Rous, the Puritan incumbent of Stanton Downham, Suffolk,
attended the lecture, it was still held on Monday as it had been for
sixty odd years, and the "combination" still met for consultation at
the time of the lecture. Predictably, the sermon Rous heard was of
questionable orthodoxy.[65] Not until 1636 could Laud report that

Bishop Wren had finally "regulated" the lecture at Bury, although whether Wren did so to the "very good content" of the local parishioners is doubtful.[66] It is less surprising that the Laudians should have had to "regulate" such combinations than that Laud should have seen them as a viable alternative to the independent town preacher. Laud was an able administrator, but imagination was perhaps not his most conspicuous quality. One is left with the impression that Laud and his fellow bishops found it easier to destroy popular institutions than to find substitutes capable of commanding general support. Lacking any alternative of their own to the Puritan town preacher, they seized on another Puritan institution in the vain hope that they could somehow bend it to their purpose.

Despite the apparent advantages for a parish of a group lectureship, and despite the episcopal approval it generally received, there is no reason to suppose that it became the exclusive form of lectureship in market towns and rural villages. Unfortunately, evidence of a systematic kind does not exist that would permit even a rough approximation of the number of town and rural parishes with lectureships of one kind or another, for the episcopal visitation records of the time do not note the presence of a lecture preached by the clergy of the neighborhood. However, from the visitation of 1583 on the call books for the diocese of London do record the names of independent lecturers, those ministers whose sole function was to preach, and this evidence indicates that approximately one out of eight parishes in the diocese (exclusive of the archdeaconry of London) had an independent lecturer at some time between 1583 and 1637. More to the point, by the mid-1630's, when Laud and Bishop Juxon, his successor at London, should have had ample time to "regulate" the independent preachers out of existence, there were still lecturers at Dedham and Colchester, Castle Hedingham and Watford, Ealing and at least another ten parishes in the diocese outside London.[67]

4

Corporation Lectureships

ALTHOUGH no statistics exist to confirm the proposition, there can be little doubt that the parish lecture in one form or another was the most common variety of lecture in England. Still, particularly during the crisis years of the 1630's and 1640's, contemporary observers credited the town and borough corporation lectureships with an importance far greater than their number could have justified. The royalist author of *Mercurius Civicus*, for one, wrote that part of the Puritan conspirators' plot was "to place some of their emissaries in all corporations (those nurseries of schism and rebellion)." The anonymous author of *Lex Talionis*, a pamphlet of 1649, listed three things that had been "the bane of monarchy": trained bands, corporations, and weekly lectures.[1] Some years earlier, in the course of his prosecution of the Feoffees for Impropriations in 1633, Attorney General Noy had put his finger on the aspect of the Feoffees' activities that worried the authorities most: "I shall call them a Confederacy or Conspiracy, and this against the Church, and they declare their vast appetites to have all Impropriations and advowsons that they can come by and still in good towns which send forth Burgesses to the Parliament, the Deputies of the realm."[2]

As early as 1630 the young Peter Heylyn, at the time a Fellow of Magdalen College, had perceived the subversive nature of the Feoffees' activities; in a sermon in July of that year at St. Mary, Oxford, Heylyn became the first to expose this aspect of their design. Later he was to write of it:

The project took beginning ... when Preston governed the affairs of the Puritan faction; at which time it was resolved amongst them to set up stipendiary lecturers in all or most market towns, where the people had commonly less to do, and consequently more apt to faction and innovation than in other places, and of all market towns to choose such as were privileged for sending burgesses to the High Court of Parliament.[3]

Heylyn seems to have had an uncontrollable propensity for generalizing from insufficient evidence, or perhaps simply an extraordinary talent for inspired guesswork, for he came to his conclusion concerning the Feoffees after "resorting frequently to a town in Gloucestershire, where one of these new Lectures had been founded by them."[4] The town was evidently Cirencester, where the Feoffees had purchased the impropriation of St. John Baptist in 1626. The curate, Alexander Gregory, may have lectured; he was, in any event, paid the profits from the impropriate property plus a yearly stipend.[5]

About one thing, however, Heylyn's information was clearly adequate: Cirencester was a Parliamentary borough. Between 1625 and 1631 the Feoffees had purchased or been given in trust various properties (advowsons, impropriate tithes, etc.) in 26 parishes scattered across England.[6] Eleven of these parishes were in the Parliamentary boroughs of Hertford, Cirencester, High Wycombe, Shrewsbury, Dunwich, Bridgnorth, Haverfordwest, Aylesbury, Worcester, Great Marlow, and Lyme Regis. Yet the Feoffees did not immediately begin to wield the influence their position in these boroughs warranted. By 1631 they had had the opportunity either to present to a living or to place a lecturer in only four boroughs: Hertford, Cirencester, High Wycombe, and Bridgnorth. At that time, then, it was doubtless the threat posed by the Feoffees, rather than their actual accomplishments, that frightened the authorities.

However, by the time Heylyn preached his sermon exposing the activities of the Feoffees, the number of borough corporations that were hiring town lecturers could amply justify alarmist speculations. "Corporations," as Christopher Hill comments, "tended to be Puritan, or at least anti-Laudian," and he goes on to list sixteen corporations that exercised ecclesiastical patronage, fifteen of which were Parliamentary boroughs—Boston, Ipswich, Lincoln, Northampton, Coventry, Warwick, Bedford, St. Albans, Gloucester, Newcastle, Norwich, Kings Lynn, Yarmouth, Shrewsbury, and Plymouth.[7] Hill concludes by suggesting that "apparently the ownership of advowsons by corporations was not nearly as extensive as their practice of appointing lecturers; but where such patronage existed it was of great political significance once the ruling urban groups had lost confidence in the government's conduct of affairs."[8]

No one, so far as I have been able to discover, has attempted to confirm Hill's supposition by a systematic survey of the records of town corporations.* Yet even the most cursory survey of printed materials

---

* Such a survey, if made in conjunction with a study of the religious views of borough Members, particularly those elected to sit in the Long Parliament, might yields some significant evidence. The corporations of fourteen of the fifteen Parliamentary boroughs mentioned by Hill sponsored town lectures of one kind or another at some time before 1640.[9] The exception, St. Albans, definitely had Puritan lecturers at St. Michael's Church, at least during much of Elizabeth's reign, but the lecture was apparently given under the aegis of the Bacon family of nearby Gorhambury, rather than of the corporation.[10] In addition to the fifteen towns Hill mentions, there were at least another 59 Parliamentary boroughs that evidently had lecturers during the period.[11] Of the total of 74 boroughs, at least 52 had lectureships controlled by the town corporations. For some of the remaining 22 boroughs, there is insufficient evidence to determine the nature of the lectureships. In others, such as Guildford, Surrey, and Peterborough, Northamptonshire, the lectures were preached by a combination of local ministers and were thus indistinguishable from the lectures given by groups of ministers in small market towns. And in at least one borough, that of Tavistock, Devon, the lecture was initiated by the local Puritan vicar.[12] By the time the Long Parliament met, 201 English boroughs had the right to elect representatives to the House of Commons, and more than one-third of them (36.8 per cent) had been host to one or more lectureships. More significant, at least one-fourth of the total number of boroughs had town preachers, lecturers appointed by the corporation, and among these were almost every major urban center in the country with the exception of London, ranging from Norwich, Great Yarmouth, and Lincoln in the East to Exeter, Bristol, Plymouth and Gloucester in the West, from Southampton on the south coast to Carlisle and Berwick in the far north. It is no wonder that the disaffected town corporations became a likely scapegoat for the defeated royalists in the 1640's. The major towns had turned their backs on the Established Church, and by implication the Crown, long before loyalty to the Crown itself came into question.

It can, of course, be argued that these statistics, though suggestive, prove no more than the pervasiveness of the town lectureship. However, an examination in some detail of even this small sample from published material does, I believe, lend support to Hill's contention

---

well show how an important aspect of Puritan influence worked and provide a partial understanding of the institutions that made the events of the 1640's in some sense a Puritan revolution.

that corporations, and in this case Parliamentary boroughs as well, tended to be puritanical. More specifically, the evidence seems to suggest that in many instances corporation lectureships were initiated by decidedly radical Protestants or Puritans seeking to promote their religious convictions.

Although there is no reason to suppose that every town corporation invariably hired Puritan preachers, the evidence does point to an equally significant trend. As urban elites found the Established Church unresponsive to their need for a preaching ministry or unable to meet it because of the poverty of urban livings, they gradually began to modify and adapt the complex ecclesiastical structure inherited from the Middle Ages to their own ends.* Sometimes without even a nod toward the ecclesiastical authorities, almost always as a result of lay initiative, the town preacher emerged as the dominant clerical figure in the urban scene. The town, not the parish, was his province, and he was answerable less directly to the archdeacon and bishop than to the town magistracy. Although in one way the English Reformation simplified the ecclesiastical system greatly by eliminating the religious orders that were in many instances immune from direct episcopal control, in another way it led to a new fragmentation by starting the drive for a preaching ministry. The town preacher was still a clergyman, of course, and still subject to episcopal discipline; but his very existence owed nothing to the Church, and the Church in attempting to control his activities confronted not an isolated parish priest but a town corporation that Church and State could ill afford to alienate.

To be sure, the description presented so far of the town lecturer as an independent preacher hired by the corporation to provide sermons for all the inhabitants is an oversimplification. At Shrewsbury, for example, the corporation succeeded in 1577 after some six years of negotiations in purchasing the advowson and impropriation of St. Mary's from the Crown. From that time on the town paid the curate £20 a year to officiate the cure, and sums starting at £52 a year to preach a town lecture. In 1591 an alderman, John Okell, gave £100

---

* The corporation of Newcastle under Lyme, for example, apparently did not establish a lectureship but supplemented the tithe income of the curate from 1601 on to secure the services of a licensed preacher. Thomas Pape, *Newcastle-under-Lyme in Tudor and Early Stuart Times* (Manchester, 1938), pp. 30, 117–18, 230, 231.

toward an endowment for the lecture, the first in a series of gifts that was to free the town of most of the cost of that institution.[13] This comparatively simple situation became slightly more complicated early in the seventeenth century when a new lectureship was founded at the parish of St. Alkmond's by the initiative not of the town, but of a successful Ironmonger, Roland Heylyn, who had left Shrewsbury in 1576 to become an apprentice in London. The published records do not reveal whether Heylyn intended this lecture, which he endowed with £20 a year, for the benefit of the town or only of the parish, but at any rate the lecturer was to be elected by the corporation. Of Heylyn's many benefactions to his native town, this one in particular may have been motivated by a definite religious conviction—a conviction perhaps best evidenced by the fact that he served as presiding officer and treasurer of the Feoffees for Impropriations from 1627 until his death five years later.[14]

Newcastle upon Tyne had a more complex system of lectureships. By the end of the 1630's, when the published records begin, there were lectureships in each of the town's four parishes. In the case of the parishes of St. Andrew's and St. John's the town ordinarily paid the incumbents £40 a year each to supplement what were probably poor livings, in return for which the "lecturer" agreed to preach a Sunday afternoon sermon. The lectures at All Saints and St. Nicholas seem to have been shared by an independent "Lecturer in Newcastle" and the vicar of St. Nicholas; the two delivered three sermons a week between them. All served and received their stipends "during the pleasure of the mayor and common council of this town."[15]

The city of Oxford developed a unique arrangement for its lectureships in order to take advantage of its considerable resources of preaching talent at the university. Anthony Wood attributes the founding of the city lectureships to the fact that "the citizens had sermons but seldom delivered to them in their public church of St. Martin."[16] When the first city lectureship was begun is uncertain, but there is evidence that as early as 1573 the mayor and council were maintaining a Tuesday sermon.[17] When the Sunday sermons at St. Martin's were instituted is equally obscure, but on 13 November 1579 the council ruled "that all freemen of this City shall every Sunday and holiday come to the sermon at Carfax with their wives and families as many as may be spared."[18] What was apparently still a relatively fluid situation hardened into its final form early in 1586 when the council decided to hire two preachers, one a Fellow of Trinity, the other a Fellow of New College, to alternate in giving sermons at Carfax on Sunday mornings. The Sunday morning sermons apparently sufficed for the city's needs until early in 1613, when the council decided to hire two additional preachers to give an afternoon sermon at the same church.[19] No other corporation seems to have secured so great a variety of preaching at the cost of so few sermons.

For the town corporation the lectureship offered advantages beyond the guarantee of an adequate supply of sermons. Principally, it offered a measure of control that could not, for example, be exercised over the incumbent of one of the corporation's benefices. In the latter instance control ceased with the exercise of patronage; once having been duly instituted to a living, the incumbent could be removed only by one of the church courts for a breach of the canons, the injunctions, or other regulations of the Church of England.* Even so, removing the incumbent was difficult, for the benefice had come to be regarded as his freehold property.[20] Archbishop Bancroft dealt with this difficulty in his orders for the enforcement of the new canons of 1604 by directing the bishops to proceed to deprivation on proof of a beneficed clergyman's nonconformity, for as far as beneficed clergymen were concerned, he wrote, "It would not much trouble them, nor work the conformity that is desired, to put them to silence, if they might enjoy their benefices [i.e., the income of the living]."[21] Bad conduct (drunkenness or incontinence, for example) or lack of the ability to preach were more objectionable to a puritanically inclined town corporation than nonconformity, but the remedies available to the town were few and inadequate. A nonpreaching incumbent was well within the law so long as he read the homilies and found someone else to preach the requisite quarterly

---

* Harassment was, of course, always a possibility. Attorney General Noy made just such a charge against the Feoffees: "But this is not the worst; as soon as they get any impropriation or advowson, they go about to weary the present incumbents and labor by all means to get them out." Isabel M. Calder, *Activities of the Puritan Faction of the Church of England, 1625–33* (London, 1957), p. 55. At Newcastle under Lyme, where the town treated the curate as a town preacher, the capital burgesses stopped the curate's pay during a quarrel between the curate and the corporation. Thomas Pape, *Newcastle-under-Lyme in Tudor and Early Stuart Times* (Manchester, 1938), p. 118.

and monthly sermons. Bad conduct rarely led to more than censure or at most suspension, neither of which permitted the town to obtain a more suitable minister.

Lecturers were much more vulnerable. The ecclesiastical courts, as Bancroft pointed out, could "suspend them 'ab officio,'" which was "in effect a deprivation to them,"[22] and town corporations could apparently terminate their tenure at will. The following minute of the town council of Nottingham, dated 15 December 1617, is typical: "It is agreed that Master Caldwell, the preacher, shall have £10 fee from the town for this year in regard of his great pains which he continually taketh; and the same to continue further and longer time, if he stay in the town.... And this order for the payment thereof to have continuance for as long time as this company shall think fitting."[23] A similar minute made by the corporation of Oxford is hedged not only by the qualification that the stipend will be paid "for and during the will and pleasure of Mr. Mayor and of the council of this City and no longer," but also by the stipulation that "this to be no precedent for any succeeding preachers."[24]

Some towns, not content merely to control the purse strings, insisted on further regulations and conditions. At Ipswich, for instance, two lecturers were hired from 1577 on. In the early 1580's the town experienced some difficulty in collecting the benevolence for one of the preachers, Dr. Norton, who had been the senior lecturer since 1577.[25] By 1585 Norton had become a problem not only because it was impossible to collect all of his wages but also because he and the other lecturer, the radical Puritan William Negus, had become involved in a quarrel that "spread in the Great Court into parties, and some foul words were spoken."[26] The upshot was that the council ordered Norton to leave in April; in October he was given a testimonial "that his departure was to satisfy scruples concerning nonresidency, that his life was blameless, that his doctrine is orthodox." It is a fact that Dr. Norton was beneficed at Aldborough; it is a good guess that the scruples against nonresidency were originally those of the rigorous Mr. Negus and his party among the magistrates. Negus left the same year to become the rector of Leigh, to which he had been presented by Lord Rich. His successor at Ipswich, Robert Wright, was required "if he travel," to substitute "a godly, sufficient, and orthodox supply," and more important, not to "take any other pastoral or ecclesiastical promotion without the consents of the Bailiffs for the time being."[27]

This regulation was by no means unique. At Lincoln the temporary dominance of the council by the Puritan faction in 1600 brought about a swift change in the lectureship. In May the council ruled that to be elected preacher of the city, a man must "have no benefices, and lie and be continually amongst the citizens," thus apparently disqualifying the incumbent lecturer. In September, by a majority of one, the council elected John Smith, a young Fellow of Christ's College, Cambridge, and the future Baptist leader, to fill the vacancy created by the new regulation.[28]

As far as the ecclesiastical opponents of the lectureships were concerned, it was precisely this entire dependence on the laity that made the lectureships so thoroughly objectionable; not only would the lecturer be of necessity a "popular" preacher (i.e., pleasing to his auditory), but his very lack of connection with a parish church made it virtually impossible to ensure his conformity to prayer book practices.[29] In 1633 Archbishop Laud learned to his dismay that Richard Fishborne, a London Mercer, had left a trust to set up a lectureship in Huntingdon with the provision that if for any reason the trustees were dissatisfied with the lecturer, "he shall at a month, or a fortnight's warning, give over the place, without any relation to bishop or archbishop"; Laud's reaction was to petition the King "that no layman whatsoever, and least of all companies or corporations, may, under any pretence of giving to the Church or otherwise, have power to put in or put out any lecturer or other minister."[30] Four years earlier, in 1629, Laud and Harsnet had met to propound certain considerations to the King for the "preventing of such mischiefs" as were caused "chiefly by the multitude of irregular lecturers, both in city and country, whose work it was to undermine as well the doctrine as the government" of the Church. They had attempted at that time to meet just this problem in the only way possible without infringing the rights of the civil magistracy.[31] The relevant clause in the 1629 Instructions reads: "That if a corporation maintain a single lecturer, he be not suffered to preach, till he profess his willingness to take upon him a living with cure of souls within that corporation; and that he actually take such benefice or cure, as soon as it shall be fairly procured for him."[32]

It would be difficult even to guess how effectively this instruction was enforced. At Ipswich, Samuel Ward, who had been the "single lecturer" since 1605, could have taken a living only by giving up his lectureship, for in 1607, when the town elected him lecturer for life, the following provision had been added at the bottom of the minute: "If he take a pastoral charge, this retainer shall be void."[33] After three decades of preaching, Ward was summoned before the High Commission on 3 November 1634 and charged with 43 offenses. A year later, on 26 November 1635, he was convicted of "preaching publicly at Ipswich against the set form of prayer, saying that the using of [it] ...was confining of the Spirit"; of preaching "against the book of Common Prayer"; of preaching "disgracefully against bowing and other reverend gestures in the Church, saying that a man may teach a...baboon to do it"; and of uttering "speeches derogatory to the discipline and government of the Church of England, as namely that our Church was ready to ring the changes in matters of religion."[34] In short, the court, faced by the complete nonconformist, charged him with almost every conceivable "scandalous" tenet and position, and concluded by suspending him from his lecture. Yet, though he held no living, the court did not charge him with flouting the royal Instructions.

Similarly, when John Workman, corporation lecturer at Gloucester for thirteen years, was sentenced before the Court of High Commission in 1635, he was convicted of crimes that ranged from preaching "in the open pulpit, that how many paces a man made in dancing, so many paces he made to hell," to preaching that "the election of a minister ... doth properly belong to the people." He was also charged with praying "for the States of Holland and the King of Sweden or other great general beyond the seas before the King's majesty that now is over us." Workman was duly suspended and excommunicated, but no mention was made of the fact that he had lectured for years without ever holding a benefice.[35] Perhaps in the case of radical Puritans like Ward and Workman, such a charge was superfluous. Still, had the bishops enforced the Instructions and suspended the two from their lectureships in 1630, many of the "scandalous and erroneous" sermons would never have been preached.

The 1629 Instructions may not have been a complete dead letter in Laud's own diocese. On 14 May 1630 Laud received a letter from the bailiffs of Colchester asserting that their lecturer, Richard Maden, had accepted the vicarage of St. Peter's. His preaching license, however, had been issued for St. Botolph's and St. James's, and the bailiffs desired permission to remove their lecture to St. Peter's parish.[36] It is not certain whether permission was ever granted. What does seem certain from the evidence is that Maden held the vicarage from 1628 to about 1630 and again from 1632 to 1635. The famous Puritan William Bridges lectured in the intervening years.[37] Apparently the town had made the vicarage an adjunct of the lectureship to be held only so long as the preacher gave the town lecture. Had the spirit of the Instructions been observed, the vicarage would have provided the lecturer with a benefice and income independent of the town's control. Instead, since the living was in the gift of the town corporation, the lecturer's acceptance of the vicarage increased his dependence on the magistrates. One would be hard put to prove in the circumstances that the corporation was not sincere in its compliance, but it may not be unfair to assume that the purpose of the bailiffs' apparent cooperation with Laud was to evade the force of his regulations. Colchester was, after all, a town notorious for its Puritan proclivities.[38]

Town lectureships did not, of course, exist to vex Archbishop Laud, nor did town magistrates ordinarily go out of their way to antagonize or subvert the established order of which, it must be remembered, they were very much a part. Colchester may have observed the letter of Laud's directions in order to violate the spirit, but the evidence even in that Puritan stronghold is at best circumstantial. On occasion a borough might defy a bishop in order to try to protect its preaching minister. After Bishop Goodman prohibited John Workman from preaching the Gloucester lecture in 1633 the city council ordered that Workman "shall have his allowance of £20 yearly ... so long as he shall be pleased to inhabit and live in this city, whether he preach or not," but a suit brought against the chief magistrates in the Court of High Commission led to their capitulation two years later.[39]

Most urban governments seem to have studiously avoided direct confrontation with higher powers in Church and State. Whatever their private feelings and religious predilections, town magistrates were themselves men of substance and authority in their own communities and had an obvious stake in the perpetuation of orderly procedure and legitimate authority. The astute mayor and chamber of

Exeter, rather than defy Bishop Cotton when he rejected their choice of a preacher for the Bodley lecture in 1616, appealed instead to his more sympathetic superior, Archbishop Abbot.[40]

A few years later the mayor and jurats of Rye found themselves in a considerably more delicate situation, but a combination of luck and tact seems to have enabled them to emerge from the incident relatively unscathed and with their lectureship intact. The source of the trouble was the refusal of the local curate to permit the newly appointed lecturer access to his pulpit—not an unusual problem in itself, but exacerbated in this instance by the fact that both the lecturer, Thomas Warren, and the curate, James Wittaker, had factional support within the town. To make matters worse, higher authorities were likely to become involved in the feud, for the Lord Warden of the Cinque Ports, who had assisted the town in initiating the lectureship, could be expected to support the lecturer, and Archbishop Abbot would presumably support the recalcitrant curate, for the curate was the archbishop's chaplain. The mayor and jurats wrote first to Lord Zouch, the Lord Warden, on 24 October 1623, "beseech[ing] your Lordship that you would be pleased to be a means that the lecture may still continue," and five days later to the archbishop, requesting that he use his influence with his troublesome chaplain. Within a month Lord Zouch had written to the Bishop of Chichester requesting his support of the lecture, and by the following January a solution of sorts had been reached through the bishop's good offices: Wittaker was dismissed and Warren was installed as both curate and lecturer. During the ensuing months the magistrates damped the fires of internal faction while Lord Zouch blocked a suit in the Star Chamber brought by the disappointed Wittaker against Warren and his supporters in the town. As for the townspeople, they returned to such perennial problems as the defense of their shipping against piracy and the protection of their fishing rights.[41]

For all the deference town magistrates normally showed their superiors in Church and State in dealings over lectureships, they nevertheless dealt from a position of strength. The Crown might dissolve the Feoffees and Laud might humble the Gloucester magistrates, but neither Crown nor hierarchy was willing or able to solve the problem at the source of these troubling events. The nub of the problem was, of course, the expense of providing a preaching ministry, and so long as the solution was left to the townsmen themselves, there was bound to be that "lay dependency" so hated by Laud.

Given the dimensions of the problem, the Church's inability to deal with it is no surprise. A preaching clergy, as everyone knew, meant an educated clergy, and the pittance that might suffice for a mere reading curate would never satisfy a competent minister. William Harrison, himself a clergyman, but no Puritan, suggested in the course of a description of the clergy in the middle years of Elizabeth's reign that £30 a year or less would not serve for even a "mean scholar."[42] As late as the middle 1640's the borough of Leicester petitioned Parliament for an augmentation from sequestered episcopal lands, for as the petition noted, "There are five ancient parish churches in the said borough all of them impropriate, in none of them sufficient means to maintain an able minister, and in two of them not ten pounds per annum for serving the cure."[43] The 1586 Puritan survey of the beneficed clergy of Lincoln claimed for the town "unpreaching ministers twelve, whereof four are double beneficed and two readers. Not one preacher."[44] The survey was admittedly written from *parti pris*, but it was probably accurate at least in this instance, for there is evidence that a minimum of three livings in Lincoln—two vicarages and one rectory—had annual incomes of less than £6 each.[45] When the borough ordered the chief magistrates to provide "as shortly as may be" for a "virtuous and learned preacher ... to teach the inhabitants the word of God," they offered a salary of £20 yearly, more than three times the value of the three poorest livings in the city, and by 1590 the lecturer was paid a stipend of £40.[46]

Clearly nothing prevented town corporations from providing a remedy for the pervasive poverty of urban benefices. However, the evidence suggests that many towns preferred to pay a decent salary to a lecturer whom they could hire and fire at will, and who would preach to their liking, rather than augment the livings of the beneficed clergy in their midst. This contention is perhaps best illustrated by a letter from the Privy Council sent to the mayor and aldermen of Bristol on 16 March 1592/3. "We are credibly given to understand," the Council wrote,

that the state of the ministry in that city of Bristol is very mean and poor, and that in regard of the smallness of the livings very few of them are found of ability and sufficiency to discharge the places whereunto they are called, every single benefice being for the most part at this time not worth yearly above eight or nine pounds. . . . And whereas we are also informed that out of the common purse of the city, in regard of the zeal and care had of the truth, there is given a voluntary contribution to maintain three preachers, the better to hold the people in obedience to God and her Majesty, and that divers of good wealth and sufficiency within the city are very hardly or not at all to be drawn . . . to enlarge the maintenance of the poor ministers.

The Privy Council went on to order that the corporation make an assessment on all "inhabitants of ability" as a means to provide an "increase of the maintenance of the poor ministers as specially those who are preachers."[47] A reasonable and tactful enough request, one would have thought, particularly since no suggestion was made of forcing the town to abandon the lectureships. Its effectiveness can be measured by the following figures, which date from a few years later: the annual sum collected on the assessment was about £44, or an average of not quite £3 per parish, whereas during the same year the three lecturers were paid £30 each.[48] The Privy Council had been obeyed in a formal sense, if not fully in spirit.

It is the spirit, the religious feeling behind the lectures, that remains most elusive, although the town records are not as mute in this regard as the parish records of London. An occasional petition or minute in the town records reveals something of the motivations and expectations that led townsmen to found, support, and tenaciously defend their lectureships. When the corporation of Gloucester provided for a twice-weekly lecture in 1619, the minutes noted that insufficient care had previously been taken "for the settling and establishing of the public preaching of God's Word." In 1625 Benjamin Coxe was appointed "to read a weekly lecture in the parish church of Barnstaple to and for the instruction of the inhabitants thereof in the ways of their salvation." In 1629 the corporation of Liverpool sought the support of the Bishop of Chester for a twice-monthly lecture, on the grounds that Liverpool was "a market town and a town of great resort and many papists inhabiting thereabouts."[49] Even if the expression of these sentiments is regarded as purely a matter of form, it is significant that they should have been considered the appropriate ones. At times such claims were made for the beneficial workings of God's Word in the mundane urban society that quite evidently even the most hard-headed businessman among the city fathers must have felt the public monies were well employed. When the ministers and schoolmasters of Leicester recommended obtaining the appropriately named Mr. Angell "especially for keeping of a constant lecture one day in the week," they stated in their petition that they doubted not "but his able performance of these duties will greatly tend to the honor of God, the comfort of us all, and the great profit and credit of this corporation."[50]

Sometimes the records purport to give not an account of things hoped for, but testimony of the actual efficacy of a lecturer's preaching. Thus the mayor, aldermen, and assistants of Southampton wrote of their lecturer that they had found "four years experience of his doctrine, life and conversation to be such and so religious that he hath done great good in this place by his extraordinary zealous and laborious preaching, whereby he hath bred great reformation in many of the inhabitants."[51]

At other times the records seem to suggest that the lecture may be the product of the enthusiasm of a zealous minority who appeal to the good judgment, if not the natural inclination, of a more worldly majority. At Nottingham a group of citizens petitioned the mayor "with the rest of your brethren" to enforce attendance at the lecture, "for as much as we have a most godly exercise of preaching on the Friday once a week, and lest the same should decay amongst us through our negligence in not coming as we ought to do, and specially of the chiefest of our town, which ought to be most present." They reminded the magistrates further that "the service of almighty God" was "most carefully before all worldly matters to be considered"[52]—a sentiment, one suspects, no more to be denied with impunity by politicians in those days than appeals to the sacredness of motherhood and country are to be denied today.

Despite the effectiveness of such pressures, it was not always easy to raise the lecturer's stipend. Perhaps the worldly majority was following its natural inclinations at such times, or perhaps the zealous minority was having trouble sustaining its original enthusiasm. Whatever the reason, corporations were frequently forced to invoke sanctions to ensure that their lecturer would be paid. In 1582, when the lecture at York was only two years old, the town council found it necessary to order

that billets . . . shall be made forthwith to the constables of every parish of all such arrearages as they are behind to the preacher for his fees, and if any free citizen refuse to pay, then he ... [is] to be brought before the wardens of the ward; and if they will not thereupon pay, being able, that every such citizen [is] to be, by consent of my Lord Mayor, committed to ward, there to remain until such time as he ... will do so.[53]

In this case there had probably never been any real enthusiasm for the lecture to begin with, for it had been urged on the town by the powerful voice of the Earl of Huntingdon. Yet even the town of Ipswich, where a radical Protestant temper ran strongly, was forced to turn from entreating "foreigners as [well as] burgesses for their liberal contribution" to distraining the goods of such a man as the recalcitrant William Barber "for his proportion assessed; viz: four yards and a half of broadcloth, valued at 23s. 4d. by two prizers."[54]

What these town records almost never give direct voice to is unequivocal partisanship in religious matters. Certainly we cannot assume automatically that the presence of a lectureship implies a puritanically inclined corporation, for if we did, it would be difficult to explain why some corporations apparently had to be prodded into establishing lectures. The magistrates at Reading seem to have exhausted the local demand for sermons in 1604, when the vicar was hired at £6 a year to preach once a quarter as well as "upon the day of election of the new mayor and upon the day in which the new mayor shall take his oath, from henceforth." The corporation did establish a monthly lecture in 1618, but only at the behest of the Bishop of Salisbury, who requested the corporation's assistance "in promoting so necessary a measure." In 1625 Reading finally established a Sunday afternoon lecture, this time as a result of the promptings of the pious Calvinist bishop John Davenant, who appears to have taken the measure of the corporation, for he gave the magistrates no excuse to plead poverty. His letter proposed that the lecture be assigned either to one man or to "divers neighboring ministers within the deanery gratis"; on putting the matter to a vote, thirteen were in favor of, and none against, assigning the lecture to "divers gratis."[55] Not too much should be read into the laconic language of official minutes. The town's lack of enthusiasm may reflect its objection to the bishop's interference rather than any objection to a lecture *per se*, and the alacrity with which the offer of free sermons was accepted may reflect only the attractiveness of a bargain. In the last analysis Reading remains something of an enigma.

The religious attitudes of other towns are considerably less ambiguous. At Northampton the very wording of the records reveals that the lectureship was unquestionably of Puritan origin, for the order establishing the lectureship is part of a measure that was clearly aimed at reorganizing the local church on a Presbyterian basis. In the first clause of the measure the "singing and playing of organs before time accustomed ... is put down." The second requires that there be "in the chief church every Tuesday and Thursday from nine of the clock until ten in the morning read a lecture of the scriptures." The third requires a Sunday sermon after morning prayer, which all townsmen were to attend unless they had a sermon at their parish church. The sixth states that the youth of the town were to be examined after evening prayer "in a portion of Calvin's Catechism"—a radical provision by any standard. Most significant, however, were the orders calling for "an exercise of the ministers ... about the interpretation of Scriptures" every Saturday, and for "a weekly assembly every Thursday after the lecture by the mayor and his brethren, assisted with the preacher, minister, and other gentlemen ... for the correction of discords made in the town as for notorious blasphemy, whoredom, [and] drunkenness."[56] Even with episcopal support such a little Geneva could not survive. In 1579 the Privy Council took note of "the ecclesiastical disorders and scandals of Northampton," rusticated the chief minister, who was also town lecturer, to a remote parish in Devon, and suppressed the prophesyings and disciplinary meetings.*

More typical than Northampton's radical measure is a letter from the corporation of Leicester to the Earl of Huntingdon in which the townsmen state "that being deprived by the just judgment of God for our sins, of our faithful, godly, and learned preacher, Mr. Johnson, ... we have been destitute sithence of the blessed benefit of a resident preacher, faithfully to divide with us the everlasting bread of our salvation." This language would certainly not come amiss from a Puritan, but what establishes the Puritan complexion of the council beyond much doubt is the fact that they expect to receive a sympathetic hear-

---

* *The Records of the Borough of Northampton*, ed. J. Charles Cox (London, 1898), II, 390–91. The corporation evidently remained Puritan; in 1638 Dr. Samuel Clarke wrote rather ruefully to the Dean of Arches: "I long since advised the mayor and his brethren that the Thursday lecture and sermons on Sunday in the afternoon should be forborne in these infectious times. They then raised a report of me that I was about to starve their souls." *Ibid.*, p. 395.

ing from Henry Hastings, perhaps the most dependable aristocratic patron of the Puritans in his generation. Moreover, they expect him to help them obtain the services of one of the most notorious Puritans in the country, Walter Travers, "a man, as we are credibly informed, of singular godliness and approved learning."[57]

The supposition that the Leicester Puritans were behind Mr. Angell's appointment in 1627 as town lecturer is confirmed not simply by the phraseology of the petition mentioned earlier, but also by other circumstances surrounding the appointment. Docketed immediately after the petition is a letter from Sir William Heyricke to the mayor urging the choice of a lecturer who "is conformable to the church established, a grave man and a good scholar and sound divine, and not factious, wherein I pray you remember to set aside all private affection and join all together for the public good."[58] It seems reasonable to conjecture that Sir William had heard about Mr. Angell's candidacy, knew him to be a Puritan, and was attempting to block his appointment. The impression that Mr. Angell was the town Puritans' candidate is reinforced by the fact that one of those petitioning on his behalf was Francis Higginson. Higginson, an Emmanuel graduate and a friend of Arthur Hildersham and Thomas Hooker, had long been one of the popular ministers in the town and in fact had himself been offered the post of town preacher. He had refused, however, because he had grown more radical with the years, was no longer prepared to conform, and would in consequence be unable to procure the preaching license that a new post would require. Instead he recommended John Angell, a schoolmaster in Leicester and supposedly a conformable man; shortly afterwards, no longer finding even Leicester a safe haven, Higginson left England for the New Jerusalem across the seas.[59]

Finally, there is the evidence of John Angell's subsequent career. In 1634, seven years after Angell's appointment as lecturer, Archbishop Laud reported in his annual account that "in Leicester the dean of the arches suspended one Mr. Angell, who hath continued a lecturer in that great town, for these divers years, without any license at all to preach; yet took liberty enough."[60] How long he remained suspended is unknown. A minute in the town records of 12 January 1636/7 requests him to resign from his schoolmastership, but the

Chamberlain's Accounts for the same year show that he was still paid for keeping the library. At any rate, he had been restored to his lectureship by 1641, for he was given a quart of sack in July when he preached in favor of the Protestation of the House of Commons. Angell was evidently a Presbyterian, for he refused the Engagement in 1650 and was forced out of his lectureship. Within the year he was appointed lecturer at Grantham by the Mercers' Company of London, a post he held until his death in 1655.[61]

If, then, the mere presence of a corporation lectureship is not a sufficient ground for supposing that the town is a Puritan stronghold, or even that the lectureship is a product of a peculiarly puritanical desire for a ready supply of sermons, the circumstances surrounding the lectureship may provide more conclusive evidence of the religious motivations behind it. In particular, there are three circumstances relating to a lectureship's origin or subsequent history that permit it to be characterized as Puritan with some degree of certainty: first, the active support of a known Puritan patron; second, the opposition or interference of the hierarchy, particularly of a Laudian bishop; and third, the puritanical inclinations of the lecturers hired.

Henry Hastings, third Earl of Huntingdon, ranked perhaps second after his brother-in-law, the Earl of Leicester, among the Elizabethan grandees who used their patronage and influence in court and country to protect the nascent forces of Puritanism; of the two, however, he was probably the more consistent champion.[62] He was assuredly the greatest patron of town lectureships of his age, and as his brother wrote following his death, "He never set a straying foot in any place where he did not labor at the least to settle the preaching of the word to the people." Huntingdon concerned himself about the lecture at Leicester at least as early as 1566, when an act changing the time of the Wednesday and Friday lectures was "made by the advice and consent of the right honorable Henry, Earl of Huntingdon."[63] As late as 1590 a minute records that the lecturer's stipend was raised from £20 to £30 a year "by the earnest suit and labor of the earl of Huntingdon."[64]

When Huntingdon became Lord President in the North, he said he was determined to do all he could "to get good preachers planted in the market towns of this country."[65] He was instrumental in "planting" the lectureship at York despite the natural inertia and conserva-

tive hostility of a city that according to Claire Cross still had strong
Catholic sympathies. In 1579 Huntingdon suggested that the city
provide its own preacher; in 1580 the mayor, the aldermen, and representatives of the twenty-four "agreed that with all convenient speed
a well learned man shall be gotten and provided to be preacher for
this city."[66] Huntingdon probably encountered less resistance at Newcastle, where he succeeded in persuading the corporation to hire his
own chaplain, Richard Holdsworth, in 1585. Holdsworth was no conformist. In 1584 he had been suspended for refusing to subscribe to
Whitgift's Articles, and in the same year he had been among the Lincolnshire "preachers" who petitioned that "we may be restored to our
flocks and people in such sort as with all peace of conscience we may
go forward with the Lord's work in building up his house in our several places." Yet by 1585 Huntingdon had appointed Holdsworth his
household chaplain in the north and had launched him on a new
career.[67]

Sometimes an aristocratic patron was called on only as an adviser.
In 1599 the Chamber at Exeter, having decided to hire a preacher,
consulted the Countess of Warwick and Lady Paulett, and on their
recommendation engaged the services of Edmund Snape, former colleague of Cartwright and leader of the Northampton classis—an appointment "very acceptable to God Almighty and the commonwealth
of this city" but scarcely one calculated to please the Bishop of Exeter.[68]
Snape's short tenure of office (he was gone by late 1604, when he appears as a lecturer and curate at St. Saviour, Southwark) may mean
that he was unable to secure a preaching license from the bishop.[69]

If the religious convictions of a patron can provide some positive
evidence for ascertaining the views that led to the founding of a lectureship, episcopal and royal interference offers evidence of at least a
negative kind: that is, even though it is not certain that the corporation
in such a case was particularly sympathetic to Puritanism, or that Puritans were appointed lecturers, it is clear that the institution itself was
regarded with great suspicion and could only be tolerated when subjected to the closest episcopal supervision. One further qualification
needs to be made. Most of the instances of episcopal intervention that
this admittedly incomplete examination has turned up have been
the work of bishops associated with Laud's wing of the hierarchy.
Whether these bishops objected more to the institutional aspect of the

lectureships—to the degree of lay control they implied—or to the fact that the lectureships were frequently exploited by Puritans is difficult to ascertain. Perhaps it is also immaterial, since the bishops found both highly distasteful.

The most ambiguous case is that of Doncaster, largely because the evidence is incomplete. In a minute of 13 December 1639, four aldermen were ordered to negotiate with the Archbishop of York concerning the stipend to be paid to James Hutchinson, "who is commended to us by his Majesty to be our lecturer." Four days later the corporation wrote a letter to the archbishop expressing regret that the archbishop was not satisfied with their offer to pay Hutchinson the same salary as their former lecturer, a Mr. Bell. However, the corporation went on to say, "Being rather willing to overcharge ourselves for the present rather than not give your lordship good satisfaction, we have met together again and in this case of necessity are agreed that our corporation shall pay to the said preacher the annual stipend of £50 until he be otherwise provided for." This apparent spirit of accommodation is somewhat qualified by a plaintive wish "that God do send us a new vicar who, we hope, will be able to teach us without any charge to us."[70] Such a necessarily diplomatic letter could hardly hint at an objection either to outside interference or to the extra expense, which came on top of recent assessments for Ship Money. Whether the initial intervention by the King and archbishop had been brought on by the Puritan character of the previous lecturers we cannot tell.

Plymouth, by contrast, was subjected to massive interference in the early 1630's, and for obvious reasons. The incident that seems to have opened the way for the combined intervention of King and bishop was the appointment of Thomas Ford as lecturer in 1631.[71] On June 12 of that year, Ford, at the time in residence at Magdalen Hall, Oxford, had preached at St. Mary's against the Arminian conversion of the communion table into an altar. For this and similar sermons, he and two other Oxford preachers were summoned before the vice-chancellor and then cited to appear before the Privy Council at Laud's behest. On August 23 all three were ordered to leave the university. Ford went home to Devonshire and would have been promptly installed as lecturer of Plymouth but for the vigilance of Laud, who obtained a royal order forbidding his election.[72] Having failed to obtain Ford, the corporation proceeded in 1632 to appoint another local

Puritan, Alexander Gross. This time the King and bishop not only blocked the election of the corporation's nominee but decreed that the corporation's next choice would be Thomas Bedford.[73] It was probably as a result of this interference that the corporation, which had purchased the advowson of St. Andrew from the Crown in 1572, granted Gross a reversionary interest in that vicarage.[74] When the living fell vacant, however, it went not to Gross, but to Aaron Wilson, a London rector, lecturer, and royal chaplain who had recently been appointed Archdeacon of Exeter. The corporation had its revenge in 1642 and 1643, when Wilson and Bedford were removed and George Hughes, one of the leading Presbyterians in the West, was elected both vicar and lecturer.[75]

A few years later, at the end of the 1630's, the combined assault of Crown and hierarchy on one of the lecturers at Newcastle upon Tyne brought to light the growing power of the various Puritan groups in the borough, a power that was seen, not unreasonably, as a threat to the security of that northern outpost. Puritans had been preaching in Newcastle at least since the 1580's, when the Earl of Huntingdon had recommended Richard Holdsworth and John Udall to the town authorities, but Arminian preachers had occupied the pulpit of the chief parish church, St. Nicholas, since 1623. On the whole Newcastle's Puritan and Arminian factions had managed to coexist more or less peacefully, if uneasily, until fear of a subversive alliance between the Puritans and the Scottish Covenanters across the border exacerbated intramural relationships. In March 1639 charges were brought against Dr. Robert Jenison, who had been lecturer at All Saints for more than twenty years, for his nonconformity and seditious preaching.[76] In August, Sir John Marley of Newcastle wrote to the Dean of Durham in London

that unless it be prevented and that speedily, the Puritan faction in our town, which has much troubled us, is likely to multiply, for it is reported Dr. Jenison is coming home, but that is not great matter, he may be looked to; but what is worse, there is an intention to make Robert [Beckwith] mayor at Michaelmas next, who is the doctor's half brother and strong for that faction, and I am sure most who know him think him good for little else.[77]

Such warnings did not fall on deaf ears. Early in September, Secretary Windebank wrote to Archbishop Neile that the King thought Jenison's return to Newcastle would "too much countenance the factious party," to which Neile rather plaintively replied that although he knew Jenison's return to be dangerous, "yet how to deny a man to live at his own habitation where his wife and children are I know not."[78]

The government could do little to prevent the Puritan Beckwith's election to the mayoralty. Jenison, however, was easily suspended, and hot upon his suspension came an order from the King commanding the corporation to elect Dr. George Wishart, a Scot expelled from St. Andrews by the Covenanters, in his place. "Herein his Majesty expects you fail not, but that you show that conformity and obedience which his princely care of the town requireth." The town magistrates were not disposed to yield entirely. At the end of their order of 18 December 1639, in which they agreed to comply with the royal wishes, they added the proviso "that the said Doctor Wishart shall ... hold ... the said place ... during only the suspension of the said Doctor Jenison and no longer."[79]

By intervening in the affairs of Newcastle, the King and bishop brought into the open the town's growing Puritanism; by persecuting Jenison, a popular preacher, they seem only to have strengthened and hardened Puritan opposition. Late in January 1640 Yeldard Alvey, the Arminian vicar of St. Nicholas, Newcastle, reported optimistically to Neile that "Dr. Jenison, they say, is preparing speedily to go for Holland, to Amsterdam, and Mr. [Anthony] Lapthorne being silenced, there is good hope that now the neck of the puritanical faction is broken." Such hopes were not to be borne out by events. In the previous December the town council had retaliated for the expulsion of Jenison by discharging Thomas Stephenson, the lecturer in Alvey's parish, and electing a Puritan preacher in his stead. By October 1640 the invading Scots had driven Alvey out of town, and in April 1641 both Alvey and Wishart were cited by the House of Commons as delinquents.[80]

Newcastle was by no means the only northern town to experience royal and episcopal intervention. Between Archbishop Neile's active government and the Crown's nervous repression at the end of the 1630's, a number of centers of Puritan strength were discovered among the town and borough corporations of the region. As Neile confessed to John Shaw immediately after Shaw became the lecturer at All Saints, York, "I have ... nothing against you, but I heard ... that you are brought in by the Lord Mayor of York [John Vaux] to head the

Puritan party against me, but I tell you ... I will break Vaux and the Puritan party."[81] Besides York three of the major towns in the West Riding—Leeds, Halifax, and Bradford—had Puritan lecturers; in the East Riding the Parliamentary boroughs Beverley and Hull did also. At Hull, though the mayor complained to the ecclesiastical authorities in 1638 about the practices at Holy Trinity, the radical Puritan curate and the more moderate lecturer, Andrew Marvell, had strong backing in the town and survived the harassment of the church courts.[82] Farther north, at Berwick, Secretary Windebank commanded Bishop Morton late in 1639 in the King's name to dismiss John Jemmett, the lecturer, whether or not a legal case could be made against him: "You [are] forthwith [to] cause him to be silenced and to depart from thence, and in case you can find sufficient matter to call him into further question that you cause articles to be exhibited against him in your Court of High Commission, and there proceed legally against him." The waiving of legal niceties at that late date is not very surprising; as Neile's chaplain wrote to a local vicar, "What you do against Puritans, God reward you for; I think the generation of them is most dangerous to this church and state, especially having a Scottish example of anarchy and confusion to follow."[83] Even before the Long Parliament met, the temper of politics had risen, and frequently the Puritan town preacher was the focus of political contention.

The final criterion for determining the religious complexion of a corporation lectureship, and by implication (with some degree of certainty) the preference of the town itself, is, of course, the religious views of the lecturers hired. Presumably a town that persistently chose Puritans to lecture was indulging its taste for puritanical preaching. Ipswich provides an interesting example. There would be a strong case for presuming that Ipswich was a Puritan stronghold even without evidence concerning the lectureships, for the town was located in a region, bounded on the north by Lynn, Norwich, and Yarmouth, and on the south by Sudbury, Coggeshall, Dedham, and Colchester, that already had a long-standing reputation for religious radicalism by Elizabeth's reign.[84] Of a piece with such a supposition would be Ipswich's election of Sir Francis Walsingham as High Steward in 1581 and in general its close and friendly relations with Colchester, the nearby center of Essex Puritanism. There can be little question that by the early seventeenth century Puritan sentiments predominated.

Samuel Ward, who was elected lecturer in 1605 and confirmed in that office for life in 1607, was a graduate of Sidney Sussex, a Puritan seminary like Emmanuel. He was first inhibited from preaching in 1622 for publishing an anti-Spanish cartoon, but no doubt the corporation was aware of his Puritanism before that incident. In the spring of 1634 Sir Nathaniel Brent, Laud's vicar-general, reported that "the town is factious, and yet the better part are conformable in reasonable good measure. Mr. Samuel Ward is thought to be the chief author of their nonconformity."[85] How small in number Brent's "better part" must have been (assuming that the magistrates did not simply tell Brent what he wanted to hear) can be seen by the town's reaction to Ward's suspension. In 1636 Laud reported to the King that "the bishop was ready to have allowed them another [lecturer], if they would have sought him; but they resolve to have Mr. Ward or none, and that (as is conceived) in despite of the censure of the court."[86]

A brief look at the sixteenth-century appointments to the Ipswich lecture suggests that Samuel Ward's election was merely a continuation of a long-standing policy of hiring radical Protestants. Roger Kelk, the first lecturer appointed in Ipswich after Elizabeth's coronation, had been one of the Marian exiles at Zurich and in 1559 had replaced a Catholic as Master of Magdalene College, Cambridge; he was among those who signed the letter from the heads of Cambridge colleges to Cecil in 1565 deprecating the return to ritualism that they feared would follow the enforcement of Parker's Advertisements.[87] Kelk's successor at Ipswich, Robert Norton, was forced to withdraw from the lectureship as a consequence of a dispute with William Negus and his party in the town, who accused Norton of pluralism because he held a living in addition to his lectureship. Although Norton was obviously not nearly so radical as the unaccommodating and uncompromising Presbyterian William Negus, who was at that time the second, and junior, town lecturer, he may have had some sympathies with radical Protestantism, for he was the translator of some sermons by the Zwinglian divine Rodolph Gaultier.[88] The Robert Wright who was elected to succeed Norton in 1585 is probably the Puritan of that name who sought Presbyterian orders in Antwerp rather than episcopal ordination. On his return to England after having served as minister to various merchant and military groups in the Low Countries, Wright became chaplain to Lord Rich of Rochford and a member of the Braintree classis. He may have been a friend

of Negus, who was a member of the nearby Dedham classis and could
have introduced him to Ipswich.[89] He was followed in 1592 by another
noted Puritan, John Burgess, then at the beginning of a long and
troubled career that was to lead from ejection from his Buckinghamshire living in 1603 and trouble with the Court the following year for
a questionable sermon delivered before the King, to medical training
in Leyden and a chaplaincy with Horatio Vere's troops, and back to
more lectureships and livings in England.[90] The next lecturer at Ipswich, John Askew, was a local rector and a graduate of Caius College,
Cambridge; he remained but a short time (1604–5), apparently refusing to "resign his pastoral charge" as the town required.[91] On
Askew's departure the corporation promptly elected Samuel Ward.
During no more than ten years, then, out of the eighty between 1560
and 1640, were there lecturers at Ipswich who cannot be identified
with some assurance as Puritans.

Not all corporation lectureships present such a tidy picture of Puritan dominance. At Oxford, for example, the pattern, if it can be called
that, was far more complex. In 1582 the Earl of Leicester, as Chancellor, warned the university authorities against "the suffering of secret
and lurking papists amongst you, who seduce your youth," and suggested that the seduction was all the easier for "the want of instructing
your youth in the principles of religion." One result of this admonition was the divinity lecture at St. Mary's; another, according to
Anthony Wood, was the morning lecture at Carfax, founded by the
citizens and preached by "two zealous Calvinists," Richard Potter and
John Pryme.[92] Potter promptly received a living in Wiltshire and was
replaced within the year by John Favor, who lectured fortnightly until
1591, when he resigned. In 1593 Favor went north to the vicarage at
Halifax, where he supported two lecturers and in general acted as
protector of Puritan nonconformity in the West Riding until his death
in 1623.[93] However, neither Richard Swaddon, who replaced Pryme in
1590, and who was later Archdeacon of Worcester and chaplain to
Queen Anne, nor Richard Field, who followed Favor the next year,
and who later lectured at Lincoln's Inn, were Puritans of any stripe.
The next two lecturers, Humphrey Hargrove and Francis Mason,
seem to have been ecclesiastical careerists of some talent; they were
both subsequently royal chaplains.[94] Robert Brisendon, who held one
of the lectureships from 1595 until his death in 1609, may have been a

Puritan, for he was a friend and disciple of John Reynolds, the "precise" President of Corpus Christi.[95]

The seventeenth-century lecturers at Carfax were also very much a mixed lot. Thomas Baugh and Thomas Westly, both of whom lectured in the decade after 1609, went on to preaching careers in London, the former at St. Sepulchre's and the latter at the Savoy, but apparently neither was a Puritan. Nor was Daniel Price, who served first as rector and then lecturer at Carfax from 1606 to 1615.[96] One of the first of the two afternoon lecturers appointed in the spring of 1616 was Richard Corbett, who later became Bishop of Norwich.[97] According to a modern historian of Oxford, H. E. Salter,

> Until 1620, when Baylie was appointed, there is no indication in the list of lecturers that the City differed from the University in ecclesiastical matters. ... But with the appointment of Baylie in 1620 and Graby in 1626, and still more with others who were apponted in the next reign, the City began to show a preference for the Puritanical kind. As the University became more hostile to Calvinism the City showed a new friendship for it.[98]

Thomas Baylie, who Wood claims preached the tenets held by the Fifth Monarchy men, was certainly a Puritan of some sort and later served as one of the Wiltshire representatives at the Westminster Assembly. Robert Graby was supposed to have been the only chaplain of New College not expelled by the Parliamentary Commissioners.[99] And as Salter suggests, others can be cited who contributed to the new militancy Puritanism achieved in the early 1620's. As early as 1617 Paul Hood, "of the Puritan party in 1640," was hired as an afternoon lecturer; Edward Terry, afternoon lecturer from 1620 to 1621, was also a Puritan and the father of one who was ejected in 1662. Alexander Harry, one of the morning lecturers, may have been a Puritan; on leaving his lectureship at Carfax, he went to London, where he lectured at both St. Mary at Hill and St. Michael Cornhill from 1628 to 1630, when he left either to escape Laud or simply to accept a Cornish rectory.[100] Robert Luddington and Henry Tozier, afternoon lecturers in the middle twenties and early thirties respectively, were both Puritans. Luddington, in fact, was a Congregationalist.[101] But Salter's contention can be supported only so far, for there were still other lecturers who cannot be said to have been Puritans. On the contrary, Giles Widdowes, who was lecturer in the morning in 1619 and again from 1625 to 1641, was the author of *The Schismatical Puritan,* a book sympathetic to Laud's views, and was purported to have led his parishioners at Carfax in a dance on Whitsunday as a protest against Puritan Sabbatarianism. As late as April 1639 the town elected William Hobbes to the lectureship; he had been in trouble some years before for preaching that it was possible to fall from grace—scarcely a Puritan tenet.[102]

Whether the example of Oxford or Ipswich is the more truly representative is a question that cannot be settled conclusively on the basis of the present research. Whether it is really necessary to prove that all or most corporation lectureships were staffed by Puritan lecturers all or most of the time in order to establish the Puritan character of the institution is another matter. Even at Oxford the first two lecturers in the 1580's were Puritans, and the motives attributed to the citizens in initiating the lecture were a desire for frequent preaching and a reaction against resurgent Romanism—surely sentiments shared by the Puritans. Where evidence is available, town lectureships can often be traced to puritanical origins: to the encouragement of Puritan patrons like Henry Hastings; to a long tradition of religious radicalism and strong local Puritan sentiment, as at Ipswich, Bury, Colchester, and Yarmouth; or finally, to a local reform effort initiated by the "godly" party, whether as an adjunct to a complete Presbyterian system, as at Northampton, or whether in a less doctrinaire way as part of a piecemeal effort at civic reforms, as at Lincoln. Also, despite the long tenure of Giles Widdowes as lecturer at Oxford (and the length can surely be explained in part by the fact that he was the incumbent at St. Martin's), three out of the four lecturers during most of the 1620's and 1630's were Puritans. It may well be that after the initial enthusiasms of the 1580's gave way to the rigorous repression of Whitgift and Bancroft, town councils of no more than ordinary piety were satisfied simply to hire competent preachers, and certainly by the 1580's it was no longer necessary to hire a Puritan to obtain a preaching minister. This period of quietism, then, lasted until about 1615, when new pressures and fears of a political and ecclesiastical nature revived a sense of urgency and militancy in town councils, which again began to demand a like-minded militancy in their clergy. If William Perkins may be taken as the ideal Puritan clergyman of the quietest years, John Preston is the hero of the activist years that follow. Something approximating this pattern is what seems to emerge from a study of the London lectureships.

Finally, the direct interference of the Laudian bishops and of King Charles himself, during the 1630's in particular, suggests not only that the lecturers were frequently regarded as nonconformists and the institution as much too remote from tight ecclesiastical supervision, but also that the authorities saw the lectureships as a major cause of urban disaffection. When Laud reported in 1634 that Godfrey Goodman, Bishop of Gloucester, had "put down some lecturers, and set up other some, which he conceives he did without offense, being upon different occasions," Charles wrote in the margin, evidently with some acerbity, "I must be satisfied that the occasions were very necessary, otherwise he shall answer it."[103] By the seventeenth century this feeling that lectureships, particularly urban ones, were Puritan and therefore dangerous was not confined to Arminian clerics and their royal supporter. In his old age King James, who had no doctrinal objection to Puritanism, had come to much the same conclusion. In 1624 the citizens of Norwich sent up a complaint against Bishop Harsnet to the House of Commons because, among other things, "He forbade the morning preaching in the city, saying it was needless and there was preaching enough, and so compelled the whole city, consisting of 32 parishes wherein are contained betwixt 30 and 40,000 people, to come to Christ Church to the sermon or be without." James's comment, made at the prorogation on May 29, is instructive:

And now my Lords Bishops ... that as with one hand you labor to suppress papists, so with the other you be careful to sweep out Puritans. I like none of them nor their humors, for I think that is all one to lay down my crown to the Pope as to a popular party of Puritans. I would not have you scared with a speculation they have given in against the Bishop of Norwich, ... I commend my Lord of Norwich for suppressing of popular lectures within his diocese. I mean such as are nowadays most frequented, being supplied and held up by such ministers as have not *curam animarum* where they preach, for such must flatter and cogg and claw the people and therefore I will never allow them.[104]

Outside the ranks of the Arminians it may be doubted whether many of the bishops, to say nothing of ordinary Englishmen, felt that either Puritanism or "popular lectures" presented as great a menace to monarchy as Counter-Reformation Catholicism. Yet James's charge to his bishops proved more prophetic than even that wily king could have imagined, sensitive as he had been since youth to even the most distant rumblings of rebellion. When war came, the Catholic aristocracy and gentry proved almost embarrassingly loyal. The same could not be said of the Puritans, difficult as it may be to define precisely the relationship between religious attitudes and loyalty to King or Parliament in the 1640's. One need not go so far as Peter Heylyn, who described the town lectureship as the Presbyterians' answer to the suppression of the prophesyings in the 1580's, in order to see the institution as in some sense a product of dissatisfaction with the status quo.[105] Attorney General Noy's denunciation of the Feoffees for Impropriations as perpetrators of a vast conspiracy to subvert Church and State may well have been wide of the mark; after all, he had a case to make in court. However, what evidence is available concerning both the origins of the various corporation lectureships and the lecturers who staffed them does suggest that the alarm with which both King Charles and Laud regarded them was justified, at least in part. Certainly one must maintain a healthy skepticism of ex parte accusations; nevertheless, it is probably a mistake to assume that contemporaries were blind to what was going on around them.

The principal and obvious difficulty with using contemporary statements as evidence, however, is their general lack of precision. Sir William Dugdale's assertion is typical in its statistical vagueness and in its failure to specify who was involved and when:

Under a seeming devout and holy pretense, to advance and promote the preaching of the gospel, they got in a *number* of lecturers into *most* of the corporate towns and populous places of this realm (according to the pattern of Geneva), especially into the city of London, whom they maintained by voluntary contributions to the end they might be engaged to preach such doctrine as should (upon occasion) prepare the people for any disloyal attempt, and dispose them to rebellion when opportunity served.[106] [Italics mine.]

Opportunity served in the autumn of 1640, when the elections for the Long Parliament were held. A contemporary with a taste for statistics might have noted that 61 per cent of the total number of members elected to the House of Commons initially supported the Parliamentary cause, though eventually the King gained the support of 46 per cent.[107] And if a contemporary had examined the electoral record of the 74 boroughs that had had town preachers or other lecturers, he would have found that 70 per cent of the members elected by these boroughs followed the Parliamentary cause. Of the members who were residents of the 74 boroughs and therefore might be presumed to have been exposed to the influence of the preachers, 80 per cent were loyal to Parliament.

There would appear, then, to be some statistical basis for such comments as Dugdale's and Bishop Sheldon's. Of *Charles I*, Sheldon is reported to have said, "Nothing has spoiled the late king's affairs so much as the credit that the factious lecturers had in all corporations, for this had so great an influence on their elections that he ascribed all the war to that half-conformity."[108] Yet there are manifest difficulties both with the statistics and with contemporary observations. First of all, the 74 boroughs that had lectureships represent less than half the number with elected representatives to the House of Commons in 1640. Moreover, in all probability some boroughs that had lectureships have been omitted for lack of evidence. Hence the 74 boroughs may be only a sample, and the sample may not be representative. Second, even if we assume that all urban lecturers were Puritans, there obviously were other reasons besides the Puritan cause for adhering to Parliament against the King. There is, then, no *necessary* connection between the presence of a lectureship and loyalty to Parliament.

Finally, and perhaps most important, analyses like Bishop Sheldon's raise the question of cause and effect. Did the "factious" lecturers corrupt the corporations, or were the corporations already disaffected in some measure, if not necessarily engaged actively in plotting rebellion, when they chose to hire Puritan lecturers? Nothing emerges more clearly from an institutional study of the lectureship than the fundamental fact of lay initiative and control. Had Archbishop Laud and King Charles understood that lectureships were not the cause of urban unrest, but the expression, they might have dealt with the disaffected corporations more effectively. As it was, their policy of harassing Puritan preachers and suppressing urban lectureships served only to alienate urban leaders further from Crown and Church.

PART II

The London Lectureships

I know thou hast
All cities, in this Kingdom, over-past
In plentifully preaching of God's word;
And that thou bountifully dost afford
Large voluntary pensions to that end.

—GEORGE WITHER

5

An Anatomy of the Lectureships

GEORGE WITHER'S encomium on London preaching, and by implication on the London lectureships, is well deserved, and though written in the third decade of the seventeenth century, could be applied with equal justice to an earlier time. In fact, nearly two generations earlier, in 1571, a preacher at Paul's Cross had exclaimed, "But surely when I come out of the country hither to the city, methink I come into another world, even out of darkness into light, for here the word of God is plentifully preached."[1] In its preaching, as in so many other respects, London was without rival. Nowhere else were there so many lectureships packed into so small an area; nowhere else did the lectureships appear so early and develop so rapidly. Yet what was remarkable about the London lectureships was less a matter of their sheer quantity than of how they grew. Unlike the town and borough corporation lectureships, those in London developed neither from the wishes and actions of a single patron nor from the organized effort of a ruling corporation. Rather they seem to have been a relatively spontaneous phenomenon, a product of local sentiment expressed through the actions of parish vestries.

One attempt was made during Elizabeth's reign to organize the London lectureships on a city-wide basis. The initiative came from the highest quarter, and secular and ecclesiastical authorities combined to give their blessing. Yet with all this in its favor, the scheme faced opposition from the outset and was finally abandoned after the initial negotiations foundered. Not enough evidence remains to reconstruct the reasons for this failure with any certainty, but even so the surviving documents are illuminating.

On 14 August 1581 the Privy Council summoned a number of important ecclesiastics to Court for consultation "touching some matters which tend to the advancement of Christian religion and suppression of popery, being by the sending over of Jesuits and Seminary priests very much increased at the present within this realm."[2] Apparently as a consequence of the meeting John Aylmer, Bishop of London, for-

warded a series of instructions on behalf of the Lords of the Council
to the Lord Mayor of London. These instructions called for setting up
a lecture to be preached twice a week by a learned cleric in every "convenient division" of the city (perhaps one to a ward, of which there
were 26). The lecturers would be supported by a contribution levied
on the parishes, the amount of which would be assessed by the Lord
Mayor and aldermen in consultation with Aylmer. The Lord Mayor
was also to have a catalog of all the learned preachers in the city compiled to facilitate the selection of lecturers.[3] Who initiated these proposals is not certain. Strype attributes them to Aylmer, who was assuredly concerned with the ministry of the city.[4] Gareth Owen, a modern student of the Elizabethan ecclesiastical scene, suggests that the
initiative may have come from Sir Francis Walsingham, and certainly
Walsingham pursued the matter with considerable interest.[5]

Be that as it may, the reply of Sir John Branch, the Lord Mayor, on
6 September 1581 was completely discouraging. He complained that
since his office was already so time consuming and financially burden-
some, additional obligations were most unwelcome; that the Court of
Aldermen refused to act on the matter without consulting the Common Council; that a number of parishes already supported lecturers, a
list of which he appended, besides the four lecturers at Christ Church
Newgate and the preachers at the Temple, the Inns of Court, and St.
Paul's Cathedral; and that in addition the city supported a number
of divinity scholars at the two universities. Finally, not content with
pleading their general chargeableness—both the aldermen and the
mayor evidently assumed that they would be expected to contribute
heavily toward meeting the costs of the scheme—the Court of Aldermen also wished to register a complaint with Aylmer about his chaplain, Laurence Deios, who in a Paul's Cross sermon "had publicly de-
famed them to their faces" by claiming, significantly, "that if the
appointing of preachers were committed to them, they would appoint
such as would defend usury, the family of love, and puritanism." They
demanded that Deios "should make reparation of their good fame."[6]

Aylmer's reply, written two days later, seems surprisingly defensive.
He acknowledged the "great burdens" of city office, promised that his
chaplain would "attend and ... satisfy" the offended aldermen, and
concluded by requesting only that the city make some contribution toward the Paul's Cross sermons—a considerable comedown from a net-

work of city lectureships.[7] The following day the Lord Mayor received a letter directly from the Privy Council supporting the original instructions and directing the mayor and the aldermen to "put their helping hands hereto."[8] Finally, late the following January, the Council wrote reminding them

to advise and consult ... how they might be furnished of a more sufficient number of learned preachers able to confute their enemies in matters of religion, ... and further to advise of some good order for the entertainment of them in reading of lectures of divinity in such places within the city where most need was, ... [and] to have a care that the same may speedily be executed, according as it is expected.[9]

With this parting salvo from the government the correspondence seems to end.

In a letter to Cecil, Aylmer attributed the failure of the scheme to "the might of mammon," an explanation undoubtedly of some substance insofar as it is hard to imagine a less powerful corporation ignoring the direct orders of Council and bishop so successfully, and with apparent impunity.[10] The implication that the city was too committed to the worship of wealth to support a ministry of the gospel is more open to question.[11] In any case, the mayor's contention that local enterprise had already supplied an adequate ministry is of far greater interest here. The list of parish lecturers the mayor appended to his letter unfortunately does not appear to have survived, but it can be reconstructed.

THE DIMENSIONS OF THE INSTITUTION

The St. Antholin's lectures began or were resumed by the autumn of 1559; by 1566 they were preached on the five weekday mornings by three lecturers.[12] By 1560 a lecture was preached at Christ Church Newgate on Wednesday and Friday. Moreover, the year before the Lord Mayor's survey the parish had succeeded in converting the collegiate foundation attached to this church to the use of five lecturers.[13] There was a lecture at St. Botolph Aldersgate by 1564, and one given early Sunday morning more or less continuously from that date until 1588 at St. Giles Cripplegate by the Puritan Robert Crowley.[14] Before the 1560's were out there is evidence that four more parishes—St. Lawrence Jewry, St. Mary le Bow, Holy Trinity Minories, and St. Andrew Holborn—had lectureships.[15]

In the following decade lectureships were founded in more than twice as many parishes: at St. Mary Whitechapel in 1570, at St. Benet Gracechurch Street, St. Clement Danes, and the Temple in 1571, at St. Dunstan in the East by 1572, at St. Margaret Lothbury and St. Mary Aldermanbury in 1573 (and one was resumed at St. Michael Paternoster Row at least by that year), at St. Peter Cornhill in 1574, and at Gray's Inn* and St. Michael Cornhill in 1575.[16] By the end of the decade eight more parishes had lecturers: St. Helen Bishopsgate, St. Lawrence Pountney, St. Mary Magdalen Milk Street, St. Mary Woolnoth, St. Margaret New Fish Street, St. Mary Woolchurch, and St. Martin Ironmonger Lane by 1577; and St. Saviour, Southwark, by 1578.[17] Five more parishes—St. Alphage, St. Martin Orgar, Allhallows Staining, St. Katherine Coleman, and St. Mary Aldermary—and Lincoln's Inn began to employ lecturers in 1580 and 1581.[18]

At least 30 parishes, then, plus the Temple, Lincoln's Inn, and Gray's Inn, were hiring lecturers by September of 1581, when the Lord Mayor replied to Bishop Aylmer. The true volume of preaching was even greater than this figure might imply, for many parishes expected their lecturers to preach several times weekly, and hence from these 33 pulpits lecturers actually delivered at least 54 sermons a week.[19] Thus it is conceivable, although there is no evidence one way or the other, that the Privy Council and Bishop Aylmer dropped the plan for city lectureships because they finally accepted the thrust of the Lord Mayor's argument, concluding, in short, that there was no lack of preaching in the city. It is also possible that if Aylmer's chaplain did in fact express doubts about the orthodoxy of any preachers the mayor and aldermen might appoint, he was not speculating about the future but simply generalizing tactlessly about the past performance of London parish vestries.†

Considerable as the accomplishments of the London vestries were up to 1581, they proved to be but a prelude to the efforts yet to come. During the first two decades of Elizabeth's reign 27 parishes initiated lectures.‡ From 1580 to 1589 some 29 more followed suit, a rate of

---

* Lectures given at the Inns of Court are included in this study because they were intended for and controlled by a lay body, as were the parish lectures, in contrast to the cathedral lectureships, which were frequently meant specifically for the clergy.

† The London lecturers' religious views are discussed in Chapter 6.

‡ This figure includes the Temple and Gray's Inn. Hereafter the Inns of Court will be treated as parishes for statistical purposes without special mention.

growth unequaled by any other decade.[20] After the eighties the spread of the lectureships among the London parishes slacked off but did not stop. During the 1590's only seven new parishes introduced lectures, a drop in the rate of growth from 115 per cent to a mere 12 per cent. Nevertheless, the seven new lectures represented a rise in the percentage of London parishes that hired lecturers from about 43 to 49 per cent of the 129 parishes studied.[21] In other words, these figures mean that by 1600, in a city of little more than a square mile in area and with a population of just under a quarter of a million, approximately one hundred sermons were preached each week by lecturers, not to mention the sermons required by law of the incumbents and those given at funerals and baptisms for the more prominent inhabitants.[22]

However, for many Londoners an adequate preaching ministry evidently still remained an unrealized goal, and the opening decades of the new century witness a period of renewed activity. During the first decade of the seventeenth century, nine new parish lectureships were founded;[23] during the next decade, 20; and by the end of the 1620's, another 24. To all intents the peak was reached in 1630, when 116 London parishes, or about 90 per cent, had records of hiring lecturers.[24] By late 1628, then, when Bishop Laud was examining the results of his first survey of the London lectureships, the lay-sponsored lectures all but duplicated the parochial system under his care. It is hardly surprising that he should have been instrumental in drawing up the 1629 Instructions, and that he should have "resolved to do his duty" by vigorously enforcing them within his jurisdiction, notwithstanding the "open clamors" of the Puritans.[25] A bishop committed to freeing the Church from all lay control short of the King's must have found the situation in London intolerable.

One important qualification must be introduced at this point. Whereas these figures, based as they are on the date of foundation or first appearance of a parish lecture, can be used legitimately to establish roughly comparative rates of growth, they cannot be used to determine the actual number of parishes with active lectureships at a given time. In other words, whereas it is true that by 1600 almost half of the London parishes had hired lecturers at one time or another during the preceding 40 years, it cannot be assumed that by 1600 half of the London parishes had active lectureships. Indeed, in the opening years of the new century there is evidence of active lectureships in only 44 London parishes, about 34 per cent of the total; some of London's lecture-ships had obviously been discontinued. As might be expected, the difference between the number of parishes with a history of lecture-ships and the number with active lectureships increases steadily from the early 1580's on.

Lectureships were discontinued for a variety of reasons. In some cases, for example, they simply lapsed after the suspension of a lec-turer. Thus when George Cheston, along with a great many other London nonconformists, was suspended by Bishop Aylmer in 1584 or 1585, his lectureship at Allhallows Staining, which he had held from at least 1581, and his lectureship at St. Katherine Coleman both lapsed with or soon after his departure.[26] Although Cheston managed to re-gain his license (he was lecturing at the Minories by 1595), the lecture-ships at Allhallows and St. Katherine's do not seem to have been re-sumed during Elizabeth's reign.[27]

In other cases lectureships became too expensive to maintain. Two years after the parish of St. Bartholomew by the Exchange first set up a lecture in 1583 the vestry authorized an assessment of the parish householders in order to raise the lecturer's salary of £20 a year.[28] The assessment was clearly the highest paid by the parishioners for any purpose during this period, the rate for individual parishioners ranging anywhere from two to thirty times the amounts assessed for the Parliamentary fifteenth in 1587. Evidently the financial burden proved too great even for so wealthy a parish, and on 17 July 1586 the vestry ordered a new, lower assessment "after the rate of the clerk's wages for ... the answering as well of such money as did lack for ... paying of the preacher."[29] After this overly ambitious attempt to fund the lecture, nothing more is recorded about it until early in 1595, when Thomas Cater's legacy of £50 permitted the parish once again to consider hiring a lecturer. Within a few years additional bequests had been left to the parish for the lecture, and its existence thereafter was uninterrupted.[30]

Given the wide range of problems that beset parishes in their quest for a preaching ministry, the fact that many lectures survived as long as they did is testimony to the strength of the demand for preaching. In Table 1 the cumulative number of London parishes that had at some point initiated lectureships is compared to the average number with active lectureships in the years covered by this study. The figures

TABLE 1

London Parishes with Lectureships, 1560–1662

Period	No. of parishes that initiated lectureships (cumulative)	Parishes with active lectureships Average no.	Per cent[a]	Period	No. of parishes that initiated lectureships (cumulative)	Parishes with active lectureships Average no.	Per cent[a]
1560–64	3	3	100%	1610–14	81	49	60%
1565–69	8	8	100	1615–19	92	58	63
1570–74	17	15	90	1620–24	97	59	60
1575–79	27	23	85	1625–29	116	107	92
1580–84	44	38	86	1630–34	116	90	77
1585–89	56	48	86	1635–39	117	89	77
1590–94	58	42	72	1640–44	119	79	64
1595–99	63	42	67	1645–49	119	59	49
1600–04	69	44	64	1650–54	120	50	41
1605–09	72	43	60	1655–62	120	59	49

Sources: Episcopal visitation call books, parish vestry minutes, and churchwardens' accounts.

[a] This figure, the percentage of the cumulative number of lectureships still extant, provides a rough measure of institutional efficiency.

are only approximate at best, for the inevitable gaps that plague all attempts to quantify data from the centuries before modern statistics were kept are also present here. In particular, it seems worthwhile to mention certain gaps that affect to some degree all the statistics presented in this study. First, the Southwark parishes, although included in Bridge Ward Without, do not appear in the visitation records for London, since they were ecclesiastically part of the diocese of Winchester. Second, of the Southwark parishes, parish records of any usefulness have survived only in the case of St. Saviour's. Third, thirteen London parishes are peculiars of either the archbishop or the dean and chapter of Canterbury, and therefore do not appear in the visitation records of the diocese of London. Fourth, parish records of one kind or another exist for only about 80 (61 per cent) of the 129 parishes included in this study.[31] Finally, even within a document series the quality of records varies considerably: for example, whereas the visitation records for 1586 list 93 of the London parishes, those of 1592 list only 33.[32]

On the whole, it seems safe to assume that figures based on the local and diocesan records for London tend to err by minimizing quantities, although the degree of distortion can be expected to vary with the unevenness of the data. In Table 1 the number of parishes with active lectureships tends to be minimized still further in comparison with the figures on cumulative increase because it is necessary to have a continuous series of data on the lectures included in the former list, whereas a single mention or reference is sufficient for lectures in the latter. The figures for 1628 are the one obvious exception. In that year Laud's primary visitation coincided with his survey of the London lecturers; hence the figure of 107 parishes that had lectures during the years between 1625 and 1629 must be very nearly correct. However, since there are no surviving visitation records for the period from 1615 to 1628, the increase in the number of parishes with active lectureships between the early and late 1620's may have been more gradual than Table 1 suggests.

With all due allowance for these limitations in the data, the London lectureships clearly constituted a formidable institution. After 1580 there were active lectureships in at least one out of every four London parishes, and from 1610 to the Restoration the number never dropped as low as one out of three. Considering how small and poor many London parishes were, this was a remarkable achievement.

In 1575 Thomas Norton, the Remembrancer of London, reminded the Lord Mayor that his first duty was "to have care of God," for "it is He that ministereth and prosperously governeth all good meanings; it is He that guideth all well doings; it is He that giveth all good success." In particular the Lord Mayor was to advance religion by giving "good countenance to the supportation of favor, help, and credit to the preachers that shall come warranted to distribute so great a benefit, whereby the people of your charge shall learn the right way of honoring God, salvation of their souls, guiding of their lives, and yielding of their obedience and duties."[33] One might infer from the failure of the Council's initiative in 1581 that Norton's plea went unheeded, but the evident proliferation of parochial lectureships must then be explained away. In fact, there can be no doubt that many Londoners, both magistrates and substantial citizens, shared Norton's concern, but they acted on that concern in their livery companies and parish vestries rather than in the Court of Aldermen. Had the Council's plan succeeded, Londoners would have shared control of their preachers with their bishops; as it was, by working through the vestries London's substantial laity virtually excluded any uninvited or undue outside influence. In 1581 Aylmer complained about the "might of mammon" in London, but a later generation of bishops must have viewed the product of that might with very different feelings. Indeed the evidence suggests that enterprising Londoners were well on the way to solving the problem of how to obtain a preaching ministry by the time the Privy Council and the Church were willing to acknowledge that the problem was a critical one. For Aylmer and his successors, in fact, the real problem was not how to increase the number of preachers in the city, but how to discipline the preachers who were already there and how to control an institution that owed little to either the Church or the Crown.

MOTIVES OF THE LAITY

The parish vestries of London have left behind a mass of evidence concerning the multitude of institutional arrangements they used to found and perpetuate their lectureships. By contrast, statements of their motives for having lectureships are extremely rare. Undoubtedly this is due in part to the nature of the sources: vestry minutes record only what was propounded for discussion and finally decided, not verbatim reports of every word spoken; churchwardens' accounts, which contain a yearly statement, usually in a summary form, of the expenditures and receipts finally approved by the vestry, reveal even less.

Undoubtedly the lack of evidence is also due in part to the fact that the principal motive for setting up a lectureship seemed self-evident. "The primary *raison d'être* of the lectureship," writes Gareth Owen, was an effort by the laity "to remedy preaching deficiencies within the Church."[34] Not only was there an obvious and unassailable rationale for lectureships, but there is no evidence that the London vestries saw their actions either as innovative or as subversive to the good order of the Church. The Londoners who dominated the vestries were substantial men, accustomed to responsible positions in the greatest city in the realm; it is difficult to imagine that they saw any of their actions as a threat to the status quo. The city's growing Puritanism must have simply reinforced their self-confidence. Hence when some members of Lincoln's Inn wrote to William Cecil asking his support for their lectureship, they thought it sufficient to state, "We have been a long time desirous to have a preacher in our house, like as in other houses of court."[35] And even the most elaborate statement of motive I could discover, one recorded by the parish clerk of St. Botolph Aldgate, is no more than a laconic note: "Motion was made to have a preacher chosen to lecture in the said parish weekly, whereby the parishioners might be the better instructed in the word of God."[36]

It might be supposed that with the rise in clerical standards during Elizabeth's reign, the parishioners could have been better instructed without the help of lecturers. Certainly the considerable improvement in the London clergy's educational qualifications, for which Elizabeth's bishops deservedly took some credit, was a major ecclesiastical accomplishment. The proportion of the London incumbents who were graduates of one of the universities was only about 47 per cent in 1560; by 1583, halfway through the reign, about 61 per cent were graduates; and by 1601, 75 per cent.[37] The proportion who were licensed to preach rose even faster, from approximately 44 per cent in 1560 to 79 per cent in 1586, and finally to 88 per cent in 1601.[38] It is not surprising, then, that an increasing number of lecturers were drawn from the ranks of the incumbents themselves. Whereas incumbents held only 14 per cent of the lectureships in 1566, they held 20 per cent in 1583 and 43 per cent in 1598. The rapid increase between 1583 and 1598 can be partly accounted for by the financial attractiveness of a lectureship to a qualified incumbent. At the same time, Whitgift's efforts to ensure the conformity of all the clergy—lecturers as well as incumbents—did much to reduce the proportion of preachers who accepted a lectureship but declined a living in order to escape the ecclesiastical net.

Clerical standards continued to rise under the Stuarts, and by the 1630's the nongraduate had virtually disappeared from the new admissions to livings in the diocese of London. The first extant Subscription Book for the diocese lists 235 admissions to livings and grants of preaching licenses between August 1631 and December 1639.[39] About 3 per cent of this number claimed only a bachelor of arts degree; 71 per cent had their master's degree; 25 per cent were either bachelors or doctors of divinity. That the remaining 1 per cent have no degree listed after their names may be a clerical error. Even the new curates were remarkably well educated by the reign of Charles I. Of the 75 clergymen admitted to curacies in the diocese from September 1627 to December 1632,[40] only 7 per cent had no degree, whereas 23 per cent had their bachelor's and 70 per cent their master's degree.

If greater clerical competence alone could have satisfied the demand for a "sufficient, preaching ministry," the lectureship would have declined rapidly in the seventeenth century, and the few lectures that survived would have been given by the incumbents. Neither occurred in reality, for two fairly obvious reasons. First, despite the plethora of legislation on the subject, the Church never succeeded in solving the problem of pluralism. Rising clerical standards only complicated the problem, for well-qualified clergymen expected suitable livings. Furthermore, the bishop's own cathedral clergy were frequently the worst offenders. In 1634 the dean and eight prebendaries of Canterbury held fifteen livings and five chapels. In the diocese of Norwich 23 per cent of the clergy were pluralists in 1593; in Oxford and Worcester 20 per cent were pluralists as late as 1640.[41] Some 46 per cent of the London clergy were pluralists according to the Puritan survey of 1586, and of those sequestered or forced to resign in the 1640's, 38 per cent held more than one benefice with cure of souls.[42]

One obvious solution for the laity, when faced with a nonresident pluralist, was to hire a lecturer. When even this recourse was denied them, they registered complaints like the following, contained in a petition from the parishioners of St. Giles Cripplegate to the House of Commons in 1641:

The parish is very great, consisting of 40,000 souls, or thereabouts, having no constant preaching minister amongst them, although the living be worth seven hundred pounds, *per annum*, to the present incumbent William Fuller, Dr. of Divinity, who ... is a non-resident. ... [When] on Thursday ... John Sedgwick, ... an orthodox minister of the Church of England, together with a congregation of about four hundred persons ... waited at the church door of St. Giles aforesaid, expecting the opening of the church doors for the continuance of a weekly lecture, ... they were compelled to depart ..., being kept out, by the command of William Fuller.[43]

Even had all incumbents been resident and licensed to preach, a second problem remained: the conscientious parson was too busy to satisfy the demand for preaching easily. Besides reading morning and evening prayers on Sundays and the litany on Wednesdays and Fridays, a parson was frequently expected to officiate at baptisms, marriages, and funerals, to say nothing of catechizing, visiting the sick, and assisting the churchwardens in administering relief to the poor. It was only reasonable that a parson expected to preach sermons beyond those legally required should have the additional incentive the lecture stipend provided. If the parishioners demanded not one but two or three extra sermons weekly, it was usually necessary to hire either an independent lecturer or a reading curate. At St. Botolph Aldgate, where the twice-weekly lecture had been given for some time by the curate, the vestry finally decided early in 1597 to hire a lecturer, "for that it was thought that one man can not well supply the place both of lecturer and curate."[44]

Puritans were not the only ones to feel the need for a constant, preaching ministry, but they felt it more acutely. What the Puritan laity expected from their lecturers is expressed eloquently in a letter from Francis Hastings to Archbishop Whitgift requesting Whitgift's permission for the continuance of the Puritan William Bradshaw's lecture at Chatham:

I will undertake to your Grace for him, that he shall not offer any disturbance to the peace of our Church, either in word or action, but shall painfully bestow himself in the place, to preach Christ crucified, and to arm his people with some measure of knowledge, to stand Christianly and courageously for the truth of Christ, and to resist all errors broached against that Holy doctrine.

Hastings concluded his plea with what he evidently regarded as a more compelling ground for a ruler of the Church to support a lecture: "I make bold to tender this suit..., because I find plenty of practicing by seminaries and Jesuits to corrupt and pervert the people's hearts both in knowledge and obedience, and that through the penury of preaching in some places it may prove dangerous."[45]

Obviously, the mere fact of being the incumbent of a living did not necessarily disqualify one as a "painful" preacher; a reasonably conscientious resident parson who was willing to preach could probably satisfy all but the most puritanical vestries. However, only a minority of the London vestries possessed the advowsons to their parish livings, and short of the power to appoint their own ministers there was no way of ensuring plentiful and "painful" preaching. Hence, even had a growing number of London livings not gone to Arminians during the 1620's and 1630's, there is no reason to suppose that the improved educational standards of the parochial clergy, or even an incumbent's willingness to preach, would have eliminated the *raison d'être* of the lectureship.

RECRUITMENT AND ELECTIONS

Early in 1577, at a vestry meeting of the parish of St. Christopher le Stocks, "request was made that there might be some learned man appointed to read a lecture in the parish twice a week, and for the maintenance thereof a collection should be made of the benevolence of the parishioners."[46] With some such formula most parishes for which evidence survives recorded their decision to hire a lecturer. By this act the vestry became the patron of an ecclesiastical preferment, the value of which varied according to the importance of the auditory and the size of the stipend. But although most of the recorded decisions initiating a parish lectureship are similar, no single method was generally followed for recruiting and appointing the lecturers. Responding to local needs, and lacking any outside control, vestries improvised according to the exigencies of their own situation.

The simplest solution to the problem of recruiting was to avoid it altogether by appointing the parson to read the lecture. Thus at St. Margaret Lothbury the first minute mentioning the lectureship simply records that at a meeting held 27 July 1573 it was "agreed by the consent of Mr. Parson [James Stile] and the parishioners...to have a lecture every Wednesday and Friday."[47] Following the rector's suspension the next year and his resignation of the living the year after, the lectureship was transferred to his successors until 1592, when the rector, William Welles, announced that he "would read no more lecture and that if the parishioners would provide one to read a lecture in this our church, our said parson would...give leave for another to read or preach any day or days that they would appoint, reserving Sunday for himself, which offer the parish did accept." Whether they tried to find "such a one as they...should think meet" and failed cannot be ascertained from the records. What is certain is that the lecture lapsed until after Wells's death, when the new rector agreed to revive it.[48] The vestry of St. Dunstan in the East pursued an equally unadventurous policy, although they seemed to have desired greater control over the selection process. In a vestry minute it was agreed that whoever the parson appointed curate "shall have the lecture (if the vestry allow one) and the house entire unto him, and our parson for his part hath promised to provide the parish of a sufficient man, a graduate, and if it be possible a single man."[49]

Many parish vestries took a bolder course. At a vestry meeting at St. Margaret New Fish Street on 12 August 1582 the following minute was recorded: "For the choice of a preacher to read our lecture, these two stood for the lecture: Mr. Edmunds, Mr. Ryder."[50] Mr. Ryder received three hands; the popular Puritan preacher Thomas Edmunds received seventeen and was duly elected lecturer. Edmunds had been rector of St. Margaret's briefly ten years before, which may account for both his candidacy and his success in the election.[51] The usual procedure followed by vestries that elected their lecturers from a slate of candidates was, first, to declare the position open and appeal for nominations. The candidates were then invited to preach trial sermons, and only then did the parish hold the election. Thus a vestry minute of St. Saviour's dated 6 December 1614 orders "that the choice of a preacher shall be deferred till some other time, and that in the meanwhile, if there be no suitors to supply the place, the churchwardens shall provide a sufficient man to preach." At the vestry held on 22 February, "Mr. Thomas Sutton . . . was chosen to be our preacher and lecturer," and at a later vestry "it is ordered that 40 s. shall be distributed by the churchwardens . . . amongst the preachers which were sent for and requested to preach betwixt Mr. Dr. Symond's departing . . . and Mr. Sutton's election in his room."*

The means by which candidates came to be nominated is not always

---

* LCCRO, P/92/S/450, pp. 463, 466. In his pamphlet *Tom of All Trades; or The Plain Pathway to Preferment* (London, 1631), a compendium of advice for the gentry father of small means and many sons, Thomas Powell describes the process by which city preferment was to be obtained from the suitor's point of view. For all its derisory tone, Powell's advice may not be too wide of the mark: "In parishes and companies of tradesmen incorporate, some very few rule the roost. Your alderman of the ward, his deputy, your common councilman, yea, sometime that petty epitome of wardmote inquest, that little busy morsel of justice (the beadle of the ward), will make a strong party in the election, if he be put to it. The probatory sermon that must be made upon such trial before such an auditory would be according to the capacity in general, but more especially according to the humor and addiction of those whose wits the rest have in singular reverence, as Mr. Francis Fiat, a good understanding fishmonger (I assure you); you may give the style of right worshipful to them, though the best man of the company be but a wine cooper, and his judgment better in claret than in *contioclerum* a great deal. If your son upon his trial can but fit their palates smoothly, which is hard to do, in regard that they are so hollow-mouthed, let him be sure, though he miss the benefice for want of preparation, yet ten to one but they will strain themselves to bring him in as a lecturer, which is a thing they reverence far beyond the parson of the parish by many degrees." Reprinted in W. H. Dunham, Jr., and Stanley Pargellis, eds., *Complaint and Reform in England, 1436–1714* (New York, 1938), pp. 560–61.

clear. Sometimes, apparently, a preacher was nominated without his knowledge and consent. At a vestry meeting, held 17 December 1624 at St. Mary Aldermanbury, Robert Harris was elected lecturer with orders to preach twice on Sundays and once on a weekday during the ensuing year.[52] Three weeks later Harris, who was at the time employed as lecturer at St. Saviour's, was explaining to his annoyed and suspicious vestry "that true it was he heard that he was chosen elsewhere but without his consent, and said he was settled here and would here continue so that he might be provided for according to the qualities of his charge, and he said he was no ways engaged at Aldermanbury."[53]

Among the Puritan clergy, at least, recommendations from other members of the brotherhood seem to have been obtained frequently, either preceding the nomination or following it, but in any case before the election. When the lectureship at Chatham fell vacant, the vestry agreed to refer the matter to Laurence Chaderton, the master of Emmanuel College, who was at the time in Kent. Chaderton recommended William Bradshaw, and after the "piously affected party" in the parish had confirmed the merits of Chaderton's choice, they blocked any attempt to expand the slate of candidates by requesting Chaderton, now back in Cambridge, to make no further suggestions and by urging Bradshaw to make "no delay in coming to them." The maneuver succeeded and Bradshaw was invited to preach a trial sermon. "His meek and discreet carriage" being "by the generality observed, by the wiser sort well weighed, he was by joint consent agreed upon."[54]

The Puritan preacher Henry Smith was elected to the lectureship at St. Clement Danes on the strength of both a recommendation and a further testimonial. "Touching my calling thither," Smith wrote afterward, "I was recommended to the parish by certain godly preachers, which had heard me preach in other places in this city." At this point William Cecil, a parishioner and Smith's uncle by marriage, wrote to Smith's former teacher, Richard Greenham, requesting "a testimonial and character." Greenham replied that Smith was "well exercised in the holy Scriptures, religious and devout in mind, moderate and sober in opinions and affection, discreet and temperate in his behavior, industrious in his studies and affairs, and, as he hoped, of an humble spirit and upright heart, joined with the fervent zeal of the glory of God and health of souls."[55] Henry Smith was, in short, a very paragon of Puritan religiosity, although it may be doubted whether any further testimony to his excellence of character was necessary once he had the Lord Treasurer's backing. Perhaps Cecil's concern had been to assure himself of the soberness of Smith's opinions and the temperateness of his behavior, for Cecil had had his fill of fire-eating Puritans.

Sometimes a less elaborate procedure was followed whereby the former lecturer or the present incumbent assumed a pivotal role. Thus William Gouge was recommended by Arthur Hildersham to his old friend Stephen Egerton as a suitable assistant to Egerton and as lecturer at St. Anne Blackfriars.[56] When William Hubbuck prepared to leave his lecture at St. Botolph Aldgate on being preferred to a Leicestershire rectory, "Mr. Paget, an old lame man being a preacher, did preach in the parish ... at the request of Mr. William Hubbuck." A vestry minute of a month later notes that Eusebius Paget, a frequently suspended nonconformist, had been duly elected.[57] Sometimes, as at St. Dunstan in the West in 1648, the incumbent said nothing until the nominations were in, at which time it was requested "that between this and this day sevennight he would declare his opinion of the fitness of them or any other that he shall hear of to be put in nomination for the lecturer before they go to election."[58] At other times even the recommendation was preceded by preliminary wire-pulling. A letter from Michael Robarts of Jesus College, Oxford, to Archbishop Ussher provides a glimpse into the labyrinthine world of Puritan influence:

The thought of my own unworthiness maketh me doubt the success of my late letters, wherein I was a petitioner to your grace for favor of some help in the procurement of a lecture near Oxford, by means of Mr. Damport,* preacher of Coleman Street. Upon knowledge of your lordship's mind in my behalf, I persuade myself he will do it. Therefore I am still willing to beg a few lines to that intent, if there be not a resolution to the contrary.[59]

In all probability, however, parochial inclinations and friendships carried elections far more commonly than elaborate systems of influence. The churchwardens of St. Lawrence Pountney testified before the Consistory Court in 1619 that after the death of their former lec-

---

* John Davenport, the Puritan vicar and lecturer at St. Stephen's.

turer, four local preachers, "knowing that Mr. Lloyd was dead and that the place was void, were desirous to obtain the place and came at several times and offered to give them a sermon for a trial of their gifts." Ultimately three others preached as candidates for the lecture, but all except one of the seven were local men, and in addition one was the brother-in-law of an important parishioner.[60] Besides the great number of ministers employed in London, others came as visitors, as chaplains of the great, or as seekers of preferment. Furthermore, ministers frequently preached in pulpits other than their own and invited other ministers to preach in their absence. A parishioner who attended his church with any regularity would thus come to have a wide acquaintance among the local clergy at the very least. During the winter of 1598–99 a parishioner of St. Botolph Aldgate could have heard sermons preached by a chaplain to Lord Thomas Howard, a preacher from Deptford, one of the archbishop's chaplains, the minister of St. Katherine Cree, the parson of St. Nicholas Cole Abbey, a preacher from Suffolk, and the lecturers of St. Nicholas, of St. James Clerkenwell, and of St. Magnus the Martyr.[61]

If there were many ways of recruiting and nominating lecturers, the election itself was usually quite straightforward. Once the slate of candidates had been read off, the vestry, either with the parson, as at St. Bartholomew Exchange, or more commonly without him, proceeded to vote. Votes were cast usually by a show of hands, although occasionally "by a mark with a pen," as at St. Lawrence Pountney.[62]

To these patterns of recruitment and election the procedures followed in the handful of London parishes where the advowson had been either leased or purchased by the vestry were a notable exception. Since the incumbent was frequently the lecturer in these parishes, his election as incumbent tended to disguise his preferment to the lectureship. The election of Robert Harris to the perpetual curacy of St. Mary Aldermanbury in the winter of 1624–25 illustrates the point. In 1621 the parish, which had previously leased the rectory and advowson from the Crown, purchased them outright. By 1623 the incumbent curate, Thomas Downing, who had been appointed by the Crown in 1617, was at odds with the vestry, apparently because he refused to permit them to settle an independent lecturer in the parish. By November 1624 the quarrel had reached a point where no reconciliation seemed possible, and the vestry was determined "to try their right whether the parish have the right to place or displace their Curate at their pleasure." Sir Henry Martin, the chancellor of the diocese, patched up a compromise in which "Mr. Downing upon better deliberation was contented to surrender his supposed right" and the parish agreed to pay him an annuity of £20 for life.

A week later the parish held its first election. The method used was to all appearances indistinguishable from that commonly used to elect a lecturer. First, a parish committee reported that "having taken information of sundry sufficient ministers, amongst the rest, they in their opinions thought fit to recommend Mr. Harris of St. Mary Overies [St. Saviour's] to be their curate, yet so that they left it to the several parish either to accept of him, or else to nominate any other they should think fit." Seven were put in nomination, but Robert Harris was elected unanimously. When an agreement was finally reached with Harris three weeks later, the terms were such that for all practical purposes the parish had hired a stipendiary lecturer rather than a curate. In return for a salary of £120 a year it was agreed that Harris would "weekly for three-quarters of the year (namely from Michaelmas to midsummer) supply three sermons among us: two upon the Sunday and one upon the weekday by the name of a lecture, ... [and] for the other quarter: viz., ... he is only to supply two sermons on the sabbath day."[63] Those Anglicans who feared that the Puritans would "shrink up" all religion into preaching were not far wrong.

By the 1630's there were only thirteen London parishes in which the advowson was under the vestry's control, but their importance was far out of proportion to their number.[64] In effect these parishes provided working models of a congregationalist polity within the Established Church. They also provided a haven for some of the most famous nonconformist preachers of the day. At St. Mary Aldermanbury, Robert Harris, a future member of the Westminster Assembly, was succeeded by three other famous Puritans—Thomas Taylor, John Stoughton, and Edmund Calamy. For 70 years Stephen Egerton and William Gouge preached from the pulpit at St. Anne Blackfriars; John Davenport, later pastor of New Haven, and the Independent John Goodwin preached at St. Stephen Coleman Street as vicars and lecturers from 1624 to 1660.[65] At the conclusion of a hearing before the High Commission on 14 June 1632, the Bishop of Rochester remarked, apropos the vestry of St. Augustine Paul's Wharf, which had built pews above the communion table, "The power of vestries and churchwardens, this is to hatch a lay presbytery."[66] In what light the bishops regarded those vestries that held the power to appoint their own ministers can be safely left to the imagination.

The elections described so far can in the main be fairly called free. Such pressures and influences as were sometimes brought to bear, whether or not they were invited by the vestry itself, never constituted a serious threat to the vestry's freedom of choice. By no means, however, was this always the case. A common source of interference was the parish incumbent, although usually a vestry had little difficulty in coping with him. When, for example, the parish of St. Olave Jewry came to choose the first lecturer to preach the new Wednesday lecture established by a bequest from Dame Mary Weld, the parson, Thomas Tuke, was deliberately excluded from standing for it.[67] At the same vestry it was recorded that Tuke gave his "consent and liking" to the lecture's being delivered from his pulpit, an optimistic assumption that was not to be borne out by subsequent events. A year later, however, the vestry discovered that a modus vivendi could be reached on the basis of a thinly disguised bribe:

Forasmuch as Mr. Tuke, minister, ... hath made request unto the parishioners for the sum of £12 to be ... conferred upon him ... for the payment of his debts and supply of his other needful occasions, which they have assented unto, it is now recorded that in consideration thereof he hath ... agreed ... that the divinity lecture ... shall henceforth ... be freely read ... without his interruption and also that the choice of the person to read the same lecture shall also forever hereafter rest wholly in the election of the parishioners without molestation or intermeddling herewith.[68]

The vestry's first appointment to the lectureship was Theodore Herring, curate under William Gouge at St. Anne Blackfriars and later rector of Doddinghurst in Essex until his death in 1645.[69] As for Thomas Tuke, he was imprisoned and sequestered from his living on 23 March 1642/3 for supporting Laudian ceremonialism and for praying that "the devil confound all traitors, rebels, and turbulent spirits."[70]

A resident parson was relatively easy to deal with, one may suppose, because he had some stake in staying on good terms with his vestry. When interference emanated from higher quarters, however, there was little a vestry could do but accept the inevitable with such good grace as they could muster. A vestry minute of 18 January 1657/8 records without comment: "It was resolved, that in obedience to his highness, the Lord Protector's, order . . . , Mr. Edward Pearce was permitted to preach in the parish church of Margaret's Westminster on the Lord's Day in the forenoons, and Mr. Seth Wood in the afternoons."[71] Most London parishes escaped such unwelcome attentions, for the very extent of the intervention necessary to control the city pulpits would have proved self-defeating. Such a massive invasion of local rights would have alienated public opinion far more rapidly and profoundly than the occasional antigovernment sermons that were the price of nonintervention. On the other hand, parishes like St. Margaret's, to which the members of the House of Commons resorted during Parliamentary sessions, were a logical object of governmental concern. An excellent case study is provided by a similar suburban parish, St. Martin in the Fields, which was heavily populated by courtiers and bureaucrats.

The first incident of outside interference seems to have occurred about the year 1615, and the only extant evidence is a letter from the parish to Thomas Howard, Earl of Suffolk, endorsed "certificate to the Lord Treasurer about the lecture." Apparently Hamlet Marshall had been installed as parish lecturer by the Lord Treasurer's "special direction." It is not certain whether the Lord Treasurer had acted in his personal or his official capacity; the latter is likely, for even great peers did not ordinarily deal with city parishes in such a high-handed fashion. That the peer spoke for the King is further suggested by the fact that Hamlet Marshall became a royal chaplain-in-ordinary either then or soon after.[72] The parishioners had reacted to this interference by reducing their contribution to the lecture, until by the Lord Treasurer's "honorable commandment . . . to use our best endeavor for his better maintenance," a special collection had been ordered. However, in ordering the collection the churchwardens made the reservation that "we do only in respect of your Lordship, albeit there are special objections to the contrary, besides a dangerous precedent," namely, that they were already well supplied with preaching, and that they felt it prejudicial to pay more for one sermon a week than the parson's cure was worth.

Marshall resigned sometime in 1616. When the parishioners went to a new election in January 1617, they successfully ignored the Earl of Pembroke's candidate and with the approval of their parson elected the radical Puritan John Everard.[73] This was to be the last really free election for years; in all likelihood the notoriety the parish gained as a result of Everard's constant sermonizing against the Spanish match and of his equally frequent suspension led to the close supervision that ensued. When Everard left for Kensington, the vestry elected the innocuous John Andrews "upon the nomination of Doctor Montfort [the parson] and with the good liking of the Lord Bishop of London." The next election, in 1627, was subject to massive interference from so powerful a source that no attempt to disguise the interference could quite succeed. Bishop Mountaigne of London "upon his sacred Majesty's command" had "placed as lecturer in the church Mr. Peake, his Majesty's chaplain." Through the "mediation" of the Earl of Salisbury this hasty action was revoked, and the parish received "his Majesty's most gracious promise" that the freedom of the parish to elect the lecturer would not be infringed "by any authority." The parish was at least permitted to save face, but "in testification of our gratitude to his Majesty" Humphrey Peake was nominated and elected.[74]

The royal promise was in the circumstances perfectly worthless. In 1633 the parish received two letters—one from King Charles to Bishop Laud and a covering letter from Laud to the parish—that were copied into the vestry minute book without comment. The letter from the King to Laud reads in part as follows:

Whereas we understand that Humphrey Peake ... is to leave the place of lecturer ..., and that considering the greatness of that parish, and the quality of the auditors, we hold fit that place should be supplied by a person of worth and learning; we therefore hereby recommend unto you Alexander Levingstone ... to be forthwith admitted ..., and do ... require you to make known our purpose to the parish herein, and that we expect their readiness to give us this satisfaction.

If Charles's letter presents a clear example of *force majeure*, Laud's letter was unusually diplomatic and apologetic, for he at least recognized that the parish controlled the purse strings. "Now because the maintenance ariseth from the parish where he takes his pains," Laud wrote, "I am not willing to do anything without your liking"; but, he added, the purpose of his letter was "to pray you to satisfy his Majesty's desires ... who I know will take it very well."

With the coming of the Civil War the parish returned to more or less free elections, subject only to local aristocratic pressure. In 1645, for example, the Earls of Northumberland, Pembroke, and Salisbury and Lord Edward Howard recommended the master of Trinity College, Cambridge, as a suitable candidate, "which noble favor to us all was by some of the meaner sort slighted and disputed, but overswayed by the whole vestry and better sort of the knights and gentlemen of the parish."[75] Few at the time would have been prepared to argue that the dominance of the "better sort" in any way compromised a free election.

There is one case on record of successful opposition to a royal nominee, although the pretext on which the nominee was rejected was such a brazen fabrication that its success is difficult to account for. On 27 April 1613 King James wrote to the Masters of the Temple recommending Alexander Simpson as a suitable, able, and learned man for such "an auditory of judicious and eminent persons." Although other pretexts were advanced, the central argument of the reply was that "there is no such place of lecturer amongst us as hath been informed to your highness." On the following February 11, the Middle Temple parliament recorded that Abraham Gibson had been elected lecturer for a year. The Temple had in fact had a lecturer since 1571; the "judicious and eminent" lawyers had lied to the King and gotten away with it.[76]

DUTIES AND REGULATIONS

After the election of a new lecturer, most vestries customarily recorded the terms of the lectureship in the form of a covenant such as the following with the lecturer-elect: "It was condescended and agreed by the whole consent of the same vestry very bountifully and willingly to give to Master William Ashbold, parson, ... the sum of [£10 a year] ... for that Master Ashbold ... hath promised most certainly to ... read a lecture twice a week."[77] Many parishes, though not all, recorded elections annually as a constant reminder of their right of patronage. Usually such an election was nominal, if it actually took place at all. For example, Thomas Hodges, who was initially elected to lecture at St. Olave Jewry in 1631, was confirmed in that position for the next three years in the following manner: "It is likewise ordered and thought meet that ... as there is no competitor for the lecture with Mr. Hodges ... and that there is no cause of exception against him, that the said Mr. Hodges shall continue reader of the ... lecture ... for this next year ensuing."[78] Frequently the parish required the lecturer to give several months' warning if he decided to resign from the lecture, and such parishes usually reciprocated if they wished to replace him.[79] Frequently, too, the parish expected the lecturer to resign any extraparochial benefice that he might hold, for a lectureship was no place for a nonresident pluralist.*

The principal duty of the lecturer was, of course, to preach, ordinarily one or two times a week, but sometimes as many as four times.[80] If there was only one lecture a week, it was commonly held on Sunday afternoon, either before or immediately after evening prayer. Almost 72 per cent of the lectureships recorded in the 1629 London survey were held on Sunday afternoons.[81] However, lectures could be preached at any time. By 1628 the St. Antholin's lectures were given every morning but Sunday.[82] From 1602 on, the parish of St. Bartholomew Exchange had a lecture on Sunday mornings and another on Wednesday afternoons. In addition, beginning in 1617 there was a Tuesday afternoon sermon supported by a bequest from William Jones, Haberdasher, and beginning in 1628 a Friday evening sermon supported by a bequest from Richard Fishborne, Mercer.[83] Between 1642 and the Restoration, many vestries required their lecturers to preach on Fast days and Thanksgiving days as well as on regular lecture days.[84]

The lecture sermon was normally an hour long. When Thomas Cobhead, the preacher at St. Botolph Aldgate, deviated from this standard on the evening of 2 February 1586/7, the parish clerk was sufficiently struck by the event to record in his memoranda book, "He continued in the pulpit two hours and a half." In one important respect the lecture sermon tended to differ from the more infrequent monthly and quarterly sermons required by law and from the occasional sermons preached for anniversaries and funerals. Most sermons were exegetical, but since lecture sermons were more frequent and more regular than other sermons, some preachers made a practice of expounding a series of related texts over a period of several weeks. For example, the Puritan lecturer at St. Botolph Aldgate, Eusebius Paget, preached

---

* Vestry Minutes of St. Lawrence Jewry, 28 Aug. 1633, GLMS 2590/1, p. 295. However, there seems to have been no objection to a lecturer's holding several lectureships in different parishes.

on John 19:1–33 from 17 June to 30 September 1599. How strictly the preacher kept to his text was, of course, another matter altogether. The parish clerk of St. Botolph's noted rather testily that when David Dee, rector of St. Bartholomew the Great, preached at St. Botolph's one Sunday after evening prayer, he "followed never a whit of the text."[85]

One of the directions contained in the 1629 Instructions required "that every lecturer do read divine service according to the liturgy printed by authority, in his surplice and hood, before the lecture."[86] The positive function of this measure was to ensure the conformity of the lecturer. The negative function was to prevent the Puritan lecturer from preceding his sermon with an extemporaneous prayer. For the Puritans this regulation was a minor disaster. As Samuel Ward, the Ipswich lecturer, complained, "The using of a set form of prayer was confining of the Spirit ... ; there was not that life to quicken either hearer or speaker in the reading of ... a prayer, though penned never so elegantly."[87] Still, the government can hardly be blamed for attempting to regulate preachers like Nathaniel Bernard, lecturer at St. Sepulchre's, who quickened his hearers by praying before the sermon, "Oh Lord, open the eyes of the Queen's Majesty that she may see Jesus Christ, whom she hath pierced with her infidelity, superstition and idolatry."[88]

One can only speculate about the reaction of the London lecturers to this new regulation. As for the vestries, at least two promptly took measures that effectively circumvented both the letter and the spirit of the Instructions. The Vestry Minutes of Allhallows the Great for 31 March 1630 mention a decision made at the previous meeting, which unfortunately is not recorded in the minute book: "It was agreed upon at that vestry before that Mr. Harrison, curate of this church, should have quarterly 10s. paid by the churchwardens for reading prayers ... at Mr. Dr. Dennison's lecture on Tuesdays, which he preacheth, he himself reading sometimes." The Churchwardens' Accounts for 1630 record the first payment of £2 a year to Harrison; the last recorded payment to the reader for this service occurs, as might be expected, in 1641, although Dennison continued to lecture until 1649, the year before his death. There is no evidence of whether Dennison ever read service before the lecture. Indeed, the final phrase in the vestry minute may have been added for the benefit of the rector, Sampson Price, an orthodox divine and royal chaplain who was present at the vestry. As for Stephen Dennison, he was at least an occasional conformist, for he was the perpetual curate at St. Katherine Cree, where he also lectured.[89]

The parishioners of St. Botolph Aldgate used the same device to evade the new requirement. Their lecturer was Thomas Edwards, who later claimed in his *Gangraena* that "he never had a canonical coat, never gave a penny to the building of Paul's, took not the canonical oath, declined subscription for many years," though, he added, "I practiced the old conformity." Having already surmounted considerable difficulties in order to obtain Edwards, the parishioners were apparently not prepared to lose him over his scruples at wearing a surplice. The Churchwardens' Accounts for 1631 record an item of 3/1 "paid Mr. Bracegirdle [the curate] for reading prayers for Mr. Edwards."[90]

In addition to their preaching, all lecturers had been required since the Council's order of 1580 to "minister the holy sacraments in their own person, in what place soever they receive any portion for preaching." Canon 56 of the 1604 Constitutions elaborated on this requirement by ordering that every lecturer "shall twice at the least every year read himself the divine service upon two several Sundays publicly, and at the usual times both in the forenoon and afternoon, ... and shall likewise as often ... administer the Sacraments of Baptism, ... and of the Lord's Supper, in such manner and form, ... as are prescribed by the Book of Common Prayer."[91] Nothing further was generally demanded of the lecturer either by the parish or by the ecclesiastical authorities, and in fact evasion of the canonical requirements may have been widespread. When the Puritan preacher Francis Marbury was elected lecturer at St. Saviour's in 1602, he

did precisely except against any covenant or promise to undertake any further matter at any time either about reading of divine service, administration of the Sacraments, or other rites of the Church whatsoever; only for the avoiding of scruple in the cause he said that, if the Ordinary required him thereunto, he would for once read the divine service, but if upon any further terms he were urged to any more, he would not accept of the place.[92]

There is, of course, no way to estimate how common such practices were, for it was a rare parish that would formally minute an illegal covenant.

For all their onerous duties, lecturers also sometimes enjoyed unusual privileges. St. Mary Aldermanbury paid an extra £10 a year for an assistant to help with the catechizing because the incumbent curate already preached a Sunday afternoon lecture. St. Peter Westcheap ordered that the rector, the Puritan Daniel Votier, "should have for his better means ten pounds yearly more than now he hath during the time of his lectures in the afternoon," which sum was to help him pay the rent for his house.[93]

Quite apart from these exceptional expenditures, parishes regularly had to buy candles to illuminate the church for the lecture, and to pay small additional sums for the services of the clerk and the sexton. St. Bartholomew Exchange attempted to pay these petty sums out of contributions for the parish poor that were collected at the church door before the lecture began, only to find that "strangers (of which our congregation upon lecture days consisteth mostly) taking notice hereof, that it is to pay our clerk and sexton for their wages for their attendance upon our lectures, do withhold their charity."[94] Strangers from other parishes presented a vexing problem, for the more famous or popular the lecturer, the greater the influx of outsiders. It is easy to sympathize with the evident exasperation of the vestry at St. Botolph Aldgate, which informed its lecturer, Eusebius Paget, that "if for the great access of other parishioners, the inhabitants cannot enjoy their pews, then we are to retain Mr. Evan Thomas or some other [lecturer]."[95] However, the petty annoyances and minor expenses incidental to the lectureship pale into insignificance when compared to the single overriding problem of financing the lectureship itself.

FINANCES

The cost of a constant preaching ministry was high. This the bishops never tired of reiterating as their main defense of pluralism. "Pluralities," wrote Whitgift in 1584, "could not be taken away without discouraging the best sort of Ministers and taking away the reward of learning." Bancroft's modern apologist writes with equal conviction, "Without pluralities the Church could not have retained those learned and efficient men upon whom rested the whole weight of the ecclesiastical fabric."[96] Even admitting the logic of this question-begging argument—and the Puritans never did—the real difficulty lies in determining with any precision what was regarded as an adequate living. It was all very well for Whitgift to argue that no "man of reason will think that eight pounds yearly is able to maintain a learned Divine." What is required is evidence of a positive kind.[97]

In the middle years of Elizabeth's reign William Harrison, who had held a London benefice, wrote that any living worth £30 a year or less would not keep a "mean scholar." In the 1620's Bishop Earle commented rather cynically that at best a young preacher's "friends and much painfulness may prefer him to £30 a year." Plainly £30 was no longer considered adequate. By the Interregnum, times had changed radically. In 1652 Anthony Harford, a minister from Dartmouth, spurned the vestry's offer of the living of St. Michael Cornhill on the grounds that the living was neither "fixed," since it was sequestered, "nor competent, that I might live like a Christian." The parish had offered Harford a tax-free stipend of at least £100 a year, in addition to free housing. The price of living "like a Christian" had clearly risen.[98]

According to Christopher Hill's figures, the average value of London rectories rose from about £19 to about £84 a year between 1535, the date of the *Valor Ecclesiasticus*, and 1650, and that of London vicarages from a little more than £20 to £125 a year. Between 1500 and 1640 the cost of living rose approximately 650 per cent.[99] In other words, despite a considerable increase, the income of the average London living never kept pace with inflation. A few examples of actual, as opposed to average, incomes will show why not only unbeneficed ministers and underpaid curates but even parsons might compete for the extra income a London lectureship afforded. In 1565 the perpetual curate of St. Saviour, Southwark, was paid a salary of £20 a year plus the "vales" or "casualties"; as late as 1605 his income was still the same. In 1589 the parish of St. Lawrence Jewry, which farmed its own tithes, paid both the impropriate rector, Balliol College, and the vicar £20 a year. Following the sequestration of the living in 1643, the vicar received £100 a year, only £40 of which he could claim as his by right, for the remainder came as a benevolence of the parish. The parish of St. Stephen Coleman Street, which had purchased the rectory in 1589, was legally obliged to pay the vicar only £11 a year, and all augmentation to this princely sum was given, as the vestry repeatedly recorded, only "in manifestation of their love."[100]

By any standards curates' wages were notoriously bad. When, owing to the nonresidence of their rector, the parish of St. Stephen Walbrook hired a lecturing curate in 1635, the vestry paid him £8 a year for officiating the cure and £40 for lecturing.[101] At St. Dunstan in the East, where the churchwardens farmed the tithes for the nonresident rector, the vestry hired a curate at the pitiful wage of £4 a year in 1586; the following year, however, the twice-weekly lecture was conferred on the curate, giving him an additional £16. As late as 1658 St. Bride's paid its reading curate only £6 a year, whereas the resident preaching minister received £120.[102]

Against this background the value of a lecture stipend begins to have some meaning. It is necessary to remember further that the lecturer was paid only for preaching and not for all the hours of labor involved in officiating a cure, although admittedly the lecturer was expected to be painstaking in preparing his sermon. Finally, the lectureship was not regarded as a cure of souls. Hence lecturers could, and frequently did, hold a benefice or curacy either in the same parish or elsewhere without having to obtain the faculty required of a pluralist. And for the popular preacher there was always the possibility of obtaining several lectureships.

Since local initiative and autonomy prevailed, lecture stipends varied greatly according to such factors as the wealth of the parish, the number of sermons the lecturer was expected to preach, and the vestry's assessment of the lecturer's worth. The relatively poor parish of St. Stephen Walbrook, where in 1645 tithes amounted to no more than £35 a year, paid its lecturer only £3/6/8 in 1583. In the same year the lecturer at St. Mary Woolnoth received £10, and the lecturer at the wealthy parish of St. Helen's, £12.[103] At times a combination of factors affected wages. At St. Bartholomew by the Exchange, for example, the lecturer's salary jumped from £30 to £50 a year in 1628 for several reasons. First, and most obvious, the new lecturer preached the Wednesday morning lecture in addition to the Sunday afternoon sermon. Second, whereas the rector, who had previously preached the Sunday lecture, was a pluralist, the new lecturer was a recent Cambridge graduate who held neither curacy nor benefice. Finally, whereas the rector, John Grant, was an orthodox divine of some conviction who refused to take the covenant in 1643 and was subsequently sequestered, the new lecturer, Samuel Torshall, was a young Puritan of talent. In fact, Torshall soon attracted the attention of the famous preacher John Downham, through whose influence he gained the living of Bunbury, Cheshire.[104]

All increases in lecturers' salaries cannot be accounted for by the local parochial situation. To a much greater degree than the average

London benefice, lecture stipends rose in response to inflationary pressures. Admittedly it is difficult to generalize, and the rise was usually uneven. At St. Lawrence Jewry, for example, the lecturer's stipend rose from £10 a year in 1570 to £20 in 1594, £24 in 1603, £40 in 1604, £60 in 1631, and £100 in 1643—a level that the vestry was, however, unable to maintain. Each of the early morning lectureships at St. Antholin's paid £6 a year in 1576, £10 in 1603, £16 in 1619, £20 in 1624, and £30 in 1630. The Lincoln's Inn divinity readership, one of the most lucrative preaching positions in London, paid £40 a year in 1581, £60 in 1610, £80 in 1628, and £200 in 1647, although it is only fair to add that the munificent sum paid in 1647 reflects the eminence of the preacher, James Ussher, Archbishop of Armagh, rather than any economic consideration. In 1657, following Ussher's death, the lecturer's stipend dropped to £100.[105]

Of course, there are numerous exceptions where little or no rise is discernible. The lectureship at St. Margaret Lothbury, which had paid £10 a year in 1581, paid £20 in 1596, but the salary remained the same thereafter. In particular, the lectureships financed by a bequest tended to pay a fixed income. Lady Weld's bequest for a Wednesday lecture at St. Olave Jewry provided for an annual salary of £20 in 1623, when the first lecturer was chosen. Not until 1648 was the stipend raised, and then only an additional £5 a year was offered. By contrast, the generous endowment left by William Jones for his lecture afforded so high a salary that even in 1660 only the salaries paid to lecturers at the Inns of Court rivaled it. From the lecture's inception in 1615 the lecturer received £100 annually, in return for which he preached one sermon a week. Truly this lecture deserved to be called the "Golden Lecture."[106]

If one examines the lecturers' stipends, the upward trend is readily apparent. Table 2 is based on the salaries paid by the 40 parishes for which some sort of continuous financial record still exists. It is also instructive to compare lecture stipends with food prices. Between the decades 1583–92 and 1653–62, food prices rose approximately 70 per cent.[107] Between roughly the same dates lecture stipends tripled. It is true that in the decade before the Restoration food prices had fallen by about 5 per cent, and lecture salaries had declined similarly. The drop in wages, however, seems to have been connected not with the drop in prices but with the fact that most London parishes had over-

TABLE 2

Average Yearly Salaries of London Lecturers, 1570–1659

Period	Salary	Period	Salary
1570–79	£11/6	1620–29	£33
1580–89	16	1630–39	37/7
1590–99	16/4	1640–49	51
1600–09	21/8	1650–59	48/6
1610–19	29/7		

extended themselves in the 1640's. At St. Lawrence Jewry, for example, the vestry paid the vicar £60 for his services in 1633, and the lecturer an equal amount; ten years later each received £100. Not surprisingly, by 1650 the parish was in debt and the salaries in arrears.[108] At any rate, lecture salaries on the whole (assuming that the base wage paid in the 1580's was a fair return at the time) more than kept pace with the inflationary tendencies of the period.

Except for the unusually popular or fortunate preacher, few clergymen, Puritan or otherwise, could have hoped or wished to make a lifetime career of lecturing. For the clergyman already beneficed in the city, a lecture provided an opportunity both to supplement the income from his living and to earn the esteem of his parishioners. For the young ordinand recently graduated from the university, the lecture offered better monetary returns than a curacy, as well as the opportunity to make a reputation as a preacher and hence to attract the notice of prospective patrons. For others the lecture was usually a temporary expedient, a stopgap between more secure or better-paying positions. After the Puritan James Stile was forced to resign the rectory of St. Margaret Lothbury following his suspension in 1574, he lectured for a few years at St. Margaret New Fish Street and at St. Saviour's, but the income from these two lectureships amounted to only £11 a year in 1580.[109] By 1582 he had resigned from both, apparently to become chaplain to Sir Philip Sidney. With Sidney's death in 1586 he became one of the early morning lecturers at St. Antholin's, only to leave this position the next year to become chaplain to Sir Francis Walsingham. By 1589 he was back lecturing, this time at Allhallows Barking.[110] Obviously Stile could not manage to live on his lecturing, but as difficult as it was for a nonconformist like him to find a more permanent post, he could not afford to give up his lecturing for very long.

There are, of course, exceptions. By judiciously combining lecture-ships a few preachers managed to earn quite a comfortable living. Dr. Thomas Crook, a brother-in-law of Laurence Chaderton and a member of the London classical movement, held no benefices from 1582 till his death in 1598; however, with a lectureship at Gray's Inn and at St. Mary Woolchurch he earned the adequate income of £60 in 1583 and perhaps £70 a year by the 1590's. At the end of the 1620's another Puritan, Nathaniel Waker, equipped with a preaching license good for the whole diocese of London, managed to earn a salary of about £100 a year by lecturing concurrently at St. Antholin's, St. Lawrence Jewry, and St. Michael Cornhill. Although this kind of financial successs was by no means confined to Crook and Waker, it remained exceptional.[111]

The particular financial machinery underpinning a lectureship might be quite complex, but in the simplest terms all lectureships were financed by contributions, by bequests, or by a combination of the two. Throughout the period from 1560 to 1662 the vast majority of London parishes paid for their lectures by imposing levies of various kinds on their own parishioners; hence the various mechanisms employed at the parochial level will be described first.

The minute of the vestry of St. Christopher le Stocks that records the parish's decision to hire a lecturer goes on to order that "for the maintenance thereof a collection should be made of the benevolence of the parishioners to the intent it might be known what the sum would amount unto, for the doing whereof there was appointed Mr. Boyd and Mr. Allen to travail with the parishioners and to set down in writing what every man is willing of his own benevolence to give yearly towards the same."[112] Such an arrangement was often made to finance a lecture at first, but it seemed to work only so long as enthu-siasm for the lecture remained high. At St. Helen Bishopsgate 25 parishioners made payments totaling £10/9/8 during the fiscal year that ran from Michaelmas 1576 to Michaelmas 1577. However, eleven parishioners were behind in their payments, and the parish was heavily dependent on one donor, Sir Thomas Gresham, who contributed £2 a year. Despite the obvious weaknesses of the procedure, the parish did not change it, but reduced the lecturer's stipend instead. Even so, it was an exceptional year when money was not drawn from the parish stock to meet the deficit in the collection for the lecturer.[113]

The problem of annual deficits was one that few parishes ever solved satisfactorily. In 1615 the vestry of St. Christopher le Stocks hit upon a new expedient for raising the £30/6/8 needed for its lecturer. The sum was to be "raised upon the parish rateably according to each man's assessment to the poor"—a method estimated to bring in £40 a year. Yet the parish fell £2 short of the lecturer's stipend in 1617.[114] The situation at St. Peter Westcheap was considerably more desperate. In 1626, when the parish paid the parson, Daniel Votier, £20 for lecturing, a deficit of £11/6/10 had to be made up from the parish stock. The vestry attempted a remedy on 3 August 1627 by ordering an annual supplement from the parish stock, but they cautiously limited the supplement to £10. Finally, in 1632, "all former orders to this purpose being frustrate," the vestry regularized the deficit by granting the lecturer £10 a year from the parish stock in addition to whatever was collected by voluntary contribution.[115]

Other parishes adopted other methods. The vestry of St. Martin Ludgate seemed convinced that the manner of collection, rather than the system of voluntary benevolence, was at fault. In 1615 the parish constables were substituted for the special collectors who had previously served. In 1621, owing to complaints that the constables had "been very negligent and remiss in their duties herein," the vestry decided to try using the preceding year's churchwardens as collectors. By 1625 a return had been made to specially chosen collectors. At least one parish, St. Dunstan in the East, cut its losses by simply lowering its sights. When the first lecturer was chosen in 1572, the vestry offered him the considerable salary of £30 a year in return for two sermons weekly. Six years later the vestry reduced the stipend to £20 but agreed that no lecturing need be done between midsummer and Michaelmas. And finally, in 1587, the vestry hired a curate who would preach twice weekly for £16 a year.[116]

The practice of financing lectureships by voluntary contributions was not so much unworkable as inefficient. As long as a parish was willing to back its benevolence with the resources of the parish stock, deficits could be carried indefinitely. St. Mary Woolnoth and St. Michael Crooked Lane, two parishes that farmed their tithes and may have had, as a consequence, a more efficient system of collection, even ran up small surpluses on their lecture receipts.[117]

The most favorably placed parishes in London were the handful that had succeeded either in leasing or in purchasing their rectories, for parishes in this enviable position could finance their lectures directly from tithe receipts. During the 1580's the parish of St. Lawrence Jewry managed both to purchase the advowson and to lease the parsonage from the impropriate rector, Balliol College. Since the vestry now had the right to elect the vicar and hence was able to secure resident, preaching incumbents, it became customary to confer the lectureship on the vicar. The vicar's wages are interesting to observe, for they offer a clue to the relative weight attached by the laity to the two functions of his office. In 1589 the Churchwardens' Accounts record payments of £20 to Balliol College as rector, £20 to the vicar for officiating the cure, and £10 to the vicar for lecturing. While the first two payments remained stationary (they had, of course, been specified in the original lease), payments for the lecture rose to £13/6/8 in 1590, £20 in 1594, £24 in 1602, and £40 in 1604, by which time tithe receipts amounted to between £60 and £70 a year.[118] It might be argued that the salary increases for lecturing simply disguised an augmentation to the vicar's stipend for officiating the cure. This seems unlikely, however, since an annual benevolence would have accomplished as much, and since the stipendiary augmentations were tied to the requirement to preach.

There is every evidence that the laity of London was willing to reward the clergy adequately when two conditions were met: when the laity was able to exercise some measure of control over the selection of their clergy and when the clergy they selected were willing to preach. The second condition was equally as important as the first. In 1649, for example, a time when the vestry of St. Mary Colechurch acted as trustee of the sequestered parsonage, the minister was offered an annual stipend of £100 for preaching twice on Sundays. If he consented to preach only once on Sunday, however, he was to receive only £52.* At St. Saviour's, where the vestry controlled the selection

---

* GLMS 64, fol. 45v. The statement set forth here is, of course, only generally true; individual parishioners might and did object to paying for a preaching clergy. In a libel and defamation suit, a parishioner of St. Ethelburga was accused of saying, when reproached by the lecturer for refusing to contribute to the support of the lecture, "Thou art a base fellow and not worthy to come to church, and I would rather see a man shit over a pulpit than hear thee preach." Consistory Court Deposition Book, 1627–30 (testimony given in *Twigden vs. Mease*, 31 Oct. 1628), LCCRO, DL/C/231, no fol.

of both the incumbent and an additional lecturer, the two offices
tended to become confused in the minds of the parishioners. Both the
curate and the lecturer came to be called "preachers" in the vestry
records; both were invited to attend the vestry and assist in its deliberations (a privilege not ordinarily granted to lecturers); both received the same salary; and the putative lecturer was expected to assist the perpetual curate, when necessary, in the ordinary duties of the
cure.[119] The vestry was plainly more interested in obtaining the desired results than in preserving the ecclesiastical niceties.

Endowments, the second means by which lectureships were financed, present another aspect of the thrust toward a preaching clergy
selected by and dependent on the laity, only in this instance the London merchant or his wife acted directly and personally rather than
through the parish vestry. In light of W. K. Jordan's work, the importance of the charitable endowment and bequest in shaping the
social institutions of the period need hardly be stressed anew in this
study.[120] Although the endowment never became the dominant means
of financing the city lectureships, it not only supported but also tended
to stabilize an institution that otherwise lacked a permanent financial
base.

After 1576, when William Parker, a London Draper, left among his
many benefactions the sum of £120 to the Puritan parish of St. Antholin's for a lecture twice weekly, a continuous stream of bequests
flowed from the merchant community of the city. In all at least 76
donors left bequests to establish or augment the stipends of the London parish lecturers.[121] The distribution of these gifts over the years
was uneven in the extreme: whereas half the known lectureships had
been founded by 1600, almost five times as many bequests were made
under the first two Stuarts as under Elizabeth. Yet the practice of
leaving bequests for lectures got its impetus from the last generation
of Elizabethans. After 1584 the number of lectureship endowments
approximately doubled every fifteen years, from the 6 bequeathed by
1584, to 12 by 1599, 26 by 1614, and 49 by 1629.

Perhaps more significant than the overall rate of growth, however,
are the variations in the rate from one period to another. Five bequests
are recorded for the years 1580 to 1584; thereafter only two bequests
are noted for each five-year period until 1600. During the early years
of the seventeenth century, the rate of giving accelerated: nine bequests

were made in the first decade, twelve in the second, and sixteen each in the third and fourth. In the ten years from 1625 to 1634 a total of twenty bequests were added. A comparison of these figures with those in Table 1, in the first section of this chapter, reveals an approximate correspondence. In both sets of data the early 1580's witnessed the greatest activity of Elizabeth's reign. Merchant donors seem to have been even more sensitive than the generality of parish vestries to the official hostility reflected in Whitgift's repressive policies. In both sets of data the 1590's are years of relative stagnation, and the last years of Elizabeth's reign a period of renewed activity. Between 1605 and 1610, although the number of active lectureships continued to rise, the number of new parishes hiring lecturers and the number of new bequests fell off, perhaps in reaction to the repressive measures taken by Bancroft following the promulgation of the new canons. After 1610 both sets of data reveal a new increase in activity, culminating in a massive Puritan effort from 1625 to 1634 to challenge Laud's ascendancy.

The correspondence, approximate though it is, seems more than coincidental, and for good reasons. The donors of lecture bequests came from the same elements of the urban society as the leaders of the parish vestries. The same ecclesiastical and political climate that led vestries to establish or revive parish lectureships might also lead wealthy citizens to make bequests for their support. The sudden decline in the number of bequests after 1635 was not, as it might seem, a cowardly quitting of the field at the crucial hour. By that time the successful prosecution of the Feoffees for Impropriations and the known hostility of Laud and King Charles to lecture foundations jeopardized all such endowments, and few London businessmen, it may be imagined, would risk investing in a foundation that might be confiscated or dissolved by the Crown.[122]

Lectureship bequests were not only unevenly distributed through time; they were also unevenly distributed among the London parishes. The St. Antholin's lectureships attracted by far the heaviest investment. Aside from gifts channeled through the Feoffees for Impropriations during the years they controlled the finances of the early morning lectures at St. Antholin's, and aside from the continuous stream of small contributions not individually listed in the Churchwardens' Accounts, at least 23 bequests are known to have been received by the parish. St. Bartholomew Exchange was the next most favored parish, with 14 bequests toward the maintenance of its four weekly lectures; it was followed by St. Mary le Bow, with seven, and Allhallows Bread Street, with five. Put another way, the six most favored parishes shared at least 55 bequests among them, whereas the other 25 London parishes known to have received lecture bequests shared only 33.[123]

At no time, then, could more than a minority of London parishes have depended on endowments to finance their preaching. By 1584 only 11 per cent of the parishes that had established lectureships up to that time were in a position to finance them, either wholly or in part, from endowments; by 1604 the proportion had scarcely changed, but by 1625 it had risen to 18 per cent, and by 1635 to 22 per cent.[124] At the Restoration the proportion had increased only by four per cent. However, if comparison is made with the average number of parishes with *active* lectureships in a given period, the proportion is slightly higher, as Table 3 shows.[125]

It is fairly certain that the donors of most of these bequests were motivated by puritanical sentiments.[126] Margaret Astell was probably an exception, for when she left an annuity of £40 in 1639 for the preacher of a Friday evening lecture at St. Lawrence Jewry, her trustees were instructed to do their best to see that the vestry of St. Lawrence elected not only a pious and learned preacher, but also one conformable to the Establishment.[127] It was seldom, however, that a benefactor left this much concrete evidence one way or the other of his religious views. Even William Jones, whose benefactions stretched from London to Monmouth, and who was unquestionably a Puritan, left little direct evidence of his religious bias in his will. The preamble, for example, employs a formula common to the vast majority of wills from this period: "First I bequeath my soul to God who gave it me, and my body to be buried in Christian-like burial, hoping that of his mercy he will through the merits of Jesus Christ raise both my body and soul unto everlasting life at the last day of Judgment." More revealing than this standard passage is the fact that two of the men to whom £1000 is entrusted for distribution among poor preachers are the well-known Puritan divines Stephen Egerton and Richard Sedgwick, the latter appearing also among the overseers.[128] The will of Thomas Ridge, citizen and Grocer, which includes a bequest of £100 to St. Benet Gracechurch for an "able and sufficient preacher" to lecture weekly on Sundays, offers similar evidence, for the four overseers

TABLE 3

Parishes with Active Lectureships and Parishes with Endowed
Lectureships, 1580–1639

Period	Average no. of parishes with active lectureships	Parishes with endowed lectureships	
		Average no.	Per cent
1580–84	38	5	13%
1600–04	44	8	18
1620–24	59	17	29
1630–34	90	25	28
1635–39	89	27	30

were all Puritans and popular London lecturers—William Charke, Stephen Egerton, Edward Phillips, and Anthony Wotton. It was probably with their consent that the parish disregarded the provision of Ridge's will specifying that the £100 should be dispensed in ten equal installments during the ensuing decade and instead lent the capital at 8 per cent interest to one of the parishioners, the interest to be spent on a perpetual lecture.[129]

Further hints of a donor's religious predilections are often to be found in the conditions prescribed for paying the money. When William Garret, Merchant Taylor, bequeathed £100 to the parish of St. Mary Aldermanbury in 1586 for the maintenance of a lecture "by the advice of the chief parishioners," he provided "that if the religion then professed should alter, and the lecture service should not be used, then the interest thereof should be yearly distributed among the poor"—insurance, presumably, against the possible success of the Counter-Reformation.

By the end of the 1620's the greatest threat to the successful execution of a lectureship bequest no longer seemed to come, as it had in William Garret's day, from the external forces of militant Catholicism, but rather from what was regarded as the internal subversion of victorious Arminianism. In 1630 Bernard Hyde provided in an indenture made with the Salters' Company that they were to choose not only a "godly and learned preacher" for his Tuesday lecture at St. Dunstan in the East, but equally important a preacher "steadfast in the religion of the church of England." Any possible ambiguity is removed by the final provision that "if the said weekly lecture should be by authority suppressed or discontinued," then the funds were to be employed toward other charitable uses.[130]

Besides protecting their endowments from the depredations of unsympathetic bishops, some donors also recognized the need to guard against hostility closer to home. In her will of 22 February 1622/3 Dame Mary Weld, who gave £300 for a lecture to be preached at St. Olave Jewry "by some godly, zealous and learned preacher," provided that if the minister "shall not permit and give way that the said lecture may be performed," then the lecture was to be moved to another parish as the vestry should order. Other, less drastic, solutions were found to the problem. When Lady Camden, widow of Baptist Hicks, bequeathed £30 yearly each to St. Lawrence Jewry and St. Mary Magdalen Milk Street "towards the maintenance of a learned and able minister, of good life and conversation," she tactfully provided that £4 from this sum should be paid yearly "to the vicar of the said parish, for allowing such preacher to preach in the said parish church."[131]

Almost all the London donors were members of the London business community, or the wives or widows of businessmen, although by no means all were important merchants or members of the great livery companies. The most notable exception was a cleric, Dr. Thomas White, vicar of St. Dunstan in the West for almost half a century and founder of Sion College. Among his other benefactions White, who was himself a popular preacher, gave £18 a year toward the support of the lecture at his own parish church. Although the historian of Sion College claims that there is "no firm ground for classing him as a Puritan," there are some grounds, flimsy though they may be. One of the two overseers of White's last will, dated 4 October 1623, was the famous Puritan John Downham, previously mentioned as the preacher of the "Golden" lecture at St. Bartholomew Exchange, and, according to White's will, his "good neighbor in London." Forty years before, White had numbered among his friends Sir Walter Mildmay, the founder of Emmanuel College, and Giles Wigginton, a Presbyterian divine.[132]

Bold and imaginative as the London merchants may have been in using their wealth to establish lectureships, they were still businessmen, and careful with their investments. From William Parker, whose bequest to the St. Antholin's lectures in 1576 was entrusted to the

Drapers' Company, to Throckmorton Trotman, whose bequest for an early morning lecture at St. Giles almost half a century later was entrusted to the Haberdashers, merchants frequently left money to their livery company in trust for charitable uses.[133] As careful as some vestries were in the handling of their parish stock and other funds, few could compete with the great companies in financial expertise.

What could happen when a vestry bungled its investments is easily illustrated. On 16 January 1643/4 the parish feoffees of St. Mary Magdalen Milk Street learned of Lady Camden's will, in which the sum of £600 was conveyed to them to purchase land that would bring in £30 a year to support the weekly lecture. The feoffees invested not only the £600 but also an unspecified amount from the parish stock in an Essex farm that was expected to yield £40 a year in rent. The next year, at the vestry held on 6 August 1645, the feoffees sadly informed the parish that "the rents are since fallen." A year later the churchwardens were sent down to survey the property. Among their tasks was to make certain that the six gallons of sack sent annually as part of the rent was sewn into canvas, for the year before the carter and his porters had drunk it all and filled the cask with water. The churchwardens were no more successful in the long run than the feoffees. In 1655 the rent was badly in arrears, and a new committee had to be dispatched into Essex to take some "appropriate" action.[134]

This unhappy experience was not unique. In 1628 the vestry of St. Olave Jewry, having invested Lady Weld's gift of £300 for their lecture in a house and land at Stanford le Hope, Essex, found that the rents were "much fallen" and "the housing grown ruinous." They wisely decided to sell, but lost more than £35 in the process. St. Swithin's had so much trouble with their own feoffees over the investment of Lady Slany's lecture bequest that in 1623 the churchwardens were authorized first to pay £3/1/10 for a suit in Chancery to recover the property, and then to dispense an additional £10 "towards the preferring of a bill in parliament to have an act to pass for the land to be settled forever upon the lectures."[135]

For the prudent London donor, particularly if a large or complex bequest was involved, the city company offered at once wider connections and influence, greater experience in handling investments, and the continuity necessary for the wise management of an estate. When Lady Weld, whose gift for a lecture at St. Olave Jewry has been men-

tioned before, bequeathed £2,000 for a revolving fund to be employed
for the purpose of buying impropriations "for ever, if it shall please
Almighty God ... unto the World's End for the increase of learned
preachers," she vested the fund with the Haberdashers' Company.[136]
By its very nature her bequest was one that could not have been administered by a vestry.

In the case of the William Jones bequest, parts of the charities—the
lectures at St. Bartholomew Exchange, at Newland, Gloucestershire,
and at Monmouth, for example—could have been administered locally by vestries. However, the parts were so interrelated, and the totality
so complex, that the decision of this wealthy Merchant Adventurer to
place the bulk of his endowments in trust with his livery company
seems inevitable. On 5 March 1612/13, almost two years before his
death, Jones informed the Haberdashers of his proposals, and for the
next few years the company's court of assistants was kept busy carrying them out.

As the money came pouring in, first from Jones himself and later
from his executors, it was lent out temporarily to members of the
livery or to the East India Company at 7 per cent interest. Funds were
dispatched to Monmouth to purchase timber for the almshouses, and
bricklayers were recruited in London to build the almshouses and the
free school. The company investigated and later invested £4,000 of
the trust in the purchase of part of Hatcham manor in Surrey from
Sir John Brook, who as one of the conditions of the sale obtained a
special license under the Great Seal to convey the land in mortmain
to the company as governors of the Monmouth charities. Finally, the
company appointed the lecturer, the usher, and the schoolmaster, who
came with recommendations from respectively William Jones himself,
the Recorder of London, and the Lord Chancellor and the Lord Chief
Justice. Even before the Monmouth foundations were in full working
order, the company became engaged in setting up similar foundations
at Newland ,where Jones had endowed a lectureship and sixteen almshouses, and where it was necessary to stave off a group of parishioners,
led by Sir William Throckmorton, who challenged the company's
right to appoint the lecturer and the alms people. By comparison the
negotiations incidental to settling Jones's lecture at St. Bartholomew's
and to naming the nine poor Haberdashers who were to receive £8
a year apiece were simple matters indeed. Admittedly this was the
largest and most complex charity administered by the Haberdashers,

but obviously even the least complicated bequest benefited from the expert supervision the livery companies customarily provided.[137]

In a sense the laity of London, who otherwise lacked any substantial share of ecclesiastical patronage, gained through their parish lectureships a position somewhat analogous to that of the country squire who presented the parson at his family church. Similarly, the patronage acquired by the city companies as trustees put them in a position somewhat analogous to that of the great landed aristocrat who, in addition to employing a family tutor and chaplain, might present to livings scattered over half a dozen shires. Again, this phenomenon can be illustrated from the records of the Haberdashers. Besides William Jones's three lectureships and Lady Weld's impropriations, the company also dispensed ten scholarships to students of divinity at the universities, including two scholarships each to Emmanuel and Sidney Sussex, as well as funds to support four poor preachers and a lecture at Bunbury, Cheshire. Furthermore, in handling its patronage the company showed none of the deference expected of the mercantile community in an aristocratic society. The Bunbury lecture is a case in point.

In 1594 Thomas Aldersey gave the company certain properties at Bunbury, Cheshire, for the support of "a preacher and a minister to be his assistant." In 1603, the preacher's place falling vacant, the company appointed William Hinde, a disciple of Dr. John Reynolds of Oxford. By 1606 Hinde had been suspended, but rather than replace him the company temporized in the hope "that the Lord Bishop of that diocese will upon the suite of some good friends restore the said Mr. Hinde again to the exercise of his ministry." Twelve years later, in 1618, the company received a letter from the Bishop of Chester complaining of Hinde's "nonconformity to the ceremonies appointed in the Church." With a fine audacity the company ordered that "a letter be written to his lordship entreating his further pains to persuade with Mr. Hinde, and that if he cannot prevail, . . . then because we cannot by the patent and Mr. Aldersey's statute displace him for such his nonconformity, that therefore his lordship will be pleased for the good of the parishioners to afford him the liberty of his ministry." His lordship was undoubtedly not pleased, but Hinde continued at his post until his death in 1629, when the company appointed as his successor another Puritan, Samuel Torshall.[138]

Although not all the Haberdashers' patronage was used for the benefit of London Puritans, much of it was, and to considerable effect. It will suffice here to indicate something of the variety of assistance that the company rendered to the city's Puritan clergy. In 1584, on the petition of William Wager, the Puritan rector and lecturer of St. Benet Gracechurch, the company granted his son Edward one of Mrs. Barrett's Cambridge exhibitions, worth £5 a year, "so long as he shall remain in the said college in honest name and fame without promotion, and study divinity to the good liking of the company." Ten years later Edward resigned the exhibition and returned to the city to become curate and lecturer at St. Lawrence Pountney.[139] Thomas Sanderson, another of the company's scholars, received from them a benevolence of £3/6/8 in 1588 "for his better furnishing of him with books for his study." In 1594 Sanderson became vicar and lecturer at St. Lawrence Jewry.[140]

Another type of patronage was made available to the company in 1631 by Mary Paradine, whose bequest provided, among other things, pensions of 50 shillings yearly for each of four poor preachers. One of these pensions was granted the following year to Samuel Fawcett, "a poor minister and painful teacher of the word of God in the parish church of St. Mary Staining ... whose means is very small and his charge great." Fawcett became something of a company protégé. In 1637 the court of assistants granted him a benevolence of £10 "for rebuilding of the parsonage house that lately fell down," and in 1652 he was appointed the William Jones lecturer at Newland.[141] It would be difficult to assess the total effect of the city companies' patronage on the life of the London clergy until much more research had been carried out in the companies' records. It can be said, however, that at least 21 London lecturers or their sons benefited in one way or another between 1583 and 1660 from the Haberdashers' pensions and university exhibitions, lectureships, and livings.

Moreover, it is possible to measure at least approximately the financial effect of the endowments on the cost of the London parish lectureships. Only a minority of the London lectureships had been endowed in the first place, and of these, only a handful heavily enough to become self-supporting. Hence most parishes with endowed lectureships continued to collect lecture contributions from their parishioners. St. Swithin's is a case in point. In 1617 Thomas Whetenhall gave the parish £10 a year toward the establishment of a weekday lecture, and in 1620 Lady Margaret Slany, widow of a wealthy Skinner, left the parish 200 marks to secure an annual income of £6/13/4 to augment the Whetenhall lecture. In 1627 the parish received an additional £4 a year from the executor of Lady Harte's will. According to the 1629 Survey of Lecturers, Richard Cooke, the rector, delivered the Whetenhall Tuesday evening lecture, for which he should have received £20/13/4 .There is no record of what he was actually paid. But the parish also hired a curate, the Puritan Ithiel Smart, who preached a Sunday lecture toward which the parishioners collected £21/14/2, and for which he was paid £30 a year, according to the 1629 Churchwardens' Accounts.[142] Similarly, at St. Peter Cornhill the parishioners supported an unendowed Sunday lectureship in addition to a Thursday lecture that carried a stipend of £20 a year from the estate of Dame Lucy Edge. Despite the endowment the parishioners were asked to contribute toward making up a sufficient stipend within a year of the lectureship's establishment.[143]

Even the St. Antholin's lectures, the most heavily endowed in the city, were not self-sustaining as late as the 1620's, for the ambitions of the parish continually outran the available income. Between the 1560's and the 1620's the lecturer's stipend rose from £6 to £20 a year, and the number of preachers hired increased from three to five. In 1624, the last year for which the Churchwardens' Accounts provide a detailed record of the lectureship receipts and expenditures, the lectureship accounts almost balanced. The total receipts were £107/10, whereas the total salaries paid the five lecturers amounted to £108/16. Of the total receipts, £40 came from the Chamber of London, and the remainder from the various endowments and properties accumulated in the past. During the same year £15/6 was collected from the parishioners, and two new gifts were received, having a total capital value of £130, which in turn were invested along with two other, smaller gifts received some years before in the purchase for £160 of a lease on some nearby urban property. Obviously the St. Antholin's lectures were a major financial undertaking; it is equally obvious, however, that without the £40 granted by the Court of Aldermen—a gift that ceased in 1629—the small surplus produced by the collection of £15/6 would have been a considerable deficit.[144]

To place the role of the lectureship endowments in a larger perspective, it is necessary to turn from the details of parish finance to a con-

TABLE 4

Estimated Annual Cost of the London Lectureships, 1570–1659

Period	Average annual cost [a]	Period	Average annual cost [a]
1570–79	£200	1620–29	£2,700
1580–89	700	1630–39	3,400
1590–99	700	1640–49	3,500
1600–09	900	1650–59	2,600
1610–19	1,600		

[a] Rounded off to the nearest £100.

sideration of the total cost of the institution itself. The costs given in Table 4 have been estimated by multiplying the approximate number of active lectureships by the average yearly lecturer's salary for a given decade. Admittedly these figures are rough at best, but they do permit some estimate to be made of the proportion of the annual cost accounted for by the endowments. In his recent study of London charity W. K. Jordan estimates that London donors left almost £50,000 in capital to support lectureships between 1570 and 1660. Slightly less than half of this endowment was granted to parish lectureships in London and Middlesex. By 1600 only about £3,800 of the £50,000 total had been contributed. Assuming that about half of this endowment went to support London lectureships, and assuming that the capital sum yielded a 5 per cent return, something like £95 a year was available in London by 1600. Thus endowments accounted for only about 14 per cent of the total annual cost of the London lectureships during the last decade of the sixteenth century. Even by 1660, if the same assumptions are made, endowments accounted for not quite one-half the annual cost.[145]

Almost all London parish vestries welcomed endowments for their lectureships, since contributions solicited from parishioners were always undependable.[146] In this connection the heroic efforts of the St. Antholin's collectors to gather sufficient funds in 1604 "that the yearly contribution might cease" are readily understandable.[147] Nevertheless, from first to last most parish lectureships continued to depend on the willing support of the parishioners. Doubtless vestries found dependence on the unpredictable generosity of parishioners a source of weakness, but this dependence was also a source of strength, for the need to contribute toward the preacher's maintenance encouraged a sense of responsibility for the lectureship's survival. Moreover, this dependence was ultimately the only insurance that the institution would continue to answer local needs and respond to local controls.

SANCTIONS AND CONTROL

In 1641 a perceptive anonymous critic made the following remarks about the consequences of lay control of the London lectureships:

Where either the minister is not able, or not willing, the people's bevenolence being uncertain to the lecturer they make choice of, they [the lecturers] are forced to humor the people, often unworthily, and to make sides and factions against the minister, to his great discontent and discouragement.... They would have preachers every hour in their pulpits, but as they have beggars at their doors, clothed in rags and bowing down to them for morsels of bread, and their sermons like so many suits for a farthing; their preachers must be all of the mendicant order, and above all other orders and ranks of men, live upon their alms and benevolence, that bear no further goodwill to preaching than as it may be a shooting-horn to their esteem and gain, this being their godliness and that their God.[148]

It is undoubtedly true that some lecturers made it their study to please, and that popularity might be gained as well by flattery as by preaching the pure Word of God. It is also true that the mere presence of another clergyman might prove a source of "discontent and discouragement" to the incumbent, even when the lecturer did not "make sides" against him. When, for instance, John Herring, the Puritan vicar of St. Bride's, spoke to the vestry on 20 September 1661, "forewarning them of meddling to provide any minister for the Sabbath days in the afternoons," he claimed in justification that a lecturer would "withdraw his people from him."[149]

The anonymous critic quite rightly pointed out that both difficulties might be removed simply by providing, first, that "the maintenance of a lecturer ... be made certain ... and not to be paid at pleasure, or called back, when the people will," and second, that "no particular man be brought in, against whom the minister hath good exception." Attractive as such a solution may have been to the clergy, whether orthodox Anglican or Puritan, it had little appeal for the laity. From a vestry's point of view, to adopt such a policy would be tantamount to surrendering the fundamental means of control, which rested in the final analysis on the power to appoint the lecturer independently of outside pressures and on the continued precariousness of both the lecturer's tenure and his stipend. On rare occasions a parish might demand explicit safeguards against interference by the incumbent; the 1624 Churchwardens' Accounts of St. Pancras Soper Lane, for example, record "a bond wherein Mr. Worme, our parson, is bound not to raise his tithes, but to suffer Mr. Goodall, the lecturer, to preach." But there was little need to exact such legal guarantees from the lecturer, for ordinarily the sanctions inherent in the institution itself provided sufficient control.[150]

Since the independent lecturer, unlike the lecturing incumbent, lacked any semblance of title or right enforceable by law, he had little choice when the parish tired of his preaching but to leave the lectureship. In only one instance is there any evidence of an independent lecturer's defying the wishes of the vestry, and then only because of an ambiguity surrounding the right of appointment. Stephen Watkins, who had preached the Friday morning lecture at St. Antholin's at least since 1648, was not reappointed at the vestry held on 2 December 1654; the reasons for the vestry's decision are not stated. In any event Watkins immediately threatened to take the matter into court. The parish responded by ordering the churchwardens to "manage the business, and to defend the parish's right as to choice of lecturers." Since Watkins apparently based his claim on the supposed right of the feoffees for the lectureship to appoint the lecturers, the vestry persuaded the rector and only resident feoffee, Charles Offspring, to present two candidates, Watkins and Zachary Crofton, for the disputed lectureship. The vestry then proceeded to elect Crofton. Three weeks later Watkins was warned that another lecturer had been chosen "according to the custom of the parish" and that he would no longer be paid for preaching. In September the vestry learned that Watkins had petitioned the Lord Protector, who had in turn referred the case to the Lord Mayor and other commissioners; in October the senior churchwarden reported that the commission had asked for proof of the parish's right to elect lecturers. The vestry refused to comply, on the grounds that the commission had denied their request for a copy of Watkins's petition. Having reached this impasse, the commission evidently dropped the matter. Watkins must have continued to press his claim, however, for a vestry early in 1658 recorded a petition signed by four of the St. Antholin's lecturers who denied that they either supported Watkins's claim or considered themselves or their titles to their lectureships in any way involved in the quarrel. Only one outcome was ever conceivable. Finally, on 14 August 1660, Watkins presented the vestry with a signed statement in which he freely acknowledged "that there is a power and good authority in the minister, churchwardens, and parishioners...and their successors yearly to elect their weekly morning lecturers...at their own judgments and pleasures."[151]

In parishes where the lectureship was customarily conferred on the incumbent, vestries experienced much greater difficulty in continuing to exercise any significant degree of control. Once conferred, the lectureship tended to become identified with the living; thus an office originally granted at the pleasure of the parish came to be held as a right. Nevertheless, a new presentation to the living always provided the parish with an opportunity to reassert its rights, and it was a weak parish that let such a chance go by.

The Crown appointment of Robert Harland to the perpetual curacy of St. Mary Aldermanbury offers a particularly apt illustration. Since 1541 the parish had leased both the rectory and the advowson from the Crown, so that intervention by the government was in any case unusual, and since 1573 the parish had conferred the lectureship on the curate, whom they elected. In September 1591 Michael Salford, who had been curate and lecturer since 1588, was dismissed by the vestry with his consent. In December the parish farmers of the rectory received a letter from Lord Treasurer Burghley commanding them to place Robert Harland "in the room of the curate there," and "to provide with the consent of the parishioners" whatever stipend had formerly been paid for the lecture. The parish readily acquiesced to the appointment, "the rather for his honor's sake to whom this parish acknowledges themselves greatly bound for his Lordship's sundry favors extended towards them." But the lectureship was another matter altogether: "And touching other consideration for reading a lecture (being a matter voluntary) they can set down no certainty, but it is not to be doubted but that upon Mr. Harland's well usage of himself, and pains taking therein, there will be collected of a number of well-disposed persons that were a competent yearly sum to his good contentment." This was more than an empty gesture. Fifteen years later Harland still made his annual request of the vestry "to understand the pleasure of the parish whether they be pleased to continue the former contribution for the reading a lecture," to which the vestry replied after due deliberation "that the said lecture shall continue during the pleasure of the parish."[152]

Once installed in the parish lectureship, the incumbent could ordinarily depend on retaining his preaching post as long as he remained in the benefice. To remove the parson and substitute an independent lecturer was to run the risk of having the pulpit denied to the usurping preacher, if indeed the parish ever succeeded in electing a lecturer without the parson's consent.

Early in 1644 the vestry of St. Peter Westcheap attempted to displace their rector from his lectureship, only to come up against his obstinate refusal to cooperate in any way. For reasons that remain obscure, the parish and Daniel Votier, their Puritan parson, were at loggerheads. According to the vestry, at least, Votier would neither specify the injuries of which he complained nor refer the matter to arbitration. At any rate, the vestry requested that he resign from his lecture so that they could hold a new election. This he absolutely refused to do on the grounds "that he could not spare the means for a lecture." Faced with this refusal, the vestry took the drastic step of presenting their grievances to the Committee for Plundered Ministers and of petitioning for Votier's sequestration, an event that actually took place in July 1644. On the following January 6 the vestry elected an independent lecturer. This incident in no way disproves the initial premise, for the vestry succeeded in removing the parson from the lectureship only by removing him from the benefice itself.[153]

In their control of finances the parish had a more flexible weapon to use against a recalcitrant incumbent. Theoretically, ecclesiastical discipline was the province of the hierarchy alone, but economic sanctions wielded by a vestry were no less real for lack of official approval or recognition. The parish clerk of St. Lawrence Jewry recorded on 4 October 1590 that "as there is some controversy stirred betwixt our vicar and the parishioners, they do not consent to make any contribution for a lecture until the same be quieted." And the vestry had the effrontery to add, "If it please himself to preach of his own accord [without pay], they shall the better like thereof." Since the vicar's living was worth only £20 a year, and since his stipend for the lecture amounted to an additional £14, he stood to lose a substantial part of his income. Apparently the controversy was quickly and amicably ended, for several months later the vestry ordered that the lecture be resumed on the following Michaelmas.[154]

In a somewhat similar situation the vestry of St. Lawrence Pountney acted with equal determination, though with considerably greater tact. Their aim was not simply to discipline the incumbent but "upon disliking of the parishioners" to force him to resign. The parish had leased the rectory since 1561 and had the right of presentation, but even a perpetual curate had security of tenure unless he was lawfully deprived by his bishop. Hence it is not surprising that the curate, Robert Lloyd, ignored the vestry's warning that he was to depart in six months. A year later the vestry sent Lloyd the following message:

Mr. Lloyd, you shall understand it was agreed by an assembly of the parish yesterday ... that we should certify you once again that you might forbear your preaching, if you please, for that we are not able to undergo that charge of fourteen pounds a year no longer ..., for that we are so far in debt, by reason of the great charge we have been at of late in repairing of our church, and the great charge we are put unto by yourself in the multiplying of suits against us.

Since the lecture, at £14 a year, paid better than the cure, at £10, Lloyd had little choice but to resign. The vestry's plea of poverty, however, was no more than a subterfuge, for when Lloyd resigned a few months later, his salary both for preaching and for officiating the cure had been paid in its entirety.[155]

There is no evidence that London parish vestries abused the powers inherent in their control of the parish lectureships. Sanctions seem to have been rarely invoked, and then only after considerable provocation. Nevertheless, when Laud wrote that lecturers "by reason of their pay are the people's creatures," he was describing not some perversion of the institution but its central reality.[156] Had there been no basic dissatisfaction with the Elizabethan Settlement—had Puritanism never arisen—the opening up of a new sphere to the natural workings of lay patronage would have presented few problems to either Crown or Church. But given a vigorous minority who dissented strongly from the prevailing ideology of the Established Church, it was perhaps inevitable that this dissent should find expression in the new institution of the lectureship. Where, as in London, the vast majority of the parish livings were in the gift of the Church and the Crown, the lectureship offered the obvious means by which the Puritan laity could redress the balance of patronage in their favor.

In a sense, then, the reforms proposed by the anonymous London critic in 1641 were beside the point. The fundamental problem was not that of obtaining lecturers who would "preach the word faithfully and without flattery."[157] Lecturers were not hired to toady to the laity but "to preach Christ crucified." They were hired because many of the laity had come to believe in the centrality of the Word, and hence to believe that a minister's prime function was to preach. When a Northamptonshire mercer was asked by the High Commission in 1634 why he held it essential to depart from his parish church when the minister preached but once on a Sunday, he replied "that it was necessary for salvation (though not of absolute necessity) to have two sermons on the Lord's Day, preaching being the ordinary means ordained by God to salvation."[158]

Faced with such an attitude, the Established Church had only two alternatives: either to provide for a preaching ministry within the institutional framework of the Church, or failing that, to leave the initiative for making such a provision to the laity. The inability of the Church to act on the first option led inevitably to an abdication of control, for lay initiative implied lay dependency. Hence the reforms proposed by the London critic were based on a false premise. The real alternative to dependence on the laity was not some ideal freedom from external control, but dependence on whatever agency still retained power, sanctions, and disciplinary machinery—in short, the Church. To remove the lectureship from lay control would have been to destroy the basis of the institution itself.

6

The Careers of the Lecturers

THE London lectureships were bound to have a significant impact on the careers of the English clergy. With well over a hundred parochial benefices, to say nothing of curacies and other positions open to the clergyman seeking a living, London would have
been a major center of ecclesiastical patronage even had there not been
any lectureships, but given the number of lectureships and given the
relatively rapid turnover of lecturers in many of them, this new type
of preferment came to form an important source of patronage for
the clergy from the 1580's on. More to the point, the lectureships
made London a city of preachers, and hence a city open to Puritan
penetration. But for its lecturers, London would have been a city in
which the ambitious Anglican—frequently a pluralist or a prebendary
or a royal or episcopal chaplain—was the most conspicuous clerical
figure. As for the Puritans, they would have been no more than a tiny
minority, maintaining a toehold by virtue of the dozen or so livings
in the gift of sympathetic vestries, laymen, and corporations and companies. What follows, then, is an attempt to assess both the Puritans'
success in exploiting the vast reservoir of preferment opened by the
lectureships and the impact of the lectureship on clerical careers, Puritan and orthodox Anglican alike.

Between 1560 and 1662 at least 700 clergymen held lectureships at
one time or another in London. It is probable that a contemporary of
the period could have added considerably to that number, for quantities of records have vanished in the intervening years. Even where the
records survive, they sometimes prove to be tantalizingly uninforma-
tive. Churchwardens' accounts may note the expenses incidental to the
parish lectureship without ever mentioning the name of the lecturer;
visitation records may identify a lecturer by his surname only, leaving
the modern student with the baffling task of determining precisely
which one of half a dozen London clergymen of the same name he is
dealing with.[1] Finally, while some of the London lecturers were men
of fame or notoriety, others who lived quietly in relative obscurity

have become with the passage of years little more than a statistical quantity. Hence the statistics and generalizations that follow are only tentative and should be regarded with a certain amount of skepticism.*

Of the 700 lecturers, a figure that includes lecturing incumbents and curates as well as full-time lecturers, at least 52 per cent (368) were almost certainly Puritans and another 8 per cent (54) probably were. This should not be taken to mean that all of the remaining 278 were orthodox churchmen, however, since the religious views of some were impossible to determine. Nor were all of those who have been identified as Puritans nonconformists, although the records of the church courts have been extremely useful in determining the religious views of many otherwise obscure clergymen. Finally, it cannot even be assumed that all of the clergy whose livings were sequestered in the early 1640's were orthodox Anglicans and royalists; a few were Puritan royalists, a few were Puritan pluralists who lost one of their livings, and the livings of one or two, like Daniel Votier, the Puritan rector and lecturer of St. Peter Westcheap, were sequestered for reasons that apparently had nothing to do with the political and religious controversies of the time. In short, no single criterion has proved an infallible index for distinguishing a Puritan clergyman from an Anglican.

Happily, in many instances various kinds of corroborative evidence are available. For example, whereas John Archer, lecturer at St. Antholin's and at Allhallows Lombard Street in the late 1620's, can be identified as a Puritan on the evidence of his trial at Fulham Palace alone,[2] other evidence can be produced to the same effect. On 23 December 1630 John Humphrey, the Deputy Governor of the Massachusetts Bay Company, wrote from London to Isaac Johnson of Charlestown, "The Bishop of London hath silenced many godly men of late; this last Monday Mr. Archer is by him silenced for all England, the cause is taken from his judgment declared in a Sermon (which I think you hear) that we ought not to bow our knee at the name Jesus."[3] In addition William Prynne, the Puritan lawyer, mentions Archer as among those suspended or suppressed by Laud.[4] Admittedly, I have

---

* Further, I was unable to examine all the extant records, e.g., the records of Allhallows Barking, which had not been deposited at the Guildhall, and those of Christ Church Newgate, which are among the St. Bartholomew Hospital archives.

called many lecturers Puritans on the basis of far less evidence than I can muster for Archer, but in no instance has the evidence been merely a statistical probability. For example, no lecturer has been called a Puritan merely because he was a graduate of a predominantly Puritan college, such as Emmanuel at Cambridge, or because he lectured at a parish that normally hired Puritan preachers, such as St. Antholin's.

Once the doctrinal and disciplinary views of a lecturer have been established with some certainty, there is no need, in a study of this kind, to go into the further question of why some lecturers were Puritans while others remained contentedly within the orthodox Anglican fold. The experiences that led some future lecturers to become Puritans were presumably no different from those that led ordinary clergymen to become Puritans, a matter that has been sufficiently explored elsewhere.[5] Nevertheless, it may be worthwhile to point out the probable importance of preaching in many a Puritan's spirtual history. The "martyrologies" and "lives" of the better-known Puritan saints abound in stories of remarkable conversions whereby the fortunate, often after long years of painful introspection, suddenly became aware of the gift of saving grace and election. For many of the converts the first consciousness of the workings of the spirit came during or after hearing the Word plainly but effectually preached. John Preston, who lectured at Lincoln's Inn during the last six years of his life, attributed his conversion to the eloquent preaching of John Cotton of Boston, who in turn dated his change of heart to a sermon preached by Richard Sibbes, and Sibbes, who later lectured in London, owned his conversion to another Cambridge preacher, Paul Baines.[6] For most of the Puritan lecturers, however, spiritual biographies, or indeed biographies of any kind, are completely lacking.

It is almost as difficult to find evidence of the lecturers' social origins. What information there is comes in most instances from university admission and matriculation records, but those of the Cambridge colleges in particular rarely reveal more than the status of the student within his college—a notoriously unreliable indication of social status, since young men with no claim to gentility were sometimes admitted as pensioners or even fellow commoners while sons of gentle families matriculated as lowly sizars. At any rate there does not appear to be any obvious difference between the family background of Puritan and that of Anglican lecturers, except that among the growing number of lecturers who were themselves the sons of clergymen Puritans outnumbered Anglicans almost two to one.*

Whatever their background, it is evident that ambitious divines from all parts of the country were attracted to London. It has been possible to trace the birthplaces of 412 of the London lecturers (59 per cent of the total number of known lecturers).[7] They came in varying numbers from every shire in England except Monmouth, from Scotland, Ireland, and Wales, and in the last decades of the period, from Massachusetts. John Nicholson, who was chaplain to the Earl of Kent and lecturer at Holy Trinity Minories from 1587 until his death in 1593, was the only lecturer whose birth can be traced to distant Cumberland.[8] At the other end of the scale, 95 lecturers (23 per cent) were born in London and Middlesex, and another 32 per cent in the next seven counties: Yorkshire, Northamptonshire, Essex, Norfolk, Kent, Leicestershire, and Gloucestershire. The other 30 counties together account for less than half of the total (45 per cent).

It is not difficult to discover why a clergyman born in London or Middlesex might return home. In the first place, London had certain attractions for any clergyman. Quite apart from the number of livings and lectureships available, London as the chief metropolis and capital city also offered contact with important patrons. Many bishops, great patrons in their own right, spent at least some of their time in London, and there was always the possibility of attracting the attention of a member of the gentry or nobility whose friendship or approbation might lead to a chaplaincy or benefice. Bishop Earle described Paul's Walk in the early years of King Charles's reign as the "Market of young Lecturers, whom you may cheapen here at all rates and sizes."[9]

Undoubtedly simple familial ties played their part in drawing Londoners back to their native city, but in many cases family influence on the workings of patronage seems to have provided an underlying motive. For example, Andrew Castleton, the son of the Puritan rector and lecturer of the same name at St. Martin Ironmonger Lane, returned in 1617 from Cambridge, where he had gone first to Emmanuel and then to Queen's (he may have studied under Preston), be-

* The fathers of at least 78 lecturers can be identified as clergymen; 49 were Puritans and 29 Anglicans. In this and all subsequent calculations, lecturers are classified as Puritans only if there is substantial evidence to that effect. The 8 per cent who were probably, but not definitely, Puritans have been classified as non-Puritans.

cause a faculty had been obtained allowing him to succeed his old and blind father as rector of St. Martin's.[10] He also continued to preach the Sunday afternoon lecture, as his father had done before him, until his death in 1632, but in this case the lecture was simply an appurtenance of the living. Thomas Gouge left Cambridge soon after his appointment as Fellow at King's College in 1628 to take up a curacy and lectureship at St. Anne Blackfriars, a position he undoubtedly obtained through the influence of his father, William Gouge, the incumbent of St. Anne's and one of the most prominent London Puritan clergymen. It is likely that the post at St. Anne's was regarded as a temporary expedient until better preferments became available; at any rate, in 1637 Thomas Gouge was admitted to the perpetual curacy of Teddington, Middlesex, and the year after in quick succession to the rectory of Coulsden, Surrey, and to the vicarage of St. Sepulchre in the City, a living he held until his ejection in 1662.[11]

The career of George Downham, the son of another prominent London lecturer, as well as the grandson of one bishop and the nephew of another, followed a similar pattern. Like his father, John, and his uncle, George, the Bishop of Derry, he was educated at Christ's College, Cambridge, which he left in 1635 or early 1636. In September 1636 young George, who seems to have had no immediate prospects of preferment, was granted a small pension from Mrs. Paradine's bequest by the Haberdashers' Company, probably at the suggestion of his father, who gave the William Jones lecture at St. Bartholomew Exchange and in general advised the company in matters of ecclesiastical patronage. In 1637 Downham was elected curate and lecturer at St. Stephen Walbrook, and a year later left London on being preferred to the rectory of South Repps, Norfolk.[12]

For other lecturers of London origin, family influence and connections seem to have been important only during the earliest part of their careers. The well documented career of the Puritan Thomas Gataker, Jr., who lectured at Lincoln's Inn from 1602 till 1611, illustrates this point. Thomas was born in 1574 in the parish of St. Edmund Lombard Street, where his father, a former chaplain to the Earl of Leicester, was rector. At St. John's, Cambridge, where he matriculated in 1590, he met Richard Stock, a future London lecturer, and was tutored by Henry Alvey, who was at the time senior Fellow, a close associate of William Whitaker, the Master, and the leading Presbyterian at the college. Six years later Gataker became one of the first fellows of the recently founded Sidney Sussex, where he shared rooms with William Bradshaw, another Puritan of growing reputation.[13] The following March, at the particular request of Alderman Gourney's widow, he was granted an exhibition of £5 a year from a bequest left by Gourney and administered by the Haberdashers' Company; it is conceivable that the Gourneys had been friends of Thomas's father before his death three years earlier.[14] Thomas first returned to London as the tutor to the family of Sir William Cooke, whose wife was a near relative; later, however, he was recommended as lecturer to Lincoln's Inn by the Master of Sidney Sussex, James Montague. When he left the lectureship in 1611 to take up the rectory of nearby Rotherhithe, it was at the urging of his old friend, Richard Stock, now rector of Allhallows Bread Street.[15] Thus, though family connections played their part in Gataker's career, friendships formed at the university seem to have been a more decisive influence.

Other lecturers returned to London for reasons that seem to have had little or nothing to do with the fact that they had been born there. The Anglican and royalist Matthew Griffith, for instance, gained his lectureship at St. Dunstan in the West in 1631 through the influence of John Donne, who was vicar of St. Dunstan's as well as dean of St. Paul's. It may have been due to Donne's influence, too, that Griffith had been presented to the rectory of St. Mary Magdalen Old Fish Street in 1624, for that living was in the collation of the dean and chapter of St. Paul's.[16] The first preferment of another Londoner, John Poynter, was a curacy and lectureship at St. Mildred Bread Street. Although there is no direct evidence, it is possible that he gained this post not through any local connections but through the good offices of John Dodd, an influential Puritan and a close friend of William Gouge. Poynter certainly knew Dodd, for after leaving Oxford he boarded with Dodd at Canons Ashby and later spent a year in Leyden with Dodd's son, Timothy, before returning for his ordination and his first London preferment. It seems more than coincidental that Poynter's next position was at Hanwell, Oxfordshire, a living Dodd had once occupied for the space of twenty years.[17]

At times the possible reasons for a lecturer's return to London are so many and complex as to defy any simple explanation of his motives. Ezechial Culverwell's return to a London pulpit late in life is a case in point. Culverwell was the son of Nicholas Culverwell, Haberdasher, of the parish of St. Martin Vintry. One of his sisters married Laurence Chaderton, the Master of Puritan Emmanuel; a second married William Whitaker, the future Master of St. John's; and the third was the mother of the London Puritan lecturer William Gouge. There is some obscurity about Culverwell's education and early career, but he appears to have been trained at Oxford and to have received his M.A. in 1577. Shortly afterward he became vicar of Felstead, from which he was suspended for nonconformity in 1583 or 1584 by Bishop Aylmer. He must have conformed soon after or in some other way regained his license to preach, for the 1589 and 1592 Visitation Call Books list him as lecturing at Felstead, and during the same years he was active in the nearby Braintree classis. In 1592 he was presented to the living at Stanbridge Magna, which he managed to hold until his final deprivation in 1609. He never again held a living, and the standard authorities are silent about the last twenty years of his life.[18]

Nevertheless, it is possible to catch glimpses of Culverwell's subsequent career. Almost certainly he returned to London after his deprivation, although there is no way of knowing precisely why he did so or how he managed to support himself. The Culverwells may still have had City property. He also may have continued to preach; at least with his many connections among the London clergy, he must have had the opportunity. William Gouge, his nephew, who had gone to school at Felstead, was already lecturing at St. Anne Blackfriars, where Stephen Egerton was rector. Egerton and Culverwell had probably been acquaintances, if not close friends, since the 1580's, when they had both been involved in the classical movement; in 1603 they both contributed commendatory prefaces to an edition of Richard Rogers's *Seven Treatises*. Richard Stock, rector and lecturer at Allhallows Bread Street and formerly a favorite pupil of Culverwell's brother-in-law, William Whitaker, may have lent his pulpit to Culverwell, for the will of one of Stock's parishioners, William Priestly, a Merchant Taylor, mentions both Stock and Culverwell as "preachers."[19]

In any event, Culverwell was in London at least by 8 December 1612, when James Ussher, at the time Vice-Chancellor of Trinity College, Dublin, wrote that he spent the day of Prince Henry's funeral at London with John Dodd and Culverwell "in humbling ourselves before God." In 1616 Ussher's London correspondent, John Heartwell, reported consulting Culverwell about the printing of Ussher's sermons, and Heartwell notes further that he had dinner with Dodd, Culverwell, and John Burgess, a Puritan who preached briefly at Bishopsgate.[20] Four years later Richard Brooke, a Haberdasher of St. Augustine's parish, where Stock had lectured twenty years before, remembered in his will his "friends" Egerton, Stock, Gouge, Culverwell, Anthony Wotton, then lecturing at Allhallows Barking, and John Vicars, rector of St. Augustine's and former curate and lecturer at St. Michael Cornhill.[21] All these men had lectured at one time or another, and all were undoubtedly friends or at least acquaintances of Culverwell. Given his many connections among the clergy, it is hard to believe that Culverwell never preached from a London pulpit during his last twenty years in the City; given his important lay sympathizers in the merchant community, it is hard to believe that his occasional preaching would not have been winked at by the churchwardens.

One last effort seems to have been made to secure a regular London pulpit for Culverwell. In 1626 the Churchwardens' Accounts of St. Botolph Aldgate, a parish that had gone without a Puritan lecturer since Eusebius Paget left about 1604, recorded the expenditure of two shillings "for charges about Mr. Culverwell's lecture"; the following year the accounts recorded other small expenditures for "when we went to the Lord Bishop about the preacher." Yet Culverwell was not lecturer at St. Botolph's in 1628, probably because Bishop Mountaigne refused to license such a well-known nonconformist. On 14 April 1631 Culverwell was buried in the Puritan parish of St. Antholin's.* His precise motives in returning to London ultimately elude us, though obviously London had several attractions—family connections, merchant patrons, and friendships with the holders of many important pulpits.

London's attractions for the native born are readily understandable, but why so large a proportion of the London lecturers were native

---

* GLMS 9235/2, no fol. Dorothy A. Williams tentatively identifies "Mr. Culverwell" as Richard Culverwell, rector of St. Margaret Moses, but though he seems to have been a Puritan, he was a conformist and should have experienced no difficulty in obtaining a license. D. A. Williams, "London Puritanism: The Parish of St. Botolph without Aldgate," *Guildhall Miscellany*, II (Sept. 1960), 30. For Ezechial Culverwell, see the *Dictionary of National Biography*.

Londoners is more puzzling. By 1600 slightly more than 5 per cent of England's population lived in the metropolitan area, and throughout the period under consideration the City grew rapidly. Since London's mortality rate was abnormally high, however, most of its growth must be attributed to the constant stream of immigrants from the provinces. It is surprising, then, that as many as 23 per cent of London's lecturers between 1560 and 1662 were born in London or Middlesex. W. K. Jordan has demonstrated that only slightly more than 10 per cent of the 403 great merchants of London who were donors of charitable bequests between 1480 and 1660 were natives of London or Middlesex. Further, he notes that only slightly more than 8 per cent of the Lord Mayors during the same period were London born. Of the liveried merchant donors whose birthplace is known, about 11 per cent came originally from London or its environs; of the shopkeepers and retailers, only about 4 per cent; and of the professional classes, only 7 per cent.[22] The percentage of lecturers of local origin is, therefore, almost twice that of any of the classes of donors whose origins Jordan has analyzed.

Actually the discrepancy is not so great as it seems. Clearly for many lecturers the years of preaching in London were only a brief interlude in their careers. Thus after leaving London John Poynter went first to Hanwell, then to Wootton Wawen in Warwickshire, to Horton, Oxfordshire, to Warwick, to Huntingdon, to Bures St. Mary in Suffolk, and finally, in 1654, to Houghton Conquest in Bedfordshire.[23] A contemporary of Poynter named Philip Edlin, a graduate of Emmanuel but not a Puritan, held first the rectory of North Cray, Kent, which he left after three years, in 1631, for the rectory of Alverstoke, Hampshire; in 1635 he was presented to the rectory of St. John Zachary in London, and on 4 February 1642/3 he was admitted to the rectory of Bushy, Hertfordshire, with the connivance of the sequestered rector. In July he was removed from both livings for "malignancy" on the orders of the House of Commons, but a year later he was rector of Pinner, Middlesex, the village of his birth. In 1650 he was officiating at Denham in Buckinghamshire, and two years later he was presented under the Great Seal to the London rectory of St. Michael Bassishaw, where he officiated and lectured on Tuesday evenings until his death in 1657. For statistical purposes Edlin numbers among the lecturers born in London and Middlesex, but only during the last five years of a thirty-year professional career did he preach from a London pulpit.[24] Although few clergymen held as many livings as Edlin, many lecturers did move on to other preferments in the course of their careers. A London lectureship was the last preferment for only 42 of the 95 lecturers who were native sons. The proportion of the London born who not only returned there to preach but remained there was, then, only 10 per cent of those whose birthplace is known, a percentage quite compatible with that of the various mercantile and professional groups noted in Jordan's study.

In this respect, as in many others, London was parasitic, taking more from the rest of the realm than it returned. London not only drew on the rest of the country for more than three-fourths of its lecturers but managed to retain the services of a majority of them. Of the 538 lecturers whose last preferment is known, 283 (54 per cent) held their last preferment in London. Further, as might be anticipated, more Puritans stayed to preach in London than orthodox Anglicans; though Puritans constituted only 52 per cent of the total number of lecturers, they constituted 65 per cent of those whose last preferment was in London. Most clergymen of whatever stripe went where they could find the best available preferment. The Anglican lecturer had little reason to stay in London unless his lectureship was coupled with a good benefice. But to a Puritan who had been deprived of his living elsewhere, a London lectureship might represent his last opportunity to preach. Other Puritans, who had come because they had been sought after, felt bound to their London followers by ties of obligation and friendship. Had London vestries only wanted more sermons and had they been indifferent to the style and ideology of those who preached them, there would have been no need to hire Puritans, for by the 1590's at the latest there were enough properly licensed Anglicans to answer the City's needs. That so many Puritan preachers came and stayed to lecture reflects more significantly the nature of the demand than of the supply.

Few of even those lecturers who regarded London as only a way station in their careers seem to have returned to their native shires. At least 29 London lecturers were from Yorkshire, but only nine London lecturers found their last preferment in Yorkshire, and only five of them were natives. Eleven London lecturers came from Gloucestershire, but only five found their last living in that western shire. Ten came from Lancashire, but only one London lecturer, so far as can be ascertained, spent his last years as an active minister there. By contrast, whereas only 55 future lecturers came from Essex, Kent, Hertford-shire, or Surrey—the four counties closest to the city—90 former London lecturers spent the last years of their active careers in those shires. Of those London lecturers whose place of birth is known, 42 per cent came from within 50 miles of the City; of those whose last preferment is known, 73 per cent were within that radius.

The educational background of the London lecturers offers a more fruitful field for investigation. A trained intellect, if not necessarily a university degree, was essential for a preacher hired by a laity that had become dissatisfied with a non-preaching ministry—with what the Puritans referred to opprobriously as "dumb dogs" or "mere read-ing clerks." Some sections of the London laity might prefer a witty sermon preached by Lancelot Andrewes or John Donne to one in the plain style of Richard Sibbes or Thomas Adams, but in either case more than an outpouring of natural eloquence or enthusiasm was ex-pected.

The London lecturers were very much a part of the educated elite within the Church of England. At least 82 per cent of them are known to have attended a university, and all but ten of these attended Oxford or Cambridge.[25] The actual percentage was undoubtedly higher, since in some instances where only the surname is known, for example, or where the lecturer had both a common surname and a common given name, it has been impossible to determine which of a number of grad-uates of the same name was the lecturer. For only about 5 per cent (38) of the lecturers is there good reason to suppose that they did not at-tend a university at all. In an age when most sermons were exegetical, when the primary purpose of the preacher was to expound and apply a Biblical passage, the educational attainments of the clergy were of some consequence. When Londoners considered the trouble and ex-pense they incurred in order to obtain a preaching clergy, they could at least console themselves with the fact that they were getting a better return for their money than the Church as a whole.

Of the Puritan lecturers in London, 90 per cent had definitely at-tended a university, and another 5 per cent probably had. Whereas for many of the Anglican clergy the university simply provided the training and the worldly connections necessary for a successful clerical career, for many of the future Puritan clergy the years spent at Oxford and Cambridge were crucial. As Lawrence Stone has pointed out, it was the success the Puritans had in penetrating the universities that "turned Puritanism from the sectional eccentricity of a few great households in the countryside and groups of artisans and small traders in the towns into a nation-wide movement affecting all classes of society."[26] Puritan fellows, masters, and professors not only gave a radical ideology respectability by associating it with the educational establishment but also supplied much of whatever coherence and continuity the rather invertebrate Puritan movement had. Equally important, many preachers had first consciously identified themselves with the godly brotherhood while at the university.

To be sure, a few future preachers came to the university already committed to the Puritan movement, but many more were recruited there. William Gouge, for one, seems to have been destined from birth to become a potent force in Puritan circles. His mother was one of the Culverwell sisters; he had his early schooling at Felstead, Essex, where his nonconformist uncle Ezechial Culverwell was vicar; and by the time he reached King's College he had already been reproached for being an "arch-Puritan."[27] In contrast John Cotton, who was equally endowed with godly parents, fancied for himself a brilliant academic career and a reputation as a "witty" preacher. "When he heard the toll for the funeral of Mr. Perkins," writes his biographer, Cotton Mather, "his mind secretly rejoiced at his deliverance from that powerful ministry by which his conscience had been so oft beleaguered," for he believed "through a vain persuasion, that if he became a godly man, 'twould spoil him for being a learned one." Nevertheless, Cotton eventually succumbed to the preaching of another Puritan, Richard Sibbes, who was then a Fellow of St. John's and who later went on to become Master of St. Catherine's and also one of the most famous London lecturers.[28]

What was important for many of the future Puritan clergy, then, seems to have been not so much what they learned from tutorials and university lectures, from the formal content of higher education, as the experience of hearing the great preachers of the university towns. In the sixteenth and seventeenth centuries, as now, many students were introduced to a new mental climate at the university, and being at an impressionable age and for the first time away from the traditional world of family and neighborhood, many experienced the self-questioning and uncertainty that went with independence. For many, then, religious conversion, often brought on by a sermon, marked the end of a period of unsettledness, a change signalized by the adoption of a Puritan life style and a preaching career. Thus it was that when Chaderton was about to retire from his long tenure as lecturer at St. Clement's, Cambridge, 40 clergymen petitioned him to continue, declaring that they owed their own conversions to his preaching.[29]

Roughly the same proportion of the future London lecturers trained at each university were Puritans—59 per cent at Cambridge and 56 per cent at Oxford. The distribution of future Puritan lecturers among the colleges is very much as one might have anticipated. At Cambridge the two Puritan seminaries—"the pure house of Emmanuel," founded in 1584 by Sir Walter Mildmay, and the smaller but equally "pure" Sidney Sussex, established twelve years later—led all the rest. All nine of the future lecturers who attended Sidney were Puritans; 49 of the 56 lecturers trained at Emmanuel were definitely Puritans also. So were seven of the eight who attended St. Catherine's and 14 of the 18 at Magdalene. Together Emmanuel, Christ's, and St. John's, among the largest of the colleges at Cambridge, trained almost as many of London's Puritan lecturers as all the colleges of Oxford (109 to 110).

As might be expected from the number of Puritans they produced, both Christ's and St. John's, much older colleges than Emmanuel, had strong Puritan traditions. Owing to the teaching and preaching of a distinguished series of Puritan fellows, Christ's became the most influential center of Cambridge Puritanism in the middle years of Elizabeth's reign, a position of primacy it only gradually lost to Emmanuel in the early years of the seventeenth century. Edward Dering, a Fellow in the 1560's, was followed by the two future Separatists John Smith and George Johnson; Laurence Chaderton and William Perkins, a Fellow from 1584 to 1602, were less radical but exercised a more pervasive influence in the university. From 1609 to 1620 Valentine Cary, Master of Christ's, led a definite reaction to Calvinism and to Puritan tenets in general, and in the early years of his rule several of his more vociferous critics were forced from their fellowships, among them William Ames, Perkins's most famous disciple, and Nicholas Rush.[30] The year before Cary's election Thomas Taylor, a former Fellow and Hebrew lecturer, had been silenced by

Harsnet, the Vice-Chancellor, for a sermon at Great St. Mary's in which he had attacked Bancroft's repressive policies; Taylor was later elected curate and lecturer at St. Mary Aldermanbury, London, where his preaching stood as "a brazen wall against popery and Arminianism."[31] Despite these reverses, the memory of Perkins died slowly at Christ's College; John Milton was there in the late 1620's, and more of the future Puritan lecturers of London went to Christ's between 1609 and 1640 than had gone there during the years when Puritanism was a dominant force at the college.[32] As for St. John's, it numbered William Fulke, Henry Alvey, and Richard Sibbes as former fellows. Fulke, one of the Puritans patronized by the Earl of Leicester, went on to become Master of Pembroke in 1578; Alvey arranged for the last provincial conference of the classical movement to be held at St. John's in 1589; and Sibbes, who was of a later generation, became both lecturer at Gray's Inn and Master of St. Catherine's in Cambirdge.[33]

Queen's, though a less eminent center of Puritanism than Christ's, long provided a congenial home for thoroughgoing Calvinists. Robert Some, a supporter of Cartwright, was a Fellow and was later Vice-President from 1562 until his election as Master of Peterhouse in 1589; Humphrey Tyndall, Master of Queen's from 1579 to 1614, was a close friend of Whitaker and helped formulate the Lambeth Articles. During the first twenty years of the seventeenth century, Queen's briefly became a notable nursery of Puritanism; in those years Oliver Bowles, a Puritan and one of the most able tutors at the university in his time, was succeeded by his more famous pupil, John Preston, Fellow from 1609 until 1622.[34] It may be of some significance that six of the nine future Puritan lecturers of London who went to Queen's received their early university training during the years when Preston was Fellow and tutor.

Oxford played in all respects a secondary role in the education of the London lecturers, for only one-third of them received their academic training there. Further, whereas the 364 lecturers who had attended Cambridge were distributed among fifteen colleges, the 195 Oxford graduates were distributed among 25 Oxford colleges and halls. Hence the number attending any given Oxford college was small, and it may well be questioned whether a statistical analysis based on such small quantities is of very much significance.

In two instances, however, correlations of some interest emerge. Of the 26 London lecturers who were trained at Magdalen Hall, 20 (77 per cent) were Puritan, and all but two received their first degree after 1605, when John Wilkinson, a vigorous Puritan, became Principal. Under Wilkinson, who remained until 1648, when he was succeeded by his brother Henry, Magdalen Hall became the leading center of Oxford Puritanism. Although the Puritan Christopher Rogers was Principal of tiny New Inn Hall at a later period, from 1626 to 1662, his influence had much the same effect as Wilkinson's.[35] All nine of the lecturers who were graduates of New Inn Hall were Puritans, and all had been there when Rogers was Principal.

For some of the Puritan lecturers the influence of masters and fellows may have been much less important than the connections and friendships made during their college years. Richard Sedgwick, who was trained at Peterhouse, Cambridge, during the mastership of Robert Some, was already puritanically inclined when he arrived at Cambridge. The story is told that his uncle, who raised him, "hating the power of godliness, and wedded to games and sports," disowned Sedgwick on the grounds that no Puritan should inherit his lands. Although his years at Cambridge seem only to have confirmed him in his religious attitudes, a former Peterhouse graduate, Stephen Egerton, was to play a decisive role in his later life. Egerton had been at Peterhouse in the years immediately after the expulsion of the early Puritan leader of that college, William Charke, in 1572.[36] When Egerton arrived in London ten years later, he promptly joined the circle of London ministers engaged in fostering the classical system. Two other Peterhouse men had preceded him in this move: Charke, Cartwright's disciple, who was one of the leaders of the London classis, and Richard Gardiner, lecturer at St. Helen's, who also played a minor part in the movement. Another acquaintance of Egerton's was his fellow Peterhouse graduate and contemporary Thomas Man, who was later lecturer at Christ Church Newgate; both Egerton and Man were suspended for refusing to subscribe to Whitgift's Articles.[37]

Egerton was, in effect, a link between the older Puritan generation of Peterhouse graduates and the younger preachers of Sedgwick's age. When Sedgwick lost his first living in Kent for his outspoken criticism of the prebendaries of Canterbury, it was Egerton who obtained for him the post of chaplain with the family of Sir Edward Anstow, a

Surrey gentleman. A few years later, about the time of Elizabeth's death, Sedgwick was again in trouble, this time for his preaching at Battersea, where he assisted Percival Wyborne, one of the last survivors of the Marian exile. Again Egerton rescued him by recommending him to the Merchant Adventurers, with whom Sedgwick served first at Stade and then at Hamburg, where he met William Jones, his future benefactor.[38] Sedgwick returned to London in 1615 and served briefly as the first preacher of the Monmouth lectureship established by Jones's bequest to the Haberdashers. In 1617 Sedgwick returned to London to take up a curacy and lectureship at Wapping Chapel, a post he held until his death in 1643.[39] Few careers illustrate so well the wide variety of individuals and groups who came to the support of the Puritan clergymen of the period. Yet one suspects that, above all, friendships made at the universities proved decisive in the later careers of many Puritan lecturers.

An academic degree was by no means a requirement for obtaining a preaching license, and of course a university education was no guarantee of intellectual distinction. Richard Baxter, one of the finest Puritan writers and preachers of the seventeenth century, never attended a university and was largely self-educated. Nevertheless, for statistical purposes a university degree provides a rough-and-ready index of intellectual attainment. R. G. Usher has said that "the causes of the growth and influence of the Puritans..., must be sought elsewhere than in any moral and intellectual superiority over the clergy who were loyal to the Establishment."[40] Although a statistical study of the London lecturers can neither prove nor disprove Usher's point, and certainly sheds no light on the presence or absence of moral superiority, it can reveal something concerning the Puritans' intellectual attainments.

One-third of the London lecturers who attended a university had entered by 1600, and two-thirds entered after that date. At least 90 per cent of the Puritan lecturers had been to a university; only 4 per cent definitely had not. Among the rest of the lecturers, at least 79 per cent had been to a university and in all probability a much higher percentage, since only 7 per cent appear not to have gone to a university at all. Finally, there is no appreciable difference between the periods before and after 1600 in the percentages of the lecturers who had no univer-

TABLE 5
Academic Record of the London Lecturers

Degree	Pre-1600[a]	Post-1600 Puritans	Post-1600 Anglicans
No degree	10%	3%	2%
B.A.	14	13	9
M.A.	46	62	50
B.D.	12	9	10
D.D.	16	18	28
Other (D.C.L., M.D., etc.)	2	1	1
TOTAL	100%	100%	100%

[a] Lecturers have been placed in the two periods according to whether they entered the university before or after 1600.

sity education.* Hence it is almost certain that more than 90 per cent of all the London lecturers had had some exposure to higher education.

Other groups of clergymen were not as well educated. According to the reports of the bishops in 1603, as analyzed by Usher, 41 per cent (3,352 out of 8,179) of the clergy in the Province of Canterbury had been to one or another of the universities and possessed preaching licenses as well; in parts of Norfolk, Suffolk, and Cambridgeshire as many as 50 per cent of the clergy had university degrees.† Although there is no reason to doubt that the academic competence of the clergy continued to improve in the years after 1603, the London lecturers could have had few peers academically.[41]

The percentages of London lecturers, both Puritan and Anglican, who earned the various academic degrees are given in Table 5. Within

* The discrepancy between these percentages and the 82 per cent previously cited as the percentages of those with a record of attending a university is attributable to the fact that for some lecturers it is possible to discover that they held a degree but not where they earned it.

† R. G. Usher, *The Reconstruction of the English Church* (New York, 1910), I, 207, 253. However, in Usher's table (p. 241) the figure 8,179 is given as parishes, not clergymen. Since some parishes had curates as well as incumbents, the percentage of educated clergy may well have been lower. Further, the bishops' figures appear to have been considerably inflated; for an example, see *The State of the Church*, ed. C. W. Foster (Lincoln Record Society, Vol. XXIII, 1926), p. lvii. Mark H. Curtis has postulated that by the early seventeenth century the universities were turning out trained

TABLE 6

Academic Record of the London Incumbents

Degree	1560 (47% had degrees)	1601 (75% had degrees)	1640 (92% had degrees)
B.A.	18%	14%	0%
M.A.	36	46	62
B.D.	16	23	1
D.D.	23	17	36
D.C.L.	7	0	1
TOTAL	100%	100%	100%

Source: The data for 1560 and 1601 are based on a table in H. Gareth Owen's "London Parish Clergy in the Reign of Elizabeth I" (unpublished Ph.D. thesis, London University, 1957), p. 91. The data for 1640 are based on information given in A. G. Matthews's *Walker Revised* (Oxford, 1948) on the 108 city incumbents whose livings were sequestered in the early 1640's. The data for 1640 are therefore not strictly comparable to those for 1560 and 1601, since in 1640 about a dozen London incumbents were Puritans and did not have their livings sequestered.

the group who entered a university before 1600 there is no significant difference between the academic attainment of the Puritan and that of the Anglican lecturers. Within the group who entered a university after 1600, however, significantly more Anglican than Puritan preachers went on to take degrees beyond the master of arts (39 per cent compared to 28 per cent).

The improvement in the level of academic competence of the London incumbents, shown in Table 6, is even more dramatic. Although the lecturers represented an educated elite during much of Elizabeth's reign, the City incumbents caught up with them during the early years of the seventeenth century, and by the eve of the Civil War the city incumbents had surpassed them. When parishioners were invited to petition the House of Commons for the removal of "malignant" clergy in the early 1640's, the charges leveled against the City incumbents ranged from pluralism and nonresidence to ceremonialism and moral offenses, from the failure to preach at all to the preaching of "Arminian" tenets; but the charge of sheer ignorance, so common in Puritan tracts and petitions during Elizabeth's reign, could no longer be made, at least in London.[42]

clergymen at a faster rate than livings became available. "The Alienated Intellectuals of Early Stuart England," *Past and Present*, XXIII (1962), 25–43.

If Puritan and Anglican lecturers had much the same educational background—a similarity that was reasonable enough so long as the ability to preach was considered to depend in part on learning—their subsequent ecclesiastical careers had some important differences.

Out of the total number of London lecturers the careers of only 486 (69 per cent) are known in sufficient detail to provide a basis for analysis. Since the fortunes of both London's lectureships and its lecturers varied considerably between 1560 and 1662, the period covered by this study has been divided into five parts: first, the years of initial growth from 1560 to 1580; second, the years of crisis from 1580 to 1600, initiated by Whitgift's Articles of Subscription and his attempt to enforce conformity and uniformity, and later marked by the destruction of the classical system, which not only affected the fortunes of the Puritan preachers adversely but also quite apparently brought the growth in the number of active lectureships in the City virtually to a standstill; third, the years of slowly resumed growth from 1600 to 1619, a period that began with the new Canons and the rigors of Bancroft's efforts to enforce them, but concluded with a decade of renewed growth in the number of active lectureships; fourth, the years between 1620 and 1640, a period analogous in some ways to the 1580's and 1590's, when the number of active lectureships increased rapidly and when militant Puritanism faced the threat posed by Laud and his bishops; and finally, the years of war and Interregnum, which began with the vindication of the lectureship by the House of Commons and ended with the disaster of "black" St. Bartholomew's Day in 1662. For the purpose of analysis, each lecturer has been placed in the twenty-year period during which he first lectured in London.

This analytic framework creates a number of problems, not all of which have been solved satisfactorily. First, there is no particular magic in the twenty-year periods. An historical justification of sorts has been offered for them, but obviously the years between 1560 and 1662 could be divided other ways on other bases. Second, the careers of many lecturers fall untidily into two periods. Notwithstanding the difficulties, the need for subdivisions of some sort is obvious. The claim that 52 per cent of the London lecturers were in all likelihood Puritans, for example, though true enough, is misleading without further qualification. A majority of the lecturers can be identified as Puritans during the early years, but between 1580 and 1640 the proportion falls to less than half, whereas during the final 22 years it climbs again to at least three-fourths.

It may seem misleading, too, to call the lectureship a Puritan institution when a majority of the London lecturers between 1580 and 1640 were probably not Puritans at all. Granted that the growth and decline of the lectureship as an institution corresponds closely to the changing fortunes of Puritanism, the failure of the laity to staff their lectureships with Puritan preachers still casts doubt on the significance of the connection. Nevertheless, it must be borne in mind that the Puritan clergy were a minority within the Anglican Church, although how small or large a minority is anything but evident. R. G. Usher, who defines only true supporters of the classical movement as Puritans, argues that there were only about 300 in 1603. Assuming that there were about 9,000 clergymen in the Church of England, Usher's estimate means that less than 4 per cent of the clergy were Puritans. By contrast, Daniel Neal, an eighteenth-century Dissenter himself, determined by a questionable process of extrapolation from figures compiled on a partisan basis that about 1,500 (17 per cent) of the clergy in 1604 were Puritans. If, as G. B. Tatham has postulated, there were at most 1,000 Puritan clergymen in 1640, then they constituted only about 11 per cent of the clergy at that date.[43]

Clearly there is a large element of unadulterated guesswork in any such calculation, but if it is safe to assume that no more than 10 or 15 per cent of the clergy ever considered themselves members of the godly brotherhood, then considerable, if not heroic, efforts must have gone into the organization of lay patronage and clerical recruitment to achieve as high a proportion of Puritans among the lecturers in London as 35 per cent during Whitgift's years, to say nothing of 47 per cent during the years of Laud's ascendancy. By the 1630's the contrast between the lecturers and the incumbents of London must have been evident to any observer, for during the 1640's some 96 of the 124 London benefices were sequestered.[44] Hence among the lecturers the proportion of Puritans must have been at least twice that found among the incumbents.

Although the proportion of Puritan lecturers to Anglican changed over the years, London's lecturers shared a number of similarities throughout most of the period under consideration.[45] The average lecturer was in his early thirties when he first came to preach in London. Given the fact that the professional careers of most clergymen began at about 25, the canonical age for ordination as a priest, some years normally intervened between ordination and election to a London lectureship. Hence through much of the period a majority of the London lecturers had held some kind of preferment before preaching a lecture, and most lecturers later went on to a vicarage or rectory, or sometimes several, before the end of their careers. Of course there were always exceptions. A few came to their first London lectureship at a very early age indeed; Jeremiah Holliday was only 21 when he began his lecture at St. Mary Somerset in 1612 and he could only have been in deacon's orders. At the other extreme, Thomas Taylor was 50 when he first lectured at St. Mary Aldermanbury, with only six more years to live, and James Ussher, Archbishop of Armagh, was 66 when he began his lecture at Lincoln's Inn in 1647.[46] London vestries undoubtedly preferred men with at least a budding reputation, but comparatively few men well into their careers were willing to compete for or accept the rigors of a lectureship unless a London benefice went along with it.

Beneath these similarities, however, some significant differences can be discerned. A larger proportion of the Puritan preachers than the Anglican held lectureships independently of other preferment in the same parish. Until 1580 the position of an independent lecturer held real advantages for the scrupulous Puritan: once he was ordained and equipped with a preaching license, no further contact with ecclesiastical officialdom was needed. Early in 1580, however, the Privy Council ordered all clergymen to administer the sacraments periodically "in what place soever they receive any portion for preaching"; in 1583 all independent lecturers were warned for the first time to attend the episcopal visitation, where their preaching licenses could be scrutinized and their conduct inquired into; and finally, in the following year came Whitgift's Articles of Subscription.[47] After 1584 some measure of compromise, some degree of conformity, became inevitable for a lecturer who wished to continue very long at his post. But for the Puritan who was not prepared to take the path to Separatism, some degree of compromise was inevitable anyway, and there is no evidence that the species of occasional conformity implied by the measures of the early 1580's destroyed the attractiveness of the independent lectureship.

Even had the Puritan clergy not scrupled at the use of an unreformed prayer book or at the wearing of vestments offensive to tender consciences, the distribution of the patronage of city livings was such that only a small minority of the London Puritan clergy could ever hope to obtain preferment there. More than two-thirds of all benefices in London were in the gift of either the Church or the Crown, whereas only about 30 were in the gift of the laity.* Many Anglican clergymen, for their part, came to a lectureship not by seeking it but by having it offered to them, as an adjunct of their benefice, by a vestry eager to have additional preaching and willing to supplement the parson's income as an inducement. Hence the fact that more Puritans than Anglicans preached independent lectures was not entirely a matter of choice. Given the peculiar distribution of patronage in London, many Puritans had to accept lectureships without other preferment if they expected to preach in London at all.

The other two major differences between the Puritan and the Anglican lecturers are functions of the different role preaching played in their respective ideologies. Before 1640 at least half of London's Puritan preachers went on to another lectureship at some time during their careers. Barring the period from 1560 to 1579, fewer than one-third of the Anglicans ever preached a second lecture. The second major difference follows logically from the first. The typical Puritan lectured a greater number of years in the course of his career than did the typical Anglican, who was more likely to proceed to one or more benefices after his initial London lecture.

Although the careers of few men correspond precisely to the statistical norms, some illustrations can be given from the lives of real preachers. During the first period (1560–1579) the career of William Charke, a Presbyterian radical, approximated the statistical average. Like 63 per cent of his Puritan brethren, he had held no ecclesiastical preferment prior to his first London lectureship at Gray's Inn in 1575. He was hardly in the first flush of youth, however, for he had been a Fellow of Peterhouse from 1566 until 1572, when he was expelled for an anti-episcopal sermon, and had then served as chaplain to two aristocratic patrons. Hence by 1575 he must have been close to 34 or 35, the average age for a Puritan preacher coming to his first lectureship. Like the vast majority of Puritan lecturers in this period, he did not go on to hold a benefice (only 24 per cent did), but he did go on to

---

* By 1603 the mayor and aldermen presented to four parish livings, livery companies to five, individual laymen to sixteen, and parish trustees to another six. H. Gareth Owen, "The London Parish Clergy in the Reign of Elizabeth I" (unpubl. Ph.D. thesis, London Univ., 1957), p. 241.

other lectureships (as 70 per cent did), first at Lincoln's Inn, where he preached from 1581 until he was suspended by Whitgift early in 1593, and later briefly at St. Mary Aldermary, where he was again inhibited in 1597. In his rather checkered career he had managed to lecture eighteen years, two years more than the average.[48]

The career of a younger man, Francis Fletcher, closely follows the pattern for the Anglican preacher of those early years. Like the majority of his Anglican colleagues, Fletcher had had no preferment before his first London lecture, and typically again, his first lecture at Christ Church Newgate in 1574–75 was an independent lectureship. He managed to secure admission to the rectory of St. Mary Magdalen Milk Street in 1576, only to have it sequestered several months later, apparently for his failure to pay his first-fruits and tenths. But the vestry came to Fletcher's rescue by appointing him lecturer; hence he, like 54 per cent of his Anglican colleagues, held more than one lectureship during his career. Again, like the vast majority (92 per cent) he went on to other preferments—a Buckinghamshire rectory in 1579 and finally a Yorkshire vicarage in 1596. In all he lectured about five years, two years less than the average Anglican lecturer during this period.[49]

The typical lecturer's career changed considerably in the next twenty-year period, the years of Whitgift's dominance in ecclesiastical affairs. Approximately three out of four Puritans and two out of three Anglicans had held some preferment prior to their first London lectureship; the first lectureship for a very large majority (83 per cent) of the Puritan preachers was independent, as it was for a smaller majority of the Anglicans (62 per cent). Three out of four lecturers went on to other preferments, but whereas half the Puritans lectured again, less than 20 per cent of the Anglicans did. The Puritan Henry Holland, who later edited Richard Greenham's sermons, was probably in his late thirties when he left his vicarage at Orwell and came to London in 1592. Holland preached at St. Martin Orgar until 1594, when he was presented to the vicarage of St. Bride's, where in all probability he also lectured until his death in 1603.* In all Holland lectured

---

* Holland apparently left his living at Orwell to follow the example of his older and more prestigious friend Richard Greenham, who had resigned his living at Dry Drayton, some eight miles from Orwell, in order to take up a lectureship at Christ Church Newgate in 1591. Greenham is unusual in that late in life he gave up a benefice worth £100 a year for the rigors and insecurity of a London lectureship. He left Drayton after a ministry of 21 years there, apparently at the urging of friends who thought his great preaching talents wasted on a country parish. Greenham was also exceptional in

some ten years, about the average for the Puritan preacher of this period. The Anglican Evan Griffith, who arrived in London about the same time as Holland, was unusual in that he probably had not held a living before he was appointed lecturer and schoolmaster at St. Martin Vintry in 1591 or 1592. He was already in his thirties, however, for he had been 29 when he matriculated at New Inn Hall in 1588. Griffith continued to preach at St. Martin's for six years, an average length of tenure, and then apparently left on being presented to a Welsh rectory.[50]

Richard Stock's career is fairly typical for a Puritan preaching in London during the first twenty years of the seventeenth century. Like 62 per cent of the Puritan lecturers in this period, he had held a preferment before coming to London. On leaving Cambridge he had been chaplain to Sir Anthony Cope, and in 1596 he had been presented to an Oxfordshire rectory. Stock's first lectureship, like those of 68 per cent of the Puritan lecturers, was independent, but like more than three out of four Puritan lecturers, he later went on to a benefice and, like half of them, to another lectureship. Stock first preached at St. Augustine's, and then in 1604 became curate to Thomas Edmunds, an old Puritan and former lecturer who was rector of Allhallows Bread Street. Stock also preached the newly endowed lectureship at Allhallows and in 1611 succeeded Edmunds as rector. By the time of his death in 1626 Stock had lectured at least a quarter of a century, about twice the average length of time.[51]

The typical Anglican lecturer of those years preached for a shorter period and rarely held more than one lectureship. Like his Puritan counterpart, he had held a preferment before lecturing and went on to other preferments. Often he was parson or curate of the parish he lectured in. John Dix, a Cambridge graduate like Stock, had been admitted to the rectory of St. Bartholomew Exchange in 1591, and in 1597 became rector of St. Andrew Undershaft, a benefice he held in plurality with that of St. Bartholomew's until his death in 1613. He was also a prebendary of St. Paul's and of Bristol, and sub-almoner to

---

that he managed to gain a license to preach in London without subscription. He lectured at Christ Church until his death in 1594. H. Gareth Owen, "The London Parish Clergy in the Reign of Elizabeth I" (unpubl. Ph.D. thesis, London Univ., 1957), pp. 170, 626; Benjamin Brook, *Lives of the Puritans* (London, 1813), I, 415–18; *Dictionary of National Biography*.

the Queen. He was, in short, a very competent careerist. He preached a lecture at St. Bartholomew's from 1602 to 1609, but it is hard to imagine that he saw in his lecturing the fulfillment of his career, as Richard Stock had.[52]

The average Puritan lecturer of the 1620's and 1630's was a little younger than the lecturer of Stock's generation when he first preached in London, and for about half of the Puritan lecturers an independent lectureship was their first preferment. Like their predecessors, three out of four went on to a benefice, and about half held more than one lectureship in the course of their careers. However, most lectured for a shorter time than the preachers of Stock's generation, for many lost their lectureships and livings during the 1630's. Joseph Simonds was in all probability considerably under the average age when he arrived in London in 1625, for he had received his B.A. from Emmanuel and his ordination only the year before. He first lectured at St. Martin Orgar and then in 1626 at St. Martin Ludgate; in 1627 he moved on to a lectureship at Allhallows London Wall, where he preached twice a week. In 1632 he was presented to the rectory of St. Martin Iron-monger Lane, which he deserted late in the decade for exile in Rotterdam after having become an Independent. Simonds returned to London in 1646 or 1647 to become minister of St. Mary Abchurch. He is probably the Simonds elected lecturer at St. Michael Cornhill in 1647 and may have lectured there for several years. Although he held four lectureships, he lectured all told for only about eight or nine years at a time when the average Puritan preacher lectured for eleven.[53]

The typical Anglican lecturer of the 1620's and 1630's, like the typical Puritan, was about 31 or 32 years old. Slightly more than half had had no preferment before lecturing in London, but like their predecessors they preached in a parish in which they were either the curate or parson. Four out of five went on to other preferments, but fewer than one out of three ever lectured again. William Proctor, a Master of Arts from Oxford, was about the average age when he was elected curate and lecturer of St. Mary Magdalen Milk Street late in 1625; given his age, he may have had a previous preferment, but if so, no record of it seems to have survived. By 1629 Proctor was anxious to leave his position, and the vestry was apparently anxious to have him go, but he did not succeed until late in 1631, when he was admitted to the rectory of Stradishall, Suffolk. Proctor stayed in Suffolk until he was ejected in 1644 by the Earl of Manchester on charges that ranged from upholding Bishop Wren's injunctions to card-playing, swearing, and drunkenness. He had lectured for about six apparently not very satisfying years, the average for an Anglican lecturer in London during this period.[54]

During the turbulent period from 1640 to 1662, the typical lecturer's career changed drastically. The average lecturer was older when he arrived at his first London lectureship than lecturers during the previous century, for he had typically begun his professional career in the 1630's or earlier. Three out of four Puritans had had some other post before coming to their first London lectureship, and three out of four preached independent lectures. Particularly in the 1640's, when the sequestrations had begun and livings were plentiful, many preachers soon left their lectures for a benefice. Many of those who first preached in the 1650's, however, found their careers cut off by the Restoration and the repressive policies that followed. During 1661 and 1662 a number of Puritans who had lost their livings elsewhere to returning Anglicans flocked to London and lectured briefly before the ejections of 1662. Hence though three out of five lecturers in this period went on to other preferments, the average number of years spent lecturing was lower than at any other time (it was seven years), and only two out of five lectured again. The career of Peter Witham fits the dominant pattern almost precisely. Born in Essex in 1597, he was graduated from Sidney Sussex and had served a number of Essex cures before coming to London in 1646, when he became rector of St. Alban Wood Street. Late in the following year he was elected to Lady Camden's Tuesday lecture at St. Lawrence Jewry, where he continued to preach until midsummer 1655. He had been admitted to the rectory of St. John Baptist in 1652, where he remained until he was ejected in 1662.[55]

The average age of the Anglican lecturers during these years was 42, for many of them were survivors of the sequestrations of the 1640's and were as grateful for the opportunity a lectureship provided as their Puritan brethren had been in the days of Anglican supremacy. Seven out of ten went on to other preferments, gained either under the tolerant regime of the Cromwellian Triers or after the Restoration, but only one in five ever lectured again. The career of Zachary Cawdry, son of the vicar of Melton Mowbray, closely approximates the predominant pattern. A successful academic, Cawdry lost his fellowship at St. John's, Cambridge, and his proctorship for continuing to use the Prayer Book and for his support of the King. In 1649 his rectory at Barthomley, Cheshire, was sequestered for the same causes. However, in 1654 the Triers admitted him to the rectory of Woodford, Essex, and in 1657 he was elected to one of the St. Antholin's lectureships, which he held until 1661, when he was restored to his Cheshire living.[56]

It is important to define the average career, no matter how artificial it must inevitably be, and to realize that the professional lives of real men approximated it. In the absence of such a device the exceptional careers of the famous preachers tend to overshadow the ordinary careers of ordinary clerics. At the same time, a description of the average London lecturer's career does tend to disguise two significant aspects of the reality of those times. First, it disguises the substantial minority in all five periods who lectured for a year or two and then vanished from the London scene. Perhaps these men deserve only passing mention here, for as individuals their impact on London must have been minimal. However, the second minority, those who lectured in London for a major part of their professional careers, are too important to ignore, for their impact on their London auditors must have been very great indeed. Not all by any means were Puritans, for though preaching was a Puritan specialty, it was not a Puritan monopoly. As Anglican ideology developed in reaction to the critique of militant Puritanism, the sermon was relegated to a minor position, inferior in its function to the sacraments. But individual men are always more complex and more subject to conflicting motives and demands than any official ideology. William Ashbold, one of the first generation Anglicans (he matriculated at Magdalene, Cambridge, in 1562), briefly held a Cambridgeshire vicarage at the end of the 1560's. His real career as a London preacher began with his election to the lectureship at St. Dunstan in the East in 1572, where he continued to preach twice weekly until 1583. Two years after his election at St. Dunstan's, he became rector of St. Peter Cornhill, where he was also appointed to the twice-weekly lecture. He must have been an ambitious, as well as a capable, preacher, for in 1587, when he was admitted to the rectory of St. Michael Cornhill, he agreed to preach a twice-weekly lecture there also. He gave up the lectureship at St. Michael's after a year, but he continued to preach at St. Peter's until two years before his death in 1622. Ashbold had preached for close to half a century.

A generation later another Anglican followed in Ashbold's footsteps. Richard Worme, who was also a Cambridge graduate, and who was a nonresident at his first living at Henney Magna, Essex, served as curate and lecturer at St. Dunstan's from 1604 to 1610. He gave up the lecture at St. Dunstan's in 1606, when he became rector of St. Michael Paternoster in the Royal, only to take on the Mercers' lecture at St. Michael's from 1606 until his death in 1636. Like Ashbold, Worme had no scruples about pluralism. From 1610 on he held the rectory at St. Pancras along with his rectory at St. Michael's.[57] As far as one can tell at this distance in time, Ashbold and Worme had no recognized role in shaping Anglican policy or even the style of Anglican preaching. Yet their careers are not without significance, for they must have occupied a kind of middle ground in a Church increasingly polarized by the forces of Puritanism and Arminianism.

The Puritan counterparts of Ashbold and Worme played a larger role. Only a comparative handful of the great London preachers were important intellectuals, but if few made a contribution to Puritan ideology comparable to that of a Cartwright, a Perkins, or an Ames, many made a contribution that was no less important as living exemplars of that ideology and tradition. If Londoners responded negatively to the Arminianism and ceremonialism that attracted so many of the young clerics in the first half of the seventeenth century, it was in part because they had compelling examples of another kind of churchmanship constantly before them. Further, the significance of the example these men set was recognized beyond the Puritan community. It was the Anglican Thomas Fuller, and not one of the Puritan martyrologists, who wrote of William Gouge, "He preached so long, till it was a greater difficulty for him to go up into the pulpit, than either to make or preach a sermon; and died aged seventy-nine years, leaving the examples of his humility, faith, patience, etc., to the imitation of posterity."[58] These were the preachers many London vestries deliberately recruited, and having secured their services, kept in harness until they died. Again, it is the Anglican Fuller who testifies to the importance attached to these men by the godly laity. Of Richard Stock he wrote, "He omitted not to preach twice every Lord's day, with the approbation of all that were judicious and religious," for "his preaching was most profitable, converting many and confirming more in religion; so that, appearing with comfort at the day of judgment, he might say, 'Behold, I and the children that God hath given me.' "[59]

Among the numbers of restless and sometimes hunted Puritan divines who preached briefly in London and then passed on to other, perhaps greener, fields, these men provided an element of stability and continuity. Some London parishes early established a reputation for religious radicalism that attracted a continuous stream of Puritan lecturers: St. Antholin's above all, but also Christ Church Newgate, Holy Trinity Minories, and St. Saviour's, which hired a series of godly preachers from the 1570's until 1625. Other pulpits must have gained their reputations from their preachers: St. Anne Blackfriars, where Stephen Egerton and William Gouge between them preached from 1583 to 1653; Whitechapel, where Richard Gardiner was rector and lecturer from 1570 until his death in 1617, and where the tradition of Puritan preaching was carried on by Richard Sedgwick, curate and lecturer at Wapping Chapel from 1617 to 1643; St. Bartholomew Exchange, where John Downham preached from 1616 to 1650; St. Katherine by the Tower, where the future Congregationalist Samuel Slater preached from 1625 until his ejection in 1661; and Allhallows Barking, where Anthony Wotton lectured from 1598 until his death in 1626. The clerical dynasty of the Gatakers, father and son, lectured 66 years; Thomas, Sr. lectured at Christ Church Newgate from 1579 to 1593, and Thomas, Jr. lectured first at Lincoln's Inn from 1602 to 1611 and then across the river at Rotherhithe from 1611 until his death in 1654.

By their example these men perpetuated the tradition of Puritan preaching at the strategic center of the kingdom, but their importance to the movement did not end there. The great Puritan preachers were not pulpit prima donnas performing in isolation, but a community based on shared ideology and cemented by personal connections; this community was the vital link between the London laity and the preaching brotherhood throughout the country. Henry Holland, who has already been mentioned, edited and published Richard Greenham's sermons. The sermons of John Randall, who lectured at St. Andrew Hubbard from 1600 to 1622, were edited for the press by his old friend and fellow preacher William Holbrooke, who lectured at Bromley and West Ham, Middlesex, and at St. Andrew's after Randall's death. John Downham, Richard Sedgwick, and Thomas Gataker, Jr. all shared a common patron in the Haberdashers' Company; and Sir Anthony Cope, whose offer of a chaplaincy had assisted the young Richard Stock, offered the rectory at Hanwell, Oxfordshire, a dozen years later to another Puritan, Robert Harris, who later lectured briefly at St. Lawrence Jewry and at St. Saviour, Southwark. Joseph Symonds, whose lecturing career has already been described, first came to London to serve as assistant to Thomas Gataker, Jr. at Rotherhithe.[60] Examples of relationships like these could be multiplied many times over for any period between 1560 and 1662, for the Puritan movement found its cohesion not in any generally recognized leadership but in shared beliefs and in the richness of the communal life these beliefs fostered. Personal connections provided pulpits for the preachers and sustained them in times of adversity when their preaching got them in trouble with the ecclesiastical or governmental authorities. For all the informality of their associations, the Puritans proved more than a match for the official church in their ability to organize patronage and pulpits for their own ends.

7

The Response of the Bishops, 1560-1628

IN a Paul's Cross sermon preached in 1609 an Anglican divine charged that lecturers were "never well but when they have their sickles in another man's harvest..., [and] like ivy winding about the oak,...they wind themselves into favor with great ones, thereby standing themselves in credit." These "oily mouthed Absaloms," he warned, would "bring the people out of love with their true Father... their David."[1] The authorities, particularly the bishops, did not stand idly by while the Puritans preached away Church and State, but as early as 1621 Henry King, the Bishop of London's son, wondered whether the city preachers, whose "hot spirits, like Cannons overcharged, recoil against all discipline," might not "do more mischief than deliberation or Justice can suddenly solve."[2]

To the Puritans, who of course saw the events of these years in a different light, any subversion that had been done was largely the work of the bishops. Once the system of press censorship broke down, they launched a major counterattack not only against individual bishops but against the institution of episcopacy itself. In 1641 an anatomist of the "notorious pranks and shameful wickedness" of Bishop Wren charged that "nothing could be so pleasing and acceptable to cursed Canterbury [Archbishop Laud] as...to persecute all religious people,...to hinder all good preaching,...[and] to forbid all lectures and afternoon sermons"; behind Laud's scheme to ensure that "there might be none left that would teach the Word sincerely" was, he claimed, the ultimate intention "thereby to make way for popery."[3] Whereas the charge that Arminianism was a stalking horse for Roman Catholicism was frequently leveled against Laud and his followers, a more general indictment was leveled against the bishops collectively. *The First and Large Petition of the Citie of London* asserted in its "particulars of the manifold evils, pressures, and grievances, caused...by the prelates," that the bishops' purpose in "thrusting out of many congregations their faithful, diligent, and powerful ministers" was "the subjecting and inclining of ministers under...their authority, and so by degrees exempting of them from the temporal power."[4]

Such an attack was calculated to appeal to a wide spectrum of opinion, for the Puritans were not the only Englishmen who feared Catholic subversion and hated the overweaning, prelatical bishops for their aggrandizement of power. Indeed, to the Puritans' way of thinking, they spoke for all religious and patriotic Englishmen. Hence it was blandly assumed as self-evident that the bishops, not the "zealous and godly ministers," were the ones who were subversive to all truth and good order. An Essex petition of 1641 simply stated, "It is obvious to the judicious that the prelates have been the original cause of all the divisions and schisms in the Church, as well since the Reformation, as before."[5]

Although it is impossible at this late date to assess the relative validity of these accusations, and pointless to deal out praise or blame to those who are in any event well beyond reach, two more or less indisputable facts can be extracted from this welter of charge and countercharge: first, at least some Puritan preaching, and particularly that of the city lecturers, was seen by some contemporaries as a danger to the Established Church and State; and second, the bishops at least attempted to restrain and discipline, if not to persecute and destroy, their opponents in the pulpit.

However, there are obvious limits to the usefulness of contemporary opinion. It does, of course, reveal the attitudes contemporaries adopted toward what they were certain were the facts of the situation, but if we are to assess the effectiveness of episcopal attempts to discipline the London lecturers, we must look elsewhere for evidence. The questions to be answered in this connection are obvious. What policies were actually adopted toward the lecturers? What sanctions were available for carrying out these policies? And finally, how effectively were such sanctions employed?

There may be some merit in considering the last question first, in order to indicate in a general way the dimensions of the problem the authorities faced. Table 7 presents estimates of the total number of lecturers and of the number of Puritan lecturers preaching in London each year between 1560 and 1628. Thus it offers a crude index of the relative success of the bishops' repressive policies. The same reservations mentioned in Chapter 5 in relation to numerical data on

TABLE 7
Lecturers in London: Yearly Estimates, 1560–1628

Year	Total	Puritan	Year	Total	Puritan	Year	Total	Puritan
1560	3	3	1583	36	26	1606	36	19
1561	3	3	1584	36	25	1607	41	23
1562	4	4	1585	40	29	1608	37	21
1563	4	4	1586	41	24	1609	37	18
1564	5	4	1587	38	23	1610	37	18
1565	7	5	1588	38	24	1611	39	17
1566	11	5	1589	44	25	1612	47	18
1567	8	3	1590	43	27	1613	45	16
1568	5	3	1591	41	23	1614	47	17
1569	9	5	1592	45	27	1615	55	21
1570	9	6	1593	40	21	1616	55	25
1571	10	5	1594	42	20	1617	56	26
1572	11	6	1595	41	21	1618	52	26
1573	12	6	1596	37	19	1619	50	25
1574	14	6	1597	35	21	1620	52	26
1575	9	4	1598	40	22	1621	53	27
1576	13	6	1599	37	20	1622	63	35
1577	18	11	1600	36	20	1623	61	37
1578	17	10	1601	40	21	1624	63	36
1579	19	13	1602	42	26	1625	67	37
1580	20	12	1603	38	21	1626	73	43
1581	29	17	1604	34	17	1627	77	47
1582	30	20	1605	31	17	1628	121	59

lecturers and lectureships apply here as well, since the statistics have been compiled on the basis of the same sources. In Table 7, except for the years 1628 and 1629, the number of lecturers represented as present in London in any given year is in all probability an underestimate.

Quite apart from the question of quantitative accuracy, however, such statistics still leave important questions untouched. It would be easy enough to assert, for example, that after 1584 the number of Puritan lecturers preaching in London ceased to grow, if it did not actually decline, because in 1584 Whitgift's Articles of Subscription were added to the weapons in Bishop Aylmer's arsenal for the control of nonconformity. The question nevertheless remains whether this new sanction was in fact the cause, and if so, to what degree continuity was maintained in spite of it. Theoretically, at least, it is possible that all the Puritans who lectured in London in 1583 were swept out in 1584 and 1585, and that the maintenance of relatively the same number of preachers in the years ensuing should be credited to a massive job of recruiting. Finally, most elusive is the degree to which episcopal control succeeded in enforcing conformity on those who survived the rigors of periodic visitations and the actions of the various ecclesiastical courts. Some 40 to 45 Puritan lecturers were still in London at the end of the 1630's. One could argue that this figure represents the limits of Laud's and Juxon's success and the dimensions of their failure. On the other hand, one could argue that only the tame remnants survived, that their bolder and more fiery brethren of the 1620's and early 1630's had been silenced or driven into exile by the long purge. In many instances there is no way of discovering now whether the survivors were actually conforming or whether they had simply escaped detection.

THE FIRST DECADES

Although in 1557 the Cardinal Archbishop, Reginald Pole, tried to discover whether any secret Protestant preachings or lectures had survived the Marian reaction in his own diocese of Canterbury, the Elizabethan Establishment of a few years later was slow in dealing directly with the problem of lectures.[6] Shortly after coming to the throne, Queen Elizabeth issued a proclamation limiting the subject matter of sermons to the Gospel and Epistle for the day and the Ten Commandments, since, as the proclamation said, assemblies to hear sermons, "specially in the city of London," gave rise "amongst the common sort [to] not only unfruitful dispute in matters of religion, but also contention and occasion to break common quiet."* The In-

---

* *Documentary Annals of the Reformed Church of England*, ed. Edward Cardwell (Oxford, 1844), I, 209. A month after the Queen issued the proclamation John Jewel wrote, "Some think the reason of this to be, that there was at that time only one minister of the word in London, namely Bentham, whereas the number of papists was very considerable; others think that it is owing to the circumstances that, having heard only one public discourse of Bentham's, the people began to dispute among themselves about the ceremonies, some declaring for Geneva, and some for Frankfurt. Whatever it be, I only wish that our party may not act with too much worldly prudence and policy in the cause of God." *The Zurich Letters*, ed. Hastings Robinson (Cambridge, Eng., 1842), pp. 7–8. Jewel was still in Strasbourg and so may have been mistaken about the Crown's motives, but more significant is Jewel's belief that, whatever the motives, the policy was wrong. Like the Puritans later on, Jewel was evidently less disturbed by public controversy than by the prospect of remaining silent in the face of error. Preaching the saving word was more important than preserving the public peace.

junctions of 1559 regulated the number of sermons to be given, specified those authorized to grant preaching licenses, and ordered that all
"admitted to preaching or ministering ... shall ... wear such seemly
habits ... as were most commonly ... received in the latter year of the
reign of King Edward the Sixth, not thereby meaning to attribute
any holiness ... to the said garments."[7]

When the first ecclesiastical storm broke over London a few years
later, the Establishment's adversary was not the lecturers specifically,
but all those "ecclesiastical persons" who would not accept the authorities' definition of what constituted "seemly habits." The problem of
enforcing outward uniformity was obvious from the first; the recognition that the lecturers were a special case came later, when it became
clear that nonconformists were employing this specialized ecclesiastical function to escape from the ministerial duties and dress they abhorred.

The metropolitan visitation articles of 1559 required churchwardens
to present anyone who preached "not being lawfully licensed," but
the earliest London lecturers were not seriously affected by the requirement, for most had no difficulty in obtaining a proper license.[8]
However, when the blatant irregularities of the more vociferous Reformers precipitated the Vestiarian controversy in the middle years
of the next decade, the more precise London lecturers found themselves deeply involved. More than two years after Archbishop Parker's
Advertisements were published at the Queen's command, the ecclesiastical commissioners finally put an end to all delays and equivoca-
tions by summoning the London clergy before them at Lambeth on
26 March 1566; there the commissioners commanded them to conform forthwith.[9] The 37 who refused were suspended and threatened
with ultimate deprivation. Among them were six of the eleven London lecturers. Three of the six, Robert Crowley, John Gough, and
John Philpot, had been among the leaders of the London nonconformists, and Crowley and Gough had been among those who had
signed a supplication to Archbishop Parker and the commissioners
a year before requesting permission not to wear the vestments prescribed in the Advertisements.[10] The three had lectured at St. Antholin's since 1560, and since all held London livings in addition, they
were doubly vulnerable. Suspension was sufficient to remove Richard
Allen, who held no other preferment but his lectureship at Christ
Church Newgate; he had been in trouble before and is reputed to

have given up the ministry for husbandry in disgust.[11] John Bartlett, who lectured at Crowley's parish, St. Giles Cripplegate, was similarly eliminated by suspension. The sixth to go, Giles Boskell, vicar and lecturer at St. Lawrence Jewry, presents a doubtful case; he resigned his living during the summer of 1566, but it is possible that his resignation was brought about by the commissioners.[12]

The number permanently silenced was small, but the immediate effect on Puritan strength in the city was catastrophic. As Thomas Wood, a lay leader of the Reformers, complained to Secretary Cecil, the result was to silence many "godly men at one instant, amongst which were divers that travailed in preaching the word with more zeal ... than many others of greater calling, by means whereof all exercises almost of interpretation of the scriptures [i.e., lectures] used every morning and evening in sundry churches within this city are utterly overthrown."[13] For all but Gough and Allen, who lectured briefly at the Minories before passing from sight, and the irrepressible Crowley, the purge of 1566 marked the end of their London ministry. Had subsequent Puritan lecturers been so limited and rigid in their response to ecclesiastical pressure, the history of the London lectureships as a Puritan institution might have ended there. Hence both Crowley's flexibility and his endurance, as well as the hierarchy's tolerance of him, were most significant for the future.

Crowley, whose enthusiasm for reform dated back to Edwardian days, had announced as early as 1564 that he would not wear the "conjuring garments of Popery"; he then compounded his difficulties in April 1566 by barring the door of his church to a group of surpliced clergy who attempted to enter during his suspension. When examined before the Archbishop and the other ecclesiastical commissioners, he remained intransigent, apparently threatening to continue preaching unless he was deprived. Perhaps wisely, Parker denied him his martyrdom and instead placed him under house arrest.[14] Before the year was out Crowley was back at St. Giles, where he took over the lectureship vacated by the suspension of Bartlett. Subsequently, in 1569, he either was deprived outright or resigned. However, he was back at St. Giles again in 1578 and continued to lecture there until his death in the Armada year. During his years away from St. Giles, he returned to his first vocation as a printer.[15] In 1574 he preached before the Lord Mayor, and in 1575 he was collated to the vicarage of St. Lawrence Jewry by the Bishop of London. The vestry promptly elected him lecturer, but this was only the beginning of his most intense period of preaching. In 1576 he returned to his lecture-ship at St. Antholin's; in 1577 he lectured at St. Margaret New Fish Street and at St. Saviour, Southwark, in addition. Although he re-signed all these posts on his return to St. Giles in 1578, he is recorded as lecturer at St. Margaret Lothbury in 1583.[16]

It is impossible to do more than speculate on the causes of Crow-ley's survival, although it is safe to assume that his popularity as a preacher does not suffice as an explanation. He must have made im-portant friendships during his years in exile in Frankfurt, for he was appointed Archdeacon on Hereford promptly on his return in 1559; it is known that in the early 1560's he counted the Earl of Leicester among his friends. The fact that he was requested to preach before the Lord Mayor, Sir James Hawes, in 1574 may indicate another source of patronage. He is recorded as having visited Field and Wilcox while they were in prison for their activities as organizers of the Ad-monition in 1572, but he was also appointed with Field, Charke, and Herne to dispute with some imprisoned Catholic priests in 1582.[17] Finally, although he must have known most of the participants in the London Presbyterian movement in the 1570's—he clearly knew John Field, the chief organizer—he did not become involved in the Presbyterian conferences. It is probable, therefore, that this fierce old precisian mellowed with age, and that the new radicalism of the 1570's passed him by.

For a year or two after the disaster of 1566, a Londoner seeking Puritan preaching would have found it only at Crowley's St. Giles and at Holy Trinity Minories. John Browne, a former exile and a protégé of the Countess of Suffolk, and a Mr. Lockar, a completely obscure preacher, were lecturers at the Minories in 1567; Nicholas Standon, who was one of the Puritan incumbents deprived in 1566, preached and may have lectured there in 1567 also. The next year John Field arrived to lecture there, fresh from Oxford. Field either went on to lecture at St. Giles Cripplegate or held the St. Giles lec-tureship concurrently with his lecture at the Minories until he and Wilcox were arrested for their part in presenting the Admonition to Parliament in 1572. Giles Sinclair (or Saintloe), another deprived minister, may have lectured at the Minories along with Field, and in 1569 Richard Allen, a minister suspended from the lectureship at Christ Church Newgate, followed in their footsteps.

Late in 1569 two more radicals appeared in the parish. Nicholas Crane and William Bonham had been preachers to the congregation discovered meeting at Plumbers' Hall by the authorities in 1567. Bishop Grindal had made Crane's and Bonham's release from Bridewell conditional on their promise to conform. After the promise was signed, in May of 1569, the two went on to their lecturing at the Minories, only to be inhibited from preaching shortly after and returned to prison for disregarding the conditions of their parole.[18] Neither ever held another preferment within the Established Church, but on their release in 1571 they joined that circle of radical ministers— Standon, Sinclair, Seth Jackson, who had lectured at the Minories in 1570, Wilcox, and most important, John Field—whose "brotherhood" was the London conference of later years in embryo. The future of the Puritan lectureships was not to be in the hands of these intransigent figures, although many of the younger radical preachers who did hold lectureships in the 1570's and early 1580's were to become associated with this group.*

In spite of this inauspicious beginning, the institution flourished in the 1570's, and the number of Puritan lecturers grew steadily, if rather slowly. Although the Canons passed by Convocation on 3 April 1571 reveal an increasing awareness of the problems presented by Puritan preaching, the power to license preachers remained the principal regulative device. The Canon on Preachers specified that "no license to preach shall hereafter stand in force, but that which hath been ob-

---

* R. G. Usher, ed., *The Presbyterian Movement in the Reign of Queen Elizabeth* (Camden Society, 3d ser., Vol. VIII; London, 1905), pp. xxviii, xxxvi, 5. By the late 1570's the young radical preachers were less willing than Thomas Cartwright to tolerate the "dregs of popery" remaining in the ceremonies of the Church. Whereas Cartwright in 1577 argued that compromise was necessary for the sake of preserving a preaching ministry, for "woe is to them, if they preach not the gospel," ten of the "brethren" including Field, Wilcox, Standon, Crane, and Sinclair among the London preachers, replied that no compromise was permissible "in the maintenance of so good and just a matter." They went on to suggest to Cartwright that his silence would be more welcome than his public refutation of his former, less compromising position, that it was "better not to write any whit at all" than "to set yourself against yourself and against the Church and brethren also, to whom the defense of God's glory is so dear." *The Seconde Parte of a Register*, ed. Albert Peel (Cambridge, Eng., 1915), I, 137–39; Patrick Collinson, *The Elizabethan Puritan Movement* (London, 1967), pp. 85, 134.

tained after the last day of April . . . 1571." It added hopefully that "preachers shall behave themselves modestly and soberly in all their life." The Canon, however, also asserted that nothing in the Thirty-nine Articles, the Book of Common Prayer, or the Book of Consecration was repugnant to Scripture or sound doctrine and demanded, in consequence, that all preachers "not only in their preaching, but also by subscription confirm the authority and truth of those articles" on pain of excommunication.[19] The effectiveness of this measure was somewhat compromised by the fact that independent lecturers were not summoned to attend the regular visitations. Thus a properly licensed lecturer was immune from episcopal supervision unless the churchwardens or the incumbent presented him to the authorities.

It is probably safe to say that the Puritans' limited success in the 1570's was due both to the loopholes in the system of ecclesiastical discipline and to the cautious, moderate behavior of at least some of the lecturers. Eleven of the eighteen Puritans who lectured in London during the 1570's experienced no difficulties with the authorities, and another three who did managed nevertheless to regain their licenses and to preach another day. Thomas Barbor's immunity during the years when he lectured at St. Helen Bishopsgate (1576–78) can perhaps be attributed to the loophole in the system that permitted independent lecturers to escape ecclesiastical supervision, for he cannot be classed as a moderate. He had joined the London conference led by Field and had previously signed, as a Fellow of St. John's, the testimonial requesting Cartwright's return to Cambridge. In the early 1580's he lectured at St. Mary Woolchurch and at St. Mary le Bow, from which he was suspended in 1584 for his failure to sign Whitgift's Articles of Subscription. Whitgift offered to lift Barbor's suspension in 1587 on the condition that he sign a protestation promising to subscribe to the Articles and obey them, but Barbor refused and did not preach in London again.[20]

On the other hand, the immunity of the Puritan lecturers who were beneficed in the city can be attributed only to their moderation, though certainly some were more moderate (and discreet) than others. For example, although Thomas Wilcox declared that William Wager "hath many times been hot in words against the popish regiment and ceremonies," Wager must have confined such utterances to safe and friendly audiences, for this Puritan pluralist seems never to have been either inhibited or suspended from his lectureships during the years of his active preaching from 1571 until his death in 1591.[21] Christopher Blythman, who became curate and lecturer at St. Mary Aldermanbury on 17 February 1576/7, was only slightly less moderate, or careful, or both. In 1583 he had joined other London ministers in signing a very qualified subscription to Whitgift's Articles, and at the episcopal visitation of that year it was noted that he was not properly admitted to his lectureship. However, he did succeed in obtaining the proper instruments, for the 1586 Visitation Call Book noted that his license was in order.[22] Richard Gardiner, rector and lecturer at St. Mary Whitechapel from 1570 and lecturer at St. Helen Bishopsgate from 1578 to 1581, was scarcely a moderate at all, though he must have been discretion personified. He was a recruit to the London classis in the middle 1570's and continued to attend meetings held by various other London and Cambridge nonconformist groups right through the 1580's. Nevertheless, he appears to have escaped disciplinary action until late in 1606, when he was presented to the Consistory Court for administering the sacraments to himself while he was standing and to some of his parishioners while they were seated. The upshot of this detection is not recorded, but he held on to his living and lectureship until 1617, when he died at the age of 76.[23]

Even those caught by the disciplinary net seem to have been of a more prudent breed than the lecturers of the 1560's. George Cheston, for example, a member of the London classis, was in trouble for his lecturing at the radical parish of Holy Trinity Minories in 1577. Nevertheless, he was back lecturing in London in the early 1580's, first at Allhallows Staining and then at St. Katherine Coleman. Cheston appears to have made a strategic withdrawal in late 1583 or early 1584— at any rate in time to escape the repression that followed the enforcement of Whitgift's Articles. It may have been during these years that he was chaplain to Ambrose Dudley, Earl of Warwick. In any event, although he did not officially hold any lectureships during the remainder of the 1580's, he apparently continued to preach occasional sermons in London churches; in 1595 he was back lecturing at the Minories.[24]

James Stile, another lecturer in trouble in the 1570's, may have learned to be cautious as a result of this initial difficulty. In 1573 Stile was presented to the rectory of St. Margaret Lothbury by the

Lord Chancellor at the request of Lord Grey, and at the same time the vestry appointed him to the lecture. The following year he was in trouble for preaching out of his parish without the proper license. His living was sequestered in 1575, and he resigned it in 1576. However, he continued to hold the rectory of St. Nicholas Acons until he resigned that, too, in 1579.[25] In the meantime he lectured both at St. Margaret New Fish Street and at St. Saviour, Southwark, until 1582, when he was presented to the rectory of St. Nicholas Cole Abbey. While there he lectured briefly at St. Antholin's; in 1589 he resigned from St. Nicholas, apparently to take up a lecturing post at Allhallows Barking. Although he appears to have stayed out of trouble after 1574, the fact that he twice resigned livings in order to lecture suggests that he may have had qualms about officiating a cure. How much of his immunity can be credited to his patrons—he was chaplain to Sir Philip Sidney, and after Sidney's death to Sir Francis Walsingham—cannot be determined.[26]

Eight London parishes hired lecturers between 1565 and 1569; between 1575 and 1579 some 23 parishes had active lectureships, and the number of lecturers had risen correspondingly from the seven known to be lecturing in 1565 to nineteen in 1579. The events of 1566, which had dealt a profound blow to the Puritan incumbents in London, had no long-range effect on the lecturers. Of those lecturing in London in the early 1560's, only Crowley survived in the 1570's, but the first radical lecturers had been replaced almost immediately by a younger generation—Field, Edmunds, Barbor, Cheston, Gardiner, and others like them. At least five radicals are known to have been lecturing in 1566; in 1579 there were at least thirteen. The real test for the Puritan lecturers was to come not under Bishop Grindal and Archbishop Parker, but under their tougher successors, Bishop Aylmer and Archbishop Whitgift.

THE FIRST CHALLENGE

Whatever immunity the independent lectureship afforded the Puritan who objected to the Prayer Book and to wearing a surplice vanished in 1580. In 1579 the Queen's government had dealt with the rumor being spread through the pulpits that Elizabeth was thinking of changing her religion by having Archbishop Grindal order all ministers "to preach the gospel of Christ in all purity and singleness,

without entangling and confounding themselves in secular matters."*
Four months later the Council again wrote to Grindal, at the instigation, it was claimed, of John Aylmer, Bishop of London, and this time
the independent lecturers came under direct attack:

Whereas her majesty is credibly informed, that divers and sundry preachers ... do only apply themselves to the office of preaching, and upon some
light conceit to the dishonor of God [and] the breach of her majesty's
laws ... do separate themselves from the executing of the one part of the
office of a priest, ... we are ... to require your lordship to take a view of
all such ... as do so disjoin the one part of the function from the other,
and do not at certain times in the year as well minister the holy sacraments ... in what place soever they receive any portion for preaching; and
yourself ... to compel them to execute both.[27]

Bishop Aylmer followed up this policy in January 1581 by convoking
a consistory of the London clergy at which inquiries were made concerning not only those who preached without administering the sacraments, but also those who refused to wear the surplice, who referred
continuously to their non-preaching brethren as dumb dogs, and who
continued to touch on questions of foreign policy in their preaching.[28]
Beginning with the diocesan visitation of 1583, lecturers were regularly summoned to attend so that their licenses could be examined
and their conformity inquired into.[29]

Although Bishop Aylmer's suggestion to Lord Treasurer Burghley
that ecclesiastical apparitors might best spend their Sundays spying
on the ministers and preachers in every parish evoked from Burghley
only the countersuggestion that Aylmer and the other ecclesiastical
commissioners might well moderate their proceedings, such checks
in Aylmer's campaign were only temporary. In 1583 Aylmer received
far more important assistance, for in that year the aged Grindal,
whose sympathy for much of the Puritan program had led to his
sequestration in 1577, was replaced by the vigorous and orthodox
Whitgift. In August Archbishop Whitgift's election was confirmed,
and in September, just before his first provincial visitation, he drew

---

* At the time the rumor was circulating, Elizabeth was negotiating the abortive
marriage treaty with the Duke of Anjou. *Documentary Annals of the Reformed
Church of England*, ed. Edward Cardwell (Oxford, 1844), I, 435, 437–38; John Strype,
*The History of the Life and Acts of the Most Reverend Father in God, Edmund Grin-
dal* (Oxford, 1821), pp. 359–62.

up a series of articles with Elizabeth's consent, providing the bishops at last with a hammer strong enough to break the anvil of Puritan nonconformity. All who preached or ministered were required not only, as in the past, to wear the vestments prescribed by Parker's Advertisements and to say service and administer the sacraments at least four times a year, but also to subscribe to three articles before admission to any preferment. The first, which merely affirmed the royal supremacy, was readily acceptable to the Puritans. The third, which stated that everything contained in the Thirty-nine Articles was "agreeable to the word of God," posed no problems so long as it was taken to pertain only to the doctrinal articles authorized by the statute of 1571. But the second article, which stated that the Book of Common Prayer and of Ordination "containeth nothing . . . contrary to the word of God, and that the same may be lawfully used," was entirely unacceptable.[30]

With these articles any hope of accommodating the Puritans by orienting the Established Church toward moderate reform was lost, if it had not already been lost years before when Grindal failed to gain royal support for his policy of encouraging prophesyings. However, though Whitgift's Articles may have helped to make nonconformity a permanent feature of the Church, they were by the same token decidedly effective in achieving their immediate purpose. When the Puritans' lay supporters in the country and at Court objected to the suspension and deprivation of zealous preaching ministers merely for nonsubscription, Whitgift retaliated by drawing up a list of 24 questions, covering the gamut of nonconformist practices, on which the suspected ministers were examined by the *ex officio* oath.* It was certainly one way to ensure that those who were suspended or deprived were charged with more than nonsubscription. Sir Francis Knollys might point out that the best defense against "undermining Jesuits" was "plenty of diligent zealous preachers" and might beseech Whitgift "to open the mouths of all zealous preachers, that be sound in doctrine, howsoever otherwise they refuse to subscribe to any tra-

---

* John Strype, *The Life and Acts of John Whitgift* (Oxford, 1822), I, 268–71; III, 81–87. The questions did not deal specifically with lecturers, but since all lecturers had to read the Prayer Book service and administer the sacraments four times a year, the fact that the questions principally concerned vestments, the administration of the sacraments, and the use of the Prayer Book service suggests that lecturers could not escape such an examination unscathed, at least not if they were nonconformists.

dition of man, not compellable by law"; the Lord Treasurer might complain that Whitgift's questions were "so curiously penned, so full of branches, and circumstances, as I think the Inquisitors of Spain use not so many questions to comprehend and to trap their prey." All was to little effect.[31] Whitgift occasionally beat a tactical retreat, but his strategy remained the same.[32]

The lecturers were caught between the upper and nether millstones, between Whitgift's Articles and Aylmer's rigorous visitations.[33] Between 1580 and 1583 the number of Puritans lecturing in London had more than doubled; after 1583 the growth came to a halt. Altogether, more than forty Puritans lectured at some time or another during the 1580's, but fewer than twenty of them were still able to command London pulpits in the next decade. Nevertheless, damaging as these constant attacks were on the morale of the London Puritans, the extent of the actual damage done, of the lecturers cited, suspended, and inhibited, should not be exaggerated. Only thirteen lecturers appear to have been troubled for their preaching in London.

Two were caught preaching without the proper license at the visitation of 1583. However, both Christopher Blythman, curate and lecturer at St. Mary Aldermanbury, and Francis Scarlet, lecturer at Blackfriars, managed to obtain permission to preach, for Blythman went on lecturing until his death in 1588, and Scarlet succeeded in gaining admission to the rectory of St. Bartholomew the Less.[34] The two, along with six other London lecturers—Arthur Bright, preacher at St. Augustine's, George Close, curate and lecturer at St. Magnus, John Halton (or Houghton), lecturer at St. Antholin's, Hugh Smith, lecturer both at St. Saviour's and at St. Michael Cornhill, William Welles, lecturer at Christ Church Newgate and at St. Stephen Coleman Street, and Thomas White, who succeeded Arthur Bright as lecturer at St. Augustine's—all appear to have escaped the full effect of Whitgift's Articles by making a qualified subscription on 13 February 1583/4.[35] They signed the first clause on the royal supremacy without reservation. For the second, concerning the Prayer Book, they wrote, "We are content to use it, for the peace of the church, or if we be found offending in any part thereof to submit ourselves to the penalty of it." As for the Thirty-nine Articles, "We do consent wholly to the book of Articles agreed upon by the Archbishop and Bishops, for so much as concerneth faith and sacraments therein."[36] In the face of the storm that arose over the refusal by groups of ministers from Norwich, Kent, and Suffolk to subscribe in any form, Whitgift may well have felt that the manifest obedience of the London ministers, despite their reservations, was sufficient unto the times.[37] In any event, none of the eight was molested further.

Only three London lecturers appear to have been suspended for nonsubscription; they were, however, men of the first rank among the Presbyterian Puritans. One, as we have seen, was Thomas Barbor, an old supporter of Cartwright and an early member of the London conference. Both he and Thomas Edmunds, rector of Allhallows Bread Street and lecturer at St. Margaret New Fish Street, were forced, along with others, by the use of the *ex officio* oath, to expose the membership and policies of the classical movement in the course of a series of interrogations before the High Commission in 1590 and 1591. Edmunds, a moderate who feared the radical and divisive nature of John Field's leadership, was eventually released and permitted to return to his living; Barbor dropped from sight after the classical movement was destroyed following the exposures of 1591.[38]

Stephen Egerton, the second of the three, had lectured at St. Anne Blackfriars only a year when he joined Field in refusing to subscribe, among other reasons because the book "alloweth a reading and insufficient minister and ministry." He was back at his lecture by 1586 but was again suspended and imprisoned for three years at the time the classical movement was exposed. On his release he returned to his lecture a third time and in 1598 became in addition the curate of St. Anne's, a post he retained, except for the interruption of a further imprisonment from 1604 to 1607, until his death in 1622.[39]

John Field, the third, had already been inhibited from preaching in 1574 when he was suspended from his lectureship at St. Mary Aldermary for nonsubscription in 1584. Field, the theoretician of the radicals, recognized quite correctly that Whitgift's acceptance of qualified subscriptions would split the Puritan ranks down the middle, and he bent his efforts during his last years toward maintaining a solid front among the nonsubscribers. He failed in this, and two years after he died the disciplinary system, a cause he had championed during the last twenty years of his life, collapsed in ruins.[40]

The bishops' effort to secure uniformity continued throughout the rest of the decade. At Bishop Aylmer's 1586 visitation Richard Salt, curate at Christ Church Newgate and lecturer at St. Martin Ludgate, was cited as unlicensed, and Thomas Gataker, a former chaplain to the Earl of Leicester, who lectured at Christ Church Newgate and was rector of St. Edmund Lombard Street, was admonished for permitting unlicensed ministers to preach at his church during his absence.[41] In the same year Walter Travers's famous debate with his brother-in-law, Richard Hooker, which had been conducted from the pulpit of the Temple, where Travers was lecturer, was brought to an end by Whitgift's prohibition; this time neither the petitions of the Benchers nor the Lord Treasurer's patronage was able to save Travers.[42] Also in 1856 two Scots, John Davidson, lecturer at St. Olave Jewry, and Duncan Anderson, lecturer at St. Botolph Aldgate and at Holy Trinity Minories, were inhibited, in Duncan Anderson's case specifically because he was not licensed. Davidson at least was closely associated with Field and the "London brethren," and on returning to Scotland wrote a reply to Bancroft's *Dangerous Positions*. Anderson managed to stay on in London for a few years, preaching at St. Botolph Aldgate until 1587 and then at St. Margaret Pattens, St. Mary Aldermanbury, and St. Katherine Cree.[43]

Some of the lecturers came to London after getting in trouble elsewhere, but not all found London a haven for nonconformists. Richard Allison, who in 1584 had signed an Essex petition to the Council protesting the necessity for subscription, lectured at St. Nicholas Acon in 1589; he went on subsequently to hold several London livings.[44] Edmund Curtis, who had been deprived of his Sussex living in 1581, lectured briefly at St. Helen Bishopsgate in 1585 and was curate at St. Mary Aldermary in 1586, after which he disappears from view.[45] John Wilson, lecturer at Skipton, Yorkshire, actually came south and lectured at Allhallows Barking while the High Commission was proceeding against him at York for his nonconformity. He was soon caught in Bishop Aylmer's net for preaching a "seditious" sermon at St. Michael Cornhill, but he started back north before Aylmer's apparitor could apprehend him. This game of hide-and-seek came to an end a few months later when Wilson returned to London in order to request a preaching license, an act of impertinence that was met by a summons to appear before Whitgift.[46]

The Puritans' lay patrons had not stood idly by as the bishops whittled away at Puritan nonconformity during this crucial decade. If they ultimately lost the war in Court, they still won an occasional battle in the country. After his deprivation in Rutlandshire, Humphrey Wild-bloud came to London to seek support from his patron, Sir Thomas Cecil, who appears to have succeeded temporarily in securing his restoration. However, Wildbloud was back in London in 1589, lecturing at the Minories. He was rescued from this exposed pulpit by Lady Ann Bacon, who presented him to the vicarage of Redburn, where he was again deprived for his nonconformity in 1592. He remained in the neighborhood as one of Lady Ann's chaplains at Gorhambury and as lecturer at St. Michael's in St. Albans until 1601, when a new living was obtained for him at Pinner, Middlesex, where he remained until his death in 1625.[47] Henry Smith, who gained an immense reputation as a preacher during his four years as lecturer at St. Clement Danes, owed the lifting in 1588 of Aylmer's suspension to the intervention of his uncle by marriage, Lord Burghley, who was at the time a parishioner of St. Clement's. Aylmer had ample reason for objecting to Smith's lecture; first, Smith had been popularly elected by the congregation and was admitted without the bishop's license; second, he was alleged to have preached against the Prayer Book; and third, he had not subscribed. Smith denied the second charge, and his manner of subscribing to the third was so qualified that it made a mockery of Whitgift's intentions. He acknowledged the royal supremacy, omitted all mention of the Prayer Book, and as for the Thirty-nine Articles, yielded his consent only to those on faith and doctrine "ratified ... according to a statute." He concluded by requesting that Aylmer not "urge upon me any other subscription than the law of God and the laws positive of this realm do require."[48]

   Not every appeal to powerful friends produced happy results for the lecturer. John Hansdon was deprived of his living at Bury St. Edmund's in 1581, but despite letters on Hansdon's behalf from Burghley, Lord North, and Sir Robert Jermyn, who complained to the Bishop of Norwich that he had handled the case "very indiscreetly," Bishop Freake remained adamant. Hansdon was elected to the lectureship at St. Saviour's in 1585 but was inhibited in 1587 and failed to regain his preaching license.[49] In 1581 the Council forced Bishop Aylmer to accept William Charke as lecturer at Lincoln's Inn, even though Charke had been expelled from Peterhouse ten years before for an anti-episcopal, pro-Presbyterian sermon. Nevertheless, there were limits to the power of influence. Charke, who continued to play an active part in the schemes of the London Presbyterians, was finally silenced in 1593 by Archbishop Whitgift. He remained in London, giving occasional sermons in Puritan parishes. In 1597 he again had a lectureship, this time at St. Mary Aldermary, but he was again inhibited.[50]

The flickering out of Charke's career in the 1590's is fairly characteristic of the fortunes of the Puritan lecturers in that decade. Their numbers declined slightly: whereas during the 1580's about twenty-five Puritans could be found lecturing from London pulpits in any given year, the average dropped to about twenty during the 1590's, and fewer survived to preach in London in the new century. The lectureship had become a permanent part of the ecclesiastical landscape, but it no longer held the peculiar advantages that had made it so attractive to the nonconformists before 1580. The institution itself had never been under attack, only its abuses. That "few of the leading nonconformists still held their lecturing positions by 1590" was a result of the hierarchy's efforts to impose uniformity, not of any effort to limit preaching as such.[51]

A generation was passing. Crowley and Field both died in 1588. Cheston and Charke were silenced, except for Cheston's brief return to Christ Church Newgate in 1595 and Charke's to St. Mary Aldermary in 1597. Thomas Edmunds continued as rector of Allhallows Bread Street but lost his lectureship at St. Margaret New Fish Street when he was summoned before the High Commission to testify about the classical movement. Richard Gardiner at Whitechapel, Thomas Crook at Gray's Inn, and Stephen Egerton at Blackfriars were the other survivors among Field's "London brethren."[52] Members of other defunct classes also appeared to lecture in London in the 1590's. Brian Atkinson of the Kettering classis lectured briefly at Holy Trinity Minories in 1591 and 1592 before going on to other lectureships and preferments; John Dodd, a former member of the Oxford classis, was vicar and lecturer at St. Stephen Coleman Street from 1598 until 1609, when he went on to a long and stormy career at Coggeshall; and Richard Greenham, a venerable Purital leader and a former member of the Cambridge classis, spent his last years preaching at Christ Church Newgate, although he never subscribed.[53]

In fact, what appears to have saved the London community of Puritan radicals from impotent silence during this last decade was the steady influx of mature nonconformists from the provinces. John Fulthorpe, who had been suspended from his living at Sudbury St. George in 1584, appeared preaching at the Minories in 1596 until he was suspended again; he was followed at the Minories by his son, who was apparently made of the same stuff, for he was subsequently cited in Colchester for not wearing a surplice. Another suspended minister, John Hurleston (or Hudleston), finished his career lecturing at Tottenham and at St. Augustine's in the City; he was buried in the puritanical parish of St. Stephen Coleman Street in 1602.[54] A third nonsubscriber, Thomas Man, preached both at Christ Church and at St. Lawrence Pountney. Richard Gawton, a former colleague of Field and Wilcox and one of Lady Ann Bacon's protégés, preached at St. Mary Aldermary in 1596 and 1597 before following Humphrey Wildblood's steps at Redburn, Hertfordshire.[55] Finally, "old lame" Eusebius Paget, who had been in trouble in 1573 in Northamptonshire for refusing to use the Prayer Book, in 1576 for his part in organizing the Northamptonshire and Warwickshire classes, and again in 1584 in Cornwall for preaching against the Prayer Book and for refusing to subscribe, subsequently took up schoolteaching at Heston and then at Deptford. While Paget was there the lecturer at St. Botolph Aldgate, William Hubbuck, asked him to preach in his absence, with the result that Paget succeeded Hubbuck on his departure in 1598. Paget was inhibited briefly but somehow managed to obtain a license. What apparently worried the vestry of St. Botolph's, however, was not his difficulties in obtaining a license, but the fact that his popularity brought outsiders to the church in such numbers that parishioners were crowded out of their own pews.[56]

Many years later Peter Heylyn wrote that the "Puritans and Presbyterians in both kingdoms were brought so low when King James first obtained the Crown of England that they might have been suppressed for ever, without any great danger, if either the king had held the Reins with a constant hand or been more fortunate in the choice of his Ministers."[57] At least as far as Presbyterianism was concerned, Heylyn was undoubtedly right. Presbyterianism as an organized movement collapsed with Field's death and the destruction of the classical system in the early 1590's.[58] However, if the London lectureships are admissible as evidence, not only conforming Puritans but even notorious nonsubscribers were able to secure pulpits in the capital itself in the years just before James's accession.

The effects of Aylmer's and Whitgift's harassment of the London preachers are easy to exaggerate. It was one thing to destroy a nascent Presbyterian movement among the clergy, but quite another to destroy the drive for an evangelical ministry sponsored by the laity. Aylmer and Whitgift managed to bring the lectureship within the range of episcopal supervision and to forge new weapons for dealing with the intransigent nonconformist, but the old problems remained. There were new articles to be enforced, but the ordinary disciplinary machinery of visitations, detections, and so on remained much the same; clumsy at best, the system worked with tolerable efficiency only when a vigorous Bishop of London forced the pace. Between the device of qualified subscription and the willingness of many of the younger generation to practice occasional conformity much of the sting was removed from Whitgift's policies. Suspensions, deprivations, and the exposure of a Presbyterian underground centered in London had taken their toll, but the evidence suggests that as far as the London lecturers were concerned, the result was only to arrest any further increase in their number. There were 40 lecturers in London in 1585, 29 of whom were Puritans; a decade later there were 41 lecturers, 21 of whom were Puritans. The stresses of the 1580's were in a sense tangential to the issue of the lectureships, for neither Aylmer nor Whitgift could offer any positive solution to the problem created by the laity's demand for a preaching ministry.

STAGNATION

It is true, nevertheless, that during the opening years of the new reign, the Puritans suffered a series of reverses comparable only to those sustained in the 1580's. Hard upon the fiasco of the Hampton Court Conference came that great compilation of (among other things) anti-Puritan legislation, the Canons of 1604. Not only were all previous measures against nonconformity codified in the Canons, but an attempt was made to close the remaining loopholes. All ministers instituted to any living or lectureship were to be properly licensed, and the granting of licenses was conditional upon unqualified subscription to the three articles, a subscription that must be taken "willingly and *ex animo*" (Canons 36 and 37). Nonconformity among subscribers was to be punished by suspension, to be followed by excommunication should the nonconformist remain obstinate (Canon 38). All previously licensed preachers who failed to conform were first to be admonished, and then, if they did not conform within a month, to have their licenses voided (Canon 54). Unlicensed ministers might preach neither in their own cure nor elsewhere, but "only study to read ... the Homilies already set forth" (Canon 49). Ministers from other parishes were not to be admitted to preach without showing their licenses, and the churchwardens were charged with recording the names of all "strange" preachers, the day they preached, and the name of the bishop by whom they were licensed (Canons 50 and 52). Every minister with cure of souls, even though "he chiefly attended to preaching," and every "stipendiary preacher that readeth any lecture," was required to read the prescribed Sunday service at the appointed times and to administer the sacraments of baptism and communion twice yearly on penalty of suspension and removal (Canon 56). Finally, before any lecture could be preached, the lecturer was required to use a set form of prayer to the following effect: "You shall pray for Christ's holy Catholic Church ..., for the King's most excellent Majesty, ... for the ministers of God's holy Word and Sacraments, as well archbishops and bishops, as other pastors and curates ..., always concluding with the Lord's Prayer" (Canon 55).[59]

As expected, the Puritans and their sympathizers howled in protest. Members of the House of Commons argued that canons lacking statutory confirmation had no force in law and petitioned that the Canons "may be commanded never hereafter to be put in execution"; the House of Lords read and engrossed "an act restraining the executing of canons ecclesiastical not confirmed by Parliament." A pamphleteer saw in the Canons a vicious plot "to displace and keep out such painful and godly Ministers, as make scruple of the Ceremonies." Instructions were drawn up specifying those legal remedies available to the nonconformist who came under episcopal disciplinary action. In September 1604 King James confirmed the Canons, declaring that he found them "very profitable ... to the whole Church of this our Kingdom, and to all the true members of it."[60]

Three months later Bancroft, now archbishop, issued directions for a "uniform kind of proceeding with the disobedient and obstinate ministers." This time, unlike 1584, the lecturers were specifically provided for. "Concerning those that utterly refuse both conformity and subscription," the directions pointed out, the interest those "commonly

called lecturers ... have in their places is only by license from their ordinary, and they are no longer to enjoy them *nisi quamdiu se bene
gesserint*, so as upon such their refusal," the bishop was to "suspend
them *ab officio*, which is in effect a deprivation."[61] This time there was
to be no initial rigor followed by strategic retreat and compromise.
On 12 March 1605 Bancroft admonished the bishops that they "should
not desist by depriving one, two, or three at once, until you have
purged your diocese of them."[62]

Richard Vaughan, the Bishop of London, appears to have been a
willing executor of Bancroft's policy. In any event, he could not be lax
on his first visitation, for the articles had been drawn up by Bancroft
before he became archbishop. As far as the lecturers were concerned,
the visitation articles of 1604 followed the Canons faithfully. The
bishop demanded to know whether any without a cure "taketh upon
him to preach or read lectures ... who is not licensed to preach or read
there, or who doth not once a year [a deviation from the Canons that
could have made little difference in substance] at the least administer
the Sacraments in your said church ... according to the book";
whether any had preached "in derogation of the book of Common
Prayer ..., or against the present estate of the ecclesiastical government"; whether the parson was licensed to preach, and if so, how
many sermons he preached yearly; and whether "your preacher in his
prayer which he maketh at the entrance into his sermon use at all
times" the prescribed prayer, particularly that part "for the archbishops and bishops, as by law is also appointed."[63] It is, of course, one
thing to draw up strict articles and quite another to administer them
vigorously, but in this instance there can be little question about
Vaughan's intentions. A few months after the articles were published,
John Chamberlain wrote:

Our puritans go down on all sides, and though our new bishop of London proceed but slowly, yet at last he hath deprived, silenced, or suspended
all that continue disobedient, in which course he hath won himself great
commendation of gravity, wisdom, learning, mildness, and temperance,
event among that faction.... Yet those that are deprived wrangle, and will
not be put down.[64]

If legislative and administrative fiat were sufficient, Bancroft's reign
should have seen either the elimination of clerical Puritanism or its
taming to the point of impotence. What, then, were the results? S. B.

Babbage's recent study has proved that R. G. Usher's figures for deprivations were seriously in error. There were closer to ninety than sixty in all of England, and Babbage notes fourteen deprivations in London rather than Usher's five or six.[65] Of the fourteen men deprived in the diocese, three were city ministers, and of the three only one, David Dee, rector of St. Bartholomew the Great, had lectured at all. However, there is some reason to doubt whether Dee, who had lectured at Christ Church Newgate from 1584 to 1595, was actually deprived for nonconformity. The records of the London Consistory Court suggest other reasons. Early in 1602 he was presented under the suspicion of being "an incontinent person, a haunter of taverns, ... [and] a great userer." To be sure, it was alleged that when he read the Prayer Book, "he doth mumble it up so indistinctly and speaketh so irreverently, that the common people can hardly understand what is read," which may indicate that Dee was a nonconformist, or may indicate simply that the churchwardens wanted to ensure the effectiveness of their accusation. Dee was presented again early in 1606 from St. Bride's for marrying a couple without banns or license, a practice he continued after he was deprived.[66]

As for the City lecturers, the record looks on the surface very much like that of the preceding decade. There can be no question about the nature of episcopal activity either during the last years of Bancroft's rule as Bishop of London, or under bishops Vaughan and Ravys, his immediate successors, but the ultimate effect of this activity is perhaps less obvious.[67] The immediate results appear to have been negligible. For example, Edmund Snape, who lectured briefly at St. Saviour's in 1605, was forced to leave when he failed to obtain a preaching license. However, the Bishop of Winchester had more to do with the departure of this old survivor of the Northampton classis than the Bishop of London.[68] Anthony Wotton, a former chaplain to the Earl of Essex and a divine of considerable reputation in Puritan circles, was suspended by Bancroft from his lectureship at Allhallows Barking in 1604 for praying that "the king's eyes might be opened," but he was soon restored and continued his lecture until his death in 1626.[69] Finally, in 1604, Stephen Egerton, the lecturer at St. Anne Blackfriars, was suspended for the third time, and three years later he was restored again.[70]

In 1606 three more lecturers were presented for nonconformity.

Richard Gardiner, who as rector and preacher at St. Mary White-chapel had lectured there since 1570, was presented for his irregular administration of the communion. Although a Barrowist deposition as early as 1593 had mentioned his preaching in favor of a Presbyterian discipline, this appears to have been Gardiner's only trouble with the courts. He apparently satisfied the vicar-general, for he was not deprived and remained at St. Mary's until his death in 1617.[71] Two lecturers, William Symonds and John Trundle, were cited from that always troublesome parish Christ Church Newgate for nonconformity in 1606. Both were to certify of their "reading public prayer and ministering the sacraments in the surplice according to the Canon." On February 22, Symonds was ordered to conform at St. Saviour's, where he also lectured, and he apparently did so, for he remained at St. Saviour's until 1614, when he left the City for a Lincolnshire living.[72] Trundle, for his part, continued to procrastinate. In February 1607 he admitted that despite his inhibition he had preached at Southwark (undoubtedly Symonds's doing) and elsewhere in the City, but he "entreateth some deliberation to think," for "as yet [he] cannot resolve to conform himself." He was suspended until he would certify his willingness to conform, which he never did. In 1608 he was discovered preaching at a Brownist conventicle at Christ Church Newgate.[73]

From 1604 to 1606, then, a total of six lecturers were in trouble of one kind or another. One was forced to depart; one was suspended permanently (but Trundle may already have been a Separatist); two were suspended but restored; and two were cited but neither inhibited nor suspended. During these same years almost twenty Puritans were lecturing in London.

Much the same pattern continued under Bishop Thomas Ravys. Once again the two lecturers at Christ Church were in trouble: Humphrey Hartnes was suspended for marrying a couple in secret, and Anthony Erbery for nonsubscription. Hartnes was restored and continued at Christ Church until he left to become curate to Samuel Ward at Munden Magna, Hertfordshire.[74] Erbery's case dragged on for several months, since he insisted that he was properly licensed by Bishop Vaughan, which was apparently true, but continued to refuse subscription. He appears to have worn out the court, for the last record of the case notes merely that he was admonished to appear before the bishop at Fulham when "it shall please my Lordship to send for him." In 1635 he was in trouble before the High Commission for his activities at his Somerset living.[75] Edward Topsell, curate and lecturer at St. Botolph Aldersgate, and John Downham, rector and lecturer at St. Margaret Lothbury, were both ordered to produce their licenses, but this has no special implications, for quite orthodox Anglicans were required to do the same.[76]

Other lecturers were in more serious trouble in 1608 and 1609, the last years of Ravys's episcopate. William Parr, lecturer at Egerton's parish, St. Anne's, Robert Blincoe, lecturer at St. Bride's, and Henry Graye, lecturer at St. Giles in the Fields, were all ordered to certify that they read public prayer and administered both the sacraments in the surplice. Parr died in 1609, apparently before certifying his conformity; Blincoe, who was inhibited, made his submission a month later; and of Graye, who had already been suspended once before by the Chancery Court at York, there is no further information.[77] Andrew Castleton, who had been rector and lecturer at St. Martin Ironmonger Lane since 1577, was apparently suspected of nonconformity, for he was ordered to "observe the ceremonies of the Church ... according to the Canons"; he was not, however, suspended or deprived.[78]

All in all, the fate of the Puritan lecturers in London during the years of Bancroft's ascendancy presents a confusing picture. Almost half of those who preached in the City during these years were cited before the courts on one pretext or another, but only a handful seem to have been permanently suspended or driven away. To what degree the rest actually conformed is, of course, impossible to tell. However, if it is not possible to measure the degree of conformity exacted by the church machinery, there is ample evidence of its failure in particular instances.

It is true, for example, that Stephen Egerton gave up his lecturing after his third restoration in 1607, but it had taken three suspensions and twenty years to accomplish so much. Furthermore, Egerton's replacement, William Parr, was no improvement to the hierarchy's way of thinking. The authorities managed to silence Parr within a year, only to be faced by his replacement, William Gouge, a divine trained in his early years by Ezechial Culverwell, one of those deprived by the High Commission in the spring of 1609. Gouge had been recommended to Egerton by Arthur Hildersham, a Puritan divine of great reputation and considerable connections who had been deprived in 1605.[79]

It could, of course, be argued that since Gouge had subscribed and was properly licensed, his puritanical background is irrelevant to the question at hand. The evidence suggests, however, that though he subscribed he did not conform, and further that it took the authorities three years to catch up with him. In January 1611 Thomas Edwards, the vicar-general, questioned Gouge about the way he administered communion. Gouge admitted that he "had received it himself both sitting and standing and kneeling, knowing it in itself to be indifferent, and hath ministered it to others . . . in like manner." Gouge submitted to the correction of the judges and was admonished to conform. However, the vicar-general evidently doubted whether the lesson had been sufficiently driven home, for in October not only Gouge but the churchwardens were summoned to hear a further admonishment on the same subject.[80] It may be that Gouge got off lightly because of his willingness to submit and subscribe, but it is peculiar that no certification of conformity was demanded.[81] It may be, too, that the court knew better than to trust any certificate from the churchwardens of Blackfriars. In any case, the whole episode smacks of just that sort of compromise on all sides that had followed the promulgation of Whitgift's Articles, and that Bancroft had so obviously hoped to prevent.

Furthermore, Gouge's was not an isolated or exceptional case. To cite only one more example, Edward Spendlowe had been lecturer for 32 years at St. Antholin's when in 1628 the court noted that he was not licensed and ordered him to produce his letters of ordination. He had been ordained exactly 50 years before by Bishop Aylmer, but apparently the last time he had been properly licensed and admitted to a preferment had been in 1580, when he was presented to the vicarage of Redburn, Hertfordshire, by Lady Ann Bacon.[82] It would seem that neither Bancroft nor Vaughan nor Ravys was thorough enough in his visitations to discover this obvious and routine dereliction of duty. For that matter, their immediate successors could not claim any greater efficiency.

The Consistory Court records suggest a definite falling off of disciplinary action against the clergy in general and the lecturers in particular in the decade following Bancroft's death in 1610. This may have been due to the fact that John King, who succeeded George Abbot as Bishop of London in 1611, had himself been a popular London preacher—King James called him "the king of preachers"—and consequently looked on the lecturers' activities with greater sympathy.[83] In any event, of the 37 or 38 Puritans lecturing in London during this decade, only four were cited before the Consistory Court. Richard Cooke, the rector and lecturer at St. Swithin's, was ordered in 1613 to "show what license he had to preach," but Cooke, who continued his lecture at least until 1622, was apparently not a Puritan. James Hiat, who was a Puritan—he lived long enough to be ejected in 1662—and who was the lecturing curate at St. Mary Magdalen Milk Street, was ordered in 1616 to show by what authority he officiated the curacy at St. Andrew Wardrobe, but he, like Cooke, apparently had no trouble producing the necessary papers. Evidently he left London before 1622, since by that year he was lecturing at Liverpool, but there is no reason to suppose that he was driven from the City.[84]

The remaining three Puritans were in deeper trouble. In 1618 Jeremiah Holliday, who had lectured at St. Antholin's a few years earlier, and who had been curate and lecturer at St. Mary Somerset since 1612, was cited for failing to wear the surplice and for omitting the sign of the cross in baptism. Holliday submitted and was ordered to conform in all respects under penalty of the law. Late in 1617 John Davenport, who was to become famous for his preaching at St. Stephen Coleman Street in the 1620's, was caught lecturing and officiating at St. Mary Aldermanbury without being either licensed or admitted. He was suspended but then, on his humble petition, restored. Although he was not yet a thoroughgoing nonconformist, Davenport was notably careless about the proprieties. In 1622 he was cited again to show by what authority he was teaching school in the parish of St. Martin in the Fields. Finally, on 14 November 1618, Henry Burton, who had not yet gained his later notoriety, was ordered to show his preaching license for his lecture at St. Matthew Friday Street; he presumably had little difficulty producing one, for he was at the time Clerk of the Closet to Prince Charles and had only recently been ordained.[85]

Altogether the records for the decade after 1610 do not suggest any pressing concern with the Puritan lecturers. It is perhaps indicative of the relaxed state of ecclessiastical discipline that Elias Crabtree, who was cited in 1617 "for serving the cure [at St. Peter Cornhill] without license," should have experienced no difficulty in gaining admission to the curacy and lectureship at St. Lawrence Pountney three years later. Crabtree was a Puritan and later, at least, a nonconformist, for he was subsequently proceeded against by the High Commission in 1632 and ordered by Laud to conform and to produce a sermon that "doth express his true intent to the same."[86] One lecturer, it is true, left his London lectureship rather abruptly in 1618, but not because of any disciplinary action. William Loe, a royal chaplain who was preaching at St. Michael Cornhill, found it advisable to retire to the Continent, where he became pastor at the English Church at Hamburg for a short time, as a consequence of some obscure troubles with William Laud, then Dean of Gloucester.[87]

THE CRITICAL YEARS

The years after 1618 were a time of gradually deepening crisis for the Puritans. In 1618 King James issued the Book of Sports, dealing a heavy blow to Sabbatarian opinion, which had "got footing again in divers places by the cunning of the Puritan Faction, the ignorant confidence of some of their Lecturers, and the misguided zeal of some public Ministers of Justice."[88] At the same time the Bohemian fiasco proved to be only the opening battle of a long war, and the King's seeming indifference to the fate of his daughter and son-in-law was observed with increasing anxiety by the Puritans, who saw the Thirty Years' War not as an exercise in power politics but as a great confrontation between the godly and Antichrist.[89] In 1635 John Workman, a Gloucester lecturer, would be convented before the High Commission because he "hath usually prayed for the States of Holland and the King of Sweden or other great general beyond the seas, before the King's Majesty that now is over us."[90] However, the Elector's reverses were not the only source of worry for Protestant Englishmen, for they were soon faced with a crisis closer to home in the proposed Spanish match.[91] Increasingly, too, the Puritans were forced to recognize the growing power of the Arminian wing of the Church, particularly within the episcopate.

In later years Peter Heylyn claimed that after Bancroft's death "the English Puritans began to put forth again, not pushing at the Liturgy and Episcopal Government (as in former times), but in pursuance of the Sabbatarian and Calvinian Rigors. . . . In both which, they received some countenance from King James himself, but more from the connivance (if I may not call it the encouragement) of the new Archbishop."[92] As usual, Heylyn exaggerated, for though Archbishop Abbot did not view the Puritans as the menace that the Arminians did, and though he did on occasion protect individual Puritan preachers, it is difficult to cast either him or King James in the role of active supporters of Puritanism. Further, if the Puritan lecturers of London can serve as an index of the movement as a whole, their number did not begin to increase rapidly until about 1616. In fact, there appear to have been fewer Puritans lecturing in London in the five years after Bancroft's death than in any five-year period since 1583. This may, of course, indicate only that in those peaceful years of lax administration Puritan preachers went undetected and hence are now indistinguishable from the general run of Anglican lecturers. The fact that the total number of lecturers increased between 1610 and 1615 from 37 to 55 while the number of Puritan lecturers remained about the same suggests such a conclusion.

On the other hand, an alternative explanation is possible. It is conceivable that at a time when controversy was at a minimum, when no great issues divided public opinion, fewer London vestries bestirred themselves to hire Puritan preachers in particular; similarly, at such a time some puritanically inclined ministers might have found little cause for militancy and small reason not to conform. Certainly John Davenport, who first lectured in London in this period, showed no sign of his later radicalism; as late as 1624 he could assure his friends at Court of his willing conformity.[93] Yet within ten years he not only refused to conform but departed for New England.

Davenport was but one of many London lecturers whose Puritanism either blossomed or resumed its course after 1620. According to Heylyn the blame for the new upsurge rested squarely on Bishop Mountaigne, a man, so he claimed, whom King Charles characterized as "unactive, and addicted to voluptuousness, and one who loved his ease too well to disturb himself in the concernments of the Church."[94] However, Bishop Mountaigne's articles for his first visitation in 1621 cast doubt on such an assessment, for if anything they were even more searching than Bancroft's articles of 1604. With regard to preachers, the bishop not only wanted to know whether all admitted to preach were properly licensed and by whom, whether every "strange" preacher had subscribed his name according to Canons 50 and 52, whether all lecturers read divine service and administered the sacraments at least twice yearly, and whether all preachers used the prescribed prayer before or after every sermon; he also wanted to know whether all preachers "do raise and deliver out of the texts chosen by them, such pertinent notes as tend to teach obedience, and to edify the understanding of their auditory in matters of faith and religion, without intermeddling with any State matters not fit to be handled in the pulpit."[95]

King James himself was willing enough to have the clergy, "as also the lecturers," intermeddling when it came to preaching up a voluntary contribution for the recovery of the Palatinate. However, he noted sententiously, other "abuses and extravagancies of preachers in the pulpit have been in all times repressed in this realm by some act of Council, or State." He therefore issued the Directions of 1622, limiting the subject matter of sermons. Preachers under the degree of bishop or dean were prohibited from touching on any subject not at least implied by the Thirty-nine Articles or the Book of Homilies, and in particular they were not to discuss the controversial aspects of the doctrines of election, predestination, reprobation, and grace. Further, preachers were prohibited from indulging in "indecent railing speeches against the persons of either Papists or Puritans," and more important, from presuming to define or treat in any way the Crown's prerogatives. On the more positive side, the Directions commanded preachers to take the texts of their sermons from the Creed, the Ten Commandments, the Catechism, or the Lord's Prayer, and encouraged catechisms in preference to Sunday afternoon sermons. Finally, a new licensing procedure was set forth. Lecturers were to be licensed by the Court of Faculties "by recommendation of the party from the bishop of the diocese under his hand and seal, with a *fiat* from the Lord Archbishop of Canterbury, [and] a confirmation under the Great Seal of England."*

Archbishop Abbot found himself in the embarrassing position of having to justify the Directions, even though he apparently had had no

---

* *Documentary Annals of the Reformed Church of England*, ed. Edward Cardwell (Oxford, 1844), II, 193–97; John Rushworth, *Historical Collections* (London, 1721), I, 64–65. This last provision, which had the obvious intent of making it virtually impossible to obtain a preaching license, appears to have been a dead letter, for there is no evidence in the extant subscription books for the diocese of London that any such elaborate system was followed in practice. GLMS 9539A/1 and A/2.

hand in drawing them up (Heylyn attributes them to Laud). He knew very well, too, that in the view of "some few churchmen and many of the people" the Directions "tend to the restraint of . . . preaching, and do in some sort abate the number of sermons, and so consequently by degrees do make a breach to ignorance and superstition."[96] Unlike Abbot, who was too much of an old-fashioned Anglican to be insensitive to the reaction of ordinary Protestant Englishmen, King James left no doubt about the seriousness of his intentions. At the prorogation of Parliament in 1624, he commended Bishop Harsnet of Norwich, who had come under attack "for suppressing of popular lectures within his diocese," by which, said the King, "I mean such as nowadays are most frequented, being supplied . . . by such ministers as have not *curam animorum* where they preach, for such must flatter and cogg the people, and therefore I will never allow them."[97]

When one descends from the heights of policy to the mundane world of diocesan administration, a different picture presents itself. At least 75 Puritans lectured in London during the 1620's. In the years before Laud became bishop only ten appear to have experienced any kind of difficulty with the ecclesiastical authorities, in addition to two others who had to leave their lectureships because they could not secure licenses.

During the last years of Bishop King's episcopate, two Puritan lecturers were cited. On 5 December 1620 Robert Dumvill, curate and lecturer at St. Peter Cornhill, was ordered to show by what authority he officiated the cure, whereupon he produced a license conveniently dated the day before and was excused. He continued to lecture until 1622, at which time he disappeared from the records until 1636, when Nathaniel Brent, who was conducting Laud's metropolitan visitation, noted that he had questioned Dumvill, then vicar of Leyton, Essex, for "divers inconformities."[98] In October 1620 Richard Worsley, then curate, lecturer, and schoolteacher at St. Mary le Strand, was required to show by what authority he performed these functions. Worsley produced licenses to preach and teach, but they were licenses for the diocese of Oxford. Nevertheless, he was properly licensed when summoned in 1628 as curate of St. Bartholomew the Less. In 1631 he was in trouble again for accusing his parson of being about to bring in popery, a development he appears to have blamed ultimately on King Charles. His wife, it must be added, claimed that he was "distracted."[99]

John Everard, who lectured at St. Martin in the Fields from 1617 until 1622, was undoubtedly one of the targets of the King's Directions. In 1621 he had been imprisoned in the Gatehouse for "glancing ... at the Spanish match" in one of his sermons. He was committed again for a questionable sermon in 1622, this time in the Marshalsea, and again early in 1623. Apparently powerful friends intervened for him each time. Shortly afterward he became chaplain to Lord Holland and moved his lectureship to Kensington, where he was preaching at the time of the 1628 visitation.* The case of Dr. Edmund Wilson, lecturer at St. Andrew Holborne, who was also accused of seditious preaching, was less clear-cut. Bishop Mountaigne, who was ordered by King James to examine Wilson, reported that he had preached nothing seditious. Another sermon of Wilson's, for which he was also examined, appears to have been little more than an attack on the loyalty of papists. Whether or not he ever was suspended, he was apparently suspected of being a Puritan.[100]

Despite the testimony of Bishop Mountaigne's searching visitation articles, the records of the London Consistory Court during his episcopate lend a measure of credibility to the charge that he was too lazy to exert himself "in the concernments of the Church," at least as far as the Puritan lecturers were concerned. Six were cited, but none was inhibited or deprived. This apparent leniency cannot, however, be interpreted to mean that all six dutifully conformed. Rather the evidence suggests that neither the bishop nor his vicar-general had any pressing concern for clerical conformity.

On 26 August 1622 John Blackwell and Samuel Hoard were summoned to present the instruments entitling them to officiate the cure at St. Christopher le Stocks; Blackwell was both curate and lecturer,

---

* WPLMS F.2001, fols. 107r, 166v; WPLMS F.2, p. 398; *The Letters of John Chamberlain*, ed. Norman E. McClure (Philadelphia, 1939), II, 350, 449, 486; *Dictionary of National Biography*; GLMS, 9537/13, no fol. Thomas Scott attributed the following sentiments to Count Gondomar, the Spanish ambassador, whom he blamed for Everard's arrest: "There was not a sermon preached at Paul's Cross, or indeed in any other church of the city or place in the kingdom, that did not touch the hem of my master's garment ... but I had my leam-hounds ready in every corner to draw after them dryfoot, and fetch the authors *corum nobis*, to their cost, as one Dr. Everard of St. Martin's was for his bold and malapert inveighing and continually preaching against us and the match silenced by my only means." *The Second Part of Vox Populi* (n.p., 1624), p. 17. Though there is no reason to suppose that Scott's account of Gondomar's actions has any substance in fact, it does indicate that Protestant opinion generally was highly inflamed at the time and that Everard was not alone in preaching against the proposed marriage.

and Hoard, another lecturer, was cited as a curate as well. No action seems to have been taken. In 1625 Hoard, who was chaplain to Robert, Earl of Warwick, was presented to the rectory of Moreton, Essex, by the earl.[101] Blackwell, who also lectured at St. Saviour's, died in 1625 and was succeeded as curate at St. Christopher's by his brother, Andrew, who had lectured there since 1622. Andrew, in turn, was summoned on 7 February 1623/4 to show his letters of ordination and admission. Again no action followed, although in 1628 Laud's survey revealed that Andrew Blackwell did not possess a valid license to preach.[102] At the same court Theodore Herring, curate in Gouge's parish of St. Anne Blackfriars, was also cited. Whether Herring ever appeared is not recorded. He was also lecturer at St. Olave Jewry during these years; in 1628 he left the City for an Essex rectory.[103]

The court made a more substantial catch three weeks after Herring's case when Richard Sedgwick, lecturer at Wapping Chapel, was cited "for what the whole divine service was not read usually upon Sundays and holidays in the chapel in Wapping, nor in such manner and form as is prescribed in the book of Common Prayer." The chapel appears to have been altogether irregular, for in addition the curate was ordered to conform and the churchwardens were ordered to erect a rail around the communion table, a task they still had not accomplished two months later because, they claimed, nothing short of a warrant from the court would enable them to collect sufficient funds. Sedgwick himself had a past, sketched earlier in this study, that would have justified the court's pressing for a more searching inquisition, but despite his reputation and despite the evident irregularities in the parish, the Consistory Court dismissed Sedgwick with a mere admonition.[104]

The final case to come before the court in the years before Laud's translation to the Bishopric of London is entirely consistent with those already mentioned. On 8 December 1627 Meredith Mayday (or Maydy), who had been active in various clerical posts about the City for twenty years, was presented for preaching at St. Sepulchre's without a license. Once again no action seems to have been taken by the court; in any event the following year found him lecturing at Christ Church Newgate. He was finally silenced by Laud in 1630 for touching "upon the point of election" in a sermon, in contempt of the King's Directions of 1622.[105]

Though the case is not mentioned in the Consistory Court records, Mountaigne did suspend one Puritan lecturer at the very end of his term in London. Hugh Peter, who at the beginning of his long and notorious career lectured briefly at St. Sepulchre's to audiences he estimated as numbering in the thousands, preached a sermon in 1626 at Christ Church Newgate at the request of his patron, the Earl of Warwick, in the course of which he expressed the hope that the Queen would abandon idolatry. News of this event reached Mountaigne, who questioned Peter but apparently released him because of Warwick's influence. However, Peter was back before the bishop late in 1627, at which time the interrogation turned to the more fundamental questions of Peter's orthodoxy and conformity. By December he was suspended and had withdrawn to the Netherlands.[106]

Another two lecturers had to give up their posts after failing to secure episcopal approval under Mountaigne, but only one of these Anglican victories can be attributed to him. The futile attempt in 1627 by the parish of St. Botolph Aldgate to secure the famous old nonconformist Ezechial Culverwell as their lecturer has already been described; the incident does suggest that the bishop's tolerance or laziness did have its limits.[107] The other preacher forced to leave his London lectureship was Robert Harris, who resigned his lecture at St. Saviour's, Southwark, on 5 January 1624/5, when he failed to obtain a dispensation from the Archbishop of Canterbury. Harris, who had already gained a considerable reputation for his preaching at St. Paul's and at St. Lawrence Jewry, could not have been seriously inconvenienced by the loss of his post at St. Saviour's, since he was already beneficed at Hanwell, Oxfordshire. He returned to a London pulpit in 1642, after having been chased from his living by royalist troops following the battle of Edgehill; this time there were no bishops or archbishops to say him nay.[108]

Finally, there is the case of Zachary Symmes, an Emmanuel graduate whose father and grandfather before him had been "painful" preachers of the reformed faith. According to Cotton Mather, Symmes, who had been one of the early morning lecturers at St. Antholin's since 1621, "after many troubles from the bishops' courts, for his dissent from things whereto his consent had never been required by the great Shepherd and Bishop of our souls ... removed from thence in the year 1625 to Dunstable, where his troubles from the bishops' courts continuing, he at length transported himself with his family into the American wilderness." Although no trace survives of Symmes's harassment, at least in the correction books of the Consistory Court, it is certain that his move to St. Peter's, Dunstable, was engineered by the recently organized Feoffees for Impropriations, who had acquired the impropriation of St. Peter's in 1625 and had then managed to obtain the resignation of the former, and to them unsatisfactory, incumbent.[109]

One of Archbishop Ussher's London correspondents wrote in 1618, "The affairs of the Church here are much after one style; the better sort of preachers, some stand and are hid or winked at, and some go down the wind."[110] Since three Puritan preachers—John Burgess, John Dodd, and Ezechial Culverwell, all friends of Ussher—had been mentioned earlier in the letter, there can be little doubt about the identity of the "better sort of preachers." Taken as a whole, the evidence for the decade following 1618 suggests that in London many more were "winked at" than ever "went down the wind." Further, this was true not only of the preaching incumbents, but also of those independent lecturers "as have not *curam animorum* where they preach," whom King James vowed he would never allow. At least fourteen Puritan lecturers who held neither cure nor curacy preached in the city between 1620 and 1628 quite untroubled by the disciplinary machinery of the church courts.[111]

Lecturers for whom the lectureship was a stepping-stone or stopgap until a more permanent preferment came their way must have made a relatively slight impact on the ecclesiastical politics and spiritual life of the City. Daniel Cawdry, the son of a Puritan nonconformist and a gradaute of Sidney Sussex, preached at St. Lawrence Jewry only a year and a half before going on to the rectory of Great Billings, Northamptonshire.[112] Other lecturers, like John Preston at Lincoln's Inn and Richard Sibbes at Gray's Inn, were not only popular preachers—the chapel at Lincoln's Inn had to be expanded within a year of Preston's appointment—but also men of such stature and reputation that their presence in these important pulpits could scarcely be ignored. At the same time, their very eminence brought with it the powerful patrons and the firm connections in Court, country, and university that must have given them virtual immunity from episcopal interference.[113]

Quite apart from the fact that there is no evidence of any systematic attempt to eliminate the independent lecturer in London during these years, it might well be asked whether the lecturers posed any greater danger to the orthodoxy and discipline of the Church than the preaching incumbents. From 1620 to 1628 fourteen Puritan parsons lectured in the City, and another six combined a lectureship with a curacy. Both the independent lecturers and those who held a cure with souls had been subject to the same ecclesiastical discipline since 1580. Moreover, apart from the occasional career lecturer—John Downham, Anthony Wotton, or Edward Spendlowe, for example—those lecturers who also held a benefice were a more permanent element in the ecclesiastical scene than the independent lecturers. And with few exceptions, continuity of tenure meant leadership.

Although there was no organization in the 1620's similar to John Field's "London brethren" of forty years before, a wide variety of common concerns brought the Puritan preachers together on many occasions. For example, Richard Sibbes and John Davenport, the vicar and the lecturer at St. Stephen Coleman Street, edited and published a number of John Preston's sermons at Lord Saye's request. John Downham, lecturer at St. Bartholomew Exchange, not only published some of the sermons of Thomas Sutton, lecturer at St. Saviour's from 1615 until his untimely death in 1623, but married his widow as well.[114] A few years earlier several Puritans had taken part in a controversy between Anthony Wotton, lecturer at Allhallows Barking, and George Walker, rector of St. John the Evangelist and later lecturer at St. Benet Fink and St. Helen Bishopsgate.[115] Among Walker's supporters at two Puritan meetings where Wotton's opinions were discussed were John Downham, Richard Stock, and William Gouge. Wotton was defended successfully by another group of Puritans, which included among others John Randall, rector and lecturer at St. Andrew Hubbard, and Thomas Gataker, Jr., the former lecturer at Lincoln's Inn.

The Feoffees for Impropriations were assisted in their efforts to speed the progress of Puritanism by two independent lecturers: Hugh Peter, from St. Sepulchre's, and Thomas Foxley, from St. Antholin's.[116] However, the clerical leadership among the Feoffees came from among the more substantial group of beneficed Puritans. Richard Sibbes, preacher at Gray's Inn and Master of St. Catherine's, Cambridge, was an exception, but the others—Richard Stock, John Davenport, and Charles Offspring, rector of St. Antholin's—were all beneficed. When Stock died in 1626, he was replaced by William Gouge, rector and lecturer at St. Anne Blackfriars.[117] In 1622 Gouge, Sibbes, and Davenport, having failed to persuade King James to come to the aid of the Palatine Protestants, turned, as the Feoffees would later, to private enterprise. Early in 1627 the three and Thomas Taylor, the lecturing incumbent of St. Mary Aldermanbury, signed a circular letter soliciting voluntary support for the "godly preachers" and their widows and families in the Palatinate, an effort that earned Sibbes and Taylor a reprimand from Laud and the High Commission a year later.[118]

Activities like these must have been only the more obvious of those in which the London Puritan lecturers were involved, just as Davenport, Gouge, Sibbes, Preston, Stock, and Taylor were only the more conspicuous leaders among an army of preaching brethren. Years later it was claimed that "their faction" had emissaries "to give notice where men of their tribe preached, so that not any one of their ministers could come to London . . . but found entertainment in the city." Vast as the clerical connections of the London "faction" were, however, their equally extensive connections among the laity were a far more important source of strength. The hierarchy might thunder, but with frustrating regularity the Puritan preachers escaped the full force of episcopal displeasure by finding shelter under the protection offered by their lay patrons. As an anonymous observer wrote, "The lay brethren continued the practice of their faction in Queen Elizabeth's days in clapping silenced ministers and nonconformists and lecturers on the back, and following their sermons, setting them at the upper end of the tables, and seeking by all means to procure them credit and favor with the people."[119]

A few examples will illustrate the extent to which the lecturers were indebted to their lay patrons. When Hugh Peter came to London in 1626, he continued to visit the Earl of Warwick and to preach at Warwick's chapel at Little Leighs, Essex. However, Peter owed his lectureship at St. Sepulchre's not to his old patron but to a wealthy chandler who paid him £30 a year for his preaching. When Bishop Mountaigne refused to grant John Davenport admission, pending royal approval, to the vicarage and lectureship at St. Stephen Coleman

Street, to which he had been elected by the vestry, Davenport sought support at Court through his friend Mary, Lady Vere, whose brother-in-law was Sir Edward Conway, one of the principal Secretaries of State.[120] Richard Sibbes was elected divinity reader at Gray's Inn largely through the influence of Sir Henry Yelverton, the Solicitor General; years later in his will Sibbes remembered his friend John Pym. John Preston, the most politically minded of the preaching brotherhood, had a veritable galaxy of important friends, ranging from the Northamptonshire Knightleys and Lord Saye and Sele to the royal favorite, the Duke of Buckingham.[121]

The lay members of the Feoffees for Impropriations themselves represent a fair sampling of the support that came from the legal and mercantile communities. Alderman Roland Heylyn, sometime sheriff, served the Feoffees for six years; on his death he was replaced by Nicholas Rainton, Haberdasher and at the time Lord Mayor. One of the lawyers, John White, and three of the merchants, Francis Bridges, Richard Davis, and George Harwood, were members of the Massachusetts Bay Company, and so was the preacher John Davenport. Christopher Sherland, another of the lawyers, was a member of the Providence Island Company and a Member of Parliament in 1628. When he died in 1632, his funeral sermon was preached by Richard Sibbes, and his replacement as Feoffee was Sir Thomas Crewe, twice Speaker of the House of Commons. Another Feoffee, John White of the Middle Temple, the Winthrops' family lawyer, was to be the Member of Parliament for Southwark in 1640 and chairman of the Committee on Religion.[122]

By 1628, the year Preston died, London had 121 lecturers, almost half of whom were Puritans. The years of marking time that had followed the death of Archbishop Bancroft were long in the past. London's lecturers, like their predecessors in the 1580's, were once more men with a mission, and they now led a much larger, if more loosely knit, movement. The issue of Presbyterian discipline, which had never gained much support from the laity, was no longer a rallying point even for the clergy. In its place the preachers, like the "country" party among the laity, were united by what they feared and hated—a pusillanimous foreign policy that seemed prepared to bow to the interests of Rome and Spain abroad, the growing power of Arminianism and ceremonialism that apparently aimed at undoing the Reformation at home, and above all, the increasingly unresponsive monarchy that had condoned, even fostered, these two abominations. If the preachers no longer had great allies at Court like Leicester and Walsingham, they were tied by friendships, patronage, and common purposes to the powerful legal and mercantile elites of London. Altogether they presented a more formidable challenge to the Established Church than any Bishop of London had ever faced before.

8

Laud and the Lecturers

NEITHER George Abbot, the Archbishop, nor George Mountaigne, the Bishop of London, appears to have viewed the Puritan lecturers as a sufficiently obnoxious element within the Church to
merit any considerable expenditure of their energies. However, for
one who saw the lecturers as a menace to the integrity of Church and
State, the problem of arriving at adequate sanctions must have been a
baffling one by 1628. Control by licensing, subscription, and Directions, enforced by frequent visitations, by promoted cases, and by the
ex officio oath, had all proved inadequate. And the number of London
lecturers, which had remained roughly constant for 40 years after 1580,
had begun to increase rapidly in the 1620's.

One solution to the problem was simply more rigorous and efficient
administration, but such a solution assumes that the only threat came
from the nonconformists. On the contrary, since the middle years of
Elizabeth's reign there had been no lack of Puritans willing to argue
that compromise on the troublesome points of conformity was a lesser
evil than the abandonment of their flocks. As regards the surplice,
Cartwright himself had declared, "The truth is, that I dare not be
author to any, to forsake his pastoral charge for the inconvenience
thereof."[1] Half a century later Francis Quarles, writing of Judgment
Day, was to make much the same point:

> O what an answer will be given by some!
> We have been silenced; canons struck us dumb;
> The Great Ones would not let us feed Thy flock
> Unless we played the fool and wore a frock;
> We were forbid unless we'd yield to sign
> And cross their brows, they say a mark of Thine.

"Ah, cruel shepherds!" added Quarles, "could your conscience serve /
Not to be fools and yet to let them starve?"[2]

However, the youthful conformist might find with greater experience and changed circumstances that his conformity was no longer

tolerable. In 1624 John Davenport could write that he had "baptized many, but never without the sign of the Cross," and that he had "administered the Sacrament of the Lord's Supper, but at no time without the surplice, nor to any but those that kneeled." "Besides," he concluded, "I have persuaded many to Conformity, yea mine own Father." Eight years later when John Cotton was in hiding in London, Thomas Goodwin, Philip Nye, and John Davenport all visited that famous and "very judicious" nonconformist in order to argue him into conformity. But the upshot was the conversion of Davenport to Cotton's principles, and in 1633 Laud reported rather querulously to King Charles that Davenport, "whom I used with all moderation, and about two years since thought I had settled his judgment, having him then at advantage enough to have put extremity upon him, but forbore it," had declared against conformity and departed, Laud believed, for Amsterdam.[3] Many divines were, in effect, radicalized by the events of the 1620's and 1630's, although only a small minority followed Davenport to the New Jerusalem across the seas. To expect the ecclesiastical machinery of previous decades to wring conformity from men whose militancy increased with the years, and to expect unity to result was to indulge in the fondest of dreams.

A second alternative, embodied in the Directions of 1622, had equally grave disadvantages. For one thing, the attempt to turn Sunday afternoon lectures into catechetical exercises was doomed to failure, for it lacked any real sanctions. Against the royal and episcopal encouragement proffered to those who catechized rather than preached—a remote and speculative commodity at best—was placed the solid monetary advantages of a lectureship as well as the immediate benefits of a friendly vestry and congregation. For another, the attempt to restrict the subject matter of sermons to safe, noncontroversial doctrine and application presented both substantive and procedural difficulties. Obvious substantive problems were raised by such phraseology as that in the injunction that forbade the advancing of propositions not "comprehended and warranted in essence, substance, effect, or natural inference" in the Thirty-nine Articles or the Homilies. One man's natural inference could too easily be another's unwarranted assumption. Further, those very "deep points of predestination, election," etc., were for the Puritans not steeped in obscurity but full of the most "comfortable doctrine." Finally, the existing means of enforcement were by their very nature haphazard and inefficient at best. Supervision depended on auditors willing to report the preacher's offense, and sanctions could be invoked only after the sermon had been preached.

King James had suggested a more drastic solution in his praise of Bishop Harsnet's outright suppression of "popular lecturers" in the diocese of Norwich. Suppression, however, if confined as the King proposed to independent lecturers, left untouched the Puritan leaders, the Davenports, Taylors, and Gouges, who were beneficed. Further, unless some correspondingly popular substitute were provided, the policy of suppression would leave unsatisfied the laity's demand for frequent sermons, a demand to which the lectureship had been the logical response.

King Charles's answer was simpler; it was to translate Bishop Mountaigne to Durham and to bring in William Laud. According to Heylyn, Charles

> looked upon the City as the Retreat and Receptacle of the Grandees of the Puritan Faction; the influence which it had, by reason of its Wealth and Trading on all parts of the Kingdom; and upon the Correspondence and Conformity thereof, the welfare of the whole depended: No better way to make them an example of Obedience to the rest of the Subjects, than by placing over them a Bishop of such Parts and Power as they should be unable either to withstand or afraid to offend.[4]

If this was to be the policy, Laud was an obvious choice. He may have been lacking in sublety, in imaginativeness, and in any profound interest in doctrine, perhaps even in that intangible warmth and human sympathy that might have made him a magnetic figure, but he was nevertheless fiercely loyal, honest to a degree beyond most of his contemporaries, and whatever his private worries and doubts, fearless and efficient in his conduct of business. He had, moreover, a policy.

The Church, as he saw it, was challenged on two fronts. First, the patrimony of the Church had been sadly diminished, owing primarily, he thought, to the avarice of self-seeking bishops. Second, and more important, the Church had suffered a loss of power, a loss brought about partly by the neglect of her shepherds, the bishops, who abandoned their charges in order to maneuver for further preferment at Westminster, "partly by the great increase of Chaplains in the Houses of many private Gentlemen, but chiefly by the multitude of Irregular lecturers both in City and Country, whose work it was to undermine as well the Doctrine as the Government of it."[5]

Shortly after the dissolution of Parliament in 1629, Laud, having consulted Bishop Harsnet, forwarded a series of "Considerations for the Better Settling of the Church-Government" to the King.[6] Among other things, he asked that the King have a special care for the lecturers, who "by reason of their pay are the people's creatures and blow the bellows their way," which was "sedition." Laud had at least recognized that the real problem was "the people," at whose behest the lecturers preached. However, Laud, like a physician, was prepared to treat only the symptoms, apparently in the expectation that God or King Charles would somehow deal with the real cause of the disease. He suggested "that afternoon sermons in all parishes may be turned into catechizing," "that every lecturer do read divine service in his surplice before the lecture," that lectures given in market towns "be read by a combination of grave and orthodox divines near adjoining," that corporation lecturers not be allowed to preach until they took on a cure of souls in the town, and that bishops "encourage" their trustworthy clergy "to be present at such lecture sermons as are near them, that so the bishop may have knowledge." Many an embattled Puritan had retreated in the face of episcopal harassment to the safe cover of a tutorship or chaplaincy with a sympathetic layman. This practice, too, Laud proposed to limit by restricting private chaplaincies to the homes of the nobility. Further, Emmanuel and Sidney Sussex, as "nurseries of Puritanism," were to be provided with orthodox masters when opportunity offered. Clearly Laud's was to be a policy of "Thorough" with a vengeance.

Clearly, too, Laud was not inclined toward half-hearted measures. Suppression was to be tried where possible. Where it was not, discouraging additions to the requirements of the Canons of 1604 and the Directions of 1622 were heaped on the lecturer. No longer was the set prayer sufficient, for the lecturer who might otherwise have hoped to escape with twice-yearly displays of conformity now had to read divine service before entering the pulpit. The Directions of 1622 already restricted the subject matter of sermons. Now Laud proposed to enforce this limitation by setting ministers to spying on their neighboring colleagues. These were brutal and drastic proposals, scarcely calculated to increase their author's popularity, but Laud was not the man to shrink in the face of difficulties.

The Puritans' response was predictable. "What less could be aimed at in [Laud's measures] than suppressing the Divine Ordinance of Preaching, or at least a dreadful diminution of the number of Sermons, And what could follow thereupon, but negligence in the Priests, ignorance of the People, Popery and Superstition in the meantime gaining ground on both?"[7] Laud acknowledged "that in the time of the Gospel, God appointed the Foolishness of Preaching ... to be a Means ... by which he will save those that believe." But those were other times. "If the Distempers of the Pulpit should grow in any National Church so high, so Seditious, so Heretical and Blasphemous, so Schismatical and Outrageous, as many of them have been of late in this distracted Church of ours," he wrote, then some substitute had to be found for sermons "which do in a manner teach nothing but Disobedience to Princes and all Authority, under a false pretense of Obedience to God."[8] Laud was at least prepared to take the political implications of Puritan preaching seriously; the efficacy of his countermeasures, however, was another matter altogether.

In December 1629, a few weeks after Laud submitted his proposals, King Charles issued them as royal instructions to both archbishops.[9] A few changes had been incorporated (a town lecturer, for example, need not possess a cure at the time he accepted a corporation lectureship, but only "to profess his willingness to take upon him a living"), but essentially the "Considerations" were published without substantial modification. Laud, who had already conducted a preliminary survey of the London lecturers, promptly summoned all the lecturers from the City and suburbs to a meeting, at which he argued the good that would come from their obedience.[10] On 4 January 1629/30 he instructed his archdeacons to submit a list of all lecturers within their archdeaconries by February 3, and to leave a copy of the new Instructions concerning lecturers with every incumbent, along with an order that another copy was to be delivered to the churchwardens.[11]

The visitation of 1628 and Laud's first survey must have given him an unparalleled picture of the dimensions of his task. In that year, as Table 8 shows, there were approximately 121 lecturers in London, at least 59 of whom were Puritans. In numbers alone his task was far more awesome than Aylmer's or Bancroft's had been, for he faced three times as many lecturers as either of them.

TABLE 8

Lecturers in London: Yearly Estimates, 1628–40

Year	Total	Puritan	Year	Total	Puritan
1628	121	59	1635	88	48
1629	111	58	1636	91	51
1630	102	57	1637	99	52
1631	90	52	1638	88	45
1632	89	51	1639	83	45
1633	88	46	1640	73	42
1634	86	45			

Laud had not waited for the publication of the Instructions in order to begin bringing the London lecturers into some measure of order and discipline. The Visitation Articles for his primary visitation in 1628 do not differ in any important respect from those of Bishop Mountaigne's third visitation, held the preceding year, but the results as manifested in the activity of the Consistory Court reveal a substantial increase in the rigor of their administration. Seventeen lecturers were cited at four sessions of the court held on December 10 and 16, 1628, and on January 3 and 30, 1628/9.[12] In all but two cases, however, these preachers were cited as curates rather than as curates and lecturers; in Laud's initial list most of them appear as lecturers alone. Since most of these preachers were relatively obscure men, they were asked with few exceptions simply to show their licenses and letters of admission. Nevertheless, the number of irregularities revealed must have been fairly disturbing.

Eight lecturers were found to have no license at all. One was Andrew Blackwell, who had been lecturer at St. Christopher le Stocks since 1622 and curate since 1624, and who had already been questioned in 1624 regarding his admission to the cure. He was ordered to produce his letters of ordination and a proper license under pain of the court, and must have succeeded in doing so, for he remained at St. Christopher's at least until 1631 and was properly admitted lecturer at St. Mary at Hill in 1633.[13] Similarly a Mr. English, curate and lecturer at St. Stephen Walbrook, who also lacked a license, may have obtained the required documents, for he was still at St. Stephen's at the time of Laud's second survey in 1629.[14] By contrast, nothing more is heard of Jasper Finnes, curate and lecturer at St. Martin Vintry; or of Mr. Thorpe, curate and lecturer at St. Michael Bassishaw, unless he is the John Thorpe who is listed as curate at St. Botolph Billingsgate in 1637. The Mr. Smith described as an unlicensed curate and lecturer at St. Michael le Querne in 1628 is another shadowy figure, but he may be identical with the Mr. Smith who was preaching the Sunday afternoon lecture at St. Botolph Billingsgate in 1629.[15] Daniel Smart, the curate and lecturer at Holy Trinity Minories since 1626, was found to be unlicensed in 1628 but remained at his post until 1630. John Wilson, curate and lecturer at St. Katherine Coleman since 1625, finally obtained a license to the curacy as a result of the court's demands on 19 January 1628/9.[16] The most startling case, that of Edward Spendlowe, has already been mentioned. He was cited as an unlicensed curate at St. Edmund Lombard Street at the December 10 session of the court. Spendlowe had been curate at St. Edmund's at least since 1598 and had been lecturer at St. Antholin's since 1594. What the vicar-general must have thought when confronted with Spendlowe's case staggers the imagination. The evidence suggests that Spendlowe was not unduly inconvenienced, however, for he was still lecturing at St. Antholin's in 1629, and a new curate was not admitted at St. Edmund's until 1632.[17]

Among the remaining nine, who were not cited as unlicensed but were nevertheless required to show their letters of ordination and admission, at least five can be identified as Puritans. Only one of these, Richard Worsley, who was in trouble for seditious preaching in 1631, experienced any further difficulties under the Laudian regime.[18] As for the others, Thomas Gouge, who served as curate and lecturer at his father's parish, was simply ordered to show by what authority he officiated the cure; he evidently succeeded in satisfying the court, for he remained at St. Anne Blackfriars until 1631.[19] William Holbrooke, who defended the Puritans in a Paul's Cross sermon in 1609 against those known "to vaunt what [they] have done in vexing the godly," had been in trouble in 1613 for holding an unauthorized lecture at St. Leonard's, Bromley. He then went on to lecture at West Ham and was cited for nonconformity there in 1617. By 1620 he was lecturing concurrently at St. Andrew Hubbard, where he was also curate, and from which he was cited as unlicensed in 1628. He was still at St. Andrew's and presumably at West Ham in 1630.[20]

The fourth curate of this group, John Poynter, had lectured at St. Mildred Bread Street for two years when he was cited as unlicensed by the Consistory Court in 1628. For a number of years before he took orders in 1625, Poynter had boarded with John Dodd at Canons Ashby, and though no action was taken against Poynter in 1628, he removed to Hanwell, Dodd's old parish, in 1629 and was lecturing at Wootton Wawen, Warwickshire, in 1630. Four years later, on the advice of Dr. Robert Harris, the former lecturer at St. Saviour's and an old friend of Dodd, Poynter applied to the Mercers' Compay for their lectureship at Huntingdon. This was the lectureship established by a bequest from Richard Fishborne, a former native of Huntingdonshire, who died in 1625. With this lectureship in mind Laud had complained to King Charles in 1633 about the power of lay corporations "to put in or put out any lecturer" as they wished, but despite King Charles's promise to support Laud's efforts to overthrow such lay dependency, the Mercers succeeded in 1634 in appointing Poynter to the lectureship, where he remained until driven out by royalist troops. He then went on to other preferments, several in the gift of Oliver Cromwell, until the Restoration put an end to the career of this distinguished Independent.[21] The fifth curate was Henry Vessey, who had begun his lecture at St. Ethelburga in 1627, shortly after his ordination the previous year. He remained there until at least 1632, when he went on to become curate to Henry Mason, rector of St. Andrew Undershaft and a Puritan moralist whose writings were pronounced "learned and solid" by Sir Simonds D'Ewes. In 1643 Vessey was admitted to the vicarage of Boreham, Essex, where he died in 1648.[22]

Of the fourteen Puritan lecturers summoned before the Consistory Court of the diocese of London in the winter of 1628, only three—Finnes, Thorpe, and Poynter—left London immediately afterward. Had Bishop Laud done no more than draw up the Instructions and stiffen the routine administration of the diocesan court, which was in any case the responsibility of his vicar-general, his reputation as the scourge of the Puritans would be not only unfair but inexplicable.*

---

* Strictly speaking a distinction should be made between the Consistory Court, over which the bishop's official principal presided, and the Court of Audience or Chancery Court, over which either the bishop or his chancellor or commissory general presided. However, the London records are all catalogued as records of the Consistory Court. The Consistory Court Correction Books, which are used extensively in this study, should probably be classified as records of the Court of Audience or Chancery, in that they contain promoted and *ex officio* proceedings, whereas the Consistory Court Act Books seem to contain causes between parties, which were the routine work of the Consistory Court. For a description of the bishop's courts and their functions, see Ron-

Laud's jurisdictional powers, however, were not limited to his ordinary courts: he could and did handle some cases directly, and he had in the Court of High Commission, of which he was a member, far more impressive disciplinary machinery than that available in his diocesan courts. Some eighteen Puritan preachers of London ran afoul of Laud either in causes that he heard personally at Fulham Palace or in causes that he heard in his capacity as a commissioner. It is to these that we must turn for evidence of the success with which Laud carried out his twofold policy of regulation and suppression.

Soon after Laud became Bishop of London, the four Puritans who had signed the letter urging aid to the poor ministers of the Palatinate—Gouge, Davenport, Sibbes, and Taylor—were referred by the High Commission to Laud so that he could deal with them personally at Fulham Palace. Apparently the four escaped with no more than a reprimand for intruding into matters of high policy. William Gouge later testified to the leniency with which Laud dealt with him when he was again brought before the bishop on a complaint concerning his manner of administering communion.[23] Others were neither so cautious nor so diplomatic as Gouge, and suffered accordingly.

Shortly after becoming lecturer at St. Sepulchre's, an Emmanuel graduate, Nathaniel Bernard, prayed at St. Antholin's on 3 May 1629, "Oh Lord, open the eyes of the Queen's majesty, that she may see Jesus Christ, whom she hath pierced with her infidelity, superstition, and idolatry." Such an open breach of the 1622 Directions could hardly go unnoticed by Laud, who promptly hauled the unfortunate Bernard before the High Commission. Bernard was eventually released on making his submission and returned to his lecture. However, he appears to have learned little from his experience, for three years later to the month he preached "a schismatical and seditious" sermon at St. Mary's, Cambridge, that matched his prayer for the Queen in its explicitness. His theme, "God's ordinances for his public worship are the glory of any nation," was unexceptionable enough, but he boldly proceeded to ask, "Is there not a generation of profane men among us who are afraid and ashamed to preach twice on a Lord's day; to preach plainly, powerfully, and spiritually to the souls and consciences

<hr>

ald Marchant, *The Puritans and the Church Courts in the Diocese of York, 1560–1642* (London, 1960), pp. 4–10; and Margaret Bowker, *The Secular Clergy in the Diocese of Lincoln, 1495–1520* (Cambridge, Eng., 1968), pp. 19, 26.

of their people, lest they should be accounted Puritans?"[24] As if this was not dangerous enough, the conclusion was so offensive that the words still rankled ten years later when Laud recalled "his unjust and scandalous application of them to me, which deserved them not."[25] Bernard had said in part:

They who go about to deprive a nation of them [God's ordinances] either wholly, or of their purity, go about to make the nation base and inglorious, and are the enemies and traitors of that nation. Hereby we may learn how to account of those among ourselves (if any such there be), who endeavor to quench the light and abate the glory of our Israel, by bringing their Pelagian errors into the doctrine of our Church established by God, as high altars, crucifixes, bowing to them, and worshiping them, whereby they very shamefully symbolize with the church of Rome, to the irreparable shipwreck of many souls. How can we think that such men are not the enemies of their church and nation?[26]

Whether or not these men were the enemies of Church and State, they certainly were not friends of Nathaniel Bernard. By May 31 the detection had been registered in the London Consistory Court and Bernard had been inhibited. The case was then transferred to the High Commission, where he was excommunicated, fined, and imprisoned until he should recant. On July 21 the Consistory Court ordered the churchwardens of St. Sepulchre's to discontinue the lecture because "divers men have preached and in their sermons committed divers misdemeanors" since Bernard's inhibition. Whether Bernard would ever have preached the required recantation will never be known, for he died in New Prison before 31 January 1632/3.[27]

A month after Bernard's scandalous prayer, Henry Burton, rector and lecturer at St. Matthew Friday Street and already a familiar figure to the High Commission and Privy Council, was suspended by Laud. Burton was made of tougher stuff than Bernard, and although his "malice and boldness" later led to his famous trial along with Bastwick and Prynne in 1637, Burton survived his imprisonment and was restored to freedom by the Long Parliament in 1641.[28] During the same summer of 1629, Laud's episcopal register notes the relaxation of the suspension of another Puritan preacher, James Nalton, who then returned to his curacy and lectureship at St. Mary Colechurch. Nalton, the son of a London minister, went on to a Warwickshire rectory in 1632, but was back in London in 1643, when he was admitted to the sequestered rectory of St. Leonard Foster Lane.[29] It was probably during this year or early in 1630 that Thomas Edwards, whose election as lecturer at St. Botolph Aldgate had been celebrated with bell ringing and wine, experienced some difficulties of an unspecified nature with Bishop Laud. Only a few months before his election he had been forced to preach a sermon recanting some questionable sentiments expressed in an earlier sermon given while Edwards was one of the university preachers at Cambridge. Whatever the causes of his trouble with Laud, no lasting reformation was effected, for the Churchwardens' Accounts for 1631 note payments to Mr. Bracegirdle, the curate, for reading prayers for Edwards, a clear violation of the clause in the 1629 Instructions requiring lecturers to read divine service in surplice and hood before entering the pulpit. Nevertheless, Edwards continued to lecture at St. Botolph's undisturbed until an antiprelatical sermon preached at the Mercers' chapel in 1640 brought him before the High Commission.[30]

The following year, 1630, witnessed neither any sudden reformation on the part of the Puritan lecturers nor any slackening in Laud's dogged attempt to secure a disciplined and orthodox church. Meredith Mayday, who has already been mentioned, was prohibited in that year from preaching within the diocese. Mayday's prohibition, however, did not apparently constitute a firm precedent. On 22 October 1630 Abraham Grymes, lecturer at St. Nicholas Acons and at St. Katherine Cree, was suspended by Laud for a sermon preached at St. Martin in the Fields in which "he took occasion to treat of the name of Jesus, and . . . did ask, why should the name of Jesus have more reverence than the name of Christ?" Grymes appears not to have taken his suspension very seriously, for a report on Essex nonconformists, dated 25 November 1630, contains the following item: "One Mr. Grymes, a lecturer in London, preached in Brentwood and affirmed that bowing the head at the name of Jesus was flat idolatry." In spite of this flagrant flouting of the order inhibiting him, Grymes was released in December, following his submission.[31]

On 23 December 1630 John Humphrey, Deputy Governor of the Massachusetts Bay Company, wrote to Isaac Johnson of Charlestown that "the Bishop of London hath silenced many godly men of late; this last Monday Mr. Archer is by him silenced for all England." Archer, who had been properly licensed to preach anywhere in the

City on 28 September 1627, lectured at both Allhallows Lombard Street and St. Antholin's; his interrogation before Laud and Arthur Duck, the vicar-general, is carefully recorded in the episcopal register.[32]

Unlike many Puritan preachers, Archer was willing to catechize, but as Laud pointed out, the form drawn up by Archer did not even approach that prescribed by the Book of Common Prayer and thus violated both the Church's canons and the King's late Instructions. In fact, the excerpts recorded in the episcopal register testify to the high level of theological sophistication Puritans expected of their children, and suggests that some Puritans were quite as prepared to use catechizing as the sermon to convey their theological position. Archer was also charged with preaching "against the bowing at the name of Jesus" and with expressing himself "in a most doubtful and ambiguous manner" when Laud enjoined him to explain the canonical view to his congregation. Laud asked Archer point-blank "whether he held it lawful to bow at the name Jesus, and whether he had read over those Fathers which his lordship had formerly quoted to him out of Dr. Andrewes', the late Lord Bishop of Winchester's, books, to which he answered that he had and found no authors that did allow thereof." Archer was promptly suspended, but four months later the suspension was relaxed, following his submission. Within a month the Feoffees for Impropriations, who were also the collectors for the St. Antholin's lectures, had obtained for Archer the vicarage of All Saints, Huntingdon, at the request of Gabriel Barbour, a feoffee and the donor of the advowson, and with the ready consent of the townspeople. It is no wonder that Laud's diary for 1630 records, as the second item in a list of things he hoped to accomplish, the destruction of the Feoffees. As for Archer, he remained at Huntingdon until 1637, when, having had his fill of Laud's church, he left England to become pastor of the English congregation at Arnheim.[33]

Sometime during 1630 or 1631 Thomas Foxley, another St. Antholin's lecturer, was questioned by Laud but released after promising to conform. In 1635 or 1636 he appeared before the High Commission, and at about the same time his lecture at St. Martin in the Fields, which he had preached since 1629, was discontinued, ostensibly because of the plague. Foxley appeared before the High Commission again in 1640 but was released within a year by order of the House of

Commons.[34] Early in 1632 Elias Crabtree, who had been curate and lecturer at St. Lawrence Pountney for twelve years, was articled against in the High Commission and required by Laud to preach a sermon expressing his true intent to conform, which he apparently did, since he remained at St. Lawrence until he was admitted to a sequestered Norfolk living in 1648. Later in 1632 William Martyn, a St. Antholin's lecturer since 1629, petitioned Laud to lift the suspension imposed on him for a sermon preached at St. Leonard Foster Lane. The petition was presumably granted, for Martyn was admitted curate and lecturer at Highgate Chapel on 7 March 1634/5, a preferment he held concurrently with his St. Antholin's lecture during the later 1630's.[35]

William Prynne mentions three others questioned or suspended by Laud during these years: a Mr. Ward, a Mr. Jones, and James Gardiner. It is impossible to identify Mr. Ward with any certainty, but he may possibly be the Richard Ward who was lecturing at St. Antholin's and at St. Benet Gracechurch in the later 1630's.[36] Mr. Jones, who was punished by the High Commission "for scandalous abusing the Queen under a form of praying for her, and for divers other articles that were against him," may be the John Jones who was curate and lecturer at St. Michael Bassishaw from 1624 until sometime in the early 1630's, and who then reappears lecturing at St. Pancras Soper Lane in 1634, at St. Lawrence Jewry in 1635, and later at St. Margaret Lothbury.[37] James Gardiner was also an active independent lecturer, preaching at St. Bartholomew Exchange from 1623 until 1628, at St. Mary Hill in 1627 and 1628, at St. Peter Cornhill from 1628 to 1633, and at St. Clement Eastcheap, where he was also curate, from 1634 to 1639, when he finally left London for an Essex rectory.[38] Finally, Arthur Jackson, the Puritan parson and lecturer at St. Michael Wood Street from the early 1620's until the late 1640's, was remonstrated with by Laud for his refusal to read the Book of Sports, but Jackson, "a quiet and peaceable man," was apparently not suspended.[39]

In his annual account of his province for the year 1632 Archbishop Abbot was able to announce, to the King's certain pleasure, that "of Arminian points there is no dispute; and ordinations of ministers, for aught that I can learn, are canonically observed; the rules for lecturers are strictly kept." Abbot concluded sonorously, "There is not in the Church of England left any inconformable minister, which appeareth; and yet the lord bishops of London and Lincoln have been forced to deprive two or three, whom no time can tame, nor instruction conquer." The Puritans took a different view, needless to say. A year or two later Samuel Ward, the famous lecturer of Ipswich, bemoaned the silencing of so many godly ministers and warned his fellow townsmen to beware an alteration in religion. "The Church of England was ready to ring the changes," he announced, "religion and the Gospel stood on tiptoes, ready to be gone." "Oh, how be our weekly lecturers suppressed in divers countries," wailed Nehemiah Wallington, the pious turner of St. Leonard Eastcheap; the "lordy prelates"

have likewise lately shut up the mouths of sundry of our most godly, powerful, painful ministers, out of mere malice to religion and the people's salvation, contrary to the very laws of God and the realm; strictly prohibited, under pain of suspension, in sundry dioceses, all afternoon sermons on the Lord's Day, that so the profane vulgar might have more time to dance, play, revel, drink, and profane God's sabbaths.[40]

The historian may perhaps be pardoned if he questions the grounds for both the archbishop's optimism and the Puritan's hysterical prognostications. Certainly Laud could have had few illusions about the success of his campaign. His annual account to King Charles in 1633 records, in his usual businesslike fashion, the excommunication of Nathaniel Ward, rector of Stoneham, Essex; the process against John Beddle, rector of Barnstone in the same shire, who conformed; and the departure of John Davenport for Amsterdam. Clearly celebrations of victory were premature, although Laud could record a few gains. In 1632 he was able to note in his diary his victory over the Feoffees. In 1633 he obtained from the King an order against the ordaining of ministers without an ecclesiastical title. Ostensibly this measure was an answer to "complaints . . . concerning the multitude of both unlearned and unworthy ministers, which pester the church and are always the causes of great scandal." Actually, as Heylyn noted, the measure was "much inveighed against," for "neither any lecture, nor any possibility of being entertained as a chaplain in the houses of noblemen or others of the inferior gentry, could be allowed for a title, and consequently no orders to be given hereafter under those capacities."[41]

However, Heylyn's claim that "from henceforth we hear but little of such vagrant Ministers and Trencher-Chaplains (the old brood being worn out)" is patently absurd.[42] Two months after Archbishop Laud dispatched his letter from Lambeth, John Sprint, who had held no preferment previously, was admitted lecturer at Hampstead and was issued a preaching license valid for the whole diocese. This Puritan preacher never did hold a benefice and remained a lecturer until his ejection in 1662.[43] Between 1634 and the end of 1639 at least three Puritans and one Laudian were admitted to London lectureships as their first preferments: one of them, Edmund Brome, had been ordained by the Bishop of Norwich in 1632, but another, Lazarus Seaman, who obtained deacon's orders in 1628, does not appear to have been ordained a priest when admitted to lecture at St. Martin Ludgate in 1634; Seaman was also chaplain to Algernon Percy, Earl of Northumberland. Seaman may have avoided the whole issue of ordination without title simply by avoiding ordination.[44] Be that as it may, it is true enough that most preachers who first lectured in the City during the later 1630's also held curacies, probably as a result of Laud's campaign against the independent lecturer. As an awkward attempt to limit the sphere of lay influence, however, the measure seems to have been something of a failure.

More certainly a failure was Laud's attempt to make obvious and lasting inroads in the ranks of London's Puritan lecturers. Approximately 70 Puritans lectured in London during the six years of his regime. Of these 70 only eighteen seem to have been questioned for their nonconformity, and of the eighteen only one, Meredith Mayday, was prohibited from preaching in the diocese; another, Nathaniel Bernard, died in prison, and a third, John Davenport, left his post for safety overseas. It might be argued, of course, that a brief suspension or other minor disciplinary action was sufficient to bring these men to conformity, but the number of recidivists in the group— Gouge, Burton, Edwards, and Foxley—does not permit any such assumption. To be sure, only 46 Puritan lecturers appear to have been in London in 1633, as against 58 in 1629, a decline that can undoubtedly be attributed, insofar as it does not reflect merely a lack of information, to the uncongenial atmosphere created by Laud. Still, these 46 managed to preach about 60 sermons each week within an urban area of only a square mile or so, a situation that Laud could scarcely have regarded with equanimity.

Some years ago H. R. Trevor-Roper offered one explanation for the absence of a spectacular purge:

Laud could not afford to be as rigid as he is sometimes represented to be in his treatment of lecturers. The insufficiency of orthodox and beneficed clergy could not be remedied all at once, and, like his own bishops later, he frequently had to sacrifice the orthodoxy which he preferred to the moderate Puritanism which was the most he could get. So a vague pledge of conformity was generally sufficient to secure the restitution of a suppressed lecturer.[45]

Such a degree of accommodation and compromise as this explanation implies hardly seems in character. Further, since the lectureship patronage was entirely in the hands of the laity, Laud could exercise little control over the religious complexion of the lecturers. There were no legal grounds for refusing a Puritan's admission to a lectureship, so long as he was properly ordained and willing to subscribe. Moreover, there was no lack of available orthodox divines. As Mark Curtis has pointed out, by the early seventeenth century Oxford and Cambridge were turning out graduates trained for the ministry at a faster rate than livings became available, and London in particular experienced no dearth of orthodox churchmen in the 1630's.[46] The point is simply that the presence or absence of orthodox candidates was immaterial; parish vestries that preferred Puritan preachers did not on the whole hire orthodox Anglicans, certainly not Laudian churchmen, no matter how able or well qualified.

It seems more likely that Laud was trapped by his own preconceptions. His aim was unity in the Church, and unity was to be obtained primarily by uniformity in rites and ceremonies: hence his hated ceremonialism and his insistence on outward conformity. It was an administrator's, rather than an ideologue's, answer to the problem of unity, and it contained an obvious weakness. Laud could on occasion be both petty and harsh, but he does not seem to have deliberately twisted his own rules. When faced with a Puritan lecturer who submitted, who acknowledged his error and consented to recant or reform, Laud had very little choice but to let him go with an admonition to conform in the future.[47]

William Gouge's letter to Laud in 1631 reveals the essentials of the bishop's quandary. In it Gouge expresses his high esteem for Laud's favor; deplores and denies the libelous report that he has traduced the bishop or his policies; and appeals to Laud's well-known fairness in refusing to condemn on hearsay evidence. He has always observed Laud to be prudent, moderate and courteous, and patient and forbearing in his dealing with nonconformists. He singles out for special praise the fact that Laud has never been known to deprive any but those who absolutely refused to conform. And he concludes by observing that all England is aware of Laud's special grace to himself. One can easily imagine what Laud made of this disingenuous letter, and how intense his frustration must have been in the face of such insolent compliance. In the course of his visitation at the end of 1632, a delegation from Colchester requested the admission of William Bridges of Emmanuel to be their lecturer; Laud is reported to have angrily replied, "When you want one, you must go first to Dr. Gouge and to Dr. Sibbes, and then you come to me: I scorn to be so used. I'll never have him to lecture in my diocese."[48]

When Abbot died, in 1633, Laud became Archbishop of Canterbury, and his protégé, William Juxon, succeeded him as Bishop of London; but there was no real change in policy. In 1634 Laud was able to inform the King that "the bishop of London visited his diocese this Year, the city and Middlesex in person," and in the course of "his visitation he found divers complaints about inconformity to the Church discipline; but the proofs came home only against four, three curates and a vicar." None of the four appears to have been a City lecturer. One London lecturer, Henry Roborough, the preacher at St. Leonard Eastcheap, was before the High Commission during the spring and early summer of 1634, but the extant Act Book gives no clue of the nature of the case against him. Roborough, at any rate, was still preaching at St. Leonard's in the 1640's and eventually replaced the sequestered parson, Abraham Colfe. Early in the following year Anthony Burgess, a Fellow of Emmanuel, having failed to secure a preaching license and admission to the curacy of St. Mary Magdalen Milk Street, was forced to give up his lectureship there after a month. Before the year was out he was admitted to the living at Sutton Coldfield, Warwickshire, and in 1643, when he returned to London as a member of the Westminster Assembly, he was promptly elected vicar of St. Lawrence Jewry.[49]

The year 1635 was to give substance to the widespread complaints about "inconformity" that Juxon had reported to Laud the year before. Out of five London lecturers dealt with by Juxon "for breach of the canons of the Church in sermons, or practice, or both," three had held livings before.[50] John Viner, who had replaced Nathaniel Waker as lecturer at St. Lawrence Jewry in 1633, continued to hold his benefice at Kinnersley, Herefordshire, despite the request of the vestry of St. Lawrence that he give it up. When he left the lecture in September 1635, it may have been as much a result of his trouble with the vestry as of his trouble with Juxon. Nevertheless, after withdrawing to Kinnersley for a short time, he was back in London, lecturing at St. Botolph Aldgate, a privilege for which the vestry was forced to bribe the incumbent into acquiescence at the rate of £20 a year.[51] Viner does not seem to have been in trouble again; possibly the orthodox parson had too great a financial stake in Viner's survival to risk reporting him to the authorities. Another lecturer questioned by Juxon, John Goodwin, was Davenport's successor as vicar and lecturer at St. Stephen Coleman Street, and had previously been rector of East Rainham, but he, unlike Viner, had resigned his living before coming to London. Goodwin was again to be in trouble with Juxon in 1638 and 1639 for "some over-nice curiosities" preached "concerning the imputation of Christ's righteousness" in clear violation of the 1622 Directions. These sermons represented the latest stage in a long debate over a number of disputed theological points that had preoccupied London Puritans since 1614, when George Walker had first questioned the orthodoxy of Anthony Wotton's faith. Goodwin's mistake had been to carry the controversy into the pulpit. He nevertheless managed to retain his preferments until differences with his parishioners at St. Stephen's brought about his departure in 1645.[52] The third lecturer questioned by Juxon, John Stoughton, had, like Goodwin, replaced an eminent predecessor when he became perpetual curate and lecturer at St. Mary Aldermary in 1632 on the death of Thomas Taylor. Stoughton had previously held a Somerset living, but despite the appeals of John Winthrop, who hoped to entice Stoughton to the safer shores of New England, he was to remain at St. Mary's until his death in 1639.[53]

The other two convented before Juxon in 1635 were younger men. Andrew Molen (or Moleigne) was admitted curate and lecturer at St. Swithin's in 1633 and remained there until 1647, when he became the intruded minister at St. Giles in the Fields. Sydrach Simpson, curate and lecturer at St. Margaret New Fish Street since 1629, managed to survive Juxon's harassment in 1635, but in 1638 he followed the well-worn path of the Puritan Independent and left for Holland, although he was back again lecturing at St. Margaret's and at St. Anne Blackfriars in 1641.[54] All five preachers, so Laud claimed, "promised amendment for the future, and submission to the Church in all things, [and] my lord [Juxon] very moderately forbore further proceeding against them."[55]

During the same year Juxon suspended two lecturers who "willfully persisted" in their nonconformity. One, John Wood, "a wild turbulent preacher, and formerly censured in the high commission court," may be the lecturer of that name who had preached at St. Andrew Holborn since at least 1628. If so, Wood must have ceased his obduracy, and Juxon must have relaxed his suspension, for Wood was still at St. Andrew's in 1637.[56] The other suspended preacher was Edward Sparrowhawk, an Emmanuel graduate who had previously held a Suffolk curacy. When he came to London cannot be determined, for his name does not appear in the subscription book, and he may not have been properly admitted. In any event, he was suspended from his lecture and curacy at St. Mary Woolchurch in 1635 for preaching against bowing at the name of Jesus. Sparrowhawk withdrew to Coggeshall, Essex, where John Dodd and his son Nehemiah were vicar and curate respectively. Two years later he was reported to be maintaining conventicles at Coggeshall and to have preached the delivery of the Christian people from "the heavy impositions and cursed adorations" inflicted upon them. John Dodd himself had preached that "he thought in his conscience that the cause of the plague was the mixture of religion and the idolatry and superstition that was pressed in amongst us." The informant noted the rather ominous fact that the people of Coggeshall had refused to pay both the first and second levies of Ship Money, the "heavy impositions" Sparrowhawk had inveighed against.[57]

For all the disciplinary activity of 1635, the goal of unity, of a church united by its seemly practice of a uniform liturgy and by its submissive loyalty to a king who ruled by divine right, remained as elusive as ever. At the end of three years of conscientious rule Juxon was still faced with approximately the same number of Puritan lecturers in London as he had found when he succeeded Laud in 1633. Nevertheless, Laud and Juxon seemed prepared to go on patching their leaky vessel as long as it stayed afloat.

At Juxon's visitation in 1636 Dr. Cornelius Burgess, a royal chaplain and the rector and lecturer at St. Magnus since 1625, preached a sermon to the clergy at St. Alphage, in which he condemned the bishops for conniving to spread Arminianism and popery. Although he was convented before the High Commission for these "divers insolent passages," he was back lecturing and officiating in his parish in 1639.[58] Also in 1636 George Hughes, who had been lecturer at Allhallows Bread Street since 1628, was suspended by Laud, presumably in the High Commission. Hughes briefly contemplated emigration but was persuaded to remain by John Dodd of Fawsley, who obtained for him a chaplaincy with Lord Brooke at Warwick Castle. He also became chaplain to the Earl of Bedford, who presented him to the living at Tavistock, and in 1642 the House of Commons admitted him to the lectureship at Plymouth.[59] The Puritans were still capable of looking after their own. With a regularity that must have dismayed their episcopal opponents, Puritan preachers retreated before episcopal discipline only to reappear when the storm broke, embittered by their former treatment and prepared to preach more radical change than any had contemplated previously.

Archbishop Laud wrote in his annual account for 1637 that Juxon still "complains of some inconformable men which his chancellor hath met with in this his last visitation." But, he added, "they have received such censure as their faults deserved, or else submitted themselves." However, a survey dated November 1637 of the various clerical irregularities found in London suggests how much remained to be done. It noted that many communion tables still had not been railed in and that some still stood in the chancel; that communion was administered to many in their pews, which were so constructed that they could not receive it kneeling; and that baptisms, which should have taken place after the second lesson, were generally conducted following the Sunday afternoon sermon. Specifically, John Goodwin of St. Stephen's, Adoniram Byfield, curate and lecturer at Allhallows Staining, and Joseph Simonds, who had lectured at a number of London parishes before becoming rector of St. Martin Ironmonger Lane, were all charged with irregularities; Henry Burton's curate was said to "pray before and after sermons loosely and factiously, as for the conversion of the Queen, for a neighbor minister in persecution," etc.; and James Palmer, vicar and lecturer at St. Bride's since 1616, was accused of omitting at times the prayer for the bishops and the rest of

the clergy and of occasionally neglecting to wear his gown and surplice when he read service. Palmer, Byfield, and Goodwin all remained in London, but in 1638 Laud reported that Symonds had "utterly fallen from the Church of England, hath abandoned his benefice,
and gone beyond the seas; and so deprived in September last past."[60]

Obadiah Sedgwick, curate and lecturer at St. Mildred Bread Street
since 1630, seems to have been the only London lecturer among those
censured by Juxon in 1637 "as their faults deserved." He was suspended but two years later was presented by Robert Rich, Earl of
Warwick, to the vicarage of Coggeshall, Essex, the living where John
Dodd had presided since he left St. Stephen Coleman Street in 1609,
and which four years earlier had sheltered Edward Sparrowhawk. By
the end of 1641 Sedgwick was back at St. Mildred's preaching against
episcopacy.[61]

By 1638 Laud's regime had had a whole decade in which to work
a reformation in London. Although there were still more than 40
Puritan lecturers in the City, Heylyn wrote, admittedly with less than
his usual perspicacity:

Little trouble could be feared from the Lecturers, as they now were Regulated. The greatest part of those who had been Superinducted into other
Men's Cures...had deserted their Stations, because they would not read
the Common Prayers in their Hoods and Surplices...; such as remained,
being founded on a constant or certain Maintenance, or seeing how little
was to be gotten by a fiery or ungoverned Zeal, became more pliant and
conformable.

With an optimism that proved to be unjustified he concluded, "Not
a Lecturer of this kind found to stand out in some great Dioceses to
keep up the spirits of the faction and create disturbances." Clearly
Heylyn had described what should have been the state of affairs had
the Laudian system really worked, but a glance at Laud's annual accounts for the remaining years of the decade is sufficient to expose the
fatuity of any such sanguine assessment. The best Laud could say about
his own diocese of Canterbury in 1638 was that he had not found
"either any increase or decrease of papists or puritans in the diocese."[62]

As for London, not quite all the independent lecturers had "deserted their Stations" or lapsed into docility, for in 1638 John Cardell,
lecturer at Allhallows Lombard Street for two years, was briefly
suspended.[63] However, the real troublemakers were the lecturing incumbents, those with the most to lose. George Walker, rector of St.

John Evangelist and lecturer at St. Helen Bishopsgate, was imprisoned by the Star Chamber for a sermon in which he set out to prove that it was "sin to obey the greatest monarchs in things which are against the command of God." Walker was released by the Long Parliament in 1641 and returned to his rectory and lectureship, where he remained until his death in 1651.[64] In 1639 Laud noted that Daniel Votier, parson of St. Peter Westcheap, had been charged with "divers inconformities, and promised reformation, as Mr. Symonds also did, but being now called into the high commission, order is to be taken for the officiating of his cure, till it shall appear whether he will desert it or no, for he also is gone beyond the seas." John Goodwin at St. Stephen's was again in trouble for a sermon on the imputation of Christ's righteousness.[65]

In fact, by 1639 the bankruptcy of Laud's policy was evident for all to see, but the archbishop, with that lack of imagination that was part of his strength, refused to recognize it. In June 1638 it had been reported that at All Saints, Northampton, "Some very lately cut the rail ... that was about the Lord's board in pieces, and brought down the Lord's table into the middle of the chancel." By 1639 this kind of reaction to the storm that had broken in the North had become general. "Many that were brought to good order for receiving of the holy communion, where the rails stand before the table, are now of late fallen off, and refuse to come up thither to receive," Laud reported to the King, "and the same is now commonly fallen out in divers other dioceses." To this evidence of the collapse of his work he responded like a latter-day King Knut, commanding the tides. "But this," he wrote, "God willing, I shall take care of, and order as well as I can, and with as much speed."[66]

God was evidently not willing, but there is something impressive, if also rather grotesque, about the last days of the Laudian regime. While Church and State prepared to battle for their very existence, Daniel Votier returned to England and was "forthwith attached" by the court of High Commission on 11 June 1640, "and brought to finish his answer to the articles formerly objected against him" in 1638. A month later the troublesome Thomas Foxley was again brought before the same court, as was Thomas Edwards, for a seditious sermon preached at Mercers' Chapel.[67]

The convocation met during these same months, and at its conclusion published the first new canons promulgated since 1604. The

Canon "Of Preaching for Conformity" is indicative of the defensive position in which the Church found itself.

Whereas the preaching of order and decency according to St. Paul's rule, doth conduce to edification; it is required that all preachers (as well beneficed men as others) shall positively and plainly preach and instruct the people in their public sermons twice in the year at least, that the rites and ceremonies now established in the Church of England are lawful and commendable; and that they the said people and others ought to conform themselves in their practice to all the said rites and ceremonies, and that the people and others ought willingly to submit themselves unto the authority and government of the Church, as it is now established under the king's majesty. And if any preacher shall refuse or neglect to do according to this canon, let him be suspended.[68]

Why it should have been imagined that new canons could accomplish what years of rule had failed to bring about is difficult to conceive. Having contributed in large measure to the creation of a revolutionary situation, Laud and his colleagues evidently hoped to legislate it out of existence.

Subsequently, Bishop Juxon drew up and published articles for his triennial visitation, which, needless to say, never took place. As might be expected, Juxon was concerned to discover whether there were any "who doth affirm and teach that the Thirty-nine Articles . . . are in any part superstitious or erroneous, or such as he may not with a good conscience subscribe unto"; who teach and affirm that the form of worship prescribed in the Prayer Book "is corrupt, superstitious, or unlawful worship of God, or containeth anything repugnant to Scriptures"; or who teach "that the rites and ceremonies of the Church . . . are wicked, antichristian, or superstitious, or such as being commanded by lawful Authorities, may not with good conscience be approved [or] used . . . by men who are zealously and godly affected."[69]

The lecturers as usual were to be subjected to careful scrutiny. In addition to the standard queries concerning licensing and dress and the use of the prescribed prayer and service, Juxon wanted to know whether the lecturers "impugn or confute any doctrine formerly delivered in the same, or in any church near adjoining" without his bishop's advice and permission. Following the three articles on lecturers, Juxon concluded with an omnibus question: "Doth your Lecturer conform himself to the Laws, Ordinances, and Rites Ecclesiastical established by the Church of England?" In the article on catechizing it is further asked: "Are the afternoon Sermons in your parish (if you had any formerly) turned into Catechizing by way of questions and answers according to the King's Instructions?"[70] Although the outright abolition of the Sunday afternoon lecturer seemed clearly implied by the 1629 Instructions, in this instance King Charles was more generous and accommodating than the Laudians. In 1639 Laud had passed along a question from the Bishop of Peterborough, who "craves to receive direction, whether he shall command them to catechize only, and not preach, because your majesty's instruction seems to be strict on this point." Charles had replied, "So that Catechizing be first duly performed, let them have a Sermon after that, if they desire it." Apparently on the very eve of revolution Laud and Juxon had no intention of taking advantage of the compromise contained in the King's instruction, even though it would have enabled them to meet the Puritan objection that they aimed not at catechizing as such but at the suppression of preaching.[71]

Juxon's policy toward the lecturers, as implied in his articles, was not novel. He evidently felt neither a need to add to the measures introduced since 1604, nor a need to modify or retract them in the light of the events of 1640. Had Laud been successful in regulating the lecturers where he could not suppress them, it might be argued that no more was needed than to codify and enforce measures that had already proved their worth. In view of the failure of Laud's policy, this rigid adherence to the past seems only one more sign of the bankruptcy of the regime. It could neither advance, for no new ideas were forthcoming, nor retreat; the determination to rule remained, but the capacity, the ability to meet new challenges with new policies, was gone.

Juxon's articles do contain one innovation. Whereas it had been sufficient in 1622 to limit the subject matter of sermons and to forbid preaching on high policy or disputed theological points, Juxon now asked whether "your Parson, Vicar, Curate, or Lecturer (if you have any) ... preach the Doctrine of obedience and the King's authority according to the Canons published and set out by the late holy Synod."[72] Recognition of the royal supremacy and loyalty to the Crown had been professed by Puritan and Separatist alike since the earliest days of Elizabeth's reign.[73] That it should now be in question is indicative of the widespread malaise of the times.

Futile though such a measure was, however, its concerns were real ones; conspiracy was very much in the air. Had Juxon's visitation taken place, many parishes, if they had made true returns, would have had to answer in the affirmative the following query from the visitation articles: "Doth any Priests or Ministers of the Word of God ... meet together in any private house or elsewhere to consult upon any course to be taken by them or by any other, ... which may any way tend to the impeaching or depraving of the Church of England, ... or any part of the Government or Discipline in the Church of England now established?" In September, it was claimed, Calybute Downing, vicar of Hackney, was set "to feel the pulse of the city." Preaching before the assembled brotherhood of the Artillery Garden, he maintained "that for the defense of religion, and reformation of the church, it was lawful to take up arms against the king."[74]

A month before, on August 6, while Pym's friends were meeting at Gray's Inn and Warwick House, the leading Puritan preachers of London met at John Downham's house at St. Bartholomew Exchange to organize a petition against the canons and the "etcetera oath." Those mentioned as attending, with "divers others," were Downham, who had preached the William Jones "Golden Lecture" since 1616; Cornelius Burgess, rector and lecturer at St. Magnus; Edmund Calamy, the famous Essex preacher who had succeeded John Stoughton as parson and lecturer at St. Mary Aldermanbury in 1639; John Goodwin, Davenport's successor as vicar and lecturer at St. Stephen Coleman Street; Arthur Jackson, rector and lecturer at St. Michael Wood Street; Richard Browne, rector of St. Gabriel Fenchurch; and Charles Offspring, rector and lecturer at St. Antholin's.[75] The purpose of the meeting soon lost its importance as it was overtaken by events, but the meeting itself had great symbolic significance. With the exception of Gouge and Downham, the great leaders of the 1620's—Preston, Sibbes, Taylor, Stock, and Davenport—had all passed from the scene. The twelve intervening years of Laud's rule had served only to create a new leadership and to harden it in the crucible of repression. In 1640 the Puritan brotherhood of preachers again took the offensive, strengthened by their years of trial, and prepared not only to challenge the Laudian church, but also to act as the chief agents molding public opinion in support of Parliament.[76]

In the final analysis Laud's policy failed because it was based on a false premise. The Puritan lecturer was not the cause of disaffection in the Church, but the result. The Reformed faith created a need for an educated and preaching clergy, and when the public authorities failed to satisfy that need, free enterprise and voluntary associations stepped in to meet the demand. Had Puritanism been entirely a clerical movement, repression might have succeeded; alternatively, had lay support come chiefly from the lower ranks of the social order, the Puritans might have survived, as the Separatists did, only as a semi-underground movement existing precariously on the fringes of society. However, since that distant day when Thomas Wood, the friend of the Hastings family and of the Earl of Leicester, had berated Secretary Cecil for permitting Parker's expulsion of the City Puritans, influential support had never been lacking. This is not to imply that religious fervor and ideological commitment were insignificant; the point is simply that fervor and commitment without powerful lay support, however capable of producing inspiring martyrs, would not have produced the Puritan movement as we know it.

Certainly the Puritan preachers knew to whom they owed their survival. After preaching his inflammatory sermon at the Artillery Garden, Downing, "for fear of being questioned (for as yet it was not lawful to preach treason), retired privately to the Earl of Warwick's house in Essex, the common rendezvous of all schismatical preachers."[77] And a safe retreat was by no means the only kind of support that lay patrons provided. An aspiring preacher from London might have his university career partly financed by a livery company exhibition. The clerical friends of the master or fellows of his college might find him his first preferment, or, failing that, he could return to the City and compete on the strength of his preaching ability for one of the preferments in lay control. Even at the end of his days the Puritan preacher might find solace among his lay friends. When John Preston knew he was dying, he withdrew from his London lectureship to the home of Sir Richard Knightley at Fawsley, Northamptonshire, where he was visited by Lord Saye and where his spiritual needs were ministered to by John Dodd, one of the Puritan patriarchs.[78]

Only two alternatives open to Laud offered any real chance of success in dealing with the Puritan lecturers in London or anywhere else, and both were beyond his power. One was to launch a frontal attack on the system of lay patronage, which would have placed him in conflict not only with the aspirations of vestries, merchant companies, and town corporations, of powerful aristocrats, gentry, and merchants, but also with the fundamental property rights of the laity. The other was to drive a wedge between the Puritan preachers and their lay supporters. This is what in fact happened later, as a result of the disillusionment of the wars and Interregnum and the astute maneuvering of the Anglican leadership at the Restoration. But Laud had no such leverage, and in the end his constant harassment alienated the very conservative opinion that should have been the bulwark of the Established Church. The most fitting epitaph to his efforts to control or suppress the Puritan lecturers was pronounced in a speech in Parliament in 1641, not by Lord Saye or one of the other Puritan grandees, but by Lucius Cary, Viscount Falkland, who shortly afterward gave his life for a cause he scarcely believed in. He is reported to have said of the Laudian bishops:

A little search will find them to have been the destruction of Unity under the pretense of Uniformity; To have brought in Superstition and Scandal under titles of Reverence and Decency; To have defiled our Church by adorning our Churches; To have slackened the strictness of that Union which was formerly between us and those of our Religion beyond the Seas, An Action as unpolitic as ungodly; Or we shall find them to have resembled the Dog in the Manger, to have neither preached themselves, nor employed those that should, nor suffered those that would; To have brought in Catechizing only to thrust out Preaching, and cried down Lectures by the name of Factions, either because ... their industry in that duty appeared as a reproof to their neglect of it, or with the intention to have brought in darkness, that they might the easier sow their tares while it was night.[79]

But the Laudians, for all that they had "cried down lectures," had not destroyed them, and what "tares" the bishops had succeeded in sowing had constantly been exposed in the bitter invective that came from the Puritan pulpits in London itself. There were more Puritan lecturers in the City in 1640 than in any year before 1626. The attempt to limit controversy in the pulpit had simply given it focus, and the attempt to repress the preachers had succeeded only in heightening their militancy to the point where some were prepared to preach revolution.

9

The Years of Puritan Triumph, 1640-62

THE commencement of the Long Parliament ushered in the last great age of the lectureship. As late as 11 June 1640 the Court of High Commission, in an atmosphere of business-as-usual, ordered that Daniel Votier, who had recently returned from exile, should be attached and "wrought" to finish his answers to the articles first brought against him two years before "within the time usual in such like cases."[1] The answers of the suspended rector and lecturer of St. Peter Westcheap were never perfected; the records of the court break off; and within a few months the Long Parliament met and rang down the curtain on the court, the new canons, and the rest of the panoply of Laudian power.

The new Parliament's first act was to propose a public fast, an occasion duly observed in the House of Commons with sermons preached by the eminent Puritans Cornelius Burgess and Stephen Marshall. Essentially those first fast-day sermons, soon printed by order of Parliament, called for a new covenant with God, but in the epistle dedicatory to Burgess's sermon, addressed to the House of Commons, the two preachers advanced a "joint and earnest suit" of their own. While praying that God would steer all their "weighty consultations by His own counsel, to His own glory," to make them "the most successful and glorious House of Commons that ever sat in the High Court," the two preachers saw that glory "chiefly" in the protecting and perfecting of "our true palladium, the true religion," and the chief means to that end in the "erecting, maintaining, protecting, and encouraging of an able, godly, faithful, zealous, profitable preaching ministry" and in a "faithful, judicious, and zealous magistracy" to "back such a ministry."[2]

An answer to part of their suit was not long in coming. Within a week the committee of religion, chaired by Sir Edward Dering, was appointed "to receive complaints from oppressed ministers"; even before the first fast day the House of Commons had ordered the release of Henry Burton, although it would be another two years before he was restored to his lectureship.[3] As Thomas Knyvett wrote home to a friend in Norfolk on 24 November 1640, "Now reformation goes on again as hot as a toast," and he added, "If thou didst but hear what sermons are preached to the Parliament men, thou wouldst bless thyself."[4] In effect, from the opening of the Long Parliament those Puritans who commanded London pulpits were for the first time free to preach without fear of episcopal censure.

Positive policies to encourage a preaching ministry were another matter; they came only piecemeal and gradually. The House of Commons had already been receiving petitions for some months requesting the restoration of suspended and deprived ministers or the punishment of "malignants" when on 6 September 1641 it granted the parishioners of Stepney permission to "set up a lecture at their own charge every Sunday." Two days later on a motion by Oliver Cromwell this precedent was set forth as a general principle. The House ordered that "it shall be lawful for the parishioners of any parish in the kingdom of England and dominion of Wales to set up a lecture and to maintain an orthodox minister at their own charge, to preach every Lord's day, where there is no preaching, and to preach one day in every week, when there is no weekly lecture."[5] Thereafter a veritable stream of petitions poured into the House of Commons requesting permission to start a lectureship or sanction for a particular lecturer. Between September 1641 and July 1643 the House of Commons issued orders concerning 27 lecturers or lectureships in London alone.[6] The House not only issued orders establishing lectureships but on several occasions met attempts by incumbents to block new lecturers from their pulpits by committing the recalcitrant clergymen to the custody of the sergeant, "there to remain at the pleasure of the House." With the coming of the sequestrations and deprivations of "delinquents" and "malignants" in 1642 under the aegis of the Committee for Plundered Ministers, intervention in parochial affairs took on massive proportions.[7]

By 1642 the consequences of these interventions were measurable. The total number of lecturers in London had risen from 75 in 1641 to 93 a year later, and the number of Puritan lecturers had risen to a new high of 72. The impact of this revolution is illustrated by the events that took place at the parish of SS. Anne and Agnes Aldersgate during the early 1640's. This parish appears not to have had a lecturer until 1641, when the vestry hired the Puritan Samuel Bolton, then lecturing at St. Saviour's, at a yearly stipend of £20. The vestrymen had first tried to hire a lecturer in 1639, when they sought to obtain the services of Christopher Love, a young divine who had just come down from Oxford to serve as chaplain to Sheriff Warner. They had failed then because Bishop Juxon refused to license Love on the understandable ground that Love declined to be episcopally ordained. In 1642 the vestry again ran into trouble over their lecture, this time owing to the opposition of their rector, Richard Cluet, and had to obtain an order from the House of Commons in order to install John Rawlinson as lecturer. The rectory was sequestered the following year, and in 1645 Christopher Love, by now a popular Presbyterian preacher, was admitted minister. Having finally obtained their man, the vestry ceased to employ an independent preacher and instead paid Love £20 a year for the lecture until his death in 1651.[8]

The events at SS. Anne and Agnes were atypical in only one respect. The parishioners had sought as their preacher the young Christopher Love at a time when the typical Puritan lecturer was a man of considerable experience and mature years. As Clarendon bitterly observed with pardonable exaggeration, "All pulpits were freely delivered to the schismatical and silenced preachers, who till then had lurked in corners or lived in New England."[9] That London experienced an unprecedented influx of Puritan clerical talent could be credited largely to the Long Parliament, for during these years the House of Commons both directly sponsored a small number of prestigious divines and, by summoning the Assembly of Divines, created a pool of clerics in the City that the local vestries were not slow to draw on.

Parliament itself established an early morning lecture at the Abbey church, where seven of the most distinguished Puritans of the time— Edmund Staunton, Philip Nye, Stephen Marshall, Herbert Palmer, Jeremiah Whitaker, and Thomas Hill—took turns preaching the daily sermon.[10] All were members of the Assembly of Divines and preachers of substantial reputation. Staunton had begun his clerical career in 1623 as lecturer at Witney, Oxford, and as the incumbent at Kingston-on-Thames, where he was known as "the searching preacher," he had also participated in the local group lectureship. Nye had previously preached in London itself, first at Allhallows Staining, where he was also curate from 1627, and then concurrently at St. Michael Cornhill from 1629 until about 1633, when it was reported that he was considering following John Davenport to New England.[11] Stephen Marshall, Nye's father-in-law, had succeeded the famous Richard Rogers at the Wethersfield lecture in 1618. In February of 1642/3, a few months before Marshall was appointed to the morning exercise, the House of Commons had recommended that the vestry of St. Margaret, Westminster, appoint him their regular lecturer.

Herbert Palmer had also lectured early in his career, obtaining in 1626 or 1627 a license to preach at St. Alphage, Canterbury, from Archbishop Abbot. As a result of Palmer's preaching from this rather exposed pulpit, "the city was well seasoned with savory salt, and much preserved from the innovations and corruptions, both in doctrine and worship, which in those days was creeping in apace," despite the attempts of the Dean and Archdeacon ("cathedralists . . . who preferred pompous ceremonies before the power of godliness") to suppress the lecture. While taking part in the morning lecture at the Abbey, Palmer also lectured at St. James Duke's Place, and though he was appointed Master of Queen's College, Cambridge, in 1644, he apparently remained in London until his death in 1647.[12] Thomas Hill's career was much like Palmer's: he had lectured at St. Andrew, Cambridge, before coming to London, he preached an ordinary parish lecture at St. Martin in the Fields at the same time that he participated in the morning exercise, and in 1645 he was appointed to a college mastership (Emmanuel, and then Trinity). Jeremiah Whitaker, who apparently had not lectured prior to his nomination to the Assembly of Divines, nevertheless had had well over a decade of ministerial experience and seems to have come to London determined to make amends for the years he had lacked an important pulpit, for he preached twice weekly in Southwark, where he was lecturer at St. Mary Magdalen, Bermondsey, and once at Christ Church Newgate, all in addition to his weekly sermon at the Abbey.[13]

Parliamentary patronage was also extended to one of the most extraordinary Puritan figures of the period, Cornelius Burgess, whom the Commons appointed to a lecture at St. Paul's Cathedral in December 1643. Burgess had been a royal chaplain and a pluralist, continuing to hold the vicarage of Watford after his presentation to the rectory of St. Magnus in 1625, where he also lectured. Contrary to appearances, however, Burgess was no Laudian nor even a very orthodox Anglican churchman, a fact he demonstrated most provocatively in a sermon delivered to his fellow clergymen during the 1635 visitation, in which, Laud complained, he "uttered divers insolent passages against the bishops and the government of the Church."[14] As mentioned earlier, Burgess and Marshall were appointed by the House of Commons to preach on 17 November 1640, the first day set aside for prayer and fasting. According to Robert Chestlin, a London royalist divine, Parliament was regularly intimidated during the following months by "the tumults out of the city, lead up by Doctor Burges and Captain Ven to the Parliament doors, to see that the godly party ... in the House might not be outvoted."[15] Whether Parliament was intimidated or not, it rewarded Burgess with a cathedral for a pulpit, to which was annexed the princely income of £400 a year from the lands of the dean and chapter, the largest salary paid for a lecturer in this period.*

In many respects the divines patronized by Parliament were typical of the recruits to the London lectureships in the 1640's. Forty-three members of the Assembly of Divines had either lectured in London at some time in the past or lectured there during the 1640's. Seventeen had lectureships or other preferments in London prior to their nomination to the Assembly, but of these six had been in London only since the summoning of the Long Parliament.[16] Simeon Ashe, for example, who was active both as a preacher and as a leader of the London Presbyterians during the 1640's and 1650's, had first come to London in 1640 as the Earl of Manchester's chaplain. He lectured briefly at St. Bartholomew Exchange in 1641; on 15 March 1641/2, in response to a petition from the parishioners, the House of Commons recommended that Ashe serve as the Sunday afternoon and Tuesday lecturer at St. Bride's, a post he held until 1646, when he was appointed to deliver the Sir Wolstan Dixie Sunday and Tuesday lectures at St. Michael Bassishaw. In 1651 Ashe gave up the Dixie lectureship, which paid only £10 a year, to become Sunday afternoon lecturer and assistant to the curate, Edmund Calamy, at St. Mary Aldermanbury. Even after

---

* A. G. Matthews, *Calamy Revised* (Oxford, 1934), p. 87; *A History of St. Paul's Cathedral and the Men Associated with It,* ed. W. R. Matthews and W. M. Atkins (London, 1957), p. 168. The salaries paid to the lecturers participating in the morning exercise at the Abbey church were almost as munificent, being £300 a year. *Dictionary of National Biography,* s.v. Stephen Marshall.

he became the intruded rector at St. Augustine's in January 1654/5, he continued to lecture at either St. Michael's or St. Peter Cornhill until, as Calamy wrote, "he went seasonably to heaven ... [and] was buried the very even of St. Bartholomew's day [1662]." Ashe's career was unusual only in that he held so many lectureships and in that once having come to London, he never returned to his vicarage at Rugeley, Staffordshire.[17]

More typical of the experienced preachers who staffed the London lectureships in the 1640's was John Wincop, who came to London as chaplain to the Earl of Salisbury and was subsequently appointed to the Sunday morning lecture at St. Martin in the Fields, a parish that also employed Thomas Case, another recent recruit to London and a future member of the Assembly of Divines, to preach in the afternoon. Wincop sat in the Westminster Assembly as a representative of Hertfordshire, to which he returned as soon as his presence was no longer required in London.[18]

In addition to the seventeen preachers who were already in London, another nineteen who subsequently lectured in London first came to the City at the invitation of the Westminster Assembly.[19] London must have enjoyed a greater concentration of distinguished Puritan clergymen between 1643 and 1648 than at any other time between 1560 and 1660, and this influx of Puritans must have minimized to some degree the impact of the sudden vacancies in many pulpits caused by the sequestrations of the royalist clergy. Not all these men were strangers to London; to those who had preached briefly in London before, their return must have seemed a most triumphant vindication both of themselves and of the Puritan cause. Robert Harris, who succeeded the famous "Decalogue" Dodd at the rectory of Hanwell, Oxfordshire, in 1607, seems to have lectured at St. Lawrence Jewry during the summer of 1619 and was definitely lecturer at St. Saviour, Southwark, from September 1623 to January 1624/5, when he resigned because of his failure to obtain a "dispensation" from the Archbishop of Canterbury, or so he told the vestry of St. Saviour's. Thereafter he remained at Hanwell until he was driven out by royalist troops after the battle of Edgehill; he was nominated to the Assembly and appointed minister of St. Botolph Bishopsgate, where he preached until he was appointed one of the preachers and visitors to the University of Oxford.[20]

Another former lecturer, Anthony Burgess, a younger man, had not had to wait so long for his return. As a Fellow of Emmanuel of five years' standing, Burges had been elected curate and lecturer at St. Mary Magdalen Milk Street at a vestry meeting on 13 January 1634/5; a month later the parish clerk noted "an order for giving Mr. Burges a gratuity or love token . . . in regard Mr. Burges is returning tomorrow to Cambridge, having been almost a month in London, endeavoring to be licensed, . . . and having bestowed his pains amongst us in preaching three Sundays, twice every day." Burges returned to London in 1643 as one of the Warwickshire representatives and was elected vicar and lecturer of the sequestered living of St. Lawrence Jewry. He later returned to his Warwickshire living at Sutton Coldfield in 1648, where he remained until he was ejected in 1662.[21]

If the sitting of the Westminster Assembly led to an unusual concentration of distinguished divines in the City, few remained past its rising. Of the nineteen who took London lectureships as a result of their presence at the Assembly, only four continued to preach in the City after 1648, and of the four, one, Christopher Love, was executed for his part in a royalist-Presbyterian plot in 1651, and a second, Jeremiah Whitaker, died in 1654.[22] Some soon left for new livings elsewhere. John Lightfoot, the famous biblical scholar, left his living at Ashley, Staffordshire, to his younger brother at the time of his summons to London, where he then briefly held the rectory and the Sunday lectureship at St. Bartholomew Exchange before going on to a Hertfordshire rectory in 1644 and the mastership of St. Catherine, Cambridge, in 1650. Others left to return to posts neglected but never abandoned during their sojourn in London. Matthew Newcomen, who had succeeded John Rogers as lecturer at Dedham in 1636, was appointed Sunday afternoon lecturer and assistant to his brother-in-law, Edmund Calamy, at St. Mary Aldermanbury in 1643. Apparently he retained his London position until 1648, when he returned to Dedham until his ejection in 1662.[23]

Only about one-fifth of those who lectured in London at some time in the 1640's were still lecturing there by the 1650's. Death carried off a handful of London's most faithful lecturers in the 1640's and early 1650's: Josias Shute, a popular preacher, though a royalist, who had lectured at St. Mary Woolnoth from 1611 until his death in 1643; the Puritan Richard Sedgwick, who also died in 1643 and who had preached at Wapping since 1617; the notorious Henry Burton, who had begun his lecture at St. Matthew Friday Street in 1618 and who died there in 1647; Stephen Dennison, who lectured at St. Katherine Cree from 1622 until his death in 1650; John Downham, who held the "Golden" lecture at St. Bartholomew's from its inception in 1616 until his death in 1651; and, finally, William Gouge, who had begun his lecture at Blackfriars in 1608, when Stephen Egerton, a supporter of Cartwright, was rector, and who continued to preach from the same pulpit for 45 years until he went to his well-earned reward in 1653.[24]

The loss of the royalist clergy that occurred during the early 1640's accounted for less than 10 per cent of the overall decrease in the number of lecturers during the decade. The high turnover in lecturers was due fairly obviously to the fact that at the very moment when episcopal opposition ceased and the House of Commons set out to encourage and sanction the founding of new lectureships—when, in short, some permanence in tenure might have been expected—sequestrations made vast numbers of livings and university posts available to the talented Puritan divine. The Westminster Assembly, the machinery of Parliamentary patronage, and the presence of hostile armies in the provinces assured London of a steady supply of exceptionally experienced lecturers, particularly in the years between 1643 and 1648. In the 1650's there were both fewer lecturers of long experience in London and fewer lectureships, for many parishes had discovered that their ministers were willing both to remain in residence and to preach.

Hence what Laud had failed to bring about in the 1630's the very success of the Puritans brought about in the 1640's. As Table 9 shows, from a peak reached in the years 1642 and 1643 the number of lecturers declined until 1650; in 1643 there had been more Puritans lecturing in London than ever before, but by 1650 there were no more than there had been in 1635, hardly a banner year for the Puritan preachers. But for the new recruits brought to London by the Assembly of Divines or driven to the City by the marching armies, the decline would undoubtedly have occurred earlier and have been more precipitous. Once the wholesale sequestrations began with the outbreak of war in 1643, more livings became available than there were preachers to fill them. Chestlin claimed in 1648 that 115 London clergymen had had their livings sequestered or had withdrawn to safer quarters; A. G. Matthews's list, which includes curates and the

TABLE 9

Lecturers in London: Yearly Estimates, 1640–62

Year	Total	Puritan	Year	Total	Puritan
1640	73	42	1652	57	46
1641	75	53	1653	59	47
1642	93	72	1654	62	46
1643	88	79	1655	60	45
1644	75	71	1656	65	48
1645	77	73	1657	64	48
1646	66	62	1658	62	48
1647	67	61	1659	64	49
1648	67	58	1660	67	56
1649	59	51	1661	48	40
1650	53	48	1662	42	35
1651	58	49			

handful of clergymen who voluntarily gave up a living held in plurality, numbers 132.[25] In 1646 a Londoner complained that "there were thirty-two parish churches, utterly destitute of any pastor."[26] By the middle of the decade it had become difficult to recruit lecturers, for by then even livings, by comparison both more profitable and more secure, were going begging.

Further, the lectureship lost much of its *raison d'être* when it became possible to obtain a minister who would agree to preach twice on Sundays and once on fast days. The perpetual curacy of St. Botolph Aldersgate provides a typical example. A lecture had been given there since 1565, first by a separate, independent lecturer, and then, since 1598, by the incumbent curate. Thomas Booth, curate since 1620, was accused by a group of parishioners in a petition to the House of Commons, dated 5 October 1641, of denying them permission to take down the communion rails. In December of 1642 the parishioners received permission to choose a lecturer, and Elidad Blackwell, an Emmanuel graduate and later minister of St. Andrew Undershaft, briefly preached there.[27] When the curacy was sequestered the following year, John Conant, who had been driven from his lecture at Limington, Somerset, by the royalists, was admitted as both curate and lecturer. Conant left in 1646 to become chaplain to Lord Chandos, who paid him £80 a year to lecture at Uxbridge.[28] In 1647 the parish secured the services of Thomas Jaggard, another Emmanuel graduate, who had deserted his rectory in 1643 and withdrawn to Parliamentary territory. By the time a convention was signed between the parish of St. Botolph's and Jaggard, on 9 January 1647/8, the Sunday afternoon lecture had become a regular duty of the minister and the voluntary contribution for the lecturer an augmentation of the living.[29]

At St. Nicholas Acons the last recorded lecturer before 1655 was William Jenkyn, who preached there in 1639 and 1640. On 4 November 1655 the vestry elected Daniel Maning "our lecturer for the afternoon of each Sabbath day, who being then present did freely consent thereto." It is probable that previously the Sunday afternoon sermon had been given by the incumbent, as was generally the practice in the City during the Interregnum. However, John Meriton, who was admitted their minister in 1653, was also the Sunday afternoon lecturer at St. Martin in the Fields; no doubt it was this conflict of obligations that led the vestry of St. Nicholas to revive their lectureship.[30] Something similar seems to have occurred at Allhallows Lombard Street. In 1646 the Churchwardens' Accounts note expenses for "fetching the ministers and other service in the time of the morning lecture here." This lecture may have been given by a Mr. Lee, who is mentioned as preaching a weekly lecture the following year. However, in 1647 John Cardell, former lecturer and, since the sequestration, minister of the parish, was inducted into the living, following the death of John Weston, the sequestered rector, and no more is heard about the morning lecture until its revival in 1660. That year Henry Wilkinson, a well-known Presbyterian and former member of the Westminster Assembly, lost his canonry at Christ Church, Oxford, and returned to London to lecture at Allhallows until Bartholomew's Day of 1662.[31] Thus the decline in the number of lecturers after 1643 does not mean that there was no more lecturing to be had in certain parishes; rather it means merely that many ministers assumed the preaching of Sunday afternoon and weekday sermons as a regular part of their pastoral duties.

Two other developments date from the hour of the Puritan triumph. An observer of the ecclesiastical scene in London in 1645 might have anticipated that within a year or two Puritan preachers would monopolize the city's lectureships. Yet, as Table 9 shows, the Anglican lecturers remained a sizable minority throughout the Interregnum. It was also during these years that the apparently united front with which the Puritans had confronted their episcopal opponents began to show signs of fragmentation, marked in London by the occasional emergence of conflict between Presbyterians and Independents for the control of parish pulpits.

On 15 April 1655 John Evelyn recorded in his diary that he and his family had come up to London "to celebrate the Feast of Easter, Dr. Wild preaching at St. Gregory's on 20 John, 13, a Resurrection Sermon; the H[oly] Sacrament followed, the ruling powers conniving at the use of the Liturgy, etc., in this Church alone." What the authorities connived at was the incumbency of John Hewet, a known royalist and an "excellent preacher," according to Evelyn. But even an excellent royalist preacher could be tolerated only so far. Hewet, who had been vicar of St. Gregory's since 1653, was executed in 1658 for his part in a royalist plot.[32]

John Evelyn was mistaken in assuming that the "ruling powers" countenanced the use of the Prayer Book at St. Gregory's alone. Two years earlier a royalist newsletter from London, dated 3 June 1653, noted that "in many parts the Common Prayer is in great request again"; a month and a half later another letter observed that "conventicles for Common Prayer are frequent and much desired in London."[33] As early as 1652 Cromwell had made overtures to the moderate Anglicans in a move apparently aimed at bringing them within the limits of official toleration. Although these negotiations failed, the discreet use of the Anglican liturgy was winked at for several years. In London Prayer Book services were conducted not only at St. Gregory's but also at St. Peter Paul's Wharf, at St. Benet's, and at St. Mary Magdalen Milk Street.[34]

If there is an element of irony in the fact that the harried Anglican found greater freedom under Cromwell and the Independent army than under the rigorous rule of the Parliamentary Presbyterians, there is also a kind of perverse justice in the fact that during these years of comparative toleration Anglicans sought preferment to those very lectureships that had blighted all efforts of the Established Church to achieve uniformity before 1640. With few exceptions the Anglican lecturers of the 1650's had not lectured in the years before their persecution, and again with few exceptions these lecturers had belonged to the increasingly powerful Laudian wing of the Anglican clergy. The reappearance of Anglicans as lecturers hired by vestries also offers some indication of the real strength of Anglican sentiment among the London laity, although such evidence must obviously be used with caution. Nathaniel Hardy's lecture at St. Dionis Backchurch offers an interesting case study in the complexities of the London ecclesiastical scene during the years of Puritan dominance and suggests just how perilous it is to infer the existence of an Anglican congregation from the presence of an Anglican lecturer.

In 1660, as a reward for his loyalty, Nathaniel Hardy was appointed Dean of Rochester and chaplain to the King. At the beginning of the civil wars, however, when this London-born cleric returned from Oxford as a Master of Arts of several years' standing, he attached himself to the ranks of the London Presbyterians. By 1643, his preaching abilities being recognized, he was appointed successively to the lectureship at St. Mary at Hill and that at St. Dionis Backchurch, where he was the candidate of the predominantly Presbyterian congregation. His reputation had reached sufficient proportions by 1645 that he was chosen to attend the Uxbridge negotiations—a decisive event in his career, for while at Uxbridge he was converted to the orthodox tenets of Anglicanism by the persuasive Dr. Henry Hammond.[35] Despite this radical turnabout, of which Hardy gave notice on his return to London by preaching a recantation sermon, he remained at his lecture post and continued to participate in the activities of the London classis. Nevertheless, his return to his Presbyterian congregation did not represent any second thoughts about his conversion, and in 1655 he along with George Hall and John Pierson, two noted Laudians and future Restoration bishops, was given "liberty to preach a lecture sermon weekly in the parish church" of St. Clement's in Eastcheap.[36]

St. Clement's appears to be one of those parishes where there was an important group of Anglicans among the parishioners. In 1647 the moderate Thomas Fuller lectured there, although there is nothing to suggest that the parish had had a settled lectureship previously. In 1651 the vestry recorded that "whereas it was then declared that Mr. Thomas Fuller did resolve, according to his promise, to return to preach his weekly lecture ..., the persons then present did give their free consent." In a proviso indicating that Fuller's lectureship was supported by a group outside of the vestrymen, the latter went on to rule "that the friends and auditors of the said Mr. Fuller may be accommodated with convenient pew room."[37]

St. Gregory's, the parish Evelyn attended during his sojourns in London, was almost certainly Anglican, although as late as 1651 the vestry had chosen the Presbyterian Daniel Cawdry, a former member of the Westminster Assembly and a preacher who had lectured in London in the 1620's, as their Sunday afternoon lecturer.[38] In 1653, however, at about the same time that Hewet became vicar, the vestry elected as their lecturer George Gillingham, who had been sequestered from his Hampshire living for delinquency in 1646. Gillingham, like Cawdry, had preached a London lectureship in the 1620's.[39] Although it was reported in 1656 that "Dr. Hewet continues yet silenced" and that there was "No Communion at St. Gregory's on Whitsunday," Gillingham continued to preach his lecture unmolested until the Restoration permitted him to return to his rectory at Chalton, Hampshire, his canonry at Windsor, and his other preferments.[40]

A similar pattern seems evident at St. Mary Magdalen Milk Street. The dominant voice from the pulpit during the 1640's had been that of the vigorous Presbyterian Thomas Case, who began his lecture at St. Mary's in 1641 and then became parson in 1642, when the rector, John Jones, was sequestered. When Case was in turn deprived in 1649 for refusing the Engagement, he was succeeded both as minister and lecturer by his own curate, another Presbyterian, Thomas Manton.[41] It was on Manton's departure in 1655 that a minor ecclesiastical revolution took place. The vestry, meeting on 30 January 1655/6, chose as their minister Thomas Cartwright, who might be described as crypto-Anglican: he took the Covenant when he matriculated at Oxford in 1650, but he also sought episcopal ordination a few years later from Bishop Skinner, who was living in retirement nearby. At the same time that Cartwright was appointed, John Hewet, the Anglican incumbent at St. Gregory's, was chosen lecturer. A year later the vestry appointed John Jones, their sequestered rector, to the lectureship, and in 1658 on Jones's death, Cartwright himself lectured briefly.[42] At the end of that year another about-face occurred: either the vestry was intimidated by the general reaction against toleration that began in 1656 and 1657, or it fell once more under Puritan control. Whatever the reason, in late 1658 the vestry returned to appointing Puritan lecturers, the last two being Francis Warham, an Independent, and the famous Richard Baxter.[43]

In June 1657 the House of Commons urged Cromwell to remove the "notorious delinquent" Dr. Thomas Warmestry from his lecture-

ship at St. Margaret, Westminster; in December of the following year
Richard Cromwell ordered the mayor and aldermen of London to
enforce the regulations against Prayer Book services.[44] The end of
toleration, however, did not lead to any systematic purge of Anglican
lecturers, and in fact one of the most unusual Anglican appointments
occurred in these troubled years. At a St. Antholin's vestry held on
16 December 1657, Zachary Cawdry was appointed lecturer, the first
Anglican to hold such a post in this most Puritan of London parishes
for almost 30 years. Further, he was reappointed annually until 1661.
In 1647, when Cawdry was both Fellow of St. John's and a university
proctor, he had been in trouble both for using the Book of Common
Prayer and for praying in the college chapel for the King's success and
the confusion of his enemies.[45] Altogether at least sixteen Anglicans
lectured in London between the early 1650's and the final years of
reaction and instability that marked the end of the decade, and some,
like Thomas Warmestry at St. Margaret, Westminster, and Bruno
Ryves at Lincoln's Inn, commanded pulpits of real importance.[46]
Nevertheless, the significance of this development should not be exaggerated. Some Anglicans had always lectured, and the economic
motive must have played a greater role than ever before in encouraging them to seek lectureships, for unemployment was high among the
loyal Anglican clergy in the years following their sequestrations. Be
that as it may, it is hard to avoid the conclusion that for the lay Anglicans of the period, the most significant effect of Cromwell's policy
of toleration was not to make Anglican preaching available again but
to permit orthodox Prayer Book services in a few parishes.[47]

Lectureships had always depended on the lay support of either a
congregation or an individual donor. Lay initiative brought the return of Anglican preachers and ministers to a handful of London
parishes in the 1650's; lay initiative was also responsible for the small
number of Independent preachers who gained lectureships in predominantly Presbyterian London between 1640 and 1660. Prior to 1640
the presence of a common enemy in the bishops had largely overcome
the ideological and ecclesiastical differences that divided the Presbyterian from the Independent Puritan. In fact, for many Puritans during the 1630's the whole question of ecclesiastical polity must have been
in abeyance. "We . . . thought it best to follow our business and live
in quietness and let the bishops alone," Richard Baxter noted, until

"roused by the terrors of [the "et cetera"] oath to look about us and understand what we did." However, with the emergence of the five dissenting members in the Assembly of Divines in 1643, all hope of unanimity was lost.[48]

Controversy in the Assembly and in the press did not necessitate a battle for the control of parochial pulpits, and a number of Independents held parish lectureships in London in the 1640's without producing any discernible trouble or dissension. Of the five dissenting members, for example, four preached ordinary lectures.* Thomas Goodwin, who might be said to have been the leader of the Independents, was appointed by the vestry of St. Michael Crooked Lane to lecture fortnightly on Sunday afternoons, which he did from 1646 to 1648; Sydrach Simpson, who had lectured at St. Margaret New Fish Street in the 1620's and 1630's until he was driven out by Laud's harassment, returned to lecture at St. Margaret's in 1641; Jeremiah Burroughs, a Norfolk divine, lectured both at Stepney and at St. Giles Cripplegate until his death in 1646, when he was succeeded by another of the dissenting members, William Bridges, who not only lectured at Stepney, but also went on to succeed Simpson at St. Margaret's and to a third lectureship at Allhallows Staining in 1647 and 1648.[49]

Real troubles arose, however, when parishes and vestries were themselves divided in allegiance and when this division was reflected in their appointments to ministerial and lecture posts. For example, shortly after a group of "underwriters" hired Henry Burton to preach a catechetical lecture at St. Mary Aldermanbury in 1645, this old opponent of Laud found himself locked out by the churchwardens at the instigation of the rector, Edmund Calamy, also an old opponent of Laud but a leading Presbyterian as well.[50]

A contretemps that occurred at St. Stephen Coleman Street in the same year led to a more profound split in that parish. John Goodwin, the vicar and lecturer, had been elected to those posts by the vestry in 1633 after the departure of John Davenport. Although a conforming Puritan at the time of his election, Goodwin rapidly followed in

* The fifth member, Philip Nye, lectured at Westminster Abbey from 1646 to 1660; he and John Loder also officiated before a gathered congregation at St. Bartholomew Exchange in the later 1650's, the "one taking possession of our pulpit, the other of our pews," as the vestry complained in 1659. A. G. Matthews, *Calamy Revised* (Oxford, 1934), p. 369; *The Vestry Minute Books of the Parish of St. Bartholomew Exchange in the City of London, 1567–1676*, ed. Edwin Freshfield (London, 1890), Part II, p. 70.

Davenport's footsteps and became an Independent at some point in the late 1630's, while at the same time adding to his troubles by engaging in controversies with orthodox Puritans over the issue of Christ's righteousness. However, Goodwin's difficulties did not extend to his relationship with his parishioners until 1644, when, after several abortive attempts had been made by the vestry to negotiate a settlement, a group of parishioners petitioned the Committee for Plundered Ministers for his sequestration, ostensibly on the grounds that no agreement could be reached on who should and should not be excluded from the sacraments. Actually Goodwin had collected a number of followers, and after his sequestration he withdrew with his Independent congregation to St. Mary Abchurch.[51] Although the vestry of St. Stephen's then installed William Taylor, the Puritan minister at Stratford at Bow, as vicar and lecturer, the matter had not yet come to an end. In 1647 a group of parishioners petitioned Parliament for the return of Goodwin as lecturer, and in 1649 the vestry recorded that "it hath pleased the all-wise God by the hand of the present supreme authorities of the nation to reinstate his faithful servant, Mr. John Goodwin . . . where he is willing to bestow his labors, so it may be without prejudice to that church of Christ, to whom he is united and with whom he hath walked hitherto in another place."[52]

Goodwin's restoration, however, did not involve simply a return to the *status quo ante*. William Taylor retained both vicarage and lectureship, and at the Restoration the vestry attempted unsuccessfully to regularize his appointment on a permanent basis. The vestry had merely agreed in 1649 that Goodwin's congregation "may have the same liberty and accommodation in the public meeting place of Coleman Street, as . . . was granted them by the people at Abchurch Lane parish." Five months later, when Goodwin moved "that the parish would make allowance for a lecturer on the Sabbath days in the afternoon," the request was denied, presumably because the lecture would have competed with Taylor's regular afternoon sermon. It is perhaps indicative of the differing status of the two congregations that whereas collections for the poor and seats in the church were to be shared, Taylor's parishioners did insist that the agreement made with Goodwin's congregation in no way compromise their original property right to their pews. It is also interesting to note that although Isaac Pennington, the most important vestryman, does not appear on the list of those chosen to assist Goodwin in deciding who was worthy to partake of the sacrament, he heads the list of those appointed to assist William Taylor in the same function.[53]

The protracted and acrimonious debate that took place in the late 1650's at St. Botolph Aldgate between the Presbyterian incumbent and the Independent lecturer had no such peaceful resolution, owing in part to the personalities of the antagonists. Zachary Crofton, the Presbyterian curate, was a zealous, fiery spirit, and a born fighter. Although he owed his appointment to St. Botolph's in 1655 to the Protector, he is alleged to have remarked about this exercise of patronage, "An honest man may accept the courtesy of a thief on the highway."[54] Shortly before his appointment to St. Botolph's he had left St. James Garlickhithe, where he had been minister and lecturer, after reaching a complete impasse in his relations with the vestry there. The feud at St. James had erupted in 1654, chiefly over the matter of Crofton's income. After much dispute, the vestry finally ordered that "inasmuch that he . . . hath so much aspersed this parish abroad and at home, and hath one or more benefices besides, and . . . hath his choice of divers others at present, that in case he shall not give way for the said ministers to preach for the said election [of a new minister] that then the churchwardens are to lock up the church doors." This "turbulent and contentious preacher," as a later vestry minute refers to Crofton, continued to harass St. James at least until the early months of 1657, but by that time he was deeply embroiled in a battle at St. Botolph's with the lecturer there, John Simpson.*

Simpson, a native Londoner, had returned to the City after completing his Oxford education in the late 1630's. At what point he became a Baptist and an Antinomian is unclear, but he was both from the early 1640's, when he began his lectures at St. Dunstan in the East

---

* Initially Crofton had demanded of the parishioners of St. James that there "be a more ready submission to his ministry," that he be paid £80 a year plus casualties, and that he be made permanent parson. The first condition the vestry willingly granted, but the real issue turned on Crofton's income. The parish granted him the tithes, but Crofton insisted on gaining control of the various leases to parish property, which had been in dispute between the vestry and the parson for more than forty years and which the vestry had no intention of granting to a mere stipendiary minister. GLMS 4813/1, fols. 113r, 116v–117v, 119r, 123r, 128r. For a sketch of Crofton's early career, see A. G. Matthews, *Calamy Revised* (Oxford, 1934), p. 144; and J. A. Dodd, "Troubles in a City Parish under the Protectorate," *English Historical Review*, X (1895), 41.

(the parish of his birth) and at St. Botolph's.[55] Although frequently in trouble with the authorities, to all appearances he did manage to live on good terms with his vestries, as, of course, a lecturer had to if he depended solely on this precarious form of employment. This is not to imply, however, that he was not a competent controversialist, capable of holding his own against Crofton. When Crofton, who put great stock in catechizing, published a pamphlet entitled *Catechising God's Ordinance,* Simpson is reported to have announced to the parishioners of St. Botolph's that "to learn a catechism is not to worship God; as well buy your children rattles or hobby horses."[56]

During 1657 Crofton began a sustained effort to take over Simpson's Sunday afternoon lecture. The battle that followed for control of the pulpit was exacerbated by the already existing divisions within the parish, which was split three ways among the Anglicans, Presbyterians, and Independents. Crofton had antagonized the Anglicans not only by his insistence on ecclesiastical discipline, particularly his insistence on excluding the unworthy and "profane" from the sacrament, but also by the fact that he had displaced the former minister, the Anglican John Mackarness, who had been removed as a result of a petition to Cromwell signed by the Puritan parishioners. At the same time, Crofton had aroused the ire of what he called the "furious anabaptistical spirits" by holding catechisms and by frequently admonishing the parish to remain after morning service for baptisms—"baby-sprinkling," as Simpson termed it.

In 1657, when Crofton challenged Simpson's right to the lecture, the "well-affected" petitioned Cromwell successfully to have Simpson's lecture confirmed. When Cromwell became Protector a few months later, Crofton claimed that the former order was null and void, and announced that he intended to preach the afternoon sermon. While he held the pulpit, surrounded by his supporters, Simpson's party, an alliance between the Independents and some of the Anglicans, secured another order from the Lord Protector and Council. Although Crofton reluctantly gave way, he continued to denounce Simpson from the pulpit; Simpson's faction retaliated by petitioning for Crofton's removal on the charge of seditious preaching. The spleen of the factions seems to have been inexhaustible, and presumably the controversy could have continued indefinitely if it had not been for the Restoration, which put an end to this teapot tempest. Crofton enjoyed a brief period of victory after Simpson, along with other Fifth Monarchists, was arrested in 1660. But shortly afterward Crofton himself lost his living on the return of the sequestered curate, the Laudian Thomas Swadlin. Crofton briefly kept a foothold in the city, preaching a lecture at St. Antholin's to which he had been appointed in 1657; he drew huge crowds with his anti-episcopal sermons until May 1661, when he was imprisoned in the Tower "for matters of High Treason."[57]

By 1660 any quarrels between Presbyterians and Independents over the control of pulpits had become largely academic, for in London, as elsewhere, the Puritan lecturer's mere survival had become his most pressing problem. To be sure, the return of the Anglican incumbents did not prevent vestries from continuing to hire Puritan lecturers, and for a brief time in 1660 the supply of Puritan lecturers in London was augmented by the influx of lecturers deprived of livings elsewhere.* However, this sudden increase was not to last. During the next two years the Puritans, already divided among themselves, were repeatedly outmaneuvered by an Anglican leadership bent on revanchist policies, and this time that leadership found in the new Act of Uniformity the final solution to the Puritan problem. Although in the process a united Protestant church was sacrificed and an internal opposition was destroyed at the price of creating an external body of dissenters, the Act of Uniformity did solve by amputation the problem of internal discipline as no other measure had in the preceding century.

Despite the demoralizing effect of the reverses they suffered during the first two years of the Restoration, the Puritans presented a remarkably united front as they approached St. Bartholomew's Day in 1662, the day on which the Act of Uniformity went into effect. Only about 10 per cent of the 1,760 ministers ejected between 1660 and 1662 later

---

* For example, John Biscoe, an Independent and in 1657 the preacher at Abingdon, Berkshire, left for London in 1660, where he lectured briefly at St. George, Southwark. Joseph Foster, *Alumni Oxonienses: The Members of Oxford, 1500–1714* (Oxford, 1891), I, 129; George Yule, *The Independents in the English Civil War* (Cambridge, Eng., 1958), p. 134. Other examples were Charles Humphrey, rector of Cleobury North, Shropshire, who left in 1660 on the return of the sequestered rector, and who lectured at St. John Zachary until 1662 (A. G. Matthews, *Calamy Revised* [Oxford, 1934], p. 284), and Thomas Wadsworth, who left a Surrey living on the return of the Anglican incumbent and lectured in London at St. Antholin's, St. Margaret New Fish Street, and St. John the Baptist Walbrook until 1662 (GLMS 1045/1, p. 57; *Dictionary of National Biography*; Matthews, *Calamy Revised*, p. 505).

conformed to the reconstructed Anglican Church.[58] Of the 62 Puritans who lectured in London between the Restoration and 24 August 1662, only seven conformed.[59]

The subsequent careers of the ejected lecturers properly belong to the history of dissent, but something should be said about the lives of the last generation of Puritan lecturers while they yet remained within the national church. Six of the London lecturers died within months of the King's return. William Taylor, a Yorkshireman born in 1615, had been driven from his Cirencester preferment after the town had been stormed by royalist troops in 1642. He went to London and became lecturer at suburban Stratford at Bow. His preaching career in London proper dated from 1645, when he replaced John Goodwin as vicar and lecturer at St. Stephen Coleman Street. During the 1650's he preached additional lectures at St. Giles Cripplegate, at St. Peter Cornhill, and at St. Margaret Lothbury. This noted Presbyterian who had edited some of Christopher Love's sermons and whose funeral sermon was preached by William Spurstowe died in 1661, shortly after the vestry of St. Stephen's failed to regularize his status as vicar.[60]

Few, in Edmund Calamy's phrase, went so "seasonably to heaven," but few had so truncated a career as John Collins, a Harvard Master of Arts of 1652 who came to England, was appointed to preach in Scotland in 1654, returned to London and was elected one of the lecturers at St. Antholin's on 16 December 1661, and had perforce to vacate the position before the new appointments were made at the vestry meeting of 13 September 1662.[61] For many, however, the Restoration did end careers, at least within the Established Church, that had barely begun to fulfill their early promise. George Griffiths' career began at the age of 28 or 29, when as a recent Master of Arts of Emmanuel College, he was appointed preacher at the Charterhouse in 1648. Apparently his preaching soon commended him to other patrons, for in 1650 he was appointed by the Haberdashers to succeed John Downham as the William Jones lecturer at St. Bartholomew Exchange, a singular honor for a preacher of only two years' standing. By 1652 he was assisting the company with the examination of candidates recommended for various preferments in the company's gift; in 1654 he became one of the Commissioners for the Approbation of Ministers; and in 1658 he was appointed one of the lecturers at Westminster Abbey.[62] In 1661 he lost his appointment at the Charterhouse, and at the meeting of the Court of Assistants of the Haberdashers' Company on 27 September 1662 he tendered his resignation from the Jones lectureship "for diverse reasons by him shewed," the chief of which was doubtless that as an Independent he could not conscientiously take the oath required by the Act of Uniformity. With a generosity rare in the period he recommended as his successor Francis Raworth, an even younger man and a former lecturer at St. Antholin's, who after his dismissal in 1661 conformed and was rewarded not only with the William Jones lectureship but also with the vicarage of St. Leonard, Shoreditch. Griffiths went on to a second career as a congregational minister in London, apparently preaching regularly until well into his eighties; Raworth fell prey to the plague in 1665.[63]

Raworth's conformity was by no means an isolated act, and by no means were all who conformed time-serving hacks. Some had conscientiously taken so moderate a position through all the twists and turns of the period that conformity must have been all but inevitable. Edward Reynolds, who was described a bit acidly by Richard Baxter as "a solid, honest man, but through mildness and excess of timorous reverence to great men, altogether unfit to contend with them," seems to have been just such an accommodating person; he was, moreover, a conscientious and capable preacher, succeeding Preston as lecturer at Lincoln's Inn in 1628, and following Richard Viner as vicar and lecturer at St. Lawrence Jewry in 1656, where he was elected unanimously by a vestry that thought sufficiently of his abilities not to "put any other minister in nomination with Dr. Reynolds."[64] A Merton graduate, he had managed both to preach against Peter Heylyn in 1627 and to become a royal chaplain. In the early 1640's he held a moderate Anglican position but sat in the Westminster Assembly and took the Covenant. At the Restoration he conformed again and was promptly elevated to the bishopric of Norwich. He pursued a moderate course at the Savoy Conference and was moderate thereafter in his treatment of dissenters.[65] In an age of fierce partisanship his life presents rather an unheroic picture, but the popularity he enjoyed with his London vestrymen suggests that moderation in doctrine and action was regarded as a virtue by many of the laity.

Other Puritan conformists seem to have fallen into Baxter's category of "the old ministers, called Presbyterians formerly," some of whom "were very able, worthy men," and some of whom also "had wives and

children and poverty, which were great temptations to them."[66] Some
were young and committed themselves gradually but irrevocably to
the restored Establishment. John Meriton, who, if the records are to
be believed, was admitted sizar at St. John, Cambridge, at the age of
sixteen on 18 October 1652, left for London several months later; on
22 January 1652/3 the vestry of St. Martin in the Fields chose him as
their Sunday afternoon lecturer.[67] Three years later, when he could
not have been more than twenty, Cromwell presented him to the
rectory of St. Nicholas Acons. Although he was purportedly a staunch
Presbyterian, he managed to be reinstated at St. Nicholas in 1660. The
following year he was episcopally ordained, and the year after, despite
his initial objection to the Act of Uniformity, he conformed. Nevertheless, he seems to have been one of Baxter's "able, worthy men," for
in addition to his various other preferments, which were certainly
sufficient to render him financially secure, he preached the lecture at
St. Mary at Hill from 1661 to 1683.[68]

Thus the Act of Uniformity represented the final triumph of Laud-
ianism over the lectureships Laud had tried vigorously, even desper-
ately, to control in his lifetime.[69] Despite the sweeping expulsion of
the Dissenters in 1662, however, it was some years before the government mastered its fear of the pulpit. In October 1662 the King was led
to issue new "Directions Concerning Preachers" by the

> busy diligence of some unquiet and factious spirits who instead of preaching
> the pure word of God, and building up the people in faith and holiness,
> have made it a great part of their business to beget in the minds of their
> hearers an evil opinion of their governors, ... and to season them with such
> unsound and dangerous principles, as may lead them into disobedience,
> schism, and rebellion.

As late as 1665 Archbishop Sheldon asked his bishops about the number and loyalty of the lecturers within their dioceses.[70] The endowed
lectureship, which in particular had been constructed to withstand the
vicissitudes of time, survived in the event not only the hostility of the
ecclesiastical hierarchy but even the demise of the Puritan movement
that had brought it forth. The episcopal visitation of London in 1664
revealed that lectures were still being preached in at least 26 or 27
parishes. Some 300 years later a few still survived as archaic reminders
of the century when the lectureship had been the Puritans' answer to
the demand for a godly preaching ministry.[71]

Conclusion

EVEN so narrow a study as that of a single institution, the lectureship, has a significant bearing on some of the larger issues of the time. At the very least the history of the lectureship suggests the tremendous organizing ability, the almost protean creativity, of Puritan activism, particularly in the social and political spheres. While the English Catholic community, subjected to repression and rent by divisions, gradually lapsed into quietism, the Puritans survived their failure at Court and in convocation, and surmounted the defeat of Elizabethan Presbyterianism, with the divisions this movement and Separatism had created, to go on to a new regrouping of their forces in the early years of the seventeenth century.

The Puritan connection was never powerful enough to win the battles over ecclesiastical policy at the national level; all the petitions of the Puritan laity and exhortations of the clergy never succeeded in winning over the English monarchs. Nevertheless, the web of Puritan influence was sufficiently potent to offer local patronage and protection. Where lay Puritans could make their weight felt within a traditional institution—whether it was Parliament, a town corporation, a parish vestry, or simply an influential family—they used these institutions as a platform for their views or as a source of patronage for the clergy within their ranks. When existing institutions proved unequal to the task, new ones were called into being. Most failed. John Field's classical movement commanded the wholehearted support neither of all the Puritan clergy nor of any large section of the Puritan merchants and aristocrats, who could only have been alienated by the clerical elitism of Field and his followers and by their failure to work through channels—their refusal, in other words, to "tarry for the magistrate." The clerical Feoffees for Impropriations, by contrast, had support from the highest ranks of the London legal and mercantile community, and that support was built into the very structure of the organization. The Feoffees failed because the threat they posed to the ecclesiastical establishment was too patent to be overlooked, even by one less watchful and less sensitive to the interests of the Church than Archbishop Laud.

Yet the apparent failure of many of the Puritan platforms and policies, and of the schemes concocted to bring them about, is deceptive in several senses. Puritans thrived on failure. They advertised their defeats and issued dire warnings of the imminent demise of godly England, if not of the end of the world. Given their struggle to lead lives that bore witness to their election, and given their perception of themselves as called upon to create a commonwealth in accordance with God's will, it is perhaps not surprising that they learned to live with failure. But this is not to say that they adopted a spirit of accepting passivity. In reading their diaries we are less conscious of what they had accomplished in their busy lives than of the morbid introspection with which they catalogued their shortcomings. We note the gloomy prognostications in their sermons but are apt to overlook the exhortations to action.

In 1629 Thomas Hooker, the silenced lecturer at Chelmsford, preached in his farewell sermon: "God is going, his glory is departing, England hath seen her best days, and now evil days are befalling us; God is packing up his Gospel, because nobody will buy his wares, nor come to his price. Oh lay hands upon God and let him not go out of your coasts; he is going, stop him, and let not thy God depart."[1] The exaggeration is pardonable, but it was Hooker, not the Gospel, that was departing. A few years later, in 1634, at the same time that a Lancashire Puritan was writing to a London friend that the "course of injustice" was likely to prosper, and that he hoped God would prepare them "to suffer for their master," a very different sense of the realities of the time was displayed in a letter written by a Buckinghamshire parson, John Andrews, to the chancellor of his diocese. For the Anglican parson begged to be excused from the onerous task of preaching at Laud's visitation, not because he had no sympathy for Laudian churchmanship, but because such an overt gesture of support would bring him small thanks from a community in which "the greatest number (both of priests and people) in those parts are foully tainted" with Puritanism.[2] It is true that Hooker, among many others, had been silenced, but before he was deprived of his pulpit he had at least preached to an audience that had valued his ministry and his word; Andrews would not preach at all for fear of the hostility of his Puritan neighbors. Which represented the greater failure—the silenced Puritan who could not preach or the spokesman for the Established Church who dared not?

The Puritans failed in their own eyes at least in part because they set for themselves such impossible goals—changed men living in a transformed community, the godly commonwealth. But if they failed to reach their city on the hill, their passage across the dusty plains of mundane history was not without profound consequences. No people believed more in the efficacy of the Word than they, and if the Word ultimately failed to bring quite the revolution they hoped for, it nevertheless left a revolution in its wake, one as profound in its social as in its personal implications.

In 1575, when the Puritan preacher John More had been silenced and deprived, and thus prevented from continuing his popular lecture at St. Andrew's, Norwich, Bishop Freake had appointed a local conforming divine to take his place. The bishop's compromise, however, proved to be less than satisfactory. Not only did the parish clerk refuse to ring the church bells to announce the lecture hour, but he refused to lead in the singing of the psalm that customarily preceded the sermon. This cold welcome was followed at the conclusion of the lecture by such "spiteful" remarks from some members of the congregation as "turncoat," and More's hapless substitute found himself accused of preaching false doctrine and of betraying the Word. As for the bishop at whose command the substitute had preached, he "had no more authority than a common minister." Freake, infuriated by such public flouting of his authority and exasperated by the mayor and aldermen, whom he "found . . . very cold in Reformation," nevertheless managed by dint of threatening to appeal to the Privy Council to have the more obstreperous leaders of the Norwich commonalty imprisoned for their insubordination. However, as Nathaniel Bacon was informed by Francis Windham, who attempted to mediate between the angry bishop and the stubborn Norwich magistrates, "It is to be marveled at how many came to them to prison, and how they were banqueted." In conclusion Windham observed, "Surely this will breed some further consequences in time, I fear, if nothing be done to it."[3] And surely in time such episodes did have further consequences, in one community after another across England.

In the course of the English Reformation the Crown had ostensibly brought the religious life of the realm within the ambit of monarchical direction. Although Church and State continued to exist as distinct organizational and jurisdictional entities, ruled by separate hierarchies of civil and ecclesiastical magistrates, both were aspects, at least in constitutional theory, of a unitary commonwealth under an omnicompetent Crown. In actuality, however, many of the smaller communities within the realm organized local society as a single unit comprehending both the civil and the religious aspect of life under the watchful supervision of the local elite—a commonwealth in miniature; in this process the lecturer played an important part. For several generations after the official Crown-sponsored Reformation came to a close, these local reformations went on apace, and since the local reformation touched most immediately the lives of most Englishmen, it constituted for many the only true reformation.

If the history of the lectureships demonstrates anything, it is the existence of a powerful drive among the laity to control the Church, at least at the parochial level. This thrust was not unrelated to Puritanism as such, since the latter justified and gave confidence to the godly laity, but the drive for control was perhaps even more fundamental. The men who ran the London vestries clearly wanted a preaching ministry, but whether the preacher was Puritan or Anglican appears in many parishes to have been a secondary consideration. The hierarchical structure of the Established Church, with its set relationships of command and subordination, must have seemed to many laymen both distant and formal; the immediate reality was the presence of an educated and confident laity who followed the thought of the preacher critically, who expected substantial emotional and intellectual fare from the pulpit, and who were not much interested in preserving the niceties of traditional relationships in order to get it.

Just as the clerical elitism and authoritarianism of Laudian prelacy offended and threatened the lay aristocracy, who espoused the concept of an Erastian Church, so those aspects of Puritanism that tended toward clerical elitism and authoritarianism might in theory have set the Puritan preacher on a collision course with the local magistracy. But in fact the theocratic aspects of Puritanism and the repressive elements of its discipline were not much in evidence during the long years when the Puritan clergy were an embattled minority, or at least no more in evidence than the local lay elite desired. For the power of patronage and of the purse gave the governing elite a dominant position, leaving the preacher with at best a junior partnership in the efforts to reform the life and manners of the local community. The preacher might supply the ideology and the method for such a reformation, but without the cooperation of the magistracy the effects of his preaching were likely to be as ephemeral as the tenure of the preacher was likely to be brief.

When the Crown and the Laudian Church sought to bring the preachers to a measure of conformity and attempted to regulate, if not to destroy outright, the lectureships, they were tampering not with a recent innovation but rather with an institution that in many places had been rooted in the life of the community for several generations. Any attack on local institutions inevitably breached local rights and privileges, but an attack on the preachers was not simply a threat to local particularism. The preachers, if Puritans, were part of a national movement with common roots in the two universities and with friendships and connections among both the laity and the clergy throughout the realm. Further, the preachers had articulated the grievances of the local communities and had supplied an ideology in opposition to the patriarchalism of the Laudian Church and the Caroline monarchy. Finally, if any threat to local autonomy and privilege was to invite opposition, an attack on the preachers was infinitely more dangerous, for they were teachers of the way of salvation, conveyors of the saving Word, which was the bread of life itself.

That Puritanism as a movement commanded the allegiance of only a minority of Englishmen is undoubtedly true, but it is also largely beside the point, for there is little reason to suppose that the majority gave the Established Church, as defined by succeeding generations of prelates and supreme governors, more than their lukewarm acquiescence. In fact, the history of the lectureships suggests that what many of the local and national elites wanted was much closer to what the Puritans sought to provide than to anything the Established Church had to offer during the period between the coronation of Queen Elizabeth and the mid-seventeenth-century revolution. How else is one to explain the proliferation of town and parish lectureships despite the indifference, or indeed the open hostility, of both Crown and Church? And how else is one to explain the fact that the lectureships were staffed and supported by men who in many instances cannot be considered Puritans by any definition?

When Burgess and Marshall called upon the Long Parliament to supply a preaching ministry backed by a godly magistracy, they were not proposing a Puritan novelty; they were in fact sounding a note that had been a commonplace since the beginnings of the Protestant Reformation in England. A story told by another seventeenth-century worthy makes much the same point. In praising Queen Elizabeth as the very personification of the godly magistrate, Edward Leigh recounted the following incident:

She once in her Progress, visiting the County of Suffolk, all the Justices of the Peace in that county met her Majesty, every one of them having his Minister next to his body, which the Queen took special note of, and thereupon uttered this Speech: That she had often demanded of her Privy Council why her County of Suffolk was better governed than any other County, and could never understand the reason thereof, but now she herself perceived the reason; It must needs be so (said she) where the Word and the Sword go together.[4]

That such sentiments were attributed to Elizabeth is undoubtedly more a matter of Puritan wish-fulfillment than a matter of fact, but if the conviction that the Word and the Sword should go together was no more than a vision, it was a vision held by many responsible Englishmen for the better part of a century.

Appendixes

APPENDIX A

Parliamentary Boroughs with Lectureships
1560–1641

Parliamentary boroughs that had lectureships at some time between 1560 and 1641 are listed here under the following geographical headings: Southeast, East, Midlands, Southwest, West, and North. The list is based largely on printed sources, a partial list of which is appended to each entry, and is undoubtedly incomplete, since it was not possible to find relevant printed records for all boroughs. For abbreviations used in this appendix, see p. 313.

SOUTHEAST

Southampton, Hants.: *The Third Book of Remembrance of Southampton, 1514–1602*, ed. A. L. Merson (Southampton, 1955), II, 106.
Canterbury, Kent: William Prynne, *Canterburies Doome* (London, 1646), pp. 371–72.
Rochester, Kent: *D.N.B.*, s.v. Percival Wyborne.
London, Middx.: see Chapter 5.
Westminster, Middx.: James F. Maclear, "The Influence of the Puritan Clergy on the House of Commons: 1625–1629," *Church History*, XIV (1945), 275.
Guildford, Surrey: William Prynne, *Canterburies Doome* (London, 1646), p. 151.
Southwark, Surrey: LCCRO, P/92/449 and 450, *passim*.
Lewes, Sussex: PRO, SP 16/261, fol. 83r.
Rye, Sussex: MSS. of Rye Corporation, in *H.MSS.C., 13th Report, Appendix, Part IV* (London, 1892), pp. 162, 170.

EAST

Cambridge, Camb.: Irvonwy Morgan, *The Godly Preachers of the Elizabethan Church* (London, 1965), pp. 28–29.
Colchester, Essex: Harold Smith, *The Ecclesiastical History of Essex under the Long Parliament* (Colchester, n.d.), pp. 23, 30–36.
Maldon, Essex: Visitation Call Books for 1589 and 1637, in GLMS 9537/7, no fol., and 9537/15, fol. 19v.
Hertford, Herts.: William Urwick, *Nonconformity in Herts.* (London, 1884), p. 525.
St. Albans, Herts.: William Urwick, *Nonconformity in Herts.* (London, 1884), pp. 103–19.
Huntingdon, Hunts.: Christopher Hill, *Society and Puritanism in Pre-Revolutionary England* (London, 1964), pp. 93–94.
Boston, Lincs.: Cotton Mather, *Magnalia Christi Americana* (Hartford, Conn., 1820), I, 235.
Grantham, Lincs.: *The Works of John Smyth*, ed. W. T. Whitley (Cambridge, Eng., 1915), I, xl.

Grimsby, Lincs.: *The Works of John Smyth*, ed. W. T. Whitley (Cambridge, Eng., 1915), I, xl.

Lincoln, Lincs.: J. W. F. Hill, *Tudor and Stuart Lincoln* (Cambridge, Eng., 1956), pp. 99–116.

Stamford, Lincs.: Patrick Collinson, *The Elizabethan Puritan Movement* (London, 1967), p. 217.

King's Lynn, Norf.: Henry J. Hillen, *History of the Borough of King's Lynn* (Norwich, 1907), I, 246.

Norwich, Norf.: *Minutes of the Norwich Court of Mayoralty*, ed. William L. Sachse (Norfolk Record Society, Vol. XV; Norwich, 1942), pp. 48–50.

Great Yarmouth, Norf.: John Browne, *History of Congregationalism in Norfolk and Suffolk* (London, 1877), pp. 23, 122–37; PRO, SP 16/261, fols. 4r–v.

Aldeburgh, Suffolk: *H.MSS.C., Various Collections*, IV (London, 1907), 307.

Bury St. Edmunds, Suffolk: *Diary of John Rous*, ed. M. A. E. Green (Camden Society, Vol. LXVI; 1856), p. 68.

Dunwich, Suffolk: *H.MSS.C., Various Collections*, VII (London, 1914), 87, 91–92.

Ipswich, Suffolk: Nathaniel Bacon, *Annalls of Ipswiche* (1654), ed. William H. Richardson (Ipswich, 1884), esp. p. 255.

Orford, Suffolk: *H.MSS.C., Various Collections*, IV, 266.

Sudbury, Suffolk: John and J. A. Venn, *Alumni Cantabrigienses*, Part I, *From Earliest Times to 1751* (Cambridge, Eng., 1922), Vol. IV, p. 429, s.v. John Wilson.

MIDLANDS

Bedford, Beds.: Patrick Collinson, *The Elizabethan Puritan Movement* (London, 1967), p. 141.

Abingdon, Berks.: *Selections from the Municipal Chronicles of the Borough of Abingdon*, ed. Bromley Challoner (Abingdon, 1898), p. 146.

Reading, Berks.: *Reading Records: Diary of the Corporation*, ed. J. M. Guilding (London, 1895–96), Vols II, III, *passim*.

Derby, Derbs.: *D.N.B.*, s.v. John Crompton; W. K. Jordan, *The Charities of London, 1480–1660* (London, 1960), p. 288.

Leicester, Leics.: James Thompson, *The History of Leicester* (Leicester, 1849), pp. 256, 268, 288–90, 354, 406.

Northampton, Northants.: *Records of the Borough of Northampton*, ed. J. Charles Cox (London, 1898), II, 386–400.

Peterborough, Northants.: *Peterborough Local Administration: Parochial Government...1541–1689*, ed. W. T. Mellows (Northamptonshire Record Society, Vol. X; 1936), pp. 54–56.

Nottingham, Notts.: *Records of the Borough of Nottingham*, Vol. IV, *1547–1625*, ed. W. Henry Stevenson (London, 1889), esp. p. 147.

Banbury, Oxfs.: William Potts, *A History of Banbury* (Banbury, 1958), p. 136.

Oxford, Oxfs.: Carteret J. H. Fletcher, *A History of the Church and Parish of St. Martin (Carfax) Oxford* (Oxford, 1896), pp. 22–25, 94–109.

New Woodstock, Oxfs.: *The Works of the Most Reverend Father in God, William Laud, D.D.*, ed. William Scott and James Bliss (Oxford, 1847–60), V, ii. 330.

Stafford, Staffs.: Walter N. Landor, *Collections for a History of Staffordshire* (London, 1916), pp. 77, 247.

Coventry, Warws.: Benjamin Poole, *Coventry: Its History and Antiquities* (London, 1870), pp. 211–12.

Warwick, Warws.: Irvonwy Morgan, *The Godly Preachers of the Elizabethan Church* (London, 1965), p. 91.

Tamworth, Warws.: PRO, SP 16/261, fols. 83r–84v.

SOUTHWEST

Bodmin, Cornwall: Mary Coates, *Cornwall in the Great Civil War and Interregnum, 1642–1660* (Oxford, 1933), pp. 326–27.

Launceston, Cornwall: Mary Coates, *Cornwall in the Great Civil War and Interregnum, 1642–1660* (Oxford, 1933), pp. 326–27.

Liskeard, Cornwall: A. L. Rowse, *Tudor Cornwall* (London, 1941), p. 334.

St. Ives, Cornwall: Mary Coates, *Cornwall in the Great Civil War and Interregnum, 1642–1660* (Oxford, 1933), pp. 326–27.

Barnstaple, Devon: R. J. E. Bogges, *A History of the Diocese of Exeter* (Exeter, 1922), p. 399.

Exeter, Devon: W. T. MacCaffrey, *Exeter, 1540–1640* (Cambridge, Mass., 1958), pp. 197–98.

Plymouth, Devon: Richard N. North, *History of Plymouth* (Plymouth, 1890), pp. 241–48.

Tavistock, Devon: Edmund Calamy, *The Nonconformists' Memorial*, ed. Samuel Palmer (London, 1802), II, 56–57.

Dorchester, Dorset: Frances Rose-Troup, *John White: The Patriarch of Dorchester, 1575–1648* (New York, 1930), pp. 320, 394n, 398.

Bristol, Gloucs.: John Latimer, *Sixteenth-Century Bristol* (Bristol, 1908), pp. 103–4.

Cirencester, Gloucs.: Isabel M. Calder, *Activities of the Puritan Faction of the Church of England, 1625–33* (London, 1957), pp. xv, xxi.

Gloucester, Gloucs.: *Calendar of the Records of the Corporation of Gloucester*, ed. W. Henry Stevenson (Gloucester, 1893), p. 451.

Tewksbury, Gloucs.: John Stow, *A Survey of the Cities of London and Westminster*, ed. John Strype (London, 1720), Vol. I, Part I, p. 288.

Bridgewater, Somerset: William Prynne, *Canterburies Doome* (London, 1646), pp. 377–78.

Marlborough, Wilts.: *V.C.H., Wiltshire*, III, 38.

Salisbury, Wilts.: *V.C.H., Wiltshire*, VI, 149.

WEST

Chester, Cheshire: Ronald Marchant, *The Puritans and the Church Courts in the Diocese of York, 1560–1642* (London, 1960), pp. 16, 19, 226.

Monmouth, Monms.: W. K. Jordan, *The Charities of London, 1480–1660* (London, 1960), p. 286.

Bridgnorth, Salop.: Isabel M. Calder, *Activities of the Puritan Faction of the Church of England, 1625–33* (London, 1957), pp. xvi, xxi, 53.

Shrewsbury, Salop.: Hugh Owen and John B. Blakeway, *A History of Shrewsbury* (London, 1825), I, 392; II, 270–72, 373, 411–14.

Worcester, Worcs.: *The Works of the Most Reverend Father in God, William Laud, D.D.*, ed. William Scott and James Bliss (Oxford, 1847–60), V, ii, 343; *C.S.P.D.*, *1639–40*, pp. 70, 189, 190.

NORTH

Carlisle, Cumbs.: *Some Municipal Records of the City of Carlisle*, eds. R. S. Ferguson and W. Nanson (London, 1887), pp. 284, 288.

Lancaster, Lancs.: *Materials for the History of the Church of Lancaster*, Vol. IV, ed. William O. Roper (Chetham Society, Vol. LIX; 1906), p. 773.

Liverpool, Lancs.: George Chandler, *Liverpool under Charles I* (Liverpool, 1965), pp. 92–93, 121–22.

Berwick, Northumb.: *C.S.P.D.*, *1639–40*, pp. 77, 104–5, 393.

Newcastle on Tyne, Northumb.: *Extracts from the Newcastle upon Tyne Council Minute Book, 1639–1655*, ed. M. Hope Dodds (Newcastle, 1920), *passim*.

Beverley, Yorks.: *H.MSS.C.*, *Report on the MSS. of the Corporation of Beverley* (London, 1900), pp. 185–86.

Hull, Yorks.: Ronald Marchant, *The Puritans and the Church Courts in the Diocese of York, 1560–1642* (London, 1960), pp. 118–21.

Ripon, Yorks.: *The Works of the Most Reverend Father in God, William Laud, D.D.*, ed. William Scott and James Bliss (Oxford, 1847–60), V, ii, 320.

York, Yorks.: *York Civic Records*, Vol. VIII, ed. Angelo Raine (Yorkshire Archeological Society, Vol. CXIX; 1953), *passim*.

London Parishes, Outparishes, and Liberties

LONDON PARISHES

Allhallows Barking
Allhallows Bread Street
Allhallows Honey Lane
Allhallows Lombard Street
Allhallows London Wall
Allhallows Staining
Allhallows the Great
Allhallows the Less
Christ Church Newgate
Holy Trinity Minories
Holy Trinity the Less
St. Alban Wood Street
St. Alphage
St. Andrew Holborn
St. Andrew Hubbard
St. Andrew Undershaft
St. Andrew Wardrobe
SS. Anne and Agnes Aldersgate
St. Anne Blackfriars
St. Antholin Budge Row
St. Augustine Watling Street
St. Bartholomew Exchange
St. Bartholomew the Great
St. Bartholomew the Less
St. Benet Fink
St. Benet Gracechurch
St. Benet Paul's Wharf
St. Benet Sherehog
St. Botolph Aldersgate
St. Botolph Aldgate
St. Botolph Billingsgate
St. Botolph Bishopsgate
St. Bride Fleet Street
St. Christopher le Stocks
St. Clement Eastcheap
St. Dionis Backchurch
St. Dunstan in the East

St. Dunstan in the West
St. Edmund the King
St. Ethelburga
St. Faith under St. Paul's
St. Gabriel Fenchurch
St. George Botolph Lane
St. Giles Cripplegate
St. Gregory by St. Paul's
St. Helen Bishopsgate
St. James Duke's Place
St. James Garlickhithe
St. James London Wall
St. John the Baptist Walbrook
St. John the Evangelist Friday Street
St. John Zachary
St. Katherine by the Tower
St. Katherine Coleman
St. Katherine Cree
St. Lawrence Jewry
St. Lawrence Pountney
St. Leonard Eastcheap
St. Leonard Foster Lane
St. Magnus the Martyr
St. Margaret Lothbury
St. Margaret Moses
St. Margaret New Fish Street
St. Margaret Pattens
St. Martin Ironmonger Lane
St. Martin Ludgate
St. Martin Orgar
St. Martin Outwich
St. Martin Vintry
St. Mary Abchurch
St. Mary Aldermanbury
St. Mary Aldermary
St. Mary at Hill
St. Mary Bothaw
St. Mary Colechurch

St. Mary le Bow
St. Mary Magdalen Milk Street
St. Mary Magdalen Old Fish Street
St. Mary Mounthaw
St. Mary Somerset
St. Mary Staining
St. Mary Woolchurch
St. Mary Woolnoth
St. Matthew Friday Street
St. Michael Bassishaw
St. Michael Cornhill
St. Michael Crooked Lane
St. Michael le Querne
St. Michael Paternoster
St. Michael Queenhithe
St. Michael Wood Street
St. Mildred Bread Street
St. Mildred Poultry
St. Nicholas Acons
St. Nicholas Cole Abbey
St. Nicholas Olave
St. Olave Hart Street
St. Olave Jewry
St. Olave Silver Street
St. Pancras Soper Lane
St. Peter Cornhill
St. Peter in the Tower
St. Peter le Poor
St. Peter Paul's Wharf
St. Peter Westcheap

St. Sepulchre
St. Stephen Coleman Street
St. Stephen Walbrook
St. Swithin
St. Thomas the Apostle
St. Vedast Foster Lane

OUTPARISHES AND LIBERTIES

St. Clement Danes
St. Giles in the Fields
St. James Clerkenwell
St. John's Chapel, Wapping
St. Leonard Shoreditch
St. Margaret, Westminster
St. Martin in the Fields
St. Mary le Strand/Savoy
St. Mary Whitechapel

SOUTHWARK

St. George the Martyr, Southwark
St. Mary Magdalen, Bermondsey
St. Olave, Southwark
St. Saviour, Southwark
St. Thomas Hospital, Southwark

OTHERS

Bridewell Chapel
Gray's Inn
Lincoln's Inn
The Temple

Parishes in the Diocese of London
with Lectureships, 1583–1637

The following list contains those parishes and chapels within the Diocese of London, exclusive of the City of London, that had active lectureships at some time between 1583 and 1637. It is based on the visitation call books in Guildhall Library manuscripts 9537/5–15. Because of the difficulty in determining whether the call book designation "Concionator" or "Predicator" means that the incumbent gives a lecture or that he simply possesses a preaching license, only those parishes noted as having independent lecturers are included. The list is therefore very much a minimal one, since it omits parishes where the incumbent or a group of local incumbents lectured.

PARISHES
Barkway
Boxted
Broomfield
Bursted Magna
Bushey
Castle Hedingham
Chelmsford
Chelsea
Chesterford Magna
Chigwell
Chipping Barnet
Coggeshall
Colchester, Allhallows
Colchester, St. James
Colchester, St. Michael
Dedham
Dengie
Dovercourt
Ealing
Earls Colne
East Thorpe
Epping
Felstead

Finchingfield
Gestingthorpe
Gilston
Hackney
Halstead
Hamstead
Hanwell
Hatfield Broad Oak
Hendon
Hounslow
Ickenham
Idlestree
Isleworth
Islington
Kensington
Knightsbridge
Maldon
Mountnessing
Newington
Padwinter
Rayleigh
Rochford
Romford
Ruislip

Sabridgeford
St. Albans, St. Michael
Shalford
Southminster
South Weald
Staines
Stepney
Stortford
Teddington
Theydon Bois
Tottenham
Uxbridge
Waltham
Watford
Wenden
West Brentford
West Ham
Wethersfield

CHAPELS
Hammersmith
Highgate

Parishes in the City of London with Lectureships

The parishes in the City of London that had lectureships are listed below in the order of the lectureships' appearance. Where there is no evidence concerning the date of a lectureship's actual origin, a question mark precedes the date at which there is first evidence of its existence. The principal sources for this list are the visitation call books, parish vestry minutes, and churchwardens' accounts listed under Manuscripts Consulted, pp. 375–80.

St. Antholin Budge Row, 1559
Christ Church Newgate, 1560
St. Botolph Aldersgate, 1564
St. Giles Cripplegate, 1565
St. Lawrence Jewry, ?1566
St. Mary le Bow, ?1566
Holy Trinity Minories, ?1567
St. Andrew Holborn, ?1569
St. Mary Whitechapel, 1570
St. Benet Gracechurch, 1571
The Temple, 1571
St. Clement Danes, ?1571
St. Dunstan in the East, 1572
St. Margaret Lothbury, 1573
St. Mary Aldermanbury, 1573
St. Michael Paternoster Row, ?1573
St. Peter Cornhill, 1574
St. Michael Cornhill, 1575
Gray's Inn, 1575
St. Helen Bishopsgate, 1576
St. Lawrence Pountney, 1576
St. Mary Magdalen Milk Street, 1576
St. Mary Woolnoth, ?1576
St. Margaret New Fish Street, 1577
St. Martin Ironmonger Lane, 1577
St. Mary Woolchurch, ?1577
St. Saviour, Southwark, ?1578
St. Alphage, 1580
St. Martin Orgar, 1580
Allhallows Staining, 1581
Lincoln's Inn, 1581

St. Mary Aldermary, 1581
St. Katherine Coleman, ?1581
St. Bartholomew Exchange, ?1582
St. Anne Blackfriars, 1583
St. Augustine Watling Street, 1583
St. Clement Eastcheap, 1583
St. Magnus Martyr, 1583
St. Peter Westcheap, 1583
St. Stephen Coleman Street, 1583
Allhallows Barking, ?1583
St. Michael le Querne, ?1583
St. Botolph Aldgate, 1584
St. Martin Ludgate, 1584
St. Olave Jewry, 1585
St. Margaret Pattens, 1586
St. Martin Vintry, ?1586
St. Mary le Strand, 1587
St. Sepulchre, ?1587
St. Andrew Undershaft, ?1588
St. Mary Magdalen, Bermondsey, ?1588
St. Katherine Cree, 1589
St. Bride Fleet Street, ?1589
St. Mary Colechurch, ?1589
St. Michael Bassishaw, ?1589
St. Nicholas Acons, ?1589
St. Edmund the King, ?1590
St. Matthew Friday Street, ?1590
St. Andrew Hubbard, ?1595
St. Andrew Wardrobe, ?1596
St. Dunstan in the West, ?1597
St. Gabriel Fenchurch, ?1598

St. James Clerkenwell, ?1598

St. Stephen Walbrook, 1601

St. Benet Paul's Wharf, ?1601

St. Martin in the Fields, 1602

St. Peter Paul's Wharf, 1602

Allhallows Bread Street, ?1604

St. Nicholas Cole Abbey, ?1604

St. Swithin, ?1605

St. Nicholas Olave, ?1607

St. Giles in the Fields, ?1609

St. Mary Somerset, 1611

Bridewell Chapel, ?1612

St. Margaret Moses, ?1612

St. Mildred Bread Street, ?1612

St. Peter le Poor, ?1612

St. Thomas the Apostle, ?1612

Allhallows the Less, ?1613

St. James Garlickhithe, ?1613

St. Katherine by the Tower, 1614

St. Christopher le Stocks, 1615

St. John Zachary, 1615

St. Leonard Shoreditch, ?1615

St. Michael Queenhithe, ?1615

St. Olave Hart Street, ?1615

St. Michael Crooked Lane, ?1617

St. John's Chapel, Wapping, ?1617

Allhallows Lombard Street, 1618

St. Botolph Billingsgate, ?1618

St. Gregory by St. Paul's, ?1618

St. Mildred Poultry, ?1618

St. Michael Wood Street, ?1621

Allhallows Honey Lane, 1622

St. Ethelburga, ?1624

St. Pancras Soper Lane, ?1624

St. Mary Magdalen Old Fish Street, ?1624

St. Faith under St. Paul's, 1625

St. Leonard Eastcheap, 1625

Allhallows the Great, 1627

Allhallows London Wall, ?1628

St. Bartholomew the Great, ?1628

St. Benet Fink, ?1628

St. Dionis Backchurch, ?1628

St. James Duke's Place, ?1628

St. James London Wall, ?1628

St. John the Baptist Walbrook, ?1628

St. Leonard Foster Lane, ?1628

St. Mary at Hill, ?1628

St. Olave Silver Street, ?1628

St. Olave, Southwark, ?1628

St. Vedast Foster Lane, ?1628

St. Mary Staining, ?1628

St. Martin Outwich, ?1628

St. Botolph Bishopsgate, ?1629

St. Margaret, Westminster, ?1629

SS. Anne and Agnes Aldersgate, ?1637

St. George Botolph Lane, ?1640

St. Thomas Hospital, Southwark, ?1642

St. George the Martyr, Southwark, ?1654

Statistics on Endowed Lectureships in London

The table below summarizes individual lectureship bequests from 1570 to 1659. In addition to these, seven bequests were made after 1660, and thirteen were made at unknown times.

Period	No. of donors	Cumulative listing	Period	No. of donors	Cumulative listing	Period	No. of donors	Cumulative listing
1570–74	0	0	1600–04	6	18	1630–34	12	61
1575–79	1	1	1605–09	3	21	1635–39	4	65
1580–84	5	6	1610–14	5	26	1640–44	2	67
1585–89	2	8	1615–19	7	33	1645–49	3	70
1590–94	2	10	1620–24	8	41	1650–54	4	74
1595–99	2	12	1625–29	8	49	1655–59	2	76

In the following list the London parishes are arranged by the date at which the first endowment for a lectureship in that parish is recorded:

St. Antholin Budge Row, 1576
St. Michael Paternoster Row, 1582
St. Mary Aldermary, 1582
St. Benet Gracechurch, 1583
St. Bartholomew Exchange, 1584
St. Michael Bassishaw, 1592
Christ Church Newgate, 1600
Allhallows Bread Street, 1604
St. Michael Cornhill, 1605
St. Mary le Bow, 1610
St. Anne Blackfriars, 1616
St. Mary Whitechapel, 1616
St. Stephen Coleman Street, 1616
St. Swithin, 1616
St. Mildred Poultry, 1623
St. Olave Jewry, 1623

St. Dunstan in the West, 1624
Allhallows the Less, 1625
St. Faith under St. Paul's, 1625
St. Margaret New Fish Street, 1626
St. Margaret Pattens, 1626
St. Pancras Soper Lane, 1626
St. Peter Cornhill, 1630
St. Mary at Hill, 1630
St. Helen Bishopsgate, 1634
St. Lawrence Jewry, 1639
St. Magnus the Martyr, 1639
St. Mary Magdalen Milk Street, 1642
St. Nicholas Cole Abbey, 1646
St. Gregory by St. Paul's, 1651
St. Olave Hart Street, 1653

The cumulative number of parishes with lectureships and of parishes with endowed lectureships can be summarized as shown in the table on the following page.

Period	Parishes with lectureships	Parishes with endowed lectureships	Period	Parishes with lectureships	Parishes with endowed lectureships
1565–69	8	0	1615–19	92	14
1570–74	17	0	1620–24	97	17
1575–79	27	1	1625–29	116	22
1580–84	44	5	1630–34	116	25
1585–89	56	5	1635–39	117	27
1590–94	58	6	1640–44	119	28
1595–99	63	6	1645–49	119	29
1600–04	69	8	1650–54	120	31
1605–09	72	9	1655–59	120	31
1610–14	81	10			

Statistics on the London Lecturers' Careers

The number of London lecturers who attended each of the various universities is given below. Lecturers who attended several colleges or universities in the course of their careers are listed under the institution from which they received their first degree, or, if no degree was taken, where they matriculated or were first admitted. No information could be found on the university training of 131, or 18 per cent, of the 700 known lecturers.

University	Total	Puritan	University	Total	Puritan
Oxford			Cambridge		
Magdalen Hall	26	20	Emmanuel	56	49
Christ Church	16	8	Christ's	56	31
Magdalen	15	8	St. John's	49	29
Brasenose	15	11	Trinity	41	18
St. John's	14	4	Queen's	21	9
Exeter	12	5	Pembroke	20	5
Queen's	10	7	Magdalene	18	14
New Inn Hall	9	9	Caius	15	7
Trinity	8	4	King's	15	9
Balliol	8	3	Jesus	14	5
Merton	5	2	Corpus Christi	13	4
Lincoln	5	1	Peterhouse	13	9
Wadham	5	4	Clare	11	7
Corpus Christi	5	4	Sidney Sussex	9	9
Broadgates	4	1	St. Catherine's	8	7
New College	4	2	Unknown	5	2
Gloucester Hall	4	1	SUBTOTAL	364	214
St. Mary's	4	3			
Pembroke	4	1	Trinity, Dublin	3	2
Hart Hall	3	2	St. Andrew's, Scotland	4	2
University	2	1	Edinburgh, Scotland	1	0
St. Alban Hall	2	2	Harvard, Mass.	2	2
Oriel	2	0	GRAND TOTAL	569	330
All Soul's	1	0			
St. Edmund Hall	1	1			
Unknown	11	6			
SUBTOTAL	195	110			

Places of birth and of last preferment for those who lectured in London between 1560 and 1662 are given opposite. Place of birth is unknown for 288, or 41 per cent, of the 700 known lecturers, and place of last preferment is unknown for 162, or 23 per cent.

Place	Birth		Last preferment	
	Total	Puritan	Total	Puritan
England				
London and Middlesex	95	57	283	184
Yorkshire	29	19	9	4
Northamptonshire	25	12	9	2
Essex	18	9	39	20
Norfolk	18	7	10	6
Kent	17	11	22	8
Leicestershire	13	9	7	6
Gloucestershire	11	9	5	2
Suffolk	10	7	9	4
Warwickshire	10	9	5	4
Hertfordshire	10	7	19	14
Lancashire	10	3	1	1
Buckinghamshire	10	6	6	4
Surrey	9	6	10	5
Cheshire	9	5	6	1
Wilshire	8	5	4	3
Somerset	8	5	5	3
Lincolnshire	7	3	6	3
Hampshire	6	3	4	2
Bedfordshire	6	3	5	1
Worcestershire	6	3	3	0
Shropshire	6	5	4	4
Devon	5	4	3	1
Cambridge	5	1	8	7
Berkshire	5	3	4	2
Oxfordshire	4	2	11	8
Nottinghamshire	4	3	2	2
Huntingdonshire	3	2	4	1
Herefordshire	3	3	2	1
Sussex	3	2	8	5
Cornwall	3	2	3	1
Durham	3	2	3	2
Staffordshire	3	3	3	2
Rutland	2	2	1	1
Westmorland	2	1	0	0
Derbyshire	1	1	0	0
Northumberland	1	1	1	1
Cumberland	1	0	0	0
Dorset	1	1	2	1
Monmouthshire	0	0	1	1
SUBTOTAL	390	236	527	317
Wales	10	6	1	0
Scotland	7	3	1	1
Ireland	3	2	3	1
Continent	1	0	0	0
New England	1	1	6	6
SUBTOTAL	22	12	11	8
GRAND TOTAL	412	248	538	325

A summary of the London lecturers' careers is given below. The term Anglicans here includes all lecturers who cannot be identified positively as Puritans. An independent lectureship is one that was not held simultaneously with a curacy or with the benefice in the same parish, as opposed to a combined lectureship, which is one that was held simultaneously with another preferment. All figures have been rounded off to the nearest whole number.

	1560–79	1580–99	1600–19	1620–39	1640–62
Total number of lecturers	51	121	107	222	199
Affiliation of lecturers					
Puritans	56%	36%	40%	47%	78%
Anglicans	44	64	60	53	22
Lecturers with known careers					
Puritans	65%	82%	90%	93%	86%
Anglicans	62	69	75	60	71
First preferment was London lecture-ship					
Puritans	63%	23%	38%	55%	24%
Anglicans	54	36	40	52	23
First London lectureship was independent					
Puritans	65%	83%	68%	53%	76%
Anglicans	62	62	35	47	60
First London lectureship was combined					
Puritans	35%	17%	32%	47%	24%
Anglicans	38	38	65	53	40
Had other preferments after first London lectureship					
Puritans	24%	74%	79%	74%	59%
Anglicans	92	79	79	83	70
Had other lectureships after first London lectureship					
Puritans	71%	51%	50%	51%	43%
Anglicans	54	19	27	27	20
Average age at time of first London lectureship					
Puritans	35	34	33	31	36
Anglicans	34	30	32	32	42
Average number of years lectured in total career					
Puritans	16	10	14	11	7
Anglicans	8	7	10	7	4

Notes

Notes

Printed sources are cited in full at the first reference in each chapter. Manuscript sources are cited by archival call number, and both the call number and the title of the manuscript document referred to are given under Manuscripts Consulted, pp. 375–80. The following abbreviations are used in the Notes:

A.P.C.: *Acts of the Privy Council*
C.J.: *Journals of the House of Commons*
C.S.P.D.: *Calendar of State Papers, Domestic*
C.W. Accts.: Churchwardens' Accounts
D.N.B.: *Dictionary of National Biography*
GLMS: Guildhall Library Manuscript
H.MSS.C.: *Historical Manuscripts Commission*

LCCRO: London County Council Record Office
LPLMS: Lambeth Palace Library Manuscript
PRO: Public Record Office
V.C.H.: *Victoria County History*
V.M.: Vestry Minutes
WPLMS: Westminster Public Library Manuscript

INTRODUCTION

1. John Donne, *The First Anniversarie: An Anatomie of the World* (London, 1612), ll. 210–13, 426.

2. See G. R. Elton, *The Tudor Revolution in Government* (Cambridge, Eng., 1953); Lawrence Stone, "The Educational Revolution in England, 1560–1640," *Past and Present*, XXVIII (1964), 41–80; and Michael Walzer, *The Revolution of the Saints* (Cambridge, Mass., 1965).

3. Matthew Hutton to Lord Burghley, 6 Oct. 1573, in *A Collection of State Papers Relating to Affairs in the Reign of Queen Elizabeth*, ed. William Murdin (London, 1759), II, 262.

4. That such differences were central has been ably argued recently by John F. H. New in *Anglican and Puritan* (Stanford, Calif., 1964), *passim*.

5. For the significant role played by the laity in Puritanism from the inception of the movement, see *Letters of Thomas Wood, Puritan, 1566–1577*, ed. Patrick Collinson (*Bulletin of the Institute of Historical Research*, Special Supplement no. 5; London, 1960), and Patrick Collinson, *The Elizabethan Puritan Movement* (London, 1967). On the whole the laity has been neglected in studies of Puritanism, but see such important recent works as W. K. Jordan, *Philanthropy in England, 1480–1660* (London, 1959); *Suffolk and the Great Rebellion, 1640–1660*, ed. Alan Everitt (Suffolk Records Society, Vol. III; Ipswich, 1960), Introduction; Claire Cross, *The Puritan Earl* (London, 1966); and Roger Howell, *Newcastle upon Tyne and the Puritan Revolution* (Oxford, 1967). Collinson brings out very clearly the great difficulties experienced by the Puritan clerical leadership, even within the Presbyterian movement, in achieving any kind of coherent direction and recognized organization and control; see both *The Elizabethan Puritan Movement* and his earlier article, "John Field and Elizabethan Puritanism," in

S. T. Bindoff *et al.*, eds., *Elizabethan Government and Society* (London, 1961), pp. 127–62.

6. Richard Sibbes, *The Collected Works,* ed. Alexander B. Grosart (Edinburgh, 1863), V, 339, as quoted in Jerald C. Brauer, "Reflections on the Nature of English Puritanism," *Church History,* XXIII (1954), 102.

7. See Robert M. Kingdon, *Geneva and the Coming of the Wars of Religion in France, 1555–1563* (Geneva, 1956).

8. See H. G. Koenigsberger, "The Organization of Revolutionary Parties in France and the Netherlands during the Sixteenth Century," *Journal of Modern History,* XXVII (1955), esp. p. 336.

9. *Ibid.,* p. 336.

10. For the Attorney General's accusation, see Isabel M. Calder, *Activities of the Puritan Faction of the Church of England, 1625–33* (London, 1957), pp. 52–53.

11. Christopher Hill, *Society and Puritanism in Pre-Revolutionary England* (London, 1964), chs. 2, 3; Irvonwy Morgan, *The Godly Preachers of the Elizabethan Church* (London, 1965), chs. 1, 2.

Epigraph to Part I: Edward Dering, *XXVII Lectures, for Readings, upon Part of the Epistle to the Hebrews* (London, 1576), Heb. 5:8–9, as quoted in John F. H. New, *Anglican and Puritan* (Stanford, Calif., 1964), p. 125, n. 68.

CHAPTER I

1. *Creeds of the Churches,* ed. John H. Leith (New York, 1963), p. 273.

2. John Jewel, *An Apology of the Church of England,* ed. J. E. Booty (Ithaca, N.Y., 1963), pp. 27, 28.

3. *Ibid.,* p. 31.

4. Richard Hooker, *Of the Laws of Ecclesiastical Polity* (Everyman's Library ed.; London, 1907), II, 200.

5. *Creeds of the Churches,* p. 203.

6. John F. H. New, *Anglican and Puritan* (Stanford, Calif., 1964), pp. 64–69.

7. *The Two Books of Homilies,* ed. John Griffiths (Oxford, 1859), pp. 3–4.

8. *An Admonition to the Parliament* (1572), reprinted in W. H. Dunham and Stanley Pargellis, eds., *Complaint and Reform in England* (New York, 1938), p. 236.

9. John Strype, *The History of the Life and Acts of the Most Reverend Father in God, Edmund Grindal* (Oxford, 1821), p. 329.

10. Grindal to Queen Elizabeth, 20 Dec. 1576, as quoted in *ibid.,* pp. 561–62.

11. *The Seconde Parte of a Register,* ed. Albert Peel (Cambridge, Eng., 1915), I, 75.

12. Philip Stubbes, *The Second Part of the Anatomie of Abuses* (London, 1583), ed. Frederick J. Furnivall (London, 1882), p. 76; see also pp. 72–79. Although Stubbes had no quarrel with episcopacy, he was certainly a Puritan. His example points, in fact, to the danger of assuming that Elizabethan Puritanism and Presbyterianism were synonymous, for particularly among the laity Presbyterianism had little appeal. A general discussion of the nature and role of preaching for the Puritans is to be found in Horton Davies, *The Worship of the Puritans* (Westminster, 1948), pp. 182–203.

13. *The Acts of the High Commission Court within the Diocese of Durham,* ed. W. H. D. Longstaffe (Surtees Society, Vol. XXXIV; Durham, 1858), pp. 191–92.

14. This is tainted testimony, for the parishioners also certified that their minister was a royalist—"a noted malignant"—and petitioned for his removal. Adam Eyre, "A

Dyurnall," in *Yorkshire Diaries and Autobiographies,* ed. Charles Jackson (Surtees Society, Vol. LXV; Durham, 1877), pp. 19–20.

15. *Diary of John Rous,* ed. M. A. E. Green (Camden Society, old ser., Vol. LXVI; London, 1856), p. 69.

16. Martin Marprelate, *An Epistle to the Terrible Priests,* ed. John Petheram (London, 1843), pp. 38–39.

17. Lancelot Andrewes, *Works,* ed. J. P. Wilson and J. Bliss (Oxford, 1841–54), II, 542, as quoted in Charles H. and Katherine George, *The Protestant Mind of the English Reformation, 1570–1640* (Princeton, N.J., 1961), p. 336.

18. Sermon given at Paul's Cross, 31 Dec. 1626, as quoted in Millar Maclure, *The Paul's Cross Sermons, 1534–1642* (Toronto, 1958), pp. 249–50. Valentine lectured twice weekly at St. Dunstan's from 1626 until 1630, when he became rector of Deptford, Kent. GLMS 2968/2, fols. 309r, 310r; LPLMS 942, no. 16; John and J. A. Venn, *Alumni Cantabrigienses,* Part I (Cambridge, Eng., 1922), Vol. IV, p. 293.

19. William Cobbett, ed., *Cobbett's Complete Collection of State Trials* (London, 1809), III, 738.

20. *An Order Made by the House of Commons for the Establishing of Preaching Lecturers, Through the Kingdome of England and Wales* (London, 1641), p. 3.

21. *Two Books of Homilies,* pp. 3–4.

22. Sermon of 25 Nov. 1621, as quoted in Maclure, *Paul's Cross Sermons,* p. 108.

23. Quoted in John E. Neale, *Queen Elizabeth* (New York, 1934), p. 8. Peter Heylyn, Laud's chaplain, thought that catechizers might be "accounted the best sort of Preachers for the instruction of the people." *Aerius Redivivus* (Oxford, 1670), p. 282. One wonders whether Heylyn's attitude may not be explained in part by the fact that the approved style of preaching in Court circles was so "witty" and "metaphysical" that the content of the sermons was incomprehensible to an ordinary parish congregation; see Perry Miller, *The New England Mind: The Seventeenth Century* (New York, 1939), p. 359.

24. Cf. Philip Hughes, *The Reformation in England* (New York, 1954), III, 122–32.

25. Thomas Fuller, *The Church History of Britain* (London, 1842), III, 102. John Hacket, Bishop Williams's chaplain, made somewhat the same observation from a much less sympathetic point of view. Puritans, he said, "in great part were covetous, crossgrained, half-witted, and distractious, and had nothing but much preaching to make them plausible and popular." *Scrinia Reserata* (London, 1693), Part I, p. 34.

26. For the requirements concerning quarterly and monthly sermons, see *Injunctions Given by the Queens Majesty, Anno Domini 1559* (London, 1559), nos. 3, 4. Canon 45 of the 1604 Canons required that all resident incumbents with proper preaching licenses preach every Sunday; Canon 46 required that all incumbents, who could not preach, procure monthly sermons to be preached by a licensed minister. *Constitutions and Canons Ecclesiasticall ... Anno Dom. 1603* (London, 1633), n.p. Ronald Marchant speculates that the 1603 Canons worked to the benefit of the Puritans in the North, notably in Yorkshire, where they constituted about one-third of all licensed preachers; according to Marchant, their willingness to preach gained them access to the pulpits of non-preachers, who hired them for the monthly sermon. *The Puritans and the Church Courts in the Diocese of York, 1560–1642* (London, 1960), p. 28.

27. Montagu to Cosin, 12 Dec. [1624?], in *The Correspondence of John Cosin,* ed. George Ornsby (Surtees Society, Vol. LII; Durham, 1869), I, 32.

28. Montagu to Cosin, 12 Jan. 1626/7, in *ibid.,* p. 105. Montagu did not remain a lecturer for very long; on July 2 of the same year he wrote to Cosin: "I am now in the

course of my lectures come to the point of falling from grace; which, when I have dispatched, I end, and give over the lectures at Michaelmas. I shall not Calvinize it, nor yet Arminianize it, but with the Church of England, Augustine and Prosper, go the middle way." *Ibid.*, p. 125.

29. Hacket, *Scrinia Reserata*, Part I, p. 34.

30. Peter Heylyn, *Cyprianus Anglicus* (London, 1671), p. 64.

31. *The Letters and Epigrams of Sir John Harrington*, ed. Norman E. McClure (Philadelphia, 1930), p. 156.

32. John Earle, *Microcosmography*, ed. A. S. West (Cambridge, Eng., 1920), p. 49. This is a reprint of the 1633 edition.

33. John Udall, *A Demonstration of the Truth of That Discipline* [1588], ed. Edward Arber (Westminster, 1895), p. 49.

34. *Ibid.*, p. 50. See also Irvonwy Morgan, *The Godly Preachers of the Elizabethan Church* (London, 1965), p. 25, and Patrick Collinson, *The Elizabethan Puritan Movement* (London, 1967), pp. 341–42.

35. Patrick Collinson, *A Mirror of Elizabethan Puritanism: The Life and Letters of "Godly Master Dering"* (Friends of Dr. Williams's Library, Seventeenth Lecture, 1963; London, 1964), pp. 11, 8. Professor Collinson, perhaps the most perceptive student of Elizabethan Puritanism writing today, claims that Dering was "the archetype of the Puritan divine, whose life and works were a model for many who would come after him in the seventeenth century." Although Collinson asserts that "in his teaching on the ministry Dering had more in common with the first generation of Protestant reformers than with the new and more narrowly dogmatic Calvinists who were coming to the fore in the 1570's," he nevertheless points out that Dering's highly idealized conception of the ministry implied a Presbyterian position. Dering, unlike his more radical friends, "was more concerned with condemning the popish abuses of church offices than with dogmatically defining the offices themselves. This practical concern with the sins of prelacy rather than with the unlawfulness of episcopacy would always be characteristic of the main stream of the English Protestant tradition." It was also, as Collinson notes, a characteristic that appealed strongly to the anticlerical laity. *Ibid.*, pp. 2, 25–26.

36. *The Letters and Life of Francis Bacon*, ed. James Spedding (London, 1861–74), I, 40–41.

37. Stubbes, *Second Part of the Anatomie of Abuses*, p. 87.

38. *Ibid.*, pp. 87, 76.

39. Christopher Hill, *Economic Problems of the Church from Archbishop Whitgift to the Long Parliament* (Oxford, 1956), pp. 50–167. Contemporaries were well aware of the competitive aspect of the lectureships. According to Robert Chestlin, for example, "The suit for increase of tithes in City livings ... so nettled the purse-proud Londoners, accounting tithes but as a gift, or alms, that they would rather spend at law, or give to a lecturer of their own choice twice as much ... than to pay their dues to the parson." *Persecutio Undecima: The Churches Eleventh Persecution; or, A Briefe of the Puritan Persecution of the Protestant Clergy of England* (n.p., 1648), p. 11.

40. *Certaine Affirmations in Defence of the Pulling Down of Communion Rails, by Divers Rash and Misguided People, Judiciously and Religiously Answered, by a Gentleman of Worth* (London, 1641), Epistle Dedicatory. In the same year Lord Newark made a similar, much-qualified defense of prayer in the course of the debate on the right of the bishops to a seat in the House of Lords: "There is not any that sits here more for preaching than I am. I know it is the ordinary means to salvation; yet I like-

wise know there is not that full necessity of it as was in the primitive times. God defend, that sixteen hundred years' acquaintance should make the gospel of Christ no better known unto us! Neither, my lords, doth their office merely and wholly consist in preaching; but, partly in that; partly in praying and administering the blessed sacraments; in a godly and exemplary life . . . ; and partly in easing the burdened conscience. These, my lords, complete the office of a churchman." As quoted in Thomas Fuller, *The Church History of Britain* (London, 1842), III, 438.

41. [Robert Browne], *An Answere to Master Cartwright* [1585?], in *The Writings of Robert Harrison and Robert Browne*, ed. Albert Peel and Leland H. Carlson (London, 1953), p. 441.

42. [Robert Browne], *A True and Short Declaration* [1584], in *ibid.*, p. 419.

43. Robert Harrison, *A Treatise of the Church and the Kingdome of Christ* [1580?], in *ibid.*, p. 36. The judgment of Robert Browne was harsher: "Parish preachers and hired lecturers" were collectively part of "all that Popish rabble" and were no better than Scribes and Pharisees sitting in the seat of Moses. *A Treatise upon the 23. of Matthewe* [1582], in *ibid.*, p. 209.

44. John Canne, *A Necessity of Separation from the Church of England Proved by the Nonconformists' Principles*, ed. Charles Stovel (Hanserd Knollys Society; London, 1849), pp. 56–57. An anonymous biographer of the famous Puritan divine Stephen Marshall tells the following story. After succeeding Richard Rodgers as lecturer at Wethersfield, Marshall "had not continued long . . . before Mr. Pickering, . . . minister of Finchingfield, died. The fatness of the benefit helped the patron to suitors enow, but, amongst all, our Marshall was the man whom his affection made choice of . . . ; who having unluckily married himself to Wethersfield, knows not what course to take to sue out a bill of divorce. The great living, worth £200 a year, is a strong temptation . . . ; however, Wethersfield holds him to his promise, *never to leave them*. A little assembly of divines is called. . . . The casuists, knowing his mind before, conclude, that it bound him not to leave them for a *lesser salary*, but left him at liberty to take a *bigger* living when he could get it." *Life of Marshall* (1680), p. 5, as quoted in Benjamin Brook, *Lives of the Puritans* (London, 1813), III, 242.

45. The testimony of Abigail Delamar, given before the Court of High Commission, 7 June 1632, after her arrest at a conventicle at Blackfriars, suggests that Separatists did go to lectures on occasion. "[Bishop of] London: '. . . she a deep Familist and Brownist.' Abigail Delamar, 'I hold no Familism.' Archbishop of Canterbury: 'But, woman, where dwell you, in what parish?' Abigail D.: 'At Giles where Manwairing dwelleth.' Cant.: 'How often have you heard him within this 12 month?' A.D.: 'I have not heard him often, for the Parliament put him by his preaching a great while.' Cant.: 'Wilt thou go hear him next Sunday?' A.D.: 'No, but I will go in the afternoon.' [Margin: "Mr. Mew is the Lecturer there in the afternoon."] Cant.: 'Why not in the forenoon?' A.D.: 'Because then I shall hear popish doctrine.'" *Reports of Cases in the Courts of Star Chamber and High Commission*, ed. S. R. Gardiner (Camden Society, new ser., Vol. XXXIX; London, 1886), pp. 300–301. William Mew, the lecturer, was a Puritan; he lived long enough to sit in the Westminster Assembly and to be ejected in 1662. A. G. Matthews, *Calamy Revised* (Oxford, 1934), p. 349.

46. Edmund Grindal, *The Remains of Edmund Grindal, D.D.*, ed. William Nicholson (Parker Society; Cambridge, Eng., 1843), pp. 201–5, 316–19; Morgan, *Godly Preachers*, pp. 44–48, 94–95; H. Gareth Owen, "A Nursery of Elizabethan Nonconformity, 1567–72," *Journal of Ecclesiastical History*, XVII (1966), 65–76.

47. D.N.B.; for Caryl, see Matthews, *Calamy Revised*, pp. 103–4.

48. Chamberlain to Carleton, 10 March 1621, in *The Letters of John Chamberlain,* ed. Norman E. McClure (American Philosophical Society, Memoirs XII, Part II; Philadelphia, 1939), II, 350.

49. Chamberlain to Carleton, 21 Oct. 1608, in *ibid.,* I, 264.

50. Liber Correctione, 11 Jan. 1605/6, LCCRO, DL/C/304, fol. 43r; for later entries on the same case, see *ibid.,* fol. 165r, and DL/C/305, fols. 279r, 299r, 303r.

51. The "Mr. Clapham" whom John Manningham, the lawyer and diarist, heard lecture at St. Peter Paul's Wharf in late 1602 and early 1603 may have been the Brownist Henoch Clapham, who is known to have been in London in those years. *Diary of John Manningham,* ed. John Bruce (Camden Society, old ser., Vol. XCIX; Westminster, 1868), p. 158, and see also pp. 75–76, 105–6, 113, 127, 133; Champlin Burrage, *The Early English Dissenters in the Light of Recent Research (1550–1641)* (Cambridge, Eng., 1912), I, 196–200. Henry Jacie (or Jessy) was a Separatist and after 1645 a Baptist, but he held the lectureship at St. George's, Southwark, during the Commonwealth years; when he initially came to London in 1637, it was to accept a call from the Separatist congregation in Southwark, which had previously been led by John Lathrop. Matthews, *Calamy Revised,* p. 298; Marchant, *Puritans and the Church Courts,* pp. 122–23, 256; Henry Jacie/Jessy to John Winthrop, Jr., 18 June 1637, in *Winthrop Papers,* (Massachusetts Historical Society; Cambridge, Mass., 1929–47), III, 485.

52. For a series of rather subtle distinctions concerning the social status of various Puritan groups, see David Mathew, *The Age of Charles I* (London, 1951), pp. 116–22. The case of John Goodwin is suggestive. After John Davenport's departure from St. Stephen Coleman in 1633, Goodwin served there as vicar and lecturer. In 1645, having formed a separate, covenanted congregation, he was forced to withdraw to St. Mary Abchurch, and the vestry of St. Stephen's hired a Presbyterian minister. In 1649 Goodwin was invited back with his congregation to share St. Stephen's with the regular incumbent. However, part of the agreement for his return specified that the sharing of the church should in no way compromise the property rights of the regular parishioners in their pews. In other words, it would seem that the pew owners came from among the conservative, Presbyterian parishioners, not from among the members of Goodwin's gathered church. GLMS 4458/1, pp. 129, 134, 135, 161. Yet various examinations and depositions of Separatists suggest that the conventicles drew their members from the artisans and lesser professions: glovers, weavers, leatherworkers, haberdashers, coopers, shipwrights, joiners, scriveners, and apothecaries. Such men can hardly be classed among the London proletariat. See Burrage, *Early English Dissenters,* II, 24, 31–61, 323–24.

53. Cotton Mather, *Magnalia Christi Americana* (Hartford, Conn., 1820), I, 238.

54. For Cartwright's lecture in the 1580's, see Samuel Clarke, *A General Martyrologie* (London, 1651), p. 370. For Travers's lecture at the Temple, 1583–86, see *A Calendar of the Inner Temple Records,* ed. F. A. Inderwick (London, 1896–1901), I, 327, 333. For Chaderton's lecture at the Temple, 1579–80, see *Middle Temple Records,* ed. C. H. Hopwood (London, 1904), I, 224. For Gilby, see Claire Cross, "Noble Patronage in the Elizabethan Church," *Historical Journal,* III (1960), 5–8. For Field's lecture in the Minories, see E. M. Tomlinson, *A History of the Minories London* (London, 1907), p. 220; for his lecture at St. Mary Aldermary, 1581–85, see Patrick Collinson, "John Field and Elizabethan Puritanism," in S. T. Bindoff *et al.,* eds., *Elizabethan Government and Society* (London, 1961), p. 143. For Crowley's lecture at St. Antholin's, 1576–77, see GLMS 1046/1, fols. 6r, 7v; at St. Margaret New Fish Street, 1577, GLMS 1176/1, no fol.; and at St. Saviour, Southwark, 1578, LCCRO, P/92/S/449, p. 140.

55. For Ames's lecture at Dedham in 1609, see Harold Smith, *The Ecclesiastical History of Essex under the Long Parliament and Commonwealth* (Colchester, n.d.), p. 23. For Perkins and Baynes, see William Haller, *The Rise of Puritanism* (New York, 1938), pp. 64–65. For Dodd's lecture at Banbury, see Brook, *Lives,* III, 1. For the Rogerses of Essex, see Smith, *Ecclesiastical History of Essex,* pp. 24–26, 30–32, 39, 41–43. For Greenham's lecture at Christ Church Newgate, 1591–94, see H. Gareth Owen, "Tradition and Reform: Ecclesiastical Controversy in an Elizabethan London Parish," *Guildhall Miscellany,* II, no. 2 (1961), 69. For Egerton's lecture at St. Anne Blackfriars, see *Two Elizabethan Puritan Diaries,* ed. M. M. Knappen (Chicago, 1933), pp. 31, 34. For Preston's lecture at Lincoln's Inn, 1622–28, see *The Records of the Honorable Society of Lincoln's Inn: The Black Books,* ed. J. D. Walker and W. P. Baildon (London, 1897–1902), II, 234, 277. For Sibbes at Gray's Inn, 1616–35, see *Pension Book of Gray's Inn, 1569–1669,* ed. R. J. Fletcher (London, 1901), pp. 224, 325. For William Gouge's lecture at St. Anne Blackfriars, 1608–53, see *D.N.B.*

56. For the importance of Perkins's writings, see Haller, *Rise of Puritanism,* p. 91, and I. Breward, "The Significance of William Perkins," *Journal of Religious History,* IV (1966), 113–28. For Preston, see Irvonwy Morgan, *Prince Charles's Puritan Chaplain* (London, 1957), *passim.*

57. Thomas Fuller, *The Worthies of England,* ed. John Freeman (London, 1952), p. 301.

58. John Donne, *Iuvenilia, or Certaine Paradoxes and Problemes* (London, 1633), reprinted by Facsimile Text Society (New York, 1936), sig. F4r.

59. *The Autobiography of Richard Baxter,* ed. J. M. Lloyd Thomas (Everyman's Library ed.; London, 1931), pp. 26, 18–19.

60. For Rogers's comments, see *Two Elizabethan Puritan Diaries,* esp. pp. 84–85.

61. *The Life of Adam Martindale,* ed. Richard Parkinson (Chetham Society, Vol. IV; Manchester, 1845), p. 36. Cf. also *The Diary of the Rev. Ralph Josselin, 1616–1683,* ed. E. Hockliffe (Camden Society, 3d ser., Vol. XV; London, 1908), pp. 3–4.

62. Haller, *Rise of Puritanism,* p. 54.

63. *Life of Adam Martindale,* p. 104.

64. *Two Elizabethan Puritan Diaries,* p. 100.

65. The most sophisticated attempt so far made to sketch the nature of the transformation of society that took place in the sixteenth and seventeenth centuries is Lawrence Stone's "Social Mobility in England, 1500–1700," *Past and Present,* XXXIII (1966), 16–55. Two stimulating analyses of the way traditional modes of political thought came under attack are W. H. Greenleaf's *Order, Empiricism and Politics* (Oxford, 1964) and Michael Walzer's *The Revolution of the Saints* (Cambridge, Mass., 1965), esp. pp. 148–98; Walzer's book describes in particular the contribution of Puritanism.

66. The Lambeth Articles (1595), Article 5, as quoted in George, *Protestant Mind,* p. 59.

67. Entry dated 20 Feb. 1655/6, *Diary of Ralph Josselin,* p. 114. The problems Puritan ministers faced because they lacked disciplinary authority can be illustrated by any number of entries from the Minute Book of the Dedham classis. For example: "Mr. D. Cricke moved how he should deal with some obstinate condemners and railers of his doctrine. It was deferred till some more fit time." R. G. Usher, ed., *The Presbyterian Movement in the Reign of Queen Elizabeth* (Camden Society, 3d ser., Vol. VIII; London, 1905), p. 40; see also pp. 39, 41.

68. Dering to the Lords of the Council, 26 Nov. 1573, in William Murdin, ed., *A Collection of State Papers* (London, 1759), II, 271.

69. Dering to Burghley, 3 Nov. 1573, as quoted in Collinson, *Mirror of Elizabethan Puritanism*, p. 25.

70. *Diary of Ralph Josselin*, p. 10.

71. *Ibid.*, pp. 142, 11, 49, 99.

72. Cf. the debate over William Negus's decision to leave his lectureship at Ipswich for the benefice at Leigh in Usher, ed., *Presbyterian Movement*, pp. 46–47. As the Puritan scholar Samuel Ward noted in his diary, "A man must therefore labor above all things for alacrity in God's service." Unfortunately, it was very difficult to distinguish between such alacrity and worldly ambition. For Ward's own struggles in this respect, see *Two Elizabethan Puritan Diaries*, pp. 103, 105, 110, 115–16, 128. The doctrine of the calling was of little assistance in such cases, for the Puritans found it as difficult as men before and since to disentangle God's providence and calling from the dictates of ambition. See *ibid.*, p. 128, and *Diary of Ralph Josselin*, p. 10. Rather, the Puritan clerics appear to have turned from an unanswerable question to the more practical issue—to what degree the minister had engaged himself to remain with his congregation. See *H.MSS.C., 14ᵗʰ Report, Appendix, Part II: MSS. of the Duke of Portland* (London, 1894), III, 33, 145.

73. Usher, ed., *Presbyterian Movement*, pp. 45–46.

74. M. M. Knappen, *Tudor Puritanism* (Chicago, 1939), p. 333n; R. G. Usher, *The Reconstruction of the English Church* (New York, 1910), I, 280, 278, 268–69. Cf. Usher, ed., *Presbyterian Movement*, pp. xxiv–xxvi.

75. *The Seconde Parte of a Register*, ed. Albert Peel (Cambridge, Eng., 1915), I, 135–36.

76. See, for example, "A Bill Exhibited to the Parliament for Reformation of the Ministerie" [1586], in *Seconde Parte of a Register*, II, 196; Article 2 of the Millenary Petition, 1603, in J. P. Kenyon, ed., *The Stuart Constitution, 1603–1688* (Cambridge, Eng., 1966), p. 133; Article 1 of the Puritan requests made at the Hampton Court Conference, 1604, in *H.MSS.C., Report of the Manuscripts of Lord Montagu of Beaulieu* (London, 1900), p. 32; and Declaration of the Lords and Commons, April 1642, in *Diary of John Rous*, ed. M. A. E. Green (Camden Society, old ser., Vol. LXVI; London, 1856), pp. 119–20.

77. John More, *Three Godly and Fruitful Sermons* (Cambridge, Eng., 1594), pp. 66–69, as quoted in Collinson, *Mirror of Elizabethan Puritanism*, p. 9.

78. Quoted in Claire Cross, *The Puritan Earl: The Life of Henry Hastings, Third Earl of Huntingdon, 1536–1595* (London, 1966), pp. 43–44.

79. *The Zurich Letters*, ed. Hastings Robinson (Parker Society, Vol. L; Cambridge, Eng., 1842), p. 86.

80. *Records of the Borough of Leicester*, ed. Mary Bateson (Cambridge, Eng., 1905), III, 101.

81. *Diary of Walter Yonge, Esq.*, ed. George Roberts (Camden Society, old ser., Vol. XLI; London, 1848), pp. 85–86.

82. *The Autobiography of Henry Newcome, M.A.*, ed. Richard Parkinson (Chetham Society, Vol. XXVI; Manchester, 1852), p. 25.

83. Lady Katherine Paston to William Paston, March 1626?, in *The Correspondence of Lady Katherine Paston, 1603–1627*, ed. Ruth Hughey (Norfolk Record Society, Vol. XIV; n.p., 1941), pp. 90–91; Brilliana Harley to Edward Harley, 7 May 1639, in *Portland MSS.*, III, 57.

84. *Diary of Lady Margaret Hoby*, ed. Dorothy M. Meads (Boston, 1930), p. 32.

85. Robert Greene, *The Repentance of Robert Greene Maister of Arts* (London,

1592), in *Life and Complete Works*, ed. A. B. Grosart (New York, 1964), XII, 175–76, 178; *Diary of Ralph Josselin*, p. 4. If the autobiographical details are accurate, the preacher Greene heard must have been John More, Edward Dering's friend, who lectured at St. Andrew's for twenty years. Cf. Morgan, *Godly Preachers*, pp. 30–31, where, however, Morgan mistakenly cites Greene's *A Groatworth of Witte* as the source of the story. The whole of Greene's *Repentance* is a diatribe against sin, in which the author holds himself up as a horrible example of the kind of man who stopped his ears "against the voice of God's Ministers" (p. 174). That Greene, who must have had an ear well-tuned to the demands of the London market, expected such a pamphlet to sell suggests that by the 1590's the Puritans had already impressed their ethical concern on a large number of literate Londoners. The language of the pamphlet, which is close to that employed by the Puritan preachers, leads one to suppose that Greene himself was not immune to their style, even if he was deaf to their message.

86. *The Journal of Nicholas Assheton*, ed. F. R. Raines (Chetham Society, Vol. XIV; Manchester, 1848), pp. v–vi, xii–xiii, 87, 74, and *passim*.

87. Quoted by Maurice Ashley in *England in the Seventeenth Century (1603–1714)* (Baltimore, 1961), p. 18.

88. *Diary of Lady Margaret Hoby*, pp. 66, 83–84. When in London, Lady Margaret was equally assiduous in her attendance at lectures, going regularly to hear Stephen Egerton at Blackfriars, her mother's parish, and also on occasion to hear the lecture at "Westminster Church," presumably St. Margaret's. *Ibid.*, pp. 150–51.

89. *The Autobiography and Correspondence of Sir Simonds D'Ewes, Bart., during the Reigns of James I and Charles I*, ed. James O. Halliwell (London, 1845), I, 95, 137–38.

90. Lucy Hutchinson, *Memoirs of the Life of Colonel Hutchinson*, ed. C. H. Firth (London, 1906), p. 13. A prebendary of Bristol Cathedral reported to Laud in 1634 that at a local parish church a lecture was substituted for catechizing on Sunday afternoons, "the resort to which especially with contribution is made a mark of cognizance of the holy from the profane as they term them." House of Lords MSS., "Papers Relating to Archbishop Laud's Visitations," in *H.MSS.C., 4th Report, Part I, Appendix* (London, 1874), p. 144.

91. Thomas Gataker, *The Decease of Lazarus Christ's Friend* (London, 1640), Epistle Dedicatory, p. 36. See also John Shaw, *Mistris Shawe's Tomb-stone, or the Saints Remains* (London, 1658), in *Yorkshire Diaries and Autobiographies*, ed. Charles Jackson (Surtees Society, Vol. LXV; Durham, 1877), p. 435.

92. Shaw, *Mistris Shawe's Tomb-stone*, p. 435. For the policy of the Established Church, see *Injunctions Given by the Queen's Majesty, Anno Domini 1559*, nos. 33, 38, and *Articles to Be Enquired in the Visitation ... Anno 1559*, Article 39, reprinted in *Visitation Articles and Injunctions of the Period of the Reformation*, Vol. III, *1559–1575*, ed. Walter H. Frere (Alcuin Club Collections, Vol. XVI; London, 1910), pp. 20–21, 5. Cf. also Grindal, *Remains*, pp. 170–71 (*Articles to Be Enquired of, within the Province of Canturburie* [London, 1576], Article 45), and *The Works of the Most Reverend Father in God, William Laud, D.D.*, ed. William Scott and James Bliss (Oxford, 1847–60), V, ii, 411–12, 415–16 (*Articles to Be Enquired of within the Dioces of London ... 1628*, "Concerning Parishioners, and Other of the Laity," articles 10, 34, 38). In 1614, according to Walter Yonge, the Bishop of Exeter read letters he had received from the archbishop to the diocesan clergy; the archbishop had written in part that "every minister should exhort his parishioners to continue together the Sabbath day, and not to wander to other preachers who have better gifts than their own pastors, but

should content themselves with the word of God read, and Homilies." *Diary of Walter Yonge*, pp. 24–25.

93. See, for example, Sir Francis Hastings' letter to Mr. Price, parson of Newton St. Loe, Somerset, in which Hastings gives his opinion of the parson's preaching. "There be 3 things, Mr. Price, which I will make bold to lay down unto you as faults (in my judgment) necessarily to be reformed in your function and calling: the first is your not instructing of your people in some measure." As quoted in Claire Cross, "An Example of Lay Intervention in the Elizabethan Church," in G. J. Cuming, ed., *Studies in Church History*, II (London, 1965), 277. As Dr. Cross observes, "These laymen were not anti-clerical in intention, indeed they were willing to make considerable sacrifices to defend godly ministers, but they had no conception of theology as a separate study reserved for professional theologians, or the government of the Church as a department set aside for the Crown and the bishops." *Ibid.*, p. 282.

94. *The Acts of the High Commission Court within the Diocese of Durham*, ed. W. H. D. Longstaffe (Surtees Society, Vol. XXXIV; Durham, 1877), pp. 155–67.

95. John White, *The First Century of Scandalous, Malignant Priests* (London, 1643), p. 3. Cf. the third charge against Brian Walton: "He neither preacheth nor catechizeth on Sundays in the afternoons, nor will permit the petitioners to procure a preacher, though at their own charge." *The Articles and Charge Proved in Parliament against Doctor Walton, Minister of St. Martins Orgars in Cannonstreet* (London, 1641), p. 4; see also *Petition and Articles Exhibited in Parliament against Dr. Fuller, Deane of Ely, and Vicar of S. Giles Cripple-gate* (London, 1641), fol. 2v; and *Proceedings, Principally in the County of Kent*, ed. Lambert B. Larking (Camden Society, old ser., Vol. LXXX; Westminster, 1862), 197, 229–30.

96. White, *First Century*, p. 8; other ministers were accused of requiring bribes as the price of permitting lectures, e.g. Edward Finch, who "much opposed the lecture, which without intermission hath for many years been continued in the west end of the said church, ... not suffering any one to preach the same, unless he the said vicar might have extraordinary hire for permitting of it, viz. about forty pounds." *The Petition and Articles or Severall Charge Exhibited in Parliament against Edward Finch Vicar of Christ Church in London* (London, 1641), p. 4.

97. *Proceedings in Kent*, p. 203.

98. Robert Ryece to John Winthrop, 9 Sept. 1636, in *Collections of the Massachusetts Historical Society*, 4th ser., Vol. VI (Boston, 1863), p. 408.

99. As quoted in *Diary of Lady Margaret Hoby*, p. 7.

100. Knollys to Burghley, 13 June 1584, as quoted in Knappen, *Tudor Puritanism*, p. 275.

101. John Strype, *Annals of the Reformation* (Oxford, 1824), Vol. III, Part II, pp. 177–79.

102. Philip Stubbes, *The Second Part of the Anatomie of Abuses* (London, 1583), ed. Frederick J. Furnivall (The New Shakespeare Society ed.; London, 1882), p. 79.

103. [Robert Chestlin], *Persecutio Undecima: The Churches Eleventh Persecution; or, A Briefe of the Puritan Persecution of the Protestant Clergy of England* (n.p., 1648), p. 11. See also Christopher Hill, *Economic Problems of the Church* (Oxford, 1956), ch. 12.

104. *The Official Papers of Sir Nathaniel Bacon*, ed. H. W. Saunders (Camden Society, 3d ser., Vol. XXVI; London, 1915), pp. 194–96. For other correspondence relating to ecclesiastical affairs in Sir Nathaniel's neighborhood, see *ibid.*, pp. 185–200. In 1606 the townsmen of Wissett petitioned Sir Nathaniel, this time after he had al-

ready designated a minister of his own choosing (*ibid.*, pp. 191–92). There is another letter from the inhabitants of Wissett thanking Bacon for his care in providing them with a preaching minister "of good conversation of life," in the *Supplementary Stiffkey Papers*, ed. F. R. Brooks (*Camden Miscellany*, 3d ser., Vol. LII; London, 1936), pp. 17–18. When Sir Nathaniel Barnardiston, who had presented Samuel Fairclough to the parish of Barnardiston, offered Fairclough the richer living of Kedington, he apparently asked the parishioners of Barnardiston to consent to Fairclough's removal, again a recognition by a Puritan patron of the legitimate interest of parishioners in their preacher. Smith, *Ecclesiastical History of Essex*, p. 22. Perhaps we should not make too much of these examples. William Prynne's view that patrons were "commonly of good quality and better able to judge and make choice of fitting ministers than the people" was in all likelihood a common attitude. *Jus Patronatus* (London, 1654), p. 28, as quoted in Christopher Hill, *Economic Problems of the Church*, p. 72. As Hill notes (p. 71), "There was much ambivalence in the Puritan attitude towards patronage." Hill argues elsewhere that the "fundamental cause . . . of this drift towards a 'non-doctrinal' independency was economic"; it occurred in parishes with lectureships because preachers who held only a lectureship were virtually dependent on those who raised their stipend. *Society and Puritanism in Pre-Revolutionary England* (London, 1964), p. 90. Nevertheless, as Hill acknowledges (*ibid.*), there was an ideological element, and it is this that I have tried to illustrate by the examples drawn from the correspondence of Nathaniel Bacon.

105. *H.MSS.C.*, *Report on the Records of the City of Exeter* (London, 1916), pp. 92–96. Hazard (or Hassard) was soon gone, for he accepted the vicarage of Awliscombe, Devonshire, in 1617. Joseph Foster, *Alumni Oxonienses: The Members of Oxford, 1500–1714* (Oxford, 1891), II, 670. Nevertheless, the lectureship continued, and in 1631 its finances were put on a firm footing by the purchase of an impropriate rectory with the Bodley legacy and an additional sum contributed by a citizen, Thomas Moggridge. *Report on the Records of the City of Exeter*, pp. 97–99, 275–77; see also Wallace T. MacCaffrey, *Exeter, 1540–1640* (Cambridge, Mass., 1958), p. 198.

106. Laud to the Earl of Mulgrave, 10 Dec. 1629, in *Works of William Laud*, VII, 26. It is not certain that Laud got his way. The James Dent who was curate and lecturer there in the 1630's was almost certainly the James Dent who was graduated B.A. and M.A. from Sidney Sussex and went on in 1625 to become curate to a Yorkshire Puritan rector. Dent was subsequently instituted in 1640 to the vicarage of Shephall, Herts., where he remained unmolested until his death in 1647. GLMS 9537/13, no fol.; GLMS 9539 A/2, no fol.; Marchant, *Puritans and the Church Courts*, p. 243.

107. *Portland MSS.*, III, 69. Cf. Gower to Harley, 9 Nov. 1640, and Edward Perkins to Edward Harley, 23 Nov. 1640, in *ibid.*, pp. 67–68.

108. *Ibid.*, pp. 6–7. Harley appears to have acted in the capacity of an influential *amicus curiae*; other patrons were more direct. When Sir Nathaniel Barnardiston presented Samuel Fairclough to the living of Kedington, he was presenting a known nonconformist who had already been cited before Bishop Harsnet while lecturing at Lynn, and again before the High Commission while serving as parson at Barnardiston. To obviate the inevitable collision with the bishop over Fairclough's institution, Sir Nathaniel managed to procure it without Fairclough's having to appear, and hence without his having either to swear the oath of canonical obedience or to subscribe to the three articles. *D.N.B.*; Smith, *Ecclesiastical History of Essex*, pp. 22–23; Edmund Calamy, *The Nonconformist's Memorial*, ed. Samuel Palmer (2d ed.; London, 1802–3), III, 276. For a discussion of Puritan patronage in Elizabeth's reign, see, for example,

Letters of Thomas Wood, Puritan, 1566–1577, ed. Patrick Collinson (*Bulletin of the Institute of Historical Research*, Special Supplement no. 5; London, 1960), pp. xviii–xl; and Claire Cross, "Noble Patronage in the Elizabethan Church," *Historical Journal*, III (1960), 1–16.

109. *Portland MSS.*, III, 22. For Sir Edward Conway's relationship to John Davenport, see *Letters of John Davenport*, ed. Isabel M. Calder (New Haven, Conn., 1937), pp. 13–18, 20–23. Davenport was apparently able to exploit the influence of Conway, the secretary of state, through his friendship with Mary, Lady Vere, Conway's sister-in-law (*ibid.*, p. 19). Davenport's correspondence provides other examples of the intricate mechanisms of Puritan patronage. In 1628 Davenport reported to Lady Vere that "Mr. Sedgwick wrote to me for a preacher for Sir Edward Vere." Obadiah Sedgwick was a Puritan nonconformist and Lady Vere's husband's chaplain. He and Davenport may have met when they were both studying for their degrees at Magdalen Hall, Oxford, in the early 1620's. Sir Edward Vere was a distant kinsman of Horace, Lord Vere; both were soldiering in the Netherlands. Sir Edward doubtless turned to Lord Vere much as Sir Edward Conway appealed to Sir Robert Harley for help in securing a chaplain. Lord Vere in turn requested Sedgwick's assistance, and Sedgwick wrote to Davenport, whose location in London placed him at the center of the market for young preachers (*ibid.*, p. 31). Sedgwick returned to Oxford in 1630 to take his B.D. and subsequently became curate and lecturer at St. Mildred Bread Street in London. One wonders whether Davenport helped him to that post through his numerous city connections. For Sedgwick, see *D.N.B.*, where he is referred to as lecturer of St. Mildred's. The Visitation Call Book, 1637, lists him also as curate; see GLMS 9537/15, fol. 59v.

110. *Portland MSS.*, III, 32. For Porter, see Matthews, *Calamy Revised*, p. 396, and for his lecture at St. Lawrence Jewry, GLMS 2590/1, pp. 351, 357.

111. *Portland MSS.*, III, 32. For Hill, see Brook, *Lives*, III, 170–71, and *D.N.B.* For Hill's lecture at St. Martin in the Fields, see WPLMS F2002, p. 237. John Stoughton had powerful friends besides Harley. In October 1635 John Rous, the Suffolk divine, noted in his diary that Stoughton had been arrested on suspicion of being a collector of funds for New England ministers, "but within 2 or 3 dayes, *re cognita,* he returned with credit, in the earl of Holland's coach." *Diary of John Rous*, pp. 79–80. Actually, although Dr. Stoughton was released in October, he was subsequently tried before the High Commission: see J. C. Whitebrook, "Dr. John Stoughton the Elder," *Trans. of the Congregational Historical Society*, VI (1913–15), 178–84.

112. *Portland MSS.*, III, 32–33.

113. *Ibid.*, p. 30; *D.N.B.*, s.v. John Brinsley. The *D.N.B.* article suggests that Laud was behind the suit in Chancery that led to Brinsley's dismissal, but see *Works of William Laud*, V, i, 108 and footnote, which suggests that the initiative originally came from Matthew Brooks, a Yarmouth parson.

114. *Portland MSS.*, III, 69–72, 76, 79, 86, 142–45, 147, 160–62.

115. *Ibid.*, p. 79.

116. *C.S.P.D.*, *1547–80*, p. 304. For details of Leicester's patronage in the Midlands and a systematic analysis of his clerical patronage in general, see *Letters of Thomas Wood*, pp. xxvi–xxix.

117. *Yorkshire Diaries*, pp. 126–27. For a similar lectureship established by London merchants from Worcestershire, see Christopher Hill, *Society and Puritanism*, p. 93.

118. *Yorkshire Diaries*, p. 128. There appears to be no evidence of a connection between the Feoffees and this effort by a group of Devonshire merchants; see Isabel M. Calder, *Activities of the Puritan Faction of the Church of England, 1625–33* (London,

1957), *passim*, for the hearings on the Feoffees held in the Equity side of the Exchequer. Laud's *Works* have much to say about the Feoffees, but there are no references to the activity of the Devonshire merchants. Presumably the merchants simply saw the handwriting on the wall and ceased their activity before they were detected. However, Laud was aware of the connection between the London and the similar Norwich Feoffees, whose existence he noted in 1630; see *V.C.H. Norfolk*, ed. William Page (London, 1906), II, 281–82. And certainly Laud was busy in the 1630's closing down those havens that the laity had erected for their Puritan preachers. See, for example, Laud's letter of 17 June 1634 to the Merchant Adventurers of Delft (*Works of William Laud*, VI, ii, 380–81). H. R. Trevor-Roper suggests that by 1637 Laud had been largely successful in reducing the Merchant Adventurers' congregations to conformity (*Archbishop Laud, 1573–1645*, 2d ed. [London, 1962], pp. 252–53), but a memorandum by Secretary Windebank, apparently dating from 1639, indicates that the problem was a continuing one (*C.S.P.D., 1639–40*, p. 213). It was all very well to fulminate against the Merchant Adventurers abroad for receiving "factious ministers," but so long as Laud's policy led to their banishment and thus assured the merchants overseas a steady supply, the Crown's actions at home tended to negate efforts to achieve conformity abroad. After engineering in 1639 the suspension of Robert Jenison, the Newcastle lecturer, the government then bent its efforts toward driving him out of Newcastle, where his very presence was feared; by 1640 Jenison was gone, first to Amsterdam and then to Danzig. There he apparently ministered to the Eastland merchant colony until his triumphant return in 1645. *C.S.P.D., 1639*, pp. 450, 479–80, 483–84; *C.S.P.D., 1639–40*, pp. 183, 346, 385; *Memoirs of the Life of Mr. Ambrose Barnes*, ed. W. H. D. Longstaffe (Surtees Society, Vol. L; Durham, 1866), pp. 328–29, 335, 341–42; *D.N.B.*, s.v. Robert Jenison.

119. Lucy Hutchinson, *Memoirs of the Life of Colonel Hutchinson* (Everyman's Library ed.; London, n.d.), p. 65. "We must make a difference between our stricter people in England, whom your profaner sort call Precisians, and those who are superintendents over a few buttonmakers and weavers at Amsterdam. For of ours, we have many conformable to his Majesty's laws and the ceremonies of the church, carrying themselves very honestly and conscionably; among which I reckon not the professed Puritan, of whom I know many who gladly take that name and profession upon them, being tradesmen in cities and market towns, only to get custom to their shops." Henry Peacham, "The Truth of Our Times" [1638], in *"The Complete Gentleman," "The Truth of Our Times," and "The Art of Living in London,"* ed. Virgil B. Heltzel (Ithaca, N.Y., 1962), p. 225.

120. *Portland MSS.*, III, 79. R. G. Usher's estimates in *Reconstruction of the English Church* (I, 95, 110–12) give reason to doubt the accuracy of Gower's figures.

121. For Bancroft's estimate, see Usher, *Reconstruction of the English Church*, I, 338; for the data on London patronage, see H. Gareth Owen, "The London Parish Clergy in the Reign of Elizabeth I" (unpubl. Ph.D. thesis, London Univ., 1957), p. 241.

122. Owen, "London Parish Clergy," p. 253.

123. *A Letter from Mercurius Civicus to Mercurius Rusticus* (1643) in *Somers' Tracts*, 2d ed., ed. Sir Walter Scott (London, 1810), IV, 582. The same assertion is made by Chestlin in *Persecutio Undecima*, p. 23. "Dr. Gough" is William Gouge, curate and lecturer at St. Anne Blackfriars, 1608–53; his name is spelled "Gough" in the Visitation Call Book, 1636, GLMS 9537/14, no fol. "Jackson" is Arthur Jackson, lecturer and rector of St. Michael Wood Street from the early 1620's until 1643. *D.N.B.*; Matthews, *Calamy Revised*, p. 290. Daniel Votier was rector and lecturer at St. Peter

Westcheap from 1615 until his sequestration in 1643. GLMS 9537/12, fol. 4r; A. G. Matthews, *Walker Revised* (Oxford, 1948), p. 61. "Simons" is probably Joseph Simonds, rector of St. Martin Ironmonger Lane, who, however, had been deprived in 1639, following his departure for Holland, and who did not return permanently to England until 1647. *Works of William Laud,* V, ii, 362–63; Brook, *Lives,* III, 39; GLMS 4072/1, fol. 180v. "Walker" is George Walker, rector of St. John the Evangelist from 1614 to 1651. *D.N.B.; Works of William Laud,* V, ii, 332. See also Valerie Pearl, *London and the Outbreak of the Puritan Revolution* (Oxford, 1961), esp. p. 160. Besides those named in *Mercurius Civicus,* the following Puritans held benefices in London at the end of the 1630's: Cornelius Burgess, rector and lecturer at St. Magnus; Adoniram Byfield, curate and lecturer at St. Lawrence Jewry; Richard Culverwell, rector at St. Margaret Moses; John Downham, rector at Allhallows Thames Street; Charles Offspring, rector and lecturer at St. Antholin's; and William Palmer, vicar and lecturer at St. Bride's.

124. Richard Montagu to John Cosin, 17 Jan. 1624/5, in *The Correspondence of John Cosin,* ed. George Ornsby (Surtees Society, Vol. LII; Durham, 1869), I, 47. Complaints about the Puritanism of London were scarcely new. The Bishop of London had complained in 1573 that Cartwright was openly countenanced by many of the aldermen and secretly harbored in the City. John Strype, *The Life and Acts of John Whitgift, D.D.* (Oxford, 1822), I, 107; cf. *C.S.P.D., 1598–1601,* p. 128.

CHAPTER 2

1. Quoted in H. R. Trevor-Roper, *Archbishop Laud, 1573–1645* (London, 1940), p. 5.

2. See, for example, Millar Maclure, *The Paul's Cross Sermons, 1534–1642* (Toronto, 1958), pp. 78–80, 218.

3. Edmund Grindal, *The Remains of Edmund Grindal, D.D.,* ed. William Nicholson (Parker Society, Vol. XIX; Cambridge, Eng., 1843), pp. 378–79.

4. *The Journals of All the Parliaments during the Reign of Queen Elizabeth,* ed. Sir Simonds D'Ewes (London, 1682), pp. 328–29.

5. *Ibid.,* p. 329.

6. Robert Peters, *Oculus Episcopi* (Manchester, 1963), p. 34. One of these seditious and scandalous sermons was preached under the very nose of the government. Simonds D'Ewes recounts how on August 22, 1622, he heard one Mr. Claydon, a Hackney minister, cite in the course of a Paul's Cross sermon "a story out of our chronicles, of a Spanish sheep, brought into England in Edward the First's time, which infected most of the sheep of England with a murrain, and [Claydon] prayed no more such sheep be brought over from thence, hither; at which many of his hearers cried out 'Amen.'" D'Ewes added in explanation: "So much generally did all men fear that Prince Charles would marry the King of Spain's sister, as they ever hated that nation." As for Claydon, he "lay awhile in prison for his sermon, but was soon after set at liberty by the mediation of Sir John Ramsey, Knt., a Scotsman, Earl of Holderness, whose chaplain he was." *The Autobiography and Correspondence of Sir Simonds D'Ewes, Bart., during the Reigns of James I and Charles I,* ed. James O. Halliwell (London, 1845), I, 219–20. Some Puritan ministers who preceded their sermons with extemporaneous prayers interjected a political message at this point without waiting for the sermon. John Howe, curate and lecturer at Loughborough, Leicestershire, was suspended by the High Commission at Michaelmas Term in 1634 because "in his prayer before his sermon ... he prayed that the young Prince, meaning Prince Charles,

might not be brought up in Popery, whereof there was great cause to fear, which the court held to be fully proved ... and adjudged him well worthy to be severely punished ..., the rather that they much derogated from his Majesty's known pious and religious care in maintaining and propagating the true religion here established." PRO, SP 16/261, fol. 120r.

7. Maclure, *Paul's Cross Sermons*, pp. 103–4.

8. Sermon at Paul's Cross, 22 Nov. 1629, *ibid.*, p. 251.

9. G. R. Owst, *Preaching in Medieval England* (Cambridge, Eng., 1926), pp. 140–43.

10. G. R. Owst, *Literature and Pulpit in Medieval England* (Cambridge, Eng., 1933), p. 190, n. 4.

11. Maclure, *Paul's Cross Sermons*, p. 243; see also Michael Walzer, *The Revolution of the Saints* (Cambridge, Mass., 1965), pp. 233–34. Despite his harmless, if platitudinous, sermon at the Cross, Harris was unable to obtain a license to preach as lecturer at St. Saviour, Southwark, or so at least he claimed. LCCRO, P/92/S/450, pp. 527, 538. Although he denied the charge, Harris may have left St. Saviour's in order to accept the lectureship at St. Mary Aldermanbury in London, to which he was appointed on 17 December 1624. GLMS 3570/2, fols. 18v–19r. For Harris's biography, see *D.N.B.* and Benjamin Brook, *Lives of the Puritans* (London, 1813), III, 303–7.

12. Heylyn made his observation in the course of commenting on Archbishop Abbot's instructions to the clergy concerning the forced loan of 1626. *Cyprianus Anglicus* (London, 1671), p. 153. Cf. *Documentary Annals of the Reformed Church of England*, ed. Edward Cardwell (Oxford, 1844), II, 55.

13. Grindal, *Remains*, p. 253.

14. Maclure, *Paul's Cross Sermons*, pp. 215, 217.

15. *Ibid.*, pp. 219, 221, 82–83.

16. Chamberlain to Carleton, 1 July 1622, in *The Letters of John Chamberlain*, ed. Norman E. McClure (American Philosophical Society, Memoirs XII, Part II; Philadelphia, 1939), II, 443; see also *ibid.*, p. 439, where Chamberlain notes that little was to be gained by burning Paraeus's books in London, "when they are current all Christendom over." As Richard Baxter testifies, Puritan ministers who spoke on behalf of unpopular governmental measures were received with equal coolness: "When I was at Kidderminster [ca. 1642] the Parliament made an order for all people to take a protestation. ... I obeyed them in joining with the magistrate in offering the people this protestation, which caused some to be offended with me." *The Autobiography of Richard Baxter*, ed. J. M. Lloyd Thomas (Everyman's Library ed.; London, 1931), p. 38.

17. Maclure, *Paul's Cross Sermons*, pp. 209, 210, 238–39, 241.

18. *Puritan Manifestoes*, ed. W. H. Frere and C. E. Douglas (London, 1907; reprinted, 1954), pp. xxii–xxiii.

19. *A Collection of State Papers ... Left by William Cecil Lord Burghley*, ed. William Murdin (London, 1759), II, 255.

20. *Documentary Annals of the Reformed Church*, I, 438; II, 201–3.

21. *Calendar of State Papers, Venetian, 1621–1623*, p. 411.

22. For an extended and sustained analysis of the relationship of Puritan ideology to its organizational and political manifestations, see Walzer, *Revolution of the Saints*, *passim*.

23. *Diary of Walter Yonge, Esq.*, ed. George Roberts (Camden Society, old ser., Vol. XLI; London, 1848), pp. 2–4. Edmund Snape was an old Presbyterian nonconformist whom Yonge may have known or heard during an earlier period when he preached in

the West country; at the time mentioned in Yonge's diary Snape had just been forced to give up his lectureship in Southwark, having failed to gain the Bishop of Winchester's approbation. See V.M. of St. Saviour, Southwark, LCCRO, P/92/S/450, pp. 383, 391; Brook, *Lives*, I, 403–11; and *D.N.B.*

24. *Diary of Walter Yonge*, pp. 98, 97, 22, 9, 64, 50, 115–16. For Yonge's career, see *D.N.B.* and Mary Frear Keeler, *The Long Parliament, 1640–1641* (American Philosophical Society, Memoirs, Vol. XXXVI; Philadelphia, 1954), p. 404.

25. *Diary of Walter Yonge*, p. 98.

26. Thomas Lushington, *A Repetition Sermon* (1624), reprinted in *British Pamphleteers*, ed. George Orwell and Reginald Reynolds (London, 1948–51), I, 53.

27. Patrick Collinson, *A Mirror of Elizabethan Puritanism: The Life and Letters of "Godly Master Dering"* (Friends of Dr. Williams's Library, Seventeenth Lecture, 1963; London, 1964), p. 9.

28. For extensive samples of Puritan bills, supplications, petitions, and statistics on the state of the Church during the middle years of Elizabeth's reign, see *The Seconde Parte of a Register*, ed. Albert Peel (Cambridge, Eng., 1915). For Puritan activity during the Parliament of 1604–10, see R. G. Usher, *The Reconstruction of the English Church* (New York, 1910), and Stuart Barton Babbage, *Puritanism and Richard Bancroft* (London, 1962). For information on sermons preached before Parliament, see Godfrey Davies, "English Political Sermons, 1603–1640," *Huntington Library Quarterly*, III (1939), 1–22; James F. Maclear, "The Influence of the Puritan Clergy on the House of Commons: 1625–1629," *Church History*, XIV (1945), 272–89; Ethyn Williams Kirby, "Sermons before the Commons, 1640–1642," *American Historical Review*, XLIV (1939), 528–48; H. R. Trevor-Roper, "The Fast Sermons of the Long Parliament," in H. R. Trevor-Roper, ed., *Essays in British History* (London, 1964), pp. 85–138; James C. Spalding, "Sermons before Parliament (1640–1649) as a Public Puritan Diary," *Church History*, XXXVI (1967), 24–35. For evidence of Puritan lobbying, see Richard Bancroft, *Dangerous Positions* (London, 1593), as reprinted in abridged form in R. G. Usher, ed., *The Presbyterian Movement in the Reign of Queen Elizabeth* (Camden Society, 3d ser., Vol. VIII; London, 1905), p. 14; see also Walzer, *Revolution of the Saints*, p. 129.

29. Samuel Clarke, *The Marrow of Ecclesiastical History* (London, 1650), p. 431. Hugh Clarke was Samuel's father.

30. Usher, ed., *Presbyterian Movement*, p. 61.

31. *Letters of Thomas Wood, Puritan, 1566–1577*, ed. Patrick Collinson (London, 1960), pp. xxiv–xxv. Humphrey and Sampson preached their Paul's Cross sermons in 1565. Maclure, *Paul's Cross Sermons*, p. 59. Sampson later recovered his preaching license and held the Clothworkers' lecture at St. Michael Paternoster Row from 1573 to 1575. H. Gareth Owen, "London Parish Clergy in the Reign of Elizabeth I" (unpubl. Ph.D. thesis, London Univ., 1957), pp. 380, 629; Brook, *Lives*, I, 375–84.

32. The epithet "an unskillful and deceitful tubtrimmer" comes from the full title of Martin Marprelate's *Hay Any Worke for Cooper* (1589). The longer quotation is from Thomas Cooper, *An Admonition to the People of England* (1589), ed. Edward Arber (Westminster, 1895), p. 91.

33. Richard Bernard, *The Faithful Shepherd* (1621), sig. A5, as quoted in Maclure, *Paul's Cross Sermons*, p. 150. Cf. Samuel Clarke's description of William Perkins's preaching: "His sermons were not so plain, but the piously learned did admire them; nor so learned, but the plain did understand them. He brought the schools into the pulpit, and unshelling their controversies out of their hard school terms, made thereof plain and wholesome meat for his people." *Marrow of Ecclesiastical History*, p. 415.

34. *Diary of John Manningham, of the Middle Temple, and of Bradbourne, Kent, Barrister-at-law, 1602–1603,* ed. John Bruce (Camden Society, old ser., Vol. XCIX; London, 1868), pp. 74–75, 101, 15–16. I have not been able to discover who was lecturer at the Temple during Manningham's sojourn. Walter Travers was lecturer there in the 1580's, and William Crashaw, the Puritan father of the poet, from 1605 to 1612. Manningham mentions hearing an afternoon lecture by "Mr. Marbury of the Temple" (*ibid.*, p. 75), probably the Puritan Francis Marbury, who attempted in 1602 and 1603 to secure a license to preach that would permit him to lecture at St. Saviour, Southwark. LCCRO, P/92/S/450, pp. 359, 369. He subsequently became vicar of St. Pancras, Middlesex, and rector of St. Margaret New Fish Street in London. John and J. A. Venn, *Alumni Cantabrigienses,* Part I (Cambridge, Eng., 1922), Vol. III, p. 139.

35. *Tracts Ascribed to Richard Bancroft,* ed. Albert Peel (Cambridge, Eng., 1953), pp. 56–58. Bancroft specifically charged that "the most Precisians abroad in the Country will take no benefice" (*ibid.*, p. 58); although this is doubtless an exaggeration, it does testify to the significance of the lectureships.

36. Henry Parker, *A Discourse Concerning Puritans* (London, 1641), p. 10.

37. Lucy Hutchinson, *Memoirs of the Life of Colonel Hutchinson* (Everyman's Library ed.; London, n.d.), p. 64.

38. *Letters of John Davenport, Puritan Divine,* ed. Isabel M. Calder (New Haven, Conn., 1937), p. 14.

39. George Lawrence, *Laurentius Lutherizans* (London, 1642), fol. 2v.

40. When the Puritan parishioners of St. Giles Cripplegate, London, petitioned Parliament in 1641 against their vicar, William Fuller, their charge against his preaching was not that he exploited his pulpit for political purposes, but that the politics he preached was wrong and dangerous: "He hath published in the pulpit that all our estates are at the King's disposing, and that there is no difference between our Church of England and the Church of Rome in matter of substance, but in circumstances only, which might easily be reconciled." *Petition and Articles Exhibited in Parliament against Dr. Fuller, Deane of Ely, and Vicar of S. Giles Cripplegate,... by the Parishioners of Saint Giles* (London, 1641), fol. 2v. Cf. the tenth objection to the bishops in the first "Root and Branch" petition from London, which refers to "the publishing and venting of Popish, Arminian and other dangerous...tenets, as namely, that the Church of Rome is a true Church, and in the worst of times never erred in fundamentals, that the subjects have no property in their estates, but that the King may take from them what he pleaseth, that all is the King's, and that he is bound by no law." *The First and Large Petition of the Citie of London...for a Reformation in Church-government, as Also for the Abolishment of Episcopacie...* (London, 1641), p. 6. See also Paul H. Hardacre, *The Royalists during the Puritan Revolution* (The Hague, 1956), p. 39.

41. Edward Boughen, *Two Sermons ... the Second, Preached at Saint Paul's Crosse* (1635), as quoted in Maclure, *Paul's Cross Sermons,* p. 112. In 1642 Boughen was sequestered from his rectory of Woodchurch, Kent, for "popish" practices, and the House of Commons ordered a Puritan lecturer admitted. A. G. Matthews, *Walker Revised* (Oxford, 1948), p. 212.

42. *The Works of the Most Reverend Father in God, William Laud, D.D.,* ed. William Scott and James Bliss (Oxford, 1847–60), I, 8.

43. John Aston, *Journal,* in *Six North Country Diaries,* ed. John C. Hodgson (Surtees Society, Vol. CXVIII; Durham, 1910), p. 21; E. Duncan to Thomas Triplet, 3 March 1639/40, *C.S.P.D., 1639–40,* p. 542.

44. *C.S.P.D., 1639–40,* pp. 581–83. For Mew, see LPLMS 942, nos. 14, 16; Venn,

Alumni Cantab., Part I, Vol. III, p. 181; A. G. Matthews, *Calamy Revised* (Oxford, 1934), p. 349.

45. *C.S.P.D., 1639–40*, pp. 608–9; for Marshall, see also *D.N.B.*

46. *C.S.P.D., 1639–40*, pp. 561–62.

47. J. P. Kenyon, ed., *The Stuart Constitution, 1603–1688* (Cambridge, Eng., 1966), p. 12.

48. [Robert Chestlin], *Persecutio Undecima* (n.p., 1648), p. 57.

49. *Ibid.*, p. 62; cf. Edward Hyde, Earl of Clarendon, *History of the Rebellion and Civil Wars in England*, ed. W. D. Macray (Oxford, 1888), III, 194.

50. Chestlin, *Persecutio Undecima*, p. 62.

51. Matthews, *Calamy Revised*, pp. 87–88; *D.N.B.*

52. *A Letter from Mercurius Civicus to Mercurius Rusticus* (1643), in *Somers' Tracts*, 2d ed., ed. Sir Walter Scott (London, 1810), IV, 584.

53. Christopher Hill, *Intellectual Origins of the English Revolution* (Oxford, 1965), pp. 5–6.

54. Samuel Fawcett, *A Seasonable Sermon for These Troublesome Times* (London, 1641), pp. 25, 3.

55. Thomas Hobbes, *Behemouth*, in *English Works*, ed. William Molesworth (London, 1840), VI, 282; see also *ibid.*, p. 192.

56. John Hacket, *Scrinia Reserata* (London, 1693), p. 186.

57. *Mercurius Civicus*, in *Somers' Tracts*, IV, 581–83.

58. During Archbishop Laud's Essex Visitation in 1631, when the "Colchester men would have had his admission of Mr. Bridges of Emmanuel for their lecturer in Mr. Maiden's stead," Laud "was angry and said: 'When you want one you must go first to Dr. Gouge and to Dr. Sibs [two prestigious London Puritan lecturers], and then you come to me; I scorn to be so used. I'll never have him to lecture in my diocese.'" Henry Jacie to John Winthrop, 9 Jan. 1631/32, in *Winthrop Papers* (Massachusetts Historical Society; Cambridge, Mass., 1929–47), III, 59. William Haller has made much the same point: "By 1632 the Puritans had succeeded in establishing within the church a veritable though unacknowledged and unauthorized order or brotherhood of preachers, working in large measure independently of, though not in direct conflict with, constituted authority. Its members were linked together by ties of youthful association, kindred, friendship, and marriage as well as by conviction and interest. They looked mainly to Cambridge as their seminary and training-ground. They had the countenance and support of many of the peers and gentry, merchants and lawyers. . . . They did not in most instances go directly from the university to undertake the cure of souls . . . but, perhaps after an interval as chaplains and tutors in the households of sympathetic patrons, they commonly took up posts as 'lecturers.'" *Liberty and Reformation in the Puritan Revolution* (New York, 1955), pp. 11–12. I would question only whether this development need be dated as late as 1632.

59. Valerie Pearl, *London and the Outbreak of the Puritan Revolution* (Oxford, 1961), esp. pp. 69–71.

CHAPTER 3

1. *Documentary Annals of the Reformed Church of England*, ed. Edward Cardwell (Oxford, 1844), II, 203.

2. Irvonwy Morgan, *The Godly Preachers of the Elizabethan Church* (London, 1965), pp. 62–64.

3. Peter Heylyn, *Cyprianus Anglicus* (London, 1671), p. 9. Cf. Heylyn's statement that at the general assembly of the Presbyterians in 1582 "they agreed upon some order for putting the said Discipline in execution, but with as little violation of the peace of the Church as they could possibly devise. . . . It was resolved also, that instead of Prophesying, which now began to be suppressed in every place, lectures should be set up in some chief towns in every county, to which the ministers and lay-brethren might resort securely, and thereby prosecute their design with the like indemnity." *Aerius Redivivus* (Oxford, 1670), pp. 299–300.

4. M. M. Knappen, *Tudor Puritanism* (Chicago, 1939), p. 221.

5. *Table Talk of John Selden*, ed. Frederick Pollock (London, 1927), p. 71.

6. G. R. Owst, *Preaching in Medieval England* (Cambridge, Eng., 1926), pp. 94–96, 145, 148.

7. Quoted in J. F. Mozley, *John Foxe and His Book* (London, 1940), p. 66. The comparison to preaching friars was also used by a lawyer, possibly Thomas Norton, in his defense of independent preachers. Morgan, *Godly Preachers*, pp. 7–10.

8. Morgan, *Godly Preachers*, pp. 58–59; for Burdett's final sentence before the High Commission, see PRO, SP 16/261, fols. 165v–169r; for the lapse of the lectureship, see *The Works of the Most Reverend Father in God, William Laud, D.D.*, ed. William Scott and James Bliss (Oxford, 1847–60), V, ii, 340.

9. The refounding of schools previously associated with chantry foundations is a case in point. Joan Simon, "The Reformation and English Education," *Past and Present*, XI, (1957), 59–61; A. G. Dickens, *The English Reformation* (London, 1964), pp. 216–17.

10. John Wodderspoon, *Memorials of the Ancient Town of Ipswich in the County of Suffolk* (Ipswich, 1850), p. 366.

11. A. Hamilton Thompson, *The English Clergy and Their Organization in the Later Middle Ages* (Oxford, 1947), p. 135.

12. Owst, *Preaching in Medieval England*, p. 143n.

13. John Stow, *A Survey of London* (Everyman's Library ed. of the 1603 ed.; London, 1912), pp. 99, 217.

14. W. K. Jordan, *The Charities of London, 1480–1660* (London, 1960), p. 137; *Parliamentary Papers*, XX (1880), III, iii, 280.

15. Benjamin Brook, *Lives of the Puritans* (London, 1813), I, 375–84; Knappen, *Tudor Puritanism*, pp. 242–43; Joseph Foster, *Alumni Oxonienses: The Members of Oxford, 1500–1714* (Oxford, 1891), IV, 1307.

16. John Stow, *A Survey of the Cities of London and Westminster*, ed. John Strype (London, 1720), Vol. I, Part I, p. 266; *Parliamentary Papers*, XXXIX (1884), IV, 46.

17. W. S. Simpson, *Chapters in the History of Old St. Paul's* (London, 1881), p. 48; *A History of St. Paul's Cathedral and the Men Associated with It*, ed. W. R. Matthews and W. M. Atkins (London, 1957), p. 111; Morgan, *Godly Preachers*, p. 64.

18. *Visitation Articles and Injunctions of the Period of the Reformation*, ed. W. H. Frere and W. M. Kennedy (London, 1910), II, 133.

19. *Ibid.*, pp. 216–17, 311.

20. *Ibid.*, III, 316; for Canterbury, see *ibid.*, p. 239; for York, pp. 346–47; for Exeter, p. 42; for Winchester, p. 134; for St. Paul's, p. 115; for Carlisle, pp. 145–46; for Norwich, p. 316; for Salisbury, p. 31. The lectures at York Minster had been preached in the vernacular since 1547. Morgan, *Godly Preachers*, p. 66.

21. *Visitation Articles and Injunctions*, II, 377; John Strype, *The Life and Acts of John Whitgift, D.D.* (Oxford, 1822), I, 212–14; III, 64–65.

22. "Papers Relating to Archbishop Laud's Visitations," in *H.MSS.C., 4th Report, Part 1, Appendix* (London, 1874), pp. 141, 144–45, 154, 140, 129, 131.

23. *Diary of Walter Yonge, Esq.*, ed. George Roberts (Camden Society, old ser., Vol. XLI; London, 1848), p. 6. During a visit to London in 1600, Lady Margaret Hoby attended a Tuesday and a Friday lecture at the "collegiate church" of Westminster. Evidently the fact that the sermons were preached at the royal minster rather than at a parish church was not in itself objectionable to this diligent Puritan. *Diary of Lady Margaret Hoby, 1599–1605*, ed. Dorothy M. Meads (Boston, 1930), pp. 151, 153, 156.

24. *H.MSS.C., 4th Report, Part 1*, p. 136. Safe though such a system of patronage should have been from the point of view of the ecclesiastical hierarchy, it was no guarantee that the cathedral lecturer would feel any loyalty to Laud. Thomas Jackson, lecturer at Canterbury, where he also held a canonry, later testified against Laud in the latter's trial. *Ibid.*, p. 125; *Works of William Laud*, IV, 223.

25. *D.N.B.* Dering was invited in 1570 to lecture at St. Lawrence Jewry in the city, but it is unlikely that he served, since the vestry proceeded to a new election within a year. GLMS 2590/1, pp. 33, 39.

26. Brook, *Lives*, I, 194–207; John Strype, *Annals of the Reformation* (Oxford, 1824), II, 398–417.

27. Knappen, *Tudor Puritanism*, p. 240; Brook, *Lives*, I, 207–8; a detailed analysis of this complex affair is given in Patrick Collinson, *A Mirror of Elizabethan Puritanism: The Life and Letters of "Godly Master Dering"* (Friends of Dr. Williams's Library, Seventeenth Lecture, 1963; London, 1964), p. 9.

28. A possible exception is Andrew Willett, of whom Samuel Clarke wrote, "In his younger time he preached the lecture for three years together in the cathedral church of Ely, and for one year in St. Paul's in London, in both with a most singular approbation of a frequent auditory." *The Marrow of Ecclesiastical History* (London, 1650), p. 470. Clarke obviously thought of Willett as among the number of godly preachers, but others have disagreed; see, for example, *D.N.B.*

29. *Original Letters Relative to the English Reformation*, ed. Hastings Robinson (Parker Society; Cambridge, Eng., 1846), I, 65.

30. *Ibid.*, p. 81.

31. *Ibid.*, p. 76.

32. *Documentary Annals of the Reformed Church*, I, 96–97.

33. *Ibid.*, p. 97n.

34. "Bishop Bonner's Visitation Articles of 1554," in *ibid.*, p. 139. There is some evidence that "privy lectures" existed during the early years of the Reformation. While he was chancellor, Sir Thomas More discovered in the course of interrogating some suspected Lollards that "such heretics ... were wont to haunt those midnight lectures." E. G. Rupp, *Studies in the Making of English Protestant Tradition* (Cambridge, Eng., 1947), p. 3n. Apparently the Marian repression revived this practice.

35. See GLMS 1568, p. 34; GLMS 4071/1, fol. 34v; GLMS 4956/2, fol. 47r; and H. Gareth Owen, "The London Parish Clergy in the Reign of Elizabeth I" (unpubl. Ph.D. thesis, London Univ., 1957), p. 370. Owen sets forth what case there is for placing the origin of the St. Antholin's lectures in the reign of Edward VI or earlier. Cf. *V.C.H., London*, Vol. I, ed. William Page (London, 1909), p. 318.

36. GLMS 1568, pp. 223, 225. Wager, who continued to lecture at St. Benet's until his death in 1591, became nonresident at St. Benet's after 1575, when he was collated to the rectory of St. Michael Queenhithe; he also lectured briefly at St. Mary Woolnoth. Despite the double benefice, he may have been a moderate Puritan, for Thomas Wilcox of *Admonition* fame spoke highly of his antipapist preaching. GLMS 1568, p. 342; *The Seconde Parte of a Register*, ed. Albert Peel (Cambridge, Eng., 1915), II, 181, 183; GLMS 1002/1, fol. 185v; Owen, "London Parish Clergy," p. 515.

37. GLMS 4072/1, fol. 18v.

38. GLMS 4958/2, fols. 13r, 132r. He was George Cheston, about whom little is known except that he was a radical Puritan, a member of the London Presbyterian classis by the late 1570's or early 1580's, and a career lecturer who seems never to have held a living but to have held lectureships at various times at the Minories and at St. Katherine Coleman, as well as at Allhallows. R. G. Usher, *The Presbyterian Movement in the Reign of Queen Elizabeth* (Camden Society, 3d ser., Vol. VIII; London, 1905), p. 5; Edward M. Tomlinson, *A History of the Minories London* (London, 1907), pp. 166, 211; GLMS 9537/5, fol. 120v.

39. *The Diary of Henry Machyn*, ed. John G. Nichols (Camden Society, old ser., Vol. XLII; London, 1848), p. 212.

40. Nathaniel Bacon, *The Annals of Ipswich*, ed. William H. Richardson (Ipswich, 1884), pp. 235, 255.

41. *Records of the Borough of Leicester*, ed. Mary Bateson (Cambridge, Eng., 1905), III, 56.

42. *The Accounts of the Churchwardens of S. Martin's Leicester, 1489–1844*, ed. Thomas North (Leicester, 1884), pp. 55–57.

43. *Records of the Borough of Leicester*, ed. Bateson, III, 101.

44. Morgan, *Godly Preachers*, p. 57.

45. As quoted in Perry Miller, *Orthodoxy in Massachusetts, 1630–1650* (Cambridge, Mass., 1933), p. 19.

46. The Dedham lectureship was still in existence in 1909. C. Alfred Jones, "The Passing of the Dedham Lectureship," *Essex Review*, XVIII (1909), 44.

47. Heylyn, *Cyprianus Anglicus*, p. 265.

48. It was he, for example, who first discovered and publicly disclosed the activities of the Puritan Feoffees for Impropriations. *Ibid.*, p. 199.

49. A. L. Rowse, *The England of Elizabeth: The Structure of Society* (New York, 1951), esp. pp. 159–60.

50. *Calendar of the Plymouth Municipal Records*, ed. Richard N. Worth (Plymouth, Eng., 1893), pp. 250–51.

51. GLMS 2590/1, p. 22.

52. LCCRO, DL/C/312, fol. 165v.

53. Millar Maclure, *The Paul's Cross Sermons, 1534–1642* (Toronto, 1958), p. 232.

54. The court ordered that Holbrooke was to "minister the sacrament of the Lord . . . in the habit appointed and that in ministering thereof he repeat all the words appointed and observe and keep the form and order prescribed in the Book of Common Prayer and to bring a certificate thereof" to the court as proof of his conformity. Holbrooke lectured at West Ham from at least 1612 to about 1630. He evidently took his own criticisms to heart and, so far as is known, never held a regular benefice. LCCRO, DL/C/314, fol. 134. By 1620 he was also curate and lecturer at St. Andrew Hubbard. *Abstract of Wills in the Prerogative Court of Canterbury:*

Register Soame, 1620, ed. J. Henry Lea (Boston, 1904), pp. 264, 319; GLMS 1279/2, p. 29; GLMS 9537/13, no fol.

55. LCCRO, DL/C/312, fols. 165v, 207v.

56. Harold Smith, *The Ecclesiastical History of Essex under the Long Parliament and Commonwealth* (Colchester, n.d.), p. 23.

57. GLMS 9537/7, no fol.

58. *The Autobiography and Correspondence of Sir Simonds D'Ewes, Bart., during the Reigns of James I and Charles I,* ed. James O. Halliwell (London, 1845), I, 142; II, 31. D'Ewes first became acquainted with Abraham Gibson in 1614, Gibson "then preaching as their lecturer to the Temples, whom my mother affected very entirely for his pains and diligence in his calling, and for his witty and pleasant conversation," *Ibid.,* I, 63. For a summary of Gibson's career, see John and J. A. Venn, *Alumni Cantabrigienses,* Part I (Cambridge, Eng., 1922), Vol. II, p. 210. The market day lecture preached by the neighboring ministers was apparently "a thing pretty ordinary," as the Lancashire Puritan minister Henry Newcome noted. *The Autobiography of Henry Newcome, M.A.,* ed. Richard Parkinson (Chetham Society, Vol. XXVI; Manchester, 1852), p. 45. In an amusing poem Richard Corbett, the future bishop, describes a trip to Daventry, where "It was the Market and the Lecture-day,/ For Lecturers sell sermons, as the Lay/Doe sheep and oxen." *The Poems of Richard Corbett,* ed. J. A. W. Bennett and H. R. Trevor-Roper (Oxford, 1955), p. 32.

59. Cf. Bishop Williams's performance of "his turn" at the lectureship at Kettering, "a Market Town." John Hacket, *Scrinia Reserata* (London, 1693), p. 34.

60. Smith, *Ecclesiastical History of Essex,* p. 23. For an account of a later attempt (1630) to do the same thing at Chelmsford, see *ibid.,* pp. 35–36.

61. Heylyn, *Cyprianus Anglicus,* pp. 188–89; *Works of William Laud,* V, ii, 308; the Instructions were reissued in 1633 (*Documentary Annals of the Reformed Church,* II, 229–33) and again in 1634 (*Works of William Laud,* V, ii, 311–14).

62. *Works of William Laud,* V, ii, 319, 325; see also *ibid.,* p. 350.

63. William Prynne, *Canterburies Doome* (London, 1646), p. 151.

64. Patrick Collinson, *The Elizabethan Puritan Movement* (London, 1967), pp. 173–74, 182–83, 188, and *passim;* cf. *The Official Papers of Sir Nathaniel Bacon,* ed. H. W. Saunders (Camden Society, 3d ser., Vol. XXVI; London, 1915), pp. 189–90.

65. *Diary of John Rous,* ed. Mary A. E. Green (Camden Society, old ser., Vol. LXVI; London, 1856), pp. 68–69.

66. *Works of William Laud,* V, ii, 340.

67. GLMS 9537/5–15, *passim.* See Appendix C above for a listing of these parishes. Heylyn gives the number of parishes in the Diocese of London as 623 (*Cyprianus Anglicus,* p. 175); if London, the outparishes, and Westminster are excluded, one is left with approximately 500 parishes.

CHAPTER 4

1. *Somers' Tracts,* 2d ed., ed. Sir Walter Scott (London, 1810), IV, 583; Christopher Hill, *Economic Problems of the Church* (Oxford, 1956), p. 344.

2. Isabel M. Calder, *Activities of the Puritan Faction of the Church of England, 1625–33* (London, 1957), p. 100.

3. Peter Heylyn, *Cyprianus Anglicus* (London, 1671), p. 198.

4. *Ibid.,* p. 199.

5. Calder, *Activities of the Puritan Faction,* pp. xv, xxi.

6. *Ibid.*, pp. xv–xxii, 3–16.

7. Christopher Hill, *Economic Problems of the Church*, p. 57. Leeds is the only corporate town Hill lists that was not also a Parliamentary borough. Leeds did, however, hire a lecturer. M. A. Hornsey, "John Harrison, the Leeds Benefactor, and His Times," *Pubs. of the Thoresby Society*, XXXIII (1930–32), 126, 128.

8. Christopher Hill, *Economic Problems of the Church*, p. 57.

9. See Appendix A above.

10. The lecturers were Robert Johnson, William Dyke, and Humphrey Wildbloud. William Urwick, *Nonconformity in Herts* (London, 1884), pp. 103–19.

11. See Appendix A above.

12. For Guildford, Surrey, see William Prynne, *Canterburies Doome* (London, 1646), p. 151; for Peterborough, see *Peterborough Local Administration*, ed. W. T. Mellows (Northamptonshire Record Society, Vol. X, 1937), pp. 55–56. Tavistock's Wednesday lecture was founded by George Hughes, a former London lecturer who had been suspended by Laud. Hughes was subsequently given a chaplaincy by Lord Brooke and the vicarage of Tavistock by another patron. Edward Calamy, *The Nonconformist's Memorial*, ed. Samuel Palmer (London, 1802–3), II, 56–57.

13. Hugh Owen and John B. Blakeway, *A History of Shrewsbury* (London, 1825), I, 392; II, 373, 411–14.

14. In 1628 Heylyn gave the Feoffees the advowson of St. Alkmond's. *Ibid.*, II, 270–72; W. K. Jordan, *The Charities of London, 1480–1660* (London, 1960), pp. 198, 288, 374–75; Calder, *Activities of the Puritan Faction*, p. xii.

15. *Extracts from the Newcastle upon Tyne Council Minute Book, 1639–1656*, ed. M. Hope Dodds (Pubs. of the Newcastle upon Tyne Records Committee, Vol. I; Newcastle, 1920), pp. 2, 3, 4, 13, 30, 47, 67, 69, 72, 228–29.

16. Anthony Wood, *Annals of Oxford*, ed. John Gutch (Oxford, 1792–96), II, 193–94, as quoted in Carteret J. H. Fletcher, *A History of the Church and Parish of St. Martin (Carfax)* (Oxford, 1896), p. 24.

17. Fletcher is apparently mistaken in assuming that there was no lecture until the 1580's; see *Selections from the Records of the City of Oxford...: Henry VIII to Elizabeth, 1509–1583*, ed. William H. Turner (Oxford, 1880), p. 349.

18. *Ibid.*, p. 406.

19. *Oxford Council Acts, 1583–1626*, ed. H. E. Salter (Oxford Historical Society, Vol. LXXXVII; Oxford, 1928), pp. 23, 225, 244; Fletcher, *History of St. Martin*, pp. 102, 25. Fletcher mistakenly dates the Sunday morning lecture from 1617.

20. Christopher Hill, *Economic Problems of the Church*, pp. 50–52.

21. *Documentary Annals of the Reformed Church of England*, ed. Edward Cardwell (Oxford, 1844), II, 94–95.

22. *Ibid.*, p. 94.

23. *Records of the Borough of Nottingham*, Vol. IV, ed. W. Henry Stevenson (London, 1889), pp. 354–55.

24. *Oxford Council Acts, 1583–1626*, p. 193.

25. Nathaniel Bacon, *The Annalls of Ipswiche* (1654), ed. William H. Richardson (Ipswich, 1884), pp. 314, 333, 310.

26. William Negus was a member of the Dedham classis at the time. R. G. Usher, *The Presbyterian Movement in the Reign of Queen Elizabeth* (Camden Society, 3d ser., Vol. VIII; London, 1905), pp. xxix, xliii; T. W. Davids, *Annals of Evangelical Nonconformity in the County of Essex* (London, 1863), p. 116; Bacon, *Annalls of Ipswiche*, p. 342.

27. Bacon, *Annalls of Ipswiche*, pp. 343, 344, 360.

28. J. W. F. Hill, *Tudor and Stuart Lincoln* (Cambridge, Eng., 1956), pp. 110–11; "The Manuscripts of Lincoln, Bury, . . . &c," in *H.MSS.C., 14th Report, Appendix, Part VIII* (London, 1895), p. 76; *The Works of John Smyth*, ed. W. T. Whitley (Cambridge, Eng., 1915), I, xxxvii–xlvii.

29. Mercurius Civicus makes this dependence a principal charge against the Feoffees: "Lastly, for fear lest any of their creatures should fall from them, and desert the cause, as some had done . . . , wisely they provide, that their maintenance shall be dependent on the pleasure of their good masters the feoffees, alterable by addition or subtraction, according to their merits or demerits, and their persons subject to be cashiered." *Somers' Tracts*, IV, 584. Henry Parker turns this argument around and claims that the primary aim of the Laudian bishops was to free the clergy from their dependence on the laity, thus preparing the way for popery. *A Discourse Concerning Puritans* (London, 1641), pp. 11–12.

30. *The Works of the Most Reverend Father in God, William Laud, D.D.*, ed. William Scott and James Bliss (Oxford, 1847–60), V, ii, 321. For Fishborne, see Jordan, *Charities of London*, pp. 115–16.

31. Heylyn, *Cyprianus Anglicus*, p. 188.

32. *Works of William Laud*, V, ii. 308; cf. *Documentary Annals of the Reformed Church*, II, 230.

33. The price of resigning his lectureship was high, for in 1607 Ward received a salary of £73/6/8, which was raised to £100 a year in 1616. Bacon, *Annalls of Ipswiche*, pp. 424, 432, 461.

34. High Commission Act Book, PRO, SP 16/261, fols. 124v, 150r, 304v–305r; see also SP 16/261, fol. 316r; SP 16/434, fols. 109v, 307r.

35. PRO, SP 16/261, fols. 206r–207r; see also Benjamin Brook, *Lives of the Puritans* (London, 1813), II, 434–36.

36. *C.S.P.D., 1629–31*, p. 258.

37. Harold Smith, *The Ecclesiastical History of Essex under the Long Parliament and Commonwealth* (Colchester, n.d.), p. 23; Davids, *Annals of Evangelical Nonconformity*, p. 171n; John and J. A. Venn, *Alumni Cantabrigienses*, Part I, Vol. III, p. 125. Maden later served as curate at St. Helen Bishopsgate, London (1636–40), and as rector and lecturer at St. Mildred Poultry, London (1638–44), until his sequestration. GLMS 6836, fols. 136r, 154r; GLMS 62/1, fols. 5r, 6v, 12v; A. G. Matthews, *Walker Revised* (Oxford, 1948), p. 53.

38. Smith, *Ecclesiastical History of Essex*, pp. 6, 11, 23.

39. Geoffrey I. Soden, *Godfrey Goodman, Bishop of Gloucester, 1583–1656* (London, 1953), pp. 203–4.

40. *H.MSS.C., Report on the Records of the City of Exeter* (London, 1916), pp. 93–96.

41. "MSS. of Rye Corporation," in *H.MSS.C., 13th Report, Appendix, Part IV* (London, 1892), pp. 162, 170; *C.S.P.D., 1623–25*, pp. 101, 118, 147, 185, 358.

42. William Harrison, *Harrison's Description of England*, ed. F. J. Furnivall (London, 1877), I, 21–22.

43. *Records of the Borough of Leicester . . . 1603–1688*, ed. Helen Stocks (Cambridge, Eng., 1923), IV, 339.

44. *The Seconde Parte of a Register*, ed. Albert Peel (Cambridge, Eng., 1915), II, 91.

45. J. W. F. Hill, *Tudor and Stuart Lincoln*, pp. 100–101.

46. *H.MSS.C., 14ᵗʰ Report, VIII*, 68, 73. The first lecturer was a Mr. Jermyn, who left his rectory at Deddington in the hands of a non-preaching curate to accept the lectureship at Lincoln. *Seconde Parte of a Register*, II, 122. Compare the Lincoln stipend with that paid by the corporation of Beverley, Yorks.: £30 a year in 1585, £32 a year after 1590. *H.MSS.C., Report on the Mss. of the Corporation of Beverley* (London, 1900), pp. 185–86.

47. *A.P.C., 1592–93*, p. 120.

48. John Latimer, *Sixteenth-Century Bristol* (Bristol, 1908), p. 104.

49. *V.C.H., Gloucester*, ed. William Page (London, 1907), II, 32; R. J. E. Boggis, *A History of the Diocese of Exeter* (Exeter, 1922), p. 399; George Chandler, *Liverpool under Charles I* (Liverpool, 1965), p. 158. Two of the Liverpool lecturers, James Hyat and Richard Mather, were well-known Puritans. A. G. Matthews, *Calamy Revised* (Oxford, 1934), pp. 262–63; Cotton Mather, *Magnalia Christi Americana* (Hartford, Conn., 1820), I, 402–5.

50. *Records of the Borough of Leicester*, ed. Stocks, IV, 229.

51. *The Assembly Books of Southampton*, ed. J. W. Horrocks (Southampton Record Society; Southampton, 1924), III, 25. Cf. the statement made in the indenture entered into between the borough of Huntingdon and Thomas Beard, Cromwell's schoolmaster, which testifies to the power of his preaching. *D.N.B.*, s.v. Thomas Beard.

52. *Records of the Borough of Nottingham*, IV, 222. Cf. a minute of the town council of Orford, Suffolk, in 1589, which made attendance at the Friday lecture compulsory, and which was coupled with a measure for Sabbath observance. *H.MSS.C., Various Collections*, IV (Dublin, 1907), p. 266.

53. *York Civic Records*, Vol. VIII, ed. Angelo Raine (Yorkshire Archeological Society, Record Ser., Vol. CXIX; York, 1952), p. 57.

54. Bacon, *Annalls of Ipswiche*, pp. 274, 276.

55. *Reading Records*, ed. J. M. Guilding (London, 1895), II, 250; William H. Jones, *Diocesan Histories: Salisbury* (London, 1880), p. 204.

56. "The orders and dealings in the churches of Northampton . . . set up by the consent of the bishop of Peterborough, the mayor and brethren . . . and others the Queen's Majesty's justices of the peace . . . the 5th day of June 1571," in *The Records of the Borough of Northampton*, ed. J. Charles Cox (London, 1898), II, 386–87. J. W. F. Hill (*Tudor and Stuart Lincoln*, pp. 101–5), points out that in Lincoln in the 1580's the lecture formed but a part of a thoroughgoing reform program put forward by the "godly party" in the course of a factional fight within the town council. This program included strict observance of the Sabbath, reform of the grammar school, rationalizing of poor relief, control of the alehouses—in short, the typical combination of piety and social discipline found in many urban communities touched by Puritanism. Cf. also the orders agreed on at Dedham in 1585. Usher, ed., *Presbyterian Movement*, pp. 99–101.

57. James Thompson, *The History of Leicester* (Leicester, 1849), p. 288; *Records of the Borough of Leicester*, ed. Mary Bateson (Cambridge, Eng., 1905), III, 226.

58. *Records of the Borough of Leicester*, ed. Stocks, IV, 229.

59. Brook, *Lives*, II, 369–75; cf. Mather, *Magnalia*, I, 322–28.

60. *Works of William Laud*, V, ii, 325–26.

61. *Records of the Borough of Leicester*, ed. Stocks, IV, 289, 292, 311, 396. Brook, *Lives*, III, 236–37. The Grantham lectureship had been endowed by Lady Camden, Baptist Hicks's wife, by means of a trust administered by the Mercers. Jordan, *Charities of London*, pp. 290, 413.

62. Thomas Wood, who in a sense acted as the public conscience for the first generation of Puritan patrons, referred to Huntingdon as "our good Earl" in a letter to Gilby; *Letters of Thomas Wood, Puritan, 1566–1577*, ed. Patrick Collinson (*Bulletin of the Institute of Historical Research*, Special Supplement no. 5; London, 1960), p. 24. Wood's reference to Huntingdon should be compared with the tone of his letter to Leicester, 4 August 1576, in which Wood makes it clear that he is prepared to believe on the basis of a rumor "commonly reported among the godly ... that your Lordship hath been the chief instrument, or rather the only, of the overthrow of a most godly exercise at Southam." *Ibid.*, p. 10.

63. Claire Cross, "Noble Patronage in the Elizabethan Church," *Historical Journal*, III (1960), 9, 1–2n; *Records of the Borough of Leicester*, ed. Bateson, III, 118.

64. *Records of the Borough of Leicester*, ed. Bateson, III, 261.

65. Francis Peck, *Desiderata Curiosa* (1779), xlvi, 151, as quoted in Cross, "Noble Patronage," p. 9. Cf. Ronald Marchant, *The Puritans and the Church Courts in the Diocese of York, 1560–1642* (London, 1960), pp. 16, 19.

66. Cross, "Noble Patronage," p. 9; minute dated 10 June 1580 in the York Guild House Book, *York Civic Records*, VIII, 35.

67. Cross, "Noble Patronage," pp. 4, 9; *Seconde Parte of a Register*, I, 226–27; see also *ibid.*, I, 244; II, 122. Holdsworth's son-in-law, William Pearson, also became one of the city preachers; in addition to the lecture, Holdsworth held the vicarage of St. Nicholas until his death in 1596. Roger Howell, Jr., *Newcastle upon Tyne and the Puritan Revolution* (Oxford, 1967), p. 81; *Memoirs of the Life of Mr. Ambrose Barnes*, ed. W. H. D. Longstaffe (Surtees Society, Vol. L; Durham, 1866), pp. 297–98, 300.

68. Wallace T. MacCaffrey, *Exeter, 1540–1640* (Cambridge, Mass., 1958), pp. 197–98; *D.N.B.*, s.v. Edmund Snape; Venn, *Alumni Cantab.*, Part I, Vol. IV, p. 117; Usher, ed., *Presbyterian Movement*, pp. 13–20. The Merchant Adventurers of Exeter agreed to contribute £10 a year toward Snape's salary of £50 a year. *H.MSS.C., Report on the Records of the City of Exeter* (London, 1916), p. 40. Snape, therefore, must have had the backing of some of the substantial men of the community.

69. MacCaffrey, *Exeter*, p. 198; V.M. of St. Saviour, Southwark, LCCRO, P/92/S/-450, pp. 383, 391.

70. *A Calendar of the Records of the Borough of Doncaster*, Vol. IV, *Courtiers of the Corporation*, ed. W. J. Hardy (Doncaster, 1902), pp. 125–26.

71. Richard N. North, *History of Plymouth from the Earliest Period to the Present Time* (Plymouth, Eng., 1890), p. 241.

72. *Calendar of the Plymouth Municipal Records*, ed. Richard N. North (Plymouth, Eng., 1893), p. 250; Matthews, *Calamy Revised*, p. 207; Brook, *Lives*, II, 395–96; H. R. Trevor-Roper, *Archbishop Laud, 1573–1645* (London, 1940), p. 117.

73. *Plymouth Municipal Records*, p. 62; Matthews, *Walker Revised*, p. 108.

74. *Plymouth Municipal Records*, p. 43; the reversion may possibly have been granted previously (cf. *ibid.*, p. 251, where the grant is dated 24 January 1632); cf. North, *History of Plymouth*, p. 241; Brook, *Lives*, III, 228–29.

75. *D.N.B.*; Matthews, *Calamy Revised*, pp. 282–83. George Hughes made his reputation as a lecturer at Allhallows Bread Street from 1628 until his suspension by Laud in the mid-1630's. LPLMS 942, no. 14, no. fol.; Isabel M. Calder, "A Seventeenth Century Attempt to Purify the Anglican Church," *American Historical Review*, LIII (1948), 768n. The author of the *D.N.B.* article, Matthews, and Calder all give contradictory and mistaken dates for the beginning of Hughes's lectures at Allhallows,

namely, 1631, 1635, and 1632, respectively. Laud's survey indicates that he was lecturing by 1628. LPLMS 942, no. 14, no fol.

76. *Memoirs of Ambrose Barnes*, pp. 292–328; Howell, *Newcastle*, pp. 81–113.

77. *C.S.P.D., 1639*, p. 450.

78. *Ibid.*, pp. 479, 484.

79. *Extracts from the Newcastle upon Tyne Council Minute Book, 1639–1656*, ed. M. Hope Dodds (Pubs. of the Newcastle upon Tyne Records Committee, Vol. I; Newcastle, 1920), pp. 2–3. In the event, the suspension lasted seven years; Jenison, to escape "further questioning for sundry other misdemeanors" fled abroad, eventually making his way to Danzig. In 1645, with the Parliamentary supporters finally in control, the senior burgess procured an order from the House of Commons confirming the sequestration of the town's "delinquent clergy" and summoning Jenison home to both the lectureship and the vicarage, an invitation confirmed by a letter from the town council urging him "with all convenient speed to hasten to us." *Ibid.*, pp. 115, 38; Brook, *Lives*, III, 526–27. Brook, or Prynne, whom he cites as his source, is incorrect in assuming that Jenison went to New England.

80. *C.S.P.D., 1639–40*, p. 385; Howell, *Newcastle*, p. 111; Matthews, *Walker Revised*, pp. 288, 291.

81. *The Life of Master John Shaw*, in *Yorkshire Diaries and Autobiographies*, ed. Charles Jackson (Surtees Society, Vol. LXV; Durham, 1877), p. 129.

82. Marchant, *Puritans and the Church Courts*, pp. 116 (for Leeds), 225 (for Halifax), 239 (for Bradford), 270 (for Beverley), 118–21 (for Hull).

83. *C.S.P.D., 1639–40*, pp. 105, 542.

84. John Browne, *History of Congregationalism and Memorials of the Churches in Norfolk and Suffolk* (London, 1877), pp. 1–12; Smith, *Ecclesiastical History of Essex*, pp. 6–8; *Suffolk and the Great Rebellion, 1640–1660*, ed. Alan Everitt (Suffolk Records Society, Vol. III, 1960), pp. 11–12, 18–20. But note Everitt's statement (p. 14): "Despite its supposedly impregnable puritanism the port of Ipswich was still said in 1647 to 'desire the king.' "

85. Bacon, *Annalls of Ipswiche*, pp. 329, 510, 424, 432, 479, 509n.

86. *Works of William Laud*, V, ii, 340.

87. Bacon, *Annalls of Ipswiche*, p. 256; James B. Mullinger, *The University of Cambridge from the Earliest Times to the Accession of Charles the First* (Cambridge, Eng., 1873–84), II, 173, 198.

88. Bacon, *Annalls of Ipswiche*, pp. 310, 341–44; *D.N.B.*; for Negus, see Usher, ed., *Presbyterian Movement*, p. xliii.

89. Bacon, *Annalls of Ipswiche*, pp. 341, 361; Brook, *Lives*, I, 239–42; John Strype, *Annals of the Reformation* (Oxford, 1824), Vol. III, Part I, pp. 177–80, and Part II, pp. 228–37; Usher, ed., *Presbyterian Movement*, p. xxix.

90. Bacon, *Annalls of Ipswiche*, pp. 369, 411; *D.N.B.*; Millar Maclure, *The Paul's Cross Sermons, 1534–1642* (Toronto, 1958), p. 239; *C.S.P.D., 1603–10*, p. 127; Venn, *Alumni Cantab.*, Part I, Vol. I, p. 257; Browne, *Congregationalism in Norfolk and Suffolk*, p. 68.

91. Bacon, *Annalls of Ipswiche*, p. 419; Venn, *Alumni Cantab.*, Part I, Vol. I, p. 48.

92. Carteret J. H. Fletcher, *A History of the Church and Parish of St. Martin, (Carfax) Oxford* (Oxford, 1896), pp. 24–25; *Oxford Council Acts, 1583–1626*, ed. H. E. Salter (Oxford Historical Society, Vol. LXXXVII; Oxford, 1928), p. 23.

93. *Oxford Council Acts, 1583–1626*, pp. xxviii–xxix, 67; Marchant, *Puritanism and the Church Courts*, pp. 29–30, 246.

94. *Oxford Council Acts, 1583–1626*, pp. 53, 67, 78, 85; Fletcher, *History of St. Martin*, 102–4; *The Records of the Honorable Society of Lincoln's Inn: The Black Books*, ed. J. Douglas Walker and W. P. Baildon (London, 1897–1902), II, 34.

95. *Oxford Council Acts, 1583–1626*, p. 87; Fletcher, *History of St. Martin*, p. 104; Charles E. Mallet, *A History of the University of Oxford* (New York, 1924), II, 27–28.

96. *Oxford Council Acts, 1583–1626*, pp. 192, 244; Fletcher, *History of St. Martin*, pp. 104–5. The Visitation Call Book of 1612 for the diocese of London records Baugh as curate and lecturer at St. Sepulchre's (GLMS 9537/12, fol. 85v), but I can find no mention of Westly in any of the London records or in any of the lists given by Robert Sommerville in *The Savoy* (London, 1960). For Price, see Fletcher, p. 95.

97. *Oxford Council Acts, 1583–1626*, p. 254; Fletcher, *History of St. Martin*, p. 105.

98. *Oxford Council Acts, 1583–1626*, p. xxxii.

99. For Baylie, see Matthews, *Calamy Revised*, p. 40; for Graby, see Fletcher, *History of St. Martin*, p. 107.

100. *Oxford Council Acts, 1583–1626*, pp. 263, 305, 295; Fletcher, *History of St. Martin*, pp. 105, 106; Matthews, *Calamy Revised*, p. 480; Joseph Foster, *Alumni Oxonienses: The Members of Oxford, 1500–1714* (Oxford, 1891), II, 663; GLMS 1240/1, fol. 20r; GLMS 4072/1, fol. 146r.

101. *Oxford Council Acts, 1583–1626*, p. 324; *Oxford Council Acts, 1626–1665*, ed. M. G. Hobson and H. E. Salter (Oxford Historical Society, Vol. XCV, 1933), p. 37; Fletcher, *History of St. Martin*, p. 107; Matthews, *Calamy Revised*, p. 330.

102. *Oxford Council Acts, 1626–1665*, p. 99, 85; Fletcher, *History of St. Martin*, pp. 68–70, 108; *Works of William Laud*, IV, 229; Mallet, *History of the University of Oxford*, II, 364.

103. *Works of William Laud*, V, ii, 330.

104. Entries dated 7 May and 29 May 1624, anonymous Parliamentary diary, Harleian MS. 159, fols. 118, 136. I am obliged to Prof. Robert Ruigh for these quotations.

105. Peter Heylyn, *Aerius Redivivus* (Oxford, 1670), pp. 299–300.

106. Sir William Dugdale, *A Short View of the Late Troubles in England* (Oxford, 1681), p. 36. A further source of confusion is Dugdale's use of the vague "they," which apparently refers here to lay Puritans in general, though in the paragraph that follows the one quoted "they" refers specifically to the Feoffees for Impropriations.

107. For the figures on which these percentages are based, see Mary F. Keeler, *The Long Parliament, 1640–1641* (Philadelphia, 1954), p. 12.

108. *A Supplement to Bishop Burnet's History of My Own Time*, ed. H. C. Foxcroft (Oxford, 1902), p. 71.

Epigraph to Part II: George Wither, *Britain's Remembrancer* (London, 1628), printed for the Spenser Society (Manchester, 1880), p. 398.

CHAPTER 5

1. E.B., *A Sermon Preached at Pauls Crosse* (London, 1576), as quoted in Carl Bridenbaugh, *Vexed and Troubled Englishmen, 1590–1642* (New York, 1968), pp. 294–95. Bridenbaugh attributes the sermon to Edmund Bunny, Bishop Grindal's chaplain, but the preacher of the sermon has also been identified as Edward Bush; see J. W. Blench, *Preaching in England in the Late Fifteenth and Sixteenth Centuries* (New York, 1964), p. 302.

2. *A.P.C., 1581–82*, p. 169.

3. *Analytical Index to the Series of Records Known as the Remembrancia*, ed.

W. H. and H. C. Overall (London, 1878), pp. 364–65. Any surplus money from the contributions was to be used for supplying ministers to the prisons.

4. "Our Bishop was instrumental, anno 1581, in setting on foot a very useful practice in London; namely, that a number of learned, sound preachers might be appointed to preach on set times before great assemblies.... This motion was so approved of at Court, and by the Queen especially, that Mr. Beal, a clerk of the Council, was sent from above to the Bishop, bringing with him certain notes and articles for the more particular ordering of this business, which he and the ecclesiastical Commissioners were to lay before the Mayor and Aldermen." John Strype, *Historical Collections of the Life and Acts of ...John Aylmer* (Oxford, 1821), p. 57.

5. H. Gareth Owen, "The London Parish Clergy in the Reign of Elizabeth I" (unpubl. Ph.D. thesis, London Univ., 1957), p. 427; cf. the letter of Walsingham to Thomas Norton, the Remembrancer, 8 Nov. 1581, *Remembrancia*, p. 367.

6. *Remembrancia*, pp. 365–66.

7. *Ibid.*, p. 366.

8. *A.P.C., 1581–1582*, p. 199.

9. *Ibid.*, p. 307.

10. Strype, *Aylmer*, p. 57.

11. No doubt the laity ceased to look to the Church for guidance in their charitable spending, but Londoners willingly contributed to causes for which they saw a need. A case for this is made by W. K. Jordan in *The Charities of London, 1480–1660* (London, 1960), pp. 19, 20–27, and *passim*; Jordan concedes, though, that the Elizabethan era was "one of rather cautious giving by the burgher aristocracy of London" (*ibid.*, p. 23).

12. Isabel M. Calder, "The St. Antholin Lectures," *Church Quarterly Review*, CLX (1959), 50.

13. H. Gareth Owen, "Tradition and Reform: Ecclesiastical Controversy in an Elizabethan London Parish," *Guildhall Miscellany*, II (July 1961), 64, 67.

14. GLMS 1454, nos. 68, 69; John J. Baddeley, *An Account of the Church and Parish of St. Giles, without Cripplegate, in the City of London* (London, 1888), p. 13; William Denton, *Records of St. Giles' Cripplegate* (London, 1893), p. 46. Crowley was deprived briefly in 1566 and again in 1578. See Baddeley, *Account of St. Giles Cripplegate*, pp. 58–59; and Benjamin Brook, *Lives of the Puritans* (London, 1813), I, 359–60.

15. St. Lawrence Jewry by 1565 (GLMS 2590/1, p. 21); St. Mary le Bow by 1566 (Owen, "London Parish Clergy," p. 629); Holy Trinity Minories by 1567 (Edward M. Tomlinson, *A History of the Minories London* [London, 1907], p. 220); St. Andrew Holborn by 1569 (LCCRO, Lib. V.G. Huick, fol. 232r, cited in Owen, "London Parish Clergy," p. 623).

16. GLMS 9537/5, fol. 20r; John and J. A. Venn, *Alumni Cantabrigienses*, Part I, Vol. II, p. 193, s.v. Richard Gardiner; GLMS 1568, p. 233; Patrick Collinson, *The Elizabethan Puritan Movement* (London, 1967), pp. 134, 152, where evidence is given that Robert Johnson lectured at St. Clement Danes, 1571–73; *Middle Temple Records*, ed. Charles H. Hopwood (London, 1904–5), I, 182; GLMS 4887, p. 197; *The Vestry Minute Book of the Parish of St. Margaret Lothbury in the City of London, 1571–1677*, ed. Edwin Freshfield (London, 1877), pp. 4, 7; GLMS 3570/1, fol. 3v; Brook, *Lives*, I, 379, s.v. Thomas Sampson; GLMS 4165/1, p. 2; GLMS, 4072/1, fol. 24r; *The Pension Book of Gray's Inn, 1569–1669*, ed. Reginald J. Fletcher (London, 1901), pp. 22, 48.

17. GLMS 6836, p. 277; GLMS 3987/1, no fol.; GLMS 2596/1, fol. 157v; GLMS

1002/1, fol. 185v; GLMS 1176/1, no fol.; GLMS 1013/1, fol. 31v; GLMS 9537/5, fol. 114v; Venn, *Alumni Cantab.*, Part I, Vol. I, p. 306, s.v. Andrew Castleton, Sr.; LCCRO, P/92/S/449, p. 140.

18. *The Records of the Honorable Society of Lincoln's Inn: The Black Books*, ed. J. D. Walker and W. P. Baildon (London, 1897–1902), I, 432; GLMS 1432/3, fols. 2v–3v; GLMS 959/1, fol. 42v; GLMS 4956/2, fol. 132r; GLMS 9537/5, fol. 120v; Patrick Collinson, "John Field and Elizabethan Puritanism," in *Elizabethan Government and Society*, ed. S. T. Bindoff *et al.* (London, 1961), p. 143.

19. St. Antholin's and Christ Church Newgate hired several lecturers, each of whom was expected to preach five times a week; St. Mary Aldermary and the Temple expected their lecturers to preach three times a week; St. Lawrence Jewry, St. Dunstan in the East, St. Mary Lothbury, St. Peter Cornhill, St. Michael Cornhill, St. Helen Bishopsgate, St. Mary Woolnoth, and Gray's Inn expected their lecturers to preach two times a week.

20. See Appendix D above.

21. Appendix B above gives an alphabetical listing of these 129 parishes.

22. Various population estimates for the period are given in Jordan, *Charities of London*, p. 16.

23. See Appendix D above.

24. See *ibid.*

25. Peter Heylyn, *Cyprianus Anglicus* (London, 1671), p. 192. This survey, endorsed by Laud, is entitled "A Note of All the Lecturers in London When I Came to Be Bishop There, 1628" (LPLMS 942, no. 14). Whether Laud could not believe that the situation was as bad as first reported, or whether he wanted to check on progress made in limiting the number of lectureships, or whether he intended such surveys to become a regular annual affair, we cannot be certain; at any rate a second list exists for 1629 (LPLMS 942, no 16). A letter from Laud dated 4 January 1629/30 lends support to this last supposition: "Because they are so full of justice, honor, and care of the Church, I send to you the whole body of Instructions..., praying and requiring you as Archdeacon of London to send me at or before Wednesday the third of February next, both the Christian and surnames of every lecturer within your archdeaconry,... the place where he preacheth, and his quality and degree." William Prynne, *Canterburies Doome* (London, 1646), p. 371.

26. Allhallows Staining, C.W. Accts. 1581–82, GLMS 4956/2, fol. 132. The 1583 Visitation Call Book, which records Cheston as lecturing at Allhallows, also mentions that he lectured at St. Katherine Coleman. GLMS 9537/5, fols. 118v, 120v. Little is known about Cheston, but in testimony before the ecclesiastical commissioners Thomas Edmunds declared that Cheston was a member of the London classis. R. G. Usher, ed., *The Presbyterian Movement in the Reign of Queen Elizabeth* (Camden Society, 3d ser., Vol. VIII; London, 1905), p. 5. St. Katherine's had no lecturer in 1586, according to the Visitation Call Book, and the lecture at Allhallows was temporarily being given by the incumbent curate. GLMS 9537/6, fols. 117v, 115v. The lecture at Allhallows then lapsed until 1607. GLMS 4956/2, fols. 147v, 217v.

27. Tomlinson, *History of the Minories*, p. 211. The first solid evidence for the resumption of the lecture at St. Katherine's occurs in the Churchwardens' Accounts for 1625–26 (GLMS 1124/1, fol. 60r), where it is noted that the curate, John Wilson, was paid for lecturing. Wilson was in trouble in 1628 for preaching without a license; see 1628 Visitation Call Book, GLMS 9537/13, no fol., and an entry dated 10 Dec. 1628 in the Correction Book of the Consistory Court, LCCRO, DL/C/317, fol.

26v. Wilson apparently succeeded in obtaining a license, for he seems to be the John Wilson who was rector of Green's Norton, Northamptonshire, from 1631 until his death in 1636. George Hennessy, *Novum Repertorium Ecclesiasticum Parochiale Londinense* (London, 1898), p. 116; Venn, *Alumni Cantab.*, Part I, Vol. IV, p. 429.

28. *The Vestry Minute Books of the Parish of St. Bartholomew Exchange in the City of London, 1567–1676*, ed. Edwin Freshfield (London, 1890), Part I, pp. 15, 17.

29. *Ibid.*, pp. 18–19. The average lecture assessments ran five or six times as high as the assessment for the Parliamentary fifteenth.

30. *Ibid.*, pp. 33, 44, 45. At least by 1598 the curate lectured on Sunday. GLMS 9537/9, no fol.

31. The thirteen parishes that do not appear in the visitation records are Allhallows Bread Street, St. Dunstan in the East, St. Mary Aldermary, St. Mary le Bow, St. Michael Crooked Lane, St. Pancras Soper Lane, St. Vedast Foster Lane, Allhallows Lombard Street, St. Dionis Backchurch, St. John the Evangelist Friday Street, St. Leonard Eastcheap, St. Mary Bothaw, and St. Michael Paternoster. See Manuscripts Consulted for a listing of the parish records.

32. GLMS 9537/6; GLMS 9537/8.

33. Thomas Norton, *Instructions to the Lord-Mayor of London, 1574–5*, reprinted in *Illustrations of Old English Literature*, ed. J. P. Collier (London, 1866), III, 7–8.

34. H. Gareth Owen, "Lecturers and Lectureships in Tudor London," *Church Quarterly Review*, CLXII (1961), 65.

35. *Lincoln's Inn Black Books*, II, 485. This is all the records reveal, though the secretary goes on to note that the court had tried unsuccessfully to obtain the services of two noted Puritans, "Mr. Chaderton and Mr. Reynolds," and had succeeded in hiring a third, William Charke, who lectured there until he was finally suspended by Whitgift in 1593. For Charke, see *D.N.B.*

36. This sentence was recorded by the parish clerk in his memoranda book at a vestry meeting on 14 January 1596/7. GLMS 9234/6, fol. 97r.

37. These percentages are based on the figures given by Owen in "London Parish Clergy," p. 91. Some of the implications of the rise in the clergy's educational qualifications in this period, particularly the problem of finding appropriate livings for educated priests, are discussed in Mark H. Curtis, "The Alienated Intellectuals of Early Stuart England," *Past and Present*, XXIII (1962), 25–43.

38. Owen, "London Parish Clergy," p. 150. Owen attributes part of the rise in the number of incumbents with preaching licenses to the rise in the number of active lectureships, for the lectureships opened up a new source of income to priests who were properly qualified and licensed. *Ibid.*, p. 158.

39. Subscription Book, 1631–62, GLMS 9539A/2. At the beginning of the volume is a copy of the Oath of Supremacy, followed by the Oath of Allegiance: "I, A.B., do truly and sincerely acknowledge, profess, testify, and declare in my conscience before God and the world that our Sovereign Lord King Charles is lawful king of this Realm. . . ." The actual subscription was to the following statement: "Tribus articulus et omnibus eiusdem contentis, libenter et ex animo subscribo."

40. Subscription Book, 1627–42, GLMS 9539A/1. This volume contains the subscription of curates, lecturers, schoolmasters, and physicians.

41. Christopher Hill, *Economic Problems of the Church from Archbishop Whitgift to the Long Parliament* (Oxford, 1956), pp. 229, 225, 227.

42. *The Seconde Parte of a Register*, ed. Albert Peel (Cambridge, Eng., 1915), II, 180–84; A. G. Matthews, *Walker Revised* (Oxford, 1948), pp. 42–63.

43. *The Petition and Articles Exhibited in Parliament against Dr. Fuller, Deane of Ely, and Vicar of S. Giles Cripplegate, . . . by the Parishioners of Saint Giles* (London, 1641), fols. 2v, 4r; see also Matthews, *Walker Revised*, p. 48, s.v.William Fuller. The parishioners' charge of pluralism was certainly justified, for Fuller was dean of Ely and vicar of Weston, Nottinghamshire. Sedgwick was, needless to say, a Puritan. Brook, *Lives*, II, 485; *D.N.B.*

44. GLMS 9234/6, fol. 97v.

45. Quoted in Samuel Clarke, *A Generall Martyrologie* (London, 1651), Part III, p. 109.

46. *Minutes of the Vestry Meetings and Other Records of the Parish of St. Christopher le Stocks, in the City of London*, ed. Edwin Freshfield (London, 1886), p. 7.

47. *Vestry Minutes Books of St. Margaret Lothbury*, p. 4.

48. *Ibid.*, pp. 26, 34, 35.

49. V.M. 7 Feb. 1603/4, GLMS 4887, p. 313.

50. GLMS 1175/1, fol. 10r.

51. Edmunds also lectured at St. Mary Woolnoth. GLMS 1002/1, fol. 233r. For his career, see Brook, *Lives*, III, 515; Joseph Foster, *Alumni Oxonienses: The Members of Oxford, 1500–1714* (Oxford, 1891), II, 446; and *Seconde Parte of a Register*, I, 15.

52. GLMS 3570/2, fols. 18v–19r.

53. LCCRO P/92/S/450, p. 538. Harris, Puritan that he was, had to resign anyway because he was unable to procure the necessary "dispensation" from the Archbishop of Canterbury. *Ibid.*; *D.N.B.* William Bradshaw was also, without his knowledge or seeking, nominated and elected lecturer at Christ Church Newgate in 1602 (he had preached occasional sermons there before then). Clarke, *Martyrologie*, Part III, p. 119.

54. Clarke, *Martyrologie*, Part III, pp. 106–7. When Bradshaw lost his lectureship for nonconformity, he became chaplain to a Leicestershire gentleman on the recommendation of Arthur Hildersham, parson and lecturer at Ashby. *Ibid.*, Part III, p. 119.

55. Strype, *Aylmer*, pp. 100–101; see also William Haller, *The Rise of Puritanism* (New York, 1938), p. 29.

56. Haller, *Rise of Puritanism*, pp. 67–68. Hildersham and Egerton had worked together previously in securing the Puritan clergy's support for the Millenary Petition. *Ibid.*, p. 55; see also Collinson, *Elizabethan Puritan Movement*, pp. 447, 452.

57. Memoranda of 23 July 1598, GLMS 9234/7, fol. 122r. For Hubbuck, see Brook, *Lives*, II, 164–65; *D.N.B.*; Collinson, *Elizabethan Puritan Movement*, p. 446; and GLMS 9234/7, fol. 135v. Eusebius Paget, who had been suspended and deprived for nonconformity twice before, was suspended again at St. Botolph's in 1598, shortly after he had begun his preaching there. *Ibid.*, fol. 166v. Apparently this last suspension was due to his failure to obtain a proper license. Eventually he did obtain one and the lectureship was resumed. GLMS 9234/5, 2d section, fol. 33r.

58. GLMS 3016/1, p. 322.

59. Robarts to Ussher, 26 Feb. 1627, in *The Whole Works of the Most Rev. James Ussher, D.D.*, ed. Charles R. Elrington and J. H. Todd (Dublin, 1847–64), XVI, 462.

60. Consistory Court, Personal Answer Book, 1617–21, entry dated 4 Nov. 1619; LCCRO, DL/C/192, no fol.

61. GLMS 9234/5, fols. 3r–84v.

62. For St. Bartholomew Exchange, see *Vestry Minute Books of St. Bartholomew Exchange*, Part I, p. 95; for St. Lawrence Pountney, LCCRO, DL/C/192, entry dated

4 Nov. 1619, no fol. At St. Saviour, Southwark, beans were employed in balloting. LCCRO, P/92/S/450, p. 486.

63. GLMS 3570/2, fols. 9r, 15v, 17v, 18r–v, 19v–20r. A somewhat similar incident occurred at St. Lawrence Jewry in 1575, when the patron granted the next presentation to the vestry. Robert Crowley was elected vicar, and at a later vestry he was granted the lectureship. GLMS 2590/1, pp. 50–51.

64. See Owen, "London Parish Clergy," pp. 278–79. Although information is lacking for some parishes that owned or leased the right of presentation, most appear to have had lecturers of one kind or another. However, specific arrangements varied greatly from parish to parish and defy any easy categorization. For example, so far as one can tell, St. Michael Wood Street, which had purchased the rectory from the Crown during Henry VIII's reign, did not have a lecturer until the early 1620's, when the Puritan Arthur Jackson was hired to preach there; Jackson subsequently became the rector in 1625 and continued to lecture into the 1640's. *D.N.B.*; LPLMS 942, no 14. By contrast, the parish of St. James Clerkenwell, which purchased its advowson in 1598, was not able to reward its lecturer, the nonconformist Lawrence Barker, with the curacy, for the first vacancy did not occur at St. James's until 1607, four years after Barker's death. GLMS 9537/9, fol. 159v; GLMS 1453/1, fol. 1v; LCCRO, DL/C/338, fols. 1r, 122v. Although the vestry of St. Mary at Hill purchased the rectory in 1637 on the day after the incumbent's death and hence was able to exercise the right of patronage immediately, these changes impinged in no way on the parish lectureship, which had been endowed by Sir John Leman in 1632 and was preached every Thursday by Andrew Blackwell from 1633 until 1661. GLMS 1240/1, fols. 28v, 36r–v, 75r; GLMS 9539 A/1, fol. 24r. Where there was no well-established lectureship, however, the power to appoint a preaching incumbent may have had a significant bearing. At Allhallows Staining, for example, there does not appear to have been an active lectureship from the 1580's until the 1620's. The parish leased the parsonage in 1618; in 1627 the Puritan curate Philip Nye lectured on Sunday afternoons, a practice that his Puritan successor, Adoniram Byfield, continued from his appointment in 1629 on into the 1640's. LPLMS nos. 14, 16; GLMS 4956/2, fol. 258r. The wide variety of lectureship arrangements among these parishes is perhaps best illustrated by comparing Holy Trinity and St. Katherine Cree. The former hired more than twenty independent lecturers in the thirty years after 1567. E. M. Tomlinson, *A History of the Minories London* (London, 1907), pp. 220–21; Owen, "London Parish Clergy," p. 630. When the extant Vestry Minutes for St. Katherine's begin, in 1639, the parish, which had leased its rectory since 1544, had only one lecture a month, preached before communion; even these few lectures were financed by an endowment. GLMS 1196/1, fols. 5r, 23v. Essentially, of course, the presence of a lecture depended on the vestry's desire for a preaching ministry and on the parish's financial status. Whether or not the vestry had the right to present to the living was in most cases of little importance in this respect. St. Saviour's, which had leased the benefice from 1541, hired a lecturing minister from 1565 in addition to electing the curate (LCCRO, P/92/S/449, pp. 48, 53, 56); Stephen Egerton had been hired as lecturer at St. Anne Blackfriars almost a quarter of a century before the parish purchased the living and presented him as curate (Owen, "London Parish Clergy," pp. 278, 625; *D.N.B.*, which, however, incorrectly lists Egerton as minister in 1598); and at St. Mary Aldermanbury, which had leased the living in 1542, the lectureship had been initially conferred on independent lecturers (Owen, "London Parish Clergy," p. 544, n. 2; GLMS 6574, fols. 2r, 3v, 4v). Only at St. Lawrence Pountney and at St.

Stephen Coleman Street was the lecture given by the incumbent curate from the beginning. GLMS 3907/1, no fol.; GLMS 4457/2, fols. 4r, 14v; GLMS 9537/5, fol. 122v. Most of these parishes, but not all, appointed Puritans to their lectureships most of the time.

65. Biographies of most of these men, all famous preachers in their time, can be found in *D.N.B.*; biographies of the three who are not mentioned there—Stoughton, Davenport, and Goodwin—can be found in Brook, *Lives,* and in Haller, *Rise of Puritanism, passim.*

66. *Reports of Cases in the Courts of Star Chamber and High Commission,* ed. S. R. Gardiner (Camden Society, new ser., Vol. XXXIX; London, 1886), p. 307.

67. V.M. 19 Oct. 1623, GLMS 4415/1, fol. 10v.

68. V.M. 6 Oct. 1624, *ibid.,* fol. 16r.

69. LCCRO, DL/C/316, fol. 222v; Venn, *Alumni Cantab.,* Part I, Vol. II, p. 358; Harold Smith, *The Ecclesiastical History of Essex under the Long Parliament and Commonwealth* (Colchester, n.d.), pp. 38–39.

70. For a copy of the Parliamentary sequestration order, see GLMS 4415/1, fol. 113v.

71. WPLMS 2413, fol. 79r.

72. WPLMS F.6036; Venn, *Alumni Cantab.,* Part I, Vol. III, p. 147. The earliest mention in the Lord Chamberlain's Accounts seems to be a note of a letter sent to Marshall, 13 Jan. 1631/2, PRO/LC.5/132, p. 282.

73. WPLMS, F.2001, fol. 107v. For the difficulties Everard experienced because of his sermons against the Spanish match and for his career as a London preacher in general, see *The Letters of John Chamberlain,* ed. Norman E. McClure, American Philosophical Society, Memoirs, XII (Philadelphia, 1939), II, 350, 449, 486; and *D.N.B.*

74. WPLMS, F.2001, fol. 166v; F.2002, pp. 50–51.

75. WPLMS, F.2002, pp. 133–34, 237.

76. *A Calendar of the Inner Temple Records,* ed. Frederick A. Inderwick (London, 1896–1901), II, 73; *Middle Temple Records,* ed. Charles H. Hopwood (London, 1904–5), II, 576.

77. St. Peter Cornhill, V.M. 18 Oct. 1574, GLMS 4165/1, p. 2.

78. GLMS 4415/1, fol. 61r.

79. Cf. St. Saviour, Southwark, V.M. 21 May 1585, LCCRO, P/92/S/450, p. 204.

80. A petition from the parishioners of St. Mary le Bow to the Lord Mayor on behalf of their suspended lecturer noted that the "learned, virtuous, and godly preacher, Mr. Barbor," kept his "effectual and godly" exercise "four times every week." *Seconde Parte of a Register,* II, 220.

81. LPLMS 942, no. 16.

82. LPLMS 942, no. 14.

83. *Vestry Minute Books of St. Bartholomew Exchange,* Part I, pp. 45, 77, 93–94.

84. Cf. St. Martin in the Fields, V.M. 22 Oct. 1645, WPLMS F.2002, p. 235. Occasionally lectures were given less frequently than once a week: St. Alphage had a monthly communion preparation sermon, endowed at least in part by Thomas Thrush, Woolman, and treated as a lecture with elected preachers hired by the year (GLMS 1432/3, fol. 23r); St. Martin Orgar originally had a fortnightly lecture (GLMS 959/1, fol. 69v).

85. GLMS 9234/1, fol. 29r; GLMS 9234/5, 2d section, fols. 99r–152v, 197v. David Dee, a former lecturer at Christ Church Newgate, was constantly in trouble for vari-

ous irregularities. See Consistory Court, Liber. Correctione, LCCRO, DL/C/303, fol. 16v; DL/C/304, fol. 29r; and DL/C/306, fol. 346r. Dee was not the only one to deviate from his text. Before the Consistory Court in 1617 it was charged against an Essex curate and lecturer that when "preaching on the first of St. John's gospel and the fifteenth verse, [he] digressed utterly from his text and preached and taught with great eagerness that the putting a garland of flowers upon a hearse at a funeral was monstrous idolatry, and that whatsoever was done in the church that was not expressly commanded by the word of God was wicked and sinful." LCCRO, DL/C/-314, fol. 150v.

86. *The Works of the Most Reverend Father in God, William Laud, D.D.*, ed. William Scott and James Bliss (Oxford, 1847–60), V, ii, 308.

87. PRO, SP 16/261, fol. 304v. Extemporaneous prayers before the sermon had actually been proscribed by the 55th Canon of the Canons of 1604, which in addition set out the form to be used for the prayers. *Constitutions and Canons Ecclesiasticall; Treated upon by the Bishop of London, President of the Convocation for the Province of Canterbury, . . . and Agreed upon with the Kings Majesties License in Their Synod Begun at London, Anno Dom. 1603* (London, 1633), n.p.

88. William Prynne, *Canterburies Doome* (London, 1646), p. 362. The prayer was made before a sermon preached at St. Antholin's on 3 May 1629, just a few months before the Instructions were issued. See also the charges entered before the Court of High Commission against George Burdett (PRO, SP 16/261, fol. 168v), and against John Howe (*ibid.*, fol. 120r).

89. GLMS 819/1, p. 98; GLMS 818/1, no fol. In 1633 the Consistory Court warned Dennison to "carefully perform his duties in his said cure" (he had been presented for absenting himself from his living), and to "celebrate divine service and also to preach and catechize as the canons of the Church of England require." LCCRO, DL/C/320, fol. 58v. During 1634 and 1635 he was involved in a lengthy case before the High Commission; the major charges were invective preaching against his parishioners and incontinency, only the former of which was proved. He was also charged with publishing erroneous doctrine. PRO, SP 16/261, fols. 35v, 120v, 136r, 144r, 187r, 243v, 282v–284r, 291v–292r, 308r.

90. Edwards's statements are as given in Brook, *Lives*, III, 84. C.W. Accts. 1631, GLMS 9235/2, no fol. See also Dorothy A. Williams, "London Puritanism: The Parish of St. Botolph without Aldgate," *Guildhall Miscellany*, II (Sept. 1960), 32–34.

91. *Documentary Annals of the Reformed Church of England*, ed. Edward Cardwell (Oxford, 1844), I, 440. *Constitutions and Canons Ecclesiasticall*, n.p.

92. LCCRO, P/92/S/450, p. 359.

93. V.M. 26 Nov. 1628, GLMS 3570/2, fol. 26r, and cf. fol. 27r; V.M. 6 May 1624, GLMS 642/1, no fol.

94. *Vestry Minute Books of St. Bartholomew Exchange*, Part I, p. 101; cf. St. Mary Woolchurch, C.W. Accts. 1587–88, GLMS 1013, fol. 45v.

95. V.M. 29 Jan. 1599/1600, GLMS 9234/5, 2d section, fol. 222v.

96. John Strype, *The Life and Acts of John Whitgift, D.D.*, (London, 1822), I, 360; R. G. Usher, *The Reconstruction of the English Church* (New York, 1910), I, 220; cf. Christopher Hill, *Economic Problems of the Church from Archbishop Whitgift to the Long Parliament* (Oxford, 1956), pp. 224–26. A point of some importance that Usher overlooks is that by the turn of the century there may have been more university-trained clergy than there were "adequate" livings. (Usher himself, refuting Puritan charges, argues for the high qualifications of the Anglican clergy by 1600.)

The evidence suggests that the balance between supply and demand was not as easily or as precisely achieved as Usher (or Whitgift) seems to have assumed. See Mark H. Curtis, "The Alienated Intellectuals of Early Stuart England," *Past and Present*, Vol. XXIII (1962), esp. pp. 30–34.

97. Strype, *Whitgift*, I, 534.

98. William Harrison, *Harrison's Description of England*, ed. F. J. Furnivall, Part I (New Shakespeare Society, ser. 6; London, 1877), Vol. I, p. 22; John Earle, *Microcosmography*, ed. Alfred S. West (Cambridge, Eng., 1920), p. 51; GLMS 4072/1, fols. 198r–199v.

99. Christopher Hill, *Economic Problems of the Church*, pp. 111, 93.

100. LCCRO, P/92/S/450, pp. 48, 389; GLMS 2590/1, pp. 88, 341; GLMS 4458/1, pp. 4, 18, 87.

101. GLMS 593/2, fol. 167v.

102. GLMS 4887, pp. 243, 247; *Seconde Parte of a Register*, II, 181; GLMS 6554/1, fols. 190v, 161r.

103. GLMS 593/2, fol. 2r, and GLMS 593/4, no fol. (C.W. Accts. 1645); GLMS 1002/1, fol. 223r; GLMS 6836, fol. 33v.

104. *Vestry Minute Books of St. Bartholomew Exchange*, Part I, pp. 88, 91, 93. For Grant, see A. G. Matthews, *Walker Revised,* (Oxford, 1948), pp. 48–49, and Venn, *Alumni Cantab.*, Part I, Vol. II, p. 248. For Torshall, see *D.N.B.* and Venn, *Alumni Cantab.*, Part I, Vol. IV, p. 255. Downham preached the William Jones lecture at St. Bartholomew Exchange, the lecture being in the gift of the Haberdashers' Company. For Torshall's election to the living at Bunbury, also in the gift of the Haberdashers, see Haberdashers' Company MS., Minutes of the Court of Assistants, I, fol. 257v.

105. For St. Lawrence's, see GLMS 2590/1, pp. 33, 106, 284; and GLMS 2593/1, fols. 127v, 133v. For St. Antholin's, see GLMS 1046/1, fols. 6r, 80v, 133r, 150v; Isabel M. Calder, "The St. Antholin Lectures," *Church Quarterly Review*, CLX (1959), 53; *The Records of the Honorable Society of Lincoln's Inn: The Black Books*, ed. J. D. Walker and W. P. Baildon (London, 1897–1902), I, 432; II, 134, 277, 377, 417.

106. *Vestry Minutes of St. Margaret Lothbury*, pp. 14, 35, 50. For Lady Weld's lecture, see GLMS 4415/1, 2d section, fol. 10v; GLMS 4409/1, fol. 159r; GLMS 4409/2, no fol. (C.W. Accts. 1658). For the Jones lecture, see Haberdashers' Company MS., Minutes of the Court of Assistants, I, fols. 191v, 195r; cf. Hab. Co. MS., The State of the Charities, 1597, p. 317 (an indenture between the company and Downham, 8 Dec. 1641).

107. Christopher Hill, *The Century of Revolution, 1603–1714* (Edinburgh, 1961), p. 317.

108. GLMS 2590/1, pp. 284, 294, 341, 342, 398, 406; GLMS 2593/1, fols. 358v–359r.

109. For St. Margaret Lothbury, see GLMS 9537/3, no fol., and George Hennessy, *Novum Repertorium Ecclesiasticum Parochiale Londinense* (London, 1898), p. 279; for St. Margaret New Fish Street, C.W. Accts. 1577–78, GLMS 1176/1, no fol. (cf. GLMS 1175/1, fol. 10r); and for St. Saviour's, LCCRO, P/92/S/449, p. 140.

110. GLMS 9234/1, 1st section, fols. 34v, 39r, 103r; GLMS 9537/6, fol. 108v.

111. For Thomas Crook, see Venn, *Alumni Cantab.*, Part I, Vol. I, p. 424; Usher, ed., *Presbyterian Movement*, pp. xxviii, 5; *The Pension Book of Gray's Inn, 1559–1669*, ed. Reginald J. Fletcher (London, 1901), pp. 48, 50; and GLMS 1013/1, fols. 42r, 62r. Crook also lectured at St. Peter Westcheap in 1597; GLMS 645/1, fol. 248r. For Nathaniel Waker, see GLMS 9539A/1, fol. 8v; LPLMS 942, no. 16; GLMS 2590/1, p. 272; GLMS 2593/1, fols. 325r, 346r; and GLMS 9537/13, no fol.

112. V.M. 20 Jan. 1576/7, *Minutes of the Vestry Meetings and Other Records of the Parish of St. Christopher le Stocks, in the City of London*, ed. Edwin Freshfield (London, 1886), p. 7; cf. V.M. 6 Oct. 1583, *Vestry Minute Books of St. Bartholomew Exchange*, Part I, p. 15.

113. GLMS 6836, fols. 26r–v, 35r–v, 40r–v, 42r–v; cf. St. Margaret Pattens, C.W. Accts. 1626–33 (GLMS 4570/2, pp. 265–304), for a similar record of a parish constantly behind in its lectureship collections.

114. *Vestry Minutes of St. Christopher le Stocks*, pp. 23, 51.

115. C.W. Accts. 1626–27, GLMS 645/2, no fol.; V.M. 30 Aug. 1627, GLMS 642/1, no fol.; V.M. 5 April 1632, *ibid.*, no fol. At St. Magnus the Martyr the deficits were considerably larger. C.W. Accts. 1638–41, GLMS 1179/1, pp. 7–21; see also St. Michael Querne, C.W. Accts. 1636–40, GLMS 2895/2, no fol.

116. For St. Martin's, see GLMS 1311/1, fols. 94r, 102v, 106v, 112r. For St. Dunstan's, see GLMS 4887, pp. 197, 225, 247.

117. GLMS 1002/1, fols. 201r, 216v, 290v; GLMS 1188/1, pp. 14, 17.

118. GLMS 2590/1, pp. 64, 88, 89, 102; GLMS 2593/1, fols. 52r, 53r, 56r, 74v, 119v, 133v. Cf. St. Stephen Coleman Street, GLMS 4458/1, pp. 8, 18, and St. Lawrence Pountney, C.W. Accts. 1602–3, GLMS 3907/1, no fol. The right of the vestry at St. Lawrence Jewry to present the vicar was challenged early in 1594. Although later in the same year the vestry recorded the election of a new incumbent, Thomas Sanderson, it is probably significant that he had been a Fellow of Balliol College, which held the rectory, prior to his presentation. In any event, subsequent vicars were not elected by the vestry. However, a bequest from Allen Elwin, Leatherseller, of £100 for a lecturing curate ("a sufficient preaching reader"), recorded in 1605, permitted the vestry to hire a lecturer from 1614 on. GLMS 2590/1, pp. 102, 105, 137, 192, 202, 204. Whereas the vicar's stipend remained stationary at £60 a year until after 1640, the lecturer's salary rose from £40 in 1617 to £65 (£60 plus £5 from the Elwin bequest) in 1624. *Ibid.*, pp. 223, 250; GLMS 2593/1, fols. 232v, 304r.

119. LCCRO, P/92/S/450, pp. 382–461.

120. See W. K. Jordan, *The Charities of London, 1480–1660* (London, 1960), pp. 26–27, 309, and *passim*.

121. See Appendix E, p. 306 above. This is a minimum number, based primarily on information obtained from the nineteenth-century Reports of the Charity Commissioners (printed in the *Parliamentary Papers*), from the parish records, from John Stow's *Survey of the Cities of London and Westminster* (ed. John Strype [London, 1720]), and from Jordan, *Charities of London*.

122. See, for example, the reaction of Laud and Charles I to Richard Fishbourne's bequest for a lecture in Huntingdon. *Works of William Laud*, V, ii, 321.

123. See Appendix E, p. 306 above, for a list of the 31 parishes.

124. See Appendix E, p. 307 above.

125. The average number of parishes with active lectureships is derived from Table I, p. 127 above.

126. Cf. Jordan, *Charities of London*, esp. p. 284.

127. Charity Commissioners, 6th Report, *Parliamentary Papers* (1822), IX, 193–94; Jordan, *Charities of London*, p. 289. This bequest was not put into effect until 1666; see V.M. 14 Dec. 1665, GLMS 2590/1, fol. 578.

128. Haberdashers' Company MS., Will Book, 1635–1908, fols. 38r, 39v–41v. For Egerton, see *D.N.B.*; for Sedgwick, see Samuel Clarke, *A Generall Martyrologie* (London, 1651), Part I, pp. 395–98.

129. GLMS 1568, pp. 378, 384, 392, 397. For Charke and Wotton, see *D.N.B.*; for Phillips, see Brook, *Lives*, II, 162–63. For a similar restrictive provision, see John Strange's bequest of 20 marks for a weekly lecture at Christ Church Newgate, which was to run for one year only; LCCRO, DL/C/308, fol. 284v.

130. For Garret's bequest, see Charity Commissioners, 6th Report, *Parliamentary Papers* (1822), IX, 202. For Hyde's, see Charity Commissioners, 4th Report, *Parliamentary Papers* (1820), V, 104–5. Compare the similar provision in Dame Lucy Edge's lectureship bequest, also dating from the early 1630's, in Charity Commissioners, Reports on Parochial Charities of the City of London, Vol. III, Appendix 3, *Parliamentary Papers* (1880), XX, 308.

131. Charity Commissioners, 6th Report, *Parliamentary Papers* (1822), IX, 204–5, 194–95.

132. GLMS 3016/1, p. 116; Jordan, *Charities of London*, p. 287; E. H. Pearce, *Sion College and Library* (Cambridge, Eng., 1913), pp. 1, 8; *Seconde Parte of a Register*, II, 238; see also *ibid.*, I, 221.

133. For the Drapers' Company payments, see GLMS 1046/1, fol. 7v; for Trotman's charities, see Charity Commissioners, 10th Report, *Parliamentary Papers* (1824), XIII, 221.

134. GLMS 2597/1, pp. 75, 77, 82, 86, 109.

135. For St. Olave's, see GLMS 4415/1, fols. 32v, 39r; for St. Swithin's, GLMS 559/1, fol. 25r.

136. Haberdashers' Company MS., Will Book, 1535–1908, fols. 87r–90v. The Governors of Christ Church Hospital acted in the capacity of overseers and auditors. The first account book (1630–78), signed by the auditors, is still preserved among the Haberdashers' Company Manuscripts. The purchases of five impropriations are recorded in it.

137. For the details, which I have only sketched, see Haberdashers' Company MS., Minutes of the Court of Assistants, I, fols. 180v–196r.

138. *Ibid.*, fols. 72r, 154v, 207v, 256r, 257v. For Hinde, see Brook, *Lives*, II, 364. Torshall had previously lectured at St. Bartholomew Exchange and in 1626 returned to a London lectureship. LPLMS 942, no. 14; John J. Baddeley, *An Account of the Church and Parish of St. Giles without Cripplegate in the City of London* (London, 1888), p. 99.

139. Haberdashers' Company MS., Minutes of the Court of Assistants, I, fols. 12v, 65r; GLMS 3907/1, no fol.

140. Haberdashers' Company MS., Minutes of the Court of Assistants, I, fol. 36v; GLMS 2590/1, pp. 105, 106, 211.

141. Haberdashers' Company MS., Minutes of the Court of Assistants, I, fols. 272v, 292v, 357r.

142. Charity Commissioners, Reports on the Parochial Charities of the City of London, Vol. III, Appendix 3, *Parliamentary Papers* (1880), XX, 335–37; GLMS 559/1, fols. 17r, 21r, 28v, 30v, 31r; LPLMS 942, no. 16.

143. GLMS 4165/1, pp. 223, 237, 260, 268, 270, 280. Lucy Edge's lectureship was bequeathed in 1630, but the rector's opposition prevented the lecture from being given until after his sequestration in 1644.

144. GLMS 1046/1, fols. 148v–150v. For a description of the circumstances surrounding the unique grant from the City Chamber, see Dorothy A. Williams, "Puritanism in the City Government, 1610–1640," *Guildhall Miscellany*, IV (1955), 3–14. For a sketch of the financial status of the St. Antholin's lectureships, including the role of

the Feoffees for Impropriations, during the whole period, see Isabel M. Calder, "The St. Antholin Lectures," *Church Quarterly Review*, CLX (1959), 49–57.

145. See Jordan, *Charities of London*, p. 284.

146. In 1610, however, the vestry of St. Bartholomew Exchange rejected a conditional gift of £20 from Richard Maplesden because he would not grant the sum to the parish absolutely. *Vestry Minute Books of St. Bartholomew Exchange*, pp. 62–67.

147. GLMS 1046/1, fol. 79r.

148. *Good Works: If they be well handled; or, Certaine Projects about Maintenance for Parochiall Ministers, Provision for and Election of Lecturers, Erection and Indowment of New Churches in the Great Out Parishes about London* (London, 1641), Epistle to the Reader and p. 1.

149. GLMS 6554/1, fol. 228v.

150. *Good Works*, pp. 6–7. Compare the situation in 1600 at St. Alphage's, where the parson was willing for the vestry to hire a lecturer so long as the raising of the lecturer's stipend "be...nothing prejudicial to himself." GLMS 1431/1, p. 35. For the bond entered into by Mr. Worme, see GLMS 5018/1, no fol.

151. GLMS 1045/1, pp. 2, 32, 37, 45–46, 49, 63.

152. GLMS 3570/1, fols. 28r, 30r, 63r.

153. For the foregoing, see V.M. 7 March 1643/4, V.M. 11 March 1643/4, and V.M. 6 Jan. 1644/5, in GLMS 1642/1, no fol.; for the date of sequestration, see A. G. Matthews, *Walker Revised* (Oxford, 1948), p. 61.

154. GLMS 2590/1, pp. 89, 90; GLMS 2593/1, fols. 52r, 56r.

155. V.M. 14 Sept. 1617 and V.M. 22 Oct. 1618, GLMS 3980/1, no fol.; C.W. Accts. 1618, 1619, GLMS 3907/1, no fol. The vestry of St. Michael Cornhill also withdrew support for their parson's lecture until all differences between him and the parish had been overcome. GLMS 4072/1, fol. 150r. Compare a similar case at St. Stephen Coleman Street, where a benevolence rather than a lectureship was involved; GLMS 4458/1, pp. 4–14.

156. Quoted in William Prynne, *Canterburies Doome* (London, 1646), p. 368.

157. *Good Works*, p. 7.

158. *C.S.P.D., 1634–35*, pp. 22–23.

CHAPTER 6

1. For example, the C.W. Accts. of St. Michael Querne, 1586, which list amounts paid for candles for the lecture but do not name the lecturer. GLMS 2595/1, fol. 227v. The problem of identity can be illustrated by the ubiquitous John Jones, listed variously as incumbent or lecturer at St. Michael Bassishaw, 1624–29, at St. Nicholas Acons, 1617–37, at St. Pancras Soper Lane, 1634–35, and at St. Lawrence Jewry, 1635–37. GLMS 2601/1, fol. 57r; LPLMS 942, no. 16; George Hennessy, *Novum Repertorium Ecclesiasticum Parochiale Londinense* (London, 1898), p. 144; GLMS 5019/1, p. 39; GLMS 2590/1, p. 301.

2. Archer's trial at Fulham Palace is recorded in Laud's Episcopal Register. GLMS 9531/15, fols. 22r–22v, 23r. Cf. *C.S.P.D., 1629–31*, pp. 407, 485, 495, 532, 546.

3. *Winthrop Papers* (Massachusetts Historical Society; Cambridge, Mass., 1929–47), II, 340.

4. William Prynne, *Canterburies Doome* (London, 1646), p. 373. See also Benjamin Brook's *Lives of the Puritans* (London, 1813), II, 455, where John Archer is incorrectly referred to as "Henry" Archer.

5. See, for example, Alan Simpson, *Puritanism in Old and New England* (Chicago, 1955), ch. 1; Perry Miller, *The New England Mind: The Seventeenth Century* (New York, 1939), chs. 1–4; and William Haller, *The Rise of Puritanism* (New York, 1938), esp. pp. 27–28.

6. James B. Mullinger, *The University of Cambridge from the Earliest Times to the Accession of Charles the First* (Cambridge, Eng., 1873–84), II, 481–83; Haller, *Rise of Puritanism*, pp. 65–66.

7. The counties in which the London lecturers were born and in which they held their last preferments are listed in Appendix F, p. 309 above.

8. For Nicholson, see GLMS 9234/1, 1st section, fol. 68v; E. M. Tomlinson, *A History of the Minories London* (London, 1907), p. 220; John and J. A. Venn, *Alumni Cantabrigienses*, Part I (Cambridge, Eng., 1922), Vol. III, p. 257.

9. John Earle, *Microcosmography*, ed. Alfred S. West (Cambridge, Eng., 1920), p. 93.

10. Venn, *Alumni Cantab.*, Part I, Vol. I, p. 306; GLMS 9537/5, fol. 114v; GLMS 9537/7, no fol.; LPLMS 942, nos. 14, 16; Haberdashers' Company MS., Minutes of the Court of Assistants, I, fol. 196r.

11. Venn, *Alumni Cantab.*, Part I, Vol. II, p. 232; LPLMS 942, nos. 14, 16; GLMS 9537/13, no fol.; *D.N.B.* (which erroneously states that Thomas Gouge did not leave Cambridge until 1635); GLMS 9539A/1, fol. 97v; A. G. Matthews, *Calamy Revised* (Oxford, 1934), pp. 229–30.

12. Venn, *Alumni Cantab.*, Part I, Vol. II, p. 61; *D.N.B.*, s.v. George and John Downham; Haberdashers' Company MS., Minutes of the Court of Assistants, I, fol. 289r; GLMS 9537/15, fol. 64r; GLMS 593/2, fols. 168v–169r.

13. Venn, *Alumni Cantab.*, Part I, Vol. II, p. 200; *D.N.B.* Thomas Gataker, Sr., was also lecturer at Christ Church Newgate. GLMS 9537/6, fols. 110r, 117r; H. Gareth Owen, "Tradition and Reform: Ecclesiastical Controversy in an Elizabethan London Parish," *Guildhall Miscellany*, II (July 1961), 65. For Alvey, see H. C. Porter, *Reformation and Reaction in Tudor Cambridge* (Cambridge, Eng., 1958), pp. 183–206.

14. Haberdashers' Company MS., Minutes of the Court of Assistants, I, fols. 91r–v. Along with Downham the Haberdashers sometimes consulted Gataker about ecclesiastical appointments in their gift. *Ibid.*, fol. 201r.

15. *D.N.B.*; *The Records of the Honorable Society of Lincoln's Inn: The Black Books*, ed. J. D. Walker and W. P. Baildon (London, 1897–1902), II, 72, 134, 149; William Haller, *Liberty and Reformation in the Puritan Revolution* (New York, 1955), p. 37.

16. *D.N.B.*; Joseph Foster, *Alumni Oxonienses: The Members of Oxford, 1500–1714* (Oxford, 1891), II, 611. Griffith continued to lecture at St. Dunstan's until 1639. GLMS 3016/1, p. 149; GLMS 2968/3, fol. 578r. In 1640 he was admitted to the rectory of St. Benet Sherehog. GLMS 9539A/2, no fol. For his later career, see A. G. Matthews, *Walker Revised* (Oxford, 1948), p. 49.

17. GLMS 9537/13, no fol.; Matthews, *Calamy Revised*, pp. 397–98; Brook, *Lives*, III, 1; Venn, *Alumni Cantab.*, Part I, Vol. II, p. 50.

18. Foster, *Alumni Oxon.*, I, 362; the *D.N.B.* article has Culverwell educated at Emmanuel, which seems highly unlikely unless he matriculated after his suspension from the vicarage of Felstead in 1583. See also *The Seconde Parte of a Register*, ed. Albert Peel (Cambridge, Eng., 1915), II, 261; GLMS 9537/7, no fol.; GLMS 9537/8, fol. 57v; R. G. Usher, ed., *The Presbyterian Movement in the Reign of Queen Elizabeth* (Camden Society, 3d ser., Vol. VIII; London, 1905), pp. xxix, 19, 21.

19. Haller, *Rise of Puritanism*, p. 36; *Abstract of Wills of the Prerogative Court of Canterbury at Somerset House, London, England: Register Soame, 1620*, ed. J. Henry Lea (Boston, 1904), pp. 146–47. For Stock, see *D.N.B.*

20. *The Whole Works of the Most Rev. James Ussher, D.D.*, ed. Charles R. Elrington and J. H. Todd (Dublin, 1847–64), XVI, 320–21, 331–34; Millar Maclure, *The Paul's Cross Sermons, 1534–1642* (Toronto, 1958), p. 239. For Burgess, see *D.N.B.*

21. *Abstract of Wills: Register Soame, 1620*, p. 319. For Wotton, see *D.N.B.*; Brook, *Lives*, II, 347; and see also the mention of Wotton's "heresy" in the letter from Ralph Cudworth to Ussher, 17 Jan. 1617/18, in *Works of James Ussher*, XVI, 347.

22. W. K. Jordan, *The Charities of London, 1480–1660* (London, 1960), pp. 16–17, 316–18; Valerie Pearl, *London and the Outbreak of the Puritan Revolution* (London, 1961), pp. 12–15.

23. Matthews, *Calamy Revised*, pp. 397–98.

24. Venn, *Alumni Cantab.*, Part I, Vol. II, p. 86; GLMS 9537/15, fol. 59r; William Urwick, *Nonconformity in Herts.* (London, 1884), p. 395; Matthews, *Walker Revised*. p. 46; GLMS 2601/1, no fol.

25. For a summary of the statistics on university attendance, see Appendix F, p. 308 above.

26. Lawrence Stone, *The Crisis of the Aristocracy, 1558–1641* (Oxford, 1965), pp. 740–41.

27. *D.N.B.*; Brook, *Lives*, III, 165; Venn, *Alumni Cantab.*, Part I, Vol. II, p. 233. For William Gouge's father, see Porter, *Reformation and Reaction in Tudor Cambridge*, p. 232.

28. Cotton Mather, *Magnalia Christi Americana* (Hartford, Conn., 1820), I, 232–34.

29. Haller, *Rise of Puritanism*, p. 54.

30. Mullinger, *University of Cambridge*, II, 234, 301, 328–29, 473, 475–76, 509–10.

31. *Ibid.*, 508–9; *D.N.B.*; GLMS 3570/2, fol. 21v.

32. Cf. Porter, *Reformation and Reaction in Tudor Cambridge*, pp. 414–22.

33. *Ibid.*, pp. 115, 119–21, 188–94, 208–9; Mullinger, *University of Cambridge*, II, 204, 305, 322–24, 356, 480.

34. Porter, *Reformation and Reaction in Tudor Cambridge*, pp. 141, 203, 314–15, 364–65; Mullinger, *University of Cambridge*, II, 478–79, 483; Irvonwy Morgan, *Prince Charles's Puritan Chaplain* (London, 1957), pp. 13, 28–34.

35. C. E. Mallet, *A History of the University of Oxford* (New York, 1924–27), II, 300, 302.

36. Samuel Clarke, *A Generall Martyrologie* (London, 1651), Part I, p. 395. Egerton received his B.A. in 1576. Venn, *Alumni Cantab.*, Part I, Vol. II, p. 91. For Charke at Cambridge, see Porter, *Reformation and Reaction in Tudor Cambridge*, pp. 139, 141, 179–80, 191.

37. Usher, ed., *Presbyterian Movement*, pp. xxviii, xxxix, 5, 20–21. Egerton was lecturer at St. Anne Blackfriars. GLMS 9537/6, fol. 108v. Charke lectured at both Lincoln's Inn and Gray's Inn, and in 1597 at St. Mary Aldermary; he was silenced by Whitgift but continued to live in London until his death in 1617. *Records of Lincoln's Inn*, I, 432, II, 28; *The Pension Book of Gray's Inn*, ed. Reginald J. Fletcher (London, 1901), pp. 22, 48; GLMS 6547, fol. 3v; Venn, *Alumni Cantab.*, Part I, Vol. I, p. 324. For Gardiner, see *ibid.*, Part I, Vol. II, p. 193, and for his lecture at St. Helen's, see GLMS 6836, fols. 27v, 35v. He was also rector and lecturer at Whitechapel until his death in 1617. GLMS 9537/5, fol. 28r; GLMS 9537/11, fol. 172r. For Thomas Man, see Venn, *Alumni Cantab.*, Part I, Vol. III, p. 132; *Seconde Parte of a Register*, I, 244,

II, 113; for his lectureship at Christ Church, see H. Gareth Owen, "The London Parish Clergy in the Reign of Elizabeth I" (unpubl. Ph.D. thesis, London Univ., 1957), p. 626. He was also lecturer at St. Lawrence Pountney, 1592–94. GLMS 3907/1, no. fol.

38. Clarke, *Martyrologie*, Part I, pp. 396–97.

39. *Ibid.*, p. 398; Haberdashers' Company MS., Minutes of the Court of Assistants, I, fols. 192v, 193v, 200v, 207r; LPLMS 942, nos. 14, 16; GLMS 9537/15, fol. 56r. Sedgwick was cited before the Consistory Court for nonconformity in 1623 but was dismissed with an admonition. LCCRO, DL/C/316, fol. 162r.

40. R. G. Usher, *The Reconstruction of the English Church* (New York, 1910), I, 253.

41. A. Tindal Hart, *The Country Clergy, 1558–1660* (London, 1958), p. 66.

42. Cf. John White, *The First Century of Scandalous, Malignant Priests* (London, 1643), pp. 3, 8, 9, 25, 34–35, 37, 40–41; and *The Articles and Charge Proved in Parliament against Doctor Walton, Minister of St. Martins Orgars in Cannonstreet* (London, 1641), esp. pp. 2, 4.

43. Daniel Neal, *The History of the Puritans or Protestant Non-Conformists* (London, 1756), I, 395, 434; Usher, *Reconstruction of the English Church*, I, 248–56; G. B. Tatham, *The Puritans in Power* (Cambridge, Eng., 1913), p. 53. The figure of 9,000 clergymen is given by Curtis in "Alienated Intellectuals," *Past and Present*, XXIII (1962), 30–31.

44. Matthews, *Walker Revised*, p. xiv.

45. For a summary of the data on the careers of the London lecturers, see Appendix F, p. 310 above.

46. For Holliday, see Foster, *Alumni Oxon.*, II, 635, and GLMS 9537/11, fol. 97r. For Taylor, see *D.N.B.* and GLMS 3570/2, fol. 21v. For Ussher, see *D.N.B.* and *Records of Lincoln's Inn*, II, 375.

47. *Documentary Annals of the Reformed Church of England*, ed. Edward Cardwell (Oxford, 1844), I, 440, 466–71; GLMS 9537/5. See also H. Gareth Owen, "Lecturers and Lectureships in Tudor London," *Church Quarterly Review*, CLXII (1961), 66.

48. See note 40 above.

49. Owen, "London Parish Clergy," p. 626; GLMS 2596/1, fols. 157v, 163r; Venn, *Alumni Cantab.*, Part I, Vol. II, p. 149; George Hennessy, *Novum Repertorium Ecclesiasticum Parochiale Londinense* (London, 1898), p. 268.

50. For Holland, see GLMS 959/1, fols. 67r, 68r; GLMS 9537/9, fol. 158r; LCCRO, DL/C/338, fols. 114r, 118v; and *D.N.B.* For Griffith, see GLMS 9537/9, no fol.; GLMS 9234/2, 3d section, fol. 169v; and Foster, *Alumni Oxon.*, II, 608.

51. *D.N.B.*; Maclure, *Paul's Cross Sermons*, p. 224; Venn, *Alumni Cantab.*, Part I, Vol. IV, p. 164; Thomas Fuller, *The Worthies of England*, ed. J. Freeman (London, 1952), pp. 670–71.

52. *The Vestry Minute Book of the Parish of St. Bartholomew Exchange in the City of London, 1567–1676*, ed. Edwin Freshfield (London, 1890), Part I, esp. p. 45; Venn, *Alumni Cantab.*, Part I, Vol. II, p. 45.

53. LPLMS 942, nos. 14, 16; GLMS 959/1, fol. 163v; GLMS 1311/1, fol. 115v; GLMS 4072/1, fol. 180v; *The Works of the Most Reverend Father in God, William Laud, D.D.*, ed. William Scott and James Bliss (Oxford, 1847–60), V, ii, 362–63; Brook, *Lives*, III, 39–40.

54. GLMS 2596/2, fols. 48r, 57r; GLMS 2597/1, pp. 16, 23, 28; Matthews, *Walker Revised*, pp. 341–42.

55. GLMS 2590/1, pp. 365, 366, 425, 428, 447; Matthews, *Calamy Revised*, p. 540; Venn, *Alumni Cantab.*, Part I, Vol. IV, p. 443.

56. GLMS 1045/1, pp. 44, 65; Matthews, *Walker Revised*, pp. 89–90; Venn, *Alumni Cantab.*, Part I, Vol. I, p. 311.

57. For Ashbold, see GLMS 4887, pp. 197, 225, 235; GLMS 4165/1, pp. 2, 65, 164, 171; GLMS 4072/1, fols. 40v, 43r; and Venn, *Alumni Cantab.*, Part I, Vol. I, p. 43. For Worme, see GLMS 4887, pp. 313, 316, 326, 338; LCCRO, DL/C/303, p. 241; *C.S.P.D.*, *1636–37*, p. 175; and Venn, *Alumni Cantab.*, Part I, Vol. IV, p. 464.

58. Fuller, *Worthies*, p. 394.

59. *Ibid.*, pp. 670–71.

60. For Randall and Harris, see *D.N.B.*; for Simonds, see Brook, *Lives*, III, 39.

CHAPTER 7

1. Millar Maclure, *The Paul's Cross Sermons, 1534–1642* (Toronto, 1958), p. 93.

2. Maclure, *Paul's Cross Sermons*, p. 108.

3. *Wrens Anatomy: Discovering His Notorious Pranks, and Shamefull Wickednesse* (London, 1641), p. 8.

4. *The First and Large Petition of the Citie of London and Other Inhabitants Thereabouts: For a Reformation in Church-government, as Also for the Abolishment of Episcopacie* (London, 1641), pp. 3–4.

5. *To the Right Honorable the Knights, Citizens, and Burgesses of the Commons House of Parliament: The Humble Petition of Some of the Parishioners in the Parish of Chigwell in the County of Essex and Divers Others* (London, 1641), single sheet. The petition is against the Arminian cleric Dr. Emmanuel Utey, vicar of Chigwell. Utey had been curate and lecturer at St. Mildred Bread Street in 1612. GLMS 9537/11, fol. 85r.

6. Visitation Articles, 1557, Article 16, in *Documentary Annals of the Reformed Church of England*, ed. Edward Cardwell (Oxford, 1844), I, 206–7.

7. *Injunctions Given by the Queens Majesty, Anno Domini 1559, The First Yere of the Reign of Our Sovereign Lady Queen Elizabeth* (London, 1559), esp. articles 3, 4, 8, 30.

8. *Documentary Annals of the Reformed Church*, I, 242–43. For a thorough treatment of licensing and its effect on the London Puritans, see H. Gareth Owen, "The London Parish Clergy in the Reign of Elizabeth I" (unpub. Ph.D. thesis, London, Univ., 1957), pp. 162–76.

9. *Documentary Annals of the Reformed Church*, I, 321–31, 334–37; John Strype, *The Life and Acts of Matthew Parker* (Oxford, 1821), I, 428–29.

10. Owen, "London Parish Clergy," p. 375; see also Patrick Collinson, *The Elizabethan Puritan Movement* (London, 1967), pp. 74–77.

11. H. Gareth Owen, "Tradition and Reform: Ecclesiastical Controversy in an Elizabethan London Parish," *Guildhall Miscellany*, II (July, 1961), 64–65.

12. Collinson, *Elizabethan Puritan Movement*, pp. 77, 82.

13. *Letters of Thomas Wood, Puritan, 1566–1577*, ed. Patrick Collinson (*Bulletin of the Institute of Historical Research*, Special Supplement no. 5; London, 1960), pp. xi, 1.

14. Strype, *Parker*, I, 301, 434–35.

15. John J. Baddeley, *An Account of the Church and Parish of St. Giles, without Cripplegate, in the City of London* (London, 1888), pp. 58–59; William Denton, *Rec-*

ords of St. Giles' Cripplegate (London, 1883), pp. 46–47; Joseph Foster, *Alumni Oxonienses: The Members of Oxford, 1500–1714* (Oxford, 1891), I, 358; *D.N.B.*

16. GLMS 2590/1, pp. 51, 52, 58; GLMS 1046/1, fols. 6r, 7v; GLMS 1176/1, no fol.; LCCRO, P/92/S/449, p. 140; GLMS 9537/5, fol. 122r.

17. *D.N.B.*; Strype, *Parker*, I, 436; Collinson, *Elizabethan Puritan Movement*, p. 82.

18. Edward M. Tomlinson, *A History of the Minories London* (London, 1907), p. 220; Patrick Collinson, "John Field and Elizabethan Puritanism," in S. T. Bindoff, *et al.*, eds., *Elizabethan Government and Society* (London, 1961), pp. 129–31; Champlin Burrage, *The Early English Dissenters in the Light of Recent Research (1550–1641)* (Cambridge, Eng., 1912), I, 82–83; H. Gareth Owen, "A Nursery of Elizabethan Nonconformity, 1567–72," *Journal of Ecclesiastical History*, XVII (1966), 66–69; Benjamin Brook, *Lives of the Puritans* (London, 1813), I, 175.

19. *A Booke of Certaine Canons, Concernyng Some Parte of the Discipline of the Churche of England* (London, 1571), pp. 22–23. See also M. M. Knappen, *Tudor Puritanism* (Chicago, 1939), 229–30.

20. John E. Cox, *The Annals of St. Helen's, Bishopsgate, London* (London, 1876), p. 106; GLMS 6836, fols. 23v–24r, 27r; R. G. Usher, ed., *The Presbyterian Movement in the Reign of Queen Elizabeth* (Camden Society, 3d ser., Vol. VIII; London, 1905), pp. xxviii, xxxv; GLMS 593/2, fol. 2r; *The Seconde Parte of a Register*, ed. Albert Peel (Cambridge, Eng., 1915), II, 220, 262, and for the supplication of the parishioners of Bow church for Barbor's return, II, 219–20; Brook, *Lives*, I, 429; *D.N.B.*, s.v. Thomas Barbor.

21. Owen, "London Parish Clergy," p. 515. For Wager's lecture at St. Benet Gracechurch, where he was also rector, see GLMS 1568, pp. 223, 225, 342. For his lecture at St. Mary Woolnoth, see GLMS 1002/1, fol. 185v. Wager was also rector of St. Michael Queenhithe; GLMS 9537/5, fol. 115r. The Haberdashers assisted his son with an exhibition to Magdalene College, Cambridge, in 1584; Haberdashers' Company MS., Minutes of the Court of Assistants, I, fols. 12v, 65r.

22. GLMS 3556/1, fol. 204r; GLMS 3570/1, fol. 7r; George Hennessy, *Novum Repertorium Ecclesiasticum Parochiale Londinense* (London, 1898), p. 299; *Seconde Parte of a Register*, I, 221; GLMS 9537/5, fol. 113v; GLMS 9537/6, fol. 111r.

23. GLMS 9537/5, fol. 2r; GLMS 9537/6, fol. 111r; GLMS 6836, fols. 27v, 35v; Usher, ed., *Presbyterian Movement*, p. 5; Brook, *Lives*, III, 512; LCCRO, DL/C/304, fols. 352v, 360v; John and J. A. Venn, *Alumni Cantabrigienses*, Part I, *From Earliest Times to 1751* (Cambridge, Eng., 1922), Vol. II, p. 193.

24. Tomlinson, *History of the Minories*, pp. 166, 211; GLMS 4956/2, fol. 132r; GLMS 9537/5, fol. 118v; Owen, "London Parish Clergy," p. 540, n. 1; GLMS 9234/1, 3d section, fol. 7r. Cheston was not the first London Puritan to be rescued by the Earl of Warwick; Nicholas Standon had accompanied the earl as his chaplain on the expedition to suppress the Northern Rebellion in 1569. H. Gareth Owen, "A Nursery of Elizabethan Nonconformity, 1567–72," *Journal of Ecclesiastical History*, XVII (1966), 68–69.

25. *The Vestry Minute Book of the Parish of St. Margaret Lothbury in the City of London, 1571–1677*, ed. Edwin Freshfield (London, 1887), pp. 4, 7; Owen, "London Parish Clergy," p. 527; Hennessy, *Novum Repertorium*, pp. 144, 279; GLMS 9537/3, no fol.

26. Hennessy, *Novum Repertorium*, pp. 144, 345; GLMS 1176/1, no fol.; GLMS 1175/1, fol. 10r; LCCRO, P/92/S/449, p. 140; LCCRO, P/92/S/450, p. 172; GLMS 9537/6, fol. 108v; GLMS 9234/2, 1st section, fol. 103r; GLMS 9234/1, 1st section, fols. 34v, 39r, 90r.

27. *Documentary Annals of the Reformed Church*, I, 440; Strype, *Grindal*, pp. 362–63.

28. John Strype, *Historical Collections of the Life and Acts of the Right Reverend Father in God, John Aylmer* (Oxford, 1821), pp. 53–54.

29. GLMS 9537/5, *passim*.

30. Strype, *Aylmer*, p. 61; John Strype, *The Life and Acts of John Whitgift* (Oxford, 1822), I, 223, 228–30; *Documentary Annals of the Reformed Church*, I, 466–70. Parker had used these three articles in 1571 as a means for testing the conformity of a number of Puritan leaders brought before the Ecclesiastical Commission, but their use had not been generalized. Knappen, *Tudor Puritanism*, pp. 230, 266–67.

31. Strype, *Whitgift*, III, 103–4, 106.

32. For the concessions won from Whitgift by Walsingham, see Knappen, *Tudor Puritanism*, pp. 279–81.

33. Aylmer was able to increase his control and supervision of the ecclesiastical affairs of the City by appointing his son Archdeacon of London. Strype, *Aylmer*, pp. 81–84, 112.

34. For Blythman, see GLMS 3556/1, fol. 204r; GLMS 9537/5, fol. 113v; and GLMS 9537/6, fol. 111r. For Scarlet, see GLMS 9537/5, fols. 111r, 113r; and *Seconde Parte of a Register*, II, 181.

35. For Bright, see GLMS 9537/5, fols. 122v, 125r. Bright was not an independent lecturer and in fact went on to become a pluralist. GLMS 9537/9, no fol.; Venn, *Alumni Cantab.*, Part I, Vol. I, p. 218. For Close, see GLMS 9537/5, fol. 120v. Close was in trouble in 1585, but his difficulties in that year had been brought on by a slanderous statement he made about Sir Wolstan Dixie in a Paul's Cross sermon. Maclure, *Paul's Cross Sermons*, p. 214; *D.N.B.* Halton was curate and lecturer at St. Lawrence Pountney as well as lecturer at St. Antholin's. GLMS 3907/1, no fol.; GLMS 9537/5, fol. 111v. For Smith, see LCCRO, P/92/S/450, pp. 190, 204; and GLMS 4072/1, fol. 28r. For Welles, see GLMS 9537/5, fols. 113r, 122v; and GLMS 9537/6, fols. 110r, 120r. In 1589 Welles became rector and lecturer at St. Margaret Lothbury, a post he held until his death in 1596. *Vestry Minutes of St. Margaret Lothbury*, pp. 22, 26, 34. For White, who was also vicar of St. Dunstan in the West, see GLMS 9537/5, fols. 113r, 125r. White was a popular preacher and the founder of Sion College. E. H. Pearce, *Sion College and Library* (Cambridge, Eng., 1913), pp. 1–8.

36. *Seconde Parte of a Register*, I, 221. Altogether fifteen London ministers signed this statement.

37. Strype, *Whitgift*, I, 249–60; Knappen, *Tudor Puritanism*, pp. 267–74; Collinson, "John Field and Elizabethan Puritanism," in Bindoff *et al.*, eds., *Elizabethan Government and Society*, pp. 150–53.

38. For Barbor, see *Seconde Parte of a Register*, II, 219, 220, 262; *D.N.B.*; Brook, *Lives*, I, 429; and Strype, *Whitgift*, III, 271–85. For Edmunds, see GLMS 1175/1, fols. 10r, 11r; Brook, *Lives*, III, 515; and *Seconde Parte of a Register*, I, 15.

39. *Seconde Parte of a Register*, I, 284–86; *Two Elizabethan Puritan Diaries*, ed. M. M. Knappen (Chicago, 1933), p. 31; GLMS 9537/6, fol. 108v; *D.N.B.*; Brook, *Lives*, II, 290.

40. *Seconde Parte of a Register*, II, 262; Collinson, "John Field and Elizabethan Puritanism," in Bindoff *et al.*, eds., *Elizabethan Government and Society*, pp. 150–55.

41. For Salt, see GLMS 9537/6, fol. 110r; and GLMS 1311/1, fol. 83v. For Gataker, see GLMS 9537/5, fol. 113r; GLMS 9537/6, fols. 110r, 117r; and Brook, *Lives*, II, 68–69.

42. *A Calendar of the Inner Temple Records*, ed. Frederick A. Inderwick (London,

1896–1901), I, 327, 333; *Middle Temple Records,* ed. Charles H. Hopwood (London, 1904–5), I, 287; *Seconde Parte of a Register,* II, 262; *D.N.B.*

43. For Davidson, see GLMS 4409/1, fols. 2r, 4v; *Seconde Parte of a Register,* I, 284, II, 231; and *D.N.B.* For Anderson, see GLMS 9537/6, fols. 116r, 118v; GLMS 9234/1, 3d section, fol. 15v; and GLMS 9234/1, 1st section, fols. 3v, 9r. For his later lecturing career, see GLMS 9234/1, 2d section, fol. 66r; GLMS 9234/3, fol. 67r; GLMS 4570/2, p. 75; GLMS 9537/7, no fol.; and GLMS 9234/2, 1st section, fol. 25v.

44. GLMS 9537/7, no fol.; GLMS 9537/9, no fol.; GLMS 9537/10, fol. 109v; T. W. Davids, *Annals of Evangelical Nonconformity in the County of Essex* (London, 1863), p. 78; Usher, ed., *Presbyterian Movement,* p. xxxv.

45. GLMS 6836, fol. 42v; *Seconde Parte of a Register,* II, 182; Venn, *Alumni Cantab.,* Part I, Vol. I, p. 434.

46. *Seconde Parte of a Register,* II, 221–31; Ronald Marchant, *The Puritans and the Church Courts in the Diocese of York, 1560–1642* (London, 1960), pp. 20–21, 292; Brook, *Lives,* I, 339–55.

47. *Seconde Parte of a Register,* II, 92; GLMS 9537/7, no fol.; William Urwick, *Nonconformity in Herts.* (London, 1884), pp. 118, 294.

48. William Haller, *The Rise of Puritanism* (New York, 1938), p. 29; Strype, *Aylmer,* pp. 101–2; Brook, *Lives,* II, 108–11; *D.N.B.*

49. John Strype, *Annals of the Reformation* (Oxford, 1824), Vol. III, Part I, pp. 21–22, 29–30; LCCRO, P/92/S/450, pp. 204, 228, 231; *Seconde Parte of a Register,* II, 180.

50. Knappen, *Tudor Puritanism,* p. 261; *The Records of the Honorable Society of Lincoln's Inn: The Black Books,* ed. J. D. Walker and W. P. Baildon (London, 1897–1902), I, 432, II, 28. Charke had lectured at Gray's Inn during the five years before he became lecturer at Lincoln's Inn; the minutes noted that his preaching was to continue "if it be not otherwise misliked by the Privy Council or the Archbishop... or the Bishop of London." *The Pension Book of Gray's Inn,* ed. Reginald J. Fletcher (London, 1901), p. 22; GLMS 9234/6, fol. 85v; GLMS 6574, fol. 3v.

51. H. Gareth Owen, "Lecturers and Lectureships in Tudor London," *Church Quarterly Review,* CLXII (1961), 66.

52. Gardiner, who had lectured at St. Helen's from 1577 to 1581 (GLMS 6836, fols. 27v, 35v), was rector and lecturer at St. Mary Whitechapel from 1570 to 1617. GLMS 9537/5, fol. 20r; GLMS 9537/11, fol. 172v; Venn, *Alumni Cantab.,* Part I, Vol. II, p. 193; Usher, ed., *Presbyterian Movement,* p. 5. Crook preceded Charke at Gray's Inn. *Pension Book of Gray's Inn,* pp. 48, 50, 138. He gave up his lecture at St. Mary Woolnoth in 1591 but lectured at St. Peter Westcheap from 1597 until his death the following year. GLMS 1013/1, fols. 42r, 62r; GLMS 645/1, fol. 248r.

53. For Atkinson, see Usher, ed., *Presbyterian Movement,* p. xxix; and GLMS 9234/3, 3d section, fol. 109r. Atkinson went on to become curate and lecturer at St. Bartholomew Exchange and at Stanmore Parva in Middlesex. GLMS 9537/10, fol. 99v; GLMS 9537/11, fol. 73r. The John Dodd mentioned here was the father of Nehemiah Dodd, not the John Dodd of Fawsley. Usher, ed., *Presbyterian Movement,* pp. xxix, xxxix; GLMS 9537/9, no fol.; GLMS 4457/2, fols. 51v, 81r; GLMS 9537/10, fol. 103v. For his trouble at Coggeshall in 1637, see GLMS 9537/15, fols. 19r–v. Among other things, Dodd was presented for saying that the Bishop of Norwich "went about to bring the clergy into slavery." For Greenham, see Haller, *Rise of Puritanism,* pp. 25–26; Brook, *Lives,* I, 415–18; Samuel Clarke, *A Generall Martyrologie* (London, 1651), Part III, pp. 83–87; and *D.N.B.*

54. For the Fulthorpes, father and son, see *Seconde Parte of a Register*, I, 243; Tomlinson, *History of the Minories*, pp. 198, 220–21; GLMS 9234/6, fol. 294r; and LCCRO, DL/C/303, fol. 289v. Hurleston (Hudleston) was suspended at Saxelbie, Lincs., in 1584. *Seconde Parte of a Register*, I, 244, II, 121. See also GLMS 9537/9, fols. 154, 157r; GLMS 9234/7, fol. 131r; and Venn, *Alumni Cantab.*, Part I, Vol. II, p. 423.

55. Man was also suspended for nonsubscription in Lincolnshire. *Seconde Parte of a Register*, I, 244, II, 113; see also Owen, "London Parish Clergy," p. 626, and GLMS 3907/1, no fol. For Gawton, see Urwick, *Nonconformity in Herts.*, pp. 293, 295–97, 426; *Seconde Parte of a Register*, I, 137–39; GLMS 6574, fols. 4v, 5r, 10r.

56. For Paget, see *Seconde Parte of a Register*, I, 121, 123, 286–91; Brook, *Lives*, II, 253–58; *D.N.B.*; and Usher, ed., *Presbyterian Movement*, p. xxix. For Paget at St. Botolph's, see GLMS 9234/7, fols. 122r, 135v, 166v, and GLMS 9234/5, 2d section, fol. 222v. Hubbuck had been before the High Commission in 1590 for an "undutiful and seditious" sermon he had preached at Oxford. Both Knollys and Burghley sought to protect him, but without success. Hubbuck subsequently became chaplain at the Tower. Brook, *Lives*, II, 164–65; *D.N.B.*; GLMS 9234/6, fols. 97r, 107r.

57. Peter Heylyn, *Aerius Redivivus* (Oxford, 1670), p. 369.

58. Even as a theoretical proposal Presbyterianism played almost no part in the request made by the Puritan spokesmen at the Hampton Court Conference; see Mark H. Curtis, "Hampton Court Conference and Its Aftermath," *History*, XLVI (1961), 8–12.

59. *Constitutions and Canons Ecclesiasticall . . . , Anno Dom. 1603* (London, 1633). S. B. Babbage questions whether it was really possible to enforce Canons 37, 38, and 54 at all rigorously. *Puritanism and Richard Bancroft* (London, 1962), pp. 92, 110–11.

60. Babbage, *Puritanism and Richard Bancroft*, pp. 98–100, 101–2, 105–7.

61. *Documentary Annals of the Reformed Church*, II, 93–94.

62. Babbage, *Puritanism and Richard Bancroft*, pp. 122–23.

63. *Articles to Be Enquired of within the Dioces of London, in the Third Generall Visitation of the Reverend Father in God, Richard Bishop of London, Holden in the Yeere of Our Lord God 1604* (London, 1604), articles 15, 20, 9, 12.

64. Chamberlain to Winwood, 16 Feb. 1604/5, in *The Letters of John Chamberlain*, ed. Norman E. McClure (Philadelphia, 1939), I, 203.

65. Babbage, *Puritanism and Richard Bancroft*, p. 217.

66. Babbage does not give the cause of Dee's deprivation. *Ibid.*, p. 153. For Dee's presentations in 1602 and 1606, see LCCRO, DL/C/303, fol. 16v; and LCCRO, DL/C/304, fol. 29r. Dee was presented again for conducting illegal marriages in 1608. LCCRO, DL/C/306, fol. 346r.

67. See the Consistory Court Correction Books, LCCRO, DL/C/303–6, 308–9, covering the years 1601–11. DL/C/307 (March 1607/8 to May 1609) was not available for examination. In 1602 John Vicars and a Mr. Goodwin were presented to the court as preachers from St. Benet Paul's Wharf. The court ordered Goodwin to produce his license, but although Goodwin was beneficed in Buckinghamshire, apparently he was not licensed to preach in London. Vicars had a license from the Bishop of Peterborough, but there also seems to have been some question about his behavior. Neither appears in the court records again. Vicars may be identical with the former curate and lecturer of that name at St. Michael Cornhill who in 1600 became rector of St. Augustine Paul's Gate, where he remained until his death in 1633. This John Vicars appears to have been connected with the Feoffees for Impropriations. LCCRO,

DL/C/303, fol. 15r; GLMS 4072/1, fol. 61v; Venn, *Alumni Cantab.*, Part I, Vol. IV, p. 301; Isabel M. Calder, "A Seventeenth Century Attempt to Purify the Anglican Church," *American Historical Review*, LIII (1948), 762. In addition Lawrence Barker, curate and lecturer at St. Botolph Aldgate, was presented for failure to wear the surplice and to catechize. However, he had only recently come into the parish and apparently got off; in any case he died in 1603. LCCRO, DL/C/303, fol. 26r; GLMS 1453/1, fol. 1v; LCCRO, DL/C/338, fols. 1r, 122v. This seems to be the extent of the activity against the lecturers during the last years of Bancroft's episcopate in London.

68. LCCRO, P/92/S/450, pp. 383, 391; Usher, ed., *Presbyterian Movement*, pp. xxix, 13, 15–20; Brook, *Lives*, II, 409–11; *D.N.B.*

69. *D.N.B.*; Brook, *Lives*, II, 346–48. Before taking on the lectureship, Wotton had preached occasional sermons at various parishes about the City while he was Professor of Divinity at Gresham College. GLMS 9234/6, fol. 43r.

70. *Two Elizabethan Puritan Diaries*, p. 31. A letter from Sir Thomas Hoby to Viscount Cranborne defending Egerton is quoted in Babbage, *Puritanism and Richard Bancroft*, pp. 229–30.

71. LCCRO, DL/C/304, fols. 352v, 360v; Champlin Burrage, *The Early English Dissenters in the Light of Recent Research (1550–1641)* (Cambridge, Eng., 1912), II, 38; Venn, *Alumni Cantab.*, Part I, Vol. II, p. 193.

72. LCCRO, DL/C/304, fols. 165r, 185r; LCCRO, P/92/S/450, pp. 391, 462; *D.N.B.*, s.v. William Symonds; Joseph Foster, *Alumni Oxonienses: The Members of Oxford, 1500–1714* (Oxford, 1891), IV, 1452.

73. LCCRO, DL/C/305, fols. 279r, 303r; *Letters of John Chamberlain*, I, 264.

74. LCCRO, DL/C/305, fol. 296r; LCCRO, DL/C/308, fol. 188v; GLMS 9537/11, fol. 83r; Urwick, *Nonconformity in Herts.*, p. 594, n. 1.

75. LCCRO, DL/C/305, fols. 297r, 299r; PRO, SP 16/261, fol. 172v.

76. LCCRO, DL/C/306, fols. 329v, 26r. For example, one of Laud's future followers, Hamlet Marshall, who was in 1607 lecturer at St. Sepulchre's, was ordered to produce his license to preach. LCCRO, DL/C/306, fol. 20v.

77. LCCRO, DL/C/306, fols. 20v, 112r–v, 153r, 160r; LCCRO, DL/C/308, fols. 2r, 76r. For Graye, see Marchant, *Puritans and the Church Courts*, p. 304.

78. LCCRO, DL/C/306, fol. 111v; GLMS 9537/11, fol. 90r; GLMS 9537/12, fol. 9r.

79. For Gouge, see Brook, *Lives*, III, 165–67; *D.N.B.*; GLMS 9537/11, fol. 81v; and GLMS 9537/15, fol. 57r. For Culverwell's deprivation and a catalog of his previous indictments for nonconformity, see Babbage, *Puritanism and Richard Bancroft*, pp. 158–59. For Hildersham, see *ibid.*, pp. 183–86.

80. LCCRO, DL/C/309, fol. 136r; DL/C/308, fol. 308v.

81. Apparently the courts occasionally encouraged, or at least permitted, nonconformists to consult Gouge about the legitimacy of their reasons for refusing to conform. The records do not show that Gouge succeeded in persuading any nonconformist to conform, but the courts seem to have assumed that Gouge would try. LCCRO, DL/C/310, fol. 142r; GLMS 9531/15, fol. 23v.

82. LCCRO, DL/C/317, fol. 20r; Urwick, *Nonconformity in Herts.*, 293–94. Babbage's analysis leads him to similar doubts about the efficacy of Bancroft's program. *Puritanism and Richard Bancroft*, pp. 374–75.

83. *D.N.B.* For contemporary testimony to his prowess as a preacher, see *Diary of John Manningham*, ed. John Bruce (Camden Society, Vol. XCIX; Westminster, 1868), pp. 64, 79.

84. For Cooke, see LCCRO, DL/C/312, fol. 61r; GLMS 9537/10, fol. 16r; and GLMS 559/1, fols. 17r, 19r, 21r. For Hiat, see LCCRO, DL/C/323, fol. 221v; GLMS 2596, fol. 18v; and A. G. Matthews, *Calamy Revised* (Oxford, 1934), pp. 262–63.

85. For Holliday, see GLMS 1046/1, fols. 109v, 113r; GLMS 9537/11, fol. 97r; and LCCRO, DL/C/314, fol. 194r. For Davenport, see LCCRO, DL/C/314, fol. 124v, and for his lectureship at St. Stephen Coleman Street, GLMS 4458/1, pp. 18, 83. He was also curate and lecturer at St. Lawrence Jewry from 1619 to 1624. GLMS 2590/1, p. 234; GLMS 2593/1, fols. 271r, 292v; LCCRO, DL/C/316, fol. 107v. For Burton, see LCCRO, DL/C/314, fol. 251, where he is referred to erroneously as "James" Burton, and *D.N.B.*

86. LCCRO, DL/C/314, fol. 11v; GLMS 3907/1, no fol.; GLMS 3908/1, no fol.; GLMS 9531/15, fol. 26r. See also Matthews, *Calamy Revised*, p. 140.

87. GLMS 4072/1, fol. 120r; *D.N.B.* Loe was also a prebend of Gloucester Cathedral, which accounts for his involvement with Laud.

88. Peter Heylyn, *Cyprianus Anglicus* (London, 1671), p. 71; see also Christopher Hill, *Society and Puritanism in Pre-Revolutionary England* (London, 1964), ch. 5.

89. An anonymous Londoner's reaction is to be found in the pamphlet "Tom Tell-Troath," in *Harleian Miscellany*, ed. J. Malham (London, 1808–11), III, 428–53.

90. PRO, SP 16/261, fol. 206v.

91. See, for example, Thomas Scott, *Vox Coeli; or, News from Heaven* (London, 1624), esp. p. 45.

92. Heylyn, *Aerius Redivivus*, p. 389; cf. Daniel Neal, *The History of the Puritans or Protestant Non-Conformists* (London, 1754), I, 532.

93. For Davenport's letter protesting his conformity, see *Letters of John Davenport*, ed. Isabel M. Calder (New Haven, Conn., 1937), pp. 13–15.

94. Heylyn, *Cyprianus Anglicus*, p. 165.

95. *Articles to Be Enquired of within the Dioces of London in the First General Visitation of the Right Reverend Father in God, George Lord Bishop of London, Holden in the Yeare of Our Lord God 1621* (London, 1621), articles on the clergy, 16, 17, 18, 1, 39.

96. Heylyn, *Cyprianus Anglicus*, p. 92; *Documentary Annals of the Reformed Church*, II, 203.

97. Harleian MSS. 159, fol. 136.

98. GLMS 4165/1, pp. 165, 169; LCCRO, DL/C/316, fol. 22v; Harold Smith, *The Ecclesiastical History of Essex under the Long Parliament and Commonwealth* (Colchester, n.d.), p. 50.

99. LCCRO, DL/C/315, fol. 33r; LCCRO, DL/C/317, fol. 13v; *C.S.P.D., 1631–33*, pp. 121, 129.

100. *C.S.P.D., 1619–23*, pp. 547, 551, 610, 613.

101. LCCRO, DL/C/316, fol. 108r; T. W. Davids, *Annals of Evangelical Nonconformity in the County of Essex* (London, 1863), p. 155; Smith, *Ecclesiastical History of Essex*, p. 38; Foster, *Alumni Oxon.*, II, 720.

102. GLMS 559/1, fols. 24r, 27r; *Minutes of the Vestry Meetings and Other Records of the Parish of St. Christopher le Stocks in the City of London*, ed. Edwin Freshfield (London, 1886), pp. 25, 26, 27, 28; LCCRO, DL/C/316, fol. 224r; LCCRO, DL/C/317, fols. 20r, 49v.

103. LCCRO, DL/C/316, fol. 222v; GLMS 4415/1, fols. 10v, 21r; Venn, *Alumni Cantab.*, Part I, Vol. II, p. 358; Smith, *Ecclesiastical History of Essex*, pp. 38–39.

104. LCCRO, DL/C/316, fols. 162r, 170r. At the same time (21 May 1623) the

churchwardens confessed that at the only communion administered since they were last before the court, a lecturer from St. Antholin's, who is not named, had performed the rite without donning a surplice.

105. LCCRO, DL/C/317, fol. 39r. Mayday had been curate and schoolmaster at St. Antholin's in 1607. GLMS 9537/10, fol. 99v. For his lecture at Christ Church Newgate, see GLMS 9537/13, no fol. He is also listed as lecturing at St. James Clerkenwell in 1629. LPLMS 942, no. 16. For his silencing by Laud, see Heylyn, *Cyprianus Anglicus*, p. 202.

106. Raymond P. Stearns, *The Strenuous Puritan: Hugh Peter, 1598–1660* (Urbana, Ill., 1954), pp. 35–43.

107. C.W. Accts. 1626–27, GLMS 9235/2, no fol.

108. LCCRO, P/92/S/450, pp. 527, 538; GLMS 2590/1, p. 233; *D.N.B.*; Brook, *Lives*, III, 305.

109. Cotton Mather, *Magnalia Christi Americana* (Hartford, Conn., 1820), I, 415; Isabel M. Calder, "A Seventeenth Century Attempt to Purify the Anglican Church," *American Historical Review*, LIII (1948), 768–69.

110. *The Whole Works of the Most Rev. James Ussher, D.D.*, ed. Charles R. Elrington and J. H. Todd (Dublin, 1847–64), XVI, 355.

111. Immanuel Bourne, lecturer at St. Christopher le Stocks, 1617–22; Daniel Cawdry, lecturer at St. Lawrence Jewry, 1625–27; John Downham, lecturer at St. Bartholomew Exchange, 1616–51; Thomas Foxley, lecturer at St. Antholin Budge Row, 1622–c.1629; James Gardiner, lecturer at St. Bartholomew Exchange, 1623–c.1628; Thomas Kentish, lecturer at Christ Church Newgate, c.1623–1629; John Preston, lecturer at Lincoln's Inn, 1620–28; Henry Ramsden, lecturer in the city (parish not known), 1626–29; Richard Sibbes, lecturer at Gray's Inn, 1616–35; Edward Spendlow, lecturer at St. Antholin's, 1594–1632; Thomas Sutton, lecturer at St. Saviour, Southwark, 1615–23; Joseph Simonds, lecturer at St. Michael Orgar, 1625, and at St. Martin Ludgate, 1626–27; and Anthony Wotton, lecturer at Allhallows Barking, 1598–1626.

112. GLMS 2590/1, pp. 250, 262; Brook, *Lives*, I, 443. Cawdry was rector of Little Ilford, Essex, during these years but must have been virtually nonresident, for he preached twice a week at St. Lawrence Jewry. *D.N.B.*; Matthews, *Calamy Revised*, pp. 105–6. Cawdry lectured again in London in 1651, this time at St. Gregory by St. Paul's. GLMS 1336/1, fol. 30v.

113. *The Records of the Honorable Society of Lincoln's Inn: The Black Books*, ed. J. D. Walker and W. P. Baildon (London, 1897–1902), II, 234, 277; *The Pension Book of Gray's Inn*, ed. Reginald J. Fletcher (London, 1901), pp. 224, 229, 325.

114. *D.N.B.*, s.v. Richard Sibbes. For Thomas Sutton, see *D.N.B.* and LCCRO, P/92/S/450, pp. 466, 527.

115. For Wotton, see Brook, *Lives*, II, 346, 348. For Walker's lectures, see GLMS 9537/13, no fol., and GLMS 6836, fol. 135v; for his career, see *D.N.B.*

116. For Peter, see Stearns, *The Strenuous Puritan*, pp. 36–39. For Foxley's lecture, see GLMS 1046/1, fols. 143v, 146r; for his connection with the Feoffees, see Calder, "A Seventeenth Century Attempt to Purify the Anglican Church," p. 762.

117. Isabel M. Calder, *Activities of the Puritan Faction of the Church of England, 1625–33* (London, 1957), p. xi; Christopher Hill, *Economic Problems of the Church from Archbishop Whitgift to the Long Parliament* (Oxford, 1956), pp. 255–56. Offspring does not appear to have lectured until the late 1630's, and the first definite evidence of his lecture is from the 1640's; see GLMS 1045/1, p. 2.

118. PRO, SP 16/56/15; Stearns, *The Strenuous Puritan*, p. 38. For Taylor, see GLMS 3570/2, fol. 21v, and Brook, *Lives*, II, 397–98.

119. [Robert Chestlin?], *Persecutio Undecima* (n.p., 1648), pp. 55, 10. The author also claims that "these lecturers were wont in former Parliaments also to attend the House of Commons door, making their legs to the Members in transitu, praying their worships to remember the Gospel." *Ibid.*, p. 38.

120. Stearns, *The Strenuous Puritan*, pp. 35–36; *Letters of John Davenport*, pp. 13–23; *C.S.P.D., 1623–25*, pp. 354–57.

121. Christopher Hill, *Economic Problems of the Church*, p. 255; Irvonwy Morgan, *Prince Charles's Puritan Chaplain* (London, 1957), esp. p. 24.

122. Morgan, *Prince Charles's Puritan Chaplain*, pp. 111, 178–79, 197; Calder, "A Seventeenth Century Attempt to Purify the Anglican Church," pp. 761–62; Christopher Hill, *Economic Problems of the Church*, pp. 254–57.

CHAPTER 8

1. *The Rest of the Second Reply* (1577), p. 262, as quoted in S. B. Babbage, *Puritanism and Richard Bancroft* (London, 1962), p. 223.

2. Francis Quarles, *Divine Fancies* (London, 1632), Book I, poem 33, reprinted in *The Complete Works*, ed. Alexander B. Grosart (Edinburgh, 1880), II, 205.

3. *Letters of John Davenport*, ed. Isabel M. Calder (New Haven, Conn., 1937), p. 13; Cotton Mather, *Magnalia Christi Americana* (Hartford, Conn., 1820), I, 242; William Laud, *The History of the Troubles and Tryal of the Most Reverend Father in God, and Blessed Martyr, William Laud*, ed. Henry Wharton (London, 1695), p. 526.

4. Peter Heylyn, *Cyprianus Anglicus* (London, 1671), p. 165.

5. *Ibid.*, p. 188.

6. *Ibid.*; William Prynne, *Canterburies Doome* (London, 1646), pp. 368–69.

7. Heylyn, *Cyprianus Anglicus*, p. 191.

8. *History of the Troubles and Tryal of Laud*, pp. 491–92.

9. *The Works of the Most Reverend Father in God, William Laud, D.D.*, ed. William Scott and James Bliss (Oxford, 1847–60), V, ii, 307–9.

10. LPLMS 942, no. 14; Prynne, *Canterburies Doome*, p. 370; Heylyn, *Cyprianus Anglicus*, p. 192.

11. John Rushworth, *Historical Collections* (London, 1721), II, 30–31; Prynne, *Canterburies Doome*, pp. 371–72. LPLMS 942, no. 16, seems to be the record of this survey.

12. *Articles to Be Enquired of within the Dioces of London in the Third General Visitation of the Right Reverend Father in God, George Lord Bishop of London* (London, 1627); *Works of William Laud*, V, ii, 397–404; LCCRO, DL/C/317, fols. 13r–14v, 20r–v, 26r–v, 35r, 49v, 63v (foliation is at the back of the volume). In all, 33 curates were cited.

13. *Minutes of the Vestry Meetings and Other Records of the Parish of St. Christopher le Stocks, in the City of London*, ed. Edwin Freshfield (London, 1886), pp. 26–28; LCCRO, DL/C/316, fol. 224r; LCCRO, DL/C/317, fols. 20r, 49v; GLMS 9539A/1, fol. 24r; GLMS 1240/1, fol. 75r. For Blackwell's later lectureship at Allhallows the Less, see GLMS 9539A/1, fol. 102r; GLMS 823/1, no fol.; GLMS 824/1, no fol.

14. LCCRO, DL/C/317, fols. 20v, 49v; LPLMS 942, no. 16.

15. LCCRO, DL/C/317, fols. 20v, 49v, 63v. For Thorpe at St. Michael Bassishaw, see GLMS 9537/15, fol. 65r. For Smith, see GLMS 9537/13, no fol.; LCCRO, DL/C/317, fol. 14r; and LPLMS 942, no. 16.

16. For Smart, see Edward M. Tomlinson, *A History of the Minories London*

(London, 1907), p. 221; GLMS 9537/13, no fol.; LCCRO, DL/C/317, fol. 26r; and LPLMS 942, no. 16. For Wilson, see GLMS 1124/1, fols. 60r, 74r; GLMS 9537/13, no fol.; and George Hennessy, *Novum Repertorium Ecclesiasticum Parochiale Londinense* (London, 1898), p. 116. This John Wilson may be identical with the John Wilson, M.A., admitted lecturer at High Ongar, Essex, on 5 December 1638; see GLMS 9539A/1, fol. 105v.

17. LCCRO, DL/C/317, fol. 20r; GLMS 9537/9, no fol. The 1589 Visitation Call Book lists Spendlowe as curate at St. Olave Silver Street; see GLMS 9537/7, no fol. See also GLMS 1046/1, fol. 51v; LPLMS 942, no. 16; and GLMS 9539A/1, fols. 18v–19r.

18. *C.S.P.D., 1631–33*, pp. 121, 129.

19. LCCRO, DL/C/317, fol. 13r; LPLMS 942, nos. 14, 16; GLMS 9537/13, no fol.; *D.N.B.* Thomas Gouge was properly admitted to the curacy of Teddington, Middlesex, on 14 November 1637, and to the vicarage of St. Sepulchre on 6 October 1638. GLMS 9539A/1, fol. 97v; GLMS 9539A/2, no fol.

20. Millar Maclure, *The Paul's Cross Sermons, 1534–1642* (Toronto, 1958), p. 232; LCCRO, DL/C/312, fols. 165v, 166r, 207v; GLMS 9537/11, fol. 2v; LCCRO, DL/C/314, fol. 134v; *Abstract of Wills of the Prerogative Court of Canterbury at Somerset House, London, England: Register Soame, 1620*, ed. J. Henry Lea (Boston, 1904), pp. 264, 319; LCCRO, DL/C/317, fol. 26v; GLMS 1279/2, p. 29; LPLMS 942, no. 14; GLMS 9537/13, no fol.

21. A. G. Matthews, *Calamy Revised* (Oxford, 1934), pp. 397–98; LCCRO, DL/C/317, fol. 14r. For Harris, see LCCRO, P/92/S/450, pp. 527, 538. For Dodd, see William Haller, *The Rise of Puritanism* (New York, 1938), pp. 58–59. For Fishborne's lecture at Huntingdon, see *Works of William Laud*, V, ii, 321; and W. K. Jordan, *The Charities of London, 1480–1660* (London, 1960), p. 115. For Poynter's later preferments, see George Yule, *The Independents in the English Civil War* (Cambridge, Eng., 1958), pp. 134, 140, 147, 151; and Harold Smith, *The Ecclesiastical History of Essex under the Long Parliament and Commonwealth* (Colchester, n.d.), p. 297.

22. GLMS 4241/1, pp. 299, 327, 329; John and J. A. Venn, *Alumni Cantabrigienses*, Part I, *From Earliest Times to 1751* (Cambridge, Eng., 1922), Vol. IV, p. 300; LCCRO, DL/C/317, fol. 26r; GLMS 9537/15, fol. 66r; Simonds D'Ewes, *The Autobiography and Correspondence of Sir Simonds D'Ewes, Bart., during the Reigns of James I and Charles I*, ed. James O. Halliwell (London, 1845), I, 353; GLMS 9539A/2, no fol.

23. PRO, SP 16/56/15; William Gouge to Bishop Laud, 19 Oct. 1631, *C.S.P.D., 1631–33*, p. 167; Benjamin Brook, *Lives of the Puritans* (London, 1813), II, 398, III, 166; cf. Prynne, *Canterburies Doome*, p. 362.

24. Brook, *Lives*, II, 400–401; PRO, SP 16/261, fol. 1v; Rushworth, *Historical Collections*, II, 30–32, 140–41; Prynne, *Canterburies Doome*, pp. 364–65.

25. *History of the Troubles and Tryal of Laud*, p. 371.

26. Brook, *Lives*, II, 401.

27. LCCRO, DL/C/319, fols. 154r, 162v; PRO, SP 16/261, fol. 1v; Brook, *Lives*, II, 402–4.

28. GLMS 9531/15, fol. 21r; see *D.N.B.* for Burton's earlier troubles with the High Commission and the Privy Council. For Burton's lecture, see LPLMS 942, no. 16; and GLMS 1016/1, fols. 146v, 177r. The words "malice and boldness" are Clarendon's; see *The History of the Rebellion and Civil Wars in England*, ed. W. Dunn Macray (Oxford, 1888), I, 267.

29. GLMS 9531/15, fol. 21v; LPLMS 942, no. 16; Venn, *Alumni Cantab.*, Part I, Vol. III, p. 232; GLMS 9539A/2, no fol.

30. Prynne, *Canterburies Doome*, p. 373. For the payments for wine and ringers, see C.W. Accts. 1628–29, GLMS 9235/2, no fol. Edwards preached some months before obtaining his license. See LPLMS 942, no. 14; Richard Newcourt, *Repertorium Ecclesiasticum Parochiale Londinense* (London, 1708), p. 916; Brook, *Lives*, III, 82; *D.N.B.*; and *GLMS* 9235/2, no fol. It is not surprising to discover that Edwards was apparently a friend of that staunch Puritan pamphleteer William Prynne; see *History of the Troubles and Tryal of Laud*, p. 253.

31. LPLMS 942, no. 14; GLMS 9531/15, fols. 21v–22v; Smith, *Ecclesiastical History of Essex*, p. 41.

32. *Winthrop Papers* (Massachusetts Historical Society; Cambridge, Mass., 1929–47), II, 340; GLMS 9531/15, fols. 22r–v; GLMS 9539A/1, fol. 6v; LPLMS 942, no. 14.

33. GLMS 9531/15, fol. 23r; Isabel M. Calder, "A Seventeenth Century Attempt to Purify the Anglican Church," *American Historical Review*, LIII (1948), 769; Rushworth, *Historical Collections*, II, 74; *C.S.P.D., 1637–38*, p. 563. See also Brook, *Lives*, II, 455, which erroneously refers to John Archer as Henry Archer.

34. GLMS 1046/1, fol. 143v; LPLMS 942, no. 16; *C.S.P.D., 1631–33*, p. 167; *History of the Troubles and Tryal of Laud*, p. 249; Prynne, *Canterburies Doome*, p. 387; PRO, SP 16/434, fol. 229r; Brook, *Lives*, II, 498.

35. For Crabtree, see GLMS 3907/1, no fol.; GLMS 3908/1, no fol.; GLMS 9531/15, fol. 26v; and Matthews, *Calamy Revised*, p. 140. For Martyn, see LPLMS 942, no. 16; *C.S.P.D., 1631–33*, p. 491; Prynne, *Canterburies Doome*, p. 373; GLMS 9539A/1, fol. 57v; GLMS 9537/15, fol. 53v and the recto side of the folio between fols. 61 and 62.

36. Prynne, *Canterburies Doome*, p. 373; GLMS 9537/15, verso of the folio between fols. 61 and 62.

37. *History of the Troubles and Tryal of Laud*, p. 383; GLMS 2601/1, fol. 57r; LPLMS 942, nos. 14, 16; GLMS 5019/1, p. 39; GLMS 2590/1, p. 301; GLMS 9537/15, fols. 62r, 63v. On 27 October 1635 Jones was elected lecturer at a vestry meeting at St. Lawrence Jewry. It is perhaps significant that the election was made conditional on the bishop's admission of Jones to the curacy. GLMS 2590/1, p. 301. Jones succeeded in meeting this requirement on 13 November 1635. GLMS 9539A/1, fol. 61v.

38. *The Vestry Minute Books of the Parish of St. Bartholomew Exchange in the City of London, 1567–1676*, ed. Edwin Freshfield (London, 1890), Part I, p. 84; GLMS 1240/1, fol. 19v; GLMS 4165, pp. 191, 204; GLMS 9539A/1, fols. 32r, 33r; GLMS 9539A/2, no fol. The "Mr. Garner" who lectured at St. Benet Fink in 1629 is probably the same man. LPLMS 942, no. 16.

39. LPLMS 942, no. 14; *D.N.B.*; Matthews, *Calamy Revised*, p. 290.

40. *Works of William Laud*, V, ii, 309–10; Prynne, *Canterburies Doome*, p. 361; PRO, SP 16/261, fols. 304v–305r; Nehemiah Wallington, *Historical Notices of Events Occurring Chiefly in the Reign of Charles I*, ed. R. Webb (London, 1869), I, 9.

41. *Works of William Laud*, V, ii, 318–19; Rushworth, *Historical Collections*, II, 140, 213–15. For Heylyn's part in the suppression of the Feoffees, see *Cyprianus Anglicus*, pp. 199–200; for Heylyn's comment on Laud's measures of 1633, see *ibid.*, p. 241. *Documentary Annals of the Reformed Church of England*, ed. Edward Cardwell (Oxford, 1844), II, 233–36.

42. Heylyn, *Cyprianus Anglicus*, p. 241.

43. GLMS 9539A/1, fol. 28r; see also GLMS 9537/15, fol. 53v. Sprint also lectured at St. Antholin's from some time in the 1640's to 1658. GLMS 1045/1, pp. 2, 49; *D.N.B.*, s.v. John Sprint, Sr. Hennessy (*Novum Repertorium*, p. 188), lists Sprint as

perpetual curate, but neither the Subscription Book nor the Visitation Call Book for 1637 bears this out.

44. The four admitted to lectureships as their first preferments were Lazarus Seaman, lecturer at St. Martin Ludgate, 1634–36; Edmund Brome, lecturer at St. Christopher le Stocks, 1639; William Jenkyn, lecturer at St. Nicholas Acons, 1639; and the lone Laudian, Henry Kyberd, lecturer at St. Katherine Coleman, 1635–40. For Brome, see Matthews, *Calamy Revised*, p. 77. For Seaman, see GLMS 1311/1, fol. 125v; GLMS 9539A/1, fol. 31v; Venn, *Alumni Cantab.*, Part I, Vol. IV, p. 37; *History of the Troubles and Tryal of Laud*, p. 199.

45. H. R. Trevor-Roper, *Archbishop Laud, 1573–1645* (London, 1940), p. 119.

46. Mark H. Curtis, "The Alienated Intellectuals of Early Stuart England," *Past and Present*, XXIII (1962), 32–37. Approximately 92 per cent of those London incumbents whose livings were sequestered in the early 1640's had received degrees from Oxford or Cambridge, and more than a third of these were doctorates in theology; see A. G. Matthews, *Walker Revised* (Oxford, 1948), pp. 42–63.

47. See, for example, William Martyn's petition to Laud, *C.S.P.D., 1631–33*, p. 491; cf. the case of Thomas Weld, who testified that Laud "had granted him a long time to inform his judgment." Weld consulted William Gouge, among others, and on his final refusal to subscribe was excommunicated. GLMS 9531/15, fols. 23v, 24r.

48. *C.S.P.D., 1631–33*, p. 167; Henry Jacie to John Winthrop, Jr., 9 Jan. 1631/2, in *Winthrop Papers*, III, 59. Bridges, who had lectured at Colchester briefly in 1631, was at the time rector of St. George Tombland in Norwich, from which he was suspended and then reinstated by Bishop Corbett, and finally deprived by Bishop Wren in 1636. If Bridges was typical of the lecturers Gouge sponsored, Laud's spleen is understandable. For Bridges, see Smith, *Ecclesiastical History of Essex*, p. 23; Matthews, *Calamy Revised*, p. 74.

49. *Works of William Laud*, V, ii, 327. For Roborough, see PRO, SP 16/261, fols. 13v, 22v, 35r; for his lectureship see Wallington, *Historical Notices*, I, xxi, lii. Wallington implies that Roborough was also curate, but he is contradicted in this by LPLMS 942, no. 14. Brook, *Lives*, III, 531–32; Matthews, *Walker Revised*, s.v. Abraham Colfe. For Burgess, see GLMS 2597/1, pp. 37, 39; Matthews, *Calamy Revised*, pp. 86–87; and GLMS 2590/1, pp. 341, 343, 346.

50. *Works of William Laud*, V, ii, 332–33.

51. GLMS 2590/1, pp. 295, 301; Matthews, *Walker Revised*, p. 196; GLMS 9236, 3d section, fol. 101v.

52. GLMS 4458/1, pp. 83, 121–23, 125, 129, 134; Matthews, *Calamy Revised*, p. 227; *Works of William Laud*, V, ii, 356, 362; *D.N.B.*, s.v. Anthony Wotton.

53. GLMS 3570/2, fol. 34v; GLMS 9539A/1, fol. 20v; Venn, *Alumni Cantab.*, Part I, Vol. IV, p. 171; Hennessy, *Novum Repertorium*, p. 299; *Winthrop Papers*, III, 88–89. Stoughton was the only one of the five brought before the High Commission. PRO, SP 16/261, fols. 300r, 310r.

54. For Molen, see GLMS 9539A/1, fol. 26r; GLMS 559/1, fols. 35r, 48r; and Matthews, *Walker Revised*, p. 50. See also *An Answer to the Articles against Master Calamy, Master Martiall, Master Burton, Master Peters, Master Moleigne, . . . and Many Other Painfull Divines Who Were Impeached of High Treason by His Majesty* (London, 1642). For Simpson, see LPLMS 942, no. 16; and Brook, *Lives*, III, 311–12. According to *D.N.B.*, Simpson replaced John Viner as Master of Pembroke in 1650 when Viner refused the Engagement.

55. *Works of William Laud*, V, ii, 333.

56. *Ibid.*, V, ii, 333; LPLMS 942, nos. 14, 16; GLMS 9537/15, fol. 58r. John Wood, parson and lecturer at St. James Duke's Place from 1628 until his death in 1639, may be the same man. Hennessy, *Novum Repertorium*, p. 118; GLMS 9537/13, no fol.

57. Matthews, *Calamy Revised*, pp. 453–54; *Works of William Laud*, V, ii, 333; *C.S.P.D., 1636–37*, pp. 513–14; GLMS 9537/15, fol. 19v.

58. GLMS 9537/13, no fol.; *Works of William Laud*, V, ii, 337–38; Matthews, *Calamy Revised*, p. 87; PRO, SP 16/261, fol. 311v; GLMS 1179/1, p. 7; GLMS 9537/15, fol. 66v.

59. *D.N.B.* According to Calder, Hughes was not elected until 23 August 1632; see "A Seventeenth Century Attempt to Purify the Anglican Church," *American Historical Review*, LIII (1948), p. 768, n. 18. But this is not borne out by LPLMS 942, no. 14. Matthews, *Calamy Revised*, pp. 281–82; *C.J.*, III, 153.

60. *Works of William Laud*, V, ii, 348; *C.S.P.D., 1637*, pp. 518–19. For Byfield, see LPLMS 942, no. 16; GLMS 9537/15, fol. 65r; Venn, *Alumni Cantab.*, Part I, Vol. I, p. 149; and *D.N.B.* For Palmer, see Haberdashers' Company MS., Minutes of the Court of Assistants, I, fols. 130v, 167r; LPLMS 942, no. 14; GLMS 9537/15, fol. 58r; and *D.N.B.* For Simonds, see *Works of William Laud*, V, ii, 362–63.

61. GLMS, 9537/15, fol. 59v; *D.N.B.*

62. Heylyn, *Cyprianus Anglicus*, pp. 342–43; *Works of William Laud*, V, ii, 355 and *passim*.

63. GLMS 4051/1, fols. 85r, 91r. When the rector, John Weston, was removed in 1643, Cardell became minister of the sequestered living. GLMS 4049/1, fol. 11v; GLMS 9539A/2, no fol.; Matthews, *Walker Revised*, p. 62.

64. *History of the Troubles and Tryal of Laud*, pp. 237–38. For Walker's lecture at St. Helen's and his subsequent career, see GLMS 6836, fol. 135v; *D.N.B.*; and Brook, *Lives*, III, 140–42.

65. *Works of William Laud*, V, ii, 363. Votier had been rector and lecturer at St. Peter's since 1615; see GLMS 645/2, no fol., and LPLMS 942, nos. 14, 16. For Goodwin, see *Works of William Laud*, V, ii, 362.

66. *C.S.P.D., 1637–38*, p. 518; *Works of William Laud*, V, ii, 362.

67. PRO, SP 16/434, fol. 51r; see also fol. 223r. For Foxley, see *ibid.*, fol. 229r; for Edwards, see *D.N.B.*

68. *Works of William Laud*, V, ii, 626.

69. *Articles to Be Enquired of within the Diocese of London, in the Visitation to Be Holden in the Year of Our Lord, 1640* (London, 1640), "Concerning Religion," articles 1, 2, 3 (the articles run to 22 pages of black-letter print).

70. *Ibid.*, "Concerning Celebration of Divine Service, the Administration of the Sacraments, &c.," articles 7–10, 20.

71. *Works of William Laud*, V, ii, 368. Juxon's Article 20 did not, however, represent an innovation, for it faithfully followed Laud's article on the same subject propounded for his metropolitical visitation of 1635. *Ibid.*, p. 421.

72. *Articles to Be Enquired of … 1640*, "Concerning the Clergie, their Duty, Carriage, &c.," Article 1.

73. See, for example, Barrow's answers to the archbishop in *The Harleian Miscellany*, ed. J. Malham (London, 1808–11), II, 20–21.

74. *Articles to Be Enquired of … 1640*, "Concerning the Church, the Government, Authority, and Discipline Thereof," Article 10; "A Letter from Mercurius Civicus to Mercurius Rusticus," in *Somers' Tracts*, ed. Walter Scott (London, 1809–15), IV, 584.

75. PRO, SP 16/463/54. See also Valerie Pearl, *London and the Outbreak of the*

Puritan Revolution (Oxford, 1961), p. 109, where, however, Calybute Downing is confused with John Downham.

76. *Ibid.*, esp. p. 230; H. R. Trevor-Roper, "The Fast Sermons of the Long Parliament," *Essays in British History*, ed. H. R. Trevor-Roper (London, 1964), pp. 85–138.

77. "A Letter from Mercurius Civicus to Mercurius Rusticus," in *Somers' Tracts*, IV, 584.

78. Irvonwy Morgan, *Prince Charles's Puritan Chaplain* (London, 1957), p. 203.

79. Heylyn, *Cyprianus Anglicus*, p. 383. Heylyn omitted various parts of the speech, but not so as to change its meaning. For the full speech, which Falkland delivered to the House of Commons on 9 February 1640/41, see John Rushworth, *Historical Collections* (London, 1692), V, 184–86.

CHAPTER 9

1. PRO, SP 16/434a, fol. 51r.

2. Cornelius Burgess, *The First Sermon, Preached to the Honorable House of Commons* (London, 1641), Epistle Dedicatory. The story of the fast-day sermons is told by H. R. Trevor-Roper in "The Fast Sermons of the Long Parliament," in H. R. Trevor-Roper, ed., *Essays in British History* (London, 1964), pp. 85–138.

3. For Dering's committee, see *Proceedings, Principally in the County of Kent ... 1640*, ed. Lambert B. Larking (Camden Society, Ist ser., Vol. LXXX; 1862), p. 80. For Burton, see *D.N.B.*

4. *H.MSS.C., Various Collections*, II (London, 1903), p. 259.

5. *C. J.* II, 281, 283. See also William Haller, *Liberty and Reformation in the Puritan Revolution* (New York, 1955), pp. 24–25; William A. Shaw, *A History of the English Church during the Civil Wars and under the Commonwealth, 1640–1660* (London, 1900), II, 182–83.

6. For a summary of the various actions of the House of Commons, see Shaw, *History of the English Church*, II, 300–306.

7. The manner in which the House dealt with clerical opposition is illustrated by the case of St. Giles Cripplegate; see *C.J.*, II, 294, 295, 297, 484.

8. GLMS 587/1, fols. 46v, 70v, 76v, 84r; *The Records of Two City Parishes*, ed. William McMurray (London, 1925), pp. 338, 415; for Cluet, see A. G. Matthews, *Walker Revised* (Oxford, 1948), pp. 44–45; for Love, see *D.N.B.* and Benjamin Brook, *Lives of the Puritans* (London, 1813), III, 122. Brook is incorrect in asserting that Love was admitted to St. Lawrence Jewry at the same time he was admitted to SS. Anne and Agnes; see V.M. of St. Lawrence Jewry, 21 March 1648/9, GLMS 2590/1, pp. 382–83.

9. *The History of the Rebellion and Civil Wars in England Begun in the Year 1641*, ed. W. Dunn Macray (Oxford, 1888), I, 269.

10. Daniel Neal, *The History of the Puritans or Protestant Non-Conformists* (London, 1754), I, 798.

11. For Staunton, see *D.N.B.* For Nye's City lectureships, see GLMS 9537/13, no fol.; and LPLMS 942, nos. 14, 16. Nye eventually went to Arnheim instead of New England. Edward Howes to John Winthrop, Jr., 15 Aug. 1633, in *Winthrop Papers* (Massachusetts Historical Society; Boston, 1929–47), III, 135; A. G. Matthews, *Calamy Revised* (Oxford, 1934), pp. 369–70.

12. For Marshall, see Haller, *Liberty and Reformation*, pp. 34–37, 67–68; Brook, *Lives*, III, 241–53; and *D.N.B.* For Palmer, see Samuel Clarke, *A Generall Martyrologie* (London, 1651), pp. 420–40; and *D.N.B.*

13. For Hill, see WPLMS F.2002, p. 237; Brook, *Lives*, III, 170–71; and *D.N.B.* Hill was, like Marshall, an Emmanuel graduate. He was also a friend of John Cotton of Boston, and he was presented to his first benefice by the Earl of Warwick. For Whitaker, see Neal, *History of the Puritans*, II, 466; Brook, *Lives*, III, 190–96; and Shaw, *History of the English Church*, II, 303.

14. LPLMS 942, nos. 14, 16; GLMS 1179/1, pp. 7, 27; GLMS 9537/15, fols. 47r, 66v; *D.N.B.*; Matthews, *Calamy Revised*, pp. 87–88; *The Works of the Most Reverend Father in God, William Laud, D.D.*, ed. William Scott and James Bliss (Oxford, 1847–60), V, ii, 337–38. It is not possible from the extant records of the High Commission to follow the course of Burgess's case, which arose from this sermon, before the court, but see PRO, SP 16/261, fol. 311v.

15. [Robert Chestlin?], *Persecutio Undecima* (London, 1648), p. 62.

16. S. Bolton, C. Burgess, H. Roborough, A. Byfield, E. Calamy, Jer. Burroughs, J. Caryl, W. Gouge, W. Price, L. Seaman, O. Sedgwick, S. Ashe, T. Case, J. Jackson, S. Marshall, J. Wincop, and F. Woodcock. The last six had come to London since 1640.

17. Matthews, *Calamy Revised*, p. 16; *The Vestry Minute Books of the Parish of St. Bartholomew Exchange in the City of London, 1567–1676*, ed. Edwin Freshfield (London, 1890), Part I, p. 141; *C.J.*, II, 479; C.W. Accts., St. Michael Bassishaw, 1647–52, GLMS 2601/1, no fol.; GLMS 3570/2, fol. 68r; Henry I. Longdon, *Northamptonshire and Rutland Clergy from 1500* (Northampton, 1938–52), I, 89.

18. John McMaster, *A Short History of the Royal Parish of St. Martin-in-the-Fields, London* (London, 1916), pp. 168–69; James P. Malcolm, *Londinium Redivivum* (London, 1803–7), IV, 192; for Case, see *C.J.* II, 432. Wincop was in London at least until 1645. In 1650 he was reported to be preaching twice every Sabbath at his living at Clothall, Herts.; he died in 1653. William Urwick, *Nonconformity in Herts.* (London, 1884), p. 785.

19. J. Bond, W. Bridges, A. Burgess, H. Chambers, R. Clayton, J. Conant, S. Gower, R. Harris, T. Hill, J. Ley, J. Lightfoot, C. Love, M. Newcomen, P. Nye, H. Palmer, H. Scudder, J. Whitaker, H. Wilkinson, and T. Goodwin.

20. For Harris's early career and friendship with John Dodd, see *D.N.B.* and William Haller, *The Rise of Puritanism* (New York, 1938), pp. 57–59. For his lecture at St. Lawrence Jewry, see GLMS 2590/1, p. 233. The vestry of St. Saviour's suspected Harris of leaving in order to take up a lectureship at St. Mary Aldermanbury, but he denied this and seems not to have accepted the post at St. Mary's, to which he had been duly elected. LCCRO, P/92/S/450, pp. 527, 538; GLMS 3570/2, fols. 18v–19r; Brook, *Lives*, III, 304–5.

21. GLMS 2597/1, pp. 37, 39; GLMS 2590/1, pp. 341, 343, 346; GLMS 2593/2, pp. 159–60; Matthews, *Calamy Revised*, pp. 86–87. Anthony Burgess was probably a relative of John Burgess, who lectured briefly in London in 1616 at St. Helen Bishopsgate and who held the living of Sutton Coldfield until his death in 1635. John and J. A. Venn, *Alumni Cantabrigienses*, Part I, *From Earliest Times to 1751* (Cambridge, Eng., 1922), I, 257.

22. For Love, see GLMS 587/1, fols. 70v, 95r; GLMS 2590/1, pp. 382–83, 406–7; Brook, *Lives*, III, 115–38; and *D.N.B.* For Whitaker, see Shaw, *History of the English Church*, II, 303; Neal, *History of the Puritans*, II, 466; Brook, *Lives*, III, 190–96; and *D.N.B.*

23. For Lightfoot, see *D.N.B.* and *Vestry Minute Books of St. Bartholomew Exchange*, Part I, p. 146. For Newcomen, see GLMS 3570/2, fol. 48v; Harold Smith, *The Ecclesiastical History of Essex under the Long Parliament and Commonwealth* (Colchester, n.d.), pp. 212, 337, 386; and *D.N.B.* Newcomen is supposed to have received

an admonition in 1636 for failing to produce his orders (Matthews, *Calamy Revised*, p. 363), although it is difficult to see why this incident should have occurred, since Newcomen had subscribed prior to his admission to the curacy at Messing in 1632 (he was a deacon at the time), and was to subscribe again on 3 March 1636/7 as curate at Dedham, when he was issued a license to preach. GLMS 9539A/1, fols. 22v, 74r. It is also peculiar that the visitation call books of 1636 and 1637 should both list him simply as the lecturer at Dedham, although he is recorded as curate in the subscription book. GLMS 9537/14, no fol.; GLMS 9537/15, fol. 21r.

24. For Shute, see St. Mary Woolnoth, C.W. Accts. 1612–13 to 1639–40, where he signs the accounts for the last time. GLMS 1002/1, esp. fol. 469r. Shute was appointed Archdeacon of Colchester on 15 April 1642, apparently one of the number of appointments of popular divines made late in the day in order to increase the popularity of the ecclesiastical regime. GLMS 9539A/2, no fol. He had two brothers, both of whom were also preachers, and one of whom, Nathaniel, also preached in London prior to his death in 1638. *D.N.B.*; Thomas Fuller, *The Worthies of England*, ed. John Freeman (London, 1952), p. 663. For Sedgwick, see Clarke, *Martyrologie*, Part I, pp. 395–98; and Brook, *Lives*, II, 486–89. Dennison, who seems to have spent almost as much time in litigation with his parishioners as preaching to them, nevertheless held not only the lecture at St. Katherine's but also one at Allhallows the Great through most of his career. LPLMS 942, nos. 14, 16; GLMS 819/1, pp. 98, 176; GLMS 1196/, fols. 5r, 23v, 27v; LCCRO, DL/C/320, fol. 58v; PRO, Sp 16/261, esp. fol. 9r. Burton appears to have been in trouble with the authorities from the inception of his preaching career, which he inaugurated by preaching at St. Matthew's without a license. LCCRO, DL/C/314, fol. 251v. John Downham's and William Gouge's lecturing careers have already been documented elsewhere in this study.

25. Chestlin, *Persecutio Undecima*, p. 49; Matthews, *Walker Revised*, pp. 42–63. According to Matthews (*ibid.*, p. xiv) 96 London benefices underwent sequestration.

26. William Typing, *The Preacher's Plea* (London, 1646), p. 19, as quoted in Robert Barclay, *The Inner Life of the Religious Societies of the Commonwealth* (London, 1877), p. 260.

27. GLMS 1453/1, fol. 13v; LPLMS 942, no. 16; GLMS 9537/15, fol. 6ov. For Booth, see Matthews, *Walker Revised*, p. 42. For Blackwell, see Venn, *Alumni Cantab.*, Part I, Vol. I, p. 162; and Shaw, *History of the English Church*, II, 305.

28. GLMS 1453/1, fol. 31v; Matthews, *Walker Revised*, p. 42, s.v. Thomas Booth; *D.N.B.*, s.v. John Conant.

29. V.M. 10 Jan. 1646/7 and 9 Jan. 1647/8, GLMS 1453/1, no fol. For Jaggard, see Ronald Marchant, *The Puritans and the Church Courts in the Diocese of York, 1560–1642* (London, 1960), p. 257; Venn, *Alumni Cantab.*, Part I, Vol. II, p. 460.

30. Matthews, *Calamy Revised*, p. 269; GLMS 4060/1, no fol. Meriton was elected lecturer at St. Martin's on 22 January 1652/3 and held the post until 1662. WPLMS F.2003, pp. 13, 248.

31. GLMS 4051/1, fols. 123r, 127r, 186r; GLMS 4049/1, fol. 12r; Matthews, *Calamy Revised*, p. 530.

32. *The Diary of John Evelyn*, ed. E. S. de Beer (London, 1959), pp. 358, 390–91; Hewet had been at Oxford in 1643 as a royal chaplain. *D.N.B.*, s.v. John Hewet.

33. *Calendar of the Clarendon State Papers*, ed. W. D. Macray (Oxford, 1869), III, 217, 234.

34. Robert S. Bosher, *The Making of the Restoration Settlement* (London, 1951), pp. 9–12. Bosher does not specify which St. Benet's he is referring to.

35. *D.N.B.*; Joseph Foster, *Alumni Oxonienses: The Members of Oxford, 1500–1714* (Oxford, 1891), II, 649; GLMS 1240/1, fol. 45r.; Bosher, *Restoration Settlement*, p. 12.

36. V.M. 28 Sept. 1655, GLMS 978/1, no fol.

37. V.M. 5 Sept. 1651, GLMS 978/1, no fol. William Addison, *Worthy Dr. Fuller* (London, 1951), p. 158. Fuller also lectured on Wednesdays at St. Dunstan in the East from 1650 to 1655. GLMS 7882/1, pp. 390, 495.

38. GLMS 1336/1, fol. 30v. For Cawdry's lecture at St. Lawrence Jewry, 1624–27, see GLMS 2590/1, pp. 250, 262. Cawdry signed the Vindication in 1648 as minister of St. Martin in the Fields and may have left the City in 1652 or 1653 to return to his Northamptonshire living, from which he was deprived in 1662. Matthews, *Calamy Revised*, p. 105. For a copy of the Vindication including the names of the signers, see *Harleian Miscellany*, ed. John Malham (London, 1808–11), VI, 132.

39. GLMS 1336/1, fol. 38r; Matthews, *Walker Revised*, p. 183. Gillingham had been a royal chaplain at least as early as 1628. PRO, LC 5/132, p. 18. For his earlier career in London, see LPLMS 942, nos. 14, 16; and Robert Sommerville, *The Savoy* (London, 1960), p. 246.

40. Bosher, *Restoration Settlement*, p. 42; Matthews, *Walker Revised*, p. 183.

41. For Case, see GLMS 2597/1, p. 61; GLMS 2596/2, fols. 86r, 101r. Case also lectured at St. Martin in the Fields from 1642 until the Restoration (WPLMS F. 2003, pp. 144, 147) and at St. Mary Aldermanbury and at St. Giles in the Fields (*D.N.B.*). For Manton, see GLMS 2597/1, pp. 96, 110; and GLMS 2596/2, fols. 101r, 134r. Manton also lectured at St. Dunstan in the West from 1649 until St. Bartholomew's Day in 1662 (GLMS 2968/4, fol. 388r; GLMS 3016/1, p. 349) and at Westminster Abbey in 1656 (Matthews, *Calamy Revised*, p. 338).

42. GLMS 2597/1, p. 111. Cartwright, who was the grandson of the famous Elizabethan Presbyterian, received the bishopric of Chester in 1686 from James II as a reward for his unshakable loyalty and friendship; see *D.N.B.* For Jones, see GLMS 2597/1, p. 121; GLMS 2596/2, 141r, 144r; and Matthews, *Walker Revised*, p. 52.

43. Bosher, *Restoration Settlement*, pp. 40–44; GLMS 2597/1, pp. 121, 123, 124; Matthews, *Calamy Revised*, pp. 510, 39; *The Autobiography of Richard Baxter*, ed. J. M. Lloyd Thomas (Everyman's Library ed.; London, 1931), p. 160.

44. Bosher, *Restoration Settlement*, p. 43.

45. GLMS 1045/1, pp. 44, 65; Matthews, *Walker Revised*, pp. 89–90.

46. For Warmestry, see *D.N.B.* and Bosher, *Restoration Settlement*, pp. 12, 43. For Ryves, see *D.N.B.* and *The Records of the Honorable Society of Lincoln's Inn: The Black Books*, ed. J. D. Walker and W. P. Baildon (London, 1897–1902), II, 402, 414. Ryves had been rector and lecturer at St. Martin Vintry from 1628. LPLMS 942, nos. 14, 16; Matthews, *Walker Revised*, pp. 56–57.

47. Bosher, *Restoration Settlement*, pp. 11–12, 40–44. The controversy engendered within the ranks of the Anglican clergy by the suggestion that the use of the Prayer Book be dispensed with as a condition for accommodation under Cromwell's regime is described in *ibid.*, pp. 16–23.

48. *Autobiography of Richard Baxter*, p. 19; see also Haller, *Liberty and Reformation in the Puritan Revolution* (New York, 1955), esp. pp. 112–28.

49. For Goodwin, see GLMS 1181/1, pp. 98, 309; and Geoffrey F. Nuttall, *Visible Saints* (Oxford, 1957), esp. p. 13. For Simpson, see LPLMS 942, no. 16; *Works of William Laud*, V, ii, 333; and *D.N.B.* For Burroughs, see *D.N.B.* and Brook, *Lives*, III, 18–22. For Bridges, see Matthews, *Calamy Revised*, p. 74; GLMS 1175/1, fol. 83v; and GLMS 4956/3, pp. 122, 127. In the margin of Laud's note that Bridges had left his

Norwich lecture and gone to Holland (Annual Report, 1636), King Charles wrote: "Let him go: We are well rid of him." *Works of William Laud*, V, ii, 340.

50. Haller, *Liberty and Reformation*, p. 145; *D.N.B.*

51. GLMS 4458/1, pp. 83, 87, 129, 134; *Works of William Laud*, V, ii, 333, 356, 362; Matthews, *Calamy Revised*, p. 227; Haller, *Liberty and Reformation*, pp. 145–46.

52. GLMS 4458/1, pp. 135, 161.

53. *Ibid.*, pp. 125, 147, 162, 264, 225, 259.

54. J. A. Dodd, "Troubles in a City Parish under the Protectorate," *English Historical Review*, X (1895), 42–43.

55. For Simpson, see Foster, *Alumni Oxon.*, IV, 1358; Brook, *Lives*, III, 405–7; and Shaw, *History of the English Church*, II, 301, 302.

56. Dodd, "Troubles in a City Parish," pp. 43–44.

57. *Ibid.*, pp. 43–52; GLMS 1045/1, pp. 34, 65; Brook, *Lives*, III, 407–8; Matthews, *Calamy Revised*, p. 145.

58. A. G. Matthews, *Introduction to Calamy Revised* (London, 1959), p. 6.

59. Those who conformed were H. Hibbert, T. Horton, T. Hutchinson, J. Meriton (Merryton), F. Raworth, E. Reynolds, and T. Wills.

60. GLMS 4458/1, pp. 135–36, 255, 259; *The Vestry Minute Book of the Parish of St. Margaret Lothbury in the City of London, 1571–1677*, ed. Edwin Freshfield (London, 1887), p. 110; *D.N.B.*; Matthews, *Calamy Revised*, p. 479.

61. GLMS 1045/1, p. 69; Matthews, *Calamy Revised*, p. 127.

62. Haberdashers' Company MS., Minutes of the Court of Assistants, I, fols. 345v, 346r-v, 351r, 354v; Matthews, *Calamy Revised*, pp. 236–37. Matthews has Griffiths lecturing at St. Bartholomews only from 1654, but this seems incorrect. The single mention of Griffiths in the Vestry Minutes occurs in 1660; see *Vestry Minute Books of St. Bartholomew Exchange*, Part II, p. 78.

63. Haberdashers' Company MS., Minutes of the Court of Assistants, II, fols. 92v, 93r; GLMS 1045/1, pp. 41, 69, 72; GLMS 9537/16, fol. 49r.

64. *Autobiography of Richard Baxter*, p. 169; *Records of Lincoln's Inn*, II, 277; GLMS 2590/1, p. 459. The *D.N.B.* account gives incorrect initial dates for both of these preferments.

65. *D.N.B.*; *Autobiography of Richard Baxter*, pp. 168–70, 183. Cf. Bosher, *Restoration Settlement*, pp. 27, 102, 118–19, 127, 128, 151, 186–87, 193–94, 228.

66. *Autobiography of Richard Baxter*, p. 177.

67. Venn, *Alumni Cantab.*, Part I, Vol. III, p. 177; WPLMS F.2003, p. 13. *D.N.B.* has Meriton (Merryton) at St. Martin's "shortly" before the Restoration, but the Vestry Minutes show him as holding the post from 1653 until 1661 or 1662, the last mention of him being an order made at the vestry of 11 April 1661 that he continue as lecturer. WPLMS F.2003, p. 248.

68. *D.N.B.*, s.v. John Meriton; Venn, *Alumni Cantab.*, Part I, Vol. III, p. 177; GLMS 9537/16, fol. 60r.

69. Cf. Bosher, *Restoration Settlement*, pp. 2–4, 48, 235–36, and *passim*; and Christopher Hill, *Society and Puritanism in Pre-Revolutionary England* (London, 1964), pp. 122–23.

70. *Documentary Annals of the Reformed Church of England*, ed. Edward Cardwell (Oxford, 1844), II, 304–10, 324.

71. GLMS 9537/16; this visitation call book lists only 95 London parishes and chapels. See also the larger list of active lectureships, dating from later in the century,

printed in John Stow, *A Survey of the Cities of London and Westminster*, ed. John Strype (London, 1720), Vol. II, Part V, pp. 13–16.

CONCLUSION

1. Thomas Hooker, *The Danger of Desertion* (1641), p. 15, as quoted in Carl Bridenbaugh, *Vexed and Troubled Englishmen, 1590–1642* (New York, 1968), p. 450.

2. The two letters, both dating from the late spring of 1634, are to be found in *C.S.P.D., 1634–35*, pp. 14, 64.

3. *The Official Papers of Sir Nathaniel Bacon*, ed. H. W. Saunders (Camden Society, 3d ser., Vol. XXVI; London, 1915), pp. 185–86.

4. Edward Leigh, *A System or Body of Divinity* (London, 1654), Epistle Dedicatory.

Manuscripts Consulted

Archival call number follows title of document in parentheses.

GUILDHALL LIBRARY

Archdeaconry of London

Instance Book, 1636–48 (9058)
Assignation Book, 1635–36 (9059/1)
Assignation Book, 1639–40 (9059/2)
Deposition Book, 1632–38 (9057/1)

Diocese of London

Bishops' Registers
Bishops Grindal, Sandys, Aylmer, Fletcher, Bancroft, Vaughan, and Abbot, 1559–1617 (9531/13)
Bishops Bancroft, Vaughan, Ravys, Abbot, and King, 1604–1620/1 (9531/14)
Bishops Laud and Juxon, 1628–60 (9531/15)

Episcopal Visitation Call Books
Visitation Call Book, 1583 (9537/5)
Visitation Call Book, 1586 (9537/6)
Visitation Call Book, 1589 (9537/7)
Visitation Call Book, 1592 (9537/8)
Visitation Call Book, 1598 (9537/9)
Visitation Call Book, 1607 (9537/10)
Visitation Call Book, 1612 (9537/11)
Visitation Call Book, 1615 (9537/12)
Visitation Call Book, 1628 (9537/13)
Visitation Call Book, 1636 (9537/14)
Visitation Call Book, 1637 (9537/15)
Visitation Call Book, 1664 (9537/16)

Episcopal Visitations: Presentments
Churchwardens' Presentments (miscellaneous), 1633–40 (9582)

Subscription Books
Subscription Book: Licensed Curates, Lecturers, and Schoolmasters, 1627–44 (9539A/1)
Subscription Book: Beneficed Clergy, 1631–48, 1660–69 (9539A/2)

Parochial Records
Allhallows Honey Lane: C.W. Accts., 1618–1743 (5026/1)
Allhallows Lombard Street: C.W. Accts., 1614–94 (4051/1)
Allhallows Lombard Street: V.M., 1618–53 (4049/1)
Allhallows London Wall: C.W. Accts., 1566–1681 (5090/2)
Allhallows Staining: C.W. Accts., 1533–1628 (4956/2)
Allhallows Staining: C.W. Accts., 1645–1706 (4956/3)
Allhallows the Great: C.W. Accts., 1616–1708 (818/1)
Allhallows the Great: V.M., 1574–1684 (819/1)
Allhallows the Less: C.W. Accts., 1630–51 (823/1)
Allhallows the Less: C.W. Accts., 1651–86 (823/2)
Allhallows the Less: V.M., 1644–1830 (824/1)
Holy Trinity the Less: C.W. Accts., 1582–1662 (4835/1)
St. Alban Wood Street: C.W. Accts., 1584–1639 (7673/1)

St. Alban Wood Street: C.W. Accts., 1637–75 (7673/2)
St. Alphage: C.W. Accts., 1580–1631 (1432/3)
St. Alphage: C.W. Accts., 1631–77 (1432/4)
St. Alphage: V.M., 1593–1608 (1431/1)
St. Alphage: V.M., 1608–1711 (1431/2)
St. Andrew Holborn: Bentley Register, 1584–1622 (4249)
St. Andrew Holborn: V.M., 1624–1714 (4251/1)
St. Andrew Hubbard: C.W. Accts., 1525–1621 (1279/2)
St. Andrew Hubbard: C.W. Accts., 1621–1712 (1279/3)
St. Andrew Hubbard: V.M., 1600–1678 (1278/1)
St. Andrew Wardrobe: C.W. Accts., 1570–1668 (2088/1)
SS. Anne and Agnes Aldersgate: C.W. Accts.: 1636–63 (587/1)
St. Antholin Budge Row: C.W. Accts., 1574–1708 (1046/1)
St. Antholin Budge Row: V.M., 1648–1700 (1045/1)
St. Augustine Watling Street: V.M., 1601–1737 (635/1)
St. Benet Fink: C.W. Accts., 1610–1700 (1303/1)
St. Benet Gracechurch: C.W. Accts., 1548–1723 (1568)
St. Benet Paul's Wharf: C.W. Accts., 1605–56 (878/1)
St. Benet Paul's Wharf: V.M., 1579–1674 (877/1)
St. Botolph Aldersgate: C.W. Accts., 1637–79 (1455/1)
St. Botolph Aldersgate: V.M., 1601–57 (1453/1)
St. Botolph Aldersgate: V.M., 1651–78 (1453/2)
St. Botolph Aldgate: C.W. Accts., 1547–85 (9235/1)
St. Botolph Aldgate: C.W. Accts., 1586–1691 (9235/2)
St. Botolph Aldgate: Minutes of Portsoken Ward with V.M., 1622–73 (9237)
St. Botolph Aldgate: Parish Clerk's Memoranda Books, 1583–1625 (9234/1–8)
St. Botolph Aldgate: V.M., 1583–1640 (9236)
St. Botolph Billingsgate: C.W. Accts., 1603–74 (942/1)
St. Botolph Billingsgate: V.M., 1592–1673 (943/1)
St. Botolph Bishopsgate: C.W. Accts., 1567–1632 (4524/1)
St. Botolph Bishopsgate: C.W. Accts., 1633–62 (4524/2)
St. Botolph Bishopsgate: V.M., 1617–90 (4526/1)
St. Bride Fleet Street: C.W. Accts., 1639–78 (6552/1)
St. Bride Fleet Street: V.M., 1644–65 (6554/1)
St. Clement Eastcheap: C.W. Accts., 1636–1740 (977/1)
St. Clement Eastcheap: V.M., 1640–1759 (978/1)
St. Dionis Backchurch: C.W. Accts., 1625–1729 (4215/1)
St. Dionis Backchurch: V.M., 1647–73 (4216/1)
St. Dunstan in the East: C.W. Accts., 1635–61 (7882/1)
St. Dunstan in the East: V.M., 1537–1651 (4887)
St. Dunstan in the West: C.W. Accts., 1516–1608 (2968/1)
St. Dunstan in the West: C.W. Accts., 1609–28 (2968/2)
St. Dunstan in the West: C.W. Accts., 1628–45 (2968/3)
St. Dunstan in the West: C.W. Accts., 1645–66 (2968/4)
St. Dunstan in the West: V.M., 1587–1663 (3016/1)
St. Ethelburga: C.W. Accts., 1569–1681 (4241/1)
St. George Botolph Lane: C.W. Accts., 1590–1676 (951/1)
St. George Botolph Lane: V.M., 1600–85 (952/1)
St. Giles Cripplegate: C.W. Accts., 1648–69 (6047/1)

St. Gregory by St. Paul's: V.M., 1642–1701 (1336/1)

St. Helen Bishopsgate: C.W. Accts., 1565–1654; V.M., 1558–1578 (6836)

St. James Garlickhithe: C.W. Accts., 1555–1627 (4810/1)

St. James Garlickhithe: C.W. Accts., 1627–99 (4810/2)

St. James Garlickhithe: V.M., 1615–93 (4813/1)

St. James Garlickhithe: V.M., 1643–86 (4813/2)

St. John the Baptist Walbrook: C.W. Accts., 1595–1679 (577/1)

St. John Zachary: C.W. Accts., 1591–1682 (590/1)

St. Katherine Coleman: C.W. Accts., 1609–71 (1124/1)

St. Katherine Cree: C.W. Accts., 1650–91 (1198/1)

St. Katherine Cree: V. M., 1639–1718 (1196/1)

St. Lawrence Jewry: C.W. Accts., 1579–1640 (2593/1)

St. Lawrence Jewry: C.W. Accts., 1640–98 (2593/2)

St. Lawrence Jewry: V.M., 1556–1669 (2590/1)

St. Lawrence Pountney: C.W. Accts., 1530–1681 (3907/1)

St. Lawrence Pountney: V.M., 1614–73 (3908/1)

St. Magnus the Martyr: C.W. Accts., 1638–1734 (1179/1)

St. Margaret New Fish Street: C.W. Accts., 1576–1678 (1176/1)

St. Margaret New Fish Street: V.M., 1578–1789 (1175/1)

St. Margaret New Fish Street: V.M., 1583–1675 (1175/2)

St. Margaret Pattens: C.W. Accts., 1558–1653 (4570/2)

St. Margaret Pattens: C.W. Accts., 1653–1760 (4570/3)

St. Margaret Pattens: V.M., 1640–83 (4571/1)

St. Martin Ludgate: C.W. Accts., 1649–90 (1313/1)

St. Martin Ludgate: V.M., 1576–1715 (1311/1)

St. Martin Orgar: V.M., 1557–1643 (959/1)

St. Martin Orgar: V.M., 1644–1695 (959/2)

St. Mary Abchurch: C.W. Accts., 1629–92 (3891/1)

St. Mary Aldermanbury: C.W. Accts., 1570–92 (3556/1)

St. Mary Aldermanbury: C.W. Accts., 1631–77 (3556/2)

St. Mary Aldermanbury: V.M., 1569–1609 (3570/1)

St. Mary Aldermanbury: V.M., 1610–1763 (3570/2)

St. Mary Aldermary: C.W. Accts., 1630–1708 (4863/1)

St. Mary at Hill: V.M., 1609–1752 (1240/1)

St. Mary Colechurch: C.W. Accts., 1612–1700 (66)

St. Mary Colechurch: V.M., 1612–1701 (64)

St. Mary Magdalen Milk Street: C.W. Accts., 1518–1606 (2596/1)

St. Mary Magdalen Milk Street: C.W. Accts., 1606–67 (2596/2)

St. Mary Magdalen Milk Street: V.M., 1619–68 (2597/1)

St. Mary Magdalen Old Fish Street: C.W. Accts., 1648–1721 (1341/1)

St. Mary Staining: C.W. Accts., 1587–88 (1542/1)

St. Mary Staining: C.W. Accts., 1646–1718 (1542/2)

St. Mary Woolchurch: C.W. Accts., 1560–1672 (1013/1)

St. Mary Woolchurch: V.M., 1647–1726/7 (1012/1)

St. Mary Woolnoth: C.W. Accts., 1539–1641 (1002/1)

St. Matthew Friday Street: C.W. Accts., 1547–1678 (1016/1)

St. Michael Bassishaw: C.W. Accts., 1617–1716 (2601/1)

St. Michael Cornhill: C.W. Accts., 1455–1608 (4071/1)

St. Michael Cornhill: C.W. Accts., 1608–1702 (4071/2)

St. Michael Cornhill: V.M., 1563–1697 (4072/1)
St. Michael Crooked Lane: C.W. Accts., 1617–1693 (1188/1)
St. Michael le Querne: C.W. Accts., 1514–1604 (2895/1)
St. Michael le Querne: C.W. Accts., 1605–1717 (2895/2)
St. Michael Queenhithe: C.W. Accts., 1625–1706 (4825/1)
St. Michael Wood Street: C.W. Accts., 1619–1718 (524/1)
St. Mildred Poultry: V.M., 1641–1713 (62/1)
St. Nicholas Acons: V.M., 1619–1738 (4060/1)
St. Olave Jewry: C.W. Accts., 1586–1643 (4409/1)
St. Olave Jewry: C.W. Accts., 1643–1705 (4409/2)
St. Olave Jewry: V.M., 1574–1680 (4415/1)
St. Olave Silver Street: C.W. Accts., 1630–82 (1257/1)
St. Pancras Soper Lane: C.W. Accts., 1616–1740 (5018/1)
St. Pancras Soper Lane: V.M., 1626–99 (5019/1)
St. Peter Cornhill: V.M., 1574–1717 (4165/1)
St. Peter Westcheap: C.W. Accts., 1435–1601 (645/1)
St. Peter Westcheap: C.W. Accts., 1601–1702 (645/2)
St. Peter Westcheap: V.M., 1619–53 (642/1)
St. Peter Westcheap: V.M., 1654–1787 (642/2)
St. Sepulchre: C.W. Accts., 1648–64 (3146/1)
St. Sepulchre: V.M., 1653–62 (3149/1)
St. Stephen Coleman Street: C.W. Accts., 1586–1640 (4457/2)
St. Stephen Coleman Street: C.W. Accts., 1656–85 (4457/3)
St. Stephen Coleman Street: V.M., 1622–1726 (4458/1)
St. Stephen Walbrook: C.W. Accts., 1549–1637 (593/2)
St. Stephen Walbrook: C.W. Accts., 1637–1748 (593/4)
St. Stephen Walbrook: V.M., 1587–1624 (594/1)
St. Stephen Walbrook: V.M., 1648–99 (594/2)
St. Swithin: C.W. Accts., 1602–1725 (559/1)
St. Swithin: V.M., 1647–1729 (560/1)
St. Thomas the Apostle: C.W. Accts., 1612–1729 (662/1)

HABERDASHERS' COMPANY ARCHIVES

The Accompt of the State of the Company of Haberdashers [Charities] att Michaelmas 1657
Court of Assistants Minutes, Vol. I, 1582/3–1652
Court of Assistants Minutes, Vol. II, 1652–1671
Lady Welds Accompt of Receits and Disbursments about Lay Impropriations to Be Laid to Poore Viccaridges from the Year 1630–1678
Register of Benefactions, 1607
The State of the Charities, 1597
Statutes for Monmouth and Newland
Will Book, 1535–1908

LAMBETH PALACE LIBRARY

A Noat of All the Lecturers in London When I Came to Be Bp Thear 1628 [endorsed] (942, no. 14)

The Names of All Parsons and Vicars in the Severall Parishes within the Citty and
Suburbs of London as Well Exempt as Not Exempt [endorsed] (942, no. 15)
The Names of the Lecturers within the Citty and Suburbs of London 1629 [endorsed]
(942, no. 16)

LONDON COUNTY COUNCIL RECORD OFFICE

Assignation Books (Consistory Court Records)

October 1635–June 1638 (DL/C/88)
June 1638–October 1640 (DL/C/89)
October 1640–February 1643/4 (DL/C/90)

Deposition Books

1612/13–1613 (DL/C/221)

Miscellaneous Series (Correction Books)

May 1588–February 1592/3 (DL/C/302)
January 1601/2–March 1602/3 (DL/C/303)
January 1605/6–October 1606 (DL/C/304)
September 1606–December 1607 (DL/C/305)
November 1607–June 1609 (DL/C/306)
May 1609–October 1611 (DL/C/308)
November 1610–November 1611 (DL/C/309)
November 1611–December 1613 (DL/C/310)
October 1613–April 1617 (DL/C/311)
November 1612–October 1615 (DL/C/312)
January 1616/17–January 1618/19 (DL/C/314)
November 1619–July 1626 (DL/C/315)
October 1620–June 1624 (DL/C/316)
November 1627–January 1629/30 (DL/C/317)
January 1628/9–March 1630/1 (DL/C/318)
April 1631–June 1633 (DL/C/319)
June 1633–March 1634/5 (DL/C/320)
October 1635–July 1637 (DL/C/321)
April 1629–November 1640 (DL/C/322)
December 1612–October 1616 (DL/C/323)
December 1615–April 1617 (DL/C/324)
March 1621–April 1624 (DL/C/325)
December 1631–June 1635 (DL/C/326)
December 1631–July 1633 (DL/C/327)

Personal Answer Books

June 1617–February 1620/1 (DL/C/192)

Vicar-General's Books

Stanhope, Part V, 1601–5 (DL/C/338)

Parochial Records

St. Saviour, Southwark: C.W. Accts., 1572–1605 (P/92/S/592)
St. Saviour, Southwark: V.M., 1557–81 (P/92/S/449)
St. Saviour, Southwark: V.M., 1581/2–1628 (P/92/S/450)

PUBLIC RECORD OFFICE

Act Book, Court of High Commission, 1631–1635/6 (SP 16/261)
Act Book, Court of High Commission, 1639–40 (SP 16/434)
Act Book, Court of High Commission, 1640 (SP 16/434a)
Lord Chamberlain's Warrants, 1628–34 (LC 5/132)
Lord Chamberlain's Warrants, 1631–32 (LC 5/133)
Miscellaneous State Papers Domestic from the reigns of Elizabeth I, James I, and Charles I

WESTMINSTER PUBLIC LIBRARY ARCHIVES
Parochial Records

St. Clement Danes: C.W. Accts., 1609–33 (B.10)
St. Clement Danes: C.W. Accts., 1633–54 (B.11)
St. Clement Danes: C.W. Accts., 1654–70 (B.12)
St. Margaret, Westminster: C.W. Accts., 1570–1610 (5–6)
St. Margaret, Westminster: C.W. Accts., 1622–57 (13–37)
St. Margaret, Westminster: C.W. Accts., 1660–62 (40–42)
St. Margaret, Westminster: V.M., 1591–1661 (2413)
St. Martin in the Fields: A Certificate of the Churchwardens to Thomas, Earl of Suffolk, the Lord Treasurer, Concerning Payment of a Lecturer Recommended by Him (ca. 1615) [endorsed] (F.6036)
St. Martin in the Fields: C.W. Accts., 1601–24 (F.2)
St. Martin in the Fields: C.W. Accts., 1624–47 (F.3)
St. Martin in the Fields: C.W. Accts., 1647–63 (F. 4–19)
St. Martin in the Fields: V.M., 1574–1640 (F.2001)
St. Martin in the Fields: V.M., 1624–52 (F.2002)
St. Martin in the Fields: V.M., 1652–65 (F.2003)

Index

Index

Index

Charity Governance

Second Edition

Charity Governance

Second Edition

Con Alexander

& the Charities Team at Veale Wasbrough Vizards

JORDANS

Published by
Jordan Publishing Limited
21 St Thomas Street
Bristol BS1 6JS

British Library Cataloguing-in-Publication Data

A catalogue record for this book is available from the British Library.

ISBN 978 1 84661 300 5

Typeset by Letterpart Limited, Caterham ion the Hill, Surrey CR3 5XL

Printed in Great Britain by CPI Antony Rowe, Chippenham and Eastbourne

PREFACE

The first edition of this book was an attempt to identify the key elements of good governance for charities.

The governance of commercial organisations had been the subject of a number of reports, culminating in the Company Law Reform White Paper 2005 and subsequently the Companies Act 2006.

Much less published thought had been given to charities, notwithstanding their significant contribution to society in the United Kingdom, a contribution which is in many ways more deeply rooted over a longer period of time than the contribution of many commercial organisations.

Good charity governance is difficult to define, in part because charities are so diverse in what they do, but also because they have a purpose which is not as easily defined as the purpose of a commercial organisation in returning value to its shareholders.

The Charity Commission's view is that the 'hallmarks' of a well-governed charity are that:

- It is clear about its purposes and direction.

- It has a strong board.

- It is fit for purpose.

- It is learning and improving.

- It is financially sound and prudent.

- It is accountable and transparent.

These are laudable aims, but (in our experience) achieving them often requires an understanding of a range of legal, regulatory, cultural and other issues which are by no means straightforward.

This book is our response to that. It attempts to summarise and explain the most significant aspects of good governance for charities. It deals with the framework of company, trusts, charity and other branches of law that regulate how charities are formed, the powers they have, how they are operated and controlled and the way in which they are made accountable. We have, though, also tried to build on the legal framework by dealing with many of the practical issues that arise and, in particular, the approach taken by the sector's regulator, the Charity Commission, and also by HM Revenue & Customs.

This is an area which is constantly evolving. This second edition of the book has been updated to reflect a number of significant changes in law and regulation since 1 March 2007. These include (to name but a few) the introduction of the CIO, the challenge to the Charity Commission's interpretation of 'public benefit', the Equality Act 2010, the introduction of a statutory 'total return' power and the Charities Act 2011. However, in our experience of advising charities of all kinds during this time, some key points have been:

- The economic changes sparked by the banking crisis have affected many charities in ways that may not have been anticipated before 2008, ranging from cuts in central and local Government expenditure (and corresponding cuts to contracts entered into with charities) to declining returns on endowment; during a period when demand for many charities' services has increased significantly.

- The Charity Commission has not been immune to the economic changes that have affected the charities they regulate. Significant cuts in funding have lead to significant cuts in Commission staff, many of whom have developed expertise and experience over many years that (in our view) will be a real loss to the charity sector. Ironically, the Commission faces this challenge at a time when it is subject to continuing scrutiny and criticism from many quarters, not least the criticism levelled by the Public Administration Select Committee. How is the Commission to be expected to function as an effective regulator without the financial resources to support its work? The answer appears to be that it will target those charities considered to be 'at risk' at the expense of the advice and guidance that was available from it for all charities previously.

- The role of the Charity Tribunal has developed since the implementation of the Charities Act 2006. Schemes and Orders of the Charity Commission have become more amenable to challenge. This is probably a good thing in terms of the ability of those who have a bona fide interest in the activities of charities to challenge decisions of the Charity Commission. However, it may have made the Commission more reluctant to make the kinds of Schemes or Orders which might be susceptible to challenge without (at the very least) prior consultation which may not always be appropriate.

- Lord Hodgson's review of the Charities Act 2006 was completed and responded to by the Government. Many of his more far-reaching recommendations (such as in relation to the remuneration of charity trustees) were not accepted by the Government.

These are in our view some of the more relevant changes in relation to the charity sector over the last 7 years.

In updating this book, we have drawn upon our own practical experience of the sort of issues faced by charities ranging from grant makers to service providers. We have dealt with the differing legal positions of charitable companies, charitable incorporated organisations, corporations, trusts and associations in as much detail as we can in the space available. However, the two forms of charity most commonly encountered (the charitable company limited by guarantee and the charitable trust) are the main focus of this book.

Where relevant, we have used and quoted from the helpful guidance produced by both the Charity Commission and HM Revenue & Customs in relation to charities. These are excellent resources and are all available online (at www.charity-commission.gov.uk and www.hmrc.gov.uk respectively). All of this material is subject to Crown copyright protection.

We hope this book will be useful to lawyers, accountants and other professionals advising charities, particularly those who may not regard themselves as charities specialists. We also hope that it will be useful to charity trustees themselves and those employed by charities.

With this in mind, the book breaks down in the following way:

- The first four chapters are intended to provide a framework for the rest of the book, with much reference material that we hope will be useful in the context of other chapters.

   'What is a charity?' explains the legal definition of charities.

   'Types of charity' looks at the distinguishing characteristics of the various different types of incorporated and unincorporated charity.

   'Modern legal framework' explains the different legal regimes to which charities are subject.

   'The Charity Commission' explains the role of the Charity Commission as the regulator of charities.

- The next four chapters look at core governance issues:

   'Governance structures' explains the relationship between the members and trustees of charities.

'Trustees' duties and liabilities' looks at the potential personal liability of trustees in relation to their charities.

'Trustees' powers' discusses the position of a charity's trustees in relation to the exercise of any power, whether it is express, implied or statutory.

'Trustee governance' looks at the nuts and bolts of acting as a trustee and discusses issues ranging from how they are appointed and retire to delegation.

- The remaining chapters look at seven areas that, in practice, often raise issues of governance for a charity's trustees:

'Charity assets' explains the different ways in which charities hold and can deal with their assets, including permanent endowment and land.

'Investment' examines all of the issues raised by the exploitation of assets by way of investment, including the appropriate use of an investment policy and delegation of investment management.

'Taxation' summarises the key tax implications of particular activities that may be carried out by a charity, but looks in particular detail at the activities that can give rise to non-charitable expenditure and associated tax liabilities.

'Borrowing' explains all of the issues that are likely to be encountered by a charity's trustees in relation to commercial borrowing, including the restrictions on the mortgage of a charity's land.

'Trading' looks at the governance issues raised by trading by charities and their trading subsidiaries.

'Reporting and accounting' looks at the accounting framework and the way in which charity trustees report to their stakeholders and the wider public.

'Restructuring' explains the different ways in which a charity's trustees can respond to change by altering the way in which the charity is structured and deals with issues ranging from straightforward constitutional changes through to dissolutions.

About the authors

This second edition to this book has been a collaboration between the members of the charities team at Veale Wasbrough Vizards and other specialist lawyers within the firm.

Veale Wasbrough Vizards is a full service commercial law firm with offices in London, Bristol and Birmingham.

The firm is nationally recognised for its focus on the charities and education sectors. Its clients include charities in all areas of the sector; from smaller charities working in local communities through to much larger organisations working nationally and internationally; from charity start-ups to public sector spin-outs; and from universities and schools to social care and religious organisations.

Veale Wasbrough Vizards is recognised for its work with charities by the leading legal directories and Charity Finance ranks the firm as a leading adviser to the top 350 charities.

The contributing authors to this book are active charity trustees and understand the trustees' perspective and the strengths, weaknesses, opportunities and threats of and to their charities.

- **Con Alexander — lead author**

  Con has advised charities of all kinds for more than 15 years and specialises in helping clients with the governance and strategic challenges they face. He is particularly interested in the way in which organisations change over time, the importance of the relationship between trustees and senior management and collaboration between organisations. Con is rated by both Chambers and Legal 500 as a leading adviser in the field of charity law.

- **Rachel Tonkin - editor**

  Rachel advises in relation to all aspects of charity law and regulation, governance, constitutional review and other strategic projects involving charities and social enterprises. She has a particular interest in trust law issues encountered by charities, including endowments and restricted assets, investment, funding arrangements and charitable assets held by local authorities.

- **Contributing authors**

  Chapters of this book have been contributed by the following members of the charities team at Veale Wasbrough Vizards: Emma-Jane Burnell, Penelope Byatt, Laura Chesham, Jos Moule, Barney Northover, Jaime Parkes and Philip Reed. Specialists contributions to the chapters on borrowing by charities and taxation have been provided by Rob Collier and Emma Bradley.

Thanks

We would like to thank our charity clients for their ongoing and significant contribution to a vibrant and vital part of civil society in the UK and overseas and their trustees for their very many hours of voluntary work in driving that contribution.

We are very grateful to the following people for dedicating hours to researching and proof-reading during their time as trainee solicitors in the team: Emily Jenkins, Jessica King, Jenny Marley, Kate Newman, Bryony Robin and Matthew Roden. We would also like to thank Karen Usher and Jessica Cook for their continuing support and patience. Finally, our thanks go to Jon Napier for his valuable input to this second edition.

Con Alexander would like to thank Rachel Tonkin for the very significant part she has played in editing this book. He would also like to thank Hugh Craig of Bates, Wells & Braithwaite and Nigel Reid of Linklaters for their wise advice and guidance in the past and Simon Heald for his support and advice now and in the future.

Con would also like to thank Tamsin James for her love, friendship and good advice. Con's contribution to this book is dedicated to Tamsin, Olivia, Kitty and Ivor, with much love.

Abbreviations

There are a number of words and phrases we have used throughout this book and which have the following meanings:

- 'Advice' is advice given by the Charity Commission in accordance with the Charities Act 2011, s 110 (see **4.17**).

- 'Charities Acts' means the Charities Act 2011 and those provisions of the Charities Act 1992 still in force.

- The 'Charity Commission' is the Charity Commission for England and Wales (see **4.1**).

- A 'CIC' is a community interest company (see **2.77**).

- A 'CIO' is a charitable incorporated organisation (see **2.31**).

- 'Companies Acts' means the Companies Act 2006 and any provisions of the Companies Act 1985 still in force.

- An 'Inquiry' is an inquiry into a charity instituted by the Charity Commission (see **4.44**).

- An 'Order' is an order of the Charity Commission made in accordance with the Charities Act 2011, s 69 (see **4.22**).

- A 'Scheme' is a scheme made by the Charity Commission in accordance with the Charities Act 1993, s 69 (see **4.32**).

- 'Terms of Reference' are explained at **8.36**.

Our main aim in writing this book has been to prepare what we hope is a practically orientated guide to charity governance. Any comments will be gratefully received.

We have tried to state the law in force in England and Wales as at 1 January 2014.

Con Alexander, January 2014

Disclaimer

This material in this book is provided for general purposes only and does not constitute legal or other professional advice. It should not be acted upon without seeking appropriate independent professional advice.

Neither the publisher nor the authors accept any responsibility for loss occasioned to any person however caused or arising as a result of or in consequence of action taken (or not taken) in reliance on the material in this book.

CONTENTS

TABLE OF CASES

References are to paragraph numbers.

TABLE OF STATUTES

References are to paragraph numbers.

TABLE OF STATUTORY INSTRUMENTS

References are to paragraph numbers.

CHAPTER 1

WHAT IS A CHARITY?

1.1   There is no single way of identifying a charity. Most will be on the register of charities maintained by the Charity Commission, but many will not. And different legal definitions determine what a charity is for different purposes. When one adds to that the very wide range of activities carried out by charities in the twenty-first century, the task becomes more difficult.

CHARITY LAW

1.2   Having said this, the starting point for most purposes will be what constitutes a charity for the purposes of charity law. There is a statutory definition in the Charities Act 2011. There is a different (but very similar) definition for tax purposes. This is explained in more detail at **11.5**. The Charities Act 2011 definition is ostensibly straightforward. A charity is any institution which:[1]

> '(a)   is established for charitable purposes only, and
> (b)   falls to be subject to the control of the High Court in the exercise of its jurisdiction with respect to charities.'

1.3   The definition therefore requires three things:

- an 'institution';
- that is established only for charitable purposes; and
- that is subject to the control of the High Court in the exercise of its jurisdiction with respect to charities.

1.4   Each of these component parts needs to be looked at in more detail, because each of them has aspects that are not immediately obvious to anyone looking to apply the definition in practice.

INSTITUTION

1.5   There is a limited definition of what an 'institution' is.[2] The Charities Act 2011 states simply that an institution 'includes a trust or undertaking'. In

---

[1]   Charities Act 2011, s 1(1).
[2]   Charities Act 2011, s 9(3).

practice, charitable institutions can take almost any legal form. The most obvious examples include companies, trusts and unincorporated associations. The position is explained in more detail in **Chapter 2**.

CHARITABLE PURPOSE

1.6 'Charitable purpose' is defined by s 2 of the Charities Act 2011. It is any purpose that falls within a number of 'descriptions' of purposes set out in the Act and is also for the 'public benefit'. Both requirements must be met.

Statutory descriptions

1.7 The list of descriptions set out in s 3 of the Charities Act 2011 is as follows:

- the prevention or relief of poverty;
- the advancement of education;
- the advancement of religion (including a religion which involves belief in more than one god and a religion which does not involve belief in a god);
- the advancement of health or the saving of lives (including the prevention or relief of sickness, disease or human suffering);
- the advancement of citizenship or community development (including rural or urban regeneration and the promotion of civic responsibility, volunteering, the voluntary sector and the effectiveness or efficiency of charities);
- the advancement of the arts, culture, heritage or science;
- the advancement of amateur sport;
- the advancement of human rights, conflict resolution or reconciliation or the promotion of religious or racial harmony or equality and diversity;
- the advancement of environmental protection or improvement;
- the relief of those in need by reason of youth, age, ill-health, disability, financial hardship or other disadvantage;
- the advancement of animal welfare; and
- the promotion of the efficiency of the armed forces of the Crown or of the efficiency of the police, fire and rescue services or ambulance services.

1.8 This list reflects the way in which the law of charitable purposes developed prior to the passing of the Charities Act 2006, which made some significant changes to both the Charities Act 1993 and the general law of charities (the provisions of both the 1993 and 2006 Acts have now been consolidated in the Charities Act 2011). Perhaps the most significant change made by the Charities Act 2006 was the introduction of a statutory definition of charitable purposes.

1.9 In order to understand the statutory definition fully, it helps to look at a little history. Before the passing of the Charities Act 2006, the categories of charitable purposes were defined by the courts in the cases that came before them. Much of this case law was based on a series of charitable purposes set out in the preamble to the Statute of Charitable Uses 1601 (often called the Statute of Elizabeth). Over the centuries, the courts developed those purposes to reflect changes in society, with the result that four accepted heads of charitable purpose emerged. These were:

- the relief of poverty;
- the advancement of education;
- the advancement of religion; and
- any other purpose regarded as 'beneficial to the community'.

1.10 The last category (any purpose beneficial to the community) was used by the courts, and subsequently the Charity Commission under the overall control of the courts, to develop the scope of charitable purposes generally, subject to a test of 'public benefit' which itself evolved over time. Many of the charitable purposes recognised within this category (such as animal welfare and the advancement of human rights) were subsequently recognised and given a statutory basis by the Charities Act 2006, subject to a statutory test of public benefit.

1.11 The definition of charitable purpose in the Charities Act 2011 does not close the door on the development of new purposes that can be recognised as charitable. There is a statutory provision for new purposes which are analogous to or 'within the spirit of' the purposes listed in the Act.[3] The Act also ensures that any purpose not mentioned in the Act that was charitable under the law that applied previously will not lose that status.

1.12 It is important to remember that the Charity Commission regards the descriptions of charitable purposes in s 3 of the Charities Act 2011 as no more than descriptions. The Commission's guidance states that:[4]

> 'Each item listed is a description or "head" of charity rather than a fully-stated charitable purpose in itself. Under each of the descriptions lie a range of purposes, all of which fit the description, but each of which is a different purpose in its own right. The list of descriptions, taken as a whole with the purposes that underlie each description, encompasses everything that has, or may be, recognised as charitable in England and Wales.'

An institution which has charitable purposes modelled on the descriptions in the 2011 Act will therefore not necessarily be accepted by the Commission as established for charitable purposes only. For example, an institution established for the 'relief of those in need by reason of youth, age, ill-health, disability,

---

[3] Charities Act 2011, s 3(1)(m)(ii).
[4] The Charity Commission's *Guidance on Charitable Purposes*.

financial hardship or other disadvantage' may need to specify the 'other disadvantage' that it has in mind in order to be accepted for registration by the Commission.

1.13 A detailed discussion of charitable purposes is outside the scope of this book. For practical purposes, the important points to bear in mind are:

- Because an institution must be 'established for' charitable purposes, its constitution must state those purposes clearly and precisely. Where that is done will depend upon how the institution in question is set up. There is more information about this in **Chapter 2**.

- Because the institution must be established 'for charitable purposes only' it must also be clear that the purposes are limited to those that are charitable. If an institution has some purposes that are charitable and some that, while philanthropic or benevolent, are not, then the institution will not qualify as a charity.

- It must also be clear that the assets of the institution can only ever be applied for its charitable purposes. An institution's constitution should not contain any 'default' provisions which could apply surplus assets for any non-charitable purpose. Usually, a charity's constitution will set out expressly what will happen to the institution's surplus assets in the event that it is wound up and provide that they must be applied for other, similar, charitable purposes.

- The charitable purposes for which an institution is established are the single most important part of its constitution because their scope will determine what the institution can do and often how it can do it. The widest objects that an institution can have are 'such purposes as are exclusively charitable under the law of England and Wales'.

- Charities established before the implementation of the changes made to charity law by the Charities Act 2006, and which have not subsequently been updated, are much more likely to have purposes which reflect the four heads of charity that were used by the courts and the Charity Commission before then. Charities established after the changes took effect are more likely to have purposes that reflect the descriptions set out in the statutory definition.

Public benefit

1.14 The second component of the statutory definition of what constitutes a charitable purpose is the requirement that it must be for the 'public benefit'. This requirement was first introduced by the Charities Act 2006 and is now contained in the Charities Act 2011.

1.15 At the time, many commentators considered that the Charities Act 2006 had brought about a significant change in the law, by confirming that there is no presumption that charitable purposes falling within the descriptions now set out in s 3 of the Charities Act 2011 are for the public benefit. Previously, it had been thought, charities whose purposes were to relieve poverty or advance education or religion were presumed to be for the benefit of the public. However, the decision of the Upper Tribunal (Tax and Charity) in a challenge brought by the Independent Schools Council (ISC) against the Charity Commission's public benefit guidance[5] (see **1.23**) cast doubt over whether such a presumption of public benefit had in fact existed prior to the 2006 Act.

1.16 This confirmed that the historic position for those charities did not in fact fundamentally change with the coming into force of the 2006 Act. The practical point is that an institution must be able to demonstrate that the purposes for which it is established are for the public benefit, in order to be recognised as charitable.

1.17 The Charities Act 2011 does not contain a definition of public benefit or provide direction on what it means. Instead, the Act confirms that the term must be tested using the criteria developed by the courts in pre-existing case-law.[6] And while the courts will remain the ultimate arbiters of whether a particular purpose is for the public benefit, the Act also gives the Charity Commission a statutory duty to issue guidance on the public benefit requirement[7] which must be taken into account by charity trustees when they exercise any of their powers or duties to which the guidance is relevant. There is more about the Commission's public benefit guidance at **1.22**.

1.18 There has been considerable debate about whether a statutory definition of public benefit would be desirable,[8] but to date this has been resisted by the Government given the difficulties of condensing several hundred years of case-law into a straightforward definition that would reflect the diversity of the sector and would enable the law to continue to evolve.

1.19 It is clear that, when determining whether an institution is established for charitable purposes, the public benefit requirement is to be tested against the stated purpose set out in the institution's governing document (see **1.13**) not what the institution does or will do to further those purposes.[9] Therefore, if the institution's purposes are clearly stated, this gives the Charity Commission and the courts limited scope to look at what the institution does or will do when determining its charitable status. However, if there is uncertainty about what an institution's purpose is and whether it is charitable, the activities can be taken into account when determining whether the purposes will be implemented in a

---

[5] *Independent Schools Council v The Charity Commission for England & Wales* [2011] UKUT 421 (TCC).
[6] Charities Act 2011, s 4(3).
[7] Charities Act 2011, s 17.
[8] See, for example, Lord Hodgson's report following his review of the Charities Act 2006 'Trusted and Independent: giving charity back to charities' and the Public Administration Select Committee Third Report – 'The Role of the Charity Commission and public benefit: Post-legislative scrutiny of the Charities Act 2006'.
[9] *Independent Schools Council v The Charity Commission for England & Wales* [2011] UKUT 421 (TCC).

way which is charitable.[10] This has obvious implications on the registration of new charities. There is more about charity registration at **1.50**.

1.20 The public benefit requirement applies differently to charities with different charitable purposes. In particular, there is a different test of public benefit for charities established for the relief (and in some cases prevention) of poverty.[11] There is more about poverty charities at **1.37**.

1.21 What seems clear is that the law on public benefit will continue to evolve, as the requirement is tested and clarified in relation to different kinds of charities.

The Charity Commission's public benefit guidance

1.22 The Commission's first published guidance on public benefit was set out in its publication 'Charities and Public Benefit'.[12] That guidance did not, in the words of the Commission, 'constitute the law on public benefit' but was 'a guide to what the law says on public benefit and how we interpret and apply that law'. Some had, however, taken the view that the guidance was a guide to what the Commission considers the law to be rather than 'what the law says'. In fact, the status of the guidance was successfully challenged in the Upper Tribunal (Tax and Chancery Chamber) in 2011.[13]

1.23 As we have mentioned, the challenge was brought by the Independent Schools Council (ISC) (a body representing a number of associations concerned with charitable independent schools). The ISC argued that the Commission's guidance included errors of law in respect of the public benefit requirement as it applied to charities which charge fees for their charitable activities, and in particular as it applied to independent schools. The Upper Tribunal agreed and ordered the Commission to correct the relevant parts of its guidance. Although confined to educational charities, the decision obviously also had potential implications for other charities charging fees for the services they provide, such as care homes and 'private' hospitals.

1.24 The Charity Commission's revised public benefit guidance was published in September 2013, following a public consultation exercise.[14] This is general guidance aimed at all charities, to be supplemented by specific guidance for charities with particular purposes, including educational charities, charities for the relief of poverty and religious charities.[15]

---

[10] *Incorporated Society of Law Reporting for England and Wales v AG* [1972] Ch 73 as applied in *Helena Partnerships Limited v HMRC* [2011] UKUT 271 (TCC).

[11] *Charity Commission for England and Wales and Others v Her Majesty's Attorney General* (FTC/84/2011).

[12] Published in January 2008, amended in December 2011 and withdrawn in September 2013.

[13] *Independent Schools Council v The Charity Commission for England & Wales* [2011] UKUT 421 (TCC).

[14] 'Public Benefit: the public benefit requirement (PB1)', 'Public Benefit: running a charity (PB2)' and 'Public Benefit: reporting (PB3)' published in September 2013.

[15] At the time of writing, the Commission's supplemental guidance is under review.

1.25 The guidance consists of three separate guides. The first guide, PB1, explains the legal requirement that a charity's purposes must be for the public benefit and is relevant to people thinking of setting up a charity or changing an existing charity's purposes. PB2 explains the public benefit requirement in the context of running a charity. The separation of the guidance between these two guides reflects the principle we have mentioned that whether an institution is established for charitable purposes depends on what it has been established to do, not its activities. PB3 explains trustees' duties to report on public benefit. There is more on reporting at **1.46** and in **Chapter 14**.

The public benefit requirement

1.26 The guidance provides that to be 'for the public benefit', a purpose must satisfy two 'aspects'; the 'benefit aspect' and the 'public aspect'. Both 'aspects' are explored further below.

The 'benefit aspect'

1.27 To satisfy the 'benefit aspect', the Commission's guidance provides that a purpose must be 'beneficial' and any 'detriment or harm that results from the purpose must not outweigh the benefit'.

1.28 In relation to the first limb of the 'benefit aspect', the guidance says it should always be possible to identify and describe how a charity's purpose is beneficial. But this does not mean that the benefit should also be capable of being quantified or measured. Some benefits will be quantifiable, for example the level of financial support provided by a charity to its poor beneficiaries. Others will not, for example, viewing works of art.

1.29 If necessary, the benefit should be capable of being proved by evidence. In some cases, there will be little need for trustees to provide evidence to prove that a purpose is beneficial, eg it would not be necessary for trustees to prove that the provision of emergency aid in the context of a natural disaster was beneficial. However, in other cases, the Commission will ask to see some objective and expert advice in relation to the benefit, eg, the architectural merit of a particular building or the artistic merit of a collection of paintings.

1.30 The second limb of the 'benefit aspect' is that a purpose cannot be a charitable purpose where any detriment or harm resulting from it outweighs the benefit. The Commission will take into account detriment or harm where it is reasonable to expect that it will result from the purpose, but this will need to be based on evidence, not personal views. In the ISC case, it was stated that:

'The court ... has to balance the benefit and disadvantage in all cases where detriment is alleged and is supported by evidence. But great weight is to be given to a purpose which would, ordinarily, be charitable; before the alleged disadvantages can be given much weight, they need to be clearly demonstrated.'[16]

Damage to the environment, danger to public health and unlawful restrictions on a person's freedom are examples of things that might be detrimental or harmful. But there is clearly a balance to be struck: the fact that a charity provides a benefit, for example by providing transport for disabled people that also pollutes the environment, would not be sufficient to negate the benefit to the public of what the charity does.

The 'public aspect'

1.31   Again, there are two limbs to this aspect. To satisfy the 'public aspect', the purpose must firstly benefit the public in general or a sufficient section of the public and, secondly, it must not give rise to more than incidental personal benefit (what was, in the previous guidance, known as 'private benefit').

1.32   The guidance is clear that if a purpose benefits the public in general, this means that it is not limited to people with a particular need or who have to satisfy some other criteria. If a purpose does not specify who can benefit, it will generally be taken to mean that it will benefit the public in general.

1.33   If a purpose does not benefit the public in general, it must benefit a sufficient section of the public in order to be charitable. What constitutes a sufficient section of the public will vary, depending on the particular charitable purpose and who the purpose intends to benefit. The Commission's guidance puts it this way:

> 'A sufficient section of the public are called a "public class" of people. There is not a set minimum number of people who have to benefit in order to be a "public class". Whether a section of the public is or is not a "public class" is not the same for every purpose. What is sufficient for one purpose may not be sufficient for another.'[17]

1.34   The guidance confirms that whether or not a section of the public is 'sufficient' will be decided on a case-by-case basis and will be determined by what the courts have, and have not, accepted in other cases.

1.35   There are a number of different ways in which a charity may define who can benefit, depending on its particular purposes and how it advances them in practice. For example:

*   The Commission accepts that in most cases it is reasonable for a charity to benefit people living in a particular geographical area, although the area must not be so small that the people living in it do not constitute a sufficient section of the public. For example, restricting beneficiaries to

---

[16]   *R (Independent Schools Council) v Charity Commission* [2012] Ch 214 at [106].
[17]   PB1 Part 5.

villages and towns is likely to be acceptable, while restricting beneficiaries to specific streets within a town is much less likely to qualify.

- Some charities will define who can benefit from their services by reference to a common need, such as disability, poverty, old age or social or economic disadvantage. The Commission accepts that beneficiaries with a particular charitable need will usually constitute a sufficient section of the public.

- A charity may define who can benefit by reference to the gender, race, ethnic origin, religion or sexual orientation of the people it is intended to support. The Equality Act 2010, which makes it unlawful to discriminate against anyone because of these kinds of characteristics (called 'protected characteristics'), contains a specific exemption for charities. Broadly, this exemption allows a charity to restrict its benefits to people who share a protected characteristic, even though this may exclude (and therefore discriminate against) people with other protected characteristics. However, it may do so only if the charity's governing document only allows people who share a protected characteristic to benefit, and if the restriction can be justified, either to tackle a particular disadvantage faced by people who share a particular protected characteristic or to achieve some other legitimate aim in a fair, balanced and reasonable ('proportionate') way. The Commission's guidance on the Equality Act contains further information on when the charities exemption will apply. There is more on the Equality Act at **3.21**.

- A beneficiary class where all the beneficiaries are named, eg an individual or a fixed group of individuals will not be a sufficient section of the public. Neither will a group of people which is numerically negligible, except for in the case of certain 'poverty' charities. There is more about poverty charities at **1.37**.

- Some charities will deliver services to their beneficiaries via a membership structure. This may be acceptable if a sufficient section of the public can access those benefits by becoming members and the membership is a suitable way of carrying out the charity's purposes. However, the Commission's guidance is clear that a private or 'self regarding' members club which exists for the benefit of its members only will not be for the public benefit. As the guidance puts it:

  > 'Even if it has an open membership, an organisation that is "inward-looking", supported by its members for the purpose of providing benefits for the members, does not benefit a public class of people and so cannot be a charity.'[18]

- Where the 'poor' are excluded from benefiting, the benefit will not be to a sufficient section to the public. This is particularly relevant for charities which charge fees for their services. There is more about charging for services at **1.42**.

---

[18] PB1 Part 5.

1.36 In determining whether the 'public' aspect is satisfied, the Commission will also take into account whether the public benefit a charity provides gives rise to any 'personal benefit':[19]

- The Commission defines a 'personal benefit' as any benefit that someone (whether an individual or organisation) receives from a charity. 'Benefit' is not defined in this context, but will often mean a financial or economic benefit or advantage. Not all personal benefits will prevent a charity from meeting the public benefit requirement. Personal benefits which are 'incidental' are acceptable. A personal benefit will be incidental where it is a 'necessary result or by-product' of carrying out the charity's purposes. So a charity which pays for medical treatment for its beneficiaries will be conferring a personal benefit on a 'for profit' provider of the treatment, but this will be a necessary result or by-product of achieving the charity's aim of assisting its beneficiaries.

- There are many ways in which too great a degree of personal benefit could arise. A grant made to a beneficiary for the relief of poverty may do more than relieve their poverty and may enrich them to too great an extent. While paying employees is properly incidental to the pursuit of a charity's purposes, salaries which are too high in the context of the charity's own income or market rates generally may also confer too great a degree of personal benefit. A grant made to a 'for profit' business with the aim of generating work for impoverished beneficiaries of a charity may confer too great a degree of personal benefit on the owners of the business.

- In practice, whether a personal benefit is a necessary result or by-product of carrying out a charity's purposes will depend on whether it follows from an action which is only taken to further the charity's aims and the amount of the personal benefit is reasonable in the circumstances.

Poverty charities

1.37 As we have said, in general, for a purpose to be 'for the public benefit', it must satisfy both the 'benefit aspect' and the 'public aspect'.[20] The position for charities with the purpose to relieve (or in some cases prevent) poverty is, however, different.

1.38 These charities can meet the public benefit requirement by satisfying the 'benefit aspect' only, with no reference to the public aspect. This means that the beneficiaries of poverty charities can be defined by a reference to their family relationship (ie, their descent from one individual), their employment by an employer, or their membership of an unincorporated association. Beneficiaries, however, cannot be named personally.

---

[19] Also known as 'private benefit'.
[20] *Charity Commission for England and Wales and Others v Her Majesty's Attorney General* (FTC/84/2011).

Trustees' duties

1.39 Once it has been established that a charity's purposes are for the public benefit, trustees must then carry out those charitable purposes for the public benefit.

1.40 The Commission's guidance explains that not all decisions of trustees will impact on this duty. However, when making decisions that impact on the way in which people can benefit from the charity's purposes and who can benefit from the charity's purposes, trustees must make decisions:

- that ensure that the charity's purposes provide benefit;
- that manage risks of detriment or harm to the charity's beneficiaries or to the public in general from carrying out the charity's purposes;
- about who benefits in ways that are consistent with the charity's purposes;
- that make sure that any personal benefits are no more than incidental.

There is more about trustee decision making in **Chapter 7**.

1.41 There are various kinds of trustee decisions which will affect who can benefit from the charity and in what way. For example:

- A charity's trustees may decide to exercise their discretion to benefit a particular group. This will almost always be the case where the charity's governing document gives its trustees the widest possible discretion to apply its funds for any charitable purpose, but will also apply where, for example, a charity set up to advance education focuses its resources on a particular group of children defined by their poverty. The Commission's guidance confirms that trustees may decide to focus on certain beneficiaries provided that they have proper reasons for doing so, the poor are not excluded from benefit and the smaller group of beneficiaries is a sufficient section of the public for the charity's purposes.
- Where a charity provides facilities to the public, its trustees can decide to limit public access to those facilities, eg through restricted opening hours. This might be, for example, because of lack of resources, in order to properly protect heritage property or to ensure that the charity can comply with its obligations under the legislation in relation to health and safety. The Commission's guidance confirms that restricting public access will be acceptable provided this helps to carry out the charity's purposes in a better way and the amount of access overall is appropriate in the charity's circumstances. The Equality Act 2010 may be relevant in some cases, because it requires service providers to make reasonable adjustments for disabled people in the way they deliver their services. This is so that a disabled person is not put at a substantial disadvantage compared to non-disabled people in accessing the services. What is considered to be a reasonable adjustment will vary from charity to charity.

- A membership structure may be used to limit a charity's benefits to a section of the public, provided a sufficient section of the public can access those benefits by becoming members and the membership structure is a suitable way of carrying out the charity's purposes for the public benefit. The Commission's guidance requires that all those who might benefit from a charity be able to apply to join, with an objective criteria for deciding membership. A system which, for example, required an applicant to be proposed and seconded for membership by existing members is very unlikely to be acceptable. But restrictions which reflect, for example, a charity's capacity to provide facilities are likely to be reasonable, subject to there being a 'first come, first served' waiting list. So too would be restrictions which reflect the focus of a charity's objects on, for example, a particular geographical area. The key point is that, in order to provide public benefit, the membership provisions must not have the effect of turning the charity into a private members' club (see also **1.35**).

- However, some 'membership' charities have a membership which is not related to the activities they carry out. A charity which promotes a particular branch of science may restrict its membership to people with qualifications in the relevant field. Provided that the work of the charity is aimed at, for example, disseminating research to the public as a whole, the fact that it restricts its membership to a particular class of people will not be relevant to the public benefit requirement.

- Decisions in relation to the charges a charity makes for its services will impact on its trustees' duty in relation to public benefit. There is more about this below.

Charging for services

1.42 As we have explained earlier in this chapter, aspects of the Charity Commission's previous guidance on public benefit were successfully challenged in the Upper Tribunal (Tax and Chancery Chamber) in 2011. The guidance in question related to restrictions based on the ability to pay fees charged by charities for their services and the circumstances in which those restrictions would prevent charities from benefitting the public or a section of the public.

1.43 The revised guidance provides that trustees must not run a charity in a way that excludes the poor from benefit. There is no definition of 'poor' or of the charges that the poor cannot afford and the guidance acknowledges that charity law recognises that 'the poor' is a relative term which depends upon the circumstances. However, 'the poor' does not just mean the very poorest in society and can include people of modest means.

1.44 The guidance makes it clear that while the level of provision that trustees make for the poor must be more than minimal or tokenistic, it is for the charity's trustees to decide, taking into account the circumstances of their charity, what provisions should be made to enable the poor to benefit. The trustees' decisions must be within the range of reasonable decisions the trustees could properly make in these circumstances. There is more about trustee decision making in **Chapter 7**.

1.45 The guidance sets out some illustrative examples of how provision may be made to the poor[21] which include:

- educational establishments offering bursaries or collaborating with state schools, including working with or sponsoring academies;
- charities that advance the arts offering concessionary tickets, free lectures or free or reduced membership;
- charities that advance health or relive sickness offering treatment for free or at a reduced rate or providing medical training to nurses/doctors at NHS hospitals which benefit the non-paying patients at those hospitals;
- charities that provide residential care inviting local people who are elderly and in need to join the residents for outings or meals;
- charities that advance heritage or environmental protection or improvement offering free or reduced membership fees or providing free publications and newsletters about preservation and conservation projects.

Public benefit reporting

1.46 As well as a requirement to take the Charity Commission's guidance on public benefit into account in their decision-making, charity trustees are also required to report on the way in which their charity meets the public benefit requirement on an annual basis. There is more about this aspect in **Chapter 14**.

JUDICIAL CONTROL

1.47 The third and final requirement for charitable status imposed by the Charities Act 2011 is that the institution is 'subject to the control of the High Court in the exercise of its jurisdiction with respect to charities'. This fairly inaccessible phrase is aimed at ensuring that any institution claiming charitable status (and the UK tax and other advantages that come with it) is subject to the overall authority of the courts of England and Wales.

1.48 The way in which this requirement applies has been the subject of a number of court decisions.[22] From a practical point of view, it is helpful to look at the criteria that the Charity Commission uses when it is considering an application for registration as a charity, as the Commission can only register an organisation if the law which applies to the organisation is the law of England and Wales. These are not definitive (because only the courts can interpret the

---

21 'Charging for services: illustrative examples of benefits to the poor'.
22 *Camille and Henry Dreyfus Foundation, Inc v IRC* [1954] 2 All ER 466; *Gaudiya Mission v Brahmachary* [1997] All ER 1957; *His Beatitude Archbishop Torkom Manoogian, Armenian Patriarch of Jerusalem v Yolande Sonsino & Others* [2002] EWHC 1304 Ch.

requirement definitively) but reflect the decisions taken by the courts in the past and are a useful guide to their likely approach in the future.

1.49 The criteria for determining the law which applies to an organisation differ depending upon how an institution is set up. The position in relation to a company is straightforward. Normally, only a company incorporated in England and Wales (under the Companies Acts) can qualify. The position for other sorts of institution is more complicated. If the governing document itself does not make it clear which law applies, the law which applies will be that of the country with which the organisation has its closest connection. Whether this is England and Wales will depend on the extent to which:

- the organisation's centre of administration is in England and Wales;
- most of the trustees live in England and Wales; and
- most of the organisation's property is in England and Wales.[23]

CHARITY REGISTRATION

1.50 If it is a company incorporated in England and Wales or otherwise is governed by the law of England and Wales an institution with charitable purposes will qualify as a charity for the purposes of charity law. This brings with it an obligation (under s 35 of the Charities Act 2011) to apply to the Charity Commission to have its name and certain other details added to the register of charities maintained by the Commission unless the institution falls within certain categories of exempt and excepted charities. These exceptions are explained in **Chapter 4**.

1.51 In addition, any charity carrying on activities or fundraising in Scotland should be aware that there may be an obligation to register as a charity in Scotland with the Office of the Scottish Charity Regulator (OSCR). The obligation to register under Scots law (the Charities and Trustee Investment (Scotland) Act 2005) will arise if any of the following criteria are met:

- the charity wishes to represent itself as a charity in Scotland;
- the charity occupies any land or premises in Scotland; or
- the charity carries out activities significant in relation to its size, in any place of business in Scotland.

1.52 It is worth noting that there are no categories of charities exempt or excepted from registration in Scotland, so even if the charity is not registered with the Charity Commission, it may still need to be registered with OSCR in the above circumstances. In order to register with OSCR, it may be necessary to amend the references to 'charitable' and 'charitable purposes' in the charity's governing documents, as these terms have slightly different meanings under

---

[23] 'What makes a charity' (CC4).

Scots law. Fortunately, the Charity Commission and OSCR have agreed standard forms of wording that may be used in this situation, set out in the Charity Commission's guidance entitled *Standard Wording for Objects and Dissolution Clauses*.

1.53 A similar requirement applies in relation to charities carrying on activities in Northern Ireland. Registration with the Charity Commission for Northern Ireland (CCNI) will be required in certain circumstances under the Charities Act (Northern Ireland) 2008 as amended by the Charities Act (Northern Ireland) 2013.

1.54 Once an institution is registered as a charity, it is conclusively presumed to be a charity. This is stated to be 'for all purposes' but does not include tax purposes and charities will need to register separately with HM Revenue & Customs to be able to take advantage of the range of tax exemptions and reliefs available to registered charities (there is more on these in **Chapter 11**). Registration is subject in any event to any later decision by the Charity Commission to remove the charity from the register. There is a wide discretion for the Commission to remove any charity from the register which 'it no longer considers is a charity'.[24] This may be because, for example the charity's purposes are no longer charitable as a result of a change in the law or in society.

CHARITY TRUSTEES

1.55 While it is not part of the Charities Act 2011 definition, almost every charity will in practice also have one or more 'charity trustees'. These are defined by the Charities Act 2011 as 'the persons having the general control and management of the administration of a charity'.[25]

1.56 Knowing who the trustees of a charity are is essential. This is because it is the trustees who are responsible for ensuring that the charity fulfils its purposes in line with its constitution and within the legal framework imposed on charities in England and Wales. And, from their own perspective, it is the trustees who will be personally liable for any failure to meet these responsibilities. Even a brief review of the Charities Act 2011 will show the range of duties owed by charity trustees.

1.57 There is no simple rule of thumb that determines who the charity trustees of any given charity are, mainly because of the diversity of different forms of charitable institution. There is more about charity trusteeship in the context of specific forms of charity within **Chapter 2**. Essentially, however, the charity trustees of a charity are those who are responsible for what it does and how it does it at the highest level. They are sometimes referred to as those who take 'strategic' decisions. This implies that the activities of the charity will be sufficiently complex to require others to implement those decisions, but as a

---

[24] Charities Act 2011, s 34.
[25] Charities Act 2011, s 177.

practical guide this applies in the same way to smaller charities where the trustees will both take and implement strategic decisions.

1.58 The key point from a practical perspective is that the law applies a 'de facto' test to charity trusteeship. It looks at what a person actually does rather than what he is described as or the post that he holds. If the decisions that a person takes are the sort of decisions about general management and control that would or should ordinarily be taken by the trustees then it does not matter that he or she has not been formally appointed as a trustee because the law will treat him or her in the same way as any person who has.

1.59 For this reason, it is important to ensure that charity trustees are distinguished from:

* The people who set the charity up (usually referred to as the 'founders') or who have made donations to it ('donors').
* The people employed by the charity or who volunteer to do work for it.
* The members or other stakeholders in the charity.

1.60 This does not mean that people within one of these categories cannot also be charity trustees. Although a paid employee is unlikely to also act as a trustee, in many cases the trustees are also founders, donors or members. But these roles are in principle separate and distinct. Where the boundaries between the different roles become blurred, problems are more likely to arise. This is essentially a governance issue. There is more about this in **Chapter 5** and **Chapter 8**.

CHAPTER 2

TYPES OF CHARITY

INTRODUCTION

2.1   As explained in **Chapter 1,** the Charities Act 2011 definition of a charitable 'institution' says no more than that it is an institution, 'whether incorporated or not', and includes any 'trust or undertaking'. This means that, in principle at least, almost any legal form can be used to set up a charity provided that the other requirements of the Act (exclusively charitable purposes and judicial control) are satisfied. Partnerships, limited partnerships and limited liability partnerships (each of which must be established for profit) cannot be established as charities.

2.2   In practice, charitable institutions take one of a number of different forms. Before we look at this in more detail, it is helpful to understand that there is a significant distinction between those forms of institution that are 'incorporated' and those that are not.

2.3   An incorporated institution is one that has a legal existence (usually referred to as a 'legal personality') that is separate from the legal personality of the people who are its members or who control its activities or who were responsible for its incorporation in the first place. In other words, an incorporated institution is capable of interacting with the outside world in its own right, rather than via the people who control it. This has several important consequences:

- An incorporated institution can own property in its own name (in what is usually referred to as 'perpetual succession') and deal with that property using the powers it has in its constitution.
- It can enter into agreements with third parties (and sue and be sued on those agreements) in its own name.
- Because it can incur its own liabilities, its members and the other people interested in it will not usually have any liability for them.

2.4   These are essentially the hallmarks of incorporation. It follows that the consequences of unincorporated status are:

- An unincorporated institution can only own or hold property via other people. When those people change, the property must be transferred to their successors.

- It can only enter into agreements (and sue and be sued) in the names of other people.
- The people who enter into agreements or own property for or on behalf of an unincorporated institution are personally liable as a consequence.

2.5   There are a number of different incorporated and unincorporated institutions that operate in the charitable context:

Incorporated	*Unincorporated*
Companies limited by guarantee	Trusts
Companies limited by shares	Associations
Charitable incorporated organisations[1]	
Industrial and provident societies	
Friendly societies	
Corporations	

2.6   The key features of each of these forms of institution are as follows:

COMPANIES LIMITED BY GUARANTEE

2.7   A company limited by guarantee is incorporated under the legislation that governs companies (the Companies Acts). It is the most commonly used form of incorporated charitable institution, but is also often used for a wide range of other non-charitable purposes usually characterised as 'not for profit'; in other words, for purposes which are not aimed at private gain or enrichment (or at least not directly). These include trade associations, clubs and societies, registered social landlords and scientific research associations.

2.8   A company limited by guarantee has a 'two tier' governance structure. It will have one or more 'members' and one or more 'directors'. Because the company is limited by guarantee, the members have no shares in its capital and no entitlement to the dividends and other distributions of its profits and assets to which the members of a company limited by shares (the form of company which is typically used by commercial businesses) are entitled, including any surplus assets on a winding-up. But they do give a 'guarantee' of the company's liabilities in the event that the company is wound up and has insufficient assets to pay its debts. The guarantee is a requirement of the Companies Act 2006,[2] but the guarantee is usually only nominal (typically limited to £1). In other words, the members' liability is limited to this amount if the company is insolvent.

2.9   Membership confers important rights to vote on certain fundamental matters, including:

---

1   Charities Act 2011, Pt 11, ss 204–250. See **2.31**.
2   Companies Act 2006, s 3(3).

- altering the company's constitution;
- the appointment and removal of its directors; and
- winding the company up.

2.10 The directors are responsible for the day-to-day management and control of the company. For that reason, they will be its 'charity trustees' under the Charities Act 2011 as well as its directors under the Companies Acts (although the directors of a charitable company will in practice often be described as its 'trustees'). This dual role is explained in more detail in **Chapter 5**. A charitable company will usually have a minimum of two directors. The directors are usually referred to collectively as the 'board'.

2.11 A company will also usually have a secretary (although the Companies Act 2006 does not make this a requirement for a private company).[3] The secretary is responsible for assisting the directors to ensure that the company complies with its administrative obligations under the Companies Acts. In some charitable companies, the secretary will often also be the 'clerk' to the trustees, with responsibility for assisting the trustees by organising meetings, preparing and distributing agendas and papers etc.

2.12 The constitution of a company limited by guarantee established before the coming into force of the relevant provisions of the Companies Act 2006 (on 1 October 2009) is set out in its memorandum and articles of association. Technically, these are two separate documents although in practice they are almost always referred to and treated as one. The Companies Act 2006 made some significant changes to the way in which a company's constitution is structured. For companies incorporated after 1 October 2009, the memorandum of association is no more than a document stating that the first members of the company (usually referred to as the 'subscribers') wish to form, and have agreed to become members of, the company.[4]

2.13 All of the other provisions of a company's constitution are set out in its articles of association (as supplemented by any resolution passed by members or agreement made between the members of the company). The existence of any resolutions or agreements can be checked by carrying out a search with Companies House, because there is an obligation to ensure that a written memorandum of their terms is filed within 15 days of their being made.[5]

2.14 Every company must have articles of association. If none are registered when the company is incorporated, the Companies Act 2006 provides that a set of 'model articles' prescribed for limited companies (with different model articles for different types of company) will apply.[6] A company can also choose to adopt some or all of the provisions of the model articles or to adopt a set of

---

[3]   Companies Act 2006, s 270.
[4]   Companies Act 2006, s 8.
[5]   Companies Act 2006, s 30.
[6]   Companies Act 2006, s 20.

articles that expressly exclude the model articles. A similar set of provisions applies to companies incorporated before the coming into force of the Companies Act 2006.

2.15 Because the articles of a company set up after 1 October 2009 (when the relevant provisions of the Companies Act 2006 came into force) will set out the purposes for which a company is established (often referred to it as its 'objects'), a company that wishes to establish itself as a charity will need to adopt articles which expressly confirm its charitable purposes and the powers which it can use to achieve those purposes. As far as a company's objects are concerned, the Companies Act 2006 provides[7] that, unless the company's articles specifically restrict the objects, they are unrestricted. Clearly, in order to qualify as a charity, a company's objects will therefore need to be restricted to charitable purposes only.

2.16 The articles regulate how the company is managed and administered by its members and the directors. They will specify:

- How new members of the company will be appointed and the circumstances in which they will stop being members.
- Whether the members have to pay a subscription to the company.
- Whether the company will have different kinds of member with different kinds of rights in relation to the company.
- Provisions for members' general meetings and the way in which they can vote and count in the quorum.
- How the directors are appointed by the members (and often also by the directors themselves) and the circumstances in which they will stop being directors.
- Provisions governing directors' meetings and the way in which they vote and count in the quorum.
- Provisions designed to assist the directors to run the company effectively, including by appointing committees and advisory boards.

2.17 The memorandum of a charitable company incorporated before 1 October 2009 is more significant. In particular, it will spell out the purposes for which the company is established, its powers to achieve those purposes and the fact that the liability of its members is limited. Its articles will also spell out how the company is to be managed and administered by the members and directors (as in **2.16** above). A company incorporated before 1 October 2009 will continue to have a memorandum and articles of association in this form. The fact that the Companies Act 2006 prescribes a different procedure for incorporating companies does not affect the validity of the constitutions of charitable companies incorporated before the new provisions come into force.

---

[7]   Companies Act 2006, s 31.

2.18 The relationship between a charitable company's members and its directors, and the way in which the constitution regulates that relationship, is one of the most important aspects of good governance. See **Chapter 5**.

2.19 Not every company limited by guarantee will be a charity. That depends upon whether certain key parts of the constitution are adapted so that it will qualify as an 'institution … established for charitable purposes only'. In practice, the key provisions are:

- The objects of the company must be charitable (see **Chapter 1**).
- They must also be exclusively charitable. It is not possible to have non-charitable objects that are ancillary to charitable objects; they must either be expressed as powers or left out altogether if a company is to qualify as a charity.
- The constitution prevents any of the members or directors from benefitting from the company's assets. In this context, 'benefit' means financial or monetary benefit. This is because a company capable of conferring benefits on its members or directors would not be able to satisfy the public benefit requirement under the Charities Act 2011. There are some permitted exceptions from this rule for members and directors but these are generally small in scale. Benefits for the directors of a charitable company are explained in **Chapter 6**.
- The constitution must also include a provision that obliges any surplus assets on a winding up of a charitable company to be applied for similar charitable purposes rather than passing to the company's members. This is another aspect of the requirement that members should not benefit from a charitable company's assets, but it should be expressly stated.

2.20 A company limited by guarantee is incorporated and regulated by the Registrar of Companies (usually referred to as 'Companies House'). In practice, a charitable company limited by guarantee is regulated by both Companies House (under the Companies Acts) and the Charity Commission (under the Charities Acts) and must generally submit an annual report and accounts to both bodies.

COMPANIES LIMITED BY SHARES

2.21 A company limited by shares is also incorporated under the Companies Acts and is the usual legal form adopted by those undertaking trading and other commercial activities in the UK.

2.22 A company limited by shares has an authorised capital in respect of which it will issue one or more shares. In a commercial context, the shares entitle their holder to a proportion of the company's profits and its assets in the event that it is wound up and are often issued in order to raise funds for the company from those subscribing for the shares. The shareholders themselves are recorded in a register and the company will usually issue certificates to them in respect of each holding. If a shareholder wishes to transfer their shares, they must complete a form and submit it to the company, which will update its register and issue a new certificate to the new shareholder.

2.23 Companies limited by shares also have a 'two tier' structure. Every company will have at least one shareholder (sometimes referred to as a 'member') and at least one director. In addition to an entitlement to a share in the company's profits and assets, shares confer the same rights on shareholders as the rights exercisable by members of a company limited by guarantee.

2.24 The directors are responsible for the day-to-day management and administration of the company in exactly the same way as the directors of a company limited by guarantee. The relationship between the members and the directors will also be key to the governance of the company. See **Chapter 5.**

2.25 The constitution of a company limited by shares is also set out in its memorandum and articles of association. They will contain provisions very similar to those in the memorandum and articles of a company limited by guarantee, except that there will be provisions for the company's share capital, including the rights of shareholders to transfer shares and the rights of directors to issue new shares.

2.26 The articles of association will be in the model form specified by the Companies Act 2006 (or, in the case of companies incorporated before that Act came into force, the form specified by the Companies Act 1985) unless some other provision is made.

2.27 There are relatively few charitable companies limited by shares. This is primarily because the existence of share capital is a complication that most charities neither want nor need. Shareholders will not in any event be entitled to any dividend or other kind of distribution on their shares and, because shareholders are actually entitled to shares in the company, they must transfer them whenever they wish to resign as members of the company and the company must update its register. These are generally unnecessary complications.

2.28 The members of a company limited by guarantee, on the other hand, are able to join or resign as members without any significant complications. So where there is a choice between using a company limited by shares and a company limited by guarantee in order to set up a charity, it will usually be most straightforward to use a guarantee company except where there is some other compelling reason for using a share company. This is the approach generally taken by the Charity Commission to new charities in any event.

2.29 If a charitable company is to be limited by shares, its constitution will need to be adapted in much the same way as the constitution of a company limited by guarantee. In particular, there will need to be an express prohibition on any dividend or other distribution on shares. Like a company limited by shares, it will be subject to regulation by both Companies House and the Charity Commission.

Terminology

2.30   The terms used to describe the members and directors in the context of a charitable company are often confusing. The directors of a charitable company are often referred to as its 'trustees' and that is the approach we have adopted in this book. However, there are no hard and fast rules about this. Some charitable companies may refer to their directors as 'directors'. The company's constitution will usually define its directors in a particular way although they may sometimes be referred to in practice using a different description from the one set out in the constitution. Some of the more common terms that may come up in practice are as follows:

Word	*Meaning*
Director	A director of a company under the legislation which governs companies
Member	A member of a company limited by guarantee or a shareholder
Shareholder	A member of a company limited by shares
Subscriber	A member of a company when it was first set up
Trustee	Another way of describing a director of a charitable company
Governor	Another way of describing a director of a charitable company (often, but not always, a charitable school or other educational charity)
Board	One of the ways in which the directors can be described collectively
Council	Another one of the ways in which the board of directors can be described collectively
Secretary	The company secretary under the legislation that applies to companies
Treasurer	A director who has been given primary responsibility for a charitable company's finances. This is not a post required by law, but the articles of some companies provide for it
Chairman	The chairman of the board of directors (who will often also be the chairman at general meetings of members)
Company	The company itself but references in the articles to 'resolutions of the company' actually refer to resolutions of the members
Patron	Usually an honorary position which confers no rights and obligations and does not make an individual a trustee

President   Usually another way of describing a patron

CHARITABLE INCORPORATED ORGANISATIONS

2.31 A charitable incorporated organisation (CIO) is a new form of incorporated entity designed specifically for charitable activities. The legislation for CIOs was introduced into the Charities Act 1993 by the Charities Act 2006, but the CIO did not become available as a legal form for charities until further regulations were made which supplemented the statutory provisions (now found in Part 11 of the Charities Act 2011).[8] New charities could register as CIOs from December 2012 although a longer timetable was prescribed for those unincorporated charities wishing to incorporate as a CIO and incorporated charities wishing to convert.

2.32 Before the introduction of the CIO, anyone wishing to set up an incorporated charity would usually use a company limited by guarantee, adapted to ensure that it could qualify as a charity. Adaptation was required because limited companies were originally designed for commercial use, rather than charitable activities.

2.33 As a consequence, charitable companies are subject to regulation by both Companies House and the Charity Commission. The CIO is an attempt to create a new entity bringing with it the advantages of incorporation but without the burden of dual regulation and with the flexibility to create a constitution aimed specifically at charitable activities and governance.

2.34 The key features of a CIO are:

*   It is incorporated.
*   It has a 'two tier' structure made up of one or more members and one or more charity trustees (although the trustees and the members can be identical; see Charities Act 2011, s 206(6)).
*   The liability of the members for the CIO's debts can be limited to a maximum specified amount (which can be a nominal amount of £1) or excluded altogether.
*   It has a single constitution that must comply with certain requirements set out in the Charitable Incorporated Organisations (General) Regulations 2012/3012. The constitution must also be as similar to a statutory form set out in regulations made by the Charity Commission or as near to their form as the 'circumstances admit', which in practice means the constitution must follow one of the model constitutions produced by the Commission.[9]

---

[8]   Charities Act 2011, Pt 11, Ch 1; Charitable Incorporated Organisations (General) Regulations 2012, SI 2012/3012; and the Charitable Incorporated Organisations (Insolvency and Dissolution) Regulations 2012, SI 2012/3013.

[9]   Charities Act 2011, s 206(5); Charities Act 2011 (Charitable Incorporated Organisations) (Constitutions) Regulations 2012 (not yet in force at the time of writing).

- The constitution of a CIO needs to provide that none of its income or property can be paid or transferred, directly or indirectly, by way of dividend or otherwise by profit to any of the CIO's members and that no charity trustee of a CIO should obtain any form of financial benefit from his or her position, unless that benefit is authorised by the CIO's constitution, or by a statutory provision, or by the court or the Charity Commission.

2.35 The legal regime which applies to CIOs[10] is modelled on, and is broadly similar to, that governing companies under the Companies Acts and Insolvency Act 1986. There is more detail about this at **2.73**.

INDUSTRIAL AND PROVIDENT SOCIETIES

2.36 A charity may be set up as an industrial and provident society intended to be conducted for the 'benefit of the community' under the Industrial and Provident Societies Act 1965 (known as a 'Community Benefit Society' or 'BenCom').[11] There is another form of industrial and provident society which can be incorporated under the 1965 Act (which is intended to trade on a co-operative basis) but this cannot be used to establish a charity.

2.37 An industrial and provident society is an incorporated body. Like a company, it has a 'two tier' structure of members and trustees. Its members and trustees have limited liability and the society can hold assets, and sue and be sued, in its own name. Many of the provisions of the Industrial and Provident Societies Acts 1965, 1967, 1975, 1978 and 2002 (together with the Co-operatives and Community Benefit Societies Act 2003) incorporate provisions in a very similar form to the provisions of the companies legislation.

2.38 The Co-operative and Community Benefit Societies Bill, which at the time of writing, is due to be introduced and enacted in the current Parliamentary session (May 2013 to April 2014), will consolidate and replace existing legislation relating to industrial and provident societies which includes the Industrial and Provident Societies Act 1965 and 1967 and the Friendly and Industrial and Provident Societies Act 1968 and is designed to reduce legal complexity for new and existing societies.

2.39 Industrial and provident societies have traditionally been used to set up charitable housing associations (registered as 'registered providers of social housing' under the Housing and Regeneration Act 2008). Any society which is registered as a registered provider under the Housing and Regeneration Act 2008 is an exempt charity (they are regulated by the Financial Conduct

---

[10] Charities Act 2011, Pt 11, Chapter 1; Charitable Incorporated Organisations (General) Regulations 2012, SI 2012/3012; and the Charitable Incorporated Organisations (Insolvency and Dissolution) Regulations 2012, SI 2012/3013.

[11] Industrial and Provident Societies Act 1965, s 1.

Authority and, insofar as their status as a 'registered provider' is concerned, the Homes & Communities Agency acting through its Regulation Committee) rather than the Charity Commission.

2.40 Before the coming into force of the Charities Act 2006, all industrial and provident societies were exempt charities. However, this is no longer the case, as the Charities Act 2006 required all exempt charities either to have a principal regulator to oversee their compliance with charity law, or (where there is no suitable body to act as principal regulator) to lose their exempt status and be regulated by the Charity Commission. At the time of writing, it is not yet clear how charitable industrial and provident societies will be regulated in future.

FRIENDLY SOCIETIES

2.41 A friendly society is a 'mutual assurance' association of individual members who, in order to qualify as members, must be poor. A friendly society has corporate status under the Friendly Societies Act 1992 and can hold property in its own name. Charitable friendly societies are exempt charities and are currently regulated by the Financial Conduct Authority rather than the Charity Commission. However, following the coming into force of the Charities Act 2006, no principal regulator for friendly societies has been identified and therefore their status as exempt charities is uncertain (see **2.40** above).

CORPORATIONS

2.42 A 'corporation' is any other incorporated institution that can own property, and enter into agreements and sue and be sued on those agreements, in its own name. A charitable corporation may be established by Royal Charter or by Act of Parliament. Other corporations (such as local authorities) may hold property on charitable trusts, although they will not themselves be charitable because not all of their purposes will be charitable purposes. The constitution of a corporation will depend upon the way in which it has been established and will in any event vary from corporation to corporation. A corporation established by a Royal Charter will, for example, have all of the powers and capacity of a natural person.[12] A detailed analysis of the law in relation to corporations is outside the scope of this book.

TRUSTS

2.43 Trusts were originally developed as a way of protecting assets, usually in a family context, by separating their 'legal' ownership from their 'beneficial' ownership. The legal owners ('trustees') hold and control trust assets for the benefit of other people ('beneficiaries'). The trustees are under a duty to

---

[12]   *Pearce v University of Aston (No 2)* [1991] 2 All ER 469.

safeguard the assets. If they do not, the beneficiaries can seek compensation from them for any losses that they suffer.

2.44 The beneficiaries of a charitable trust are its charitable purposes. Because there is no way in which a purpose can enforce a trustee's duties, this role is taken by the Attorney-General and the Charity Commission. See **Chapter 4**.

2.45 A charitable trust is easy to establish, requiring only a single trust deed to set it up, and is regulated only by the Charity Commission. A trust can also be established by a will or by a conveyance of property or a transfer of other assets. The trust deed or a trust in a will need not be in any particular form, but will ideally address certain fundamental points:

- It will specify the charitable objects of the trust.
- It will identify the first trustees.
- The trustees' entitlement to benefit personally from the trust will be limited, with any exceptions clearly spelled out.
- The trustees' powers to apply the trust's assets (and to invest and insure them etc) will be specified.
- It will explain how the trustees must take decisions, how often they must meet, the quorum required in order to pass resolutions etc.

2.46 Not every charitable trust will be established by a clearly drafted trust deed or will. This is because all that is required in order to establish a valid charitable trust is a sufficient degree of certainty about three things. First, the charitable purposes of the trust must be certain. Secondly, that the assets which are subject to the trust are certain. Thirdly, that there is sufficient certainty that the creation of a charitable trust was intended.

2.47 Subject to the requirement that a declaration of trust over land or any interest in land must be in writing,[13] there are no technical words that must be used in order to establish a trust, provided the three certainties mentioned in **2.46** are present. In principle, therefore, a charitable trust over assets other than land could be declared orally provided there is sufficient evidence of the position. Equally, charitable trusts may be established by documents other than trust deeds and wills. Many charities are established by a conveyance or transfer of assets to be held by the transferees for particular charitable purposes. Provided the three certainties are present, a charitable trust will be established in such cases, although a Scheme of the Charity Commission is often required to supplement the powers given to the charity trustees to deal with the assets (see **Chapter 4**).

2.48 It is open to anyone who wishes to establish a charitable trust to specify terms on which the relevant assets are to be held. Charitable trusts can (and often do) state that the trustees have a power to hold and invest assets with a

---

[13] Law of Property Act 1925, s 53(1)(b).

view to applying the investment income that is produced but with an obligation to retain the capital of the assets in perpetuity. Other trusts will specify that trustees have a power (or perhaps an obligation) to apply both the capital and income of the charitable trust's assets. The terms of a charitable trust will differ from case to case and a detailed examination of the provisions of the trust's constitution will always be required in order to determine the powers and obligations of the trustees in relation to the charity's assets. There is more about this in **Chapter 9**.

2.49   There are a number of legal rules which govern the way in which gifts for charitable purposes will take effect in the event that they should fail. A detailed discussion of this area is outside the scope of this book.[14]

2.50   Most charitable trusts will have a 'single tier' governance structure simply made up of the trustees. But it would be perfectly possible to write a trust deed so that it has members who appoint and remove the trustees or exercise other powers (there are a number of charitable trusts that include provisions along these lines). See **Chapter 5**.

2.51   Because a trust is unincorporated, it can only interact with the outside world via its trustees. This means that:

•   The trustees must hold all of the trust's assets in their own names or the name of a nominee on their behalf. If the assets are held in the trustees' names they must be transferred whenever a trustee is appointed or retires.

•   The trustees must enter into all contracts that relate to the trust personally. They will remain liable even after they have retired as trustees, unless there is a provision for them to be released from their obligations.

ASSOCIATIONS

2.52   A charitable unincorporated association will exist where two or more people (usually individuals) make a legally binding agreement between themselves to act together to promote or advance one or more charitable purposes. There are no statutory formalities which must be observed in order to set up an association but the terms of the agreement between the members will usually be set out in a body of rules. The rules will vary from association to association, but will usually contain provisions relating to the admission of new members, the retirement of existing members, the way in which assets are held and who will have day-to-day management and control of the association's activities.

2.53   In many cases (although not all) an association's rules will provide for the appointment of a committee of members who are responsible for the management and control of the association's activities. They will be the

---

[14]   For further information see eg *Tudor on Charities* (Sweet & Maxwell, 9th edn, 2003).

association's charity trustees. An association set up in this way will have a 'two tier' governance structure which is broadly similar to the structure of a company or a CIO. However, an association is not an incorporated body, cannot hold assets or enter into contracts on its own and does not confer any limited liability on its members or its trustees. Because the assets of an association cannot be held in its own name, they must be held by individuals on trust for it. The rules will usually identify the people who are to act as trustees. This may be the members of a committee, although some rules will provide that assets must be held by a separate group of trustees from the trustees who make up the committee. Generally, the trustees who hold the association's assets will act only on the direction of the committee and not on their own initiative.

2.54 Because an association is not able to enter into contracts in its own name, contracts must be entered into on behalf of all of the members of the association, usually by the members of the committee. In order to ensure that contracts can properly be entered into by committee members, the rules will usually need to contain an express power of delegation (or there must be an appropriate statutory power). There is more about delegation in relation to charitable unincorporated associations in **Chapter 8**.

SCHEMES

2.55 A Scheme is the legal mechanism by which the Charity Commission can alter the provisions of a charity's constitution in certain circumstances. A Scheme will not usually be made where a charity has an existing express or statutory power to amend its own constitution. Incorporated charities will generally have an appropriate power of amendment, so Schemes are invariably made in relation to existing charitable trusts and other unincorporated charities. The making of a Scheme will not alter the fundamental legal structure of a charitable trust or any other unincorporated charity, but it may become a charity's constitutional document. While a charity cannot be established, therefore, by way of a Scheme, it may regulate the charity's governance arrangements.

NEW CHARITIES

2.56 Anyone looking to set up a new charity will need to choose which of the forms of charitable institution will best serve their purposes. It is difficult to give any definitive guidance on how to approach this question because a lot depends on what a new charity is intended to do, but there are certain fundamental considerations.

2.57 A key consideration is whether to use an incorporated or unincorporated body. This depends on a number of things.

2.58 Is liability likely to be an issue because of what the charity will do (eg provide services or undertake a particular project) or because of the assets it will own (eg land that may be contaminated)? If the answer to this question is 'yes', then using an incorporated body will confer limited liability for members and trustees in most circumstances. The trustees (and, in certain circumstances, the members) of an unincorporated body will almost inevitably be personally liable in respect of what their charity does and how it does it. That liability may be limited in other ways but these are all less certain than the limited liability of an incorporated body. See **Chapters 5** and **6**.

2.59 An incorporated body can hold assets in its own name. While the trustees of an unincorporated body can in most circumstances use a nominee to hold assets on their behalf, arrangements must be made for title to pass from trustee to trustee as they are appointed and retire. This is not difficult but adds to the burden of administering the charity properly and can cause problems if it is not done. The appointment and retirement of trustees of an incorporated body has no impact on the assets held in its name.

2.60 An incorporated body can enter into contracts in its own name. The trustees of an unincorporated body must enter into contracts that relate to it personally. Again, this is not in itself a particular problem but it adds to the burden of administering the charity and the risk that it is not done properly.

2.61 The position in relation to asset holding and entering into contracts for unincorporated charities is sometimes solved by appointing a corporate trustee or by incorporating the charity trustees under Part 12 of the Charities Act 2011 (see **Chapter 6**). While this may simplify the position in relation to asset holding and entering into contracts (and using a corporate trustee may improve the liability position of the individual trustees), creating additional incorporated bodies may add to the burden of administering the charity (although not usually significantly).

2.62 Some take the view that unincorporated bodies are easier to administer than incorporated bodies, partly because they are not subject to formal legal administrative requirements and partly because they are regulated with a 'lighter touch'. It is certainly true that the Charity Commission alone regulates most unincorporated bodies, whereas both the Commission and Companies House regulate companies. It is also true that most unincorporated bodies can operate fairly informally within the terms of their constitutions.

2.63 Having said this, the filing and reporting requirements of the Commission tend to match those of Companies House and, more generally, there is a strong argument that the precisely formulated and comprehensive requirements of the legislation that applies to companies actually provides a good and easily understood framework for effective administration, whereas an unincorporated body's constitution may not be particularly clear or easily understood. In practice, a lot will depend upon how complex the charity's affairs (and therefore its administration) are likely to be.

2.64 Some also take the view that an unincorporated body can be established more easily and cheaply than an incorporated body. This is probably true of the most simply constituted unincorporated body but the availability of good precedent documents and online advice from the Charity Commission and other sources in relation to companies makes the difference marginal in the majority of cases.

2.65 Incorporated bodies (and companies in particular) are almost inevitably more familiar to commercial entities (particularly banks and other financial institutions) that the charity may wish to engage with than unincorporated bodies. So, for example, a bank will find it easier to lend to a charitable company than a charitable trust because it routinely lends to companies and the charitable component does not fundamentally alter the way in which a company looks and behaves. This is not an insurmountable problem for unincorporated bodies, but may be an issue depending on what the charity wishes to do. So most banks will be able to open an account for a charitable trust as easily as an account for a charitable company, but may find it more difficult (and therefore more time consuming and costly) to enter into a syndicated loan agreement with it. In particular, an unincorporated body is not able to grant a 'floating charge' over its assets as security for borrowings. There is more about borrowing at **Chapter 12**.

2.66 The table below summarises the position:

Issue	*Incorporated*	*Unincorporated*
Liability	Limited liability in most circumstances	Personal liability for trustees
Asset holding	Assets held in body's own name	Assets held in names of trustees (except where trustee body incorporated)[15]
Contracts	Body contracts in own name	Trustees contract in their own names
Administration	Greater degree of regulation/well-established administrative framework	Lesser degree of regulation/less well-established administrative framework
Set-up	Arguably more complicated documents and set-up process	Arguably less complicated documents and set-up process
Recognition	Greater degree of third party recognition	Less recognisable by third parties

2.67 On balance, incorporated status is likely to be an advantage for any charity that plans to do things that may involve liability, that will own assets

---

[15] See **6.28**.

that are either complex or used operationally or carry with them some associated liabilities. The most obvious examples of this are:

- Taking a lease or buying the freehold of a property.
- Raising finance, for example, by taking a bank loan, particularly where a floating charge is to be given as security for the loan (although note that CIOs will be unable to give a floating charge as the Charity Commission does not maintain an equivalent to the register of charges maintained by Companies House for companies).
- Employing people.
- Giving advice or entering into contracts to provide goods or services.
- Organising events involving members of the public.

CHOOSING AN UNINCORPORATED BODY

2.68   That is not to say that unincorporated charities do not have their place. They are likely to be most appropriate in the following circumstances:

- Charities that do no more than hold and invest their assets with a view to making straightforward grants and donations to other charities or for other charitable purposes, usually referred to as 'grant making trusts' or 'foundations'.
- Charities established by groups of individuals for a particular purpose that does not involve any significant liability or potential liability, for example a league of friends that organises hospital visits or a charity that promotes a particular religion.
- A charity established to do no more than raise funds for a particular purpose, for example an appeal to raise funds for new hospital equipment or facilities or the 'friends of' a university, college or school looking to raise funds from alumni or parents.

2.69   Which form of unincorporated body should be used will depend upon what it is intended to do. It will generally be most appropriate to set up a grant making trust or foundation or an appeal as a trust, whereas a league of friends or other body involving participation by a group of members will generally be an association. A Scheme will only be relevant to existing charities and is not an option in relation to new charities.[16]

CHOOSING AN INCORPORATED BODY

2.70   If an incorporated body is required, the choice will usually be between a company limited by guarantee and a CIO, unless there are particular reasons for using some other form. For example, historically many housing associations

---

[16]   See further at **4.26**.

have been set up as industrial and provident societies in order to ensure that they are exempt charities, regulated only by the Financial Conduct Authority (previously the Financial Services Authority) and the Homes & Communities Agency (previously the Housing Corporation) and not also by the Charity Commission.[17] An existing charity may petition for incorporation by Royal Charter in recognition of the particular value of its work.

2.71 The main advantage of using a CIO is likely to be that it is specifically designed to be used as a vehicle for charitable activities and will be regulated only by the Charity Commission. The main advantage of using a company limited by guarantee as against a CIO is that a company is a long established legal form governed by a well-developed and comprehensive body of statute and case law. There are very few questions about the way in which such companies function that cannot be answered by reference to that body of law. By contrast, a CIO is the creation of a relatively recently enacted statute, the Charities Act 2006. The relevant provisions are now found in the Charities Act 2011 and regulations made under it, which describe what a CIO is and how it functions in, at least by comparison to the Companies Acts, a few brief provisions and which are not presently the subject of any decided case law which might supplement the statutory provisions.

2.72 The chief disadvantage of using a CIO, therefore, is likely to be that there is presently not the same degree of certainty about how it will function in most circumstances as there is about a company limited by guarantee. This may mean that, in practice, there will be a degree of caution about using a CIO rather than a company. Lawyers in particular may be reluctant to recommend the use of a CIO to their clients while it remains a relatively new legal form.

2.73 In our view, this would be an overly cautious approach to an entity specifically designed for carrying out charitable activities, particularly when the Charities Act 2011 contains a range of provisions which are aimed at ensuring that CIOs will function in a certain and reliable way and many of the provisions intended to regulate CIOs are based upon the framework of the Companies Acts and the Insolvency Act 1986. For example:

- Subject to anything in its constitution, a CIO has power to do anything which is 'calculated to further its purposes or is conducive or incidental to doing so'.[18]
- In favour of a person who deals with a CIO in good faith and has given consideration in money or money's worth, the validity of any act done by the CIO, and the power of the charity trustees of the CIO to act to bind it, cannot be called into question on the ground that the CIO either lacked the relevant powers in its constitution or because of any constitutional

---

[18] Charities Act 2011, s 216(1).

limitation on those powers unless the third party actually knew that the act was beyond the CIO's powers or contravened any limitation in the constitution.[19]

- A party to an arrangement or transaction with a CIO is not bound to enquire whether it is within the CIO's constitutional capacity or the powers of its charity trustees.[20]

- Sections 245–247 of the Charities Act 2011 give the Secretary of State a wide power to make regulations governing how CIOs operate.[21] This power is likely to be used to plug any gaps in the CIO regime as they appear.

However, in comparison to the regulatory regime which applies to companies, there are (at the time of writing) some notable 'gaps' in the legislation which regulates CIOs. For example, there is no proposed equivalent of the register of charges maintained by Companies House for CIOs, with the result that CIOs may find it difficult to secure lending arrangements.

2.74 A better reason for remaining cautious about using a CIO while it remains reasonably unusual is that it is likely to be less recognisable to third parties than a company limited by guarantee. This may cause practical difficulties, although the position may well change as more CIOs are incorporated and registered as charities.

2.75 Charitable companies and industrial and provident societies will, in future, be able to convert to become CIOs under a statutory procedure in the Charities Act 2011[22] although Parliament must pass further legislation before this is possible. The possibility of conversion would enable anyone who wishes to establish a new charity, but who is cautious about the workability of the CIO legislation, to opt for one of the more traditional approaches in the knowledge that there is a statutory provision for its conversion into a CIO should that, with the benefit of hindsight, turn out to be the best approach.

2.76 In what could be considered another notable omission from the legislation, there is no equivalent procedure for existing unincorporated charities wishing to incorporate as CIOs. Incorporation will need to take place by registering a new CIO and then transferring the unincorporated charity's assets to that body, in much the same way as incorporating as a company limited by guarantee.

---

[19] Charities Act 2011, s 218(1) and (2).
[20] Charities Act 2011, s 218(4).
[21] See eg Charitable Incorporated Organisations (General) Regulations 2012, SI 2012/3012 and Charitable Incorporated Organisations (Insolvency and Dissolution) Regulations 2012, SI 2012/3013.
[22] Charities Act 2011, ss 228–234.

COMMUNITY INTEREST COMPANIES

2.77   Community interest companies (or CICs, as they are usually referred to) were introduced by the Companies (Audit, Investigations and Community Enterprise) Act 2004. They are intended to be a legal form earmarked specifically for those who wish to pursue some sort of enterprise in the interests of the public (or 'community') rather than their own personal economic interests. In other words, a CIC is an entity which can only function on a 'not for profit' basis. The hope is that CICs will develop as a 'brand' for developing community interest in much the same way as the 'charity' brand.

2.78   CICs can be incorporated under the Companies Acts as a company limited by shares or by guarantee. The provisions of the Companies Acts apply to a CIC in the same way as they apply to any other company limited by shares or by guarantee, except to the extent that they are modified by the Community Interest Company Regulations 2005.[23] The most significant modification is the introduction of an 'asset lock'. Essentially, a CIC's assets must be held for its community interest objects and any distributions to any of its members (other than another CIC or charity) must be on 'arms' length' terms. In other words, the CIC must receive value in return for any payment it makes to a member for goods or services supplied to it. There are also specific provisions that limit the amount of any dividend that can be paid by a CIC to its members.

2.79   Prior to the introduction of the CIC, the usual way in which to establish an entity with community interests as its objects rather than personal profit was to use a company (usually limited by guarantee) with a specific provision in its memorandum precluding any distribution of its profits for any purpose other than its public or community interest objects. While the constitution of a 'not for profit' company could provide that none of its assets should be distributed to its members, this could not override the fundamental principle of company law that, subject to any agreement between them requiring unanimity, 75% or more of the members of the company could at any time resolve to alter those provisions. CICs were intended to solve this potential problem by creating the 'asset lock' we have described.

2.80   Section 22 of the Companies Act 2006 introduced statutory provisions for the 'entrenchment' of specific provisions of a company's articles, so that they can provide that they can be altered only if particular conditions are met or procedures are complied with. This could include, for example, a condition that the company's assets cannot be distributed to its members without their unanimous agreement. However, no provision for entrenchment can ever prevent all of the members of a company from agreeing to alter its constitution.[24] The asset lock provided for by the provisions governing CICs goes further than this.

---

[23]   SI 2005/1788.
[24]   Society for Promoting Employment of Women [1927] WN 145.

2.81 A CIC cannot be registered as a charity. CICs are regulated by the CIC Regulator at Companies House rather than the Charity Commission. They do not qualify for the exemptions and reliefs from tax which can be claimed by charities but are subject to a 'lighter touch' regulatory regime. It is possible that what a CIC could be established to do may be charitable. In deciding whether or not to establish a CIC or a charity, the decision to set up a charity will usually be driven by the desire to obtain the exemptions and reliefs from tax available to charities and the degree of public recognition given to the 'charity' brand (particularly where funds are to be raised from donors who will wish to see a high degree of regulation and accountability).

2.82 A CIC is likely to be more appropriate where tax is not a particular concern or where there is a desire to make limited distributions to its members (which will not be possible with a charity) and the potential disadvantage of the lower degree of public recognition likely to be given to the 'CIC' brand is outweighed by the desire for a lighter touch regulatory regime.

CHAPTER 3

MODERN LEGAL FRAMEWORK

3.1   Charities are subject to a number of different legal regimes. The position can be summarised as follows:

- All charities are subject to charity law.
- All charities are also subject to tax law.
- Every charity will be subject to the legal regime that applies to its particular legal form.
- Every charity will also be subject to the legal regimes that apply as a consequence of what it does.
- All charities will be subject to legal regimes that apply generally in the UK, including the Equality Act 2010 and the Bribery Act 2010.

CHARITY LAW

3.2   The law that applies to all charities, irrespective of the legal form that they take, is set out for the most part in the Charities Act 2011 and in a number of statutory instruments made under the Charities Acts 1992 to 2011. The purpose of the Charities Act 2011 was not to change the law but to consolidate existing charity law in order to make it easier to understand. The 2011 Act replaces and repeals most of the Charities Acts 1992, 1993 and 2006 and all of the Recreational Charities Act 1958 although it does not replace the law on certain forms of fundraising, which continue to be governed by the 1992 Act, and the law on public collections by charities, which continue to be governed by the 2006 Act.[1]

3.3   The Charities Act 2011 governs, among other things:

- the meaning of a 'charity' and 'charitable purposes' (see **Chapter 1**);
- the status of the Charity Commission and its regulatory powers (see **Chapter 4**);
- the disposition of land owned by charities (see **Chapter 9**) and the charging of charity land (see **Chapter 12**);
- charity accounts, reports and returns (see **Chapter 14**); and

---

[1]   At the time of writing, the relevant provisions of the Charities Act 2006 in respect of public collections are not yet fully in force.

- the Charity Tribunal (see **Chapter 4**).

3.4   Part 10 of the Charities Act 2011 relates specifically to charitable companies. It regulates certain aspects of the relationship between charity and company law as they apply to charitable companies. Part 11 of the Charities Act 2011 relates specifically to CIOs. Part 13 relates to unincorporated charities and gives certain powers to the trustees of unincorporated charities.

3.5   Certain 'exempt charities' are not subject to some of the provisions of the 2011 Act. Other 'excepted charities' are not obliged to register with the Charity Commission. There is more information about exempt and excepted charities in **Chapter 4**.

3.6   The 1992 and 2011 Acts are by no means comprehensive and are essentially additions to a body of court decisions that deal with the aspects of charity law not dealt with by the Acts themselves and which continue to clarify the meaning of the statutory provisions.

TAX LAW

3.7   Every charity will be subject to tax law. Tax law is governed by a number of different statutes governing different taxes. This is dealt with in more detail in **Chapter 11**.

REGIMES THAT APPLY TO DIFFERENT LEGAL FORMS

Companies

3.8   Charities established as companies are subject to the provisions of the legislation that governs all companies established in England and Wales, the Companies Act 2006. This is complex legislation, some of which is not relevant to charitable companies, but much of which is. In particular:

- Provisions relating to a company's capacity and the execution of documents (Companies Act 2006, Part 4) (see **Chapter 8**).
- Provisions regulating the information about the company that must be made available on a company's letterhead and other documents (Companies Act 2006, Part 5, Chapter 2).
- Provisions dealing with the duties of the company's directors (Companies Act 2006, Part 10, Chapter 2) (see **Chapter 6**).
- Provisions in relation to members' meetings (Companies Act 2006, Part 13) (see **Chapter 5**).
- Provisions in relation to accounts and reports (Companies Act 2006, Part 15) (see **Chapter 14**).

3.9 The Companies Act is supplemented by a large and comprehensive body of case-law that regulates those aspects of the legal position of companies which the Act does not cater for.

3.10 The Companies Act regulates the rights and duties of all company directors, including directors of charitable companies. There is more about these duties in **Chapter 6**. Directors are also subject to a body of case-law that supplements the provisions of the 2006 Act, as well as the Companies Directors Disqualification Act 1986. As the name suggests, this deals with the disqualification of directors from office where they are convicted of offences or carry out certain other acts which make them unfit to hold office (see **Chapter 8**).

Charitable incorporated organisations

3.11 CIOs are governed by the provisions of the Part 11 of the Charities Act 2011 as supplemented by Regulations. These deal with, amongst other things, how CIOs are constituted, the conversion of other legal entities into CIOs, amalgamations of CIOs, their winding up and insolvency and the powers and duties of their members and trustees.

3.12 Since registration as a CIO only became possible in December 2012, at the time of writing there is no case law that relates to them (although, as charities, they are subject to charity law).

Trusts

3.13 Charities established as trusts are subject to the patchwork of statute and case law that make up the English law of trusts. Perhaps the most important point to appreciate is that the law of trusts was developed by the courts as part of their 'equitable' jurisdiction in order to protect the interests of those often incapable of looking after their own interests. As a consequence, the statutes that apply to them are very much laid over a well-developed and reasonably complex body of case law that is much more accessible to the lawyer than the layman. This is obviously important in understanding how trusts operate, but it is equally important to the charity trustees of all charities (whichever legal form that they take) because very many of their most significant rights and duties are governed by the law of trusts rather than the law that related to charities generally or to charities established as, say, companies.

3.14 The most significant statutes that form part of the law of trusts are:

- Trustee Act 1925;
- Trusts of Land and Appointment of Trustees Act 1996;
- Trustee Delegation Act 1999; and
- Trustee Act 2000.

3.15   Not every part of each of these statutes applies to a charity established as a trust, nor to the trustees of every charity. The most significant aspects of each of them as they apply in practice are identified in this book.

Unincorporated associations

3.16   There are no statutes that relate specifically to unincorporated associations. An association is created by a contract between its members. The law of contract is made up of a body of case law supplemented by statutes that deal with specific aspects of contracts.

3.17   The law of trusts will often also be relevant to charitable associations because their assets are often held on trust for their charitable objects. This is dependent on the terms of their constitutional documents and often also on the terms on which assets are donated to them, but the law of trusts will usually be relevant.

REGIMES THAT APPLY BECAUSE OF WHAT CHARITIES DO

3.18   There are many different legal regimes that can apply to a charity as a consequence of what it does. Some examples may help to illustrate this:

- A charity that educates children (say, an independent school) will be affected by the Education Acts (in relation to the standards of education it provides), the legislation regulating the safeguarding of vulnerable beneficiaries (specifically the Care Standards Act 2000, the Education Act 2002, the Safeguarding Vulnerable Groups Act 2006 and the Protection of Freedoms Act 2012), the Data Protection Act 1998 (in relation to the confidentiality and security of personal data) and employment and health and safety legislation.

- A charity that raises funds from the public to assist those in poverty overseas is likely to be affected by the law on fundraising (in the Charities Act 1992), the VAT law that applies to certain fundraising activities, the law that relates to commercial contracts and trademark licences, the law that applies to it overseas in the places it is active, the law relating to advertising and employment and health and safety legislation as it applies to its employees and volunteers.

- A charity that employs staff has a duty under the Health & Safety at Work etc Act 1974 to ensure the health, safety and welfare of employees and others who may be affected by the actions of the charity. 'Others' would include volunteers, service users and trustees for example. In addition, the Corporate Manslaughter and Corporate Homicide Act 2007 means that it is possible for employers to be prosecuted for a gross breach of duty if someone is killed at or by work.

3.19 Neither of these lists is in any sense exhaustive and a full analysis and explanation of all of the different legal regimes that might apply to charities is outside the scope of this book. In this sense, a charity is in much the same position as any commercial entity operating in a particular area.

LEGAL REGIMES GENERALLY

3.20 There are some legal regimes which apply to charities in the UK, regardless of how they are constituted or what their activities are. Two significant regimes are the Equality Act 2010 and the Bribery Act 2010.

Equality Act 2010

3.21 The Equality Act 2010, which consolidated and replaced pre-existing discrimination legislation, provides protection from unlawful discrimination in relation to what are referred to as 'protected characteristics'. These are: age; disability; gender reassignment; marriage and civil partnership; pregnancy and maternity; race; religion or belief; sex; and sexual orientation. The Act makes it unlawful to discriminate against anyone on the basis of a 'protected characteristic' in a wide range of areas, including employment and the provision of services.

3.22 There are a number of exceptions that may be relevant to charities. For example:

- **Charities exception**
  There is a specific exception for charities in the Act which allows a charity to restrict benefits to people with a particular 'protected characteristic' even though this may exclude people with other protected characteristics if certain conditions are met. There is more about the charities exception in **Chapter 1.**

- **Men or women only fundraising**
  Participation in activities to support or promote charities can be restricted to one sex only.

- **Admission to education**
  Schools and further and higher education institutions are allowed to admit students based on gender where the school or institution is single sex.

3.23 Detailed guidance on the application of the 2010 Act and exceptions can be found on the following websites:

- Charity Commission (www.charitycommission.gov.uk);
- Equality and Equality and Human Rights Commission (www.equalityhumanrights.com);
- Government Equalities Office (www.gov.uk/government/organisations/government-equalities-office).

Bribery Act 2010

3.25 The Bribery Act 2010 will apply to all charities in the UK, but it will be particularly relevant for charities operating in jurisdictions where bribery is more culturally prevalent.

3.26 The Act makes it an offence to:

- offer, promise or give a bribe;
- request, agree to receive or accept a bribe;
- bribe a foreign official; or
- fail to prevent bribery (a corporate offence).

3.27 An incorporated charity can be liable if a trustee or senior employee commits any of these offences, which can be attributed to the charity itself. The trustee or employee would also be personally liable, whether the charity is incorporated or unincorporated. An incorporated charity can also be liable for failing to prevent bribery committed by any of its trustees, employees or agents acting on its behalf (the corporate offence). However, the charity will have a full defence if it can show that it has adequate procedures in place to prevent bribery. These procedures should be proportionate to the risk of bribery, but are likely to include risk assessments, employee and trustee training and an anti-bribery policy.

3.28 For further information, charities should refer to the guidance on the Act issued by the Ministry of Justice.[2]

---

[2] See www.justice.gov.uk.

CHAPTER 4

THE CHARITY COMMISSION

INTRODUCTION

4.1   The Charity Commission for England and Wales (the Comisiwyn Elusennau Cymru a Lloegr in Welsh) regulates all charities in England and Wales (although its regulatory role in relation to exempt charities is circumscribed (see **4.68**)). It is a statutory corporation established under the Charities Act 2011 to perform its functions on behalf of the Crown. The Commission replaced the former regulator (the Charity Commissioners for England and Wales) and is free of any control by the Government, except for any particular statutory controls and any administrative controls the Treasury imposes in relation to its spending.

4.2   The governance framework for the Commission is set out in the Charities Act 2011.[1] It consists of a chairperson and between four and eight other members, at least two of whom must be legally qualified and at least one of whom is familiar with conditions in Wales and is appointed after consultation with the National Assembly for Wales. The Commission also has a Chief Executive.

4.3   The Commission is established in line with a number of statutory objectives, general functions and duties.[2] These are considered at **4.6–4.10**.

4.4   As a result of a reduction in the Commission's budget by 33% between 2010/11 and 2014/15, the Commission acknowledged as part of its 2011 strategic review that it would need to focus on its core regulatory role and responsibilities and concentrate its resources on the activities which only it, as independent regulator, can carry out. Similar recommendations were made by Lord Hodgson in his review of the Charities Act 2006:[3]

> 'In a time of significantly reduced resources, the "friend" side of the Charity Commission's work can only be seen as an extra, and the regulatory role must come to the fore.'

---

[1]   Charities Act 2011, s 13.
[2]   Charities Act 2011, s 14.
[3]   'Trusted and independent: giving charity back to charities' published in July 2012.

4.5 In June 2012, the Commission published its Risk Framework[4] which sets out its regulatory approach to protecting the public's interest in charity. The framework focuses on how the Commission assesses and manages risk and this chapter should be read with the framework in mind.

OBJECTIVES

4.6 The Commission's objectives are:

- Public confidence – to increase public trust and confidence in charities.
- Public benefit – to promote awareness and understanding of the public benefit requirement (see **Chapter 1** for more detail on this).
- Compliance – to promote compliance by charity trustees with their legal obligations in exercising control and management and administration of their charities.
- Charitable resources – to promote the effective use of charitable resources.
- Accountability – to enhance the accountability of charities to donors, beneficiaries and the general public.

GENERAL FUNCTIONS

4.7 In addition to these objectives, the Commission has a number of general functions:[5]

- Determining whether institutions are or are not charities.
- Encouraging and facilitating the better administration of charities.
- Identifying and investigating apparent misconduct or mismanagement in the administration of charities and taking remedial or protective action in connection with misconduct or mismanagement therein.
- Determining whether public collections certificates should be issued, and remain in force, in respect of public charitable collections.
- Obtaining, evaluating and disseminating information in connection with the performance of any of the Commission's functions or meeting any of its objectives.
- Giving information or advice, or making proposals, to any Minister of the Crown on matters relating to any of the Commission's functions or meeting any of its objectives.

4.8 These general functions are effectively the broad headings under which the Charity Commission discharges the specific powers vested in it by Charities Act 2011. There is more about these at **4.11**.

---

[4]   'Risk Framework, Our regulatory approach to protecting the public's interest in charity – how we assess and manage risks' Charity Commission, June 2012.

[5]   Charities Act 2011, s 15.

GENERAL DUTIES

4.9   The Charity Commission also has a number of general duties.[6] These are:

- So far as is reasonably practicable, it must, in performing its functions, act in a way which is compatible with its objectives and which it considers most appropriate for the purpose of meeting those objectives.

- It must, on the same basis, also act in a way that is compatible with the encouragement of all forms of charitable giving and voluntary participation in charity work.

- In performing its functions it must have regard to the need to use its resources in the most efficient, effective and economic way.

- In performing its functions, it must, so far as relevant, have regard to the best regulatory practice (including the principles under which regulatory activities should be proportionate, accountable, consistent, transparent and targeted only at cases in which action is needed).

- In performing its functions it must, in appropriate cases, have regard to the desirability of facilitating innovation by or on behalf of charities.

- In managing its affairs, the Commission must have regard to such generally accepted principles of good corporate governance as it is reasonable to regard as applicable to it.

4.10   These duties are obviously sensible duties for any regulator to owe, although their generality and the extent to which they are hedged by 'so far as reasonably practicable', 'so far as relevant', and 'in appropriate cases' makes their enforceability against the Commission reasonably doubtful. The ability of third parties to challenge the Commission in respect of its acts and omissions as regulator is explained in more detail at **4.76–4.90**.

POWERS

4.11   The Charity Commission has a range of powers conferred on it by the Charities Act 2011. The most significant of its specific regulatory powers are considered at **4.13–4.56**.

4.12   The Commission also has a statutory power to do anything which is calculated to facilitate, or is incidental or conducive to, the performance of its functions. But this does not give it any power to act in the place of any charity trustee, to substitute its own views for those of a trustee nor to do anything else that means it will become directly involved in administering a charity.[7]

---

6   Charities Act 2011, s 16.
7   Charities Act 2011, s 20.

Register of charities

4.13 The Commission maintains the register of charities.[8] It includes the names and other details of all charities other than those that are exempt or excepted (there is more information about these charities at **4.68** and **4.73**). Every other charity is obliged to apply for registration by the Commission, and the Commission is obliged to register every such charity. It is also obliged to review existing registrations in order to ensure that every institution that is registered continues to be a charity or whether the Commission should exercise its discretion to remove from the register any institution which the Commission no longer considers to be a charity or which has ceased to exist or operate.[9] Maintaining an accurate and up-to-date register is part of the Commission's general function of obtaining, evaluating and disseminating information in connection with the performance of any of its functions or meeting any of its objectives.[10]

4.14 The Charities Act 2011 obliges a charity's trustees to apply for its registration and also to notify the Commission if the charity ceases to exist or there is any change to its details in the register or to its 'trusts'. 'Trusts' means the constitutional document (or documents) which establish and govern the charity (and which will vary depending on the charity's legal form).[11]

4.15 The register is undoubtedly central to the Commission's ability to regulate charities properly (albeit that there is a large number of charities which are regulated by the Commission but are not required to register). Being available online, it is an invaluable source of information for both the public and those involved with the sector. The information available is not detailed, but will usually identify the charity's objects, how it is established, who its trustees are, its 'area of benefit' (which is the Commission's way of identifying any geographical area that the charity is intended to benefit) and its annual income. Copies of all charities' constitutional documents are maintained by the Charity Commission and may be obtained by members of the public.[12]

Reports, accounts and returns

4.16 The accuracy of the register maintained by the Commission depends upon the extent to which charities comply with their obligations to supply information to the Charity Commission and, in particular, to submit the reports and accounts and annual return required by the Charities Act 2011. The accounting and reporting obligations of charities are an essential part of governance and are explained in detail in **Chapter 14**.

---

[8]   Charities Act 2011, s 29.
[9]   Charities Act 2011, s 29.
[10] Charities Act 2011, s 15(4).
[11] Charities Act 2011, ss 35, 353(1).
[12] Charities Act 2011, s 38(4).

Advice

4.17 The Commission has the power to advise any charity trustee on anything that relates to the performance of his or her duties as a trustee or the proper administration of the charity. If the trustee acts in accordance with that advice, he is presumed to have acted in accordance with his duties as trustee. This is part of the Commission's general function of encouraging and facilitating the better administration of charities.[13]

4.18 There are some restrictions on this. The advice cannot be relied upon if the trustee knows or has reasonable cause to suspect that the Commission has not been told all of the facts that are material to the advice, nor if there is a court decision on the point in question or one pending.

4.19 The Commission will not use this power where it thinks that the trustee proposes to do something he or she has no power to do (this will usually require an Order) (see **4.22** for more on Orders). In practice, advice is often sought on, for example, whether something the charity proposes to do is within its charitable objects.

4.20 Under its Risk Framework, the Commission will provide advice to charities, either under s 110 or generally, in circumstances where only it (apart from the court) can give authoritative advice and where failure to do so will seriously impact on trustees being able to comply with their legal duties. In practice, the Commission is unlikely to give advice if the trustees could take legal advice or advice from another regulatory body.

4.21 The Commission will, however, often be prepared to give advice in complex charity mergers and restructuring. Similarly, regulatory advice may be given where there are serious concerns about the administration of a charity, to support trustees to carry out their duties properly or where there is a serious risk of non-compliance with legal requirements.

Orders

4.22 The Commission has power to make Orders under the Charities Act 2011[14] where it concludes that:

> '... any action proposed or contemplated in the administration of a charity is expedient in the interests of the charity ...'

4.23 However, in practice and as noted in its Risk Framework, the Commission will:

> 'give permissions under section 105 of the Charities Act 2011 only in circumstances where the matter is outside the trustees' powers (and the trustees

---

[13] Charities Act 2011, s 110.
[14] Charities Act 2011, s 105.

cannot confer power on themselves under section 280 of the Charities Act 2011) except in cases of trustee benefit, extreme controversy, conflicts of interest or where other very significant or momentous issues arise.'

4.24 Once made, an Order authorises the charity's trustees to do whatever it is they are proposing or contemplating notwithstanding that they do not have, or may not have, power to do so. This is achieved by deeming anything done by trustees under an Order to fall within their powers.

4.25 The scope of this power is limited to things associated with the administration of a charity. In practice, an Order cannot be used where:

- It will authorise the trustees to do something that is 'expressly prohibited' by the 'trusts' of the charity. 'Trusts' means the constitutional document (or documents) which establish and govern the charity (and which will vary depending on the charity's legal form).[15] There is no statutory definition of 'expressly prohibited' but the Charity Commission will look at the constitutional documents to decide whether the action is 'subject to an express prohibition in the charity's governing document'.[16]

- It will authorise the trustees to do something that is expressly prohibited by any Act of Parliament.[17] This provision may catch any charity whose constitution is (in whole or part) regulated by an Act of Parliament. Certain Acts (relating to ecclesiastical leases) can be disregarded.[18]

- It will 'extend or alter the purposes of the charity'.[19]

- It imposes duties or directions on the charity trustees that do not relate to the powers they are given by the Order itself.

- If the trustees already have the power they need, either in the charity's constitutional documents or under statute. The Commission does not make 'comfort' Orders for trustees where the extent of their powers are clear. It may, though, consider giving advice under Charities Act 2011, s 110 in order to confirm the position.[20]

- If the trustees already have a power to amend the constitutional documents of the charity to give themselves the power that they need. Where the trustees have an express power of amendment which is sufficiently wide or where they can rely on the statutory power of amendment under Charities Act 2011, s 280 the Commission will expect them to use this power unless what they proposed to do requires something more than an amendment, for example authority for a trustee to act with a conflict of interest.

- As a matter of policy, the Commission will not make an Order if it concludes that the grant of the authority sought should be subject to a

---

15 Charities Act 2011, s 353(1).
16 Charity Commission Operational Guidance OG 501 Orders B2.6.
17 Charities Act 2011, s 105(8).
18 Charities Act 2011, s 105(8).
19 Charities Act 2011, s 105(8)(b).
20 See section on advice at **4.16** and also OG 501 Orders B1.

right of appeal.[21] This will usually be the case where what is proposed will have some effect on a third party's rights under a charity's constitution, for example to appoint trustees.

- An Order cannot be used in relation to certain consecrated buildings.[22]

4.26 If a proposal will override an express prohibition in the charity's governing document or extend or alter the charity's purposes, these changes can only be made by way of a Scheme. There is more about Schemes at **4.32**.

4.27 An Order can only be used to give charity trustees the power to do something. It cannot direct them to act in a particular way, although any power that is given can be (and often is) made subject to conditions and directions which the trustees must observe when they exercise the power.

4.28 An order can be used to give authority for a specific transaction. In some cases, the Commission might be prepared to make a 'blanket' order giving authority for multiple transactions (eg where there is a planned programme of disposals of land to a connected person).

4.29 Some of the Charity Commission's Orders are made under Charities Act 2011, s 105. This gives the Commission a broad discretion to authorise any action as long as it is expedient in the interests of the charity (subject to the limitations described at **4.25**). This section is often now used to authorise trustees to act, notwithstanding their conflicts of interest (see **Chapter 6**).

4.30 The Charities Act 2011 also gives the Charity Commission powers to make Orders in specific circumstances. Examples include:

Order	*More detail:*
Appointment of a corporate trustee of a charity under s 69	**Chapter 6**
Relieving a trustee in breach of trust from personal liability under s 191	**Chapter 6**
Disposal of charity property under s 117 (where the trustees cannot comply with the other requirements of that section)	**Chapter 9**
Charging a charity's land as security for borrowing under s 124 (where the trustees cannot comply with the other requirements of that section)	**Chapter 12**

4.31 The procedure for obtaining an Order is straightforward:

- The trustees (or someone authorised by them) should write to the Commission explaining what is required and all of the relevant

---

[21] OG 501 Orders B2.3.
[22] Charities Act 2011, s 105(10).

circumstances. It is important that the position is explained as fully as possible and all relevant circumstances disclosed, partly because the Commission has a power to discharge an Order which it considers it was misled into making[23] and partly because this is more likely to help speed up the process. Knowingly or recklessly providing the Commission with false or misleading information is in any event an offence.[24]

- The trustees will need to resolve to apply for an Order in accordance with the provisions of the charity's constitution.

- The Commission will draft the Order using its own precedents, but the trustees and their advisors will usually be given an opportunity to comment on the draft.

- There is no statutory requirement for an Order to be publicised before it is made but the Commission can ask trustees to publicise the proposal to make an Order.[25] It also has the power to publicise an Order once it has been made.[26]

    The Commission's view on this is that when considering whether the public notice requirement is necessary, the Commission needs to assess the potential risks attached to the action authorised by the Order. The Commission will need to consider issues such as the likely level of public interest in the case; the public profile of the charity, and the risk of the Commission being accused of lack of transparency.[27] Where an Order is sought in relation to a particularly contentious matter, it may be that publicity for the draft leads the Commission to conclude that it would be better for a Scheme (with an associated right of appeal) to be made.

- There is no right of appeal in relation to an Order made by the Commission. The only option for someone who objects to the making of an Order is to complain to the Commission (see **4.76** for more on this).

Schemes

4.32 A Scheme is the legal mechanism by which the Commission can change a charity's constitutional provisions. Once made, it takes effect as part of the constitution and will be either:

- a 'fully regulating' Scheme which deals with all aspects of a charity's purposes and administration and becomes the charity's governing document (although see **4.40**); or

- a Scheme that changes a distinct part of a charity's governing document.

4.33 The Commission's policy is not to make a Scheme where there is any other way of making a change to a charity's constitutional documents. So a Scheme will not be available where:

23 Charities Act 2011, s 337(4).
24 Charities Act 2011, s 60(1)(b).
25 Charities Act 2011, s 337(3).
26 Charities Act 2011, s 337(3).
27 OG 501 Orders B6.3.

- The trustees already have the power they need, either in the charity's constitution or under statute.

- The trustees have a power to amend the constitutional documents of the charity in the manner proposed.

  Powers of amendment of this kind will enable trustees to alter the way in which their charity's purposes are worded without changing their substance. Sometimes the power is clearly not capable of altering the actual words that are used (typically because there is a restriction on any change to the 'objects clause' as opposed to the charitable objects or purposes themselves). Alternatively, the power may authorise the trustees to amend the Charity's purposes with the Commission's consent.

  In the case of a charitable company, its members can exercise the power they have under the Companies Acts to alter its constitution, although the Commission's prior written consent is required in certain circumstances under the Charities Act 2011, s 198 (see **Chapter 15** for more detail on this).

  The charity may also be able to take advantage of the provisions of the Charities Act 2011, ss 275 and 280, which allow certain unincorporated charities to alter their constitutional documents by resolution, including both their charitable purposes and their administrative powers and procedures. There is more detail about the charities that can utilise these provisions at **15.9** and **15.12**.

4.34 The Charity Commission's most significant Scheme-making power is contained in the Charities Act 2011, s 69. Section 69 gives the Commission jurisdiction to make Schemes concurrently with the High Court (which has an inherent jurisdiction to make Schemes for charities). This means that, in most cases, a Scheme will be made by the Commission rather than the Court, except where an application is contentious or involves difficult questions of fact or law.[28] In those circumstances, or if the Commission thinks that there are other good reasons for doing so, the Commission has a discretion to decide not to exercise its jurisdiction.

4.35 The Schemes that the Commission can make under the Charities Act 2011, s 69 relate to:

- The cy-près application of gifts to a charity where its purposes have failed.[29] There is more about cy-près Schemes at **15.21**.

- The cy-près application of gifts to a charity where the donors are unknown or have disclaimed.[30]

- The administration of a charity.[31]

---

[28] Charities Act 2011, s 70(8).
[29] Charities Act 2011, ss 62(1), 66(1).
[30] Charities Act 2011, s 63.
[31] Charities Act 2011, s 69(1)(a).

- The appointment, discharge, or removal of any charity trustee or any officer or employee of a charity.[32]
- Vesting or transferring property or requiring others to vest or transfer property.[33]

4.36 The Commission's jurisdiction under s 69 is exercisable where:

- The Court makes an Order directing it to do so, in which case the Commission will 'settle' the Scheme; in other words draft the provisions of the Scheme so as to give effect to the directions the Court gives.[34]
- An application for a Scheme is made by a charity or by the Attorney-General.
- The Commission concludes that a charity's trustees ought to have applied for a Scheme but have unreasonably failed to do so and the trustees have been given an opportunity to make representations to the Commission; in these circumstances, the Commission can proceed as if they had received an application for a Scheme from the charity.

4.37 Charities established by Royal Charter or statute are not within the Charity Commission's Scheme-making jurisdiction. Because the authority of the Crown and Parliament is higher than the authority of the Court, they are only within the jurisdiction of the Court as a consequence of the express provisions of the Charities Act 2011, s 68 and the Commission's concurrent jurisdiction does not extend to them. However, the Charities 2011, s 73(1) does give the Commission the ability to 'settle' a Scheme for a charity which is established or regulated by any Act of Parliament.

4.38 There are certain questions that cannot be determined by the Commission using its Scheme-making power and which may, therefore, prevent it from making a Scheme for a charity. These are:

- Any question about the ownership of property where there is a dispute between a charity and a third party claiming an interest in it. This is a question that only the courts are in a position to answer.
- Any question about 'the existence or extent of any charge or trust'. This is aimed at other kinds of third party claims over assets. Again, only the courts are in a position to answer this question.

The Commission also has discretion to refuse to make a Scheme where it concludes that it is more appropriate for the courts to consider an application. This is usually where the application is particularly contentious or involves difficult questions of fact or law. See **4.34** for more on this.

---

[32] Charities Act 2011, s 69(1)(b).
[33] Charities Act 2011, s 69(1)(c).
[34] Charities Act 2011, s 69(3).

4.39 In practice, most Schemes made by the Commission will be aimed at the following:

- To alter a charity's purposes to allow the cy-près application of its assets.

- To make changes to an unincorporated charity's constitution which are likely to be contentious. This is often where the charity's constitution gives third parties certain rights in relation to it, for example to appoint trustees or exercise powers of veto, and there is a dispute between the charity and the third parties or perhaps between the third parties themselves.

- Where an unincorporated charity's trustees wish to make changes to its constitution that will override an express prohibition (so that an Order cannot be made). This would include, for example, an application to include a provision for trustee remuneration where there is a prohibition on trustee benefits.

- Where the trustees are to be directed to do something required by the Commission properly to regulate the charity.

4.40 As we have mentioned, the Commission's policy is only to make a Scheme where there is no other option available to the trustees to make the required changes. It will only make those changes that cannot be made in any other way.[35] This means that whilst the Commission is able to make a 'fully regulating' Scheme, it is more likely that the Commission will make a Scheme that changes the parts of a charity's governing document that the trustees cannot change and will expect the trustees to make the changes that they can using express or statutory powers.

4.41 In summary, the procedure for obtaining a Scheme is as follows:

- The need for a Scheme will usually emerge from discussions between a charity's trustees, senior officers or advisers and the Commission in respect of proposed amendments to a charity's governing document.

- However, before the Commission will agree to make a Scheme, it may be necessary for the trustees to provide further information and/or make a case in support of the Scheme. Again, it is important that the position is explained as fully as possible and all relevant circumstances disclosed, partly because the Commission has a power to discharge a Scheme which it considers it was misled into making[36] and partly because this is more likely to help speed up the process. Knowingly or recklessly providing the Commission with false or misleading information is in any event an offence.[37]

- The trustees will need to make a formal application for a Scheme and the trustees must resolve to make the application in accordance with the charity's governing document. The application is normally made by email

---

[35] OG 500 Schemes, Policy Statement/Overview.
[36] Charities Act 2011, s 337(4).
[37] Charities Act 2011, s 60(1)(b).

and must be made by someone authorised by the trustees to make it. It must confirm that all the charity's trustees are aware of the decision to apply for a Scheme (or provide contact details for any trustee who is not aware).

- Applicants should not prepare their own draft Schemes. The Commission will prepare a draft based upon the information available to it using its own precedents and model form Schemes. The Commission will invariably send the Scheme in draft to the applicant with a view to obtaining their comments on it and agreeing the final form.[38]

- The Commission is required under the Charities Act 2011 to give public notice of its intention to make a Scheme and invite representations from the public unless it decides it is not necessary because of the nature of the Scheme or for any other reason.[39] There is more about publication of Schemes in the context of amending a charity's governing document at **15.22**. Where the Scheme will remove any trustee against his or her will, at least one month's notice must be given to them personally (the Commission has no discretion not to give this notice).

- The Commission will add its seal to a Scheme in order to make it and will usually post the Scheme on its website.[40]

4.42 An appeal against any Scheme in respect of a charity made by the Commission using its Charities Act 2011, s 69 jurisdiction can be made using the appeals procedure summarised at **4.76** to **4.90**.

Protective powers

4.43 The Charity Commission has a range of investigatory and enforcement powers which it can use in furtherance of its general function of 'identifying and investigating apparent misconduct or mismanagement in the administration of charities and taking remedial or protective action'.[41] The most important of these are summarised at **4.44–4.55**. The Commission's risk framework underpins its approach when exercising its protective powers.

Inquiries

4.44 The Commission has the power to open an Inquiry into any charity (including an exempt charity in certain circumstances). There are no statutory grounds for this but it must be seen as an important part of the Commission's general function referred to at **4.43**.

4.45 The Commission's approach to Inquiries is set out in its guidance 'Statutory inquiries into charities: guidance for charities and their advisers' (CC 46). This confirms that the Commission will consider opening an Inquiry

---

[38]   OG 500 Schemes.
[39]   Charities Act 2011, s 88.
[40]   Charities Act 2011, s 88(5), (6).
[41]   Charities Act 2011, s 15(1).

only in the most serious, higher risk, cases. These are where there are issues of serious financial loss to a charity, serious criminality and/or illegal activity within a charity or where it suspects a charity has been set up for an illegal or improper purpose (including the use of abusive tax arrangements). This approach reflects the significant resource issues for the Commission in opening an Inquiry, as well as for the charity.

4.46 Whether the Commission opens an Inquiry depends on a number of factors including:

- the seriousness of the regulatory issues;
- indications of evidence or serious suspicions of misconduct or mismanagement;
- indications of significant risk to property;
- other factors which indicate that it is necessary to promote public trust and confidence in the charity or charities more generally.[42]

4.47 The Commission can either carry out an Inquiry itself or appoint a third party to conduct the Inquiry on its behalf (usually an accountant or solicitor). Whoever conducts the Inquiry has wide powers to gather the information that they need, including directing any person to supply accounts and statements, provide copy documents and give evidence on oath.[43] The Commission may (and usually does) decide to publish a report into an Inquiry on its website, generally with some guidance on the wider lessons to be learned from the Inquiry.

4.48 Opening an Inquiry brings into play a number of other important powers aimed at allowing the Commission to take the remedial or protective action that forms part of its general function.

4.49 Where the Commission is satisfied that there has been any misconduct or mismanagement in the administration of a charity or that it should act to protect the charity's property, it has a range of 'temporary' protective powers it can use. These powers are likely to be exercised at an early stage in any Inquiry in order to protect the charity's position pending the outcome of the Inquiry. In particular, the Commission can:

- Suspend any charity trustee, officer, agent or employee of the charity (and, if they are also a member of the charity, suspend that membership).[44]
- Appoint additional trustees.[45]
- Vest any of the charity's property in the official custodian for charities.[46]

---

[42] Section G4 of 'Risk Framework, Application of the Charity Commission's Risk Framework', Charity Commission, January 2012.
[43] Charities Act 2011, s 47.
[44] Charities Act 2011, s 76.
[45] Charities Act 2011, s 76(3)(b).
[46] Charities Act 2011, s 76(3)(c).

- Order anyone holding any property for the charity not to dispose of it without the Commission's approval.[47]
- Order anyone who owes the charity any liability not to discharge it without the Commission's approval.[48]
- Restrict the transactions that the charity can enter into or the payments it can make without the Commission's approval.[49]
- Obtain a warrant to enter premises and seize documents, computer files etc where there are reasonable grounds for believing that an order to produce them will not be complied with or that they will be destroyed or tampered with.[50]

4.50 The Commission may also decide to appoint an 'interim manager' of the charity under s 76(3)(g) of the Charities Act 2011. This is an individual (usually an accountant or solicitor but not an employee of the Commission itself) appointed to take control of a charity where there is a concern that its assets are at risk.[51] The interim manager has 3 months from his appointment to investigate the affairs of the charity and report to the Commission on the position and the proposals for rectifying the position. This may include the winding-up of the charity.[52]

4.51 Another significant protective power applies where the Commission is satisfied that there has been any misconduct or mismanagement in the administration of a charity or that it should act to protect the charity's property. In those circumstances, it can direct any charity trustee, any officer or employee or the charity itself (where it is a body corporate) to take any action the Commission thinks is expedient in the charity's interests. This includes directing the relevant person to do something outside his or her powers (which is deemed to have been done within his or her powers) but not anything which is prohibited by any Act of Parliament or 'expressly prohibited' by the charity's constitutional documents or otherwise inconsistent with its purposes. Nothing done as a consequence of any direction affects any contractual or other rights.[53]

4.52 Once the Inquiry into a charity (or an interim manager's report) has helped to clarify the position, the Charities Act 2011 gives the Commission further protective powers that enable it to implement longer term solutions to problems identified.

4.53 In particular, the Commission is authorised to exercise the powers it has to make a Scheme for the administration of the charity and to remove any charity trustee, officer, agent or employee of the charity (and, if they are also a

---

[47]   Charities Act 2011, s 76(3)(d).
[48]   Charities Act 2011, s 76(3)(e).
[49]   Charities Act 2011, s 76(3)(f).
[50]   Charities Act 2011, s 48.
[51]   Charity Commission Report 1997, paras 116–122.
[52]   SI 1992/2355.
[53]   Charities Act 2011, s 84.

member of the charity, terminate that membership).[54] These powers can be used to make any necessary change to the charity's constitution and, in conjunction with its power to appoint trustees, put it under the control of a new body of trustees. The exercise of these powers depends on the Commission satisfying itself that there has been some misconduct or mismanagement in the administration of a charity and that it should act to protect the charity's property.

4.54 'Misconduct and mismanagement' is not defined by the Charities Act 2011 and is essentially a question of fact to be decided upon by the Commission. However, the Charities Act 2011, s 76(2) specifically refers to arrangements for any person to be paid by a charity for services which are excessive in relation to the value of the charity's assets. This is one of the circumstances the Commission often pick up in their review of a charity's annual report and accounts. It is worth reading the reports into completed Inquiries posted on the Commission's website, partly because they illustrate the sort of governance failings that charities can succumb to but also because they offer an insight into the kind of activities the Commission is likely to regard as mismanagement and misconduct.

Other protective powers

4.55 The Commission has a number of other powers it can exercise to protect charities and which are not dependent on the opening of an Inquiry. These are:

- Power to remove charity trustees in certain specified circumstances, including a trustee who has stopped acting as a trustee and will not confirm whether he or she is willing to act or not.[55]
- Power to appoint charity trustees in certain specified circumstances, including where there are no trustees able to act because of death and incapacity.[56]
- Power to vest a charity's property in new trustees where the Commission removes or appoints trustees.[57]
- Power to determine who the members of a charity are if, as sometimes happens, the charity itself is no longer capable of determining who its members are.[58]
- Power to direct any person who holds or controls a charity's assets whom the Commission is satisfied is unwilling to apply them properly for the charity's purposes to deal with the assets in any way the Commission determines. The Commission must also conclude that making an order to this effect is desirable in order to ensure that the charity's assets are properly applied. The Commission can direct the relevant person to do

---

[54] Charities Act 2011, s 76.
[55] Charities Act 2011, s 80(1).
[56] Charities Act 2011, s 80(2).
[57] Charities Act 2011, s 81.
[58] Charities Act 2011, s 111.

something outside their powers (which is deemed to have been done within their powers) but not anything which is prohibited by any Act or Parliament or 'expressly prohibited' by the charity's constitutional documents or otherwise inconsistent with its purposes. Nothing done as a consequence of any direction affects any contractual or other rights.[59]

4.56 At the time of writing, the Government is undertaking consultation in relation to the Charity Commission's powers to act where there are issues of regulatory concern, in particular where there is non-compliance with charity law, misconduct or mismanagement or a risk to charity property. The consultation is on proposals to help the Commission tackle the most serious cases of abuse within charities. Depending on the outcome of this consultation, the Commission's statutory protective powers may be strengthened further.

REVIEWS

4.57 Following its strategic review in 2011, the Commission acknowledged that the charitable sector has a vital role to play in strengthening its own governance and has started to develop a series of projects with key partners as part of a review programme. Project partners are organisations with particular expertise or knowledge important to the charitable sector. Projects have included, for instance, a review of financial controls and risk awareness in charities carried out by the Institute of Chartered Accountants in England and Wales (ICAEW) and a review of governance of newly registered charities carried out by the Institute of Chartered Secretaries and Administrators.

4.58 Each project will involve reviews of individual charities assessing a particular governance topic followed by an analysis of the findings of those reviews being presented in a report to the Commission. The reviews will be carried out by project partners, rather than the Commission.

4.59 The Commission has made it clear that the reviews are not part of its statutory functions and that it will not be involved in the reviews. The Commission will not even know which charities are involved in the reviews because the selection process will be undertaken by, or on behalf of, the reviewers. The expectation is that participating charities will benefit through a free consultation on an aspect of their governance with bespoke suggestions for improvement where relevant.

GUIDANCE

4.60 The Commission has no specific power under the Charities Act 2011 to issue general information and guidance to charities, so the wide range of material it does produce must form part of its general function of encouraging and facilitating the better administration of charities and disseminating

---

[59]　Charities Act 2011, s 85.

information in connection with its functions or objectives. The material the Commission produces is available online and is generally very helpful, and often invaluable, in assisting charity trustees and their advisors. It falls into a number of different categories.

Publications

4.61 The Commission produces a very wide range of publications (these are numbered and prefixed 'CC'). They range in scope from guidance on issues of general significance such as, for example, the basics of charity trusteeship ('The essential trustee: what you need to know' (CC 3)) to more specific advice in relation to, for example, charities and public service delivery and charities and insurance.

4.62 Different publications are aimed at different audiences. Some are intended to assist the public generally and the trustees of smaller charities, while others are aimed at charity sector professionals and the trustees and employees of larger charities. They are all available on the Commission's website.

Operational guidance

4.63 In addition to its publications for public consumption, the Commission also publishes its internal guidance to its own staff on its website (under the heading 'About us/operational guidance' and numbered and prefixed 'OG'). This is a very useful resource for anyone who wants to understand how the Commission approaches particular aspects of charity law and regulation and highlights their policies and expectations as well as including examples of the sort of model documents that the Commission produces (eg model Orders and Schemes). Understandably, the guidance assumes a reasonably high degree of knowledge about charity law and regulation, but it is a recommended starting point for anyone looking in detail at a particular issue. We refer to the operational guidance throughout this book.

Specialist guidance

4.64 The Commission also publishes a range of specialist guidance for particular kinds of charities including, for example, charities providing housing and recreation ground charities. There is a full list of the specialist guidance on the Commission's website.

Decisions

4.65 The Commission publishes some of the decisions it takes in relation to charities on its website, particularly where they relate to novel areas of charity law or are of wider interest. Many relate to applications for registration as a charity and deal with what can constitute a charitable purpose.

Regulatory reports

4.66 The Commission also produces a range of review reports (often numbered and prefixed 'RR') and research reports (often numbered and prefixed 'RS'). 'RR' reports set out and explain the Commission's policy in key areas of law including, for example, 'independence of charities from the state' and 'the Recreational Charities Act 1958' whilst 'RS' reports focus on a range of issues affecting charities which help the Commission promote good practice, develop policy and produce guidance for charities. Such reports are not strictly guidance, but they are a useful summary of the research that the Commission does and the likely developments in policy in particular areas.

OTHER SPECIFIC POWERS

4.67 The Commission has a number of other specific powers. The more significant of these are:

- Power to require a charity's name to be changed.[60]
- Power to make Schemes to establish common investment and common deposit funds.[61]
- Power to authorise ex gratia payments.[62]
- Power to give directions about dormant bank accounts.[63]
- Power to order taxation of a solicitor's bill.[64]
- Power to relieve trustees and auditors from liability for breach of trust.[65]

EXEMPT CHARITIES

4.68 Exempt charities are not fully regulated by the Charity Commission, although in most other respects they are subject to charity law in the same way as charities that are not exempt. The rationale for exempting some charities is that some other body or Government department already regulates them. The full list of exempt charities is set out in Sch 3 to the Charities Act 2011. Some of the more important exempt charities are:

- universities and university colleges;[66]
- higher and further education corporations;

---

[60]   Charities Act 2011, s 42.
[61]   Charities Act 2011, ss 96–104.
[62]   Charities Act 2011, s 106.
[63]   Charities Act 2011, s 107.
[64]   Charities Act 2011, s 112.
[65]   Charities Act 2011, ss 191–192.
[66]   As specified by the Charities Act 2011, Sch 3.

- any industrial and provident society which is a registered provider of social housing under Part 1 of the Housing and Regeneration Act 2008; and

- any other institution administered by any exempt charity and established for any general or special purpose of that charity (excluding student unions).

4.69   In the past, not all exempt charities have been effectively regulated as charities because the body or Government department regulating them has not been responsible for ensuring compliance with charity law. The Charities Act 2011, however, puts the body or Government department which is the 'principal regulator' of an exempt charity under a statutory duty to do all that it reasonably can to promote compliance by the charity trustees with their legal obligations.

4.70   Where no suitable body can be identified to act as a 'principal regulator', charities will cease to be exempt and will instead become excepted. This means that the Charity Commission will be the regulator of such charities (see **4.73** and **4.74**).

4.71   The rules are changing for different groups of existing exempt charities at different times. Certain charities (eg student unions) are no longer exempt because no 'principal regulator' has been identified. Certain other charities do not yet know whether they will have a 'principal regulator' or whether they will become excepted. At the time of writing, for example, a 'principal regulator' has not been identified for charitable industrial and provident societies which are not registered providers of social housing.

4.72   The Commission's powers in relation to an exempt charity are limited. The most significant powers exercisable by the Commission are to:

- Open an Inquiry into an exempt charity provided it is asked to do so by the charity's principal regulator.[67]

- Require an exempt charity to change its name.[68]

- Require an exempt charity to produce documents and search records.[69]

- Exercise its Scheme-making jurisdiction[70] (see **4.32–4.42** for more detail).

- Exercise its powers to take remedial or protective action in relation to an exempt charity following an Inquiry.[71]

- Give its prior consent to court proceedings taken in relation to any exempt charity.[72]

---

[67]   Charities Act 2011, s 46(2).
[68]   Charities Act 2011, s 42.
[69]   Charities Act 2011, s 47.
[70]   Charities Act 2011, s 69.
[71]   Charities Act 2011, s 76.
[72]   Charities Act 2011, s 115.

EXCEPTED CHARITIES

4.73 Certain charities (usually referred to as 'excepted charities') are free of the requirement to be registered by the Charity Commission and are also excepted from the requirement to file annual reports and accounts.[73] Excepted charities are, however, fully under the Commission's supervision and are subject to charity law in the same way as registered charities.

4.74 There are three categories of excepted charity:

- Exempt charities which do not have a 'principal regulator' and have an income not exceeding £100,000 per year (see **4.70**).

- Any charity excepted by regulations made by parliament or an order of the Charity Commission and who has income not exceeding £100,000 per year. These include, for example, churches and chapels belonging to some Christian denominations and Scout and Guide groups. Since 2009, no new exceptions can be made by Parliament or the Commission except for in relation to charities that cease to be exempt charities.

- Any charity whose gross income in its financial year is £5,000 or less.

4.75 Any charity within the second two categories is entitled to be registered if it wishes.[74]

COMPLAINTS AND APPEALS

4.76 There are a number of options open to charity trustees who wish to complain about, or challenge, decisions taken by the Charity Commission or the way in which the Commission has provided a service.

Decision review service

4.77 Those who wish to make a complaint about a formal decision made by the Commission using its powers under the Charities Act 2011 can use the Commission's decision review process.

4.78 The review will look at whether the original decision was correct or whether it should be changed or discharged either in full or part. The decision received following the decision review process is the Commission's final decision. There is more information about the Commission's decision review process on its website.[75]

4.79 The review process can be used for most decisions of the Commission. These are the decisions which can be challenged in an application to the Tribunal (see **4.82**). Only the persons who would be eligible to make an

---

[73] Charities Act 2011, s 161.
[74] Charities Act 2011, s 30(3).
[75] See the guidance 'Dissatisfied with one of the Commission's decisions: how can we help you?'.

application to the Tribunal can use the decision review process, but this will generally include the charity's trustees and the charity itself (if incorporated).

4.80 If, following the decision review, the applicant is still not satisfied with the Commission's decision, they may be able to apply to the Tribunal. There is, however, no requirement to use the Commission's decision review process before bringing an application in the Tribunal.

Charity Tribunal

4.81 The First-tier Tribunal (Charity) was introduced by the Charities Act 2006 in order to provide a more cost-effective avenue specifically for appeals against decisions by the Commission to exercise (or, as the case may be, not to exercise) its statutory powers in relation to a charity.

4.82 The Tribunal's jurisdiction does not extend to the exercise of all of the Commission's statutory powers, but many of the Commission's most significant powers are subject to a right of appeal to the Tribunal. These are set out in Charities Act 2001, Sch 6. These include a decision to register, or not to register, a particular entity as a charity; a decision to remove, or not to remove, a charity from the register of charities; and a decision to open an Inquiry. Decisions to make an Order or Scheme (or not to make them, as the case may be) are also subject to the right of appeal. The most significant omission from the Tribunal's jurisdiction is a decision by the Commission to give, or not to give, Advice.

4.83 The Tribunal considers only the formal legal decisions of the Commission in relation to the exercise of its statutory powers. It does not consider complaints in relation to maladministration (due, for example, to delay). Where the Tribunal upholds an appeal against a decision of the Commission, it will generally have a number of options open to it. These include quashing the decision taken by the Commission; remitting the decision to the Commission (with or without a direction to Commission about the decision it should reach); substituting the Tribunal's own decision; or adding to the Commission's decision in some way. Which of these options is available to the Tribunal will depend upon the decision of the Commission that is being appealed against.

4.84 Some decisions of the Commission are subject to a review by the Tribunal rather than an appeal. This means that the Tribunal will look only at the way in which the Commission reached the decision (in other words, whether it followed a proper decision-making process) rather than looking at all of the facts which were available to the Commission in relation to the original decision.

4.85 Different appeals can be brought by different people but will generally include a charity's trustees and the charity itself (where it is incorporated). In some cases, other persons affected by the decision may be able to appeal.

4.86 Where a charity brings an appeal to the Tribunal, it is responsible for paying its own legal and other costs. The same will be true of the Charity Commission. There are limited circumstances in which the Tribunal will have a power to order that the Commission or the appellant must pay the other's costs. An Order can be made where the Tribunal considers that either party has acted 'vexatiously, frivolously or unreasonably'. The Tribunal can also award costs against the Charity Commission if it considers that the Commission's decision which is subject to the appeal was unreasonable in the first place.

4.87 The costs of the appellant may be reduced where the Attorney-General exercises his right to intervene in cases brought before the Tribunal (which would generally only be the case particularly where an important legal issue is being considered by the Tribunal). Where the Attorney-General intervenes in relation to a charity's appeal, the charity's trustees can expect him to argue the appeal in full, which may mean that the appellant charity can limit its own legal and other professional costs.

4.88 The Tribunal has no power to compensate a successful appellant for any loss it has suffered as a result of a decision by the Commission.

4.89 There is a right of appeal from any decision of the Tribunal to the Upper Tribunal and a right of appeal from any decision of the Upper Tribunal to the Court of Appeal.[76]

Appeals to the High Court

4.90 If it is not possible to challenge a decision of the Commission through the Tribunal, it may still be possible to challenge it through the courts. A detailed discussion on this is outside the scope of this book.

Complaining about a service

4.91 Complaints about quality of service provided by the Charity Commission are dealt with differently to complaints about a formal decision it has made. The Commission has a formal complaints procedure which charities can use. There is more information about this on the Commission's website.

Parliamentary and Health Service Ombudsman

4.92 The Parliamentary and Health Service Ombudsman deals with any complaint that the Commission has treated somebody unfairly or provided a poor service (eg because of an unreasonable delay). The Ombudsman has no power to review formal legal decisions taken by the Commission. The Ombudsman also has limited powers to recompense a complainant. He or she can make recommendations to the Commission (including a recommendation

---

[76] Charities Act 2011, s 317 and Tribunals, Courts and Enforcement Act 2007, ss 11 and 13.

that financial compensation should be paid). In practice, the Commission appears to comply with the Ombudsman's recommendations.

CHAPTER 5

GOVERNANCE STRUCTURES

5.1 The way in which a charity is constituted is fundamental to its governance. A charity's legal form will determine a great deal about the way in which it operates. It will also determine a great deal about who the charity's trustees are and the powers they can exercise and the duties that they are under.

5.2 There is more about the way in which trustees can ensure that they exercise good governance of their charity in **Chapter 8**. This chapter is concerned with the impact on governance of the relationship between the trustees of a charity and its members. By 'members' we mean anyone who has a form of relationship with a charity that enables them to exercise some right or power in relation to it. The nature of that relationship will vary from charity to charity depending on the way in which it is constituted and the specific constitutional provisions that govern membership. Some of the more obvious relationships are:

- Where the beneficiaries of a charity are also its members because they are intended to have some say or involvement in the way in which the charity is run. So, for example, the tenants of a charitable housing association are often also its members.

- Where donors to a charity are also its members because of the significance of their donations to funding its operations. This would include, for example, a charity that conserves historic sites and relies upon a wide membership of individuals interested in such sites to fund a significant part of its work.

- Where a wide membership of individuals gives a charity a certain status or legitimacy that it requires in order to carry out its work. This could include, for example, a charity providing advocacy or services for people with disabilities which has disabled people among its members.

- Where a charity relies upon volunteers for its work and wishes to encourage their continued participation by giving them some say in the way in which it operates.

- Where a charity may draw some or all of its trustees from its members.

- Where a charity is established by stakeholders who have an interest in continuing to have some say in which it operates. This would include, for example, a charity established by individual donors or a charity established by one or more other charities to advance particular charitable purposes.

5.3   Many charities will have individual members but there are no legal restrictions on a charity having corporate members. Many charities do have corporate stakeholders as members, including companies, local authorities and other public bodies and other charities. There is more about stakeholders of this kind acting as members at **5.86–5.94**.

5.4   Not every charity will have members. Charitable companies and CIOs will inevitably have them because this is one of the requirements of the legislation under which they are incorporated. Charitable unincorporated associations will also inevitably have members because they are essentially 'membership organisations', ie, they consist of a group of individuals who wish to act together with some common charitable purpose. Charitable trusts, on the other hand, have no legal requirement for members and, in practice, most do not have them.

5.5   The kind of rights that members may have as part of their membership relationship will also vary from charity to charity.

- Some members may exercise a number of important rights in relation to a charity. These can include rights to:
  - alter the charity's constitution
  - appoint and remove its charity trustees
  - wind the charity up and distribute its surplus assets for similar charitable purposes.
- These rights may derive from the legal form that the charity takes. So, for example, the members of a charitable company will have these rights under the Companies Acts. The members of other charities may have them because of provisions in the charity's constitution (for example, a charitable unincorporated association).
- Other rights conferred upon members may be much less significant from a legal point of view but are as important in governance terms. Members may not have rights to vote on the issues mentioned above, but may be entitled to receive newsletters and other information from a charity, or a right of reduced admission to its properties or facilities or the right to attend an annual meeting to discuss, but not vote on, the way in which the charity is operating.
- In some cases, the members of a charity may be entitled to both voting and other rights.

5.6   The rights that the members exercise will generally reflect the balance of power between the members and trustees intended by the people who set the charity up or who last amended its constitution. In this sense, members can play an important constitutional role in acting as a check and balance on the powers of the trustees.

5.7   Like other terms used in relation to charities, 'member' can mean different things in different contexts. In the context of charitable companies, 'member' usually means the members of a company under company law, as identified in its register of members. However, it can also refer to individuals who, while they are not company law members of the company, exercise certain rights in relation to the company. There is more about membership of charitable companies in **Chapter 2**.

5.8 While the relationship between trustees and members will vary from charity to charity there are certain models that are used more often than others.

'FLAT' MODEL

5.9 The key feature of this model (sometimes referred to as an 'oligarchical' model) is that the members are the same people as the trustees. The aim is to give the trustees an absolute discretion to control the charity where, in contrast to the membership model, there is no need or desire to involve any third party in the governance arrangements. The simplest and most common forms of the flat model are the charitable trust (which has no members) and the charitable company whose trustees are also its members (and whose articles will provide for a trustee to be a member for only so long as he or she is a trustee and vice versa). This model is also now possible with a CIO as the Charities Act 2011[1] expressly provides that the trustees of a CIO may also act as its members (and vice versa), although there is no obligation to arrange things in this way. A charitable company or CIO set up in this way will often be used in preference to a charitable trust because of liability issues (see **Chapter 2**).

5.10 This is a reasonably straightforward governance structure and one that reflects the fact that it is the trustees who are ultimately responsible for managing a charity's operations and will be liable if they fail to do so properly. However, it may not work for a charity that needs to include beneficiaries or other stakeholders as members in order to ensure that it can operate effectively. In those circumstances, the 'hybrid' model (see **5.18–5.21**) may meet its requirements without exposing it to some of the potential problems inherent in the 'membership' model.

5.11 There are a number of considerations that need to be taken into account in relation to a model of this kind. These are explained in more detail at **5.25**.

'MEMBERSHIP' MODEL

5.12 At the other extreme, the key feature of the 'membership' model is a group of members capable of exercising some oversight and control over the activities of the charity trustees.

5.13 The advantage of this model is undoubtedly that it gives the members a say in the governance of the charity and allows them, for example, to take

---

[1] Charities Act 2011, s 206(6).

action in respect of anything proposed by the charity trustees which the members consider will not be for the benefit of the charity's purposes. In that sense, the members may be the custodians of a particular ethos or approach inherent in the way that the charity operates, subject of course to the overriding requirements of charity law.

5.14 The disadvantage of this approach is that it may give the members a degree of control over a charity which may actually impede its effective operation in circumstances where:

- The members may not appreciate or understand operational circumstances to which the charity trustees are responding.
- The members may be motivated by 'personal' beliefs or aims rather than concern for the charity's purposes.
- Some members may disagree with other members about the way in which the charity should operate and use their membership powers to try to win the argument.

5.15 These are all real possibilities. Past court cases have seen a group of scientologists acting to establish control over a mental health organisation whose psychiatric practice they disagreed with, and members of the National Trust seeking to review the Trust's policy on allowing deer hunting on its land. The cost to both charities in terms of management time and legal and other expenses is likely to have been high.

5.16 The position is complicated by the lack of clarity about the legal duties of the members of most charities. There is more about this at 5.22.

5.17 The Charity Commission published a Regulatory Report in 2004 into membership charities[2] which confirms that in the region of 50% of disputes considered by the Commission relate to the sort of membership issues mentioned above. There is more about the particular problems that arise at 5.28.

'HYBRID' MODEL

5.18 The key feature of this model is that it gives the control of a charity to its trustees while allowing others to become members with limited rights. So members would have an entitlement to, say, attend an annual meeting, to receive information about the charity's operations or have privileged rights of admission to property but would have no legal right to control any aspect of the charity's governance.

5.19 In the context of a charitable company, the charity trustees would act as its company law members, but its constitution will provide for a wider class of

---

2   RS7.

members with rights specified in the constitution, or perhaps by the trustees using a power given to them by the constitution. The same effect can be achieved in relation to any other charity by vesting legal rights of control in the charity trustees and vesting other rights in a class of members.

5.20 This approach can be (and often is) used to create different categories and classes of membership. So, for example, a charity can create classes of 'full' members able to vote and other members with no, or restricted, voting rights but other entitlements. It is often preferable to give the charity trustees the power to create different classes of member and to determine the rights that they should have. This gives them the flexibility to alter the rights exercisable by different classes without altering the charity's constitution.

5.21 Using a hybrid model raises many of the issues raised by both the flat and membership models depending on the arrangements that are actually adopted. There is more information about this at **5.25** and **5.28**.

MEMBERS' DUTIES

5.22 With one important exception, the legal duties of the members of a charity are not clear. This is due to the lack of any clear case-law in this area. While there are many cases dealing with the duties of shareholders in commercial companies, they do not clearly establish that a shareholder's powers must be exercised for the benefit of a company as a whole, and there are in addition no clear precedents in the context of charitable companies. The position in relation to charitable unincorporated associations is just as unclear.

5.23 The exception is the CIO, as under the Charities Act 2011, the members of a CIO are obliged to exercise their powers in the way that they decide, in good faith, would be most likely to further the purposes of the CIO.[3] The legislation does not specify what will happen as a result of any failure to comply with this duty, but a breach is likely to allow a claim to be made to the courts for an appropriate order.

5.24 While the position in relation to the members of other forms of charity is unclear, the courts are likely to impose a duty on members. This is consistent with the approach taken by the courts in relation to charities generally (often as part of its equitable jurisdiction) and also with the statutory duty imposed in relation to CIOs by the 2011 Act (which the courts may well refer to in making a decision). It would also be consistent with the approach taken by the Charity Commission, who regard members as acting in a fiduciary capacity. It is perhaps easier to see this in the case of the many charities who have corporate members (including companies, local authorities, other public bodies and other charities) appointed because they are stakeholders of the charity. However, the

---

[3]   Charities Act 2011, s 220.

Commission takes the view that members have a fiduciary duty, regardless of whether they are an individual or a corporate member.

FLAT MODEL ISSUES

5.25 One practical problem posed by this model in practice is that trustees often do not appreciate that they are acting in two capacities, ie as trustees and as members. So, for example, decisions may be taken by members and trustees in different ways, with different notice, quorum and voting requirements for meetings. Although this dual capacity is often regarded by trustees as no more than a technicality invented by lawyers (trustees are unlikely to take a different decision in their different capacities), it can cause problems where, for example, the charity's powers are not properly exercised as a consequence. In practice, the key to this issue is ensuring that trustees receive a proper induction when they are appointed.

5.26 Another problem that can arise in relation to this model is that, unless properly drafted, the charity's constitution may not ensure that the trustees from time to time are also the members from time to time (and vice versa). Problems can arise in practice where a person ceases to act as a trustee but remains a member and is perhaps unwilling to relinquish his or her membership or moves address and cannot be located.

5.27 A further issue can arise where there is no limit on the number of members of a charity, with the result that there is no limit on the number of trustees. In general, a charity with too many trustees is likely to experience problems in decision-making and effective governance generally.

MEMBERSHIP MODEL ISSUES

5.28 On the governance issues faced by membership charities, the Charity Commission's Regulatory Report RS7 says:

> 'Membership charities, like all charities, can run into difficulties if proper attention is not paid to their governance arrangements. The scope for problems is greater in membership charities, however, because the number of people involved can make the governance arrangements more complex to manage. Differences of opinion sometimes arise which, if not well managed, can disrupt the smooth running of the charity and result in charitable resources being wasted. Analysis of a sample of Charity Commission casework showed that more cases are opened for membership charities than other organisations, including a greater proportion of cases related to internal disputes ...
>
> Our findings show that membership charities receive wide-ranging benefits from their members, and these benefits include:
>
> • enhancing the trustee board's transparency and accountability;
> • providing a greater appreciation of the needs of beneficiaries;

- improving a charity's influence within the charity sector, giving weight to an advocacy role;
- providing fundraising opportunities; and
- providing a consistent source of trustees.

However, Charity Commission experience indicates that those few charities that do run into problems with their membership are likely to have one or more of the following features:

- Trustees are not clear about their role and their legal responsibilities toward their charity's members.
- Charity members are not clear about their role and responsibilities towards the charity.
- There are insufficient or inadequate governance structures in place to manage the charity's relationship with its members.
- The trustee body puts up barriers to membership involvement, either deliberately or inadvertently.
- The charity's membership lacks diversity so the trustee board is self-perpetuating or change-resistant and unrepresentative of its potential beneficiaries.
- Members or trustees deliberately abuse voting procedures and rights.
- There are weak administrative arrangements in place leading to problems such as accusations of elections being held on the basis of inaccurate membership lists or problems with organising quorate meetings.'

5.29 There are a number of key points that will need to be addressed if a membership charity wishes to manage its relationship with its members effectively. These are set out below.

5.30 If a charity is to manage its relationship with its members well, it has to know who they are. This is often a problem in practice. While company law obliges the trustees of a charitable company to maintain a register of its members, this is a requirement that is often not observed by charities. Without the discipline of making an annual return of members and issuing them with share certificates that are a requirements for share companies, a charitable company limited by guarantee may well have records that do not show definitively who its members are. And while other charities (such as unincorporated associations) may have a constitutional requirement for a register of members to be kept, information is often out of date.

5.31 The Charities Act 2011 gives the Charity Commission the power to determine who are the members of a charity, either on the application of the charity itself or at any time after an Inquiry (see **4.44**) has been instituted.[4] This is obviously a useful fallback provision in the event that there is uncertainty or dispute about the identity of a charity's members, but not a power which is regularly used by the Commission. In practice, therefore, the key points will be that:

---

[4] Charities Act 2011, s 111.

- The charity's constitution clearly sets out the mechanism for members to become, and cease to be, members.
- Records of membership are kept up to date.
- If possible, there is a provision in the charity's constitution for the trustees to determine conclusively whether a person is or is not a member of the charity where the position is uncertain.

5.32 The charity trustees must understand the legal relationship between the charity and its members, the members' rights and duties in relation to the charity and the trustees' own duties to the members. It will be the trustees' responsibility to interpret the constitution in relation to members and they must understand how it is intended to work. The key points will be that:

- where relevant, the trustees understand the differences in status between different categories of member;
- a clear explanation of the position is provided to new trustees as part of their induction (see **Chapter 8**).

5.33 The charity's constitution must set out the provisions governing membership clearly and, in line with the general principle that the constitution should be a living document and fit for its purpose, must reflect what happens, or is intended to happen, in practice. The key points are:

- Ensure that the constitutional provisions in relation to members are up to date and, if not, revise them.
- Consider setting out the framework for the membership arrangements in the constitution but setting out the detail in a set of rules or subsidiary handbook for members that can be altered by the trustees from time to time without the need for a change to the constitution itself.
- Irrespective of where the membership arrangements are set out, ensure that, as a minimum, they cover:
  - who is eligible to be a member of the charity and, where relevant, the eligibility criteria for different types of member;
  - how membership can be terminated or suspended and any grievance procedure that can be invoked by a member in these circumstances;
  - how voting rights are to be distributed;
  - conditions and rules regarding attending and voting at the annual general meeting, including the voting and quorum provisions;
  - provisions for calling an extraordinary general meeting and the voting and quorum provisions; and
  - how alterations to the constitution or dissolution of the charity can be decided on.

5.34 Members must be given the tools to understand their rights and duties in relation to the charity. The key points are:

- The constitutional provisions in relation to membership must be explained, with an emphasis on the rights of members to vote on, say, the appointment of trustees. A handbook or set of rules is often the best way of explaining the position in a way that will be easily understood by a wide range of members.

- The charity should communicate with its members regularly and effectively in order to keep them informed about its operations and, in particular, issues which affect them as members.

- Trustees should consider whether a charity's constitution should include an express provision governing members' duties to the charity. This will obviously not be strictly necessary in relation to a CIO (whose members will have a statutory duty to act in good faith and in a way which is most likely to further the interests of the charity), but a similar provision might usefully be added to the constitution of any charity.

5.35 Where members have voting rights, the arrangements for those rights to be exercised must be clearly formulated and explained. The key points are:

- The periods of notice for annual and extraordinary general meetings must be clear and notices must be given on time and set out the business which is to be discussed at a particular meeting.

- The arrangements for giving notice must be clear and adhered to. Giving notice electronically is likely to be the most cost-effective method but this must be expressly authorised by the charity's constitution.

- The voting and quorum requirements at a meeting must be observed but must also be workable. A provision which requires a quorum of not less than one-third of the members may make sense in the context of a charity with 30 members, but much less so for a charity with 300 members. The same is true of majority voting requirements. A requirement for two-thirds of the members at the meeting to vote for a particular resolution may be workable whereas a requirement for a vote of two-thirds of all of the members may not.

- Provisions for proxy voting may help to ensure that meetings are quorate and that resolutions can be passed, but the charity's constitution must provide for them expressly (except for a charitable company where a member has a right to appoint a proxy under the Companies Act 2006)[5] and the relevant provisions must be clearly explained to members.

There is more about members' meetings at **5.38**.

5.36 A charity may wish to adopt a mediation procedure in relation to disputes with members. This should be set out in writing and made available to all members, perhaps as part of a set of rules or a handbook.

---

[5]   Companies Act 2006, s 324(1).

5.37 The consequences of allowing disputes with members to arise are potentially serious. The courts have considered a number of cases relating to membership disputes. In addition, the Charity Commission may well consider intervening in disputes in certain circumstances and using its powers in relation to Schemes, Orders and Inquiries accordingly (see **Chapter 4** for more on this). The Commission's own guidance on this is that:[6]

> 'The Charity Commission may intervene:
>
> - where concerns are expressed about serious mismanagement, for example involving a failure to observe the requirements of charity law;
> - where there is clear evidence of deliberate abuse;
> - where trustees are not acting in accordance with the provisions of the governing document;
> - where the administration of the charity has broken down to such an extent that the charity is not working effectively;
> - where there is a clear danger of the name of charity being brought into disrepute; or
> - where honest errors have resulted in problems (such as decisions of inquorate meetings being acted upon) that require us to authorise actions necessary to remedy the situation; and
> - where the use of the Charity Commission's powers are proportionate to it.
>
> Sincerely held but differing views are of no concern to the Charity Commission if trustees are acting properly. Matters of policy or administration may be disputed within the trusteeship or within the membership but they must be settled within and in accordance with the terms of the charity's governing document. Members who disagree with the direction of the charity to which they belong can make a change by exercising their right to vote, either at the AGM or by calling an EGM (which requires a sufficient number of members agreeing to it), or by putting themselves in a position to be elected on to the committee. Where none of these courses of action result in a satisfactory conclusion for a disaffected member, they should accept the majority opinion or consider leaving. A complaint to the Charity Commission should only be made where there are well-founded suspicions or evidence of malpractice.'

MEETINGS

5.38 Except in relation to charitable companies and CIOs, there is no general legal requirement that a charity need hold meetings of its members. The position will be determined by a charity's constitution, which will usually require meetings to be held and, if so, will generally spell out in some detail the way in which they are convened, the business that should be transacted at them and the voting and quorum requirements. The most important aspects of meetings are summarised below, but we should emphasise that the position will depend upon the specific provisions of every charity's constitution and will, therefore, vary from charity to charity.

---

6   RS7.

5.39 As we have mentioned, there are specific legal requirements in relation to meetings of a charitable company's members. We have summarised the main considerations below at **5.62**. The regulations which govern meetings of a CIO's are broadly based on the requirements for companies and we have summarised the key requirements at **5.83**.

5.40 The Charity Commission has published some helpful guidance on meetings in conjunction with the Institute of Chartered Secretaries and Administrators.[7] This is a useful summary and, as the Commission points out:

> 'Where business is transacted at meetings, it is essential for the good governance of charities that the meetings should be effective. Meetings provide an environment for informed decision making, clarification of responsibilities and monitoring the implementation of decisions.'

Frequency

5.41 There are no legal restrictions on the frequency with which members' meetings should be held except where the provisions of a charity's constitution specify a particular number. Any charity, whether incorporated or unincorporated will need to hold an AGM only if it is required to do so by its constitution.

5.42 If a charity's constitution does require the holding of an AGM, it will often spell out the business that needs to be transacted at it. This will generally include the approval of the charity's accounts for the previous financial year and the election or re-election of the charity's trustees by the members. The position will, however, vary from charity to charity.

Notice

5.43 In the case of an unincorporated charity, there are no legal rules that govern the periods of notice that are required at members' meetings. The notice period is governed solely by the provisions of the charity's constitution. The key points are:

- The charity's constitution will often identify who is able to call a meeting. The charity's trustees will generally be able to do so, but the constitution may also provide for one or more of the members to do so.

- The charity's constitution will often specify the number of days' notice that need to be given to members. Any reference to 'clear days' excludes the day on which the notice is received by the member and the day of the meeting itself. The same is true of references to 'days' where there is nothing else in the constitution which provides that the days on which notice is received and the meeting is held are to be counted within the notice period.

---

[7] CC 48.

- The notice must be sent to everyone entitled to receive it under the charity's constitution.

- The charity's constitution may specify how notice should be given (eg by post, fax or email). It may also specify when notice is deemed to be given (eg by specifying that notices sent by first class post are deemed to have been served on the following day). The Charities Act 2011, s 332 provides specifically for notices to be given to a charity's members by post, in which case they are deemed to be received by the time the letter would have been delivered 'in the ordinary course of post'.

- The charity's constitution will also generally state the address to which a member's notice should be given. Again, the Charities Act 2011, s 332 allows the charity's trustees to send the notice to the last address given to the charity by a member.

- The notice must, as a minimum, confirm the date, time and place of the meeting and state its purpose sufficiently clearly. The key point is whether the notice contains sufficient information about the matters that will be considered to enable members to decide whether or not to attend the meeting.

- The notice must not contravene any rules and regulations in relation to the charity. There is more about this at **5.46**.

5.44 Where a notice is not properly given, any decisions taken at the meeting will be invalid. There are a number of ways in which decisions may still validly be taken notwithstanding that notice has not been properly given:

- It may be possible to rectify an invalid notice by sending out a further notice clarifying the position, but the second notice would need to be sent within the time-limits which apply to the giving of the original notice of the meeting.

- The charity's constitution may include an express provision that an accidental omission to give notice of a meeting to someone entitled to receive it (or their failure to receive it because, for example, it has been lost in the post) will not invalidate the meeting that is held subsequently.

- If all of the people who are entitled to receive notice of a meeting waive the requirement to receive a valid notice, the meeting can still proceed. Some charities' constitutions may lower this requirement so that, for example, a specified percentage of members can agree to waive the entitlement to a valid notice.

5.45 Some charities' constitutions may not provide for express periods of notice. Those convening a meeting in the absence of such provision will need to give reasonable notice. The period of notice that applies to the meetings of a charitable company's members (14 clear days) would be a reasonable starting point. The trustees of a charity which is in this position may well wish to amend its constitution to include specified periods of notice. There is more about constitutional changes at **Chapter 15**.

Rules and regulations

5.46 A charity's constitution will often give its trustees power to make rules and regulations in relation to the way in which they convene and hold members' meetings in order to give them flexibility to work in the most effective way. This is the approach usually taken by the constitution of a charitable company (and reflects the approach taken by companies generally) but any charity can adopt a similar approach with an appropriate constitutional provision. Any rules and regulations that are made should preferably be in writing and reviewed by the trustees from time to time. This should not conflict with the provisions of the constitution itself (on the basis that the constitution can only properly be altered in accordance with whatever mechanism applies to it). Any notice given by the charity's trustees must comply with any relevant rules and regulations.

Electronic meetings

5.47 A valid meeting can only usually be held where the participants can see and hear each other (which will include meetings held by way of video conference or web camera). However, a charity's constitution can expressly widen the definition of 'meeting'. An appropriate provision could authorise meetings to be held by way of telephone conference.

Voting

5.48 Voting at members' meetings will be in accordance with the charity's constitution but, if the constitution is silent, a 'simple' majority can pass resolutions. A 'simple' majority exists where more members vote for a particular resolution than against it. A charity's constitution may also provide that a higher or 'special' majority is required in relation to a particular resolution. So, for example, a resolution to dissolve a charity will often require a two-thirds majority vote in order to pass it.

5.49 The majority generally required is a majority of the charity's members present at the relevant meeting. The charity's constitution may alter this in relation to certain resolutions. So, for example, a resolution to exercise the sort of power of dissolution we have mentioned in the previous paragraph may only be passed by a two-thirds majority of *all* of the charity's members rather than a two-thirds majority of the members who actually attend the meetings.

5.50 Detailed requirements in relation to the majority required in respect of particular resolutions are often dealt with in a charity's rules and regulations rather than its constitution. There is more about rules and regulations at **5.46**.

5.51 The charity's constitution (or any rules and regulations made under it) govern the way in which members' votes are cast and counted. If the charity's constitution is silent, voting will be on a 'show of hands'. This means that the chairman of the meeting will ask the members present to indicate how they vote by holding up their hands. This is often a quick and effective way of passing resolutions, but it does not allow for voting by members who may have different voting rights. This may be because, for example, a particular class of members is able to cast more votes on a particular issue than another class of members. The 'show of hands' method is also potentially imprecise given that the chairman must count the votes cast and may make a mistake in doing so.

5.52   For these reasons, a vote may also be taken using a 'poll'. The purpose of a vote by poll is to ensure that votes cast are recorded in writing and are counted in an accurate way which, if appropriate, reflects any weighted voting rights. There is the common law right for any member to demand a poll on a particular resolution, although this can generally be limited or excluded by express provisions in the charity's constitution.[8]

5.53   The charity's constitution or rules and regulations relating to meetings may specify who should act as chairman of a member's meeting (this will often be the chairman of the board of trustees acting in another capacity) and whether he or she should exercise a 'casting' or 'second' vote in the event of deadlock. If there is no express provision for the chairman to exercise a casting or second vote, he or she cannot exercise such a vote.

Written resolutions

5.54   If a charity cannot hold a meeting to consider a resolution, the alternative is for the necessary majority (in accordance with the charity's constitution) of the members to sign a written resolution. As a general principle, all of the members can agree to do in writing what only a majority of them could resolve to do at a meeting. A charity's constitution may contain an express provision for a written resolution of the members of the charity but, where the constitution is silent, the members can still sign a written resolution unless there is something in the charity's constitution which conflicts with, or prohibits, this approach. A charity's constitution may provide for a minimum number of members to sign a written resolution, in which case it will be valid provided their signatures can be obtained.

Quorum

5.55   A charity's constitution will usually specify the quorum that applies at a meeting. In other cases, the quorum may be set out in rules or regulations in relation to the conduct of meetings. Different quorums may apply to different meetings or to different resolutions. The quorum required will often vary from charity to charity. A charity with a significant number of individual members will wish to avoid a quorum based upon a percentage of their number which may mean that, in practice, members' meetings can never be quorate. The quorum will often be the 'lower of' or 'greater of' a fixed number or proportion of members, so that they can keep pace with changing numbers of members.

---

[8]   *R v Wimbledon Local Board* [1882] 8 QBD 459.

5.56 The number of members necessary for a quorum must be present 'in person'. An authorised representative of a corporate member will be present 'in person' for the purposes of this rule. Proxies, however, will not count unless the charity's constitution or rules and regulations in relation to meetings expressly provide that they should count.

5.57 In general, a meeting must be quorate from start to finish. However, a charity's constitution (or rules and regulations relating to the conduct of meetings) may provide a meeting has only to be quorate at the start of the meeting. If so, all of the resolutions passed at the meeting will be valid notwithstanding that it may have become inquorate part of the way through.

Other attendees

5.58 There are a number of people who may attend members' meetings in addition to the members themselves. Who can or should attend will depend generally upon the charity's constitution or the rules and regulations relating to the conduct of its meetings, but will often include:

- the secretary (if there is one);
- professional advisers to the charity;
- the charity's trustees (including the chairman of the board, who will often act as the chairman of the members' meeting); and
- senior employees (if any).

5.59 Clearly, attendance at a members' meeting does not mean that any of these people are entitled to vote on any of the business being considered by the members at the meeting, although the chairman of a meeting may sometimes consider it helpful for some attendees to speak at the meeting, perhaps in order to explain particular issues for the members.

Minutes

5.60 Whether there is an express legal requirement on a charity to maintain minutes of its members' meetings will depend upon the terms of its constitution, but the obligation to maintain good records is in any event a part of the trustees' duty to safeguard its assets. For this reason, all charities should maintain comprehensive and accurate records of the business transacted at their members' meetings. The Charity Commission's guidance states that:[9]

> 'Whatever may be the legal requirements, we recommend that accurate minutes are kept of all meetings. The minutes do not need to be a word for word record, but need to record information that is important to the charity. We recommend that each set of minutes give:
>
> - the name of the charity;

---

[9] CC 48.

- the type of meeting;
- the date and time the meetings was held;
- apologies for absence;
- the names of those present, including:
  - in what capacity they attended eg trustee, advisor etc; and
  - for what items on the agenda.

...

The minutes would usually record:

- the precise wording of any resolution together with the name of the proposer and (optionally) the seconder of the motion;
- a summary of the discussion on each item of business;
- information upon which the decision was based;
- details of the decision, ie who voted and how and, in the event of an equality of votes, if the chair used a casting vote;
- the action required;
- the names of the people who are responsible for implementing the decision; and
- the date, time and venue of the next meeting.'

5.61 The Charity Commission's guidance also emphasises the importance of preparing and approving accurate minutes. It states as follows:[10]

'It should be noted that the formal minutes, once approved and signed as an accurate record by the chairman, form the only legal record of the business of the meeting.'

COMPANY MEETINGS

5.62 As we have indicated earlier in this chapter, there is a specific body of rules derived from companies legislation and case-law which governs the way in which meetings of the members of a charitable company must be conducted. We summarise the main considerations below. These comments should be read in conjunction with our comments on meetings generally at **5.38–5.61**.

Frequency

5.63 The Companies Act 2006 abolished the requirement for private companies to hold an 'annual general meeting' (or 'AGM'). Many charitable companies still hold an AGM each year, and must do so if required by their constitution. The main purpose of the AGM is to lay the company's accounts before the members, re-appoint the company's auditors (and fix their remuneration) and deal with any retirement by rotation of the trustees.

---

[10]   CC 48.

5.64 Any meeting of the members of a charitable company other than an AGM is, under the Companies Act 2006, simply a 'general meeting' or 'GM'. However, many charities will still refer to this as an 'extraordinary general meeting' or 'EGM'. There is no requirement that a GM should ever be held, but both the directors and members have the power to call one. This is explained at 5.65.

Notice

5.65 The Companies Act 2006 spells out in detail the procedures for convening, and giving notice of, meetings of members. Broadly:

- The charitable company's trustees have the power to convene a GM whenever they think it appropriate in the interests of the charity. Most charitable companies' constitutions will give trustees an express power to convene a GM in any event.

- The trustees of a charitable company must also convene a GM on a 'members' requisition'. This is a demand by those members representing not less than one-twentieth of the total voting rights of all of the members at the date of the requisition who are able to vote at general meetings.[11]

- Notice of any meeting must be sent to anyone who is entitled, under the terms of the company's constitution, to receive notice. In general, this will be all of the members of the charitable company. The charitable company's auditors are also entitled to receive notice of any meeting.[12]

- A charitable company's constitution will usually specify that notice of a meeting must be given to its members in writing. This includes giving notice electronically, either to an email address or via a website.[13]

- The charitable company's constitution will also usually specify when notice is deemed to be given. Notices should be sent to the address recorded for a particular member in the register of members. This includes an electronic address.

- The notice must confirm the date, time and place of the meeting and state its purpose sufficiently clearly. The key point is that the notice must contain sufficient information about the matters that will be considered to enable members to decide whether or not to attend the meetings.

- The period of notice required is specified by s 307 of the Companies Act 2006 as 14 days' notice in writing. The period of notice required excludes both the day on which the notice is received by the member and the day on which the meeting is held.

- There are certain provisions for 'special notice' to be given for particular resolutions, including any resolution to remove a trustee by ordinary

---

[11] Companies Act 2006, s 303.
[12] Companies Act 2006, s 502.
[13] Companies Act 2006, s 308.

resolution.[14] The period of special notice is not less than 28 days before the meeting at which the relevant resolution is to be proposed.

5.66 Where the notice is not properly given, any decisions taken at the meeting will be invalid. There are a number of ways in which decisions may still validly be taken notwithstanding that notice has not been properly given:

- It may be possible to rectify an invalid notice by sending out a further notice clarifying the position, but the second notice would need to be sent within the time-limits which apply to the giving of the original notice of the meeting.

- The charitable company's constitution may include an express provision that an accidental omission to give notice of a meeting to someone entitled to receive it (or their failure to receive it because, for example, it has been lost in the post) will not invalidate the meeting that is held subsequently.

- The Companies Act 2006 contains a provision for a majority of members to consent to the giving of a short notice. The 'requisite majority' for this purpose is all of those members who together hold not less than 90% of the total voting rights exercisable at the meeting unless the charitable company's constitution sets a higher percentage not higher than 95%.[15]

5.67 Where a decision is taken by the members of a charitable company at a meeting which has not been validly called, the decision can effectively be ratified by a subsequent resolution of the members at a properly called meeting.

5.68 Under the Companies Act 2006,[16] the court has the power to call a meeting of a company's members. This power has been used in a 2011 case involving a company limited by guarantee which owned three mosques, in which the court was asked to make an order to convene a general meeting for the purpose of appointing directors, where a meeting could not be requisitioned by the members.

Rules and regulations

5.69 A charitable company's constitution will often give its trustees power to make rules and regulations in relation to the way in which they convene and hold members' meetings. The new rules and regulations that are made should preferably be in writing and be reviewed by the trustees from time to time. These should not conflict with the provisions of the charity's constitution. Any notice given by the charity's trustees must comply with any relevant rules and regulations.

---

14   Companies Act 2006, s 312.
15   Companies Act 2006, s 307.
16   Companies Act 2006, s 306.

Electronic meetings

5.70 A valid meeting can only usually be held where the participants can see and hear each other (which will include meetings held by way of video conference or web camera). However, a charity's constitution can expressly widen the definition of 'meeting'. An appropriate provision could authorise meetings to be held by way of telephone conference.

Voting

5.71 Voting at the meetings of members of a charitable company will be in accordance with the charity's constitution. The majority required in respect of certain resolutions will be determined by company law.

5.72 Resolutions passed by a simple majority are usually referred to as 'ordinary resolutions' in the context of charitable companies. References to 'resolutions' in the Companies Acts should be interpreted as references to 'ordinary resolutions'. A 'special resolution' of the members means a resolution passed by a majority of not less than 75%. This will include, for example, a resolution to alter a charitable company's constitution.

5.73 A charitable company's constitution will determine how members' votes are cast and counted. In general, voting will be by way of a 'show of hands'. However, there is both a common law and statutory right for members to demand that voting should be way of a 'poll'.[17] This right cannot be excluded by the terms of the charitable company's constitution. The statutory right enables five or more members or members holding not less than one tenth of the total voting right to demand a poll.

5.74 The purpose of a vote by poll is to ensure that votes cast are recorded in writing and are counted in an accurate way which reflects any weighted voting rights.

5.75 A charitable company incorporated under the Companies Act 1985 or earlier may have a provision in its constitution specifying that the chairman of the members' meeting should exercise a 'casting' or 'second' vote in the event of deadlock. In the absence of a provision of this kind, the chairman has no second or casting vote in addition to any other vote he or she may have. Companies incorporated after 1 October 2007 cannot pass a resolution using a chairman's casting vote.[18]

Written resolutions

5.76 The Companies Act 2006 provides that a written resolution is passed when the 'required majority' of members have signed it. The required majority is the number of members who would be required to vote for a particular

---

[17] Companies Act 2006, s 321.
[18] Companies Act 2006, ss 281(3) and 282.

ordinary or special resolution at a meeting. The ability to pass written resolutions of this kind is subject to a number of detailed requirements in relation to the circulation of written resolutions to all members but, provided these restrictions are observed, the ability to pass written resolutions in this way is often helpful.

Quorum

5.77 A charitable company's constitution will usually specify the quorum that applies at a meeting but, if no quorum is specified, the quorum is two members personally present.[19] In the case of a single-member charitable company, the quorum is reduced to one person.

5.78 The quorum required by a charitable company's constitution may vary depending upon the resolution that is proposed. Typically, the quorum will be the 'lower of' or 'greater of' a fixed number or proportion of members, so that they can keep pace with a changing number of members.

5.79 The number of members necessary for the quorum must be present at the meeting 'in person'. An authorised representative of a corporate member will be present 'in person' for the purposes of this rule.[20] A proxy will not be personally present, unless the charitable company's constitution expressly provides for it to count.

5.80 In general, a meeting must be quorate from start to finish. However, a charitable company's constitution may often provide that a quorum must be present 'at the time when the meeting is called to order'. This means that the quorum must be satisfied at the start of the meeting but is not necessary for the quorum to be maintained until the finish.

Other attendees

5.81 A charitable company's auditors have a right to attend general meetings.[21] Who else can or should attend will generally depend upon the terms of the charity's constitution. The position is broadly similar to the position in relation to charities that are not set up as companies.

Minutes

5.82 The Companies Act 2006, s 355 obliges every charitable company to keep minutes of all of the proceedings of its general meetings. Section 356(4) provides that any minute which is signed by the chairman of the meeting, or by

---

[19] Companies Act 2006, s 318.
[20] Companies Act 2006, s 318.
[21] Companies Act 2006, s 502.

the chairman of the next succeeding meeting, is evidence of the proceedings. The Charity Commission's guidance in relation to minutes is in CC 48 (see 5.60).

Meetings of the members of a CIO

5.83 The regulations governing the constitution and procedure of CIOs[22] are modelled broadly on companies legislation, albeit without the same detail in many areas. Rather than specifying detailed procedure which CIOs must follow in relation to meetings and decision making, the regulations set out the minimum requirements which the constitution of a CIO must satisfy in relation to holding meetings. For example, there is no automatic right for members of a CIO to appoint a proxy to attend meetings in their place or to demand a poll vote and no automatic ability to pass resolutions in writing. However, if the constitution provides for these, the regulations specify further detail which the constitution must prescribe. These will be spelled out in the constitution if applicable.

5.84 The regulations do, however, contain specific requirements in relation to giving notice of meetings, which are modelled on company procedure. 14 clear days' notice of a members' meeting must to be given to all of the CIO's members and trustees, provided that a simple majority of the members holding 90% or more of the voting rights in the CIO may consent to short notice.

5.85 The regulations do not require the constitution to include provisions for holding an AGM.

STAKEHOLDER MEMBERS

5.86 Charities with stakeholder members face a series of particular issues that will need to be addressed. By 'stakeholder members' we mean corporate members of charities who are members because they have some interest in what the charity does. These can include companies, local authorities and other public bodies and other charities. So, for example, a charity established to provide sports and leisure services under a contract with a local authority may admit the local authority as a member.

5.87 A stakeholder member will often appoint an individual (usually referred to as an 'authorised representative') to act on its behalf. The charity's constitution should provide expressly for this and set out the mechanism by which such individuals are appointed and removed.

5.88 A stakeholder member may also have the right to appoint a trustee of the charity in order to give it more direct influence over the way in which the

---

[22] The Charitable Incorporated Organisations (General) Regulations 2012, SI 2012/3012.

charity operates. Again, the mechanism by which such individual trustees are appointed and removed should be clearly set out in the charity's constitution.

5.89 Giving a stakeholder the right to be a member of a charity can cause problems where there is a conflict between the interests of the stakeholder and the interests of the charity. The stakeholder member's authorised representative may wish to give priority to the stakeholder's own interests over the interests of the charity. As explained at 5.22, the duty owed by a member to a charity is unclear, except in relation to a CIO or where there is an express duty incorporated into the constitution. Having said that, it is possible that the court will conclude that any member should act in good faith in the interests of the charity. Both the stakeholder and the charity should be made aware of the position in cases of conflict.

5.90 The problems caused by conflicts of interest are more acute where a stakeholder is able to appoint or nominate a trustee of the charity. Again, the trustee may be faced with a decision where he or she would prefer to give priority to the interests of the stakeholder over the interests of the charity. The position is likely to be particularly difficult where the appointee or nominee is an officer or employee of the stakeholder or, where the stakeholder is itself a charity, is one of its trustees. The duty of a charity trustee to act only for the benefit of his or her charity and to avoid conflicts of interest is absolutely clear, so that any decision by a trustee which is motivated by a desire to prefer the stakeholder's interests will be a breach of trust.

5.91 There are some steps that can be taken to avoid problems arising out of conflict of this kind:

- Where a charity is being set up by one or more stakeholders, some thought should be given to whether stakeholders should have an express right to appoint or nominate trustees in addition to acting as members. The alternative would be to give the stakeholder member a right to appoint an 'Observer' with a right to attend and speak at trustees' meetings with a view to explaining the stakeholder's views and reporting back to the stakeholder on the trustees' thinking in relation to the charity. An Observer has no voting rights and is not therefore a charity trustee (unless he or she actually participates in the management and control of the charity), so that there is no scope for any conflict of interest to arise. The disadvantage of this approach is that the stakeholder will generally have less influence over the charity's activities than if it were able to appoint a trustee directly.

- As part of their induction, trustees appointed or nominated by stakeholders should understand that, while they have been appointed to represent the views of the stakeholders in relation to the charity, their duty is to act in the best interests of the charity alone.

- The charity's constitution should include a mechanism for dealing with conflicts of interest that will allow trustees to declare their interests and/or not to participate in particular potentially conflicted decisions. There is more about trustees' conflicts of interests in **Chapter 8**.

5.92 The charity's constitution should clearly distinguish between a stakeholder's right to appoint a trustee of the charity and the right to nominate a person for appointment as a trustee by the charity's own trustees. Giving a stakeholder a direct right to appoint a trustee may mean that the person appointed does not match the criteria set by the charity's trustees for appointments. This issue should be addressed in the following way:

- If the stakeholder has a right to appoint trustees, the trustees should have the power to set clear criteria for appointees as part of their identification of the skills required for trustees generally.

- The trustees could also have the power to appoint additional trustees to fill any skills gap. These are usually referred to as 'co-opted' trustees. There is more information about this in **Chapter 8**.

- Stakeholders could be given the right to nominate trustees for appointment by the trustees instead of a direct right of appointment. This will allow the trustees to control the composition of the board and the skill set of the trustees.

5.93 Stakeholder involvement should be reviewed on a regular basis. As time passes and a charity develops, its stakeholders may change with the consequence that its stakeholder members should change. Those establishing new charities should consider including a mechanism for adding new stakeholder members, perhaps with the consent of a majority of existing stakeholder members. The possibility of stakeholder members ceasing to exist or changing their legal form by way of restructuring or merger should also be dealt with expressly so that it is clear in which circumstances membership rights will cease or transfer to a successor.

5.94 Stakeholders will need to consider whether there are restrictions on their own ability to become stakeholder members:

- Every stakeholder should ensure that its own constitution authorises it to act as a stakeholder in a charity.

- Company stakeholders should consider whether becoming a stakeholder member will have any implications for them under the accounting rules and practice that require the consolidation of accounts.

- Local authority stakeholders should consider the implications of the rules regulating companies in which local authorities have an interest ie, where a local authority is a member of the company or where persons 'associated' with a local authority are members or directors of it. These may have implications for the company, as well as for the authority itself. At the time of writing, these rules are contained in the Local Government and Housing Act 1989 and legislation made under it. The rules are complex and a discussion of them is outside the scope of this book. The provisions in the 1989 Act are due to be replaced by provisions in the Local Government and Public Involvement in Health Act 2007.

'FEDERAL' AND 'BRANCH' ARRANGEMENTS

5.95 Charities are sometimes set up as part of a 'federation' of other charities, generally operating in different localities. The aim is usually to carry out the work of the charity in particular geographical areas but under the influence of a national 'headquarters' charity which may provide support and assistance to the local charity (perhaps in the form of a standard constitution, assistance with governance arrangements etc).

5.96 The degree of affiliation between the local and the national charities will vary from case to case. From the point of view of good governance, it is obviously essential that the relationship between the two entities is clearly established. In practice, this will mean ensuring that there is clarity in relation to the degree of control that the national charity can exercise over the local charity.

5.97 In contrast to this 'federal' approach, some national charities operate using a 'branch' structure. There is no legal definition of a 'branch' for this purpose. The key point is that the activities carried out locally are the activities of the national charity, but are carried out by individuals on the charity's behalf, usually on the basis of delegated authority. Typically, a local 'subcommittee' of the board of trustees of the main charity will have delegated authority to carry out all of the charity's activities in a particular area. Typically, the delegation will impose a number of restrictions on their ability to operate, including, for example, their ability to spend the charity's funds or to incur significant liabilities.

5.98 Clearly, if a branch structure of this kind is to operate effectively it is essential that the terms on which the subcommittee is authorised to operate are very clear. In exercising authority delegated by the charity's trustees, the delegates themselves will be subject to the same liabilities as charity trustees. They will need to understand the implications of this for them personally.

5.99 The position in relation to the branches is made more complicated by the definition of 'branch' used by the Charities SORP 2005 for accounting purposes. A detailed discussion of this area is outside the scope of this book, but it is important to appreciate that the definition for accounting purposes is wider than the legal interpretation.

CHAPTER 6

TRUSTEES' DUTIES AND LIABILITIES

6.1   The trustees of any charity, regardless of how it is constituted, owe the same duties under the law relating to charities, trusts and trustees. So, for example, the trustees of a charitable company will owe the same duties as the trustees of a charitable trust.[1] There are obviously specific duties imposed by the Charities Act 2011 (eg to register their charity, to prepare an annual report in respect of each financial year etc), but of greater importance are the duties that underpin all of their acts as trustees. The most important duties are:

- to ensure that the charity's assets are applied only for its particular charitable purposes;
- to act within the powers they have as trustees of the charity;
- to exercise those powers only in the best interests of the charity and only for the purposes for which they have been given;
- to avoid any conflict between the charity's interests and the personal interests of the trustee or the duties he or she may owe in some other capacity;
- to act unpaid and avoid any arrangement which may result in the trustee taking any personal benefit directly or indirectly; and
- to exercise their powers personally, without delegating responsibility for decisions to anyone else.

6.2   In discharging these duties, charity trustees are under an obligation to exercise due care and skill. The trustees of an unincorporated charity are under a statutory obligation[2] to exercise such care and skill as is reasonable in the circumstances in exercising a range of powers, including powers of investment and delegation. The level of care and skill required is assessed having regard to:

- any special knowledge or expertise that the trustee has or holds him or herself out as having; and
- where a trustee acts in the course of a business or profession, to any special knowledge or expertise that it is reasonable to expect of a person acting in the course of that kind of business or profession.

---

[1]   *Re The French Protestant Hospital* [1951] Ch 567.
[2]   Trustee Act 2000, s 1.

In principle, this duty applies only to the exercise of the powers conferred on the trustees of unincorporated charities by the Trustee Act 2000, but the courts are likely to apply a similar duty of care to the exercise of other powers exercised by trustees. This is also the approach taken by the Charity Commission.[3]

6.3   The trustees of a charitable company owe a statutory duty as company directors to exercise reasonable care, skill and diligence under the Companies Act 2006. However, the assumption should be that in assessing whether a trustee has discharged his or her duty as a charity trustee, the court will look at the higher standard imposed on trustees by the Trustee Act 2000. That is consistent with the approach taken to the trustees of incorporated charities in the past. It is also consistent with the Charity Commission's approach.[4]

6.4   It is important to appreciate that, while this test does not require a charity trustee to meet wholly objective standards of skill and experience, it does not impose a wholly subjective test (which would only require the trustee to meet his own standards of skill and experience). But the test does provide that a trustee who has, or professes to have, for example, financial expertise will be held to a higher standard in relation to their charity's financial matters than a trustee without that expertise.

6.5   In addition to the duties summarised above, the trustees of a charitable company owe other duties under the Companies Act 2006 and the Insolvency Act 1986. These provisions will apply to the trustees of a charitable company in exactly the same way as the directors of any commercial company.

CHARITABLE COMPANIES – COMPANIES ACT 2006

6.6   The Companies Act 2006 imposes a number of specific statutory duties on company directors.[5] These are:

- to act within their powers;
- to exercise independent skill and judgement;
- to exercise reasonable care, skill and diligence;
- to avoid conflicts of interest;
- to declare interests;
- not to accept benefits from third parties; and
- to promote the success of the company.

6.7   Some of these duties derive from the pre-existing common law as it related to the fiduciary duties of company directors and the Act states that the

---

[3]   CC 3.
[4]   CC 3.
[5]   Companies Act 2006, ss 171–177.

duties must be interpreted and applied having regard to the common law rules and equitable principles previously established. Others re-express statutory duties imposed by previous legislation in relation to companies. Significantly, however, these duties are also consistent with the duties imposed upon charity trustees generally (as summarised above). So, for example, a director of a charitable company owes a duty to avoid conflicts of interest under both the common law rules relating to trustees and the statutory rules imposed by the Companies Acts.

6.8   One possible exception to this is the duty to promote the success of the company, which replaced the common law principle of acting in a company's best interests that applied before the Companies Act 2006. The duty on every director is that he 'should act in a way he considers, in good faith, would be most likely to promote the success of the company for the benefit of the members as a whole' and that, in doing so, he or she must consider:

- the likely long-term consequences of the decision;
- the interests of the employees;
- the need to foster business relationships with suppliers, customers and others;
- the impact of the company's operations on the community and the environment;
- the desirability of maintaining the company's reputation for high standards of business conduct; and
- the need to act fairly between the members of the company.

6.9   The duty to promote the success of the company was driven by a desire to use the Companies Act 2006 to put directors' duties in a wider social, ethical and environmental framework than had previously applied. This reflects the principle identified by the Company Law Reform Final Report (and endorsed by the Government) of 'enlightened shareholder value'. The duty is, however, modified as it applies to charitable companies. Where a company has a purpose that consists of or includes a purpose other than the benefit of its members, the reference to 'most likely to promote the success of the company for the benefit of the members as a whole' is to be read as 'most likely to achieve those purposes'.[6] In other words, in the context of a charitable company, promoting the success of the company is to be interpreted as promoting its charitable purposes.

6.10   Clearly not all of the matters specified by the Companies Act 2006 will be relevant to charitable companies. There will, for example, be no practical requirement to act fairly between the members of a charitable company in the same way as the shareholders in a commercial company, because the members have no personal financial interest in the charity.

---

[6]   Companies Act 2006, s 172(2).

6.11 There may be circumstances in which the Companies Act duties could conflict with the duties imposed on charity trustees generally. The duty to take into account the impact of the charity's activities on the community generally may, for example, conflict with the duty to act only in the best interests of the charity where its charitable purposes focus only on a particular section of the community.

6.12 In addition to these statutory duties, the Companies Act 2006 imposes a number of more administrative duties on company directors. These include duties to:

- maintain the company's statutory books and records;
- file resolutions and other corporate documents with Companies House;
- keep accounting records; and
- prepare and file an annual report and accounts.

6.13 There are more than 150 criminal offences in the Companies Act 2006 which may be committed by a company and for which a director in default may be prosecuted. The penalties range from imprisonment for up to 2 years to fines. Experience suggests that criminal prosecutions are rare. The more usual sanction for default is a financial penalty imposed by Companies House or disqualification as a director (see **6.16**).

CHARITABLE COMPANIES – INSOLVENCY ACT 1986

6.14 Where a charitable company has financial problems, its trustees will be faced with difficult judgements about the best way of managing them. In those circumstances, there are two provisions of the Insolvency Act 1986 (IA 1986) that can impose personal liability on the directors of a charitable company for 'wrongful' and 'fraudulent' trading.

Wrongful trading (IA 1986, s 214)	Where, before the start of an insolvent liquidation of the company, a director knew or ought to have known that there was no reasonable prospect that the company would avoid insolvent liquidation, its liquidator can apply to the court for an order obliging the director to contribute to the company's assets out of his or her own personal assets.
	The director can avoid liability to make a personal contribution if he or she can show that, once they had concluded, or ought to have concluded, that there was no reasonable prospect that the company would avoid insolvent liquidation, he or she took every step with a view to minimising the potential loss to creditors.

Fraudulent trading (IA 1986, s 213)	Where, in the course of the insolvent liquidation of a company, it appears that any business of the company has been carried on with intent to defraud its creditors, the liquidator can apply to the court for an order obliging anyone who was knowingly a party to carrying on the business in that way (including the directors) to contribute to the company's assets out of his or her own personal assets.
	The liquidator must show (beyond reasonable doubt given that fraudulent trading involves dishonesty) that the director took positive steps to continue to trade and incur debts when he or she knew that there was no reasonable prospect of repaying them.

6.15 The liquidator of any insolvent charitable company will assess whether there are claims against the trustees for wrongful or fraudulent trading. Liability extends to any 'shadow director'; in other words, to anyone not formally appointed as a director but in accordance with whose directions or instructions the appointed directors were accustomed to act.

6.16 The liquidator can also bring other claims against the trustees of a charitable company under the Insolvency Act 1986. These include claims for misconduct in the course of winding up,[7] false representations to creditors,[8] material omissions from statements relating to the charitable company's affairs[9] and misfeasance or breaches of duty.[10] The liquidator will also make a report to the Secretary of State for Business Innovation and Skills (BIS) on the conduct of the directors and any shadow directors of the company. That report may form the basis of disqualification proceedings under the Company Directors Disqualification Act 1986.

6.17 In practice, and in the absence of any dishonesty, the trustees of a charitable company in financial difficulty will be most concerned about liability for wrongful trading. The key steps in relation to managing this risk are:

- taking legal and financial advice at an early stage;
- ensuring that the financial information required to make judgements about the charitable company's finances is up to date and accurate; and
- assessing the situation regularly and ensuring that all deliberations and decisions are properly recorded.

---

[7] IA 1986, s 208.
[8] IA 1986, s 211.
[9] IA 1986, s 210.
[10] IA 1986, s 212.

LIABILITY

6.18 What are the consequences of a breach by a charity trustee of any of the duties outlined above? The short answer is 'personal liability'. In other words, that the trustee is personally liable to compensate the charity out of his or her own assets for the losses that would not have been suffered if the breach of duty had not occurred. This is the starting point, but the position will vary depending on the legal form that the charity takes.

6.19 A charity trustee of any charity (however it is constituted) is potentially personally liable to compensate the charity for any losses that would not have been suffered but for his or her breach of trust. Liability would be determined by the court, which will look at all relevant circumstances in deciding how far the liability should extend. In practice, no liability will arise where:

- the court exercises its discretion to relieve any trustee from personal liability where the trustee can show that he or she acted honestly and reasonably and ought fairly to be excused for the breach;[11] or

- the Charity Commission exercises its discretion (on the same basis as the court) to relieve any trustee from personal liability under the Charities Act 2011.[12]

Other instances of personal liability can arise, depending on how a charity is constituted.

Charitable companies

6.20 Members of a charitable company have a right to bring a 'derivative action' claim against the trustees for loss arising to the company (this is known as a 'derivative' action because the member's right to claim derives from the company's right to claim). The Companies Act 2006 introduced a statutory 'derivative action',[13] extending the pre-existing common law right to bring a claim.

6.21 At common law, a member of a charitable company could bring a claim on behalf of or for the benefit of the company in respect of some wrong done to it. The common law claim could be brought even if the company, its trustees and a majority of the other members did not wish to pursue it. However, the ability to pursue a derivative claim at common law was generally restricted to cases of fraud.

6.22 The Companies Act 2006 has made it easier for members to sue trustees for a broader range of conduct than under the pre-existing common law. These include any actual proposed act or omission involving negligence, default, breach of duty or breach of trust.

---

[11] Trustee Act 1925, s 61; Companies Act 1985, s 727.
[12] Charities Act 2011, s 191.
[13] Companies Act 2006, ss 260–269.

6.23 A member's ability to bring a derivative action under the 2006 Act may be a concern for the trustees in certain circumstances (although it is obviously likely to be less of a concern where the trustees and members are the same individuals). There is a safeguard against 'frivolous' claims, which is that the courts must be satisfied that a claim bought by a member discloses a 'prima facie' case before the claim is allowed to proceed. The courts will look at whether or not the member is acting in good faith, the importance a trustee promoting the success of the company would attach to it, whether the conduct complained of is likely to be authorised or ratified by the company and whether the company itself has decided not to pursue the claim. It still remains to be seen whether or not the 2006 Act will stimulate a greater number of claims by the members of charitable companies.

Unincorporated charities

6.24 Where a charity is unincorporated, a liability to a third party that is incurred by a trustee in breach of trust is likely to be his or her personal liability. This is because an unincorporated charity has no legal personality of its own and can only interact with third parties via its trustees. This means that the trustees themselves take on liabilities to third parties personally; in other words, they are potentially personally liable to meet the liabilities in question. This could be, for example, rent due under a lease taken out in the names of the trustees for the purposes of the charity.

6.25 Generally speaking, the trustees will not have to meet the liabilities out of their own assets (if they did, there would obviously be very few people willing to act as trustees) because they can indemnify themselves in respect of properly incurred liabilities out of the charity's assets. Many charities' constitutions will provide for an express indemnity. Failing that, there is a statutory indemnity under the Trustee Act 2000 in respect of properly incurred liabilities.[14]

6.26 This means that there are two circumstances in which the trustees of an unincorporated charity may have personal liability:

- Where the charity's assets are not sufficient to meet the liabilities due to a third party.
- Where the trustees do not properly incur the liability in the first place, so that the trustees cannot indemnify themselves out of the charity's assets.

Trustees may seek expressly to limit their contractual liabilities to a third party by agreeing that the third party's only recourse is to the assets of the charity from time to time. This must be expressly agreed (it is not enough to state simply that the trustees are contracting in their capacity as trustees). The trustees may also be able to insure themselves against the risk of any shortfall in the charity's assets (see **6.33**).

---

[14] Trustee Act 2000, s 31.

6.27 Where a liability is incurred in breach of trust (eg because the trustees had no power to incur it, perhaps by taking a loan when they have no power to borrow), the liability is unlikely to have been properly incurred. This means that the trustees remain personally liable for it with no recourse to the charity's assets (and notwithstanding that the exercise of the power may actually have been in good faith and for the charity's benefit).

6.28 In certain circumstances, the trustees of an unincorporated charity may wish to consider whether appointing a corporate trustee or arranging for their own incorporation under the Charities Act 2011, Part 12 may help to limit their liabilities. Each of these possibilities is explained in more detail below.

Corporate trustees

An unincorporated charity may have a body corporate acting as its sole charity trustee. This could be, for example, a professional trust company or bank appointed to act on a paid basis or a local authority. In other cases a charity may wish to appoint a sole corporate trustee in order to simplify the way in which its assets can be held or contracts can be entered into. Using a sole corporate trustee will also help to avoid exposing individuals who might otherwise act as trustees to personal liability to third parties in respect of, for example, liabilities in excess of the charity's assets available to pay them.

Where a corporate trustee is appointed, it will have all of the usual duties and liabilities of a charity trustee. Its directors (who might otherwise act as individual trustees of the charity) will not be charity trustees, although they will owe fiduciary duties to the corporate trustee in directing the way in which it functions as a charity trustee.

In the event that the corporate trustee is in breach of its duties as charity trustee, only the trustee itself will be directly personally liable (to the extent of its corporate assets) as a result. However, that is not to say that the corporate directors will not also have some indirect liability as a consequence. If the corporate trustee's breach of trust is due to breaches of duty by its directors then the corporate trustee may have claims against the directors personally in respect of the losses it has suffered as a consequence (commonly referred to as a 'dog leg' claim).

The individual directors' potential liability will be indirect but, for all practical purposes, they should assume that they owe the same duties to the charity as the corporate trustee. In other words, that they should regard themselves as charity trustees. This is confirmed by the Charity Commission in OG 38 B4.

The liability position of trustees who opt for incorporation under Charities Act 2011, ss 251-266 is different (see below).   ➜

When appointing a sole corporate trustee, charities should bear in mind that it may be necessary for the appointment to be made by a Charity Commission Scheme or Order so that the corporate trustee will have 'trust corporation' status and will be able to give a valid receipt for the proceeds of sale on the disposal of land.

Incorporation of charity trustees

Part 12 (ss 251-266) of the Charities Act 2011 provides a mechanism for the individual trustees of an unincorporated charity to opt to become an incorporated body. The effect of their incorporation is to:

- vest all of the charity's assets (and all associated rights and liabilities) in the incorporated body;
- allow the trustees to sue and be sued in the name of the incorporated body;
- allow the trustees to execute documents in the name of the incorporated body; and
- give the incorporated body all of the powers (subject to the same restrictions) of the individual trustees.

Incorporation solves many of the problems posed by unincorporated status, by allowing the charity to hold assets, enter into contracts and act generally in the name of a single incorporated body rather than the names of the individual trustees from time to time.

However, incorporation does not affect the liability of the individual trustees for any breaches of trust they are responsible for (this is expressly provided for by the Charities Act 2011, s 254). The effect of incorporation on the individual trustees' liability to third parties in respect of contracts and other liabilities incurred to others is that it does not confer limited liability in the same way as, say, the limited liability status of a company and takes effect only for the specific purposes of holding assets etc mentioned in the Charities Act 2011.

Trustees' liabilities for breach of trust and to third parties may be affected by appointing a corporate trustee to act in their place (see above).

INDEMNITY INSURANCE

6.29   Many charity trustees (and particularly prospective trustees) will want to consider whether the risk of personal liability can be managed using indemnity insurance. The key point in relation to trustee indemnity insurance is that the premiums paid by a charity are benefits to the trustees personally and, as such, are subject to all of the usual prohibitions on trustee benefits (there is more detail about this at **6.36**).

6.30 If a charity is to take out indemnity insurance for the benefit of its trustees, it must have a power to do so. The position is:

- The charity's constitution may expressly authorise it to take out indemnity insurance. This will usually be an express exception from the prohibition on the trustees benefitting personally from the charity's assets.

- If there is no express power to insure the trustees, the charity may be able to use the statutory power conferred by the Charities Act 2011, s 189 to insure its trustees against personal liability in respect of:
    - any breach of trust or duty committed by the trustees in their capacity as charity trustees;
    - any negligence, default, breach of trust or duty committed by them in their capacity as directors or officers of any incorporated charity or any 'body corporate carrying on any activities on behalf of the charity' (this provision is therefore arguably wide enough to cover the directors or officers of a trading subsidiary of the charity).

  The statutory power applies only where the trustees are satisfied that it is in the best interests of the charity to purchase the insurance. Trustees are also subject to the 'duty of care' in s 1(1) of the Trustee Act 2000 when making a decision to buy trustee indemnity insurance.

  There must also be nothing in the charity's constitution that expressly prohibits the use of the statutory power. Express prohibitions are rare and the sort of general prohibition on trustee benefits found in most charity constitutions is not an express prohibition for this purpose.

- If there is no express authority in the charity's constitution and the statutory power cannot be used (because the constitution expressly prohibits the purchase of indemnity insurance) then the trustees can apply to the Commission for consent to the inclusion of a power. The Commission will look at the circumstances in which the prohibition was introduced when considering whether it is in the charity's interests for it to be overturned. Often this may be because it is difficult to recruit new trustees without the comfort of indemnity cover. If consent is given, this will be by way of a Scheme in respect of an unincorporated charity and under the Charities Act 2011, s 198 for a change to the memorandum or articles of a charitable company. There is more detail about this in the Commission's Operational Guidance.[15] Given the statutory power to insure, it is only likely to be relevant to charities that have an express prohibition on the purchase of indemnity insurance.

6.31 The statutory power cannot be used to pay for insurance which covers any of the following liabilities:

---

[15] OG 100 A1.

- a fine imposed in criminal proceedings or a penalty payable to any regulatory authority;

- any liability arising out of criminal proceedings in which the trustee is convicted of any offence arising out of any fraud or dishonesty or wilful or reckless misconduct by him or her; or

- any liability incurred by the trustee to the charity that arises out of any conduct that he or she knew (or must reasonably be assumed to have known) was not in the interests of the charity or where he or she did not care whether it was in the charity's interest or not.

6.32 The net effect of this is that a charity cannot insure its trustees against their own breaches of trust unless they are as a result of negligent acts or omissions that the trustee did not know about and cannot reasonably be assumed to have known about.

6.33 Most express powers to purchase indemnity insurance will be subject to similar restrictions (as they would not otherwise have been accepted by the Charity Commission on an application for registration or a subsequent application for an express power). If the Commission are asked for authority to include an express power, they will expect it to be subject to the restrictions set out in the Charities Act 2011, s 189 (see eg, the Commission's model Scheme for unincorporated charities containing an appropriate power).[16]

6.34 Even where a charity has an express power to purchase indemnity insurance, trustees should consider carefully whether it will actually improve their position and be for the benefit of their charity, particularly given the restrictions on the liabilities that it can cover:

- Many of the liabilities which concern trustees can often be insured by the charity itself, for example loss to the charity's assets giving rise to a shortfall as against the trustees' liabilities. The Charity Commission recognises that, even in the context of an unincorporated charity, a distinction should be drawn between liabilities which are primarily those of the charity and those which are primarily liabilities of the trustees. On that basis, the Commission does not treat trustee reimbursement insurance (to cover any shortfall in assets against liabilities) as trustee indemnity insurance notwithstanding that the trustees will benefit personally as a consequence.

- The main advantage of indemnity insurance will be to cover negligent breaches of trust. In the context of a charitable company, the most significant example of that would be liability for wrongful trading. Notwithstanding that the Commission's guidance states that indemnity insurance can cover wrongful trading,[17] there is a question mark over the extent to which cover for wrongful trading can be obtained given the prohibition on insuring liabilities arising out of conduct that a trustee

---

[16]   OG 100 C3.
[17]   OG 100 A1.

knew or must be assumed to have known was not in the charity's best interests. Given that the test for wrongful trading is that the trustee must have known or ought to have known that there was no reasonable prospect of the charity avoiding insolvent liquidation, it is possible that cover for wrongful trading will not be provided. The key point is that the scope of the cover a charity takes out for the benefit of its trustees should be confirmed at the outset.

6.35 The Charity Commission's guidance acknowledges that indemnity insurance may often be provided under a policy which covers other aspects of a charity's activities. The important point is that, if the insurance policy as a whole provides any indemnity to trustees for their personal liability, it will amount to a benefit which needs authority.

TRUSTEE BENEFITS

6.36 As part of the requirement that all charities must be for the public benefit, charity law prohibits the provision of benefits by a charity to its trustees without express authority to do so. This is a very important aspect of every charity trustee's duty to act voluntarily and gratuitously, which is itself connected to the duty to avoid any conflict between a trustee's duties to a charity and his or her own personal interests. Put simply, the concern is that a trustee cannot act in good faith and bring independence of mind to a charity's affairs if he or she is also concerned about the charity's ability to pay him or her or provide them with other benefits.

6.37 That is not to say that a charity cannot in certain circumstances pay its trustees, but this can only happen where there is an appropriate authority in its constitution. Without that authority, it does not matter whether the charity has received value for money for services provided by its trustees, or would not have been able to obtain the services anywhere else or only on much worse terms. The trustees will be in breach of trust for making the unauthorised payments and the trustee who has received the payments will be liable to repay them in full to the charity, with an obligation on the trustees of the charity to consider enforcing that liability.

6.38 The Charities Act 2011, s 187 defines a trustee benefit as 'a direct or indirect benefit of any nature'. In practice, the benefits that are often relevant are:

- payments for services provided to a charity by a trustee;
- payments by a charity to an employee (often the chief executive) who is also a trustee; and
- payments by a charity to a trustee for acting as a trustee.

These are considered at **6.44–6.60**.

Reimbursement of expenses

6.39 Benefits do not include the reimbursement of expenses properly incurred by a trustee in acting as trustee. These can be reimbursed by the charity without any authority in its constitution (although an express authority is often included). However, expenses do not include any sort of compensation for loss of earnings or profit suffered by a trustee in spending time acting as trustee.

Benefits freely enjoyed by a trustee alongside the public or as a beneficiary of the charity are also excluded from the general prohibition.

Benefits to connected persons

6.40 It is important to appreciate that the restrictions on the provision of benefits to trustees apply in the same way to benefits made available to anyone closely associated with them. To illustrate the point, the Commission's guidance on employing the spouse or partner of a trustee says that if the trustee and his or her spouse are financially interdependent, the trustee could profit from the employment, which would be a trustee payment requiring authority. The guidance goes on to say that the same principle applies to businesses owned by the trustee, or in which the trustee is a partner, a managing director or has a financial interest, and it can also apply to employment with a subsidiary owned by the charity.[18]

6.41 There is a statutory definition of who should be considered to be 'connected' to a trustee in the context of payments to trustees. This applies only to the statutory power referred to at **6.46**, but best practice will be to assume that a similar test applies in relation to all proposed payments to trustees. The categories of connected person[19] are:

(a) a child, parent, grandchild, grandparent or sibling of the trustee;

(b) a spouse or civil partner of the trustee or of anyone within (a);

(c) anyone in partnership with the trustee or with anyone within (a) or (b);

(d) any 'institution' controlled by the trustee or by anyone within (a), (b) or (c) (whether acting alone or together). 'Control' means that the relevant person can secure that the affairs of the 'institution' are conducted in accordance with his wishes;

(e) any 'body corporate' in which the trustee or anyone within (a), (b) or (c) has a 'substantial interest' (whether alone or taken together). A substantial interest is more than 20% of the share capital or voting rights in the relevant 'body corporate'.

6.42 It is open to anyone establishing a charity to decide that its trustees (or persons connected to them) should receive payment for services provided to the charity, usually on the basis that they think it will help the charity to function

---

18 CC 11.
19 Charities Act 2011, s 188.

more effectively. So, for example, someone establishing a charity may decide to appoint a bank as one of its trustees in order to ensure a degree of professional expertise and continuity in its administration and that, in order to secure the bank's services, it should be paid for doing so. The Charity Commission accepts that this is possible, subject only to ensuring that the charity can continue to meet the public benefit requirement. The test applied by the Commission is whether the benefits that can be provided are in excess of what might be considered reasonable payment for the services actually provided. The Commission will expect there to be other restrictions on the power to pay a trustee where that power is included. These are summarised at **6.44**.

Express authorisation

6.43 Where an existing charity wishes to provide benefits to its trustees, it can only do so if it has the relevant authority. The starting point will be its constitution, which may include the relevant authority, often as an exception to a general prohibition on trustees benefitting from their trusteeship. The position will vary from charity to charity but the following benefits will typically be provided for:

- a reasonable rate of interest on money loaned to the charity by a trustee (often capped at a percentage rate above or below a bank base rate);
- a reasonable rent on property leased to the charity by a trustee;
- reimbursement of expenses properly incurred;
- payments to companies for services where the trustee owns less than 1% of the share capital (this is intended to avoid the need for authorisation where payments are made to listed companies or companies in which the trustee has only a 'de minimis' interest); and
- premiums in respect of trustee indemnity insurance.

Payment for goods and services

6.44 More modern charity constitutions may also contain provisions for the payment of trustees for goods or services provided to the charity. Powers of this kind will usually be subject to a number of conditions which require that:

- the payment for the goods or services which are supplied is reasonable;
- the trustee providing the goods or services is not involved in taking any decision in relation to their supply;
- only a minority of trustees provide goods and services to the charity at any time; and
- the trustees conclude that paying the trustee for the goods and services is in the best interests of the charity.

6.45 If there is no express power of this kind in the charity's constitution and the trustees wish to pay one or more of their number for providing goods and services, there are three options open to them:

- If the total payments to all trustees (and persons connected to them) during the charity's financial year will amount to less than £1,000 in aggregate the trustees can self-certify the position (provided there are no other reasons why the trustees should apply for authority, eg, if the Commission is addressing issues of mismanagement of the charity).[20] Conflicts of interest will need to be managed effectively and the trustees' reasons for why the payment is in the best interests of the charity should be recorded in the minutes of the relevant meeting. The payment must also be disclosed in the charity's accounts. See the Commission's Operational Guidance OG 515-7 for further details about its small payments policy.

- The trustees may be able to use the statutory power conferred by Charities Act 2011, s 185 to pay a trustee for services (see **6.46**).

- The trustees may be able to apply to the Charity Commission for an express power to make payments.

Statutory power

6.46 The statutory power under the Charities Act 2011, s 185 to pay a trustee for services is subject to a number of conditions:

- The payment due to the trustee is specified in a written agreement. This is good practice in any event.

- The payment must not be more than what is reasonable in the circumstances. This is a judgement for the trustees to make taking into account the terms of the proposed agreement. In most cases, they are likely to need comparators in order to enable to decide what level of payment is reasonable. Again, this is good practice in any event in order to ensure that the charity is getting value for money.

- The trustees must decide, before they enter into the agreement, that it is in the best interests of the charity to pay the trustee for the relevant services. See **6.47**.

- If there is more than one paid trustee (whether under the statutory power or some other power), they must be a minority of the trustees.

- The constitution of the charity must not contain any express provision that prohibits the trustee from receiving payment. The Charities Act 2011, s 185 does not define what constitutes an 'express provision', but there is a clear argument that the sort of general prohibition on benefits to trustees found in many charity constitutions will be caught. If this is right, then some charities will not be in a position to take advantage of the statutory power unless they are first able to amend their constitutions.

---

[20] CC 11 and OG 515-7.

- The trustees are subject to the statutory duty of care imposed by the Trustee Act 2000.

- The trustees must take into account the guidance given by the Charity Commission in relation to such agreements. The Commission's existing guidance is summarised at **6.47**.

- The rules apply to anyone 'connected' to a trustee in the same way as to a trustee him or herself.

6.47 The Commission will expect the trustees to have considered a number of different questions as part of their assessment of whether paying a trustee for providing services is in the interests of the charity. These are spelled out in CC 11 and provide a helpful basis for the trustees' decision making:

- **Value for money**
  The service must be needed by the charity, and the trustee concerned must be sufficiently experienced and skilled or qualified to deliver it. There may be a cost advantage in using a trustee, but this does not always mean work should be done 'on the cheap'. Quality is important, and speed of delivery might also be a factor. Trustee boards must be satisfied that the charity will be receiving value for money, and that there will be no adverse affect on its reputation, or levels of support and funding. The board must ensure that the charity can afford the cost of the service, without any adverse impact on the charity's activities.

- **Knowledge of the charity**
  A particular knowledge of the charity and its working environment can sometimes be an advantage. A trustee board may decide that for less – or no more – than the market rate, it can use the skills of a trustee who knows the specific requirements of the charity, and is perfectly competent to do the work in question.

- **Purchase of goods**
  Where goods are supplied by a trustee in connection with a service provided, again there must be a clear advantage. This will normally mean items being supplied at a favourable rate. Where quality is also a factor, there should still normally be a significant 'value for money' advantage to the charity.

- **When there is no advantage**
  Where there is an unfavourable financial comparison with an outside supplier, and no weight of special expertise or knowledge that would tip the scales, the charity should use the supplier who is not a trustee. There would be no clear advantage in using the trustee, because of the need to manage the conflict of interest.

Trustees should also consider the implications for the charity if a trustee is paid to carry out work which he or she does badly, giving rise to a claim for damages or some other contractual remedy. Will the trustee carry insurance cover to meet the cost of a claim? If not, will they be able to meet the cost of a claim out of their own resources? Taking legal action against a trustee in these circumstances may be difficult to contemplate but the trustees should consider the 'worst case' position in advance, particularly where the value of the services is high or is material to the charity's ability to operate effectively.

6.48   If a charity's constitution prohibits the use of the statutory power, but this could otherwise be relied on as authority for paying a trustee for services, the trustees may need to apply to the Commission to amend the charity's constitution.

6.49   For an unincorporated charity, this will need to be by Scheme (the trustees cannot use the statutory power of amendment under Charities Act 2011, s 280).

6.50   A charitable company will need to amend its articles of association and in some cases it may be possible to do this without involving the Commission (see CC 11 E10 for more details).

6.51   Any application to the Charity Commission will need to spell out the trustees' reasoning in relation to why payments will be for the benefit of the charity, and the work they have done to satisfy themselves of that. The trustees will also need to satisfy themselves that the services in question are not services that form part of the trustee's duties as trustee. That will obviously require an analysis of the services in question, but trustees should be aware that the Charity Commission may take the view that certain services are intrinsically trustee duties. There is unlikely to be much doubt that, for example, professional legal or accounting services fall outside a trustee's duties, but the provision of, say, business planning services might be seen by the Commission as no more than part of the trustees' role in planning the charity's strategy.

6.52   In addition, the statutory power applies only to services (and specifically excludes payments for acting as trustee or to employees who are also trustees). Payments can be made for goods but only if they are supplied in connection with the provision of services. If, therefore, the trustees of a charity wish to pay a trustee for the supply of goods they will need to consider applying to the Charity Commission for an appropriate power.

6.53   Again, this will need to be given by way of a Scheme for an unincorporated charity. A charitable company will need to obtain the Commission's consent under Charities Act 2011, s 198 to amend its articles to include an appropriate power. The power granted will be subject to the sort of restrictions that apply to the exercise of the statutory power (see **6.46**).

Other payments

6.54   Payments to trustees for acting as trustees or to a trustee who is also an employee are more contentious than payments to trustees for discrete services. There is no statutory power to make payments of this kind, so any charity that wishes to be able to do this and does not already have authority in its own constitution will need to make an application to the Charity Commission for authority.

6.55 In relation to paying a trustee for serving as trustee, the Commission will normally only give authority where the complexity of a charity's operations has led to an unusually high burden of trusteeship, involving a trustee exercising a higher degree of responsibility and supervision in a complex field of activity. The Commission says in its guidance that it may also consider a case by the trustees that they will only be able to obtain the skills, experience and diversity they need for the charity if they are able to pay a trustee for serving as trustee.[21]

6.56 In making an application, the trustees will need to be able to show why the charity will not be as effective without payment. The Charity Commission will expect the trustees to show they have considered the following factors:

- What steps have been taken to recruit trustees without payment – if none, then reasons should be given.
- Why the trustees consider there are clear and significant advantages to the charity in paying a trustee rather than, for example, spreading duties among other trustees, or increasing the number of unpaid trustees (if the governing document allows it).
- Whether the functions to be carried out are genuinely those of a trustee – as distinct from the functions of an employee or a consultant. Has the charity struck the right balance between its executive and non-executive functions?
- That the payment can be shown to be reasonable and affordable and will not affect the charity's ability to carry out its objects.
- What risks they have identified and how they will manage them.
- How the unpaid trustees will be able to review performance (including dealing with poor performance), judge value for money and, if necessary, bring the payments to an end.
- How the conflicts of interest will be managed, so that the 'conflicted' trustee can still take an effective role in the governance of the charity.

If the Commission does give authority, it will generally only do so on the basis that the number of trustees being paid for serving as trustee will be in the minority.

6.57 Payments to trustees for serving as trustees were considered by Lord Hodgson in his review of the Charities Act 2006.[22] However, his recommendation that charities with an income exceeding £1,000,000 should have the power to pay their trustees subject to clear disclosure requirements

---

[21]   CC 11.
[22]   'Trusted and Independent: Giving charity back to charities. Review of the Charities Act 2006' (July 2012).

was rejected by Government, with many commentators arguing that permitting remuneration would undermine the voluntary nature of charity trusteeship.

6.58   Where the trustees are proposing that one of their number (or a former trustee) should become a paid employee, the Commission will expect the trustees to be able to show that the post is genuinely required for the effectiveness of the charity, and has not been created or tailored to meet the needs of the trustee or former trustee or weighted towards his or her experience. Trustee boards will need to satisfy the Commission that:

- The charity has a need for the work to be carried out.
- The person has the appropriate knowledge and skills for the job.
- Payment for the job is reasonable in relation to the work being carried out: how does it compare with payment for similar duties elsewhere? Is the charity obtaining value for money?
- Conflicts of interest and the risk of an adverse effect on the reputation of the charity among its supporters and users have been considered and managed.
- (Usually) the job has been subject to an open and transparent selection process.
- (Where relevant to the charity) stakeholders have been consulted.

6.59   In certain circumstances, the trustees of a charity may wish to appoint one of the charity's employees (possibly its chief executive) as a trustee. There are certain kinds of charities which often do have employees on their board including higher education institutions, academy trusts and some church charities.

6.60   While there is no issue of trustee benefit in relation to earnings received before the start of the trusteeship, the ability for an employee-trustee to retain any future additional benefit negotiated whilst the employee is a trustee (eg a pay rise) might be subject to challenge. In the absence of express authority in the charity's governing document, authority for the arrangement from the Charity Commission will therefore need to be sought. The Commission's policy is that it will only give this authority if it is satisfied that the arrangement is in the best interests of the charity. It will also expect to see that conflicts of interest will be adequately managed.[23]

6.61   If a payment is made to a trustee without authority, any such payment is a breach of trust, even if the charity benefits from the arrangement. The trustees, or the trustee who has benefitted, may be required to reimburse the charity for part or all of the payment made in breach of trust.

---

[23]   OG 515-4.

CHAPTER 7

TRUSTEES' POWERS

7.1   In order to discharge their duties to the standard required by law, the trustees of every charity must:

- act within the powers they have as trustees;
- exercise those powers only in the best interests of the charity and only for the purposes for which they have been given; and
- exercise their powers personally, without delegating responsibility for decisions to anyone else.

7.2   An incorporated charity will have powers in its own right. These will be exercisable by its trustees (usually by an express provision in its constitution). We refer to them as 'trustees' powers' because, in practice, they are exercised by the trustees rather than by the charity.

7.3   In discharging these duties, charity trustees are under an obligation to exercise such care and skill as is reasonable in the circumstances having regard to:

- any special knowledge or expertise that the trustee has or holds him or herself out as having; and
- where a trustee acts in the course of a business or profession, to any special knowledge or expertise that it is reasonable to expect of a person acting in the course of that kind of business or profession.

There is more about this statutory duty of care at **6.2**. However, in order to ensure that they discharge it, trustees will need to ensure that they understand the sources and scope of their powers and the restrictions on, and other considerations in relation to, their exercise.

7.4   There are two reasons why this is important:

- If the trustees fail to act within their powers, or exercise them in the wrong way, they will be acting in breach of trust. There is more about the consequences of that at **6.18**.
- If the trustees purport to exercise a power that they do not have or exercise a power in the wrong way, the charity will be acting ultra vires (in other words, outside its capacity). The effect of that will depend upon the

way in which the power was purportedly exercised, but in general the effect will be to make any agreement entered into or liability incurred by the charity on the strength of the power void or, in some cases, voidable. Clearly, this may expose the charity to claims and its trustees to personal liability for any losses suffered by the charity as a consequence.

7.5   Before identifying the sources of charity trustees' powers, it is helpful to understand that, as a general principle, the powers conferred upon all charity trustees can only ever be exercised in order to promote the charity's charitable purposes. There is a fundamental difference between those purposes (the charity's ultimate objectives) and the powers (which are no more than the means by which the purposes can be achieved). So, for example, an express power for a charity to give a guarantee must be interpreted as a power to give guarantees that advance its purposes, perhaps by guaranteeing the liabilities of impoverished beneficiaries.

7.6   Charity constitutions will generally draw a clear distinction between the purposes and powers, usually by expressly stating that the powers are only exercisable in order to advance the purposes (the format of a modern charitable company's constitution is a good example of this). But even if this is not expressly spelled out, the position is the same, irrespective of whether the powers are said to be exercisable at the discretion of the trustees or not.

SOURCES OF POWERS

7.7   The powers available to charity trustees have three potential sources:

- express powers conferred by the charity's constitution;
- powers that can be implied into the charity's constitution; and
- powers conferred by law, primarily by statute.

7.8   The specific powers available to any particular charity under any of these three heads will depend upon its legal form. The position of companies, CIOs and unincorporated charities is examined below.

7.9   The powers available to a charity's trustees in relation to its assets will also vary depending upon whether they are 'trust assets'. All of the assets of an unincorporated charity will be trust assets. In general, the assets of a charitable company will not be held on trust (and will constitute its 'corporate assets'), but there are exceptions to this. There is more detail about this at **Chapter 9**.

EXPRESS POWERS

7.10   Most modern charity constitutions will spell out the charity's powers in reasonable detail. There is obviously a judgement to be made in drafting provisions of this kind because, in practice, including very detailed provisions may mean that a third party seeking to rely upon a particular power becomes concerned that the detail included does not deal sufficiently precisely with the particular issue they are considering. The best approach will be to ensure that the powers included are drafted with this possibility in mind. Using an appropriate standard form document may also give some comfort that the scope of the powers is sufficient.

Companies

7.11 For a charitable company incorporated after 1 October 2009 (when the relevant provisions of the Companies Act 2006 came into force), the company's purposes and powers are set out in its articles of association. Companies incorporated before that date will have their purposes and powers set out in their memorandum of association (unless they have subsequently adopted articles in the new form).

7.12 The Companies Act 2006 prevents the validity of any act done by a company being called into question by reason of anything in the company's constitution.[1] The Act also provides that, in favour of a person dealing with a company in good faith, the power of its directors to bind the company is deemed to be free of any limitation in the company's constitution. In other words, no third party acting in good faith need have any concern that any act is ultra vires and outside a company's capacity because it has no power to do it or because it does have a power but the restrictions on its exercise have not been observed. However, this rule applies to the acts of charitable companies in a modified form. It can only be relied upon by a person who:

- gives full consideration in money or money's worth in relation to the act in question and does not know that the act is not permitted by the company's constitution or is beyond the trustees' powers; or
- who does not know at the time the act is done that the company is a charity.

7.13 Clearly, therefore, anyone who does not meet these criteria (and many third parties who deal with charities are likely to ask for confirmation of its powers so that they will have actual or constructive notice that a charity lacks a power or that it is subject to restrictions) cannot rely upon the protection conferred by the 2006 Act. Having said that, there is an additional protection for anyone who subsequently acquires an asset originally transferred by a charity without an appropriate power. Provided that they acquire the asset without actual notice of the circumstances that affect the validity of the transfer and give full consideration for the asset, they will get good title to it.[2]

7.14 The ultra vires rule that applies to a charitable company does not affect the duty of its charity trustees to comply with the provisions of its constitution

---

[1] Companies Act 2006, s 42.
[2] Companies Act 2006, s 42.

in relation to the exercise of its powers and does not restrict their liability for failing to comply with that duty. In addition, it does not prevent any member of the company from taking action to restrain the directors from taking action that is outside the company's powers.

7.15 From the point of view of both the charity trustees and third parties, therefore, it will be essential that a charity has the express powers required to operate it in the way the trustees wish.

7.16 If there is no express power, it will usually be possible to add one or to modify any restrictions on an existing power. This requires a members' resolution and is dealt with in more detail in **Chapter 15**.

CIOs

7.17 The Charities Act 2011 gives a CIO the power to do anything that is 'calculated to further its purposes'. This power is subject to any restriction in the CIO's constitution. It remains to be seen whether CIO constitutions will generally include the range of express powers usually seen in a company's memorandum or articles, although the Charity Commission's model constitutions for CIOs contain a limited set of express powers (including powers to borrow, acquire and dispose of property and employ staff and powers in relation to investment). In practice, third parties may insist on an express power.

7.18 CIOs are subject to an ultra vires rule that is modelled on the rule that applies in relation to companies. See **7.12** for further detail on this.

7.19 The charity trustees of a CIO are in the same position as the trustees of a charitable company in relation to liability for breach of trust in acting outside their powers.

7.20 If there is no express power, it will usually be possible to add one or to modify any restrictions on an existing power. This requires a members' resolution and is dealt with in more detail in **Chapter 15**.

Unincorporated charities

7.21 The express powers of any unincorporated charity will be set out in its constitution. They will need to be construed in context. There is no statutory provision similar to the ultra vires provisions in relation to companies and CIOs.

7.22 If there is no express power, the trustees may have a sufficiently wide power of amendment to add a new power or modify an existing one. This will usually be exercisable by the trustees but the position will depend upon the constitutional provisions as they vary from charity to charity. The trustees may also be able to rely on the statutory power under Charities Act 2011, s 280 to modify their powers or procedures (although, if the charity is an unincorporated association, the resolution will need to be ratified by the members). There is more about amendments in **Chapter 15**.

7.23 If (and only if) the trustees cannot rely on an express power of amendment or the statutory power under Charities Act 2011, s 280, they may be able to apply for an Order or a Scheme of the Charity Commission to give them the necessary authority. There is more about this in **Chapters 4** and **15**.

IMPLIED POWERS

7.24 If there are no express powers that authorise something a charity proposes to do, it may be possible to imply a power into its constitution. Whether this is possible will depend upon how the charity is constituted, what its constitution says and the approach taken by its trustees and any third party with whom the charity wishes to engage.

Companies

7.25 The possibility of implying powers into a charitable company's constitution usually turns on the 'sweep-up' provision often included. This usually states that the company has the power to do 'such other lawful things as are necessary to achieve its objects'. 'Necessary' might sometimes read 'conducive' or 'expedient' or 'incidental'.

7.26 Essentially, the powers that can be implied using a provision of this kind will be limited to carrying out the charity's purposes. This is in line with the general principle of construction of the powers of charities explained at 7.5. The powers that can be implied have been fairly restrictively construed by the courts in the past (albeit in the context of an industrial and provident society, although the same principle is likely to apply).[3]

7.27 Perhaps the most one can say about the approach that can be taken to implied powers is that the position can never be determined with sufficient certainty without a decision of the court. In practice, most third parties dealing with charities will want to see an express power authorising whatever is proposed and will not be interested in debating the possibility of implying a power. The same may be true of the charity's trustees, albeit that they may often be reluctant to incur the delay and expense involved in obtaining an express power.

---

[3]   *Rosemary Simmons Memorial Housing Association Ltd v United Dominions Trust Ltd* [1987] 1 All ER 281.

CIOs

7.28 CIOs have a statutory power to do anything which is 'conducive or incidental' to their purposes. The courts are likely to take the same approach to powers implied under this provision as they do in relation to companies. So too are third parties.

Unincorporated charities

7.29 Whether powers can be implied into the constitution of an unincorporated charity will depend upon what is in the constitution. Often, there will be a provision in a similar form to the sort of 'sweep-up' clause found in a company's memorandum or articles or a CIO's statutory power to the same effect.

7.30 The courts are likely to take a very similar approach to implied powers of this kind for unincorporated charities as they do for companies (and as they are likely to do in relation to CIOs). So too are third parties.

STATUTORY POWERS

7.31 All charities have certain powers conferred by the Charities Act 2011. These are:

- power to co-operate with local authorities and other charities;[4]
- power to make ex gratia payments (with the consent of the Charity Commission);[5] and
- power to waive entitlement to property (with the consent of the Charity Commission).[6]

7.32 Unincorporated charities also have a range of powers conferred by the Charities Act 2011:

- power to spend the capital of an unincorporated charity;[7]
- power to transfer the property of an unincorporated charity;[8]
- power to replace the purposes of an unincorporated charity;[9] and
- power to modify the powers and procedures of an unincorporated charity.[10]

---

[4]   Charities Act 2011, s 297.
[5]   Charities Act 2011, s 106(2)(a).
[6]   Charities Act 2011, s 106(2)(b).
[7]   Charities Act 2011, ss 281–286.
[8]   Charities Act 2011, ss 267–274.
[9]   Charities Act 2011, ss 275–279.
[10]   Charities Act 2011, s 280.

These powers were first introduced by the Charities Act 2006. Their effect is explained in more detail at **Chapters 9** and **15**.

Companies

7.33   Companies have no additional statutory powers conferred specifically by the Charities Act 2011 over and above those mentioned in **7.31**.

CIOs

7.34   CIOs have no additional statutory powers conferred specifically by the Charities Act 2011 over and above those mentioned in **7.31**.

Unincorporated charities

7.35   In addition to the powers conferred by the Charities Act 2011 mentioned in **7.31**, the trustees of most unincorporated charities will be able to rely upon a range of statutory powers available to trustees generally. The more important of these powers are:

- Power to insure the charity's assets (including power to insure the charity against the consequences of breach of trust by its trustees, but not insurance indemnifying trustees against the consequences of their own breaches).[11]

- Power to deal with land. There is more about this in **Chapter 9**.

- Power to delegate trustees' powers.[12] There is more about this in **Chapter 8**.

- A limited power to borrow money in connection with land.[13] There is more about this in **Chapter 12**.

- Power to invest the charity's assets.[14] There is more about this in **Chapter 10**.

7.36   The statutory powers available to the trustees of an unincorporated charity are by no means comprehensive. In general, its trustees will wish to ensure that, where possible, they have express powers. Where that is not possible, the statutory powers will be a useful fallback.

Advice

7.37   Where the charity trustees do not have a particular power to do something that they wish to do, the Charity Commission will not issue them with advice under Charities Act 2011, s 110 that would deem them to have

---

[11]   Trustee Act 1925, s 19.
[12]   Trustee Act 2000, s 11.
[13]   Trusts of Land and Appointment of Trustees Act 1996, s 6.
[14]   Trustee Act 2000, s 3.

acted in accordance with their duties as trustees. Where a third party is involved, it is unlikely to want to rely on advice in any event.

RESTRICTIONS

7.38 There are a number of things that may restrict the exercise of charity trustees' powers. These are:

- restrictions imposed by the charity's own constitution;
- restrictions imposed by the Charities Acts and other statutes; and
- restrictions imposed by the law generally.

Constitutional restrictions

7.39 Any restrictions on the exercise of express powers conferred by a charity's constitution should be observed. These could include, for example, obtaining any third party consent to a sale of an asset, borrowing only up to a specified limit or buying only particular types of investment.

Statutory restrictions

7.40 There are a number of restrictions on the exercise of powers conferred by the Charities Act 2011, but the two most significant provisions are:

- The requirements of the Charities Act 2011, ss 117–123 in relation to the disposal of land owned by a charity. There is more about this in **Chapter 9**.
- The requirements of the Charities Act 2011, ss 124–126 in relation to mortgages of charity land. There is more about this in **Chapter 12**.

7.41 In addition, significant restrictions are imposed in relation to powers conferred by other statutes. The most important are:

- the restrictions on the power of investment conferred by the Trustee Act 2000. There is more about this in **Chapter 10**; and
- the restrictions on the power of delegation conferred by the Trustee Act 2000. There is more about this at **7.49**.

Other restrictions

7.42 Charity trustees must exercise the powers conferred upon them honestly and after giving proper consideration to everything relevant to the decision that they take. The courts have indicated that trustees must act in good faith and reasonably and it is the standard of the 'reasonable trustee' that they will look for in assessing whether a decision was properly taken or not.[15]

7.43 In making that assessment, the courts will look at whether the trustees armed themselves with all relevant information, whether they took (or should have taken) advice from an expert and whether they considered the right question and properly applied their minds to it. Another essential aspect of this is that the power in question is being exercised for the purpose for which it is given.

7.44 Most decisions will not, of course, ever be reviewed by the courts and they are in general very reluctant to interfere with trustees' decisions. However, the benchmark set by them is the obvious starting point for trustees in exercising their powers.

7.45 In its guidance for charity trustees on decision making,[16] the Commission confirms that trustees must follow the principles that the courts have developed for reviewing decisions made by trustees. The key points are that trustees must:

- act within their powers, ie they must only make decisions which are consistent with the charity's objects and powers;
- act in good faith and only in the interests of the charity;
- make sure they are sufficiently informed and be able to demonstrate that their decisions are based on sufficient and appropriate evidence. The Commission will expect trustees to have read any relevant Commission guidance and it may be appropriate to carry out risk assessments and take external advice;
- take account of all relevant factors. These will vary depending on the particular circumstances, but the key factor is always likely to be whether the proposed decision is in the best interests of the charity;
- ignore any irrelevant factors. In particular, the trustees must not allow personal prejudices to sway their views;
- manage conflicts of interest. There is more about managing conflicts in **Chapter 8**;
- make decisions that are within the range of decisions that a reasonable trustee body could make. The guidance is helpful here:

> 'The trustees must decide which option is in the best interests of the charity. The courts and the Commission cannot judge whether the trustees' duty was *right*, or was the *best decision* or not. We can only consider whether the decision was within the *range of decisions* that a reasonable trustee body could have made, and whether the trustees have followed proper processes and the principles in this guidance.'

---

[15] *Scott v National Trust* [1998] 2 All ER 705.
[16] 'It's your decision: charity trustees and decision making.'

ADVICE

7.46 In exercising their powers trustees must consider whether they first need to take advice on the issue that they are considering. Some statutory powers impose an express statutory obligation to take advice or at least to consider taking it. The most obvious example is the power of investment conferred upon the charity trustees of an unincorporated charity (see **Chapter 10** for more on this). Obligations may also be imposed by statute (eg the Charities Act 2011 obliges charity trustees to take advice before mortgaging or disposing of land) or by the charity's constitution (eg the constitution of a charitable company may oblige its trustee to consider taking advice on investment).

7.47 Regardless of the obligations imposed on charity trustees, the key point is that many trustees will not be in a position to take a proper decision about particular issues without taking advice. This could include, for example, issues raised by the funding requirements of a charity's final salary pension scheme, where the legal and actuarial position can be complex. Advice will obviously not be required in every case but charity trustees will need to consider whether it is necessary in relation to most substantive decisions.

7.48 There is no objection to charity trustees taking advice on areas outside their own areas of competence. The cost of that advice is a properly incurred expense payable out of the charity's funds.

DELEGATION

7.49 In addition to identifying the source and scope of their powers, charity trustees will need to ensure that they understand who is responsible for their exercise. In the majority of cases, powers will be vested in the charity trustees themselves although there are other possibilities:

- a charity's constitution may vest certain powers in its members or other third parties; and
- a charity's constitution may vest powers in the charity trustees but make their exercise subject to the consent of third parties, eg the settlor of a charitable trust or the Charity Commission.

7.50 Where a power is vested in the charity trustees themselves, they must exercise it personally in accordance with the provisions of the charity's constitution. In general, this will require a decision by the charity trustees themselves unless there is authority in the constitution for the decision to be delegated. This reflects the overriding duty on all charity trustees to act personally unless they are authorised to delegate any of their functions to someone else.

7.51 There is more about delegation in **Chapter 8**. The key point is that charity trustees must identify in whom a particular power is vested before a decision is taken. In practice, it is reasonably easy for a decision to be taken by the wrong people if the position is not clearly established at the outset. A decision taken on this basis will be invalid.

PROCESS

7.52 In exercising their powers, the charity trustees must ensure that they follow the process set out in their charity's constitution. At its most straightforward, this may mean no more than ensuring that the relevant decision is taken at a properly convened and quorate meeting where the trustees have available to them all of the advice and other information that they need to consider the position.

7.53 In other cases, the process may be more complicated. Where, for example, a members' decision is required, the constitution's requirements in relation to notice, quorum and voting must be observed. There is more about members' meetings in **Chapter 5**.

RECORD-KEEPING

7.54 There are several reasons for keeping clear and comprehensive written records of the exercise of trustees' powers. The first is that any well-governed charity will wish to have proper records of all of the most important aspects of its operations. The second is that changes in trustees and employees may mean that the reasons for decisions taken in the past may not be clear to later generations unless there is a clear written record of the position. Third, if the exercise of the trustees' power is ever challenged, the trustees will want to be able to show that it was properly exercised. Without a clear written record (including copies of any advice taken and full minutes of discussion), that may be difficult to do. In the very worst case, the courts will wish to assess whether the trustees acted reasonably and the trustees' position is likely to be very much stronger if they have written evidence to support this.

CHECKLIST

7.55 In exercising their powers, charity trustees should ensure that they have dealt with the following points:

- Do the charity trustees have an express power under the charity's constitution to do whatever it is they want to do?
- If there is no express power, can the charity trustees exercise a power in their charity's constitution or the power under s 280, Charities Act 2011 to add an express power? If not, can they apply to the Charity Commission for an Order or Scheme giving them the necessary express

power? In the case of a charitable company, can the trustees arrange for the members to amend the constitution to give the trustees an express power?

- If there is no express power, can the trustees rely upon an implied or statutory power?

- Whatever form the power takes, what are the restrictions on its exercise?

- Are the charity trustees obliged to take advice in relation to the exercise of the power in question?

- Even if they are not obliged to do so, should they take advice on the issue they are considering?

- Is the power vested in the charity trustees or in a third party?

- If the power is vested in the charity trustees, do they propose to take the decision or is it to be delegated? If it is to be delegated, is there a power of delegation and has this been exercised in accordance with the charity's constitution?

- Are there any third party consents that are required in relation to the exercise of the power?

- Has the decision-making process set out in the charity's constitution been observed?

- Have the charity trustees' deliberations in relation to the exercise of the power been properly recorded in writing?

- Have any conflicts been managed properly? There is more about conflicts at **Chapter 8.**

CHAPTER 8

TRUSTEE GOVERNANCE

INTRODUCTION

8.1 It is generally recognised that the key to the effective governance of a charity is its trustees and the way in which they discharge their legal responsibility for controlling and managing it. In the view of the Charity Commission:[1]

'Trustees matter a great deal. It is very important for any charity to have trustees committed to their task and with the skills, knowledge and experience that the charity needs.

Trustees play an essential role in the governance of charities. They also have a lot to contribute to their success. For example they can:

- serve as a means of communication with communities that a charity exists to serve;
- bring valuable professional or other experience to charities; and
- help to ensure that charities are well-managed through the appointment of senior executive staff.'

8.2 With the exception of a sole corporate trustee, every charity should have more than one trustee. While there is no legal objection to a sole trustee acting (except in certain limited circumstances[2]), the capacity for debate and discussion in relation to the management of a charity is an intrinsic part of trusteeship. This is also true of a sole corporate trustee, which will almost invariably be under the control of more than one individual.

8.3 Trustees can be described collectively in a number of different ways; common references are to a 'committee', 'council' or 'board' of trustees, but there are no legal restrictions on describing them in other ways. The term 'charity trustee' used in the Charities Act 2011 has a specific statutory meaning of 'the persons having the general control of the management and administration of the charity'.[3] A charity's constitution will usually define the

---

[1]   'Finding new trustees' (CC 30).
[2]   Only a sole trustee which is a trust corporation can give a valid receipt for the proceeds of sale of land under the Law of Property Act 1925, s 27. A corporate trustee appointed by a Scheme or Order of the Charity Commission is automatically a trust corporation under the Charities Act 2011, Sch 7, para 3(1).
[3]   Charities Act 2011, s 177.

trustees as a group in a particular way and it is usually preferable to use this definition in practice where possible. For the sake of simplicity, we use the terms 'board of trustees' or 'board'.

OTHER POSTS

8.4   There are a number of other posts commonly found within charities that do not mean that the post holder is a trustee. It is important to understand the distinction between trusteeship and the role and responsibilities of the holders of other posts. This can only be determined definitively on the basis of a charity's constitution, but some of the more common posts are:

Post	Meaning
Patron	Usually an honorary position which confers no rights or obligations on the holder (who is often a member of the 'great and good' whose association with, and support for, the charity is intended to enhance its reputation and standing).
President	Usually another way of describing a Patron and, often a 'Patron in chief'. The past Chairman of a charity may sometimes become a president of the charity after he or she has ceased to be a trustee. Again, this is usually (although not always) an honorary position with no rights or obligations in relation to the charity.
Observer	Usually an individual nominated by a stakeholder in a charity to attend trustees' meetings on its behalf in order to advise the charity on the stakeholder's views and to report proceedings to the stakeholder. Generally, an Observer will have no more than a right to attend (and perhaps to speak) at trustees' meetings. He or she will have no voting rights in relation to the charity. See **5.91** for more on Observers.
Secretary/ Clerk	Usually the person responsible for administering the trustees as a group by giving notice of meetings, keeping minutes, registers and other records etc and also for ensuring that all documents required by the Charity Commission and any other regulator are properly filed. In the context of a charitable company, the Secretary will generally be the company secretary appointed under the Companies Act 2006 (if appointed to this role as well). The Secretary may also be a trustee, but will act in a different capacity in relation to each post.

8.5   Not every charity will have posts of this kind. The position will depend upon the provisions of an individual charity's constitution.

COMPOSITION OF THE BOARD OF TRUSTEES

8.6   A number of different provisions will determine the composition of the board of trustees. These are as follows.

8.7   While there are no legal restrictions on the minimum or maximum number of trustees who may act, most charities' constitutions will set limits. There is obviously a balance to be struck between deploying a sufficiently wide range of skills and experience on the board and ensuring that it remains sufficiently compact to operate effectively. In practice, a board may prove to be too large to allow decisions to be taken effectively, particularly where not all of the members of a large board are actually able to attend meetings on a regular basis. There can then be a danger that decisions are made in practice by a smaller group of trustees to the exclusion of the others. Where a wide range of skills and experience are required but there is a desire to keep the board reasonably small, the solution will generally be for the trustees to delegate some of their powers and discretions to committees of the board. This is explained in more detail at **8.116**.

8.8   It is essential that the board of trustees can bring the right sort of skills and experience to the charity. What is required will depend upon what the charity does, but there will often be a requirement for trustees with experience of finance, accounting and law. One way of helping to ensure that the right skills and experience are available is for the trustees to identify the skill sets they consider are necessary for the charity's health and development. This can be used as the basis for the charity's policy on trustee recruitment.

8.9   In order to ensure that the mix of skills and experience on the board is continually refreshed, most charities will wish to set limits on the terms for which trustees hold office. There is currently no legal requirement that trustees should only act for a particular term and, if no term is specified, the rule is that a trustee will continue to act until he or she retires, is removed, dies, becomes incapable of acting or is otherwise disqualified from acting as a charity trustee (there is more about this at **8.30**). Many charities do adopt this approach and rely upon the good sense and discretion of their trustees in deciding when to call time. The disadvantage of this approach is that trustees can remain in office in circumstances where they have very little to offer to the charity because of changes in their own lives or changes in the way that the charity operates. Long-serving trustees can sometimes also be resistant to change and reluctant to challenge the status quo. This can leave a charity without trustees equipped to deal with changes in the environment in which it operates.

8.10   There is obviously a balance to be struck between bringing new trustees (with new skills, experience and ideas) to the board and preserving the continuity and collective experience of the board. Using terms of office fixed by the constitution is the usual way of striking this balance. The key provisions are generally:

- Setting a fixed term of office for every trustee. The recent trend in relation to terms of office appears to be between 3 and 5 years (on the basis that this strikes a balance between continuity and refreshment).

- A trustee who has come to the end of his or her term of office may be eligible for re-appointment for a further term, but the maximum number of terms may be specified. Popular choices are 2 and 3 terms.

- A 'cooling-off' period (often of a year) during which a retiring trustee cannot act may be included either between each term or, more usually, at the end of a specified number of terms. The aim is obviously to give both the retiring trustee and the charity a chance to see how they get on without each other.

- An 'override' provision which will allow the board to resolve that a trustee's term of office should continue beyond the term for which he or she is appointed where they are doing particularly valuable work on a particular project or aspect of the charity's operations and need to be able to continue to act while that work continues.

- Provisions that allow the retirement and appointment and re-appointment of trustees to be staggered, so that trustees who have acted for similar periods of time do not all retire en masse leaving a board of new trustees to start work without the benefit of their collective knowledge and experience. There is more about this at **8.11**.

Staggered retirement

8.11   Staggering the retirement of trustees can be done in a number of different ways.

- Many charitable companies will use a form of 'retirement by rotation' based upon the provisions of the Companies Acts that apply to private companies limited by shares. The idea is that a proportion of the trustees (often, but not necessarily, one-third) should retire every year, with those who have acted for the longest retiring before those appointed after them (and any trustees who have acted for the same period being identified by drawing lots). This has the effect of staggering trustee retirements and the appointment of other trustees to take their places.

- The retirement usually takes place with effect from the end of an annual general meeting ('AGM') that, prior to the coming into force of the Companies Act 2006, all companies were required to hold (except where they had an 'elective resolution' in place to dispense with this requirement). The benefit of this approach is that one event takes place annually at which trustees can retire (and perhaps be re-appointed) and new trustees can be appointed. This does assume that the power to appoint and re-appoint lies with the members attending the AGM, but the appointments can as easily be dealt with at a board meeting held after the AGM if the power to appoint trustees lies with the trustees themselves.

- The Companies Act 2006 abolished the previous requirement for all private companies to hold an AGM, unless their articles require it. Many charitable companies have taken the opportunity to amend their articles to take advantage of this procedural relaxation, especially where the members are the individuals acting as trustees for the time being. However, an AGM can still be held and many charitable companies may wish to do so, if only to deal with the retirement and appointment of trustees. If no AGM is to be held, then another way of dealing with trustee appointments and retirements will need to be identified in the constitution.

- There is no legal objection to charities other than companies holding AGMs and many may wish to do so in order to deal with the retirement and appointment of trustees. The provisions dealing with the AGM will need to be spelled out in the charity's constitution because there is no legal regime equivalent to the Companies Acts that provides a framework for the holding of meetings by other forms of charity.

- If no AGM is held, retirements can be dealt with using the same basic principle but by reference to another date. The obvious choice is a trustees' meeting, perhaps the first or last to be held in the year, although this assumes that the appointment of new trustees can take place at the same time (whether by the trustees or the members or anyone else with the right to appoint trustees). It will generally be preferable to deal with the retirement and appointment or re-appointment of trustees at the same time in order to ensure that the board retains a full complement of trustees. This may not always be practicable, but is less likely to present a problem than, say, retiring a third of a charity's trustees on 1 January in every year when there may then be an interval until they can be re-appointed or others appointed in their place.

- Good records of trustees' terms of office are essential.

CHAIRMAN

8.12 Every board of trustees needs a chairman to oversee board meetings, to provide leadership to the trustees and, where the charity has employees, often to act as the main point of contact at board level for the chief executive and other senior employees.

8.13 The chairman will inevitably be one of the trustees. Although there is no legal restriction on someone who is not already a trustee being appointed as chairman, he or she will play a very active part in the management and control of the charity at the highest level. In practice, therefore, the chairman is often already a trustee of the charity, having had an opportunity to demonstrate that he or she has the skills and experience required to perform the role well. For the same reason, the trustees themselves will almost invariably appoint the chairman. While the chairman could in principle be appointed by the members of a charity, it is the trustees who are likely to be best placed to make a judgement about who would best meet the requirements of the role.

8.14 The mechanism for appointing the chairman (if there is one) should be specified in the charity's constitution. The chairman's term of office should also be specified and will be co-extensive with his or her term of office as trustee. If he or she ceases to be a trustee, he or she will also cease to be chairman unless the charity's constitution provides to the contrary. In practice, this would be an unusual provision.

8.15 There are no legal rules that govern how long the chairman may hold office for. The position will normally be determined by the charity's constitution, which may provide that the trustees should determine the term when they make the appointment. An alternative is for the constitution to specify a term of office in the same way as it will spell out the trustees' terms of office. In practice, the term of office of the chairman needs to strike a balance between allowing the chairman to establish him or herself in the role and ensuring that a chairman who is not performing in what is likely to be the most important role at board level does not continue over the longer term. This may mean that the emphasis is on appointment for shorter periods than the trustees (perhaps on annual basis), but with no restriction on the number of times an effective chairman can be re-appointed while they remain a trustee.

8.16 Many charities will wish to make Terms of Reference (see **8.36** for more on this) for their chairman. The terms made will vary from charity to charity, but may look something like this:

Chairman

Terms of Reference

The board (the '**Board**') of trustees (the '**Trustees**') of the [Charity] (the '**Charity**') has adopted the following terms of reference in respect of the Charity's Chairman.

Role

In addition to complying with his or her general duties as a Trustee of the Charity, the Chairman's role is to provide overall leadership to the Charity in a manner which maximises the contributions of Trustees and employees and ensures that all remain focused on achieving the aims set out in the Charity's vision and mission statements.

The Chairman is primarily responsible for the three key aspects of the Charity's governance:

- How the Trustees work together as an effective Board
- How the Board sets and achieves the Charity's aims
- The relationship between the Board and the Charity's senior executives.

➡

Effective working

In order to encourage effective working, the Chairman is expected to:

- Help identify the skills and experience required on the Board.
- Ensure that there is a plan for Trustee succession and help to seek new Trustees from diverse sources.
- Arrange comprehensive Trustee induction and training programmes.
- Chair meetings effectively by using carefully structured agendas and briefing papers and encouraging participation by all Trustees.
- Ensure that the Trustees review both the performance of the Board and their own individual contribution annually.
- Establish and keep under review an appropriate governance model for the Charity, including the use of Committees of the Board.
- Ensure that terms of reference are in place for Trustees, the Treasurer and Committees of the Board.

Achieving the Charity's aims

In order to achieve the Charity's aims, the Chairman is expected to:

- Ensure that those aims are clearly identified and set out in its vision and mission statements and its guiding principles and that they are kept under review.
- Ensure that the Charity's aims reflect its legal charitable objects.
- Ensure that a business plan and budget are set annually and are properly monitored in the light of the Charity's aims and the Board's assessment of its strengths and weaknesses and the threats to, and opportunities for, it.
- Work closely with the Chief Executive to ensure that there is clarity about the Charity's aims at all levels within the organisation.
- Ensure that the efforts of the senior executives and other members of management are effectively directed within a framework of clearly structured strategies.
- Ensure that there is an effective risk management policy in place.
- Ensure that the Charity has appropriate policies on investment and reserves.
- Promote the Charity to its beneficiaries and other stakeholders, the media and the public at large, where this assists the senior executives' public relations strategy.

Effective delegation

In so far as the relationship between the Board and the senior executives is concerned, the Chairman is expected to: ➜

- Ensure that both he or she and the Chief Executive understand each other's roles.

- Act as the main point of contact on the Board for the Chief Executive.

- Ensure that terms of reference are in place for the Chief Executive and other senior executives.

- Ensure that a process for evaluating the performance of the Chief Executive and other senior executives is established and adhered to.

- Ensure that the Chief Executive is clear about the key performance indicators that the Board wishes to use to monitor the performance of the senior executives and by which the Chief Executive will be held accountable.

- Appraise the Chief Executive annually (with another member of the Board).

Conflicts of interest

The Chairman is expected to pay particular attention to the possibility of any conflict arising in relation to any aspect of the Charity's operations.

This will include any conflict for members of the Board or any senior executive.

TREASURER

8.17 Although there is no legal obligation to do so, many charities do appoint a treasurer to oversee their finances. This is entirely dependent upon the provisions in a charity's constitution. The treasurer will usually be a trustee appointed by the board. The charity's constitution should spell out the mechanism for the treasurer's appointment, his or her term of office, and the basis on which he or she can be removed.

8.18 Many larger charities will prefer to delegate the consideration of financial matters to a finance committee (and possibly also audit issues to an audit committee) rather than appointing an individual trustee as treasurer (although the two things are not mutually exclusive). Where a charity does have a treasurer, it is important to recognise that he or she does not become solely responsible for a charity's finances as a consequence (unless there is an express delegation of responsibility in the charity's constitution to this effect, which would be unusual). All of the trustees remain collectively responsible for understanding, and taking decisions in relation to, the charity's finances. The treasurer's role is usually to act as the first port of call for employees in relation to financial matters and to provide other members of the board with guidance in relation to the charity's financial affairs.

8.19 The treasurer is often an accountant or someone else with financial experience, but there is no legal requirement that they should have any particular qualifications. The charity's constitution will often set criteria.

8.20 Charities may wish to make Terms of Reference in relation to the treasurer's role. The Terms made will vary from charity to charity, but may look something like the Terms set out below (which include an option for the Treasurer to serve on a Finance Committee):

Treasurer

Terms of Reference

The board (the '**Board**') of trustees (the '**Trustees**') of the [Charity] (the '**Charity**') has adopted the following terms of reference in respect of the Charity's Treasurer.

Role

In addition to complying with his or her general duties as a Trustee of the Charity, the Treasurer's role is:

- To provide advice, information and comfort to the other Trustees on the Board on their responsibilities in respect of the financial aspects of the Charity's operations.
- To act as the main point of contact on the Board for the Finance Director, head of internal audit and any other member of management concerned with the financial aspects of the Charity's operations.
- To serve as a member of the Finance Committee.

Each of these roles is dealt with in more detail below.

Because of the wide-ranging scope of the Treasurer's role, he or she will not usually be expected to serve on any Committee of the Board other than the Finance Committee.

Because of the requirements of the role of the Treasurer he or she will usually be a qualified accountant or some other person whom the Board considers to have a high degree of financial and commercial expertise and acumen.

Board

As part of his or her duty to advise the Board in relation to its financial responsibilities, the Treasurer is expected to do the following things: ➡

- Ensure that, in close co-operation with the Finance Director, an appropriate financial policy framework is in place to guide the Board's financial decision-making (including recommending to the Finance Director how management accounts and other financial information is best presented to the Board).

- Develop a close understanding of the most important financial and other assumptions in the Charity's business plan and the annual budgetary proposals put forward by the Charity's management with a view to advising the Board on them.

- Advise the Board in relation to the budget, management accounts and the Charity's financial statements and the financial aspects of the business plan.

- Advise the Board on significant financial issues that arise and are outside the scope of the authority delegated to the Charity's management.

- Develop a close understanding of the Charity's internal financial controls with a view to ensuring that they operate effectively.

- Act as the initial point of contact for Trustees in relation to any question they may have on any of the financial aspects of the Charity's operations.

- Recommend to the Board when they may wish to consider taking professional advice on any financial aspect of the Charity's operations.

The Treasurer is also expected to advise the Board on the relationship between the financial aspects of the Charity's operations and the Board's policies on investment and reserves.

Management

The Treasurer is the day-to-day contact at Board level in relation to any financial aspect of the Charity's operations for the Finance Director and must provide support and advice to him or her on financial matters. In order to facilitate this, the Treasurer is expected to arrange meetings with the Finance Director on a regular or ad hoc basis, as he or she considers appropriate.

The Treasurer is also the point of contact at Board level for the head of internal audit and external auditor in relation to any financial aspect of the Charity's operations. The Treasurer is expected to arrange meetings with the head of internal audit and the external auditor on a regular or an ad hoc basis, as he or she considers appropriate.

The Chief Executive may also discuss any financial aspect of the Charity's operations with the Treasurer.   ➡

The Treasurer is expected to ensure that a record is kept of the matters discussed with the Chief Executive and the Finance Director, the head of internal audit and the external auditor and will report to the Board and/or the Finance Committee (as appropriate) at every Board and/or Committee meeting on the matters so discussed.

Finance Committee

In fulfilling his or her role as a member of the Finance Committee (and subject always to the terms of reference for that Committee), the Treasurer is expected to:

- Provide financial acumen and expertise to the Finance Committee.
- Plan (in conjunction with the external and internal auditors) an annual cycle of meetings of the Finance Committee and recommend the agenda of each such meeting for consideration by the Committee.
- Plan who to invite to each meeting of the Finance Committee (eg the head of internal audit, the external auditor, the Finance Director, any other employee of the Charity with responsibility for its finances) and make appropriate recommendations to the Committee.
- Recommend to the Finance Director how management accounts and other financial data relating to the Charity's operations should best be presented to the Finance Committee.
- Recommend to the Finance Committee when they may wish to consider taking professional advice on any of the matters within the Finance Committee's terms of reference.
- Make recommendations to the Committee in relation to the Charity's internal audit function.

The Treasurer is also expected to make recommendations to the Finance Committee in relation to the performance, constitution and terms of reference of the Committee with a view to ensuring that it operates at maximum effectiveness.

Conflicts of interest

The Treasurer is expected to pay particular attention to the possibility of any conflict arising in relation to any financial aspect of the Charity's operations.

This will include any conflict for the external auditor in addition to the members of the Board or any member of management.

SECRETARY

8.21 As a result of the de-regulation of company administration implemented by the Companies Act 2006, private companies are not required to have a company secretary responsible for administering the board and members' meeting and dealing with other administrative matters, including filing information with Companies House.

8.22 However, it is still open to any charitable company to opt to have a secretary and many charities will (regardless of whether they are set up as companies or not) wish to have some provision in their constitution for the appointment of a Secretary with primary responsibility for administrative matters.

8.23 The mechanism for the appointment of the secretary will be set out in the charity's constitution (with certain aspects of a charitable company secretary's appointment dealt with in the Companies Acts). There are no legal restrictions that will prevent one of the trustees also acting as secretary, although the post could as easily be given to a non-trustee, including one of the senior executives of the charity or perhaps a professional adviser. The charity's constitution should clearly set out the mechanism for the secretary's appointment and removal, any requirement that he or she should be a trustee and should provide for the board to determine the scope of their duties. In the context of a charitable company, of course, the secretary's duties will be regulated to a degree by the Companies Act 2006.

8.24 Many charities may wish to make Terms of Reference for their secretary. The Terms made will vary from charity to charity, but may look something like this (provisions relating to a charitable company are in square brackets):

Secretary

Terms of Reference

The board (the **'Board'**) of trustees (the **'Trustees'**) of [Charity] (the **'Charity'**) has adopted the following terms of reference in respect of the Charity's Secretary.

Role

The Secretary's role is to:

- Ensure the smooth running of the Board and Board Committees' activities by assisting the Chairman to set agendas, prepare papers and distribute them to the Board and to advise on Board procedures and ensure that they are adhered to.
- Advise and assist the Board with respect to their duties and responsibilities.   →

- Ensure that the Charity complies with its constitution.

- Keep under review all legislative, regulatory and corporate governance developments that might affect the Charity's operations and help ensure that the Board is fully briefed on those issues and that it has regard to them when taking decisions.

- Act as a primary point of contact for Trustees as regards information and advice in relation to proceedings of the Board.

- Ensure that every new Trustee is properly inducted into the Charity's operations and their roles and responsibilities.

- Ensure that the Charity complies with all statutory requirements of the relevant [companies and] charities legislation, including in particular:
  — [Filing forms AP01/TM01, annual returns, annual reports and accounts, resolutions of the members adopted at any general meeting or in writing and new articles of association with Companies House.]
  — Filing annual returns, trustees' details forms and annual reports and accounts with the Charity Commission and updating the Commission following changes of Trustees.

- Ensure that the Charity's [statutory] registers (in particular the registers of trustees, trustees' interests and members) are kept up to date and held at the registered office.

- Make arrangements for and manage the process of the AGM and establish, with the Board's agreement, the items to be considered at the AGM, including resolutions dealing with governance matters.

- Co-ordinate the publication and distribution of the Charity's annual report and accounts.

- Keep accurate and comprehensive minutes of all meetings of the Board and AGMs and other meetings of the Charity's members.

- Ensure that all business letters, notices and other official publications show the information required by the [companies and] charities legislation.

- Ensure that procedures are in place for the proper administration of the Charity's subsidiary companies.

- Arrange indemnity insurance cover for the trustees in accordance with the instructions of the Board.

- Ensure that the Charity's stakeholders (including its employees) are in the Board's mind when important operational decisions are taken.

- Act as an additional enquiring voice in relation to Board decisions which particularly affect the Charity, drawing on his or her experience and knowledge of the practical aspects of management including law, tax and business finance.

- Act as a confidential sounding board to the Chairman and other trustees on points that may concern them. ➜

Reporting

The Secretary is responsible to the Board and should be accountable to the Board through the Chairman on all matters relating to his or her duties as a company officer.

Where the Secretary has other executive or administrative duties in addition to those as Secretary, he or she reports to the Chief Executive (or any other member of management to whom responsibility for that matter has been delegated by the Board).

'EX-OFFICIO', 'NOMINATED' AND 'CO-OPTED' TRUSTEES

8.25 Some charities may have 'ex-officio', 'nominated' or 'co-opted' trustees. These terms are really no more than a reference to the way in which particular trustees are appointed.

8.26 An 'ex-officio' trustee becomes a trustee because he or she has been appointed to some other post or office that carries with it the right to become a trustee of the charity in question. The post or office could be with the charity itself (for example, the chief executive) or with some other organisation (for example, the Dean of a Cathedral may be an ex-officio trustee of a school associated with the Cathedral).

8.27 A 'nominated' trustee is one appointed by a third party, sometimes another charity, a university or public body. The constitution of the charity will set out the method of nomination, including whether or not the charity has the right to veto the nomination. A nominated trustee does not act as a delegate or representative of the nominating body but must act in his or her own right and only in the interests of the charity, in the same way as all other trustees.

8.28 A 'co-opted' trustee is usually appointed by the board either to fill a trustee vacancy or as an additional trustee to fill a gap in the skill set of the board. They will typically be appointed for a shorter period than trustees appointed by the charity's members or trustees in the usual way, although this will depend upon the terms of the charity's constitution.

8.29 The most important thing to appreciate about co-opted, nominated and ex-officio trustees is that they are as much trustees of the charity as trustees appointed in any other way. The fact that they may, for example, hold office for a shorter period does not affect the nature or extent of the duties that they owe to the charity. It is only the mechanism by which they are appointed that differs.

DISQUALIFICATION

8.30 There are a number of provisions that may disqualify an individual from acting as a charity trustee.

8.31 The Charities Act 2011[4] disqualifies anyone from acting as a charity trustee if they:

- have been convicted of any offence involving dishonesty or deception;
- are subject to an undischarged bankruptcy order or have made a composition with their creditors which has not been discharged;
- have already been removed as a charity trustee by the Charity Commission or by the courts on the grounds of misconduct or mismanagement of the administration of a charity; or
- are subject to a disqualification order or a disqualification undertaking under the Company Directors Disqualification Act 1986 (this provision applies to a person seeking to become a trustee of any charity regardless of whether it is constituted as a company or not).

8.32 The Charity Commission has a discretion to waive certain of these requirements. Acting as a charity trustee while disqualified is a criminal offence under the Charities Act 2011.[5]

8.33 The courts can make disqualification orders against directors of companies under the Company Directors Disqualification Act 1986 in a variety of circumstances, including:

- on conviction of an indictable offence;
- for any fraud committed in the winding-up of a company; or
- following an investigation into the company's affairs by the Department for Business, Innovation and Skills (BIS) or on an application in respect of wrongful trading or fraudulent trading (there is more about this in **Chapter 6**).

8.34 Disqualification as a director of a company will mean that the person who has been disqualified cannot act as a trustee of any charity, whether set up as a company or not, unless the Charity Commission is willing and able to exercise its discretion to allow him or her to act.

8.35 In addition to the statutory provisions, the constitution of most charities will set out a number of circumstances in which a charity trustee is disqualified from acting. This will have the effect of removing an existing trustee or disqualifying a prospective trustee. Often, the express provisions will mirror the provisions of the Charities Act 2011 but may be tailored to meet the needs of

---

[4] Charities Act 2011, s 178.
[5] Charities Act 2011, ss 181 and 183.

the charity (for example a charity working with children or vulnerable adults may include a provision that inclusion on a statutory list of persons prohibited from working with these groups is grounds for disqualification).

Some constitutions may also provide for a trustee to cease to act if, for example, all of the other trustees resolve that it would be in the charity's best interests if he or she were to be removed. There is more detail about provisions of this kind in **8.162**.

TERMS OF REFERENCE

8.36 'Terms of Reference' are usually made by the board as part of its governance arrangements for three purposes:

- to define the scope of the role of particular members of the board or other post holders within the charity, eg the chairman, treasurer or secretary;
- to define the scope of the duties delegated to committees of the board relating to particular aspects of the charity's operations; and
- to define the scope of the roles and duties of senior employees.

8.37 Terms of Reference for committees are usually made pursuant to the exercise by the board of an express power to delegate some or all of its functions to a committee. The Terms themselves must reflect the requirements in the charity's constitution in relation to delegation on this basis. There is more about this at **8.91**.

8.38 Terms of reference for individual trustees and post holders are more likely to be made on an 'informal' basis; in other words, without a particular requirement or provision for them in the charity's constitution. Having said that, many charities' constitutions will provide for the board to determine, for example, the scope of the role of the chairman or secretary, in which case creating Terms of Reference is usually an effective way of achieving this.

8.39 Terms of Reference are usually written in a more informal way than the provisions of a charity's constitution. The intention is to put flesh on the bones of the legal structure in a way that will be intelligible to the charity's trustees, any employees and others.

BOARD MEETINGS

8.40 The main focus of trustees' attention and effort will be their meetings. Because charity trustees will generally act on an unpaid basis, they may not spend a great deal of time acting as trustees other than at meetings, although certain posts which trustees may hold (eg chairman or treasurer) are likely to involve more day-to-day work.

Frequency

8.41 There are no legal restrictions on the frequency with which board meetings should be held except where the provisions of a charity's constitution specify a minimum number. The Charity Commission recommends at least one physical meeting of a charity's trustees each year and a minimum of two full trustees' meetings,[6] but the number of meetings that are required in practice will generally be determined by the scale and complexity of the charity's operations.

Board papers

8.42 One of the keys to effective discussion and decision-making at board meetings is distribution of information beforehand. There are no hard and fast rules about what charity trustees should and should not see, but the following things are likely to be relevant:

- Regular financial information, particularly where a charity's income is derived largely from operational activities rather than, say, investment income and gains. This could include, for example, management accounts.
- Where the charity's operations mean that it has employees, the trustees may wish to see short reports from the chief executive and other senior employees on particular aspects of the charity's operations.
- The trustees should see draft minutes of the previous meeting for their approval.
- Reports and papers relating to particular projects under consideration should be circulated.

8.43 In order to ensure that trustees have sufficient time to read and digest information made available before a meeting, all papers should be distributed in good time. They should be sent with a formal notice of the meeting, although information can be sent subsequently without invalidating the notice provided that the notice contains sufficient information about the matters that will be considered to enable the trustees to decide whether or not to attend the meeting. Tabling detailed papers for decision should be discouraged as trustees will not have had time to read and scrutinise the papers beforehand.

Notice

8.44 There are no legal rules that govern the periods of notice that are required for trustees' meetings except that the notice given must be reasonable in the circumstances (eg short notice in an emergency is likely to be reasonable). The notice period is governed solely by the provisions of the charity's constitution. This may specify a particular period of time or it may simply provide that meetings can be called on notice determined by the trustees from time to time.

---

[6]   CC 48.

8.45 Where a charity's constitution specifies that notice must be given in a particular way, these provisions must be adhered to. Notices can be given by email or using some other electronic means provided the charity's constitution provides for this. As we have indicated, the notice must provide sufficient information to the trustees about what will be discussed to enable them to decide whether or not to attend. The charity's constitution should ideally specify who is able to give notice of a meeting. As regards board meetings this is typically any trustee, but notice is sometimes required to be given via the Secretary (if there is one).

Rules and regulations

8.46 The charity's constitution will often give trustees a power to make rules and regulations in relation to the way in which their board meetings are convened and held in order to give them flexibility to work in the most effective way. This is the approach usually taken by the articles of charitable companies (and reflects the approach taken by companies generally) but any charity can adopt a similar approach. Any rules or regulations that are made should preferably be in writing and reviewed by the trustees from time to time. They should not conflict with the provisions of the constitution itself (on the basis that the constitution can only properly be altered in accordance with whatever mechanism applies to it). This will often be expressly spelled out in the provisions of the constitution dealing with rule making.

Electronic meetings

8.47 The general rule is that a meeting can only validly be held where the participants can both see and hear each other. This means that, unless a charity's constitution expressly prohibits it, trustees can hold meetings by electronic means, including by way of video conference or web camera. Because a telephone conference call does not allow trustees to see each other, it cannot constitute a 'meeting' unless the charity's constitution expressly provides for meetings to be held on this basis. If there is no specific power to conduct trustees' meetings by telephone conference call, some trustees may still be able to phone into a physical meeting of trustees provided that (disregarding the trustees who are on the telephone) they can form a valid quorum for the meeting.

Voting

8.48 Voting at meetings will be in accordance with the charity's constitution but, if the constitution is silent, then a simple majority can pass resolutions. The trustees of private trusts are obliged to pass resolutions unanimously unless there are provisions in their constitution to the contrary. This is not true of charity trustees, who may act by a majority. In some cases, a constitution may specify a higher majority in relation to particular decisions, or may specify that certain resolutions can only be passed with the consent of particular trustees (for example, a trustee appointed by a particular stakeholder or an ex-officio trustee). In practice, most chairmen will seek consensus in relation to trustees' resolutions but where this is not possible, the majority will rule.

8.49 The constitution should ideally specify whether or not the chairman should exercise a 'casting' or 'second' vote in the event of deadlock. If there is no express provision for the chairman to exercise a casting or second vote, he or she will have only one vote as a trustee. A tied vote with no casting vote provision will mean that the resolution is 'lost'.

Written resolutions

8.50 If a meeting cannot be held to consider a resolution, the alternative is for the trustees to sign a written resolution. Whether a written resolution needs to be signed by all of the trustees in a charity in order to be valid will depend upon the provisions of the charity's constitution. If the constitution is silent then all of the trustees must sign. If the constitution provides for a minimum number of trustees to sign then it will be valid provided their signatures can be obtained. Careful consideration should be given to including a provision in a charity's constitution that will allow a majority of trustees to pass resolutions in writing. The requirement for unanimity is usually intended to reflect the fact that the trustees do not have an opportunity to debate the resolution before it is proposed and allowing resolutions to pass by majority may mean that there is no opportunity for that kind of debate to be had.

8.51 In practice, trustees are often keen to make decisions by way of email exchange confirming that a particular decision is approved. Again, resolutions can only be validly passed in this way if the charity's constitution expressly provides for this to happen.

Quorum

8.52 The charity's constitution will usually specify the quorum requirements of board meetings. The quorum will often be a 'lower of' or 'greater of' fixed number proportion of the trustees so that the quorum can keep pace with a fluctuating number of trustees. If there is no quorum present in accordance with a charity's constitution, resolutions cannot validly be passed at the meeting. If obtaining a quorum proves difficult in practice, the approach often taken is to provide in the constitution for a lower quorum after, say, two previous inquorate meetings.

Other attendees

8.53 There are a number of people who may attend board meetings in addition to the trustees themselves:

- the Secretary (if there is one);
- any Observers (who may have a right to attend board meetings in a representative capacity, eg to represent a charity's major funder);

- professional advisers; and
- senior employees (if any).

8.54 Where other people routinely attend trustees' meetings, the board may wish to make part of the meeting 'closed' to non-trustees in order to allow debate and discussion amongst the trustees alone. This is commonly called 'reserved business'.

Minutes

8.55 Charitable companies are obliged to maintain minutes of all trustees' meetings for at least 10 years from the date of the relevant meeting. Failure to do so is a criminal offence by the trustees and any company secretary.[7] Minutes are deemed to be evidence that the relevant meeting was properly convened and held and that any appointment made at it was valid (in the absence of any evidence to the contrary).

8.56 There are no equivalent legal provisions which apply to charities that are not set up as companies, but the obligation to maintain good records is a part of the trustees' duty to safeguard their charity's assets. In that sense, the obligation on charitable companies should be regarded as the benchmark for unincorporated charities.

8.57 The Charity Commission's guidance states that:

'Whatever may be the legal requirements, we recommend that accurate minutes are kept of all meetings. The minutes do not need to be a word for word record, but need to record information that is important to the charity. We recommend that each of the minutes give:

- the name of the charity
- the type of meeting
- the date and time the meetings was held
- apologies for absence
- the names of those present, including:
    - in what capacity they attended e.g. trustee, advisor etc; and
    - for what items on the agenda.

The minutes usually record:

- the precise wording of any resolution together with the name of the proposer and (optionally) the seconder of the motion
- a summary of the discussion on each item of business
- information upon which the decision was based
- details of the decision, i.e. who voted and how and, in the event of an equality of votes, if the Chair used a casting vote
- the action required
- the names of the people who are responsible for implementing the decision

---

7   Companies Act 2006, s 248.

- the date, time and venue of the next meeting.'[8]

8.58 The Charity Commission's guidance also emphasises the importance of ensuring that the minutes are an accurate record of the business that is transacted:

> 'It should be noted that the formal minutes, once approved and signed as an accurate record by the chairman, form the only legal record of the business at the meeting. Clearly, trustees can take notes of meetings for their own purposes; these should not however be used as an afterthought to the official minutes. It is important that, if a trustee is unable to agree that the draft minutes are an accurate record of the meeting, then he or she should draw the matter to the attention of the chairman before they are approved and signed.'[9]

8.59 For this reason, it is very important that draft minutes are circulated to all of the trustees in order to ensure that they have an opportunity to review and, if necessary, suggest any changes to them. If a trustee cannot agree that minutes are accurate, then the Commission's view is that 'his or her dissension should be formally noted and recorded as a postscript to the minutes before they are signed'.

APPOINTMENT

8.60 For most charities, identifying potential new trustees will be essential in order to maintain the right mix of skills and experience on the board as existing trustees retire. Many charities plan for trustee succession in order to ensure continuity on the board. New trustees may be drawn from a number of different sources, including the charity's members and beneficiaries.

8.61 Every new charity trustee must be properly appointed in accordance with the mechanism set out in the charity's constitution. This will vary from charity to charity, but there will usually be a number of key points:

- The charity's constitution should identify who is responsible for the appointment. Is it the charity's members (if it has members)? Is it the board of trustees? Or is some third party responsible?
- There are some specific rules that apply to unincorporated charities (see 8.65).
- Regardless of who is responsible for making the appointment, is there any nominations procedure that must first be observed (for example, does the board or a third party have to nominate people for appointment by the members) and are any third party consents required?
- If the trustee is to be appointed at a meeting of the members or the trustees, has proper notice been given of the proposal in accordance with the charity's constitution?

---

[8] CC 48.
[9] CC 48.

- Have the prospective trustees agreed to act as trustees of the charity? There is more about this issue at **8.78**.

8.62 Newly appointed trustees of charitable companies must have their appointment notified to Companies House on form AP01. The new trustee has to sign his or her consent to act and the form has to be countersigned by an existing trustee or the company secretary (unless the charity is a member of the PROOF online filing scheme and notifies Companies House of such changes electronically). The charity's register of directors should also be updated to reflect the appointment.

8.63 Formal requirements for the appointment of new trustees of other charities will depend upon the provisions of their constitution. This may include requirements in relation to consent or the entry of their name in a register of trustees. For charities other than companies, there are no legal requirements obliging the maintenance of a register of trustees; although this is obviously a sensible approach from the point of view of best practice.

8.64 The appointment of new trustees of a charity need not be notified immediately to the Charity Commission. Changes will be notified using the annual return (see **14.25** for more on this) and that information will then be made available online on the Commission's website. The Commission will not normally make changes to the details of existing trustees, remove them or add new trustees between Annual Return submissions, but charities can update these details themselves by logging into the Commission's website (and it will obviously be good practice to do so to ensure the information on the register is up to date).

Unincorporated charities

8.65 There are some specific considerations that must be taken into account in relation to the appointment of new trustees of charitable trusts and other unincorporated charities.

8.66 Often the constitution of an unincorporated charity will state expressly who is entitled to appoint new trustees. However, if there is no express power, the trustees of a charitable trust or unincorporated association can exercise the powers conferred by the Trustee Act 1925, s 36. Essentially, s 36 provides that:

- In default of the express nomination of a person with the power to appoint new trustees by a charity's constitution, the existing trustees, whether continuing or outgoing (or the personal representatives of the last surviving trustee) can appoint new trustees both in place of an outgoing trustee and as an additional trustee.
- This is a power and not a duty. The trustees cannot be compelled to exercise it.

- The power to replace an outgoing trustee applies where a trustee is dead, remains out of the UK for more than 12 months, wishes to retire, is unfit, refuses to act or is mentally or physically incapable of acting.
- The power to appoint an additional trustee can be used at any time but only if the total number of trustees after the appointment is no more than four or (unless the charity trustees hold land) such higher number as may be specified by the charity's constitution.

8.67 Where there is no express power to appoint new trustees (and the power conferred by s 36 of the Trustee Act 1925 in relation to unincorporated charities is not capable of being exercised) a charity may be able to seek an order from the Charity Commission under the Charities Act 2011, s 80(2). This section gives the Commission the power to appoint a new charity trustee:

- in place of a charity trustee who has been removed by them under their s 79 powers following the opening of an Inquiry (see **4.44** for more on this);
- where there are no charity trustees at all, or where, because of any vacancy in the board or the absence or incapacity of any of the trustees, the charity cannot apply for their appointment; or
- where the Commission concludes that it is necessary for the proper administration of the charity to have an additional charity trustee because one of the existing charity trustees (who ought nevertheless to remain a charity trustee) either cannot be found or does not act or is outside England and Wales.

8.68 In addition, the Charities Act 2011, s 76(3)(b) gives the Charity Commission the power to appoint additional trustees of a charity which is presently being administered by a single charity trustee (other than a 'corporation aggregate', commonly a limited company or a Royal Charter corporation) where the Commission is of the opinion that it is necessary to increase the number of trustees for the proper administration of the charity.

8.69 The Charity Commission also has jurisdiction (under the Charities Act 2011, s 69) to exercise the same jurisdiction and powers that are exercisable by the High Court. The court has an inherent jurisdiction to appoint new trustees to charities, even when there are no vacancies on the trustee board and where there is a power of appointment in existence and people capable of exercising it.

8.70 Alternatively, an application could be made to the court itself to exercise its inherent jurisdiction to appoint new trustees. Whenever it is desirable that a new trustee should be appointed and it is 'inexpedient, difficult or impractical to do so without the assistance of the Court', the court can also appoint a new trustee, either as an additional trustee or in substitution for an existing trustee, under the jurisdiction confirmed by the Trustee Act 1925, s 41. The court will not usually exercise this power unless it is satisfied that there is no provision in the charity's constitution which provides for the appointment of trustees and the power under the Trustee Act 1925, s 36 is not available.

8.71 Unincorporated charities have no legal personality separate from their trustees and the charity's assets can only be owned and held by the trustees themselves (or some of them) unless there is a provision for them to be held by a nominee.

8.72 The difficulty posed by the appointment of new trustees of charities of this kind is that legal title to the charity's assets must be vested in its trustees from time to time. This is in order to ensure that the individuals who are a charity's trustees at any particular time can deal with the assets effectively and have full control over them. This is an intrinsic part of every charity trustee's duty to safeguard the assets of a charity.

8.73 One way of dealing with this would be for title to the charity's assets to be transferred out of the name of any retiring trustee and into the names of the continuing and any newly appointed trustee. This would mean executing transfers in relation to land and shares and other securities, assignments of debts and all other individual assets. Clearly, where a charity's trustees change fairly frequently, transferring the assets in this way can become a fairly onerous burden. In practice, it is not often done, which can cause problems for the continuing trustees when they need to deal with the charity's assets at a later date.

8.74 Transfers of this kind can generally be avoided by ensuring that every charity trustee is appointed, or retired, by signing a document that constitutes a 'deed'. A deed is a document like any other but is executed in a particular way. The person making the deed must have his or her signature witnessed and intend it to be delivered as a deed.[10]

8.75 Where trustees' appointments and retirements are done by way of deed, s 40 of the Trustee Act 1925 provides that, unless the deed contains a provision to the contrary, it will automatically vest all of the charity's assets in the new or continuing trustees. Section 40 does not apply to every asset (for example, mortgages of land or transfers of shares or securities where a form of transfer has to be registered by the company). In addition, registered land will only be transferred on production of the deed to the Land Registry so that the proprietorship register can be brought up to date.[11]

8.76 Where no deed is used, the same effect can be achieved by appointing or retiring charity trustees by resolution of a meeting of the trustees, members or other people exercising the relevant power, where the charity's constitution provides for this. A memorandum recording the appointment or retirement of the trustees will bring the provisions of s 40 of the Trustee Act 1925 into play

---

[10] The document should also state that it is intended to be executed as a deed.
[11] Land Registration Act 2002, s 27.

provided that the memorandum has been signed either at the meeting by the chairman or in some other way directed by those present at the meeting and it is witnessed by two people who were present at the meeting. Clearly, the execution of the memorandum in this way is intended to replicate the formalities for execution of a deed.[12]

8.77 The constitutions of many charitable trusts and other unincorporated charities will sometimes expressly require new trustees to be appointed (and old trustees to retire) by way of deed. Sometimes they refer simply to appointment by 'resolution of' the members or trustees or 'by the members'. Notwithstanding that there is no reference to a deed, the trustees should ensure that every appointment is dealt with either by deed or by memorandum. Ideally, every unincorporated charity's constitution should provide expressly for appointments to be by way of deed and/or memorandum.

Consent to act

8.78 The Charity Commission recommends that all new charity trustees should sign a declaration confirming that they are willing to act as a trustee. A similar declaration is required from the trustees of any charity that is applying for registration by the Commission. It may seem to be obvious that anyone who has agreed to become a charity trustee and has signed the necessary documents and complied with the necessary formalities is willing to act. But the Commission's point is really that no-one should become a charity trustee unless they have taken the time and trouble to understand the scope of their role, their powers and, most importantly, their duties.

8.79 This is an important governance issue in practice. Essentially, a trustee is only worth the skills and experience he or she is willing and able to bring to a charity. If a new trustee does not appreciate that, say, they will be required to attend four meetings a year and ends up attending only one, the other trustees may wonder (quite rightly) whether they should have appointed someone more willing to make a real contribution to the charity's work.

8.80 Obtaining the formal consent of a new charity trustee to act is one step that charity trustees can take in order to ensure that new trustees brought on board will add value to the charity. A written consent from the trustee can also serve as their declaration that they are not disqualified from acting as a charity trustee (see **8.30** above) and for the purposes of HMRC's 'fit and proper persons' test. There is more about this at **8.88**.

An example of the kind of undertaking that could be sought is as follows:

---

12 Charities Act 2011, s 334.

Trustee's undertaking

I confirm my willingness to accept the appointment and responsibility of a trustee of [charity] (the **'Charity'**).

I have read and understood the following:

- The Charity's constitution
- [The Charity's Terms of Reference for trustees]
- 'The Essential Trustee: What you need to know' – booklet CC3 published by the Charity Commission

I understand that, together with my fellow trustees, it is my duty to act within the Charity's constitution and in accordance with any code of practice relating to the Charity to ensure that the Charity fulfils its objects, which are:

- To promote the [charitable purposes]

With utmost faith, I will be diligent and exercise reasonable care and skill in carrying out my duties as a trustee of the Charity.

I confirm that:

- I am not disqualified from acting as a charity trustee
- I have not been convicted of an offence involving deception or dishonesty (or any such conviction is legally regarded as spent)
- I have not been involved in tax fraud
- I am not an undischarged bankrupt
- I have not made compositions or arrangements with my creditors from which I have not been discharged
- I have not been removed from serving as a charity trustee, or been stopped from acting in a management position within a charity
- I have not been disqualified from serving as a company director
- I will at all times seek to ensure that the Charity's funds, and charity tax reliefs received by the Charity, are used only for charitable purposes.

Signed: Date:
Name:

8.81 This undertaking helps to ensure that the new trustee has taken steps to understand what it is that he or she is taking on. However, it really only makes sense in the context of a wide-ranging induction process.

Induction

8.82 A charity trustee cannot expect to understand the nature and extent of his or her role and responsibilities without an induction. And all charity trustees are in any event under a legal duty to ensure that they familiarise themselves with the charitable purposes and assets of their charity and the provisions of its constitution. As a minimum, a new charity trustee should be given the following items:

- a copy of the charity's constitution and, if appropriate, a summary of its charitable purposes;
- an explanation of how it operates to achieve its charitable purposes, with particular attention to the core areas of its operations;
- a copy of the charity's latest report and accounts;
- a copy of any Terms of Reference for the charity's trustees adopted by the board;
- any trustee policies, including, for example, policies on expenses and conflicts of interest;
- an explanation of the charity's relationship with any trading subsidiary (if there is one). There is more about this in **Chapter 13**;
- details of the charity's key employees and their respective roles and lines of reporting;
- details of the place and date of trustees' meetings and the information which will be made available for meetings; and
- a summary of the charity's internal financial controls.

8.83 As part of a new trustee's induction, it will normally be sensible to set out some Terms of Reference for the charity's trustees generally. This will obviously also be an important document as regards the existing trustees. As with all Terms of Reference, any Terms that are set should be reviewed by the charity trustees from time to time. Terms will obviously vary from charity to charity, but an example of the sort of provisions one might expect to see is as follows:

Trustees

Terms of reference

The board (the '**Board**') of trustees (the '**Trustees**') of the [Charity] (the '**Charity**') has approved these Terms of Reference for Trustees.

Board meetings

Trustees are expected:

- To attend meetings of the Board having carefully read and considered the agenda and briefing papers. ➜

- To participate in Board meetings in a reasonable, objective and prudent manner, not allowing prejudice to impinge on the debate and decision-making process.
- To contribute actively to the Board in giving firm strategic direction to the Charity, setting overall policies, defining goals and setting targets and evaluating performance against agreed targets.
- To monitor the Charity's financial position and ensure total accountability.
- To assist in the formulation of budgets and strategic plans.
- To approve the Charity's annual report and accounts.

Trustees' responsibilities

Trustees' responsibilities are:

- To ensure that legal, financial and management duties comply with the Charity's constitution and charitable objects.
- To safeguard the reputation and ethos of the Charity by ensuring that all activities are conducted with probity and propriety.
- To ensure the effective and efficient administration of the Charity as well as its financial stability.
- To ensure the protection and conscientious management of the property and assets of the Charity and to ensure the proper investment of its funds.
- To act in the interests of all, rather than any local or sectional interest.
- To act collectively with the other Trustees, not as an individual.
- To disclose any conflict of interest.
- To maintain appropriate confidentiality.
- To honour the collective responsibility for decisions properly taken, channelling concerns or disagreements through the chairman.
- To review annually the performance of the Trustees.
- To approve the annual appraisal of the Chief Executive.
- To ensure that an annual general meeting is held every calendar year and the annual return, accounts, report and all other relevant documents and resolutions are filed within the appropriate time limit.

What trustees may also be able to offer

Trustees must be able to offer:

- An informative/educational/ambassadorial role at a local and regional level.

→

- Availability to serve on committees of the Board or working groups where relevant.
- Willingness to take part in induction and training as appropriate.
- Specific skills and contacts.
- Willingness to offer advice to other Trustees and staff drawn from personal experience.

Responsibilities to employees

Trustees' responsibilities to the charity's employees are:

- To ensure compliance with current employment and equal opportunities legislation as well as good practice and the Charity's current policy on these and related matters.
- To ensure the establishment of procedures for the recruitment, support, appraisal and remuneration of employees.
- To ensure that disciplinary and complaints procedures are in place.
- To work in close co-operation with the Chief Executive and other senior executives.

Object drift

8.84 A good example of a failure by charity trustees to appreciate the scope of their role, the nature of their powers and duties and the legal framework within which their charity operates is 'object drift'. For example, a charity may be established for the relief of poverty but starts to operate programmes which help people in poverty as a consequence of ill health. The charity operates successfully and its activities develop to the extent that it starts to help anyone in ill health regardless of their economic circumstances. Over time, the charity's activities in relation to health become more important than its activities in relation to poverty. The work it does in relation to health is very valuable but it is not work that falls within the charity's legal purposes. In principle, the charity's trustees are in breach of trust for allowing the charity to operate in this way.

8.85 In many cases, 'object drift' of this kind is due to changes in the composition of the board of trustees over time. As old trustees retire and new trustees are appointed, there is always a danger that new trustees do not properly understand what the charity does or the legal framework within which it operates and will agree (with the best of intentions) to something that the charity is legally incapable of doing, or at least not without giving rise to a breach of trust.

8.86 Avoiding this sort of problem depends upon a number of factors, but a comprehensive and effective induction of a new trustee is obviously an essential starting point.

DBS checks

8.87 There is a raft of legislation aimed at ensuring that any organisation that works with children or vulnerable adults carries out checks on the various different lists of individuals who may pose a risk to them. The statutes in question are the Care Standards Act 2000, the Education Act 2002, the Safeguarding Vulnerable Groups Act 2006 and the Protection of Freedoms Act 2012. A detailed analysis of these provisions is outside the scope of this book, but the trustees of any charity that works with children or vulnerable adults must ensure that they familiarise themselves with the framework of the legislation. This is aimed at ensuring that every individual who will work with children or vulnerable adults is the subject of a criminal records check with the Disclosure and Barring Service (DBS). The DBS maintains lists of individuals who have been convicted of criminal offences associated with children and vulnerable adults. There is more information available on the Home Office website.[13] Charities whose main beneficiaries are children or vulnerable adults may also wish to consider developing protection policies in relation to their beneficiaries. The Charity Commission has also published guidance on safeguarding vulnerable beneficiaries.[14]

FIT AND PROPER PERSONS

8.88 As we explain at **11.5**, the Finance Act 2010 introduced a new definition of charity for tax purposes. In order to be charitable, an organisation must satisfy the 'management condition', which requires it to have 'managers' who are 'fit and proper persons'. Managers are defined as the persons having the general control and management of the charity and will include trustees, but also the charity's senior executives and anyone who, in practice, controls the financial aspects of running the charity.

8.89 There is no definition in the legislation of a 'fit and proper person' and HMRC has published guidance explaining how it will apply the test.[15] Broadly, HMRC expects charities to give consideration to the suitability of individuals to act as the managers of the charity and will assume that all people appointed by charities are fit and proper persons unless they hold information to show otherwise. Provided charities take appropriate steps on appointing personnel, they can assume that they meet the management condition unless, in exceptional circumstances, they are challenged by HMRC.

8.90 HMRC recommends charities ask all new managers to read its basic guidance on the fit and proper persons test[16] and sign a model declaration which can be obtained from HMRC's website. The declaration should be kept

---

[13] See www.homeoffice.gov.uk/agencies-public-bodies/dbs.
[14] See the Commission's 'Strategy for Dealing with Safeguarding Children and Vulnerable Adults Issues in Charities'.
[15] Available on HMRC's website at www.hmrc.gov.uk/charities.
[16] 'The Fit and Proper Persons test: a basic guide for managers of charities'.

for the duration of the manager's service with the charity and for 4 years afterwards. An example of a declaration which incorporates HMRC's model declaration is set out at **8.80**.

DELEGATION

8.91   The delegation of charity trustees' powers is an area that often seems to cause problems in practice. It helps if one understands that the starting point is that every charity trustee should exercise his or her powers personally unless they are expressly authorised to allow someone else to exercise them. That is essentially what delegation amounts to; a charity trustee authorising some other person to exercise his or her powers.

8.92   Powers of delegation are important because they affect many aspects of many charities' operations. These range from the trustees of a charitable trust authorising someone to sign documents on their behalf to the trustees of a charitable company delegating consideration of a complex transaction to a specially constituted committee of the board.

8.93   Without an appropriate power of delegation that is exercised properly by the relevant charity trustees, decisions taken and acts carried out by people to whom the trustees' powers have purportedly been delegated will have no legal effect. The consequences of that will vary from case to case but the scope for potential liability for a breach of trust by the charity trustees is obvious, with some potential personal liability for the people to whom powers were purportedly delegated.

8.94   Before we look in more detail at the powers of delegation available to the trustees of charities it is important to appreciate that, as a general rule, delegation of a power does not involve the delegation of responsibility. While the court may in certain circumstances conclude that a delegate should be liable for any failure to exercise a delegated power properly in much the same way as the charity trustees by whom the power is delegated to him or her, the charity trustees will, as a general rule, remain personally responsible for the acts and defaults of the delegate. For this reason, there are three fundamental issues that should ideally be addressed in any power of delegation.

8.95   These are:

- A clear indication of whether the delegate has the authority to take decisions and carry out acts which will bind the charity trustees or whether the delegate is authorised only to advise the charity trustees, to take decisions that must be ratified by the trustees or to carry out basic administrative or ministerial functions that do no more than give effect to the trustees' decisions.

- An express provision for any delegate to report back to the charity trustees so that they understand exactly how the delegated powers are being exercised and can take steps to prevent acts and decisions which may, for example, be a breach of trust.

- The power of delegation could be made subject to a requirement that at least one of the delegates must be a trustee. This is with a view to ensuring that the trustee-delegate can monitor what his or her co-delegates are doing, report back to his or her co-trustees and take steps to prevent any acts or decisions that may, for example, be a breach of trust.

8.96 There is no strict legal requirement for provisions of this kind to be included in powers of delegation, but they make good practical sense as safeguards of the trustees' position and the position of the charity generally. The Charity Commission's preference is for powers of delegation to include at least one trustee as a delegate. In principle, this should not be necessary provided a provision for monitoring and reporting back is included and works effectively, but one can see that including at least one trustee-delegate is likely to give the trustees a more direct line of reporting.

8.97 In principle, it would be possible to construct a power of delegation in such a way that the delegates take on not only the powers but the duties of the charity trustees whose powers they are exercising. A provision to this effect would need to be very clear indeed and would result in the delegates becoming charity trustees in their own right. For this reason alone, it is generally better to assume that charity trustees will remain responsible for the acts and decisions of their delegates.

8.98 The powers of delegation available to charity trustees will depend primarily upon the way in which their charity has been set up.

Charitable companies

8.99 The constitution of a charitable company will generally contain an express provision to the effect that the business of the charity will be managed by the trustees who may exercise all of its powers. The articles will also usually include an express power to delegate any of the trustees' powers to any committee consisting of one or more persons, at least one of whom must be a trustee.

8.100 The Companies Act 2006 and Charities Act 2011 provide that, in favour of a person dealing with a company in good faith, the directors' power to bind the company, or to authorise others to do so, is deemed to be free of any limitation under the company's constitution (see also **7.12**).[17]

8.101 This power does not apply to charitable companies except in favour of a person who does not know that the company is a charity or gives full

---

[17] Companies Act 2006, s 42.

consideration in money or money's worth and does not know that the act in question is not permitted by the company's constitution or that it is beyond the powers of the charitable company's trustees. Clearly, therefore, it is essential that the trustees of a charitable company understand their powers of delegation and exercise them properly. Failing to do so is likely to make the acts and decisions of the delegate void.

8.102 The only other power of delegation available to the trustees of a charitable company is the ability to appoint 'alternate directors'. An alternate director is any person appointed by a charity trustee to act in his or her place and can only be appointed if there is an express provision for this in the charitable company's constitution. This will set out the basis on which the alternate is appointed and the scope of his or her powers. The relevant provisions will normally provide for the alternate to act in the place of the trustee who has appointed him or her where the trustee is absent. The alternate will usually cease to be an alternate director if the person ceases to be a trustee.

8.103 The power to appoint an alternate director is useful in practice where a trustee is likely to be absent for a period of time and wishes to appoint someone to act in his or her place while they are away. The power will not usually be used to delegate particular trustee powers or functions. Alternate directors are an exception to the usual rule that those appointing delegates will remain responsible for the delegate's acts and decisions. A charitable company's constitution will usually expressly provide that an alternate director is solely responsible for his or her own acts and defaults to the exclusion of any liability for the trustee who has appointed him or her.

8.104 A trustee of a charitable company cannot delegate any of his or her powers or functions to another person using a trustee power of attorney under s 25 of the Trustees Act 1925 (see also **8.113**).

Unincorporated charities

8.105 Many unincorporated charities will have an express power in their constitution authorising the delegation of trustees' powers and functions to other people. Where there is an express power, its provisions must be properly observed, particularly in relation to any conditions that apply (for example, that a majority of delegates must themselves be trustees or that any act or decision taken by the delegates must be ratified by the trustees in order to become effective). A power of delegation contained in the constitution of an unincorporated charity will often be expressed as a power to employ and appoint agents.

8.106 In addition to any express powers conferred on charity trustees by the constitution of their charity, s 11 of the Trustee Act 2000 confers a general authority on trustees (acting collectively) to delegate certain of their functions. The general authority conferred by the 2000 Act is in addition to any other powers to appoint agents and delegates exercised by the trustees but is also subject to any restrictions or exclusions imposed by the charity's constitution.

8.107 Section 11(3) of the Trustee Act 2000 provides that charity trustees may delegate the following functions:

- any function consisting of carrying out a decision that the trustees have taken (in other words, acts of a purely administrative or ministerial nature);
- any function relating to the investments of the charity's assets (there is more about this in **Chapter 10**);
- any function relating to raising funds for the charity, except by carrying out a 'primary purpose trade' (there is more about primary purpose trades generally in **Chapter 13**); and
- any other function prescribed by an order made by the Secretary of State.

8.108 Clearly, except where the function relates to investment (usually discretionary investment management) or fundraising, the general authority is limited in its scope. It cannot (subject to these exceptions) be used to delegate the power to take substantive decisions about the charity or any aspect of its operations.

8.109 The general authority can appoint any person as a delegate, including any of the trustees themselves. Two or more delegates can be appointed provided that they exercise the same function jointly. The general authority is also subject to a number of restrictions. The charity trustees have a discretion to determine the terms on which any delegate should be appointed but cannot, unless it is reasonably necessary, agree to terms which:

- permit the delegate to appoint a substitute;
- include any exemption clause restricting the delegate's liability; or
- permit the delegate to act in circumstances which give rise to potential conflicts of interest.

8.110 Charity trustees must exercise the general authority in accordance with their statutory duty of care (as to which see **Chapter 6**), particularly in relation to the selection of the delegate and the terms on which he or she is to act.

8.111 Provided the charity trustees comply with their statutory duty of care[18] in selecting the delegate and determining the basis on which he or she should act, the Trustee Act 2000 provides that they will not be liable for any of the delegate's acts or defaults.[19] This is an exception to the general rule that a charity trustee will remain liable for the acts and defaults of his or her delegate.

---

[18] See **6.2** and **7.3** for more in relation to this.
[19] Trustee Act 2000, s 23(1).

8.112 The general authority to delegate conferred by the Trustee Act 2000 relates to collective delegation by charity trustees. In other words, the board of trustees exercise the power conferred upon them collectively to delegate particular powers and functions to one or more other people. However, there are other powers of delegation that can be exercised by a trustee individually which may sometimes be relevant.

8.113 Section 25 of the Trustee Act 1925 gives any charity trustee the ability to delegate all or any of the powers and discretions invested in him or her as a trustee using a power of attorney. Any person can be appointed as an attorney, including any co-trustee. However, the delegation cannot be for more than 12 months (although that period does not have to start on the day on which the power of attorney is actually executed). And the charity trustee making the power of attorney must (within seven days of granting it) give written notice of the delegation to each of his co-trustees and any other person who has the power to appoint new trustees.

8.114 A charity trustee will remain liable for every act or default of the delegate appointed pursuant to a power of attorney. This is in contrast to the provisions of the Trustee Act 2000, where a charity trustee will only be liable for the acts and defaults of a delegate if he or she has failed to comply with the statutory duty of care in selecting the delegate in the first place.

8.115 A trustee power of attorney of this kind can be useful in certain circumstances. Where a trustee is required to execute a document but will not be available at the relevant time, a power of attorney is likely to be the most effective way of dealing with the position. However, powers can be used to delegate all or any trustee functions, not just administrative or ministerial acts and could also be used, for example, to delegate all of a trustee's powers and discretions to an attorney during a period of absence. The scope of the attorney's authority will depend entirely upon the terms of the power set by the trustee.

Committees

8.116 Larger charities with more complex operational requirements are likely to use delegation as a governance tool. By creating committees of the board with non-trustees as members, the board may be able to harness the skills and experience of a wider range of people who do not have the time, or perhaps may not be willing, to become trustees themselves or could only do so at the risk of increasing the number of members of the board until it becomes unworkable. Power to delegate to a committee of the board will usually be set out in an express provision in the charity's constitution.

8.117 Committees of the board often encountered include:

- a finance committee, with overall responsibility for a charity's finances;

- an audit committee, with overall responsibility for overseeing a charity's audit arrangements and for financial scrutiny and accountability;
- a remuneration committee, responsible for reviewing the terms on which a charity's senior employees are engaged (in much the same way as the non-executive directors sitting on a commercial company's remuneration committee); and
- a strategy committee, to engage with the charity's strengths and weaknesses and the opportunities for, and threats to, it.

8.118 The basis on which the trustees' powers are delegated to committees of the board of this kind will usually be set out in Terms of Reference. These should obviously be set by the board itself, and should also be reviewed from time to time in order to ensure that they remain appropriate. The Terms made will vary from charity to charity but examples of the sort of provisions that might be made are set out below.

Finance Committee

Terms of Reference

The board (the 'Board') of trustees (the 'Trustees') of the [Charity] (the 'Charity') has established a committee of the Board to be known as the Finance Committee (the 'Committee'). These are its terms of reference.

Membership

The Committee will be appointed by the Board and will comprise no more than [*number*] and no fewer than [*number*] members, of whom one will be the Treasurer of the Charity and a majority (including the Treasurer) will be Trustees. At least one member shall be a qualified accountant or have relevant financial experience, expertise or qualification.

The Board will appoint one of the members of the Committee as its chairman (the 'Chairman').

Attendance

It is the expectation of the Board that every member of the Committee will attend each meeting.

The Committee may ask the [Chief Executive and the Finance Director] and any other senior executive to attend meetings of the Committee either regularly or by invitation. Invitees have no right to attend committee meetings.   ➙

Voting

Only those members of the Committee who are Trustees will be entitled to vote and count in the quorum at meetings of the Committee. The quorum for each meeting shall be [*number*] Trustee-members. The Chairman will have a casting vote on an equality of votes.

The Committee will be competent to exercise all or any of the authority, powers and discretions vested in or exercisable by the Committee.

Meetings

The Committee shall meet [quarterly] on such dates as shall be determined by the Committee from time to time and at such other time as the Secretary shall specify at the request of any member of the Committee.

Unless otherwise agreed, notice of each meeting confirming the venue, date and time together with an agenda shall be sent to each member of the Committee and any other person invited or required to attend no fewer than 7 working days prior to the date of the meeting.

Minutes

The Secretary will minute the proceedings and resolutions of the Committee and ascertain, at the beginning of each meeting, the existence of any conflicts of interest and minute them accordingly.

Minutes of each Committee meeting will be sent to all members of the Committee and the Board within 7 working days of the meeting.

Authority

The Committee is authorised by the Board to investigate any activity within its terms of reference. It is authorised to seek any information it requires from any employee and all employees are directed to cooperate with any request made by the Committee.

The Committee is authorised by the Board to obtain outside legal, financial or other independent professional advice if it considers this necessary.

[The Committee is authorised by the Board to take and/or authorise all proper decisions of an executive nature relating to expenditure, finance and property brought to the Committee by a Trustee, but the Committee shall not make or authorise a decision which:

• is contrary to any policy that has been set by the Board; →

- exceeds a budgetary limit that has been approved by the Board for a particular item of expenditure by more than [£–];
- authorises the acquisition or sale of any land or investments that has not previously been approved by the Board;
- would (if acted upon) be a wilful default or breach of trust or an *ultra vires* act on the part of the Board;
- would tend adversely to affect the reputation or standing of the Charity in the community;
- would (if acted upon) reduce the accountability of the Committee to the Board;
- should, in the opinion of the Chairman of the Committee or Chairman of the Board or a majority of the Committee members present and voting, be referred to a full meeting of the Board before being acted upon.]

[Unless delegated authority has been given, all Committee decisions are subject to ratification by a full meeting of the Board.]

[An executive decision within the Committee's remit, to which 75% or more of the Committee members consent in writing, taken before a meeting of the Committee can be duly convened, shall be valid and binding and shall be reported at the next Committee meeting and shall be minuted accordingly.]

Duties

The duties of the Committee shall be to:

- develop a financial strategy for the Charity
- oversee and develop the Charity's financial procedures, policies or plans
- ensure compliance with appropriate regulations for submitting reports and returns
- approve budgets and monitor adherence to them
- review the Charity's income and expenditure to ensure its continued solvency
- oversee investment and capital financing decisions
- approve and keep under review the Charity's investment policy
- approve and keep under review the Charity's reserves policy
- ensure appropriate insurance policies are taken out
- monitor risk and ensure appropriate procedures are in place
- ensure the Charity's commercial activities and fundraising activities are carried out effectively
- safeguard the Charity's assets and ensure the optimal use of revenues →

- review any other matter, which is within the Committee's remit, as directed by the Board
- promptly report any issues to the Board.

Audit Committee

Terms of Reference

The board (the **'Board'**) of trustees (the **'Trustees'**) of the [Charity] (the **'Charity'**) has established a committee of the Board to be known as the Audit Committee (the **'Committee'**). These are its terms of reference.

Membership

The Committee will be appointed by the Board and will comprise no more than [*number*] and no fewer than [*number*] members, of whom one will be the Treasurer of the Charity and a majority (including the Treasurer) will be Trustees.

The Board will appoint one of the members of the Committee as its chairman (the **'Chairman'**).

The Committee will elect a Secretary to the Committee.

Attendance

The Committee may ask the Chief Executive and the Finance Director and any other senior executive to attend meetings of the Committee either regularly or by invitation. Invitees have no right to attend Committee meetings.

The Committee will ask a representative of the external auditors and the head of internal audit to attend all meetings. The Committee will have at least one annual meeting, or part of one meeting, with each of the external auditor and the head of internal audit without the senior executives being present.

Voting

Only those members of the Committee who are Trustees will be entitled to vote and count in the quorum at meetings of the Committee. The quorum at any meeting of the Committee will be [*number*] Trustee-members. The Chairman will have a casting vote on an equality of votes.

The Committee will be competent to exercise all or any of the authority, powers and discretions vested in or exercisable by the Committee. ➡

Meetings

The Committee shall meet [quarterly] on such dates as shall be determined by the Committee from time to time and at such other time as the Secretary shall specify at the request of any member of the Committee.

Meetings can be requested by the external or internal auditors if they consider that one is necessary.

Unless otherwise agreed, notice of each meeting confirming the venue, date and time together with an agenda shall be sent to each member of the Committee and any other person invited or required to attend no fewer than 7 working days prior to the date of the meeting.

Minutes

The Secretary will minute the proceedings and resolutions of the Committee and ascertain, at the beginning of each meeting, the existence of any conflicts of interest and minute them accordingly.

Minutes of each Committee meeting will be sent to all members of the Committee and the Board within 7 working days of the meeting.

Authority

The Committee is authorised by the Board to investigate any activity within its terms of reference. It is authorised to seek any information it requires from any employee and all employees are directed to cooperate with any request made by the Committee.

The Committee is authorised by the Board to obtain outside legal or other independent professional advice and to secure the attendance of any person at any Committee meeting with relevant experience and expertise if it considers this necessary.

Duties

The duties of the Committee shall be:

- to consider the appointment of the external auditor, the audit fee, and any questions of resignation or dismissal;
- to discuss with the external auditor before the audit commences the nature and scope of the audit;
- to review the annual financial statements before submission to the board of trustees, focussing particularly on:
  - any changes in accounting policies and practices
  - areas involving a significant degree of judgement
  - significant adjustments resulting from the audit   ➡

- the going concern assumption
- compliance with accounting standards
- compliance with legal requirements
- the clarity of disclosures
- the consistency of accounting policies from year to year

- to discuss problems and reservations arising from the audit and any matters the external auditor may wish to discuss (in the absence of the management where necessary);

- to act as the body to whom the head of internal audit reports on the internal audit function and to discuss any issue that the head of internal audit may wish to raise (in the absence of the management where necessary);

- to review the internal audit function, consider the major findings of internal audit investigations and the management's response, and ensure co-ordination between the internal and external auditors;

- to keep under review the effectiveness of internal control systems, and in particular review the external auditor's management letter and the management's response;

- to consider other topics, as defined by the Board from time to time; and

- to review, on a regular basis, its own performance, constitution and terms of reference to ensure it is operating at maximum effectiveness.

In discharging its duties, the aims of the Audit Committee are to:

- facilitate good communication between the Charity and its external auditor;

- increase the credibility and objectivity of financial reporting;

- strengthen the independence of the audit function; and

- improve the quality of the accounting and auditing functions.

Remuneration Committee

Terms of Reference

The board (the 'Board') of trustees (the 'Trustees') of the [Charity] (the 'Charity') has established a committee of the Board to be known as the Remuneration Committee (the 'Committee'). These are its terms of reference.

Membership

The Committee will be appointed by the Board and will comprise no more than [*number*] and no fewer than [*number*] members, of whom a majority will be Trustees.

➜

Those members of the Committee who are Trustees will elect a Trustee-member to be the chairman (the **'Chairman'**) of the Committee.

The Committee will elect a Secretary to the Committee.

Attendance

The Committee may ask the Chief Executive and the Finance Director and any other senior executive to attend meetings of the Committee either regularly or by invitation. Invitees have no right to attend Committee meetings.

The Committee may also ask any other person whose attendance they consider necessary or desirable to attend any meeting either regularly or by invitation. Invitees have no right to attend Committee meetings.

Voting

Only those members of the Committee who are Trustees will be entitled to vote and count in the quorum at meetings of the Committee. The quorum at any meeting of the Committee will be [*number*] Trustee-members. The Chairman will have a casting vote on any equality of votes.

The Committee will be competent to exercise all or any of the authorities, powers and discretions vested in or exercisable by the Committee.

Meetings

The Committee shall meet [quarterly] on such dates as shall be determined by the Committee from time to time and at such other time as the Secretary shall specify at the request of any member of the Committee.

Unless otherwise agreed, notice of each meeting confirming the venue, date and time together with an agenda shall be sent to each member of the Committee and any other person invited or required to attend no fewer than 7 working days prior to the date of the meeting.

Minutes

The Secretary will minute the proceedings and resolutions of the Committee and ascertain, at the beginning of each meeting, the existence of any conflicts of interest and minute them accordingly.

Minutes of each Committee meeting will be sent to all members of the Committee and the Board within 7 working days of the meeting.   ➥

Authority

The Committee is authorised by the Board to investigate any activity within its terms of reference. It is authorised to seek any information it requires from any employee and all employees are directed to cooperate with any request made by the Committee.

The Committee is authorised by the Board to obtain outside legal or other independent professional advice if it considers this necessary.

Duties

The duties of the Committee shall be:

- to consider, determine and keep under review a framework or policy for the remuneration, benefits and incentives of the Chief Executive and the Finance Director and such other senior executives as the Board shall from time to time direct;
- in determining that framework, to seek evidence of the remuneration, benefits and incentives paid to senior executives in comparable employment within the commercial and voluntary sectors;
- to consider the outcome of every appraisal of the performance of the Chief Executive and the Finance Director and such other senior executives as the Board shall from time to time direct;
- to make recommendations to the Board as to the remuneration, benefit and incentives that should be paid to the Chief Executive and the Finance Director and such other senior executives as the Board shall from time to time direct with a view to ensuring that they are encouraged to enhance their performance and are, in a fair and responsible manner, rewarded for their individual contributions to the success of the Charity and its progress towards fulfilling its objectives;
- to make recommendations to the Board as to the remuneration, benefits and incentives of newly appointed senior executives;
- to determine the policy for and scope of pension arrangements, service agreements for the senior executives, termination payments and compensation commitments;
- to consider other topics, as defined by the Board from time to time; and
- to review, on a regular basis, its own performance, constitution and terms of reference to ensure it is operating at maximum effectiveness.

Strategy Committee

Terms of Reference

The board (the **'Board'**) of trustees (the **'Trustees'**) of the [Charity] (the **'Charity'**) has established a committee of the Board to be known as the Strategy Committee (the **'Committee'**). These are its terms of reference.

Membership

The Committee will be appointed by the Board and will comprise no more than [*number*] and no fewer than [*number*] members, of whom a majority will be Trustees.

Those members of the Committee who are Trustees will elect a Trustee-member to be the chairman (the **'Chairman'**) of the Committee.

The Committee will elect a Secretary to the Committee.

Attendance

The Committee may ask the Chief Executive and the Finance Director and any other senior executive to attend meetings of the Committee either regularly or by invitation. Invitees have no right to attend Committee meetings.

The Committee may also ask any other person whose attendance they consider necessary or desirable to attend any meeting either regularly or by invitation. Invitees have no right to attend Committee meetings.

Voting

Only those members of the Committee who are Trustees will be entitled to vote and count in the quorum at meetings of the Committee. The quorum at any meeting of the Committee will be [*number*] Trustee-members. The Chairman will have a casting vote on an equality of votes.

The Committee will be competent to exercise all or any of the authorities, powers and discretions vested in or exercisable by the Committee.

Meetings

The Committee shall meet [quarterly] on such dates as shall be determined by the Committee from time to time and at such other time as the Secretary shall specify at the request of any member of the Committee.

Unless otherwise agreed, notice of each meeting confirming the venue, date and time together with an agenda shall be sent to each member of the →

Committee and any other person invited or required to attend no fewer than 7 working days prior to the date of the meeting.

Minutes

The Secretary will minute the proceedings and resolutions of the Committee and ascertain, at the beginning of each meeting, the existence of any conflicts of interest and minute them accordingly.

Minutes of each Committee meeting will be sent to all members of the Committee and the Board within 7 working days of the meeting.

Authority

The Committee is authorised by the Board to investigate any activity within its terms of reference. It is authorised to seek any information it requires from any employee and all employees are directed to co-operate with any request made by the Committee.

The Committee is authorised by the Board to obtain outside legal or other independent professional advice if it considers this necessary.

Duties

The duties of the Committee shall be:

- to identify, seek evidence of and monitor the Charity's strengths and weaknesses and the threats and opportunities to and for it in the future;
- to evaluate the skills and expertise of the Trustees with a view to identifying potential gaps in their skills and expertise and the other requirements that the Charity will need in the future;
- to make recommendations to the Board as to how any gap in the skills and expertise of the Trustees can be remedied by succession planning;
- to make recommendations to the Board as to the changes that may be required to the Charity's business plan (or any other aspects of the Charity's activities) in order to deal with the strengths and weaknesses and threats and opportunities that the Committee identifies;
- to make recommendations to the Board as regards plans for succession for the Chief Executive and the Finance Director and any other senior executive the Board considers relevant;
- to identify any risks that should be added to or deleted from the risk management policy adopted by the Board from time to time;
- to consider other topics, as defined by the Board from time to time; and

→

> • to review, on a regular basis, its own performance, constitution and terms of reference to ensure it is operating at maximum effectiveness.

EXECUTION OF DOCUMENTS

8.119 The way in which a charity executes documents often depends upon the existence and exercise of powers of delegation.

Charitable companies

8.120 The Companies Act 2006 sets out a specific regime for the execution of documents by companies, including charitable companies. Essentially, this regime is as follows:

- A 'simple' contract (that is, any contract which is not required to be executed as a deed) can be made by a charitable company in writing using its common seal (if it has one, although there is no requirement that it should have) or on behalf of the charitable company by a person acting under its express or implied authority. In practice, any charity trustee will have implied authority to make simple contracts of this kind on behalf of a charitable company. A charitable company's constitution may make express provision to this effect or the board itself may exercise an express power in the constitution to authorise one of their number to sign.

- Any document which needs to be signed as a deed can be validly executed by the charitable company by fixing its common seal (again, if it has one), by being signed by two trustees or a trustee and the company secretary (if there is one) or by a single trustee in the presence of a witness who attests the trustee's signature and signs and adds his or her own name, address and occupation.[20]

- In order for any document validly executed by a company to take effect as a deed, it will also need to be 'delivered' as a deed.

- Any charitable company can appoint an attorney to execute deeds and other documents on its behalf.[21]

8.121 The above provisions only govern companies established under the Companies Acts. For other corporate bodies, the terms of the relevant governing instrument will need to be checked for the correct method of executing a deed. For contracts not executed by deed, the Corporate Bodies' Contracts Act 1960 allows a contract to be executed on behalf of the corporate body by a person acting with express or implied authority or under its common seal.

---

[20] Companies Act 2006, s 44.
[21] Companies Act 2006, s 47.

Unincorporated charities

8.122 There is no single statutory regime that governs the execution of documents by unincorporated charities. The starting point is that an unincorporated charity can only enter into deeds and other documents by its trustees. So every contract between the charity and a third party will actually be made between the third party and the trustees of the charity at the time the contract is entered into.

8.123 This means that, in order to validly execute a document, each of the trustees of a charity must execute it (either by signing a simple contract or by executing a deed in the presence of a witness who attests his or her signature) unless the trustees can use an appropriate power to delegate responsibility for signing to one or more of the trustees or to any other person. The relevant powers of delegation are as follows:

- The charity's constitution may confer an express power of delegation or an express power in relation to the signing of documents that will enable the trustees to properly authorise one or more of the trustees or any other person to sign a particular document or deed on their behalf.

- In addition, but subject to the provisions of the charity's constitution, the general authority to delegate conferred by s 11 of the Trustee Act 2000 will be sufficiently wide to authorise the signature of any document which sets out the terms of an agreement that the trustees have already decided to enter into.

- The Charities Act 2011, s 333 gives charity trustees an express power (subject to the provisions of the charity's constitution) to confer on any two or more of the trustees a general authority, or a limited authority if the trustees consider it more appropriate, to execute documents and deeds in the names and on behalf of the trustees. Provided the documents give effect to transactions to which the trustees are a party, signature under a 'section 333' power of this kind will have the same effect as if executed by all of the trustees. Provided the document states that it is executed under a section 333 power, then it is conclusively presumed to have been properly executed by all of the trustees in favour of a person who acts in good faith and acquires (for money or money's worth) any interest in, or charge on, property as a consequence.

8.124 The section 333 power is particularly useful and many charities will wish to pass a general authority for any two or more of the trustees to sign documents and deeds on their behalf. Once given, this authority continues notwithstanding any changes to the charity trustees as if it refers to the charity trustees at the relevant time. The trustees also have the ability to restrict the basis on which documents can be signed. This could include, for example, only signing any document that has been properly approved by resolution of the charity trustees as a body.

8.125 Because a third party acting in good faith who has given money or money's worth can only rely upon a section 333 power where a document 'purports to be executed in pursuance of', such a power should be expressly referred to in any document which is intended to be signed on the charity's behalf.

8.126 A section 333 power itself can be given in writing or by resolution of a meeting of the charity trustees. Section 333 expressly provides that any power given this way is sufficient to authorise two or more trustees to sign any deed or other written instruments. This is an exception to the usual rule that any delegated authority to sign a deed must be given by deed.

EMPLOYEES

8.127 Many charities have employees whose role is to help advance their purposes in accordance with the strategy and decisions of the board of trustees. In larger and more complex charities, the role played by the charity's chief executive, finance director and chief operating officer is very often significant.

8.128 While they may have wide-ranging powers and authority, a charity's employees do not have the power or authority to take the strategic decisions that are reserved to the charity trustees alone. In other words, they have no power or authority to take decisions at the highest level that affect the way in which the charity is managed and controlled. In larger charities, the employees will have significant day-to-day powers and discretions, but the exercise of those powers and discretions will be aimed at giving effect to the strategic decisions of the trustees.

8.129 There are no hard and fast legal rules about what constitutes a 'strategic' decision. Ultimately, one can only look at the test of charity trusteeship set by the Charities Act 2011. The decisions taken by the charity trustees are those that relate to the management and control of the charity in question.

8.130 Having said this, the trustees of larger charities will often wish to ensure that senior employees have Terms of Reference that set out clearly the scope of their roles and responsibilities. These will usually be set by the board as part of the exercise of a power to employ individuals to advance the charity's purposes (and must be consistent with the employees' contracts of employment). Terms of this kind will vary from charity to charity but may look something like this:

Chief Executive

Terms of Reference

The board (the '**Board**') of trustees (the '**Trustees**') of the [Charity] (the '**Charity**') has adopted the following terms of reference in respect of the Charity's Chief Executive.

Role

The Chief Executive's role is to act as the chief executive of the Charity and, in particular:

- to take primary responsibility for the implementation of the business plan and the budget;
- to provide clear and effective leadership of the Charity's employees;
- to represent the chief public face of the Charity to its beneficiaries and other stakeholders, the media and the public at large;
- to engage actively with other charities and social enterprises, particularly those with objectives or activities similar to the Charity, with a view to ensuring that the Charity's own vision is fulfilled; and
- to assist the Board to identify the strengths and weaknesses and the threats and opportunities for the Charity.

The Chief Executive's responsibility for these matters is delegated to him by the Board but there are a number of matters that must be presented to the Board:

- specific risk management policies, including insurance and borrowing limits;
- avoidance of wrongful or fraudulent trading;
- acquisition and disposal of assets or liabilities over 5% of net assets/income;
- investment and capital projects over a similar level;
- substantial commitments including pension funding, contracts of more than one year's duration and giving security over the Charity's assets; and
- contracts not in the ordinary course of business.

Delegation

In fulfilling his or her role, the Chief Executive is assisted by the Finance Director.

In particular, the day-to-day implementation of the business plan and budget is delegated by the Chief Executive to the Finance Director. ➡

The Finance Director (and such other senior executives as the Chief Executive may decide from time to time) report to the Chief Executive at monthly management meetings and, between those meetings, on an ad hoc basis as and when the Chief Executive considers necessary.

Reporting

The Chief Executive reports on every aspect of his or her role and, in particular, the implementation of the business plan and budget, to the Board at every meeting. A report is made in writing. The Chief Executive also attends the meeting to discuss the report, other relevant issues and answer questions.

The Chief Executive also reports between Board meetings on an ad hoc basis to the Chairman of the Board.

Appraisal

The Chief Executive's performance is appraised annually by the Chairman and another Trustee selected by the Board.

The Chairman and the other Trustee selected by the Board consult the Finance Director in relation to the performance of the Chief Executive before the appraisal takes place.

Conflicts of interest

The Chief Executive must disclose any personal interest he or she may have in any agreement or proposed agreement with the Charity or in any other matter in which the Charity has an interest.

Any interests which are disclosed are recorded in a register of interests maintained by the Charity.

Finance Director

Terms of Reference

The board (the **'Board'**) of trustees (the **'Trustees'**) of the [Charity] (the **'Charity'**) has adopted the following terms of reference in respect of the Charity's Finance Director.

Role

The Finance Director's role is to act as the chief financial officer of the Charity and, in particular: →

- to take day-to-day responsibility for the financial aspects of the implementation of the business plan and the budget under the direction of the Chief Executive;
- to provide clear and effective leadership of the Charity's employees;
- to take responsibility for all aspects of the Charity's finances;
- to work with the Chief Executive to manage the Charity's assets and liabilities;
- to assist the Board to identify the strengths and weaknesses and the threats and opportunities for the Charity.

The Finance Director's responsibility for these matters is delegated to him or her by the Board but there are a number of matters that must be presented to the Board:

- specific risk management policies, including insurance and borrowing limits;
- avoidance of wrongful or fraudulent trading;
- acquisition and disposal of assets or liabilities over 5% of net assets/income;
- investment and capital projects over a similar level;
- substantial commitments including pension funding, contracts of more than one year's duration and giving security over the Charity's assets; and
- contracts not in the ordinary course of business.

Delegation

In fulfilling his or her role, the Finance Director works in conjunction with the Chief Executive.

The Finance Director is responsible for ensuring that the Charity has sufficient well-qualified employees to assist him or her to fulfil his or her role as effectively as possible.

Reporting

The Finance Director reports on every aspect of his or her role and, in particular, the financial aspects of the implementation of the business plan and budget, to the Board at every meeting. A report is made in writing. The Finance Director also attends the meeting to discuss the report and other relevant issues and to answer questions.

The Finance Director also reports between Board meetings on an ad hoc basis to the Chief Executive. ➡

> *Appraisal*
>
> The Finance Director's performance is appraised annually by the Chief Executive.
>
> *Conflicts of interest*
>
> The Finance Director must disclose any personal interest he or she may have in any agreement or proposed agreement with the Charity or in any other matter in which the Charity has an interest.
>
> Any interests which are disclosed are recorded in a register of interests maintained by the Charity.

8.131 If a charity does have employees, their relationship with its trustees will be very important, particularly at the level of the chief executive and the chairman. Trustees may be less visible in the operation of the charity than the senior employees and, notwithstanding that the trustees have ultimate responsibility for the charity, this may mean that a relationship is more difficult to establish.

8.132 Effective management will depend in part on a clear understanding of the scope of the role of the senior employees (as set out in the relevant Terms of Reference) but also in part on an effective appraisal process for senior employees (who will themselves appraise more junior staff). This task can in reality only fall to the trustees.

CONFLICTS OF INTEREST

8.133 Every charity trustee has a duty to avoid any conflict between his or her duties to their charity and their own personal interests. Charity trustees also have a duty to avoid any conflict between their duties to their charity and the duties they may owe some other entity notwithstanding that they have no personal interest in it. It is perhaps more accurately described as a 'conflict of duty' but is generally referred to as a 'conflict of interest'.

8.134 The fundamental issue is that a conflict of interest may compromise a trustee's ability to act solely in the best interests of his or her charity. The Charity Commission[22] takes the following position:

> 'It is inevitable that conflicts of interest occur. The issue is not the integrity of the trustee concerned, but the management of any potential to profit from a person's

---

[22] The Charity Commission's 'A guide to conflicts of interest for charity trustees'. At the time of writing, the Charity Commission is revising its guidance in relation to conflicts of interest, with the new guidance expected to be published in Spring 2014.

position as trustee, or for a trustee to be influenced by conflicting loyalties. Even the appearance of a conflict of interest can damage the charity's reputation, so conflicts need to be managed carefully.'

8.135 The most obvious, and most frequently encountered, example of a conflict of interest arises where a charity trustee wishes to receive any sort of benefit from the charity. The Commission's guidance makes it clear that 'benefit' includes 'any property, goods or services which have a monetary value, as well as money'. There is more about trustee benefits at **6.36**. The fundamental issue is well summarised by the Charity Commission in its Guide to conflicts of interest:

> 'The rule that a trustee cannot receive any benefit from his or her charity without explicit authority is based on the principle that trustees should not be in a position where their personal interests and their duty to the charity conflict, unless the possibility of personal benefit from which the conflict of interest arises is transparent. Transparency is achieved by requiring explicit authorisation of the benefit, and by ensuring that any particular conflict of interest is properly and openly managed.
>
> It is the potential, rather than the actual, benefit from which the conflict of interest arises which requires authority. In order to avoid the breach of trust and to ensure transparency, authority is required where there is a possibility of benefit. This will avoid accusations of impropriety, which could in turn have a damaging effect on the charity's reputation.'

8.136 This point is well made. The fact that a trustee may not actually receive any benefit from his or her charity or that the charity has received valuable goods or services in return is irrelevant. It is the potential for the trustee to benefit that is significant.

8.137 The Commission's Guide states that:

> 'Where we find, or are alerted to, an unauthorised benefit, the action we take will depend on the extent of the benefit and cumulative interest and the impact which it has on the charity. We will also take into account other factors such as the reason why the trustees did not obtain authority. We are likely to be more supportive if the trustees can show that the failure to obtain authority was an oversight. However, we will generally not take a sympathetic line where we have previously advised the trustees that the benefit needs to be authorised or where a solicitor is acting for the trustees.
>
> Where the arrangements are in the interests of a charity we will give advice on the management of conflicts of interest and the authorisation of future benefits to trustees. However, we will open a formal inquiry, with the possibility that we might use our statutory powers, in cases where trustees appear to have placed their personal or other interests ahead of those of the charity in order to derive significant benefit at the charity's expense, and where they have deliberately ignored the requirements of the law or of previous advice'.

8.138   Although, as we have indicated, most cases of conflict of interest arise in the context of benefits received by trustees, other forms of conflict can arise. This could be, for example, where there is a conflict of duties, such as where a trustee is appointed by a stakeholder member to whom he or she owes duties as a trustee or employee are owed.

Managing conflicts of interest

8.139   There are three key aspects of managing trustees' conflicts of interest. These are:

- ensuring that any trustee benefits are properly authorised (by the charity's governing instrument, by the Charity Commission or by the Court);
- ensuring that conflicts of interest and potential conflicts of interest are properly identified and disclosed; and
- ensuring that a trustee who has a conflict of interest does not participate in any decision by the board of trustees that relates to it.

At the time of writing, the Charity Commission is revising its guidance in relation to conflicts of interest, with the new guidance due to be published in Spring 2014. The new guidance is expected to clarify what is required of charity trustees in the context of managing conflicts, by the introduction of a three-step 'action plan' of (1) identifying conflicts, (2) preventing conflicts (how this is done will depend on the nature of the conflict) and (3) recording the trustees' decisions.

Charitable companies

8.140   Trustees of charitable companies are subject to a more comprehensive statutory regime in relation to conflicts of interest imposed by the Companies Act 2006. Section 175 of the 2006 Act states that:

> 'A director of a company must avoid a situation in which he has, or can have, a direct or indirect interest that conflicts, or possibly may conflict, with the interests of the company.

8.141   Section 175(4) provides that this duty is not infringed if either the situation in question cannot reasonably be regarded as likely to give rise to a conflict of interest or if the matter has been authorised by the directors. In addition, section 175(3) provides that the duty does not apply to a conflict of interest arising in relation to a 'transaction or arrangement' with the company itself. However, both of these provisions are modified by s 181 in relation to charitable companies. This section requires any conflict to be specifically authorised by the charitable company's constitution and provides that this may be done 'only in relation to the descriptions of transactions or arrangement specified in' the constitution. In addition, the charitable company's trustees can only authorise the conflict if there is a provision enabling them to do so in its constitution.

8.142 The extent to which a trustees' conflict of interest can be authorised (and a breach of duty avoided) will therefore depend upon the provisions in a charitable company's constitution. A well drafted constitution will typically authorise a range of uncontentious conflicts of interest, such as a benefit received by a trustee who is also a beneficiary of the charity or a trustee's entitlement to be reimbursed his or her reasonable expenses.

8.143 However, there are, in our view, limits on the range of conflicts of interest that can be authorised on a 'blanket' basis by a charitable company's constitution and certain kinds of conflicts should be specifically authorised by the charity's trustees on a case-by-case basis. These would include, for example, any proposal to remunerate a trustee or for a trustee's company to enter into a contract for services with the charity.

8.144 Again, a well drafted constitution will set out a very clear mechanism for issues giving rise to conflicts of this kind to be considered by those trustees who have no interest, in the absence of the interested trustee. Those trustees without a conflict are then able to decide whether to authorise the conflict and, if so, the basis on which the conflicted trustee should be allowed to continue to act. The constitution should give the un-conflicted trustees the flexibility to authorise a conflicted trustee to act by voting on the relevant issue or, at the other extreme, not to act at all (ie not to vote, count in the quorum on the vote or receive any other information in relation to the issue giving rise to the conflict). In extreme cases of conflict (for example, where there is a significant legal dispute between a charity and a trustee's company), the most appropriate approach may be for the trustees to invite the conflicted trustee to retire.

8.145 The Companies Act 2006 also imposes an express duty on trustees to declare the nature and extent of any interest, whether direct or indirect, which he or she may have in a proposed transaction or arrangement with the company. The declaration has to be made before the company enters into the transaction or arrangement in question. However, the interest need not be declared if it cannot reasonably be regarded as likely to give rise to a conflict of interest or if the other trustees are already aware of it. In addition, the trustee does not need to declare any interest where he or she is not actually aware of the transaction or arrangement in question.

8.146 The declaration can be made in any way but s 177(2) of the Companies Act specifically provides that it may be made either by giving notice to a meeting of the trustees or by giving notice in accordance with an additional statutory duty placed upon all trustees to declare any interest in any existing transaction or arrangements.

8.147 The duty in relation to existing transactions or arrangements is imposed by s 182 of the 2006 Act and is in very similar form to the duty imposed by s 177. It provides that:

'Where a director of a company is in any way, directly or indirectly, interested in a transaction or arrangement that has been entered into by the company, he must declare the nature and extent of the interest of the other directors in accordance with this section'.

8.148 The declaration must be made as soon as is reasonably practicable. A similar set of exemptions applies to the duty imposed by s 182 of the Companies Act 2006 as applies to the duty imposed by s 177.

8.149 There are therefore three ways in which a trustee can declare an interest in the proposed or existing transaction or arrangement with his or her charitable company:

- by making a declaration at a meeting of the trustees;
- by sending a written notice to all of the other trustees (provided that it is properly sent in accordance with the provisions of the Companies Act 2006, s 184 it is treated as if the declaration had been made at the next meeting of the trustees after the notice is given); or
- by giving a 'general notice' to the trustees of the charitable company that the trustee in question has an interest (as a member, officer or employee or in any other way) in a particular body corporate or firm or connected person and is to be regarded as interested in any transaction or arrangement that may, after the day of the notice, be made with the body corporate, firm or connected person in question. The general notice is not required to be made in writing. However, it is not effective unless it is given at a meeting of the trustees or the trustee in question takes reasonable steps to ensure that it is brought up and read at the next meeting of the trustees after it is given.

8.150 Any failure to declare any conflict relating to any proposed transaction or arrangement will be a breach of trust. The consequences of failing to declare a conflict relating to an existing transaction or arrangement are more significant because the Companies Act 2006, s 183 makes a failure to comply with the requirements of s 182 a criminal offence (it will also obviously be a breach of trust). However, where a charity has conflict of interest procedures in its constitution and the trustees act in accordance with those procedures, then the Companies Act 2006, s 180(4) provides that the trustees have not infringed their duties as directors if they have acted in accordance with those provisions.

8.151 Additional safeguards are imposed by the Companies Act 2006 and s 201 of the Charities Act 2011 in relation to the potential conflicts of interest of the directors of all companies. Essentially, a company's members must approve certain transactions and arrangements. If not, the transaction or arrangement in question is generally either void or voidable. The provisions in question include:

- directors' long-term service contracts;
- substantial property transactions with directors; and

- payments to directors for loss of office.

8.152 Many of these provisions are unlikely to be relevant to the trustees of a charitable company (for example, it is very unlikely that any charitable company's constitution will authorise it to pay to trustees under service contracts). The consent of the Charity Commission is in any event required for any of these transactions or arrangements even if they are approved by the charitable company's members.

Unincorporated charities

8.153 Although there are statutory rules which govern the position in relation to conflicts of interest for the trustees of charities set up as companies, the constitutions of many unincorporated charities may contain express provisions dealing with conflicts. Typically, these may include:

- provisions authorising any trustee benefits;
- provisions obliging trustees to disclose any conflict of interest or potential conflict of interest to the other trustees; and
- provisions which oblige a trustee who has a conflict of interest or a potential conflict not to take part in any decision in relation to the transaction in question.

8.154 Where there are express provisions of this kind in a charity's constitution, they must obviously be adhered to. But the trustees of a charity which does not include express provisions of this kind will still need to take the same steps in relation to conflicts of interest and potential conflicts. They may take the view, therefore, that it will be sensible to alter their charity's constitution to specifically include provisions of this kind. Specific express provisions will be required in order to authorise trustee benefits in any event. There is more about altering constitutional provisions in **Chapter 15**.

Conflict of interests policy

8.155 Regardless of the way in which a charity is set up, its trustees should consider putting in place a policy in relation to conflicts of interest. This should explain in clear and simple terms:

- The purpose of the policy in seeking to identify and manage conflicts of interest and potential conflicts.
- The conflicts of interest (and conflicts of duty) with which the policy is concerned, particularly in relation to benefits to trustees.
- A summary of any provisions which authorise trustees to benefit from the charity.
- The use of a register of interests (if the charity has one).

- An explanation of the way in which trustees should disclose their interest in relation to particular transactions (whether by way of written notice to the charity or a declaration at a trustees' meeting).

- The restrictions on a trustee's ability to vote on (and possibly also to participate in a discussion about) a transaction in which he or she has an interest.

8.156 The charity's trustees may also operate a register of interests in which a record of all other relevant interests, posts, employments and other matters is kept. This is not a legal requirement, but is a sensible part of a wider policy on managing conflicts of interest.

RETIREMENT

8.157 In general, a charity trustee can only retire if there is an express or an implied power to do so. Many charity constitutions will include express powers. But even if there is no express power, a trustee appointed for a fixed term of office will generally have an implied power (and a corresponding obligation) to retire when that term comes to an end.

8.158 In the case of an unincorporated charity, a trustee who wishes to retire may be able to rely upon the statutory power conferred by the Trustee Act 1925, s 39. This will allow the trustees to retire either on the appointment of a new trustee in his or her place or, if there is to be no such new appointment, if at least two trustees or a trust corporation will continue to hold office as trustees of the charity. If there is no trust corporation acting or fewer than two trustees will be left after his or her retirement, the trustee will not be able to rely upon s 39.

REMOVAL

8.159 A trustee of an unincorporated charity may be removed from office as a consequence of the exercise of powers conferred by the Trustee Act 1925, s 36. This will only be relevant where one or more new trustees are to be appointed in place of the retiring trustee. There is more about s 36 at **8.66**.

8.160 A charity trustee will be removed from office where he or she is disqualified from acting as a charity trustee. The circumstances in which a charity trustee is disqualified from acting are set out in the Charities Act 2011, s 178 (and summarised above at **8.30**). Many charities' constitutions will expressly include the circumstances specified by the Charities Act 2011, s 178 as grounds for the removal or automatic retirement of trustees. However, the provisions are overriding, so that they will apply to a charity trustee even if they are not included in the charity's constitution.

8.161 Where a charity trustee is disqualified from acting as a director of a company under the Company Directors Disqualification Act 1986, he or she will also be disqualified from acting as a trustee of any charity, whether set up as a company or not (unless the Charity Commission is willing and able to exercise its discretion to allow them to act). There is more about this at **8.33**.

8.162 A charity's constitution may also include other express circumstances in which a charity trustee is removed from office. Some of the more often encountered examples are:

- Where a trustee is convicted of an offence which does not involve dishonesty or deception (and will not, therefore lead to disqualification under the Charities Act 2011, s 178), the charity's constitution may give its trustees a discretion to remove the trustee who has been convicted of the offence if they reasonably conclude that it will damage the interests of the charity.
- Where a trustee fails to attend a specified number of meetings (usually two or three) the other trustees may be given a discretion to remove the absentee from office. This is usually subject to certain safeguards; the resolution may need to be unanimous and the trustees may need reasonable grounds in order to exercise their discretion. A power of this kind usually only relates to absence without the consent of the trustees, to cater for a trustee who is, for example, absent over the long term due to illness or work overseas.
- The trustees of a charity may occasionally have a power to remove one of their number if they conclude that anything he or she has done is contrary to the best interests of the charity. Again, this will often be subject to certain safeguards; typically the power must be exercised unanimously (with the exception of the trustee who is being removed) and on reasonable grounds.

8.163 In some cases, a charity's constitution may include an express power for its members (or other third parties) to remove a trustee. Typically, 'stakeholder members' of charities may have an express power to appoint and remove one or more individuals as trustees of the charity (there is more about 'nominated' trustees at **8.27**). A stakeholder member exercising a power of this kind will need to ensure that any restrictions on the power are properly observed. The legal duty owed by a member to a charity is unclear (except in relation to a CIO or where there is an express duty incorporated into the constitution). However, the Charity Commission's approach is that 'members have an obligation to use their rights and exercise their role in the best interests of the charity [of] which they are a member'.[23] In our view, the likelihood is that the court will conclude that any member should act in good faith in the interests of the charity. A stakeholder member that wishes to remove its appointee as a trustee should therefore only do so if it considers that this is in the best interests of the charity. There is more about members' duties at **5.22** and stakeholder members at **5.86**.

---

[23] RS7.

8.164 A trustee of a charitable company can be removed by ordinary resolution of the majority of its members. There is a specific procedure for removing a trustee using this power which is set out in the Companies Act 2006.[24] Broadly, the members have to give the company special notice of the proposed resolution to remove the trustee. The trustee is able to attend and speak at the meeting at which the resolution is proposed. He or she can also require the charity to circulate their written representations in relation to the proposed resolution to the members.

Removal by the court

8.165 The High Court has an inherent jurisdiction to remove any charity trustee and appoint a new trustee in his or her place. An application to remove a trustee can be made by the charity itself, or by any of the charity trustees or by any person interested in the charity (or by any two or more local residents if the charity is a 'local charity'). The application will constitute 'charity proceedings' under the Charities Act 2011, s 115. This means that the consent of the Charity Commission is required before the application can be brought, and the Commission will not authorise an application if it could deal with the removal of the trustee itself, using its own statutory powers (see **8.167** below).

8.166 Broadly, the High Court has the power to remove a charity trustee where he or she has committed a wilful breach of trust. Where there is no wilful breach of trust, the courts are likely to be more reluctant to remove a trustee.

Removal by the Charity Commission

8.167 The Charity Commission has jurisdiction to remove any charity trustee on an application by the charity or where the High Court has made an order directing a Scheme under the Charities Act 2011, s 69(1).

8.168 The Charity Commission also has the power to remove a charity trustee where:

- Within the last 5 years, the trustee:
  - having previously been adjudged bankrupt or had his estate sequestrated, has been discharged; or
  - having previously made a composition or arrangement with, or granted a trust deed for, his creditors, has been discharged in respect of it.
- Where the trustee is a corporation in liquidation.
- Where the trustee is incapable of acting by reason of mental disorder within the meaning of the Mental Health Act 1983.
- Where the trustee has not acted and will not declare his willingness or unwillingness to act.

---

[24]   Companies Act 2006, ss 168, 169.

- Where the trustee is outside England and Wales or cannot be found or does not act and his absence or failure to act impedes the proper administration of the charity.[25]

8.169 Where the Charity Commission has opened an Inquiry into a charity, it also has all of the enforcement and remedial powers conferred upon it by the Charities Act 2011, ss 79 to 85, which include a power to remove any charity trustee. The Commission's jurisdiction depends upon it being satisfied that there has been misconduct or mismanagement in the administration of the charity or that it is necessary or desirable to remove the trustee in order to protect the property of the charity.

8.170 Where the Commission exercises its powers under the Charities Act 2011 after the opening of the Inquiry to remove a charity trustee, the Commission also has the power to terminate his or her membership of the charity.[26] This provision is intended to allow the Commission to prevent a trustee who has been removed on the grounds of misconduct or mismanagement to continue to exercise his or her powers as a member of the charity in question.

DISCHARGE

8.171 A retiring charity trustee (or a trustee who is being removed) will wish to ensure that he or she is properly discharged from his office as trustee (and, therefore, his duties and liabilities in relation to the charity) once he or she has retired.

Charitable companies

8.172 The position in relation to charitable companies is straightforward. A retiring trustee will give notice of his retirement in accordance with the charity's constitution. The retirement must be notified to Companies House on form TM01 (which must be signed by one of the charity's trustees or its secretary, if it has one) or can be updated online. The charitable company should amend its register of trustees accordingly.

Unincorporated charities

8.173 An unincorporated charity has no legal personality separate from its trustees, so that they are personally liable in respect of liabilities incurred in relation to the charity and will in general hold its assets in their own names (or via a nominee). In order to obtain a discharge from their duties and liabilities, the trustees will need to comply with the requirements of the charity's constitution in respect of retirement, but will also need to ensure that:

---

[25] Charities Act 2011, s 80(1)(e).
[26] Charities Act 2011, s 83.

- there is a power for the trustee to retire;
- title to the charity's assets is vested in the continuing trustees; and
- the retiring trustee is indemnified in respect of the liabilities he or she has incurred in relation to the charity.

Power to retire

8.174 The powers of retirement available to trustees are explained at **8.157**. Where a new trustee is to be appointed in the place of a retiring trustee of an unincorporated charity, it will be important to ensure that there are at least two continuing trustees of the charity (or a trust corporation acting as trustee) in order to ensure that the retiring trustee is properly discharged. This restriction is imposed by the Trustee Act 1925, s 37 (although it is subject to anything to the contrary in the charity's constitution).

Vesting of assets

8.175 Where a trustee of an unincorporated charity retires using the statutory power conferred by the Trustee Act 1925, s 39 and he or she does so by deed, the Trustee Act 1925, s 40 provides that, unless the deed contains provisions to the contrary, it will vest all of the charity's assets in the continuing trustees. Section 40 does not apply to every asset (for example, mortgages of land, transfers of shares or securities or transfers of registered land). Assets of this kind will need to be dealt with individually.

8.176 Section 40 of the Trustee Act 1925 does not apply where a trustee retires under an express or an implied power. In practice, therefore, a trustee should retire using a deed which recites that he or she relies upon the power conferred by s 39 (and any other power, express or implied, available to them). This will bring into effect the provisions of the Trustee Act 1925, s 40, provided the retirement is by deed.

8.177 Where no deed is used, the same effect can be achieved by discharging the retiring trustee by resolution of a meeting of the charity trustees, members or other persons who have power to give the discharge.[27] In general, the power to give a discharge will be vested in the continuing trustees, but the position may vary from charity to charity.

Indemnity

8.178 As a general principle, every charity trustee is entitled to an indemnity against the charity's assets in respect of liabilities that he or she has properly incurred in relation to it. The right to an indemnity continues after the trustees' retirement. A charity's constitution may contain an express power for the continuing trustees to give an express indemnity to a retiring trustee on this basis. If there is no express power, it should be possible to imply a power (on

---

[27]   Charities Act 2011, s 334.

the basis that the legal right to an indemnity exists in any event), but this will be subject to the same restrictions as any express power. In other words, the liabilities that can be indemnified against must be 'properly' incurred. This excludes any indemnity in respect of liabilities incurred as a consequence of any breach of trust. See **6.22** for more in relation to this.

8.179 Although a charity trustee's right to an indemnity in respect of properly incurred liabilities arises automatically, many retiring trustees will prefer to see an express indemnity (appropriately qualified in relation to liabilities incurred in breach of trust) set out in a deed of retirement which is signed by both the retiring trustee and the continuing trustees.

Notification

8.180 There is no obligation to notify the Charity Commission of the retirement of a charity trustee. The fact that he or she has retired will be picked up in the charity's annual return for the period during which the trustee has retired. However, it would be best practice to update the charity's details, via the Charity Commission's website.

CHAPTER 9

CHARITY ASSETS

9.1   This chapter is intended to summarise the legal basis on which charities hold assets. As we will explain, there are a number of legal concepts in this area that are unique to charities. This is of more than simply academic interest. The basis on which a charity holds a particular asset will determine the powers and duties its trustees have in relation to it. It may mean that the asset in question can only be applied for a particular charitable purpose within a wider range of purposes for which the charity has been established. Or it may mean that the charity has no power to sell the asset or, if it does, that there will be restrictions on the way in which it can apply the proceeds of sale.

9.2   The basis on which assets are held will also have an impact on the way in which the trustees of a charity formulate their reserves policy. This is explained in detail. We also go on to explain some of the specific considerations that apply to charities holding land, including the restrictions on its disposal imposed by the Charities Act 2011.

GOVERNANCE

9.3   Understanding the way in which a charity holds it assets is an important governance issue for its trustees. Failure to observe particular legal restrictions may mean that the trustees act in breach of trust, with the potential for personal liability as a consequence (see **6.18** for more on this). As importantly, the trustees must understand the way in which a particular asset can be used as part of their strategic planning for the charity generally. For example, trustees who wish to raise finance to develop one aspect of their charity's activities by using the proceeds of sale of a particular asset will be frustrated by a restriction on their ability to sell that asset or, if it is capable of being sold, on their ability to apply the proceeds of sale. Trustees must also be able to formulate a reserves policy for their charity, something that will be difficult to do unless the basis on which assets are held is clear and understood.

UNINCORPORATED CHARITIES

9.4   In looking at the way in which charities hold their assets, there is a fundamental distinction to be drawn between incorporated and unincorporated charities. Broadly, the assets of an unincorporated charity are almost invariably held on trust. A trust is a legal relationship where one or more persons (the trustees) hold property for the benefit of others (the beneficiaries). The assets of a charitable trust are, as the name suggests, always held on trust. And while the assets of an unincorporated association can be held in a number of different ways, assets held by a charitable unincorporated association will generally be held on trust for its charitable purposes. This is consistent with the fact that the individual members of a charitable unincorporated association have no personal entitlement to its assets.[1]

INCORPORATED CHARITIES

9.5   The assets of a charitable company are almost invariably held as corporate, rather than trust, assets. In other words, the assets are beneficially owned by the company itself rather than being held on trust by it. The constitution of the company will oblige it to apply its assets for its charitable purposes. In that sense, the company's 'beneficial' ownership of the assets is qualitatively different to the beneficial ownership of a commercial company's assets. But while the company's trustees can be liable for a 'breach of trust' if they mis-apply its assets, the assets themselves are not held on a trust of the kind found in the context of unincorporated charities.

9.6   The leading case in this area confirms that, while a company may hold its assets as a 'trustee' for charitable purposes where its constitution places a binding obligation on it to apply its assets for exclusively charitable purposes, a company is not a 'trustee' in 'the strict sense' of its corporate assets. Rather, the company is in a position 'analogous to that of a trustee in relation to its corporate assets'.[2] This decision was at least partly based upon the inconsistency that the court thought would arise if a company could incur liabilities without holding any of its assets beneficially, so that they were available to meet those liabilities. This distinction is important for charities operating on the 'corporate trustee' model, where a corporate body acts as the sole trustee of an unincorporated trust (see **9.9**).

9.7   The position is less clear in relation to other charitable corporations. In particular, there has historically been some uncertainty around the basis on which Royal Charter corporations hold their assets, with some taking the view that they hold their assets on trust. The approach the court will take to CIOs remains to be seen, but the likelihood is that, given their limited liability status, this will be the same as the approach to charitable companies.

TRUST ASSETS

9.8   The fact that incorporated charities do not hold their corporate assets on trust does not mean that they cannot hold particular assets on trust. Many

---

1   *Re Morrison* (1967) 111 SJ 758; *Re Finger's Will Trusts* [1972] Ch 286.
2   *Liverpool and District Hospital for Diseases of the Heart v Att-Gen* [1981] Ch 193.

incorporated charities hold trust assets of this kind, particularly where they have been given an asset for a particular purpose or on terms that restrict the charity's ability to dispose of the asset or apply its proceeds. There is more about restrictions of this kind at **9.27**.

9.9 This is an important governance issue for the trustees of incorporated charities. At the most basic level, the powers the charity has to deal with trust assets will depend upon the terms of the trust itself rather than the constitution of the charitable company. So while a power to charge corporate assets in a charitable company's constitution may be clear, it will not apply to any trust assets held by the charity. If the trustees do something with a trust asset that they do not have power to do, they may be personally liable for a breach of trust as a consequence. In addition, assets held on trust will not generally be available to the charitable company's creditors in the event of its liquidation except where the company has contracted in its capacity as trustee in respect of the asset in question and any liabilities are properly incurred.

9.10 It is very important, therefore, that the trustees of an incorporated charity identify any trust assets held by the charity and distinguish them from its corporate assets. The first port of call will usually be the charity's accounts, which should give some guidance on the basis on which assets are held (see **9.61** for more in relation to this). Having said that, the charity's accounts are not definitive. They will generally depend upon whether the underlying legal position has been correctly interpreted. This can, in turn, depend upon whether the terms of, for example, a gift of a particular asset to the charity has been correctly interpreted.

9.11 All of this means that charity assets are trust assets where:

- the charity is unincorporated; or
- the charity is incorporated but holds the assets in question on trust.

9.12 Why is it important to recognise trust assets? We have explained the significance of trust assets held by incorporated charities at **9.8**. But there is a wider significance, which is that the terms of the trust may impose certain restrictions on the way in which the trust assets can be applied. There are two types of restriction that may apply:

- Restrictions that mean that the assets can only be applied for particular charitable purposes within a charity's wider charitable purposes (usually referred to as a 'special trust').
- Restrictions that control how trust assets can be used or applied for particular charitable purposes, rather than restrictions on the purposes themselves (usually referred to as 'endowment').

SPECIAL TRUSTS

9.13 The restrictions may mean that the assets can only be applied for particular charitable purposes within the wider charitable purposes of the charity that holds them on trust. For example, a university (an exempt charity) might hold a portfolio of investments to pay for a particular scholarship for students. This is a charitable educational purpose, but one that is narrower than the general educational purposes of the university. Therefore, the university cannot use these trust assets to pay for any other aspect of its operations.

9.14 Restrictions of this kind will usually be imposed by the person who has given the trust assets to the charity in the first place, although the charity itself may have exercised a power under its constitution to impose the restrictions itself. In some cases, it may not be entirely clear whether the terms on which the assets were given impose a legally binding restriction on the charity only to hold the assets for particular (narrower) purposes. This difficulty can arise in the context of appeals made by charities and in the context of grant funding.

9.15 Assets held on this basis are usually held on what is referred to as a 'special trust'. There is a definition of 'special trust' in the 2011 Act:

> '"Special trust" means property which is held and administered by or on behalf of the charity, and is so held and administered on separate trusts relating only to that property ...'[3]

9.16 This definition applies for the purposes of the 2011 Act but is used by the Charity Commission generally. See, for example, the Commission's Glossary of terms used in its Operational Guidance which confirms that:

> 'It follows that the objects of a special trust must be narrower than those of the main charity.'

This is consistent with the definition of 'special trust' in the 2011 Act, which goes on to say that while property held on a special trust is 'held and administered on separate trusts relating only to that property', a special trust 'shall not, by itself, constitute a charity' for the purpose of reporting under the Act.

9.17 Assets held on a special trust should be identified in a charity's accounts as a 'restricted fund'. There is more about this at **9.61**.

9.18 Assets held on a special trust can also be income or endowment. This is explained in more detail at **9.19**.

---

[3] Charities Act 2011, s 278.

INCOME AND ENDOWMENT

9.19   The other kind of restriction that may be imposed on trust assets relates to how they can be used or applied for particular charitable purposes rather than restrictions on those purposes. Charity lawyers often refer to the 'expenditure' of charity assets rather than their use or application. This reflects the terminology used by the Charities Act 2011, but the term really means no more than how the assets can be used or applied.

9.20   Restrictions on expenditure will make the trust assets 'endowment'. But in order to understand fully what constitutes a charity's endowment, it is important to understand how a charity holds other assets that its trustees are free to apply for its purposes without restriction. Assets of this kind are usually referred to as 'income'. The Charity Commission explains the position in another way by stating that income is all of the financial resources 'that become available to a charity and that the trustees are legally required to apply in furtherance of its charitable purposes within a reasonable time of receipt'.[4] This is quite correct (and there is more about trustees' duties to apply income at **9.66**), but the point is essentially this; a charity's trustees are free to apply its income for the charity's purposes (subject only to any restriction on the purposes for which the income can be applied where the relevant assets are held on a special trust) and are obliged to do so within a reasonable time of its receipt.

9.21   As is often the case in relation to charity law, the terminology used in this context can be confusing although, unusually, perhaps more so for the lawyer than the layman. This is because trust law (as it applies to private trusts) distinguishes between the 'income' and the 'capital' of assets and has developed rules to distinguish between the two things and the way in which a trust's beneficiaries are entitled to them. In the context of trust law, 'capital' means the principal of an asset, while 'income' is whatever return it produces that is not an increase in the value of the principal itself.

9.22   In a charitable context, 'income' can include assets that a trusts lawyer would categorise as capital as well as those he or she would categorise as income. So a portfolio of investments held by a charity without any restriction on its application will be 'income' notwithstanding that the portfolio is made up of capital assets and can produce both capital gains and income. This is also true of the corporate assets of an incorporated charity, although its trustees owe a different duty in respect of the application or expenditure of those assets from the duty owed by the trustees of an unincorporated charity (there is more about this at **9.68**).

9.23   As we have explained, if a charity's trust assets are not 'income' then they are 'endowment'. There is no statutory definition of 'endowment' which, as we have said, refers essentially to those assets of a charity that are under a legal restriction that requires them to be retained by the charity for its benefit and

---

[4]   Charity Commission's Glossary of terms used in Operational Guidance.

which the trustees are not, therefore, free to apply. Endowment assets take two forms; 'expendable endowment' and 'permanent endowment'. These are dealt with in more detail below.

9.24 Endowment held by a charity is broadly equivalent to the capital of private trusts. In fact, endowment is often referred to as 'capital' in the Charity Commission's published guidance.

EXPENDABLE ENDOWMENT

9.25 The Charity Commission's definition of 'expendable endowment' is as follows:

> 'An expendable endowment fund is a fund that must be invested to produce income. Depending on the conditions attached to the endowment, the trustees will have a legal power to convert all or part of it into an income fund which can then be spent.'[5]

In other words, an expendable endowment asset can be applied by the trustees of a charity, but the general duty to apply it for their charity's purposes within a reasonable period of receipt does not apply. The Commission confirms this:

> 'An expendable endowment differs from an income fund in that there is no actual requirement to spend the principal for the purposes of the charity unless or until the trustees decide to.'

The reference here to 'principal' is to 'capital' or 'endowment'. The Commission goes on to say:

> 'However, income generated from expendable endowment ... should be spent for the purposes of the charity within a reasonable time of receipt.'[6]

The reference to 'income' here must be to 'income' in the sense it is used in relation to private trusts.

9.26 Why is it important to identify expendable endowment? Essentially, because the trustees should understand they have a power to apply it at their discretion rather than being subject to the duty in respect of income to apply it within a reasonable time of receipt. This will in turn affect their judgement about the level of their charity's reserves and probably also their strategic financial planning for its operations.

---

[5] Charity Commission's Glossary of terms used in Operational Guidance.
[6] Charity Commission's Glossary of terms used in Operational Guidance.

PERMANENT ENDOWMENT

9.27 Unlike expendable endowment, 'permanent endowment' is defined by the Charities Act 2011. The definition is:

> '"permanent endowment" means, in relation to any charity, property held subject to a restriction on its being expended for the purposes of the charity.'[7]

This is the definition that applies for the purposes of the 2011 Act. The Commission's Operational Guidance expands upon this:

> 'Permanent endowment is property of the charity (including land, buildings, cash or investments) which the trustees may not spend as if it were income. It must be held permanently, sometimes to be used in furthering the charity's purposes, sometimes to produce an income for the charity.[8]

9.28 The concept of holding assets permanently on trust is unique to charity law. In the context of private trusts there is a body of law devoted to preventing what is usually referred to as the 'alienation' of assets permanently (these are the rules against perpetuities and excessive accumulations). And yet this concept is accepted in relation to charities, presumably because society has always accepted that donors to charity should be free to set whatever restrictions they choose on assets that they give away and that there will always be a requirement for charity.

9.29 In practice, charity permanent endowment is often land and is often held to be used 'in furthering the charity's purposes', usually because a donor has given it to the charity or the charity has acquired it (often in the dim and distant past) to be used for the purposes of the charity. So, for example, an almshouse charity is likely to hold its almshouses as permanent endowment assets for use by its beneficiaries. Land held subject to a requirement that it is to be used in a particular way is referred to by the Charity Commission as 'functional' permanent endowment or 'designated land' (its definition is 'land required to be used for a particular charitable purpose').[9]

9.30 The other form of permanent endowment often encountered (and used 'to produce an income for the charity') is an investment portfolio, made up of cash and investment assets. The Commission calls this 'investment' permanent endowment.

Identifying permanent endowment

9.31 How does one identify permanent endowment in the first place? This is often difficult, particularly where an asset (often land) has been held by a charity for a very long period of time, with no or limited written evidence of the

---

[7] Charities Act 2011, s 353(3).
[8] Charity Commission's Glossary for its Operational Guidance.
[9] This was previously referred to by the Commission as 'specie' land.

position. In assessing the status of charity assets, one has to take into account a presumption set out in the Charities Act 2011:

> 'A charity shall be deemed for the purposes of this Act to have a permanent endowment unless all property held for the purposes of the charity may be expended for those purposes without distinction between capital and income.'[10]

9.32 This provision applies only 'for the purposes of' the 2011 Act and not to the construction a court might place on the documents relating to a particular asset, but any application to the Commission for an Order or Scheme under the 2011 Act (as to which, see **4.22** and **4.32**) may make the presumption relevant.

9.33 Having said this, the Commission explains its approach to identifying permanent endowment in the following terms:

> 'Interpreting the governing document provisions can sometimes be problematic. If there is nothing to indicate that there is a restriction on spending capital we will usually agree that it can be spent on the charity's purposes. It is not necessary for there to be a clear power to spend capital in order to support the view that the charity's assets are all expendable and consequently not subject to a permanent endowment restriction. However, if a power to spend income is given but the governing document does not mention capital, that is an indication of the charity having permanent endowment.'[11]

This reflects guidance the Commission published previously (albeit now withdrawn) to the extent that it does not construe governing documents with any bias in favour of permanent endowment and that 'there is no presumption that a charity's property is [permanent endowment]. The first step is to interpret the charity's governing instrument in the light of the surrounding circumstances ... there must be some evidence of probative value which points to the creation of a trust for investment or use, as the case may be.'

9.34 More often than not, therefore, whether an asset is permanent endowment will depend upon the way in which the documents recording its gift or acquisition are construed. A reference to the gift of an asset 'in perpetuity' or 'forever' is likely to be very clear evidence that the gift is permanent endowment. Other cases may be more difficult to interpret and may also lead to disagreement with the Charity Commission.

9.35 A charity may hold a permanent endowment asset subject to an obligation to retain it permanently and with no power to sell or otherwise dispose of it. Alternatively, a charity may hold permanent endowment but with a power to sell it and reinvest the proceeds in other permanent endowment assets. This will often be true, for example, of a permanent endowment investment portfolio, within which investments are regularly sold and the

---

[10]   Charities Act 2011, s 353(3).
[11]   OG 545-1 E1.1.

proceeds reinvested. It would also be true of land held for, eg recreational purposes that is sold in order to buy replacement land. The Charity Commission's guidance recognises this:

'The terms of the endowment may permit assets within the fund to be sold and reinvested, or may provide that some or all of the assets are retained indefinitely (for example, a particular building).'[12]

9.36 What is the significance of a charity holding permanent endowment? In previously published guidance (now withdrawn, albeit that it remains a correct statement of the position) the Charity Commission sums the position up as follows:

'Normally, trustees cannot spend any part of the charity's permanent endowment. Not only would it be contrary to the trusts of the charity, but if they did, the capital would be depleted and therefore would generate less income, thus reducing the charity's capacity to carry out its work. Eventually the charity might simply cease to exist because of lack of funds, whereas the intention was that the help or facilities provided by the charity would last forever and thereby serve successive generations of the community.'[13]

Buildings

9.37 As we have indicated, some permanent endowment assets may be held with a power to dispose of them and apply the proceeds in purchasing other permanent endowment assets. It is worth mentioning the Charity Commission's approach to buildings in this context. Many charities hold permanent endowment land which, for one reason or another, they wish to sell. This might be because the land can no longer be used effectively for the purpose for which it is given or that its investment value (as, say development land) can, if unlocked, make a real difference to a charity's operational capabilities.

9.38 In this context, it is worth remembering that the Charity Commission generally takes the view that buildings are not normally permanent endowment assets. This means that if a charity sells a piece of permanent endowment land with a view to using the proceeds to build facilities on other land it owns, the Charity Commission is likely to treat this as the expenditure of the permanent endowment unless it can be demonstrated that the buildings are likely to have a relatively long lifespan (the Commission's guidance at OG542-2 suggests that this is likely to be a lifespan of at least 75 years). This is on the basis that buildings are 'wasting assets', with a value that will decline over time, presumably in contrast to an investment portfolio or land.

9.39 This approach can lead to some strange practical consequences. A charity may need a new building to operate effectively but cannot use the proceeds of

---

[12] Charity Commission's Glossary for its Operational Guidance.
[13] Previous OG 545-2 E2.1

sale of a piece of permanent endowment land which is held as an investment to pay for it to be built (at least not without an order for 'recoupment', as described below).

Recoupment

9.40 Where permanent endowment assets are held without a power to sell them and reinvest the proceeds in replacement property, the Charity Commission's consent will be required (usually by way of Order (see **4.22** for more on this)) to the disposal. Where a charity has a power of sale, no Order will generally be required where the proceeds of sale are to be used to purchase replacement property. However, if the asset in question is functional or designated land (land which must be used for particular purposes) and the proceeds of sale are not being used to replace it with other land, then a Scheme is needed as the sale and disposal of the proceeds will constitute a change in the trusts affecting the endowment.

9.41 Where the charity's trustees have a power to dispose of a permanent endowment asset but no power to spend the proceeds of sale on some operational activity rather than replacing the asset, the Commission's consent will also be required but will generally only be available on the basis of what is usually referred to as 'recoupment' or 'replacement'. The Commission may, on occasion, waive the need for recoupment but this is in our experience the exception rather than the rule.

9.42 The trustees of a charity that holds permanent endowment have a duty to retain it permanently. For this reason, the Charity Commission will generally only authorise the expenditure of permanent endowment on the basis that whatever is spent must be reimbursed by the charity out of its future income. In other words, the permanent endowment that is spent is treated as a loan made to the charity for its general purposes that must be replaced or 'recouped' over a particular period.

9.43 For this reason, where the Charity Commission agrees to the expenditure of a charity's permanent endowment, it will generally only do so by making an Order that provides for recoupment. This is likely to be on the 'pound for pound' replacement basis over an agreed replacement period. As an example, if the charity uses £10,000 of permanent endowment, the Commission will include in its Order a requirement for the charity to repay £1,000 over 10 years. The charity is free to use the income from the recouped capital for its purposes in the usual way. If the charity repays the £10,000 earlier it can apply to the Commission for a further Order to terminate the recoupment arrangements.

9.44 A recoupment order will generally not provide for the payment of any interest in respect of the recouped funds. The recouped funds are effectively loaned to the charity on an interest free basis.

Security

9.45 Notwithstanding the restrictions on the disposal of permanent endowment, the consent of the Charity Commission is not required to the grant of security over it, except as required by the Charities Act 2011, s 124. This is dealt with in more detail in **Chapter 12**. There is obviously a degree of contradiction here. While permanent endowment land cannot be sold to generate income for a charity without the Commission's consent, it can be charged as security for a loan which may be spent by the charity in the same way as income without the Commission's consent. This is notwithstanding that a failure by the charity to meet its obligations to the lender may result in the forced sale of the land by the lender under its security to meet the charity's liabilities.

CONVERTING PERMANENT ENDOWMENT INTO INCOME

9.46 The Commission's power to make Orders for the disposal of permanent endowment requiring recoupment is based upon the provisions of the 2011 Act that authorise it to issue directions binding on a charity's trustees which may include directions 'requiring expenditure charged to capital to be recouped out of income within a specified time'.[14]

9.47 The Charity Commission regards itself as bound to make Orders that include directions for recoupment, but may in exceptional circumstances consider whether to do so without recoupment. This is generally where the permanent endowment is being used for a purpose that has a long life expectancy. As we have explained above, this will usually be where new buildings or extensions to existing buildings are being built have an expected lifespan of more than 75 years. The Commission contrasts this to the situation where funds are used to redecorate a building, which may be in the best interests of the charity, but would have a relatively short lifespan. In those circumstances, replacement of the permanent endowment expended will be required.[15]

9.48 The Commission may also consider waiving replacement of the permanent endowment where a charity cannot afford to make repayments. As the Commission says in its operational guidance, this could happen where a charity's finances are so poor that its only hope of a long-term future would be to spend its permanent endowment, but its income would not be sufficient to afford replacement. The Commission would, however, need to be satisfied that the charity had a viable future before waiving the requirement for replacement.[16]

---

[14]   Charities Act 2011, s 105(1).
[15]   OG 545-2.
[16]   OG 545-2.

STATUTORY POWERS TO CONVERT PERMANENT ENDOWMENT INTO INCOME

9.49 The Charities Act 2011 contains statutory provisions which may authorise an unincorporated charity to spend its permanent endowment assets, except for any specie or functional land ('land held on trusts which stipulate that it is to be used for the purposes, or any particular purposes, of the charity').[17] In summary, these provisions are as follows:

- Where the trustees of an unincorporated charity with gross income in its last financial year of more than £1,000 and permanent endowment (excluding specie or functional land) entirely given by one or more individuals or institutions with a value in excess of £10,000 conclude that the trusts on which the endowment is held could be carried out more effectively if the capital of the fund could be spent as well as the fund's income, rather than just the income, they can resolve that the capital of the endowment (or a part of it) should be spent.

- The trustees must send a copy of the resolution to the Charity Commission. The Commission can then do a number of things. It can direct the trustees to give public notice of the resolution and take into account any representations made by anyone interested in the charity who responds to the notice. The Commission can also direct the trustees to provide it with additional information in relation to the resolution.

- The Commission must then consider the resolution, taking into account any evidence which is available in relation to the wishes of the person who originally gave the endowment to the charity and any changes in the circumstances of the charity since the gift was made (these include 'its financial position, the needs of its beneficiaries, and the social, economic and legal environment in which it operates').

- The Commission has three months from the date on which it receives the resolution (or the date on which public notice is given, if this is directed by the Commission) to consider whether to agree to the resolution. If it notifies the trustees that it agrees to the resolution within that period or they hear nothing from the Commission, the trustees are entitled to go ahead and spend the endowment in accordance with the resolution.

- The Commission cannot agree to the resolution if it concludes that its implementation will not 'accord with the spirit' of the original gift of the endowment or that the trustees have not complied with their obligations in respect of the statutory power to spend the endowment.

9.50 For an unincorporated charity with gross income in its last financial year of £1,000 or less or permanent endowment given by one or more individuals or institutions with a value of £10,000 or less, the power enables the trustees to resolve to spend all or part of the endowment (excluding specie or functional land) without the Charity Commission's consent. This is provided that they

---

[17] Charities Act 2011, ss 281-292.

conclude that the trusts on which the endowment is held could be carried out more effectively if the capital of the fund could be spent as well as the fund's income, rather than just the income. There is no obligation to notify the Commission that the resolution has been passed.[18]

9.51 Trustees also have a statutory power to spend endowment held on certain special trusts (see **9.13** for more on this). The power applies where the Commission has directed that a special trust be treated as a 'distinct charity' for the purposes of the 2011 Act (in other words, where a charity or its trustees hold permanent endowment for the charity's purposes but as part of a separately registered charity). Essentially, the trustees have a power to spend permanent endowment (other than specie or functional land) held on a special trust on the same basis as any other charity with endowment.[19] This can include endowment held on special trust by an incorporated charity. The procedure to be adopted in relation to the expenditure of the endowment will depend upon the level of the charity's income and the value of the endowment (as to which, see **9.49**).

CONVERTING INCOME INTO ENDOWMENT

9.52 Some unincorporated charities will have a power in their constitution to convert income into endowment. As is the case in the context of private trusts, this is usually referred to as a power of 'accumulation'. By exercising the power, the charity's trustees can accumulate income and change it into endowment.

9.53 Powers of accumulation are not common and the Charity Commission take the view that they cannot be exercised 'in default'. In other words, the power must be expressly exercised by the trustees with the deliberate intention of changing income into endowment. Income cannot be changed into endowment by a simple failure to apply it over the long term. This sort of 'thoughtless accumulation' is likely to put the trustees in breach of their duty to apply the income within a reasonable time of its receipt (see **9.66** in relation to this).

9.54 The trustees of a charity which has no constitutional power to accumulate income may occasionally seek the Charity Commission's authority for accumulation. This might be because, for example, the charity has received an exceptionally large amount of income which the trustees cannot hope to spend in line with their duty to apply it within a reasonable time of receipt. The Charity Commission gives the example of 'an exceptionally large dividend or other distribution from a company, which is technically 'income' but in common sense appears to be a return of part of the capital investment'. Where the charity's trustees have a duty to maintain a balance between capital income and trusts, a distribution of this kind may upset that balance if it is treated as income. Authority for accumulation will be given by way of a Scheme or Order.

---

[18] Charities Act 2011, s 281.
[19] Charities Act 2011, s 288.

9.55   Accumulation of income in a charitable trust is subject to the provisions of the Perpetuities and Accumulations Act 2009. This provides that income may only be accumulated for a period of 21 years starting on the first day when income must, or may, be accumulated. Alternatively, income may be accumulated for the lifetime of the settlor of the trust, but only if the charity's governing document provides for this.[20]

9.56   There are three situations where, at first glance, income may appear to be converted into endowment. It is important to distinguish these situations from accumulation because the legal analysis is that the assets remain as income. The three situations are:

- designation;
- reserves; and
- total return approach to investment.

Designation

9.57   The trustees of a charity will often earmark a part of its income for a particular purpose or project. Earmarking income in this way is usually referred to as 'designation' and the income which is earmarked as 'designated funds'. The key point to appreciate is that the designation does not in any way restrict or commit the charity to spend the income for the purpose for which it has been designated. The trustees are free to use designated funds for some other purpose if the charity's circumstances change. This is expressly confirmed by the Charity Commission:

> 'Unrestricted funds are expendable at the discretion of the trustees in furtherance of the charity's objects. If part of an unrestricted fund is earmarked for a particular project it may be designated as a separate fund, but the designation has an administrative purpose only, and does not legally restrict the trustees' discretion to apply the fund.'[21]

9.58   Designated funds must be expressly identified in a charity's accounts.

Reserves

9.59   Many charities reserve part of their income from one financial year with a view to spending it in future financial years. The legal position in relation to reserves is explained at **9.66**. The important point to appreciate is that, unless accumulated using an express power of accumulation, reserving income does not change it into endowment.

---

[20]   Perpetuities and Accumulations Act 2009, s 14.
[21]   Glossary of terms used in Operational Guidance.

Total return approach to investment

9.60 Charities with permanent endowment made up of investment assets will often wish to adopt a 'total return' basis of investment. Previously, charities could apply to the Charity Commission for a total return order authorising this. From January 2014 when regulations made by the Charity Commission under the Trusts (Income and Capital) Act 2013 came into force,[22] trustees can pass a resolution giving themselves a power to invest on a total return basis. An Order or resolution of this kind will generally have the effect of treating the investment return as endowment unless and until the charity's trustees allocate it to a 'trust for application' (essentially, treating it as income). However, the underlying legal analysis is that the income received continues to be income and is not converted into capital (unless the trustees exercise their limited power under the regulations to accumulate income). Total return investment is explained in more detail at **10.152**.

RESTRICTED AND UNRESTRICTED FUNDS

9.61 It is obviously essential that assets held on trust are accounted for in such a way that a charity's accounts gives an overall view of its financial position. For accounting purposes, a distinction is drawn between the restricted and unrestricted funds of a charity. Looking at a charity's accounts is often the best starting point for an assessment of how it holds its property and it is obviously important that the terminology used in the accounts is intelligible.

9.62 A charity's unrestricted funds are all of the assets capable of being applied by the trustees without restriction. In other words, a charity's income will be its unrestricted funds. Some unrestricted funds are described as 'designated funds' for accounting purposes. As we have explained, this means no more than that they have been earmarked by trustees as available for a particular charitable purpose, but are not subject to a legally binding restriction.

9.63 The Charity Commission defines restricted funds as follows:

> 'Restricted funds are funds subject to specific trusts which may be declared by the donor(s), or with their authority (eg, in a public appeal), but still within the objects of the charity. Restricted funds may be restricted income funds, which are expendable at the discretion of the trustees in furtherance of some particular aspect(s) of the objects of the charity, or they may be capital funds, where the assets are required to be invested, or retained for actual use, rather than expended.'[23]

---

[22] The Charities (Total Return) Regulations 2013.
[23] Glossary of terms used in Operational Guidance.

9.64 This definition is drawn from the Charities SORP 2005. The reference to 'specific trusts' must be to 'special trusts'. The reference to restricted income funds is clear. The reference to restricted capital funds is a reference to endowment.

9.65 It follows that 'unrestricted funds' are 'expendable at the discretion of the trustees in furtherance of the charity's objects'. Again, this definition is drawn from the Charities SORP 2005. See **Chapter 14** for more in relation to the SORP 2005.

RESERVES

9.66 The trustees of an unincorporated charity have duties to ensure that:

- the income of the charity is applied as income unless it is endowment; and
- the income is applied for the charity's purposes within a reasonable time of receipt (subject to any provision in the charity's constitution which authorises the accumulation of all or part of the income as capital).

9.67 The duty to apply the income of a charity within a reasonable time of receipt is based upon the case of *A-G v Alford*.[24] This is an old case, but the Charity Commission points to more recent case law in the context of private trusts which by analogy, suggest that a failure to distribute income within a reasonable time of receipt is likely to constitute a breach of trust by the trustee.[25]

Charitable companies

9.68 The duty to apply income within a reasonable time of receipt applies to trust assets held by charitable companies. It does not, however, apply to the corporate assets of a charitable company. As the Commission recognises, company law does not impose any duty on the directors of a charitable company to apply its corporate property within a reasonable time of its receipt. But in the Commission's view, this does not 'sanction its accumulation' and 'it is legitimate to expect that a charitable company's incoming resources should be used to further its objects'.[26]

9.69 The Commission bases this 'legitimate expectation' on a case relating to a commercial trading company whose members, the court held, had a legitimate expectation that they would receive dividends out of its profit.[27] Whatever the correctness of this analogy, the trustees of a charitable company will obviously do well to plan on the basis that this is the approach the Commission will take

---

[24] (1855) 4 De G M & G 843.
[25] OG 43 P1.
[26] OG 43 B2 1.4.
[27] *Re A company No 370 of 987* [1988] 1 WLR 1068.

notwithstanding that they have a greater degree of flexibility in relation to the application of income than the trustees of an unincorporated charity.

Power to hold reserves

9.70 Notwithstanding the duty imposed on the trustees of an unincorporated charity to apply its income within a reasonable time of receipt, there are likely to be many cases where, for good practical reasons, it is not possible or appropriate for all of the charity's income to be distributed promptly. The Charity Commission's guidance is that:

> 'It is recognised that trustees in the charity's interest may need to retain some reserve of income to ensure the smooth and effective operation of the charity in order to ensure the continued furtherance of its objects. This is reflected by the inclusion of the word 'reasonable' in the phrase 'within a reasonable period of receipt'. But it is clearly not 'reasonable' to retain income, to the detriment of beneficiaries which the charity should be assisting, where there is no connection between doing so and ensuring the proper administration of the trust.'[28]

9.71 The key point is ensuring that the reserve of income is made in order to ensure the 'proper administration' of the charity in question.

9.72 Some charity constitutions may give their trustees an express power to hold income in reserve, although provisions of this kind are relatively unusual. More often, trustees will need to rely upon an implied power to make a reserve. Clearly, it is likely to be impossible to imply a power where there are any other express provisions in a charity's constitution which are inconsistent with this approach.

9.73 Ensuring that they have a sufficiently wide express or implied power to hold reserves is an important consideration for a charity's trustees because, without it, holding reserves will amount to a breach of trust. But as, with all powers, it is not enough for the trustees simply to exercise their power to hold reserves of income. The power will only be exercisable by them without giving rise to a breach of trust if they consider that what they are doing is necessary and in the best interests of the charity. As the Commission says in its guidance:

> 'The holding of reserves will be authorised either by using an express or implied power to hold reserves. Trustees are justified in exercising their power to hold income reserves, whether express or implied only if, in their considered view, it is necessary in the charity's best interests. [...] If the power is used without justification then the holding of income in reserve might amount to a breach of trust.'[29]

---

[28] OG 43 B2 1.1.
[29] CC 19.

Defining reserves

9.74 Before a charity's trustees can take any decision in relation to the exercise of an express or implied power to earn income, it is important that they understand which part of the charity's income will constitute 'reserves'. The Charity Commission's approach is as follows:

> 'Reserves are that part of a charity's unrestricted funds that is freely available to spend on any of the charity's purposes. This definition excludes restricted income funds and endowment funds, although holding such funds may influence a charity's reserves policy. Reserves will also normally exclude tangible fixed assets held for the charity's use and amounts designated for essential future spending.
>
> The Charities SORP defines reserves as that part of a charity's income funds that is freely available to spend. Reserves therefore exclude endowment or restricted income funds which have particular restrictions on how the funds may be used. Trustees need to consider how the funds of the charity are held and how they are being used in order to identify those resources that are freely available to spend.'[30]

9.75 In summary, the following types of funds or assets are excluded from the definition of reserves:

- permanent endowment (see **9.27**);
- expendable endowment (see **9.25** and **9.76**);
- income which has been converted into endowment using a power of accumulation (see **9.52**);
- designated funds (see **9.57** and **9.79**);
- restricted funds (see **9.63** and **9.80**);
- the value of the total gift element of permanent endowment together with the unapplied total return where permanent endowment is managed on a total return basis (see **9.60**); and
- fixed assets held for charity use which could only be realised by disposal.

Expendable endowment

9.76 As regards expendable endowment, the practical reason for excluding it from reserves is that many charities with an expendable endowment depend upon the income it produces to fund their operations. Spending the endowment is likely to reduce the income available to the charity and may jeopardise its operations as a result. That may leave the charity to seek income from other sources or cut back on the scope of its operations. In that sense, the expendable endowment is not treated by the Charity Commission as funds 'freely available' for the charity's general purposes.

9.77 However, because expendable endowment offers trustees considerable flexibility in how they may use the funds, the Commission suggests that this

---

[30]   CC 19.

may influence the amount of reserves trustees choose to hold. As the Commission says in its guidance, the freedom to spend expendable endowment may reduce the need for reserves, especially where the charity is not wholly dependent upon the investment income provided by the expendable endowment to fund its activities.[31]

9.78 It is also important to bear in mind that income generated by expendable endowment is income subject to the trustees' general duty to spend it within a reasonable time of receipt. Reinvesting the income as part of the expendable endowment will not have the effect of converting the income into endowment (unless the trustees have exercised an express power of accumulation) (see **9.52**).

Designated funds

9.79 The practical reason for excluding designated funds from the definition of 'reserves' is presumably that a charity's trustees need the flexibility to build up funds for particular purposes or projects and on the basis that the assets held in a designated fund are at an appropriate level for the project or purpose that the trustees have in mind. On this basis, the Charity Commission accepts that designated funds can be excluded from charity's reserves. However, it states that:

> 'Designations which are never used, or the nature of which are frequently changed without funds being spent, risk bringing the charity into disrepute with donors and financial supporters. If a complaint is made to the Charity Commission about a charity's reserves, the inappropriate use of designated funds may attract regulatory attention.'[32]

Restricted funds

9.80 Restricted funds also fall outside the definition of reserves, as they can only be used for a particular purpose which is narrower than the charity's overall charitable purposes. However, as with expendable endowment, the nature and amount of a charity's restricted funds may impact upon its reserves policy. As the Commission says in its guidance:

> 'Where significant amounts are held as restricted funds the nature of the restriction should be considered, as such funds may reduce the need for reserves in particular areas of the charity's work.'[33]

Tax

9.81 There are also tax reasons why the trustees of a charity must take care to ensure that they comply with their duty to apply the charity's income within a

---

[31]   CC 19.
[32]   CC 19.
[33]   CC 19.

reasonable time of receipt. The exemptions from direct tax available to charities depend upon their income and capital gains being applied for charitable purposes only. Income that is retained by a charity without either a legal power of accumulation or proper justification will not be 'applied' for charitable purposes, with the result that exemption from tax may be lost. There is more information about this at **11.47**.

Donations

9.82 The Charity Commission acknowledges that 'people who give or leave money to charities do not usually specify whether their donation or legacy should be treated as income or as permanent or expendable endowment'. The key issue is the available evidence of a donor's intention, whether formal, informal or circumstantial. As we have mentioned, the Commission's view is that if there is no evidence, either direct or circumstantial, as to the donor's intention then the gift should be applied as income consistently with the terms of the charity's governing document'.[34] The key point for the charity will obviously be to try, where possible, to ensure that there is evidence of the donor's intention. Generally, the charity will wish to have the flexibility to treat a gift as expendable endowment, though the position will vary from case to case.

Justifying reserves

9.83 As we have indicated, the Charity Commission acknowledges and accepts that charity trustees are often justified in creating reserves of income in order to ensure that their charities are financially viable and better able to withstand financial setbacks or problems. At the same time, the Commission acknowledges the public interest in knowing that charities are actually applying their assets for their charitable purposes. As the Commission says:

> 'A reserves policy provides essential accountability to funders, donors and other stakeholders. A good reserves policy will explain how reserves are used to manage uncertainty and, if reserves are held to fund future purchases or activities, it will explain how and when the reserves will be spent. A reserves policy provides assurance that the finances of the charity are actively managed and its activities are sustainable'.[35]

9.84 The Commission's approach to reserves strikes a balance between the strategic and operational requirements of charities and the public interest in seeing that they apply their assets. The key point is that the Commission has no objection to a charity making reserves if its trustees can justify why they are doing it. As the Commission says in its operational guidance:

> 'If a charity can demonstrate to donors and others that it has good reasons to retain a particular level of income as a reserve (that is, if it can justify its position)

---

[34] OG 43 B4.
[35] CC 19.

then we consider it is acting responsibly. A charity which has no reserves does not avoid the need for justification – "nil" or "negative" shows that a decision has been taken regarding reserves and a charity in this position needs to be clear that this is right in the circumstances and it must have a policy for the future.

Justifying reserves does not mean excusing or being defensive about reserves. It means being able to demonstrate, by reference to a charity's current position and future prospects, why holding a particular level of reserves is right for the charity at that time.'[36]

9.85 The level of reserves held will need to reflect the particular circumstances of each charity. The Commission's guidance is helpful in terms of the factors the trustees will need to take into account:

'The charity''s target level of reserves can be expressed as a target figure or a target range and should be informed by:

- its forecasts for levels of income for the current and future years, taking into account the reliability of each source of income and the prospects for developing new income sources;
- its forecasts for expenditure for the current and future years on the basis of planned activity;
- its analysis of any future needs, opportunities, commitments or risks, where future income alone is unlikely to be able to meet anticipated costs; and
- its assessment, on the best evidence reasonably available, of the likelihood of each of those needs that justify having reserves arising and the potential consequences for the charity of not being able to meet them.

Trustees who hold reserves without attempting to relate their need for reserves to factors such as these will have difficulty in satisfactorily explaining why they hold the amount of reserves that they do.'[37]

9.86 Charity trustees are required by the SORP 2005 to make a statement in their annual report about the level of reserves their charity holds and why. However, in most cases, trustees will need to justify the reserve they are holding by developing a reserves policy based upon, in the Commission's words, 'a realistic assessment of their reserve needs'.

Reserves policy

9.87 The key points in relation to reserves policy are as follows:

- The policy should be agreed upon by the trustees and set out in writing, notwithstanding that it may be drafted by senior employees of the charity or a sub-committee of the trustees.
- The policy should, as a minimum, cover the following points:

---

[36] OG 43 B2.
[37] CC 19.

- Why the charity needs reserves (or does not need them as the case may be).
- What level or range of reserves the trustees think the charity needs.
- What steps the charity is going to take to establish or maintain reserves at the agreed level or range.
- What arrangements the trustees are going to make for monitoring and reviewing the policy.

- The amount of time invested in preparing and reviewing the policy should be in proportion to the scale and complexity of the charity's affairs.

- Even if the charity is not in a position to build up reserves to the level required or perhaps at all, its trustee should consider what level of reserves would be appropriate.

- An established charity with a low level of reserves will need to have a policy which makes it clear whether there are no financial problems or, as the case may be, that there are financial problems which the trustees are seeking to resolve.

- A decision to hold no reserves does not mean that a reserves policy is not required. The trustees would still need to justify why they have decided not to hold any reserves at all.

- The trustees should put together a reserves policy taking into account their understanding of its operations and finances and, in particular, its forecast levels of income and expenditure over future years, the trustees' analysis of any future needs, opportunities, contingencies or risks and the likelihood of those risks becoming a reality.

Bearing in mind the implications for raising funds from the general public and the likelihood that other funders may regard reserves as either too high (eliminating the need for additional funds) or too low (implying financial problems), it is obviously essential from the point of view of good governance that trustees invest an appropriate amount of time and effort in their reserves policy and communicate it effectively to all of those with an interest in its operations and activity.

9.88 The Charity Commission's guidance on reserves is set out in CC19 and highlights the importance of setting an effective reserves policy. It also sets out the Commission's views on the factors that should be considered by small and large charities when drawing up their reserve policies.[38]

LAND

9.89 Many charities own freehold or leasehold land, some using it for their charitable purposes ('specie' or 'functional' land), while others may hold it as an investment that produces income to support their operations.

---

[38] CC 19, Annexes 1 and 2.

Acquiring land

9.90 Incorporated charities will generally have an express power to acquire and hold both functional and investment land under their constitution. Unincorporated charities may have a similar express power but, failing that, can rely upon a statutory power to purchase functional or investment land under s 8 of the Trustee Act 2000. This power will also apply to the acquisition of land on trust by an incorporated charity but is subject to any provisions to the contrary in a charity's constitution. Except where a charity has no power to acquire land (or the trustees propose to spend permanent endowment to acquire land and buildings), the consent of the Charity Commission is not required to the acquisition of land by a charity.

9.91 Charity trustees acquiring land should familiarise themselves with the Charity Commission's guidance in this area.[39] Much of this is common sense, but trustees should bear in mind that the Commission will expect them to have considered the following issues:

- The trustees must have the power or authority to purchase or lease the land.
- The trustees will need to have taken reasonable steps to ensure that the land is suitable for its intended use and is not subject to any legal or planning restrictions which might conflict with that use.
- The trustees must also have taken reasonable steps to ensure that the charity can afford the purchase (or the rent and any other obligations under a lease) and, where it is being bought with the aid of a mortgage, the charity can cope with projected rises in interest rates.
- While there is no legal requirement to do so, the Commission 'strongly recommends' that the trustees obtain a surveyor's report which deals with valuation, the maximum price the trustees ought to have to pay, a description of any repairs or alterations the trustees will need to make and their cost and a 'positive recommendation (with reasons) that is in the interest of the charity to purchase the land'.

9.92 Specific considerations apply where a charity's trustees wish to acquire land using a mortgage. These are dealt with in more detail in the context of borrowing by charities in **Chapter 12**.

Disposing of land

9.93 An incorporated charity will usually also have express powers under its constitution to sell, lease or mortgage its land. The trustees of an unincorporated charity have all of the powers of an 'absolute owner' of land under s 8 of the Trustee Act 2000 (which can be restricted by the charity's constitution) and s 6 of the Trusts of Land and Appointment of Trustees Act 1996 (which cannot). These powers will generally be sufficiently wide to

---

[39] CC 33.

authorise a sale, lease or mortgage of land. Mortgages of land are dealt with in the context of borrowing by charities in **Chapter 12**. This chapter deals with the sale and lease of land.

9.94   Some express powers of disposal may be subject to particular restrictions. Where a disposal is stated to be subject to the consent of the Charity Commission, the Charities Act 2011, s 117 frees the charity and its trustees from this restriction. When the exercise of a power of disposal is subject to the consent of the court, an Order of the Commission may be required (see **4.22** for more on this), depending upon the power that is being exercised and the way in which the restriction is worded.

9.95   Notwithstanding that a charity may have the powers it needs, the sale or lease of land by a charity is subject to certain other restrictions:

- If the land is specie or functional land (see **9.29** for more on this) that is to be used for the charity's purposes and the charity does not have an express power to sell it, the charity can rely on the statutory power of sale provided that the trustees intend to buy replacement property with the proceeds. However, if the land is to be sold without replacing it, a Scheme (see **4.32** for more on this) will be required in order to authorise the sale (on the basis that the sale will alter the purposes of the charity). The Scheme will specify how the proceeds of sale must be spent.

- If the land is held as an investment or part of the charity's permanent endowment, an Order of the Commission will be required if the proceeds of sale are to be spent by the charity rather than being reinvested in replacement investments. No Order will be required to authorise a sale if the proceeds are used to buy replacement investments provided that the charity has a power of sale.

- The charity's trustees must conclude that the sale or lease is in the charity's best interests. Where functional land is being replaced, the new land must be at least as suitable for the charity's operational needs. Where investment land is sold, the trustees will need to be satisfied that investing the proceeds in other land or asset classes is likely to produce a better return for the charity. Where a lease is being granted, the trustees will generally need to take advice on its terms.

- The terms of the sale must be the best reasonably obtainable. This may mean that the trustees must take advice on the best way of marketing the land and the price that should be obtained (this is certainly the Charity Commission's view).

- In certain circumstances, the consent of the Charity Commission to a sale or lease may be required. This depends upon the provisions of the Charities Act 2011, s 117. This is dealt with in more detail below.

Charities Act 2011, s 117

9.96 The Charities Act 2011, s 117 provides that land in England or Wales held 'by or in trust for' a charity (other than an exempt charity) cannot be 'sold, leased or otherwise disposed of' without a court order or an Order of the Charity Commission. The words 'in trust for' ensure that land held by a third party for a charity (such as a nominee or custodian trustee) is subject to the restrictions. The words 'sold, leased or otherwise disposed of' have a wide meaning but do not include the grant of a mortgage or other security over the land.

9.97 There are two main exceptions to this general principle. The first applies to the grant of any lease by a charity for seven years or less where the charity receives no premium in return. No court order or Order of the Commission is required provided that:

- The trustees obtain and consider the advice of any person that they reasonably believe has the ability and experience to advise them competently on the grant of the lease.
- The trustees are satisfied (taking into account the advice they have received) that the terms on which the lease is being granted are the best that can reasonably be obtained in the circumstances.
- The land is not being leased to a 'connected person'.

9.98 The 'connected person' requirement is intended to prevent charity trustees from disposing of land at an undervalue to people who are able to pass on the benefit of the undervalue to the trustees or retain it for their own benefit. They are:

(i) A charity trustee or a 'trustee for the charity' (ie a nominee or custodian).

(ii) Anyone who has given any land (not just the land in question) to the charity (at any time).

(iii) A child, parent, grandchild, grandparent or sibling of the trustee.

(iv) An officer, agent or employee of the charity.

(v) A spouse or civil partner of the trustee or anyone within (i) to (iv).

(vi) Any 'institution' controlled by the trustee or anyone within (i) to (v) above (whether acting alone or together). 'Control' means that the relevant person can secure that the affairs of the 'institution' are conducted in accordance with his wishes.

(vii) Any 'body corporate' in which the trustee or anyone within (i) to (vi) has a 'substantial interest' (whether alone or taken together). A substantial interest is more than 20% of the share capital or voting rights in the relevant 'body corporate'.

9.99   The second exception relates to any other sale or lease of a charity's land. A court order or an Order of the Commission is not required provided that the trustees:

- obtain and consider a written report on the proposed disposal from a qualified surveyor instructed by the trustees and acting exclusively for the charity (there are special requirements both for the surveyor's qualifications and for the contents of the surveyor's report, which are explained below);

- advertise the property in accordance with the surveyor's advice (but if the surveyor advises that advertising or marketing the property would not be in the best interests of the charity, then the property need not be advertised);

- having considered the surveyor's report, they must satisfy themselves that the terms of the disposal they intend to make are the best that can reasonably be obtained; and

- are not selling or leasing the land to a 'connected person' (as defined at 9.98).

9.100   The surveyor must be a Fellow or Professional Associate of the Royal Institution of Chartered Surveyors (RICS). He or she will be entitled to use the letters MRICS or FRICS after his or her name. The content of the report prepared by the surveyor is specified by the Charities (Qualified Surveyors Reports) Regulations (SI 1992/2980) and includes advice on how best to sell the land and its likely value. However, the Charity Commission quite rightly encourages charity trustees to engage with their surveyor's advice pro-actively with a view to obtaining advice on any other relevant matters, in order to obtain the best deal for their charity.[40] The surveyor could, for example, be asked to assess the offers actually made for the land and give a positive recommendation if he or she believes that one offer represents the best obtainable in the circumstances. In some cases the surveyor may need, for instance, to give specific advice about the effect of a sale on the value of adjoining land retained by the charity. It may also be that trustees will need to receive more than one report, at different stages of the transaction.

9.101   In most circumstances the trustees are under a duty to accept the best price for the charity's land without regard to their own personal preferences. This includes a duty to consider a higher offer at any time before exchange of contracts unless the trustees reasonably consider that the prospective purchaser's ability to complete the purchase is doubtful. There is some helpful guidance about this from the Commission:[41]

> 'There may, however, be occasions where the trustees can, on reasonable grounds, properly accept a lower offer, provided that their professional advisers agree with that conclusion. Such cases can arise when the trustees have good reason to doubt:

---

[40]   See OG 54 B2.
[41]   OG 54 B2.

- the prospective purchaser's ability or intention to complete the purchase; or
- where the purchaser would use the land in a way that could harm the interests of the charity.

Where they accept a lower price, the trustees **must** be clear that this is to the overall advantage of the charity. The surveyor or other advisor must be instructed to assess the value of any non-monetary elements in an offer.'

Functional land

9.102 The Charities Act 2011, s 121 imposes additional restrictions where a charity wishes to dispose of any functional or specie land (see **9.29** for more on this) which its constitution requires should be used for its purposes (eg land used for recreational purposes). Unless waived by the Charity Commission, the trustees are required to give public notice of their intention to sell the land with a view to allowing anyone affected by the disposal to make representations to the charity's trustees. This must allow at least one month for representations to be submitted. The Commission's guidance says this about the notice:

> 'The form and extent of the notice will depend on the size and type of the charity. In the case of a local charity it will usually be acceptable for the trustees to put up a notice on the property itself and to insert a second notice in a local newspaper. Larger charities, or charities with specialised activities, will have to consider advertising in newspapers of wider circulation or in specialised publications connected with the charity's activities. In publishing the notices, it is recommended that trustees aim to reach as many beneficiaries, and other people who may have an interest in the charity, as is possible at reasonable cost.'[42]

There is helpful guidance available on the content of the notice and its publication and the trustees' approach to any representations received.[43]

9.103 The provisions of Charities Act 2011, s 117 do not apply (and no consent is required from the Charity Commission) in certain circumstances:

- Where a disposal is authorised by a statutory provision or a Scheme made by the Charity Commission.[44]

- Where a charity sells or leases land to another charity at less than its full value and is authorised to do so by its constitution (because it has a power to transfer the land and the transfer is the best way of advancing its charitable purposes and is not expressly prohibited by anything in its constitution).[45] In practice, this will generally mean that the objects of the two charities must be compatible.

---

[42] CC 28.
[43] OG 54 B3.
[44] Charities Act 2011, s 117(3)(a).
[45] Charities Act 2011, s 117(3)(b).

- Where a charity grants a lease to a beneficiary at less than full value (described as 'less than the best rent reasonably obtainable') and the lease is authorised by the charity's constitution.[46]

9.104 In order to give those purchasing land from charities a degree of protection, the Charities Act 2011, s 122 obliges trustees to include certain statements and certificates in the contract they make with the purchaser and the transfer of the land itself. Charities Act 2011, s 122(3) requires a contract for sale and transfer to state that the land is held by or in trust for a charity and that either restrictions apply on its disposition or that it is exempt. If the restrictions apply, the trustees must also certify in the transfer that either the Charity Commission's consent or a court order has been obtained or that the charity trustees have the power under the charity's constitution to make the disposition and have complied with the relevant restrictions so far as applicable to it.

9.105 If the trustees give this certificate but have not actually complied with the restrictions in the Charities Act 2011, s 117, the disposal is still valid in favour of the purchaser if he or she acted in good faith for money or money's worth. However, the Court has held that where the statement required by s 122 is included in a contract for sale but the requirements of s 117 have not actually been complied with, the contract itself is unenforceable.[47] As a consequence, a purchaser may seek evidence that s 117 has been complied with before exchange of contracts for the sale of land by a charity.

9.106 The Charity Commission takes the view that the certificate required by the Charities Act 2011, s 122 must be given by a charity's trustees rather than the charity itself. This is consistent with the legislation, although it is possible for trustees to delegate responsibility for signing the certificate using whatever powers of delegation they have available to them.

NOMINEES AND CUSTODIANS

9.107 Many charities use nominees and custodians to hold their assets. A 'nominee' will hold legal title to the charity's assets on its behalf, almost invariably on trust. The charity will remain beneficially entitled to the assets, but it is the nominee's name which will appear on the legal title. In the context of shares and other securities, it is the nominee's name which will appear in the relevant share register. Where the nominee holds registered land on behalf of the charity, the nominee will appear as the registered proprietor of the land at HM Land Registry.

9.108 A 'custodian' may also hold legal title to an asset on behalf of a charity, but the expression is more often used to describe a person who has physical

---

46   Charities Act 2011, s 117(3)(c).
47   *Bayoumi v Women's Total Abstinence Educational Union Limited and Another* [2003] 1 All ER 864.

custody of particular documents or other evidence of the charity's title to its assets. This could include, for example, share certificates. However, neither 'nominee' nor 'custodian' has any very precise legal definition and in practice they are often used interchangeably.

9.109 The main advantage of using a nominee or custodian is to avoid the administrative difficulties posed by vesting assets in a body of trustees whose identity will change from time to time. This is generally only an issue in relation to unincorporated charities. Because they lack legal personality, their assets must be held in the names of their trustees from time to time. When a trustee retires and a new trustee is appointed in his or her place, arrangements must be made for the title of the charity's assets to be vested in the new trustee alongside the continuing trustees. This issue can be dealt with to an extent by ensuring that trustees retire and are appointed by way of deed, but unincorporated charities still face the administrative task of changing records of legal title. Although this is really no more than an administrative burden, a failure to deal with title to a charity's assets can lead to significant problems in practice. Where, for example, a charity's trustees wish to dispose of an asset, they may find it very difficult to do so if title to it is still with individuals who have long since retired as trustees and may subsequently have disappeared or died. There is more about how a charity's assets should be dealt with in the context of the appointment and retirement of trustees at **8.72**.

9.110 This kind of administrative problem is much less of an issue in relation to incorporated charities, which are capable of holding assets in their own name regardless of changes in the identity of their trustees. Having said that, nominees and custodians may still be used by an incorporated charity, often to facilitate the rapid sale and purchase of investments where a charity has engaged an investment manager to invest its assets. There is more about this in **Chapter 10**.

9.111 Both incorporated and unincorporated charities may wish to use a custodian in any event to hold important title documents with a view to safeguarding them against loss and the delay and expense that may ensue as a consequence.

POWERS TO APPOINT NOMINEES AND CUSTODIANS

9.112 An unincorporated charity may have an express power to engage a nominee or custodian in its constitution. If not, the charity's trustees can rely upon the statutory powers to appoint nominees and custodians in the Trustee Act 2000.[48] The power can be used to appoint a person as both nominee and custodian in relation to all or any of the assets of the charity. It is in addition to, but can also be excluded by, any express power contained in the charity's constitution.

---

[48] Trustees Act 2000, ss 16 and 17.

9.113 The statutory power conferred by the Trustee Act 2000 also applies to assets held on trust by an incorporated charity. It is not available to an incorporated charity in respect of its corporate assets, although many incorporated charity's constitutions will contain an express power to appoint a nominee or custodian.

9.114 The statutory power does not apply in some specific circumstances. These are:

- It cannot be used by common investment funds or common deposit funds.
- It does not apply to any land held in the name of the Official Custodian for Charities.
- It cannot be used where the charity already has a custodian trustee under the terms of its constitution.

9.115 The statutory powers in the Trustee Act 2000 were designed to balance flexibility for charities in relation to using nominees and custodians (for the good practical reasons we have mentioned earlier) against a concern that a charity's assets held by a nominee or custodian will not be secure. In the words of the Charity Commission:

> 'A balance has to be struck between economy and convenience of trust administration on the one hand, and security for the trust property on the other.'[49]

9.116 One of the main safeguards in the Trustee Act 2000 is a provision that a charity's trustees can only appoint as a nominee or a custodian:

- a person who carries on a business which includes acting as nominee or custodian;
- a corporate body controlled by the trustees of the charity; or
- a solicitors' nominee company under s 9 of the Administration of Justice Act 1985.

9.117 Providing services as a nominee or custodian will in certain circumstances constitute 'investment business' for the purpose of the Financial Services and Markets Act 2000. Authorisation by the Financial Conduct Authority to carry on business as a nominee or custodian will obviously ensure that the first of the requirements mentioned in **9.116** is satisfied.

9.118 There are a number of other safeguards built into the Trustee Act 2000. If the nominee or custodian is to be appointed on terms of business which allow it to appoint a substitute to carry out its work on its behalf, or which limit its liability to the charity, or which allow a nominee or custodian to act in circumstances capable of giving rise to conflicts of interest, the charity's trustees must conclude that it is 'reasonably necessary to do so'. This obviously imports

---

[49] CC 42.

an objective standard into this test. Having said that, the terms of business of many professional nominees or custodians will include provisions of this kind. It may be that the trustees of the charity conclude that it is reasonably necessary to include terms of this kind if only because there are no other nominees or custodians who will not also insist on terms of this kind as part of their appointment.

9.119   There are other safeguards:

- A sole trustee cannot appoint itself as a nominee or custodian and a body of trustees can only appoint one of their number to act as a nominee or custodian if it is a trust corporation.
- The trustees must ensure that they discharge the statutory duty of care applied by the Trustee Act 2000 when selecting the nominee or custodian and in agreeing the terms on which it should act. There is more about the statutory duty of care in **Chapter 6**.
- The appointment of the nominee or custodian must be in, or be evidenced by, writing. Professional nominees or custodians (and in particular, those authorised by the Financial Conduct Authority) will not generally agree to act without a written agreement in any event.
- The charity's trustees are under an obligation to review the arrangements under which the nominee or custodian acts and whether it is appropriate to give directions to it or to determine its appointment. The statutory duty of care under the Trustee Act 2000 also applies to this duty to review the position (see **6.2** for more on this).

9.120   While none of these safeguards will apply to the exercise of a power to appoint a nominee or custodian in the constitution of an incorporated charity (except where the express power itself contains provisions of this kind), it is likely that the court would, if called upon to do so, apply similar principles to the exercise of the trustees' duties in respect of the appointment. For practical purposes therefore, the trustees of an incorporated charity should assume that safeguards of the kind we have summarised above should apply to the exercise of their express powers of appointment.

9.121   The other significant provision contained in the Trustee Act 2000 is that the trustees of a charity (other than an exempt charity) exercising the statutory power must act in accordance with any guidance given by the Charity Commission in relation to the selection of nominees or custodians using the statutory power. The Commission has this to say in relation to the guidance:

> 'The guidance only applies directly to the exercise of the powers in the act to appoint nominees/custodians. It does not apply directly to the exercise of any other power to appoint a nominee/custodian, but we recommend that charity trustees exercising such a power should nonetheless bear this guidance in mind.'[50]

---

[50]   CC 42.

9.122 The Commission's guidance also makes the point that a nominee or custodian which is routinely used by a charity's investment manager to hold investments on its behalf will still be 'selected' by the charity's trustees notwithstanding that the investment manager may (as agent) have in practice selected it to act.

9.123 The Commission's guidance in CC 42 covers four areas:

- **The relationship between the nominee and the charity.**
  As we have stated earlier in this chapter, a nominee will usually hold assets on trust for a charity. This means that only legal title to the assets is with the nominee while beneficial ownership remains with the charity. This is important, because the existence of the trust prevents creditors of the nominee claiming any asset to meet its liabilities. Where, on the other hand, a nominee is only contractually obliged to a charity, the assets it holds will be at risk to creditors' claims in the event that it becomes insolvent. The Commission's guidance is that 'charity trustees must normally avoid selecting a nominee who insists on a purely contractual relationship'. It goes on to say that it is '...important for trustees to ensure that the proposed arrangements with the selected nominee do, in fact, make it clear that the shares or other property which the nominee is to hold on behalf of the charitable trust do, in fact, belong to the trust'.

- **The qualification and location of the nominee or custodian.**
  The Commission's guidance acknowledges that a nominee or custodian engaged in the business of providing a nominee or custodian services may, but need not necessarily, be authorised by the Financial Conduct Authority. The Commission also acknowledges that trustees may exercise their statutory power to appoint a nominee or custodian who is not under their control or subject to the sort of regulations imposed by the Financial Services and Markets Act 2000 (or, in fact, any regulation at all). The Commission acknowledges that an appointment of this kind may be necessary where investments are made outside the UK but state that '... charity trustees need to consider the legal risks associated with the transfer of the trust property to the jurisdiction where the nominee/custodian is located. These risks should be factored into any decision as to whether the relevant location is or is not a suitable one for the investment of the charity's assets, and into the process of reviewing investments...'. The Commission's guidance goes on to make the point that the trustees need a clear understanding of the relevant aspects of the law in the country in which the nominee or custodian is situated. This is so that they understand what sort of legal constraints an overseas nominee or custodian is under and how its obligations to the charity can be enforced.

- **The independence of the nominee and custodian.**
  While the statutory power to the Trustee Act 2000 allows a charity to appoint the same person as both nominee and custodian, the Commission's guidance recognises that the person appointed as a discretionary investment manager may also act as a nominee or custodian (or both). The guidance reminds trustees that a nominee or custodian

should only be appointed on terms which allow it to act in circumstances that are capable of giving rise to conflicts of interest if it is 'reasonably necessary to do so'. Their guidance states: 'Charity trustees need to recognise the possible risks associated with the lack of independence in the persons responsible for the process of administering the charity's investments on its behalf'.

- **Reporting by the nominee or custodian to the charity.**
  As part of the duty on charity trustees to review the performance of a nominee or custodian appointed by them, the Charity Commission's guidance is that 'it is important for charity trustees to ensure that any nominee/custodian whom they propose to select is prepared to agree to satisfactory reporting arrangements'. The Commission also recommends ensuring that any agreement with a nominee or custodian obliges them to report to the charity on an agreed basis.

9.124 The Charity Commission's guidance makes a number of other useful points in relation to these four areas and the appointment of custodians generally. Trustees looking to appoint a nominee or custodian (whether or not as part of appointing a discretionary investment manager) should bear in mind that it is binding upon them and refer to it.

CHAPTER 10

INVESTMENT

10.1 This chapter is called 'Investment', but it deals with two different kinds of investment by charities. The first kind is 'financial' investment; in other words, the way in which a charity's trustees decide to invest its assets in order to generate the best financial return with the level of risk that they consider to be appropriate for the charity. The second kind is 'programme related' investment; in other words, the way in which a charity's trustees decide to use its assets in order to advance its objects, while potentially also generating a financial return.

10.2 Different considerations and legal duties apply to each of these two kinds of investment. However, we have decided to deal with both kinds in the same chapter because this is the way in which the Charity Commission has chosen to deal with them in its guidance 'Charities and Investment Matters: a guide for trustees' (CC 14). There is in any event a potential overlap between the two kind of investment (so-called 'mixed motive' investment, which we will explain in more detail later in this chapter) which we think makes this approach sensible.

10.3 Financial and programme related investment will not be relevant to every charity; and there will be some charities for whom neither is relevant, particularly those whose financial resources are limited. However, financial investment will be relevant to charities with endowment assets or those with sufficient surplus income to enable them to build up reserves. There is more about endowment and reserves in **Chapter 9**. Equally, programme related investment may be relevant to many charities who might formerly have made grants and are looking to adopt a new approach to the way in which they apply their assets to advance their charitable objects.

10.4 The Charity Commission reissued its CC14 guidance in 2011. One of the main changes to it was to broaden its scope beyond financial investment to include programme related investment (which had previously been dealt with by the Commission in a separate publication called 'Charities and Social Investment'). CC14 is a helpful document in many ways and we have referred to it where we think necessary in this chapter.

FINANCIAL INVESTMENT

10.5 What do we mean by financial investment? As we have indicated above, the purpose of financial investment is to yield the best financial return on a charity's assets within the level of risk considered to be acceptable – this return can then be applied to advance the charity's objects.

10.6 The legal meaning of 'investment' in this context is that it is 'property held by ... trustees for the purpose of generating money, whether income or capital growth, with which to further the work of the [charity]'.[1] So the return on an investment can be in both income or capital gains (or both).

10.7 Financial investment is no more than one of a number of ways in which a charity can seek to exploit its assets with a view to generating financial resources to support its activities. However, there are a number of methods of generating resources that should be clearly distinguished from investment, not least because the powers and duties which apply to them are different. The most significant examples are:

- Trading, usually by selling goods, services or other assets for money. There is more about how to identify a trade and the most important of aspects of trading by charities in **Chapter 13**.
- Raising funds by way of grant and donation.
- Buying assets which are so speculative that the purchaser is in reality doing little more than betting on a rise or fall in their value. The usual examples are commodities, works of art and premium bonds. This is not something that charities can properly engage in.

10.8 The distinction between trading and investment is particularly important and is often narrow. The best example of this is the acquisition of land. Land purchased by a charity with the intention of letting it at a rent will be an 'investment'. Land purchased by a charity with a view to selling it on for development at a higher price will constitute a 'trade'. The fact that land acquired by charity is subsequently sold for development does not necessarily mean that it was not bought and held as an investment rather than as a trading asset. The key issue is what the charity intended at the time it bought the land.

10.9 The usual classes of asset in which charities invest are:

- quoted shares and securities (including loan stock issued by companies and local authorities and sovereign debt);
- units in authorised unit trusts and other listed collective investment schemes;
- investment land; and

---

[1]   *Harries v Church Commissioners* [1992] 1 WLR 1241.

- cash deposits with banks, building societies and other financial institutions.

10.10 Modern investment practice has meant that more charities are now investing in other asset classes (so-called 'alternative investments'), including hedge funds and private equity funds. There is more about this at **10.98** and **10.103**.

PROGRAMME RELATED INVESTMENT

10.11 As we have indicated above, financial investment must be clearly distinguished from programme related investment, not least because different legal duties and other considerations apply to each form of investment.

10.12 Programme related investment (or PRI) describes the way in which a charity's trustees decide to use its assets in order to advance its objects, while potentially also generating a financial return. The key point is that the purpose of a PRI is to advance the charity's objects. The fact that the way in which the PRI is made may give rise to a financial return does not make it a financial investment, because this is essentially incidental to the charity's intention. As a result, the duties and other principles which apply to the making of a financial investment (see **10.51** for more on this), are not relevant to the making of a PRI.

10.13 PRIs are sometimes referred to as 'social investments'. Neither term is legally defined and they are not always used consistently or precisely.

10.14 The number and range of charities making PRIs has increased significantly in recent years, a point recognised by the increased focus on this area in CC14. It is in our view still an emerging and developing area of operation for charities. While a relatively small number have been actively involved in PRI programmes for some years, a larger number have sought to develop programmes more recently. In this sense, there is less detailed guidance and there are fewer publicly available examples of best practice in relation to running a PRI programme than in, for example, running a grant making programme. CC14 contains some useful guidance on the most important principles and legal considerations but this is an area in which, in our view, trustees and their advisers need to be reasonably confident and creative in their thinking and approach. This is recognised to a degree in CC14, which states that trustees can:

> '... explore new and innovative ways of using PRIs to further their aims bearing in mind the principles set out in this guidance.'

10.15 Superficially, a PRI may resemble a financial investment in the sense that it will generally involve making funds available on an ostensibly 'commercial' basis and is expected to produce a financial return. In fact, one way of looking at PRIs is that they are grants made on a commercial basis with the aim of holding the recipient to account in terms of the charitable return on the investment and a proper approach to financial management, and securing the potential to 'recycle' the investment return on a PRI to invest in other PRIs.

10.16 Common examples of ways of making PRIs are:

- loans (whether secured or unsecured) and loan guarantees;
- equity investment in shares;
- revenue participation or 'quasi equity' (essentially, where the charity receives an agreed share of revenue or profit in return for funding); and
- 'outcomes based' finance, eg a 'social impact bond' which generates a return under a contract to deliver identified charitable outcomes (eg the rehabilitation of those released from prison) which depends upon how successfully those outcomes are delivered.

10.17 By way of example, the poverty of a group of farmers in Africa may be attributable in part to the lack of a processing infrastructure to enable them to get their produce to market in a way that will secure them a good price:

- A local cooperative may wish to build a facility to improve the position. An English charity for whom the farmers in question are a clearly identified group of beneficiaries will have a number of choices open to it in relation to providing funding for the facility. It might simply make a grant to the cooperative, having first taken reasonable steps to carry out due diligence and to negotiate an appropriate grant agreement requiring a range of deliverables.
- The charity might also consider whether a better way of advancing its charitable objectives in line with its strategic aims would be to make a loan to the cooperative or to subscribe for shares in a special purpose company set up to build and operate the facility.
- Much will depend on the size and scope of the project in question, the level of funding required and, for example, whether there are other organisations involved in the project with their own requirements in relation to the most appropriate way of providing funding.

10.18 In essence, therefore, a PRI is any application of a charity's funds which:

- is intended to advance the charity's objectives;
- is for public rather than private benefit; and
- is expected to produce a financial return for the charity (although this is not the main reason for doing it).

10.19 As we have indicated above, the intention behind the PRI is important because it is what distinguishes the investment from a financial investment. The distinction between the two is not always clear-cut in practice, but the

Commission does recognise the existence of 'mixed motive' investments. There is more about this kind of investment at **10.52** below.

10.20   The role of a charity's trustees in relation to PRIs is (subject to their general overriding duty to act in the charity's best interests) to ensure that the PRI only allows the charity's funds to be applied for its charitable objectives and that any 'private benefit' (also referred to as 'personal benefit') arising from the PRI is (as the Commission puts it in its guidance) 'necessary, reasonable and in the interests of the charity'.

10.21   The first of these requirements reflects the requirement on every charity to ensure that its assets are only applied for its particular charitable objectives. The trustees must therefore ensure that there is a clear link between their charity's specific charitable objectives and the charitable purposes that the PRI is intended to achieve. A PRI that, for example, advances sustainable development may not clearly advance the objects of a charity that exists to support the welfare of people with disabilities (unless it is clear that the charity's disabled beneficiaries will benefit from the developmental changes that the PRI is aimed at).

10.22   The second of these requirements reflects the general legal requirement on all charities to operate only for the benefit of the public (for more on this, see **1.14**). This can be a challenging area in relation to some PRIs; we look at this in more detail below.

Private benefit

10.23   The Charity Commission's approach to public benefit is set out in its three public benefit guides[2]. All trustees must have regard to this guidance when they consider the issue of private benefit in the context of PRIs.

10.24   Many PRIs will give rise to a degree of private benefit. This is generally because a PRI involves an investment in an organisation which is not itself charitable and which may have one or more other investors who are not themselves charitable. This is likely to be particularly relevant where the organisation being invested in is established outside the UK (so that it cannot, by definition, constitute a charity under English law). However, it can equally be true of many organisations established in the UK, particularly given the rise in the number of non-charitable social enterprises which, although not charities, are involved in activities which are wholly or partly capable of being charitable.

10.25   So, for example, a charity's trustees may wish to invest in a non-charitable company which is carrying out activities which further its own charitable objects. This could be, for example, by purchasing shares in a company which has been set up to provide training for disadvantaged young

---

[2]   See www.charitycommission.gov.uk/detailed-guidance/charitable-purposes-and-public-benefit.

people to enable them to enter the job market. This is an activity which the charity itself could carry out directly – it is clearly connected to the charity's own objects of providing education and training to disadvantaged people. The difficulty, from a public/private benefit perspective, is that the company is privately owned by a group of individual shareholders whose own financial interests in the company will be advanced by the charity's investment. The company will have access to investment which is likely to allow it to increase the scale of its operations and, as a consequence, increase the scope for it to return profit to all of its shareholders, including both the charity and the individual shareholders. In this example, there is a clear and obvious benefit to the public in terms of the company's enhanced ability to deliver its services to the charity's beneficiaries. The difficulty for the trustees is the degree of private benefit for the non-charitable shareholders as a consequence.

10.26 The Charity Commission's guidance for trustees facing this kind of decision is that some private benefit flowing to other investors is acceptable if the trustees are satisfied that the private benefit is:

- necessary in the circumstances;
- reasonable in amount; and
- in the interests of the charity.[3]

10.27 Whether the PRI is necessary and in the interests of the charity should obviously form an intrinsic part of the trustees' decision-making process (there is more about this at **10.30**), but the 'reasonableness' of any amount of private benefit may be more difficult to assess.

10.28 The Charity Commission's guidance recognises that sometimes, the best way for a charity to help its beneficiaries may result in individuals or businesses making a private benefit, but also that an unacceptable level of private benefit can affect a charity's charitable status.

10.29 Clearly, there is no financial formula that can be used to assess acceptable or unacceptable private benefit in relation to any given PRI. The Commission's guidance states that any private benefit must not be 'excessive', which does not obviously add clarity to what is, or is not, likely to be acceptable. Ultimately, therefore, this is an issue that the trustees must assess using their judgement and discretion and with the benefit of all of the data that they need in order to make an informed judgement. The Commission recognises that, in some cases, the assessment required will be relatively simple. In others it will 'be complex, based on multiple factors, and the decision will be finely balanced'. As with most trustee decisions, the key is ensuring that the decision-making process that the trustees use is sound. In the words of the Commission, 'trustees are unlikely to be criticised for their decisions if they have considered the relevant issues, taken advice where appropriate and reached a reasonable decision'.

---

3   CC 14, para J8.

Managing a PRI programme

10.30 The trustees of any charity which is engaging in PRI will need to ensure that they have effective governance processes in place to enable them to assess and manage the charity's PRIs. The shape and scale of those processes will obviously depend upon the scale and complexity of the PRI programme that the trustees wish to pursue. Where the number of PRIs is small and in UK organisations, a lighter touch approach is likely to be appropriate; where the PRI programme is more extensive, involves larger amounts of investment and is focused overseas, then a more complex and sophisticated approach is likely to be required.

10.31 A more complex approach is likely to involve a number of different elements:

- Trustees may wish to adopt a formal policy which articulates their aims and approach in relation to PRIs, covering the strategic aims of the PRI programme, the charitable objectives it is intended to advance, any focus on particular beneficiary groups or geographical areas, the preferred approach to investment (eg whether by shares or loan), the levels of financial return on a PRI which are anticipated, and the likely timescale for exit from investment.

- A policy of this kind could also articulate in reasonable detail the trustees' expectations in relation to the financial profile of organisations that are eligible for consideration (eg is the focus on small enterprises with clear evidence of a 'market failure' which prevents them from accessing funding from banks etc or on larger enterprises?), the percentage shareholding the charity should generally acquire, the rights that should attach to the shares, any requirements in relation to co-investors and controls over the level of remuneration paid to the senior staff of the organisation being invested in (particularly where they are also investors in the organisation).

- The trustees should also consider articulating the approach the charity should take to a change in an organisation's activities (a key risk if it is possible for what the organisation does to move away from activities which advance the charity's objectives) and to the degree of private benefit that is likely to be inherent in many PRIs (there is more about this at 10.35).

- It may be appropriate for decisions about PRIs to be delegated to a committee of the board of trustees and/or to the charity's staff in order to ensure that expertise in relation to PRIs is deployed appropriately and increases over time.

- The decision-making process in relation to PRIs should be clearly articulated. This should cover how the 'business case' for prospective PRIs should be prepared and presented to the trustees (or a committee of the trustees if they have delegated responsibility for PRIs), the scope and extent of the financial, legal and other due diligence that the trustees will expect to happen and the proposals for monitoring and reporting in relation to a PRI (including issues such as representation on the board of the PRI for the charity).

- The trustees should clearly identify any advice that they will expect to be taken in relation to PRIs. This could include financial advice on risk, financial viability and level of return and due diligence and legal advice (which may be overseas legal advice where the PRI is outside the UK) on contracts, rights and obligations and due diligence. The Charity Commission's guidance confirms that there is no legal obligation to take such advice, but that the charity's requirements will depend on the size and scale of the PRI and the degree of risk and complexity involved.

- The ongoing processes for monitoring the performance of the PRI, in both financial terms and in terms of the charitable outcomes that it has achieved. The trustees will also want to consider the level and frequency of reporting by PRIs and by those who are responsible for managing the charity's PRIs to the board of trustees.

Not all of these elements will be relevant to every charity involved in making PRIs, but many will. The trustees should think hard about these aspects in formulating their approach and keep it under review as their PRI programme develops.

Risk assessment

10.32 The Charity Commission will expect the trustees' thinking to be informed by an ongoing assessment of the risks involved in any PRI for their charity. The main risks are helpfully identified by the Commission in the 'PRI checklist' set out in its guidance[4]:

- How reliant is the charity on getting a financial return? (as the guidance says, 'the viability of a charity may be threatened if it is reliant on a predicted level of financial return that does not materialise')
- What is the financial health of the organisation that is being invested in?
- What other factors may impact on the success of the project of the financial return (eg inflation or exchange rates)?
- What is the risk that the organisation will default on its contractual obligations and how can this be managed?
- Under what conditions can the PRI be converted into a grant or written off?
- Are there any potential reputational risks for the charity, eg by excessive private benefit to other investors?
- What are the tax implications of the PRI? (there is more about this at 10.43)

---

[4] CC 14, Annex 2.

10.33 The risk of a PRI generating excessive private benefit is most likely to arise where the PRI in question is an investment in shares or by way of loan where the organisation being invested in is not itself a charity. As we have mentioned, access to funding for the organisation which is being invested is likely to put the organisation in a better financial position, with an enhanced ability to return profit to its shareholders.

10.34 The Commission's guidance on this states that, because of the likely financial return for other shareholders, a charity should only make a PRI in shares in exceptional circumstances and specifically where 'there is a clear correlation between the social purposes that the company will achieve and the aims of the charity'.[5] In our view, there will inevitably be a correlation between the social purposes of a company which is being invested in and the charity's aims; this will be an intrinsic part of the trustees' 'best interests' decision-making. If that is true, then what does the requirement 'clear correlation' add to the trustees' thinking about the degree of private benefit?

10.35 Our interpretation of the Commission's guidance on this is that it will expect a direct connection between what the organisation being invested in does and the charity's objectives. So where the organisation carries out a range of activities only some of which meet the charity's objectives, or the objectives are only advanced by an indirect or 'knock-on' effect of those activities, the Commission is much more likely to view the level of private benefit as excessive and unacceptable.

'Exit' strategy

10.36 It will also be important for the trustees to have considered how the charity can be protected if the organisation it is investing in ceases to carry out activities that advance its charitable objects. Trustees will generally wish to consider the issue of exit from the PRI in any event.

10.37 Where the PRI is in shares which are not listed on a stock exchange, it may be that there is no market for their sale. Typically, shares in a private company of this kind will in any event be subject to a range of restrictions on the ability of shareholders to transfer their shares to third parties. There are also restrictions on the ability of English companies to buy back their shares; restrictions of this kind are often found under the law of overseas jurisdictions, primarily because they are intended to prevent a reduction in their capital.

10.38 The key issue, therefore, is generally that the trustees agree a PRI on negotiated terms which will enable them to dispose of their shares and realise their value in the event that the company in which they are investing alters its activities. This could be by arranging for the shares to be redeemable (or, depending upon the applicable legal regime, to be re-purchased) at the option of the charity in certain defined circumstances.

---

[5] CC 14, para J9.

Permanent endowment

10.39 Some permanently endowed charities may wish to make PRIs. Because investments held as permanent endowment are held on trust to produce income which is to be applied to advance the charity's objectives (and will therefore generally be financial investments), it is likely to be difficult for permanent endowment investments to include PRIs. The income generated by permanent endowment investment can obviously be used in this way, but not the capital. If this is an issue for a permanently endowed charity, there are a number of options that they might look at.

10.40 It could be that the PRI in question can properly be regarded as a financial investment which also happens to advance the charity's objectives. So, for example, a charity whose objective is to promote sustainable development may be able to make an investment in a company which is developing 'green' technology which is capable of being justified as a financial investment but will also promote development which is sustainable.

10.41 Trustees may also be able to justify investing permanent endowment in PRIs on the basis that it is in line with their ethical investment policy. The key point is that the PRI in question will still need to be properly justified as a financial investment, albeit working within the charity's ethical investment policy (there is more about this at **10.84**).

10.42 Another approach may be to look at whether it is possible to use a statutory power available under the Charities Act 2011 to remove restrictions from all or part of the charity's permanent endowment so that it can be applied as part of a PRI programme. There is more about how these statutory powers can be used at **9.49**. Alternatively, it may be possible for trustees to adopt a 'total return' approach to their permanent endowment investment. This is explained in more detail at **10.157**, but would essentially allow capital gains within the charity's permanent endowment investment portfolio to be applied in the same way as the income generated by the portfolio. The gains could, therefore, be applied to make PRIs.

Tax

10.43 Trustees will need to be alive to the tax implications of their PRI programme. As we have explained in more detail at **11.58**, charities risk losing their wide-ranging exemptions from tax if they incur 'non-charitable expenditure'. In the context of a PRI programme, the risk is that investments in shares, loans or other instruments do not constitute 'approved charitable investments' within the tax legislation. In general, HM Revenue & Customs will accept that PRIs are 'approved' investments if they are for the benefit of the charity and not for the avoidance of tax. The charity will also need to ensure that any financial return from a PRI is applied exclusively for its charitable objects.

10.44 Given that any PRI will need to be made in the interests of a charity in any event, it would be unusual for a tax liability to arise. However, the trustees need to understand and address the implications of making a PRI which does not qualify as an 'approved' investment and take this into account in formulating their policy and approach to their charity's PRI programme.

Intermediaries

10.45 In some cases, the charity may wish to make PRIs through an 'intermediary', which will receive the investment by the charity and make its own investment in a range of other organisations. An intermediary's role is generally therefore to finance (or facilitate the financing of) other organisations and to allow a charity's trustees to access market knowledge they do not have themselves. It can also in certain circumstances allow a charity to spread a risk across a larger number of investments and may also facilitate an easier exit.

10.46 The key points for the trustees of a charity considering using intermediaries as part of their PRI programme are that the charity's assets can only be used to further its objectives and that any private benefit arising from the investment via the intermediary is in line with the Commission's guidance about what is and is not acceptable.

10.47 The trustees will need to understand how the intermediary will apply the funds invested by the charity and, in particular, how the intermediary will engage with the organisations in which it invests in a way which will ensure the charity's objects are advanced and there is no unacceptable private benefit.

Reporting and accounting

10.48 Charities which are subject to statutory audit must prepare an annual report (there is more about this in **Chapter 14**). Their trustees must ensure that the report includes an explanation of the charity's policy for making PRIs and how material PRIs perform against the objectives set for them.

10.49 The charity's balance sheet must also show financial investments separately from PRIs and there are a number of requirements imposed by the SORP that applies to charities which regulate how PRIs should be accounted for. This includes where a PRI no longer fulfils the charity's objectives.

10.50 Early engagement with a charity's auditors is likely to be important where its trustees are considering setting up a PRI programme, in order to ensure that the impact on the charity's accounts is understood. The position will also need to be kept under review in the context of the trustees' annual cycle of preparing and approving the charity's annual report and accounts.

Summary

10.51 In summary, there are a number of key issues identified by the Commission's guidance for the trustees of any charity which is engaging (or proposing to engage) in making PRIs. These are:

* Does the PRI further the objectives of the charity?
* What private benefit might arise as a result?
* What advice do the trustees of the charity need to take?
* Have the trustees given sufficient thought to the terms which will regulate the basis on which the PRI is made?
* Have the trustees considered the governance arrangements that need to be put in place in order to ensure the charity's PRI programme is properly regulated?

MIXED MOTIVE INVESTMENTS

10.52 There may be occasions when a charity's trustees wish to make an investment but cannot satisfy themselves that the investment can be wholly justified either as a financial investment or as a PRI (bearing in mind the considerations set out earlier in this chapter).

10.53 If the trustees still consider that the investment is likely to be in the best interests of the charity, they may be able to justify it as a 'mixed motive' investment. A mixed motive investment is essentially an investment which the trustees of a charity make on the basis that it has elements of both a financial investment and PRI but which cannot be wholly justified as one or the other. This might be because, for example, the investment in question will clearly advance the charity's objectives but will also deliver other outcomes which are not connected with those objectives.

10.54 The trustees will need to be satisfied that the mixed motive investment in question is in the best interests of the charity and can be justified as a proper application of the charity's assets. There are some obvious situations highlighted by the Charity Commission's guidance where a mixed motive investment would not be justified, including where it did not advance the charity's objectives or delivers 'unacceptable' private benefit (which must presumably mean that it is greater in extent than the private benefit which is acceptable in the context of a PRI).

10.55 The Commission's guidance suggests that the trustees of any charity which is making a mixed motive investment should consider the following points:

* The trustees will need to consider 'how much' of the investment can be justified by the PRI's contribution to the charity's objectives and how much can be justified by the financial returns. The Commission recognises

that this is likely to be difficult to quantify (it would be difficult to identify a formula that would determine this in all cases), but it recommends it as a useful analytical exercise in justifying the investment before it is made.

- The trustees will need to consider how to monitor the mixed motive investment.

- The trustees must consider whether investment is suitable for the charity in the context of its activities and financial position generally. The Commission recommends that this includes consideration of the size of the mixed motive investment in the context of the charity's investment portfolio and the trustees' agreed attitude to risk.

- The trustees will also need to ensure that they have applied the decision-making criteria which apply to *both* financial investments and PRIs.

- The trustees will also need to consider whether any private benefit arising from the mixed motive investment is acceptable, taking into account the contribution that the activities the organisation being invested in will carry out will make to the charity's objectives.

- The trustees should also consider whether they need to take professional advice on the proposed mixed motive investment in relation to extent to which it will advance the charity's objectives, any legal issues which arise and any tax implications.

10.56 The Commission's guidance also highlights the importance of monitoring the mixed motive investment as a financial investment and as a PRI bearing in mind the different criteria that applies to each of them. The Commission recognises that the balance between them may change and develop over time. Helpfully, the Commission also recognises that, where a mixed motive investment generates a financial loss for the charity, provided the trustees have taken and recorded their decisions properly, they are likely to be able to deal with any challenges raised by the Commission in relation to their decisions.

10.57 Unlike PRIs, the SORP which applies to charities does not currently address the accounting issues that may arise in relation to mixed motive investments.

FINANCIAL INVESTMENT POWERS

10.58 As is so often the case, the investment powers which are available to a particular charity will depend upon whether it is an incorporated or an unincorporated charity.

Unincorporated charities

10.59 An unincorporated charity may have an express power of investment in its constitution. However, its trustees can also rely upon the statutory power of investment conferred by the Trustee Act 2000, s 3. This authorises them to invest the charity's assets in any kind of investment in which they could invest if they were the absolute owner of the assets. This power (usually referred to as the 'general power of investment') gives charity trustees the widest possible discretion to invest. It is subject to two conditions:

- it is subject to any restriction or exclusion in the charity's constitution; and
- it does not authorise charity trustees to invest in land.

There is more about each of these conditions below.

Restriction or exclusion

10.60 Whether a charity's constitution does 'restrict or exclude' the general power of investment will obviously depend upon what is in the constitution. Although a discussion of this does not feature in the updated CC14 published in 2011, the Charity Commission's previous guidance in this area is helpful:[6]

> 'A provision in the governing document of a charity will only be a "restriction or exclusion" ... if it is intended to prevent the trustees from making a particular form of investment which will be within the scope of the general power, or if it is intended to apply a procedural restriction to the making of an investment (for example, a requirement of consent from the person who set the charity up).'

10.61 So, for example, a positive direction in a charity's constitution to invest only in a particular way will be a restriction (albeit that a provision of this kind may not be enforceable by the court on the basis that it may conflict with the general duty of the charity trustees in relation to investment). However, a provision which is part of the definition of a power of investment that is intended to be wider than a statutory power of investment that may have been in force in the past should not be treated as a restriction or exclusion. This sort of provision will usually spell out the charity's power to invest in a range of specified investment assets, often prefaced by the words '... and in particular to invest in ...' or something similar.

10.62 The powers of investment of every charity include power to participate in common investment funds and common deposit funds unless the power is excluded by a provision in the charity's governing document specifically referring to common investment funds or common deposit funds.[7] There is more about these at **10.123** and **10.124**.

Land

10.63 Although investment in land is not authorised by the general power of investment, the trustees of an unincorporated charity can exercise another

---

6   Investment of Charitable Funds: Detailed guidance (February 2003).
7   Charities Act 20111, ss 99(2) and 103(2).

statutory power (conferred by the Trustee Act 2000, s 8) to acquire freehold or leasehold land in the UK as an investment. This power is available on exactly the same basis as the general power of investment. Clearly, land outside the UK is excluded. Charities that wish to invest in overseas property will generally need to use a collective investment scheme whose underlying assets include property overseas (see **10.123–10.124** for more on this).

Corporate assets

10.64 The general power of investment is not available to the trustees of an incorporated charity in respect of its corporate assets (see **10.65** for more detail in relation to this). However, the general power does apply in relation to trust assets held by an incorporated charity (see **9.8–9.12** for more on this). This means that any restriction or exclusion on investment set out in the incorporated charity's constitution will not operate to restrict or exclude the scope of the general power in relation to trust assets. There is more about the corporate and trust assets of incorporated charities in **Chapter 9**.

Incorporated charities

10.65 As we have explained, incorporated charities cannot take advantage of the general power of investment conferred by the Trustee Act 2000, s 3 in relation to their corporate assets. An incorporated charity must rely upon an express power of investment in its constitution. Many such charities will have an express power, often in very similar terms to the general power of investment.

10.66 In the unlikely event that an incorporated charity does not have an express power of investment or its power is not sufficiently wide to authorise an investment it proposes to make, it will generally be possible to amend the charity's constitution to include a new express power or alter an existing express power. There is more on amending charity constitutions in **Chapter 15**.

TRUSTEES' DUTIES

10.67 There are several significant aspects to the duty owed by charity trustees when making investments. These are:

- The trustees must ensure that they have an appropriate power of investment and are acting within its scope.
- The Trustee Act 2000 imposes statutory duties in respect of the exercise of any power of investment by charity trustees.
- There is also a statutory duty of care owed by trustees imposed by the Trustee Act 2000.
- The trustees must ensure that the tax implications of any investment they make are understood and taken into account in exercising their discretion.

Powers of investment

10.68 The scope of the express and statutory powers of investment available to trustees are explained earlier in this chapter. See **Chapter 7** for more in relation to the exercise of powers.

Statutory duties

10.69 In exercising any power of investment (whether an express or statutory power), a charity's trustees must have regard to the 'standard investment criteria' specified by the Trustee Act 2000.[8] There are two criteria:

- The suitability to the charity of 'investments in the same kind as any particular investment proposed to be made, and of that particular investment as an investment of that kind'. This is usually referred to as 'suitability'.
- The need for diversification of the charity's investments 'in so far as is appropriate to the circumstances' of the charity. This is usually referred to as 'diversification'.

10.70 The trustees must also review the charity's investments from time to time with a view to deciding whether, having regard to the standard investment criteria, the investments should be retained or changed.

10.71 Before they exercise any power of investment (again, whether an express or statutory power), a charity's trustees must obtain and consider 'proper advice' about the way in which the power should be exercised, having regard to the investment criteria we have mentioned. There is an important exception to this which is mentioned at **10.80**.

10.72 The trustees have a similar duty to obtain and consider proper advice when they review whether investments should be retained or changed.

Incorporated charities

10.73 The trustees of an incorporated charity are not subject to these statutory duties when they exercise their power of investment in respect of the charity's corporate assets. However, it is clear that an incorporated charity is in the position 'analogous to that of a trustee in relation to its corporate assets'.[9] On this basis, the likelihood is that a court would regard the trustees of an incorporated charity as owing duties comparable to the statutory duties imposed upon the trustees of an unincorporated charity. This is certainly the approach taken by the Charity Commission. For practical purposes, therefore, it is advisable to assume that the trustees of an incorporated charity owe duties

---

[8] Trustee Act 2000, s 4(3).
[9] *Liverpool and District Hospital for Diseases of the Heart v Att-Gen* [1981] Ch 193.

in relation to investments which are substantially similar to the duties owed by the trustees of an unincorporated charity.

Suitability and diversification

10.74 Suitability relates to both the allocation of a charity's funds between different classes of assets (usually referred to in the investment world as 'asset allocation') and the merits of individual investments within each asset class.

10.75 Diversification means ensuring that the assets invested in are sufficiently diverse to reduce the risk to the charity of significant fluctuations in the value of a particular asset class or an individual investment within each asset class.

10.76 Suitability and diversification are aimed at managing the risk to the charity of investments which fail or underperform. In the context of investment, risk is usually categorised as 'counterparty risk' and 'investment risk'. Counterparty risk is the possibility that an entity with which the charity does business in relation to investment (such as an investment manager) defaults on its obligations. Investment risk relates to the risk inherent in any investment of failure or underperformance.

10.77 Some charity constitutions will expressly provide that trustees are not under a duty to consider the suitability or (more often) the diversification of the charity's investments. The Commission previously expressed its stance in relation to clauses of this kind as being that they 'have no legal effect'. While it is certainly true that a court is unlikely to treat provisions of this kind as ousting these duties altogether, our view is that their existence is certainly one of the factors trustees can legitimately take into account in exercising their investment powers and, is likely to be one of the 'circumstances' in the context of the diversification that may be relevant to the charity.

Advice

10.78 The 'proper advice' a charity's trustees are obliged to obtain before exercising any investment power is the advice of 'a person who is reasonably believed by the trustee to be qualified to give it by his ability in and practical experience of financial and other matters relating to the proposed investment'. This need not necessarily be a person authorised to give investment advice by the Financial Conduct Authority (FCA) pursuant to the Financial Services and Markets Act 2000, although some charity constitutions make it a requirement that the adviser is appropriately authorised (and it may not be possible for anyone other than an FCA authorised person to give certain advice in any event).

10.79 There is no objection in principle to an adviser not being authorised by the FCA (unless his or her advice relates to an area that is regulated by the FCA), and it is also possible for a trustee who is appropriately qualified to advise his co-trustees. While this may be a more cost-effective option for the charity than consulting an independent adviser, trustees looking to rely on the advice of one of their co-trustees are obviously under a particular duty to consider the advice they receive objectively. And, as the Commission points out, the trustee who does give advice may be liable to the charity if the advice he or she has given proves to be negligent.

10.80 There is an important exception to the duty to seek advice where the trustees reasonably conclude that, in all the circumstances, it is unnecessary or inappropriate to do so. The key word here is 'reasonably'. It would be reasonable to expect trustees not to seek advice where the value of the funds they are seeking to invest is so small that the cost of the advice would be disproportionate. Equally, it is likely to be unreasonable for trustees to conclude that they will not take advice because they have some limited experience of making investments in their personal capacity and do not wish to incur any fees. The general duty on trustees to consider taking advice in relation to matters which they are not qualified to consider themselves is clear (see **7.46** for more on this). The fact that the advice may need to be paid for is not, of itself, a sufficient justification not to take it.

Statutory duty of care

10.81 In exercising any power of investment (and the specific duties in relation to investment imposed by the Trustee Act 2000) the trustees of an unincorporated charity are subject to the statutory duty of care imposed by the 2000 Act. The trustees of incorporated charities are likely to be subject to a similar duty. There is more about the statutory duty of care at **6.2**.

Tax implications

10.82 The wide range of exemptions and reliefs from tax available to charities can be restricted where they incur 'non-charitable expenditure'. One form of non-charitable expenditure is investment in assets outside the asset classes specified in the Income Tax Act 2007 and the Corporation Tax Act 2010.[10] This will include, for example, investments in private equity and hedge funds. Investments of this kind are only at risk of being treated as non-charitable expenditure if made for tax avoidance purposes. This will not often be the case, but it is obviously essential that a charity's trustees appreciate the significance of investing in asset classes of this kind. There is more detail about this in **Chapter 11**.

10.83 More generally, trustees should ensure that the tax implications of a particular investment are understood. Because of the 'patchwork' of exemptions and reliefs from tax available to charities, not every investment that may be made by a charity will give rise to an investment return which is free of tax. This does not necessarily mean that a charity cannot invest in assets of this kind, but the fact that they may produce a taxable return whereas other

---

[10]   Income Tax Act 2007, s 558; Corporation Tax Act 2010, s 511.

investments will not is an important factor to be taken into account by the trustees in exercising their investment powers in accordance with their duty of care.

ETHICAL INVESTMENT

10.84 Ethical investment means investing in a way that reflects a charity's values and does not run counter to its aims. This may involve one or more approaches, including 'negative screening' (avoiding investment in companies or sectors operating in a way which may be harmful to the charity's interests and objectives); 'positive screening' (which means investing in companies or sectors which reflect the charity's objectives in areas like environmental protection, health, employment, human rights or in companies which demonstrate good corporate and social responsibility in governance); and 'stakeholder activism' (where the charity is a shareholder and uses its voting rights to influence a company's policies in a way that reflects its aims and ethos).

10.85 It is important to appreciate that ethical investment is a form of financial investment and that all of the usual duties with regard to financial investment apply to it.

10.86 Charity trustees who wish to adopt an ethical investment policy are bound by the principles set out in the leading case, *Harries (Bishop of Oxford) v Church Commissioners for England*.[11] The starting point is that the trustees of every charity are under a duty to act in the best interests of the charity and that those interests will generally best be advanced by maximising (in a way which is consistent with the trustees' duty in relation to investment) the financial return for its investments regardless of other considerations, whether ethical or otherwise.

10.87 As the Commission points out:[12]

'An ethical investment policy may be entirely consistent with this principle of seeking the best return. For example, there is an increasingly held view that companies which act in a socially responsible way are more likely to flourish and to deliver the best long term balance between risk and return. The trustees are free to adopt any ethical investment policy which they reasonably believe will provide the best balance or risk and reward for their charity.'

10.88 Notwithstanding this, the *Bishop of Oxford* case recognised the circumstances in which the trustees of a charity can allow ethical considerations to carry more weight than 'financial' considerations:

---

[11] [1992] 1 WLR 1241.
[12] CC 14 – Legal underpinning.

- Where there is a clear conflict between the operations of a particular investment and the operations of the charity, the charity is able to rule it out as an investment. This will, for example, allow a charity that relieves those suffering from cancer to exclude investments in the tobacco industry.

- Investments which might cause a charity problems in practice (perhaps because they alienate beneficiaries, members, volunteers etc) can be excluded provided that the trustees consider that the risk to the charity posed by, say, alienating its supporters is greater than the risk of financial underperformance.

- More generally, trustees of a charity are free to make an ethical investment if they conclude that it will leave them in no worse financial position than any other investment. This condition is likely to become easier to satisfy as more and more professional investment managers offer 'ethical' funds and other forms of collective investment schemes that appear to offer returns comparable to 'unethical' funds.

10.89 The Commission's guidance offers some helpful practical guidance to trustees in relation to formulating an ethical investment policy:[13]

> '• Consider the aims and objectives of the charity.
> - Keep in mind the fundamental principle of maximising return. If an ethical policy is adopted, it should be set out in writing and should be clear both on positive aims and any exclusions.
> - If companies or sectors are excluded, the reasons for exclusion should be clearly thought through. The more restrictive the policy (in terms of exclusions) the greater may be the risk to returns.
> - Trustees need to evaluate the effect which any proposed policy may have on potential investment returns, and this will usually require expert advice.'

10.90 It may be, of course, that the express power of investment given to a particular charity specifically excludes investment in particular assets or particular classes of assets. So, for example, those establishing a charity to assist people who are injured by landmines may decide to state in the charity's constitution that it is not permitted to invest in shares or securities in companies engaged in the arms trade. Provisions of this kind will be binding on the charity's trustees.

SPECIFIC INVESTMENTS

10.91 As we suggested earlier in this chapter, there are a number of different investments (including 'alternative investments') that now form part of the modern investment portfolio for many charities alongside more 'traditional' asset classes. These are considered in more detail below.

---

13   CC 14 – Legal underpinning.

Derivatives

10.92 'Derivatives' is the way in which a wide range of different financial instruments are described. What they have in common is that, while they are not 'investments' in their own right, they generally relate to an investment and will give rise to a financial return (or loss) which is dependant upon the way in which the relevant investment performs.

10.93 The other factor common to the derivatives is that they are intended to protect against (or 'hedge') the financial risk which may attach to particular investments. A good example of this is an interest rate 'swap'. This is essentially an agreement which allows a party that has financial exposure to a floating rate of interest (eg under a floating rate loan) to 'swap' that rate for a fixed rate of interest. The counterparty to the swap will generally be a bank or other financial institution. The counterparty receives a premium for taking on the risk that floating rates of interest will rise above the fixed rate specified in the swap. The other party has the comfort of knowing that its financial exposure to a rise in interest rates has been capped. Other forms of derivative include currency rate swaps, options, and futures.

10.94 The Charity Commission's previous guidance stated that derivatives could only be used as ancillary to the exercise of an investment power. Broadly, this meant that the purpose of entering into the derivative was to manage risk or manage transaction costs in relation to another investment.

10.95 The revised CC14 reflects a change in the Commission's stance in relation to derivatives. As the Commission says:[14]

> 'It may well be that in some cases use of derivatives in a way which is not ancillary to the exercise of an investment power could be regarded as trading rather than investment. However, there are many derivative products and some may be so analogous to investments as to be lawful as an exercise of the investment power in their own right. This will depend on the nature of the derivative product and the considerations in using that product as an investment. In particular, they are only likely to be used if they constitute a small proportion of a large fund available for investment.'

The guidance is clear that derivatives 'are likely to be suitable only as part of a well-diversified investment portfolio because of the higher risk they can represent'.[15]

10.96 Most derivatives are complex financial instruments used by sophisticated investors which generate significant income for the banks and financial institutions which provide them. It will generally be particularly important for charity trustees to seek advice in relation to a derivative transaction they are proposing to enter into in order to understand its financial

---

[14] CC 14 – Legal underpinning.
[15] CC 14.

implications and the risks attached to it. The Charity Commission recommends that trustees take professional advice where appropriate in selecting and reviewing these types of investment.

10.97 The tax treatment of derivatives is more complex than the tax treatment of investments. Trustees should ensure that they understand the tax implications of the derivative transaction they are proposing to enter into. Professional advice will generally be required under the general duty to consider taking appropriate advice.

Hedge funds

10.98 Hedge funds have become an increasingly 'mainstream' investment asset in recent years, prompted, no doubt, by the apparently significant investment returns they are reported to produce. Investors generally are looking to include hedge fund investments as part of their portfolios and many charities are no exception to this.

10.99 A hedge fund is essentially a collective investment scheme that uses investors' funds to buy a wide range of assets, particularly assets that are not closely correlated to movements in more traditional asset classes, such as listed shares and securities.

10.100 Hedge funds are often highly 'leveraged'. In other words, their managers borrow significantly in order to buy assets. This can obviously increase the gains that a fund may make on assets that perform well. Equally, it can exaggerate the losses that a fund may experience if assets do not perform as expected. Hedge funds are also generally unregulated, often operating out of offshore jurisdictions with no (or very 'light touch') regulatory regimes. This means that obtaining reliable and verifiable information about the way in which hedge funds perform is often difficult.

10.101 Having said all this, hedge funds have, as we have explained, become more of a mainstream investment in recent years and the approach many charities take is to invest in a 'fund of funds'. In other words, a charity may invest in a collective investment scheme which itself invests in a wide range of hedge funds adopting different investment strategies, with a view to mitigating risk. Given the duties owed by charity trustees in relation to investment, this is obviously likely to be a sensible approach. However, any investment in any hedge fund (whether directly or via a collective investment scheme) is likely to carry a higher degree of risk than investing in the more 'traditional' asset classes. Charity trustees are unlikely to be able to assess the risks in investing in hedge funds or retaining their investments without taking professional advice.

10.102 Any investment in a hedge fund is not 'charitable expenditure' where it is made to avoid tax. This issue will need to be addressed by a charity's trustees before they make any investment in a hedge fund. They will also need to ensure that they understand the tax implications of the investment and any financial return it produces. Again, they are unlikely to be able to do this without taking professional advice.

Private equity

10.103 'Private equity' means buying shares in a private company, as opposed to shares which are traded on a stock exchange. Investment by charities in private equity was unusual in the past (except perhaps where a charity held shares transferred by a donor), but the emergence of collective investment schemes specialising in private equity investment has meant that private equity investment, like investment in hedge funds, is becoming more mainstream for investors generally, including charities.

10.104 The most significant issue for charity trustees looking to invest in private equity is that their ability to exit from the investment is likely to be limited because there will be no market on which shares that are bought can be traded and sold. This risk may be mitigated to a certain extent by investing in private equity via units or shares in a collective investment scheme specialising in the area.

10.105 A direct investment in private equity by a charity is likely to be difficult without taking professional advice, which may well make the investment disproportionately expensive. It will be particularly important to understand the control (if any) the charity will acquire over the private company it is investing in. This will obviously determine the charity's ability to exercise control over the way in which the company's business is operated. Charity trustees should also bear in mind that the governance and other regulatory requirements in relation to private companies will be lighter than those which apply to the shares of a public company listed on the stock exchange.

10.106 Like hedge funds, private equity investments are not 'charitable expenditure' for tax purposes where they are made in order to avoid tax. A charity's trustees will need to take professional advice on this issue before investing.

Underwriting

10.107 Charities may occasionally be invited to underwrite a new issue of shares by a listed company. Essentially, the underwriter is asked to buy newly issued shares at an agreed price in the event that they are not subscribed for by anyone else. Generally speaking, the obligation to subscribe will arise where the expected subscription price is not being met, so that the price paid by the underwriter is higher than the price for the shares in the market. The underwriter will, however, receive a fee for agreeing to underwrite the subscription.

10.108 Charity trustees would need to consider an invitation of this kind very carefully, not least because of the risk of the charity being obliged to buy a significant number of shares at a price which is higher than they can be purchased in the market.

10.109 Underwriting fees which are received are likely to be taxable. A charity's trustees should take professional advice on this point before agreeing to underwrite shares.

Stock lending

10.110 'Stock lending' is a technique used by many pension trustees and other 'institutional' investors to maximise the return from their investment portfolios.

10.111 A 'stock loan' describes the economic effect of the transaction, rather than the actual legal position. The reality is that stock lending involves the transfer of shares or other securities by one party (a 'lender') to another party (a 'borrower') on the basis of an undertaking from the borrower to redeliver exactly the same number and type of securities after a specified period. The borrower pays the lender a fee in respect of the 'loan'.

10.112 Borrowers are typically banks and other large investment houses which need particular stock to satisfy other obligations they may owe to third parties. For example, a bank may sell shares in a particular company short and not be able to comply with its delivery obligations unless it can 'borrow' shares from another source. The borrower will also agree to pay to the lender amounts equal to any dividends or other distributions paid on the borrowed shares during the loan. From the lender's perspective, therefore, a stock loan maximises the investment return from the shares it holds.

10.113 Stock loans are usually secured by the borrower, who will deliver collateral to the lender as security for its redelivery obligations. Because of the availability of collateral, the risk to the lender of a failure by the borrower to comply with its obligations should be limited to the possibility of default in respect of the collateral itself. Acceptable collateral is usually limited to cash and other near cash obligations such as sovereign debt. Having said that, there are clearly risks associated with stock lending that charity trustees should understand and consider before they agree to lend shares within their charity's investment portfolio. In particular, trustees will need to consider the terms on which they engage an agent to arrange stock loans (an agent will almost always be required on the basis that most charities that wish to engage in stock lending would have great difficulty in identifying potential borrowers or making appropriate arrangements with them).

10.114 Fees payable to the charity in respect of the stock loan are liable to tax. This may not be an issue if the trustees can conclude that the fees are an additional financial return which would not otherwise have been received in respect of the relevant shares and that the risk of the stock loan as against the net fees receivable is acceptable.

10.115 Stock loans are treated by HM Revenue & Customs as non-charitable expenditure where they are made in order to avoid tax. Charity trustees who are considering engaging in stock lending should ensure that they understand the position and are likely to need to take professional advice in order to do so.

Insurance policies

10.116 Although the Charity Commission previously took the view that purchasing life insurance policies is within the general power of investment,[16] HM Revenue & Customs will treat the premiums payable by the charity as non-charitable expenditure. On this basis, charity trustees should not generally consider purchasing life insurance policies as an investment. Gains on policies are, in any event, liable to tax. See **11.29** for more in relation to this.

Land

10.117 An incorporated charity will generally have an express power to acquire investment land under its constitution. Unincorporated charities (or incorporated charities which hold trust assets) may have a similar express power but, failing that, can rely upon the statutory power to purchase investment land conferred by the Trustee Act 2000, s 8. This statutory power is subject to any provisions to the contrary in a charity's constitution.

10.118 The Charity Commission's guidance on acquiring investment land[17] mentions a number of considerations which charity trustees should take into account when considering buying land as an investment:

- Land may require more active management than other investment assets. This would include, for example, ensuring the investment property is kept in repair and fully let to tenants.

- In comparison to cash, listed investments etc, land is illiquid.

- Managing investment land requires different skills and experience from managing listed investments.

- The cost of investing in a sufficiently diversified portfolio of investment land (particularly commercial property) may not be practicable for an individual charity acting alone.

- The ownership of investment land may impose financial obligations on the charity.

---

[16] Investment of Charitable Funds: Detailed guidance (February 2003).
[17] CC 33.

10.119   The Charity Commission goes on to say that:[18]

> 'We would recommend that this type of investment is normally only suitable for a charity which either:
>
> - has traditionally held land as an investment; or
> - has a sufficiently wide and varied portfolio of investments into which land could reasonably be introduced.'

10.120   While these comments are helpful, most of these issues may be answered (to a greater or lesser extent) by investing in collective investment schemes which specialise in property. This will usually enable a charity to invest in land (albeit indirectly) with the same liquidity as an investment in any other listed investment and with responsibility for the day-to-day management of the underlying property vested in professional managers.

10.121   Where, on the other hand, a charity proposes a direct investment in land, the Commission's guidance should be carefully considered. So too should its recommendation that trustees proposing to buy land for investment purposes should obtain a report from a qualified surveyor (although there is no legal obligation to do so).

10.122   The statutory power conferred by s 8 of the Trustee Act 2000 applies only to land in England and Wales. In the absence of an express power in a charity's constitution, it would be a breach of trust for its trustees to acquire land overseas. While the investment return from overseas land will generally be exempt from UK tax, overseas tax may be withheld, with no entitlement for credit under a double tax treaty (even if there is one in place between the UK and the relevant jurisdiction).

Common investment and deposit funds

10.123   Common deposit funds are arrangements under which charities can deposit cash with a view to generating interest on the deposit they have made. Common deposit funds are themselves charities and are set up by way of a Scheme made by the Commission under the Charities Act 2011.[19]

10.124   The Charity Commission has a similar power to make common investment schemes.[20] Common investment schemes enable participating charities to pool their assets for investment purposes, with a view to gaining access to a wider range of investments. Common investment schemes are themselves charities and are very similar in the way they are structured to any other collective investment scheme. Investing charities acquire an interest in the common investment scheme (usually 'units' or 'shares') rather than in the underlying assets of the scheme itself.

---

[18]   CC 33, para 17.
[19]   Charities Act 2011, s 100.
[20]   Charities Act 2011, s 96.

DELEGATION OF INVESTMENT MANAGEMENT

10.125 Many charities employ a professional management adviser to manage their assets. In some cases, investment managers of this kind may act on an 'execution only' and 'advisory' basis. In other words, they may advise a charity's trustees on their investment strategy and deal with the purchase and sale of investments at their direction. More often, charities will engage a 'discretionary' investment manager and authorise it to exercise its own discretion to buy and sell assets on behalf of the charity within an investment policy laid down by the trustees.

10.126 In legal terms, engaging a discretionary investment manager is a delegation of the trustees' power to invest their charity's assets. Delegation by trustees is considered in more detail in **Chapter 8**, but it is helpful to remember that the starting point is that every charity trustee should exercise his or her powers personally unless they are expressly authorised by someone else to exercise them. This means that every charity trustee is obliged to make decisions about investment personally unless they are able to delegate responsibility for investment decisions to someone else.

10.127 The powers of delegation available to trustees in relation to investment management depend upon whether the charity in question is incorporated or unincorporated.

Incorporated charities

10.128 Most incorporated charities will have a power in their constitution expressly authorising their trustees to delegate investment management to a third party. Powers of this kind will usually impose certain restrictions on the exercise of the power, including provisions in relation to the competence and experience of the investment management. If an incorporated charity does not have an appropriate power of delegation, it will usually be possible to amend its constitution to add one. See **15.26–15.34** for more detail in relation to this.

Unincorporated charities

10.129 The trustees of an unincorporated charity may also have an express power of delegation under its constitution. Failing that, s 11 of the Trustee Act 2000 gives trustees the power to delegate functions relating to the investment of charity assets. The power is conferred by the 2000 Act in addition to any powers of delegation expressly set out in the charity's constitution (or which are otherwise available to the charity's trustees under some other legal provision). See **8.106–8.115** for detail in relation to this.

10.130 The statutory power conferred by the Trustee Act 2000 can be restricted or excluded by provisions in the charity's constitution. The statutory power applies to trust assets held by an incorporated charity (but not to its corporate assets).

10.131 The statutory power is wide enough to authorise the trustees to appoint one of their number as a discretionary investment manager (although the prohibition under the Financial Services and Markets Act 2000 on anyone other than an authorised person providing investment management advice may preclude this).

Investment management agreements

10.132 Charity trustees must ensure that any agreement they enter into with any investment manager is appropriate. The trustees of an unincorporated charity who wish to rely upon the power of delegation conferred upon them by the Trustee Act 2000 must comply with a number of statutory restrictions on their discretion to agree terms with an investment manager.[21] Essentially, the trustees have a discretion to determine the basis on which any delegate should be appointed but cannot, unless it is reasonably necessary, agree to terms which:

- permit the investment manager to appoint a substitute to act in its place;
- include any exemption clause restricting the investment manager's liability to the charity; or
- permit the investment manager to act in circumstances which give rise to potential conflicts of interest.

10.133 While these restrictions do not strictly apply to the trustees of an incorporated charity entering into an investment management agreement in relation to its corporate assets, the Charity Commission makes no distinction in its guidance between the trustees of unincorporated charities and incorporated charities. The Commission's view expressed in its previous guidance was that 'these restrictions apply whether or not the statutory power of delegation is being relied upon'.[22] In other words, any charity trustee looking to enter into an investment management agreement must observe the Trustee Act 2000 restrictions we have mentioned. There does not appear to be any direct authority to substantiate the Commission's previous view and there is no equivalent statement in the revised guidance (except for a general statement that the duties set out in CC14 are based on the law relating to trusts, but directors of charitable companies are likely to have similar duties when investing their charities' assets). However, it is likely that the court would, if called upon, take into account statutory restrictions imposed on the trustees of an unincorporated charity in assessing the comparable position of the trustees of an incorporated charity. For practical purposes, therefore, all charity trustees should assume that these restrictions apply to them.

10.134 In practice, restrictions of this kind form part of the terms and conditions of business of many professional investment managers. In that sense, they are by no means unusual. On this basis, charity trustees may well conclude

---

[21] Trustee Act 2000, s 14.
[22] Investment of Charitable Funds: Detailed guidance (February 2003).

that it is 'reasonably necessary' to agree to terms of this kind on the basis that most (if not all) other professional investment managers will only agree to act on the same basis. However, that is not to say that trustees should not seek to negotiate the terms of the investment management agreement with the manager before they enter into it.

10.135 The investment management agreement must be in writing or 'be evidenced in writing'. In practice, no professional investment manager authorised by the Financial Conduct Authority will agree to act unless it has been appointed in writing.

Trustees' duty of care

10.136 In appointing a discretionary investment manager, a charity's trustees are under the general duty to exercise due care and skill we have mentioned at **10.81**. This includes the determination of whether the sort of terms we have mentioned at **10.132** are 'reasonably necessary' within the investment management agreement. Trustees looking to appoint an investment manager will generally need to consider more than one potential provider of investment management services, often through a formal tendering process, and look in some detail at comparative service levels and costs in order to comply with their general duty. CC14 contains some helpful guidance for trustees in relation to selecting an investment manager.[23]

10.137 When considering an investment manager's charges, trustees will wish to seek clarity in relation to the fee structure that applies and the actual cost to be met by the charity in relation to the investment management agreement. Generally speaking, the fee payable to the investment manager (which will often be a percentage to the value of the funds under management payable on an annual basis) will be clear. What are often less clear are the fees that may be payable in respect of the investments which make up the portfolio itself, particularly where funds are being invested in collective investment schemes. Those operating collective investment schemes are generally entitled to charge management fees which it may be much more difficult for the charity's trustees to assess.

10.138 The Commission's guidance states that trustees must be clear about what payments or benefits the manager or other parties receive under the agreement and be satisfied that these payments or benefits represent good value for the charity. The Commission says that if the charity appoints the manager by a tendering exercise, the trustees may be able to use this to satisfy themselves that the fees represent good value for money and are in the interests of the charity.

---

[23] See CC 14, para F4.

Investment manager's duty of care

10.139 Once appointed, an investment manager will owe exactly the same duties in relation to the investments it makes on the charity's behalf as the trustees themselves. This will mean, therefore, that the investment manager must pay due regard to the 'standard investment criteria' of suitability and diversification. An investment manager will not, though, be under the same obligation as the charity's trustees to consider taking advice in relation to a particular investment. This is on the basis that the manager is a person from whom the charity's trustees could properly have taken advice from if they were exercising the power of investment themselves.[24]

10.140 An investment manager does not owe the same duty of care and skill as the charity's trustees. The duty of care owed to the charity will be regulated by the investment management agreement.

Investment policy

10.141 The Trustee Act 2000[25] obliges the trustees of any unincorporated charity to prepare an investment policy before they exercise any power (whether conferred by the 2000 Act or not) to delegate responsibility for investment to an investment manager. The investment policy is intended to guide the investment manager in relation to the exercise of the functions delegated to it in the best interests of the charity. The policy itself has to be in writing and the charity's trustees are personally responsible for preparing it without delegating it to the investment manager in question. However, as the Charity Commission points out, trustees might find it helpful to prepare the policy in consultation with the investment manager to ensure its terms are workable and achievable. The investment management agreement itself must also include a provision requiring the manager to comply with the policy statement.

10.142 The duty of care we have mentioned earlier in this chapter at **10.81** applies to the trustees in relation to preparing and reviewing the investment policy.

10.143 Because the requirement to prepare an investment policy and ensure that an investment manager is obliged to comply with it is imposed by the Trustee Act 2000, it does not strictly apply to the trustees of an incorporated charity in relation to its corporate assets. However, as we have said, the Charity Commission makes no distinction in its guidance between the trustees of unincorporated and incorporated charities, taking the view that the trustees of incorporated charities are likely to have similar duties to those of unincorporated charities when investing their charity's funds. The constitutions of many incorporated charities will, in any event, require the preparation of an

---

[24] Trustee Act 2000, s 13(2).
[25] Trustee Act 2000, s 15.

investment policy. For practical purposes, therefore, all charity trustees should assume that an investment policy is required.

10.144 In any event, it is likely to be sensible for the trustees of any charity with investments to formulate an investment policy and keep it under review, notwithstanding that they do not propose to delegate investment management to a professional manager.

10.145 The Trustee Act 2000 does not specify the content or form of an investment policy. The terms of the policy will need to be reasonably specific to enable the investment manager to agree to comply with them. However, subject to that, the content of the policy is likely to be determined by the circumstances of individual charities and their particular investment objectives. The Charity Commission suggests general areas which might be dealt with in an investment policy. These are:

- The scope of the charity's investment powers. Any restrictions on the trustees' powers of investment should be clearly identified with a view to ensuring that the investment manager does not inadvertently breach them. The policy may also usefully set out the classes of investment that may be regarded as non-charitable expenditure for tax purposes.

- The charity's investment objectives, taking into account the charity's short and long term financial commitments. Trustees of charities with permanent endowment will need to ensure that the policy will enable them to distinguish between income and capital returns, unless they have adopted a 'total return' approach to investment. There is more about this at **10.157**.

- The charity's attitude to risk. The trustees' assessment of risk will mean striking a balance between the level of investment return required and the risk associated with it. As the Commission points out, as part of their duty of care, trustees must be satisfied that the overall level of risk is right for the charity and its beneficiaries. The position will need to be clearly stated to the investment manager.

- How much is available for investment, timing of returns and the charity's liquidity needs. Some charities may have particular requirements in relation to asset allocation where, for example, they have a particular requirement for liquidity. Many charities will agree a range of percentage values of the managed fund as a while for allocation between particular asset classes.

- The types of investment the charity wants to make. This might include ethical considerations, in which case the charity's ethical investment policy must clearly be spelled out, including any requirements in relation to positive and negative screening, or 'stakeholder activism'.

- Who can take investment decisions. For example, this may include the trustees, an executive or an investment advisor or manager.

- How investments will be managed and benchmarks and targets set by which performance will be judged. Particularly where an investment manager is appointed, benchmarking their performance will be essential for the charity. Identifying the right benchmark is clearly a key consideration. Many investment managers will suggest benchmarks against which they should be assessed, but it may be difficult for charity trustees with limited experience in relation to investment management to assess whether or not the benchmarks suggested are appropriate. In these circumstances, advice from an independent third party may be required.

• Reporting requirements for investment managers, to enable the trustees to keep the service provided by the charity's investment manager under regular review.

The Trustee Act 2000 obliges charity trustees to keep their investment policy under review. An investment policy should normally also state the basis on which it will be reviewed and the intervals at which this is expected to happen.

10.146 An example of an investment policy for a newly established grant making charity (without endowment assets and intending to operate overseas) is as follows:

Investment policy

Background

[*The Charity*] (the '**Charity**') is a registered charity (registered number [ ]) and a company limited by guarantee (registered number [ ]) with the following charitable objects:

> [*charitable objects*]

Investment powers

The Charity has a wide power to invest or deposit funds in any manner (subject to an obligation to invest only after taking such advice as the trustees consider is reasonably necessary).

The Charity (and [*manager*] in its capacity as discretionary investment manager) should ensure that, in managing the investments, they have regard to:

• the *suitability* to the Charity of investments of the same kind as any proposed investment;

• the *suitability* of the proposed investment as an investment of that kind; and

• the need for *diversification* of the investments of the Charity so far as is appropriate to its circumstances.   ➡

There are no factors which limit the need for diversification of the Charity's investments.

The investment powers of the Charity authorise an investment in hedge funds, subject to the requirements of suitability and diversification.

Investment restrictions

As a registered charity, investment by the Charity in any assets other than 'qualifying investments' within section 558 Income Tax Act 2007 and section 511 Corporation Tax Act 2010 may constitute non-charitable expenditure in certain circumstances and lead to the restriction of the tax exemptions available to the Charity in respect of its investment income and gains.

Any foreign withholding taxes should be taken into account in making investments.

Investment aims

The Charity's aim over the first 5 years of its lifespan is to invest its initial assets with a view to increasing their value. The return should be considered on a total return basis and the income generated will be re-invested. After the expiry of the first 5 year period, the Charity expects to start to use its investment return to support [ ] in respect of its activities within the Charity's objects.

The Charity's total lifespan is expected to be between [ ] and [ ] years.

Special preferences and constraints

Currency

The majority of the liabilities of the Charity will be in the currencies of [the countries in which it operates], although no significant liabilities are expected to arise during the first 5 years of the Charity's lifespan. The impact of this on the currency exposure of the investments must be taken into account.

Investments in fixed interest securities should be restricted to Sterling, Euro and the US dollar denominations, in government debt or corporate bonds at or above a Standard & Poor's 'A' credit rating.

Yield

There are no restrictions on the yield of the investment portfolio. →

Risk profile

The investment portfolio should carry a medium to low risk profile.

- The majority of equity investments will be in the major world companies with collective investment vehicles used to cover specialised areas such as smaller company investment.
- All investments should be readily marketable in normal stock market conditions.
- For the equity section of the portfolio no single holding should exceed 5% of the total valuation of the portfolio. Nor should any single holding produce more than 5% of the total income of the portfolio. Should either of these limits be exceeded that holding should be reduced, subject to market considerations. Larger holdings in fixed interest stocks and in collectives are permitted provided that they do not compromise the overall requirement to spread the risk of the portfolio.

Liquidity

During the first 5 years of the Charity's lifespan, liquidity will only be required to pay investment management fees and other administrative costs and expenses.

Socially Responsible Investment constraints

As the Charity wishes to invest in a way that helps to promote its objects, investment should not normally be made in companies known to be operating in the following sectors:

[ ]

Asset Allocation

Initial asset allocation / strategic range	Index	Range for Portfolio
Fixed Interest and cash	50%	[40%–60]%
International Equities	50%	[40%–60]%

Benchmark

The portfolio should be benchmarked against an index weighted 50% on the Salomon Government Bonds World Index and 50% against the FTSE World Index. These figures will be provided by [manager] as part of its half yearly reporting.

➡

> *Reviews and reporting*
>
> Valuations and performance figures are expected every half year with details of the income received and other information as required by the auditors at the Charity's year end. Additional reports on performance and strategy may be requested by the Charity from time to time. This investment policy and the delegation of the Charity's discretionary investment management will be reviewed by the Charity annually.

Review

10.147 Charity trustees are under a duty to review their investment management arrangements, as part of their duty to review their investments from time to time, changing them if necessary.[26] However, 'review' in this context does not necessarily mean seeking alternative bids for the investment management work from other investment managers.

10.148 Clearly, identifying an appropriate benchmark at the outset and ensuring performance is regularly measured against those benchmarks will be the fundamental point in relation to any review. Where necessary, a charity's trustee may need to think about obtaining professional advice from a third party if they conclude that they are not themselves in a position to make an assessment.

NOMINEES AND CUSTODIANS

10.149 As part of most investment management agreements, the investment manager will agree to hold their charity client's investments in the name of a nominee company established by the investment manager. Beneficial ownership of the investments remains with the charity, but using a nominee company will usually make buying and selling investments within the charity's portfolio much more straightforward.

10.150 The trustees of an unincorporated charity have a statutory power under the Trustee Act 2000 to appoint a nominee or custodian of any of the charity's assets.[27] This is in addition to any powers to appoint a nominee or custodian in the charity's own constitution.

10.151 The trustees of an incorporated charity cannot rely upon the Trustee Act 2000 in respect of its corporate assets, but will generally have an express power to put assets into the name of a nominee or custodian in the charity's constitution. There is more about this in **Chapter 9**.

---

[26] Trustee Act 2000, s 22.
[27] Trustee Act 2000, ss 16, 17.

TOTAL RETURN APPROACH TO INVESTMENT

10.152 Specific investment considerations apply to the trustees of any charity with permanent endowment. Permanent endowment is the term applied to any charity asset which is held on trust to retain it for the purposes of the charity. Permanent endowment will often be land used for a charity's particular purposes. However, permanent endowment may also be investment assets held with a view to generating income capable of supporting the charity's operations. See **9.27–9.36** for more detail in relation to permanent endowment.

10.153 In this sense, permanent endowment is very similar to the capital assets of a private trust which are held to generate an income for certain beneficiaries, while the endowment assets themselves are held for other beneficiaries. In the context of a charity, trustees are required to hold the balance between its present and future needs. The charity's present requirements will be met out of the income generated by the endowment assets. But the endowment assets themselves must be retained in order to maintain a capital base which can generate income to meet the charity's requirements in the future.

10.154 However, these requirements can create a discrepancy between the way in which charities with permanent endowment can apply the investment return from the endowment itself and what might be considered, in investment terms alone, the best possible approach for the benefit of the charity. The Charity Commission expressed the issue in this way:[28]

> 'Trustees are selecting investments which they judge should produce returns that, when the rules are applied to them, will break down into a mix of income needed by the charity to carry out its charitable purposes for the benefit of the current beneficiaries and of capital growth for the benefit of future beneficiaries. This reflects their duty to maintain a fair balance between capital and income interests.
>
> In theory, this approach does not seem problematic. However, the need to comply with the rules has led trustees to select investment portfolios because they will "fit" the rules for the treatment of investment returns, rather than because the portfolio's mix of investments will give the charity the best total level of economic return. A charity's scope for investment and the total level of returns it is able to realise can be negatively affected as a result.'

10.155 In other words, charity trustees may feel (and in fact are) obliged to allow the legal constraints on the way in which they can apply income and capital gains generated by their invested endowment to take precedence over the investment approach that might otherwise be taken to produce the best overall return for the charity.

10.156 The Charity Commission's previous response to this issue was to adopt a policy on 'total return approach to investment' which was intended to enable the trustees of any charity with permanent endowment to invest the

---

[28]   Consultation Document July 2000.

endowment's assets in the way that would produce the best overall financial return for the endowment, regardless of whether this was made up of income or capital gains or both. Trustees were required to apply for an Order from the Commission authorising them to adopt a total return approach to investment.

Statutory power

10.157 This policy approach by the Commission has since been replaced by the introduction of a statutory power to adopt a 'total return' approach. This change was made by s 4 of the Trusts (Capital and Income) Act 2013, which amended the Charities Act 2011 to give permanently endowed charities the statutory power and to allow the Commission to make regulations creating a statutory framework within which trustees must exercise that power. The Regulations in question (the Charities (Total Return) Regulations 2013) came into force on 1 January 2014.

10.158 The Charity Commission has published helpful guidance on the 2013 Regulations it has made.[29] The guidance explains the issue in relation to the investment of permanent endowment:

> 'A unique feature of charities is that they can hold permanent endowment and exist in the long term. This means that the trustees must invest in a way that has regard to the furtherance of the charity's aims both now and in the future. Under the standard rules, this means investing in a way that provides enough income for current needs and enough capital growth to safeguard future income.'

10.159 By 'standard rules' the Commission means the legal constraints referred to above at **10.153** which govern the allocation of investment and returns between capital and income and oblige any capital gains arising from a charity's investments to be treated as capital which must be retained for reinvestment rather than spent. As the Commission's guidance states:[30]

> 'The standard rules can sometimes cause difficulty where income from dividends, interest etc. is low and capital gains are high. These conditions can mean that a charity is less able to meet current needs due to lower income and could mean that future needs will be over-provided for.'

10.160 In essence, the total return approach envisaged by the statutory power is as follows:

- In order to exercise the statutory power, the trustees of a charity with permanent endowment must first determine the original value of the endowment (in other words, the amount of the original gift or gifts which constituted it), together with the investment return which has since

---

[29] Total return investment for permanently endowed charities (December 2013).
[30] Total return investment for permanently endowed charities (December 2013), para C1.

accrued in relation to the original endowment. This investment return (which will include both income and capital gains) is referred to as the 'unapplied investment return'.

- The 'unapplied investment return' then forms the basis of what is referred to as the 'unapplied total return', with the value of the original endowment forming what is referred to as the 'investment fund'.

- If the statutory power is adopted, the return on the assets comprised in the investment fund (and in the unapplied total return) after the adoption of the power will also form part of the 'unapplied total return'.

- The statutory power gives the trustees of the charity the ability to allocate all or part of the unapplied total return to an 'income fund' (referred to in the 2013 Regulations as the 'trust for application'). The amounts so allocated can be freely applied for the charitable purposes for which the endowment is held.

- The trustees also have a limited ability to allocate part of the unapplied total return to the investment fund; in other words, to add it back to the original endowment. However, the amount that can be allocated in this way is capped by reference to inflation.

- Any part of the unapplied total return which is not either allocated to the trust for income or the trust for investment remains as part of the unapplied total return. This continues to be treated as permanent endowment pending further decisions to allocate it to the income fund or the investment fund. The terminology used can be confusing. But, in essence, the statutory power gives trustees the flexibility to hold permanent endowment funds in a way which enables them to respond to their charity's operating requirements, while always being required to justify the balance of unapplied total return that is held with a view to carrying out its objectives in the future.

Allocating the unapplied total return

10.161 The key issue for trustees in relation to the exercise of the statutory power is likely to be which part of the unapplied total return they should apply to the income fund and which part they should apply to the investment fund and the balance that should be retained as unapplied total return. Funds allocated to the income fund can be spent to further the aims of the charity and must (as with all other income of the charity) be applied within a reasonable period of time; if they are not, the trustees will need to justify their retention in the same as they must justify holding reserves. There is more about reserves at **9.66**.

10.162 In addition, the Commission's guidance is clear that, on each occasion on which trustees allocate part of the unapplied total return to the income fund, they must look at the total amount of total unapplied return available to them, rather than just the charity's investment return received in a particular financial year.

10.163   The key driver for the trustees' decision making is their duty to further the charity's aims both now and in the future. The Commission's guidance confirms that:[31]

> 'Trustees must be able to justify the balance of funds remaining as unapplied total return after any allocations to the income and/or investment funds have been made. The justification should be based on the need to ensure that the charity will be able to carry out its aims effectively in the future, even if there is a reduction in the charity's unapplied total return caused by a fall in the value of the charity's investment assets.'

10.164   The Commission's guidance also makes it clear that, when complying with this duty, trustees need to take into account fluctuations in investment returns from year to year (taking into account the effect of anticipated inflationary increases in the cost of the charity's operations), an analysis of potential investment risks and an understanding of likely changes in the services the charity provides.

10.165   Although there is no statutory requirement for trustees to adopt a policy about the way in which the unapplied total return should be treated, the Commission clearly expects that a policy of this kind should be adopted and adhered to. Its guidance states that trustees who do not have or act in accordance with a policy 'may be open to the same level of criticism levelled against charities … who keep excessive income reserves'.

10.166   The determination of the unapplied total return at the point at which the trustees wish to adopt the statutory power is also likely to be very important. Clearly, in some cases it may be difficult for the trustees to confirm the extent to which the permanent endowment fund they hold comprises capital gains. This is because under the 'standard rules' referred to above capital gains would not generally be distinguished from the assets representing the original endowment. The Commission's guidance confirms that there is some flexibility in relation to this determination:[32]

> 'Trustees won't be expected to carry out an elaborate tracing exercise here, as it might not be practical – particularly in the case of that part of the unapplied investment return which takes the form of capital gains rather than the form of retained investment income … In many cases trustees will have to make a "reasonable estimate" as to what part of their resources represents the unapplied investment return from the investment of the endowment. We cannot recommend any particular basis for making a reasonable estimate. How far back in time it is reasonable to go in making the analysis will depend on the charity's circumstances, the amounts involved, the state of the charity's records and so on. In some cases, it will not be practical to go back to the founding of the charity.'

10.167   This will be an important judgement for the trustees of the charity. How far back in time the trustees are able to go in determining what part of the

---

[31]   Total return investment for permanently endowed charities (December 2013), para E1.
[32]   Total return investment for permanently endowed charities (December 2013), para D6.

existing endowment comprises capital gains is likely to have a direct effect on the initial value of the unapplied total return, which will in turn determine the degree of flexibility the trustees will have going forward in allocating funds to the income and investment funds and the value of the retained unapplied total return.

Trustees' duties

10.168 As we have said (see **10.163**), the key duty for trustees when exercising the statutory power is their duty to exercise it in such a way as not to prejudice their ability to further the charity's aims both now and in the future.

10.169 There are a number of other duties connected to the exercise of the statutory power under the 2013 Regulations.

10.170 The trustees must use reasonable care and skill in dealing with the permanent endowment, taking into account any special knowledge they may have or hold themselves out as having. This is in line with the duty of care placed on trustees generally by the Trustee Act 2000 (see **10.81**).

10.171 Trustees are also obliged to take proper advice in relation to the exercise of the statutory power. This is very similar to the requirement to take advice in relation to financial investments. It must come from someone whom the trustees reasonably believe to be qualified to give it by his or her ability in and practical experience of financial matters. In practice, the advice is likely to come from an investment manager, an investment adviser or potentially also a trustee, if one of the trustees has the relevant financial experience and ability (although, in that case, the trustees will need to consider the extent to which they, and the trustee concerned, are content for the advice to be relied upon). In the Commission's view, trustees who give advice are responsible for the quality of the advice which they give and that they may be liable to the charity if the advice they give is negligent.

10.172 Trustees will need to consider this requirement carefully. It may be the advice is not reasonably required because the cost of obtaining it will be disproportionate.

Accounting and reporting

10.173 Trustees should also consider their accounting and reporting obligations in relation to total return. The trustees' report will need to explain how the value of the investment fund has been established and should also explain the considerations and policies that the trustees have taken into account in their ongoing allocations of the unapplied total return to the income fund or, as the case may be, the investment fund. If the trustees do take advice, the person providing the advice must be named in the report.

10.174 The 2013 Regulations do not place any particular accounting disclosure requirements on charities in relation to total return. However, the Commission's guidance makes it clear that, under SORP principles, the statement of the charity's financial activities in its accounts must record any allocation made from the unapplied total return or investment fund.

Adopting the statutory power

10.175 In order to be able to use the statutory power, there are a number of issues that the trustees need to consider before proceeding:

- There must be a clear valuation of the permanent endowment fund, together with a decision about the value of the original investment fund (which will, as explained above, determine the value of the unapplied total return as at the date on which the statutory power is first adopted).

- The trustees must resolve to adopt the statutory power, acting in the best interests of the charity.

- The trustees will need to decide how the power will be exercised in practice. This may well be on an annual basis in line with financial planning and budgetary cycles, although it could be exercised more or less frequently than that (there is no statutory requirement in relation to this). It is important to appreciate that the power must be properly exercised on every occasion on which trustees wish to allocate funds from the unapplied total return. Advice will be required in relation to each exercise.

- In line with the Commission's guidance, trustees should consider adopting a policy in relation to the exercise of the statutory power which makes it clear how they will approach allocations, taking into account issues such as fluctuations on investment returns, inflation and the likely income requirements of the charity going forward.

Release of capital

10.176 The 2013 Regulations also give the trustees of a permanent endowment fund a limited power to release some of the original endowment (ie the investment fund) so it can be applied as income. This is subject to the duties to act in the best interests of the charity and to take proper advice.

10.177 There are a number of restrictions on the exercise of this power under the 2013 Regulations. The amount released cannot be more than 10% of the value of the investment fund at the relevant time (taking into account any previous releases) and, importantly, must be repaid or 'recouped' by the charity. The Regulations allow the charity to decide over what period and at what rate the amount should be replaced, but trustees will need to make a clear decision about this taking into account all relevant issues and taking advice where appropriate.

Total return orders

10.178 Some charities may already have an Order made by the Charity Commission giving the trustees the power to adopt a total return approach to investment. Such Orders are likely to contain provisions similar to those required by the 2013 Regulations, but the Regulations will only override an Order if the trustees pass a resolution to operate a total return approach in accordance with the Regulations. This will effectively discharge any existing Order. Having said this, if the Order contains any obligations to 'recoup' capital, these must continue to be complied with.

CHAPTER 11

TAXATION

11.1 There is a popular misconception that charities are eligible for a blanket exemption from tax in respect of all and any of their activities. In reality, the blanket is more of a patchwork, with scope for liabilities for tax to arise where particular activities or transactions are not properly considered or structured by a charity's trustees beforehand.[1]

11.2 Why is this a governance issue? The Charity Commission's view (expressed in its 1988 Report) is that charity trustees may be

> '… personally liable to account for taxation liabilities which are unnecessarily incurred directly or indirectly as a result of the inefficient administration of the charity.'

11.3 From the point of view of good governance, therefore, the duty owed by a charity's trustees in relation to tax liabilities is clear. Given the scope of activities within which liability to tax can arise (whether in relation to investment, trading or fundraising), this duty is fairly onerous.

11.4 The way in which charities are taxed is the subject of a book in itself. In this chapter, we do no more than summarise the framework for the taxation of charities with the view to highlighting some of the more significant issues that may arise in practice. In order to do this, we explain:

- what constitutes a 'charity' for tax purposes;
- how the income and capital gains of incorporated and unincorporated charities are charged to tax, subject to any exemptions;
- the exemptions from tax on the income and capital gains of charities that are available;
- the restrictions on these exemptions that are aimed at countering tax avoidance; and
- the tax treatment of donations of cash and other assets by individuals and commercial entities.

---

[1] All tax rates referred to in this chapter are as applicable for the Tax Year 2013/14.

'CHARITY' FOR TAX PURPOSES

11.5   As we have mentioned in **Chapter 1** a 'charity' is defined differently for the purposes of charity law and tax, although the definitions are very similar. The Finance Act 2010 introduced a new statutory definition of charity and other organisations entitled to UK charity tax reliefs.[2] The definition now applies for all tax purposes. To qualify as a charity for tax purposes, a body of persons or a trust must satisfy four conditions. It must:

(a)   be established for charitable purposes only;

(b)   meet the jurisdiction condition;

(c)   meet the registration condition; and

(d)   meet the management condition.

11.6   A charity must be established for charitable purposes only. This is the same meaning as set out in Charities Act 2011, s 2 for charities in England and Wales but the meaning is extended to cover charities wherever they are established.

11.7   A charity meets the jurisdiction condition if it is within the authority of the High Court in the UK or if established in another member state (of the EU) or a territory specified in regulations within the authority of a court in that corresponding jurisdiction.

11.8   A charity meets the registration condition provided it complies with the requirements to be registered under the law of the relevant country.

11.9   A charity will meet the management condition provided the persons responsible for the general management and control of the administration of the charity are fit and proper persons to hold that position. There is no statutory definition of a fit and proper person. HM Revenue & Customs has set out its views in a detailed guidance note.[3] This explains the procedures HM Revenue & Customs will follow in operating the fit and proper persons test and suggests the steps a charity should take to ensure it complies with this requirement.

EU LAW AND OTHER TERRITORIES

11.10   The scope of exemptions from UK tax are now extended to charities established under the laws of other EU jurisdictions and other territories specified in regulations. The regulations currently extend to the Republic of Iceland and the Kingdom of Norway.[4]

---

[2]   Finance Act 2010, Sch 6, para 1.
[3]   HMRC Charities: detailed guidance notes, Chapter 2, paragraph 2.1.6.
[4]   The Taxes (Definition of Charity) (Relevant Territories) Regulations 2010, SI 2010/1904.

LIABILITY TO TAX

11.11 The way in which a charity is constituted will determine the tax to which it will be liable in the event that there is no exemption available.

11.12 Charitable trusts are potentially liable to pay income tax on their taxable income and capital gains tax on their capital gains. The liability to income tax is the basic rate (presently 20%) or, where the income in question is less than £2,790 and is savings income, the starting rate (presently 10%) applies. Charitable trusts are not subject to the 'rate applicable to trusts' paid by private trusts,[5] which would bring the rate of income tax up to 50% (45% from 6 April 2013). However, a charitable trust does pay capital gains tax at the 'rate applicable to trusts' on its capital gains. The rate is therefore presently 28%, subject to an annual exemption. Trusts are generally entitled to half the annual exemption afforded to individuals.

11.13 Charitable companies, and any other charity which is a 'corporation' for tax purposes, pay corporation tax in respect of both their income and profits arising on chargeable gains. The rate of tax that applies will depend upon the level of taxable profit. Profits of less than £300,000 are charged to tax at 20%. Profits in excess of £1,500,000 are charged at 23%. Where profits fall between these two figures a 'marginal' rate of tax applies.

11.14 For tax purposes, a 'corporation' will include charitable companies limited by guarantee and by shares, CIOs, industrial and provident societies, friendly societies, corporations and also charitable unincorporated associations.

11.15 Where a charitable company is 'close', it is likely to be a 'close investment-holding company'. This means that the company is not entitled to pay corporation tax at the lower rate of 20%.[6] A company is 'close' if it is under the control of five or fewer participators or any number of participators who are also its directors. A 'participator' is any person who exercises voting rights in relation to a company. This will include not only the members of charitable companies, but also the members of any charitable unincorporated association. In many cases, a charitable company's trustees will also be its members, so that the company will be close irrespective of the number of trustees.

11.16 A charitable close company will generally be an 'investment-holding' company. This is because its charitable purposes will prevent it from qualifying for any of the exceptions in the tax legislation from the definition of 'investment-holding'. These include, for example, existing wholly or mainly for the purpose of carrying on a trade. While a charitable company may well carry on a trade, it will not exist wholly and mainly for this purpose.

---

[5]   Income Tax Act 2007, s 481(1)(c).
[6]   Corporation Tax Act 2010, s 18.

EXEMPTIONS FROM TAX ON INCOME

11.17 Part 10 of the Income Tax Act 2007 (charitable trusts etc) and Part 11 of the Corporation Tax Act 2010 (charitable companies etc) give charities a number of significant exemptions from tax on particular types of income. This reflects the scheme of the income tax legislation generally, which categorises and taxes different types of income according to their 'source'.

11.18 There are two general requirements that must be satisfied in order for each of the specific exemptions to apply. The first is that the income in question is actually the income of a 'charity' for tax purposes. The second is that the income must be 'applied to charitable purposes only'. We look at the way in which income is applied to charitable purposes only in more detail at **11.47**.

Trading income

11.19 There are a number of specific exemptions that apply to a charity's trading income. These are explained in more detail in **Chapter 13**. In general, the exemptions summarised below relate to a charity's investment income. There is more about investment generally in **Chapter 10**.

Deduction of tax

11.20 Many of the sources of income mentioned below (eg bank interest) will have tax deducted from them at source. The availability of an exemption from tax will enable the charity to reclaim the tax deducted. There is more about tax reclaims at **11.160**.

Income from land

11.21 There is an exemption from tax on rent and other profit and gains received in respect of land (whether inside or outside the UK). This includes a beneficial interest in land vested in the charity, where the legal title is held by a nominee on its behalf.[7]

11.22 There is a specific anti-avoidance provision which charges to income tax gains arising from the disposal of land by a charity.[8] Although this is an 'anti-avoidance' provision, it is wide enough to catch any land that is obtained, held or developed with the intention of realising a gain on its disposal. In practice, a charge is often triggered where charity trustees selling land with the potential for development do so on the basis that they are entitled to a share in any profits that are realised if the land is actually subsequently developed.

11.23 It is also possible that, in certain circumstances, HM Revenue & Customs may argue that a disposal of land is part of a trade of property development being carried out by the charity. Because property development

---

[7]   Income Tax Act 2007, s 531 and Corporation Tax Act 2010, s 485.
[8]   Income Tax Act 2007, s 755 and Corporation Tax Act 2010, s 818.

cannot be a primary purpose trade of a charity, any trading profits are unlikely to qualify for exemption for tax. There is more about this in **Chapter 13**.

11.24 The key issue for charity trustees in relation to any proposal to dispose of land is to seek professional tax advice on the position at an early stage.

Interest and annual payments

11.25 Section 532 of the Income Tax Act 2007 and s 486 of the Corporation Tax Act 2010 exempt all payments of interest to a charity from tax. These include, for example, interest payable on bonds and loan notes issued by companies, local authorities, governments etc. It does not matter whether or not the interest has a UK 'source'. In other words, the exemption applies whether the interest is paid by an entity that is resident inside or outside the UK.

11.26 The same provisions also exempt from tax 'annual payments', again irrespective of whether they have UK or an overseas source. Annual payments are explained in more detail at **13.68**. For the purposes of this exemption, they include royalties and gift aid donations payable to the charity.

Dividends

11.27 There is an exemption from tax for dividends received in respect of shares held by a charity.[9] This exemption also extends to all other forms of 'distribution' by a company in which a charity owns shares, irrespective of whether the company is resident in the UK or overseas. The exemption also applies to distributions from unit trusts, OEICs and other forms of collective investment schemes.

11.28 Although dividends and other distributions are exempt from tax, they will have been paid out of the company's taxed profits. Charities are not able to reclaim the tax paid by a UK resident company, which will be tax at a rate of 20% to 23%. In the case of an overseas company, the tax paid by it on its profits will be at whatever rate applies in the overseas jurisdiction (but see the comments at **11.41** for more on this).

Insurance policies

11.29 Where a charity invests in an insurance policy, a tax charge can arise when the policy matures or in certain other circumstances specified by the tax legislation. The rules governing the way in which policies are taxed are complicated, depending in part upon the type of policy in question and the terms on which it is issued.

---

[9] Income Tax Act 2007, s 532(b) and (c) and Corporation Tax Act 2010, s 486(2)(b).

11.30   The key point is that any gain in the value of the policy (which will reflect any increase in the value of the insurer's underlying investments) will be liable to tax in the hands of the charity. A tax credit is available to a charitable trust in certain circumstances, but incorporated charities and unincorporated associations do not qualify for an exemption.

11.31   There are in any event two other significant issues that need to be taken into account by a charity that is looking to invest in insurance policies. First, HM Revenue & Customs does not regard them as 'qualifying investments' for the purpose of the rules on charitable expenditure (there is more about this at **11.58**). Second, any return on the policy will be net of the tax paid by the insurer, which may mean that the net benefit to the charity is lower than the net benefit that can be received from other forms of investment.

Stock lending

11.32   The tax treatment of stock loans and stock lending fees is complex and may give rise to tax liabilities for charities. Trustees should seek professional advice before entering into stock loans.

Swaps

11.33   Where a charity enters into swap arrangements as part of its investment strategy (and HM Revenue & Customs will assess whether the charity has complied with the Charity Commission's guidance in relation to the appropriate use of swaps in this context)[10] an incorporated charity or unincorporated association can claim an exemption in respect of any profits arising from the swap. However, where the swap transaction is entered into by a charitable trust, an exemption is only likely to be available under the small trades exemption. There is more about this at **13.38**.

11.34   If HM Revenue & Customs concludes that a swap transaction is entered into as part of a trade rather than as an investment, any profits received by the charity will qualify for exemption on the same basis as any other trading income. There is more about this at **13.29**.

Futures and options

11.35   Where a charitable trust (but not a charitable company) enters into futures and options as part of its investment strategy, and the futures and options are structured in such a way that they produce a return which is both guaranteed and is substantially the same as interest, it will pay income tax on the payments unless they fall within the exemption for small trades. There is more about this at **13.38**. An incorporated charity or an unincorporated association will generally be able to claim an exemption from tax.[11]

---

[10]   HM Revenue & Customs' Tax Bulletin 66.
[11]   Income Tax Act 2007, s 526.

Underwriting fees

11.36 Underwriting fees are not generally exempt from tax. Trustees will need to take professional advice on the tax treatment of such fees.

EXEMPTION FROM TAX ON CAPITAL GAINS

11.37 Section 256(1) of the Taxation of Chargeable Gains Act 1992 exempts from tax capital gains that accrue to a charity and are 'applicable and applied for charitable purposes'. In essence, therefore, there are two general requirements that must be satisfied in order for this exemption to apply. These are essentially the same as the requirements that apply to the exemptions from tax on income. The first is that the capital gains are actually capital gains of a 'charity' for tax purposes. A 'charity' is now defined in statute. There is more about this at **11.5**.

11.38 The second requirement of the capital gains tax exemption requires that the capital gains must be 'applied for charitable purposes'. This has the same meaning as set out in Charities Act 2011, s 2.

11.39 The capital gains in question must also be 'applicable for' charitable purposes. It is difficult to see what this adds to the other two requirements given that, between them, they ensure that the exemption is only available where the charity is actually a charity (and therefore established for charitable purposes) and that the capital gain must only be applied for those charitable purposes.

11.40 Unlike the different exemptions that apply in relation to tax on different types of income, there is only a single exemption in respect of tax on capital gains. This will apply in almost every situation providing the requirements we have mentioned above are satisfied. However, it is worth mentioning that capital gains can in certain circumstances be deemed to arise. Given the practical difficulty of showing that deemed gains have been applied for charitable purposes, it is possible that HM Revenue & Customs may not allow exemption in certain circumstances. The most notable example of this is where a close company which is resident for tax purposes outside the UK realises gains. The anti-avoidance provisions in the capital gains tax legislation will deem the gains to have been realised by certain participators in the company. Where this includes a charity, an exemption from capital gains tax is unlikely to be available.[12] There is more about close companies at **11.15**.

OVERSEAS INVESTMENTS

11.41 As we have explained, the exemptions from income and capital gains available to charities will generally apply irrespective of whether the investment

---

[12] Taxation of Chargeable Gains Act 1992, s 13; Budget notice 5/01.

that generates the income or gains is inside or outside the UK. In terms of UK tax, this obviously gives a charity's trustees the flexibility to consider including overseas investments as part of their overall investment strategy.

11.42 Having said this, it is obviously important that the charity's trustees take into account any foreign taxes that may be payable in respect of particular investments. While, for example, rental income from land in an overseas jurisdiction may be free of UK tax, there is unlikely to be an exemption within that jurisdiction for rental income payable to a UK charity. Any overseas tax that is payable will obviously reduce the net returns of the charity on its investment. This is a very important consideration for trustees when they are determining their investment strategy.

11.43 In practice, relief from overseas tax will generally only be available under a 'double tax treaty' between the UK and the overseas jurisdiction in question. The UK has a very wide range of double tax treaties. While most will not refer to charities expressly, it may be possible to claim double treaty relief from overseas tax in certain circumstances. There are a number of potential issues for charities in relation to double tax treaties, not least that relief is usually only available to entities which are 'liable to tax'. While there is a good argument that charities are liable to UK tax, subject only to the wide range of exemptions and reliefs that are available, the position is not absolutely certain.

11.44 In practice, any charity looking to invest overseas will need to take advice on any foreign taxes which are payable and then look in some detail at the availability of double taxation relief.

GIFTS AND DONATIONS

11.45 While gifts and donations to a charity will form part of its income for the purposes of charity law, they are not 'income' for tax purposes. This means that, with two exceptions, there is no specific exemption from tax in respect of funds donated to a charity.

11.46 The exceptions we have mentioned are donations by individuals that qualify for gift aid relief and donations made between charities. Both of these kinds of donation are deemed by the tax legislation to be taxable income of the charity that receives them. However, both also qualify for a specific exemption from tax (they are, in fact, treated in the same way as 'annual payments'; there is more about this at **11.26**).

APPLICATION FOR CHARITABLE PURPOSES ONLY

11.47 As we have mentioned, the exemptions from tax on both income and capital gains are subject to a requirement that the income and gains in question are applied for (or 'to') charitable purposes only. This requirement relates only to a charity's income and capital gains and not, for example, to the way in which it may spend any other financial resources. There are specific rules relating to 'charitable expenditure' which are intended to deal with this wider issue. These are explained in more detail at **11.58**.

11.48 Income and gains will be applied by a charity for charitable purposes only where the way in which they are applied is authorised by the charity's constitution. Clearly, this will include grants for the charity's purposes and operational activities that advance those purposes. But it will also include expenditure on the costs of maintaining and administering the charity so that it can continue to advance its charitable purposes.

11.49 Equally clearly, income and gains will not have been applied for charitable purposes only where they are applied in breach of the charity's constitution. This would include, for example, making a payment to a trustee in circumstances where the trustee is not entitled to be paid and has done nothing in return for the charity or where the charity makes payments for purposes that are not charitable (eg funding a political party or campaign).

11.50 In principle, applying income and gains for a purpose that is charitable but is not one of the charitable purposes specified in the charity's constitution will not breach the requirement.[13] HM Revenue & Customs appears to accept that this may be the case, while reserving its position:

> 'If expenditure is clearly of a charitable nature, but it is not specifically authorised by the terms of the governing document of the charity, it will not necessarily be treated as non-charitable expenditure.'[14]

11.51 Clearly, the application of funds for a charitable purpose which is outside the charity's own purposes will be a breach of the restrictions imposed by charity law and is also likely to be a breach of trust by the charity's trustees.

11.52 Where the Charity Commission makes an Order under Charities Act 2011, section 105 which deems a charity's trustees to have power to do something they do not otherwise have a power to do, there is a good argument that any income and gains applied pursuant to the Order will have been applied for charitable purposes only. The position is different where a charity's trustees seek Advice, because this merely protects trustees from personal liability rather than deeming them to have a power that they do not otherwise have. There is more about Advice and Orders at **4.17** and **4.22** respectively.

11.53 In certain circumstances, a charity may take the decision not to spend income that it receives. Its trustees may decide, for example, to make a reserve of income that can be spent to fund future projects. Or they may have a formal power to add the income to the charity's capital assets. This is usually referred to as 'accumulation'. There is more about reserves and accumulation at **9.66** and **9.52** respectively.

---

[13] *Ofrex (George Drexler) Foundation (Trustees) v IRC* [1965] 3 All ER 529.
[14] HM Revenue & Customs' Guidance Note Annex II.7.

11.54   HM Revenue & Customs' view is that:

'Where a charity accumulates income, or builds up reserves, we need to decide if this is within the meaning of the phrase "applied for charitable purposes only".'[15]

11.55   Clearly, the concern is that the income that is held in reserve or added to capital cannot have actually been 'applied'. But the Courts have concluded previously that income that is accumulated or reserved can be treated as 'applied for charitable purposes' where this is properly done.[16] Provided, therefore, that income is properly accumulated in accordance with a power conferred upon a charity's trustees or added to its reserves in accordance with the duties imposed upon the trustees in relation to reserves generally, the income will have been applied for charitable purposes only.

11.56   HM Revenue & Customs mentions two other circumstances in which it will argue that accumulated and reserved income has not been applied for charitable purposes only:

'HMRC Charities will challenge accumulations of income on the grounds that the income has not been applied to charitable purposes:

- if income is not invested at all but kept in cash or in a current account; or
- if it becomes apparent that investment decisions are not made exclusively for the benefit of the charity, e.g. where accumulated income is being invested in a project in which there is a potential conflict of interest between the interest of the charitable trust and the interest of the trustee or provider of the trust funds.'[17]

11.57   In certain circumstances, a charity's trustees may enter into a transaction that is in breach of the charity's constitution and also qualifies as a breach of trust by the trustees. This might be because, for example, the charity enters into a transaction with one of the trustees that is not authorised by its constitution. The courts have concluded previously that where a breach of trust of this kind does not result in any disadvantage to the charity, any income or capital gains paid by the charity to the trustee will still have been applied for charitable purposes only, notwithstanding that a breach of trust may have occurred. The position will be different where the breach of trust has clearly resulted in the trustee benefiting at the expense of the charity.

CHARITABLE EXPENDITURE

11.58   As we have explained, the charitable expenditure rules supplement the requirement for the expenditure of income and capital gains for charitable purposes only. The rules are essentially straightforward:

---

[15]   HM Revenue & Customs' Guidance Note Annex II.8.
[16]   *Nightingale v Price* [1996] STC (SCD) 116.
[17]   HM Revenue & Customs' Guidance Note Annex II.8.

- The tax legislation distinguishes between 'charitable expenditure' and 'non-charitable expenditure'. Charitable expenditure is expenditure that is 'exclusively for charitable purposes'. All other expenditure (and certain things that, although not strictly 'expenditure', are deemed to be expenditure by a charity) is non-charitable.

- 'Expenditure which is exclusively for charitable purposes' is not defined by the tax legislation but, in our view, it has the same meaning as 'applied for charitable purposes only'.

- Certain things are deemed by the tax legislation to be non-charitable expenditure. These are:
  - any investment made by the charity that is not a 'qualifying investment'
  - any loan made by the charity that is not an investment and also fails to meet the criteria for a 'qualifying loan'
  - any payment to an overseas body where the charity has failed to take reasonable steps to ensure that the payment will be applied for charitable purposes
  - certain payments made on transactions with a 'substantial donor'.

  Each of these four categories of non-charitable expenditure is explained in more detail below.

- Where a charity incurs any non-charitable expenditure, the charity's ability to claim exemption from tax on its income and capital gains is restricted. The exemption the charity could otherwise claim is restricted by an amount equal to its non-charitable expenditure. This is on a 'pound for pound' basis.

- If the charity's non-charitable expenditure exceeds both its income and capital gains and any non-taxable income (including donations), the excess can be carried back to previous 'chargeable periods' and set against the income and gains and non-taxable income of previous years. It cannot be carried back for more than 6 years before the end of the chargeable period in which the non-charitable expenditure was actually incurred.

- The 'chargeable period' in respect of which a charity's relevant income and gains and non-charitable expenditure is assessed will depend upon the way in which it is constituted. The chargeable period for a charitable trust is the tax year ending 5 April. For a charity that is incorporated or a charitable unincorporated association, the chargeable period is the period in respect of which it makes up its accounts (often the period of 12 months to 31 December or 31 March in each year).

11.59 Essentially, therefore, whether or not the charitable expenditure rules give rise to a liability to tax for a charity will depend whether it has incurred any expenditure which is not exclusively for charitable purposes and, in particular, whether it has made any non-qualifying investments or loans; made payments to an overseas body without taking reasonable steps to ensure that the funds paid over can only be applied for charitable purposes; or entered into any transactions with any of its substantial donors. Each of these four items of non-charitable expenditure is examined in more detail below.

11.60 Because a charity must self-assess itself in respect of its liability to tax, it is obviously essential that its trustees understand how the charitable expenditure rules work and their implications and that they take professional advice where required.

Non-qualifying investments

11.61 A non-qualifying investment is any investment made by a charity which does not feature on a list of 'qualifying' investments set out in the Income Tax Act 2007, s 558 and 561 or the Corporation Tax Act 2010, ss 511 and 514. There is more about what constitutes an 'investment' in **Chapter 10**.

11.62 The investments mentioned in the Income Tax Act 2007, s 558 or the Corporation Tax Act 2010, s 511 are as follows:

- Any investment falling within Trustee Investment Act 1961, Schedule 1, Parts I, II or III (with the exception of Part II, paragraph 13). The 1961 Act specifies a number of 'safe' investments considered suitable for trustees in 1961. They include National Savings Certificates and UK Government bonds.

- Any investment in a common investment fund or common deposit fund. There is more about funds of this kind in **Chapter 10**.

- Any interest in land (except an interest in land which is held as security for a debt).

- Shares or securities issued by a company that are listed on a 'recognised stock exchange'. HM Revenue & Customs maintains a list of recognised stock exchanges for tax purposes. This includes shares listed on the Alternative Investment Market (or 'AIM').

- Units and authorised unit trusts and shares in an OEIC (open ended investment company).[18]

- Any deposit with a bank where the bank pays interest at a commercial rate (except where the deposit is made as part of an arrangement (usually the giving of 'back to back' security) under which a loan is made by the bank to some other person on the strength of the deposit by the charity).

- Uncertificated eligible debt security units.[19]

- Certificates of deposit.

- A loan or other investment which HM Revenue & Customs is satisfied is made for the benefit of the charity and not for the avoidance of tax (whether by the charity or by any other person). For this purpose, a loan includes a loan which is secured by a mortgage or a charge over any land.

11.63 Clearly, this final category will be very important where a charity wishes to invest in any asset that does not appear in any of the other categories we

---

[18] Financial Services and Markets Act 2000, s 237.
[19] Income Tax Act 2007, s 986(3).

have mentioned. The best examples are a direct investment in private equity (because buying unlisted shares in a company is not one of the specified categories of qualifying investment) or an interest in a hedge fund.

11.64 The first requirement for an asset to be a qualifying investment under this category is that it is made for 'the benefit of the charity'. There is no statutory definition of this test nor of what 'benefit' means, but HM Revenue & Customs will assess the position at the time the investment or loan in question is made. HM Revenue & Customs also states in its guidance that 'an investment or loan will normally be "for the benefit of the charity" where it is made to generate a flow of income or capital appreciation to enable the charity to deliver its charitable objectives and is on sound commercial terms. Whether or not an investment or loan is commercially sound should be considered by reference to the circumstances prevailing at the time it was made and HM Revenue & Customs will look at the arrangements in the round'.[20]

11.65 In our view, the test of what is for the 'benefit' of a charity includes both an objective and a subjective element, in much the same way as the statutory duty of care imposed upon charity trustees in relation to the exercise of certain powers by the Trustee Act 2000, s 1. In this sense, trustees considering whether to buy a particular asset or to make a particular loan is for the benefit of their charity should ensure that there is some objective justification for their decision. HM Revenue & Customs' guidance is that:

'There is no one test of commercial soundness, and each case must be viewed on its own facts. Where the loan is an investment loan, HMRC will normally accept it is for the financial benefit of the charity where it:

- carries a commercial rate of interest which is paid and actively pursued; and
- is adequately secured; and
- is made under a formal written agreement which includes reasonable repayment terms.'[21]

11.66 It will obviously be essential from the point of view of the charity's trustees that they ensure that a full written record of their reasons for making a particular loan or investment is kept, together with any supporting advice or other evidence. Again, HM Revenue & Customs' guidance is helpful (although in the context of investments and loans to trading subsidiaries):

'HMRC may ask to see the:

- Business plans
- Cash flow forecasts
- Other business projections

---

[20]   HM Revenue & Customs' Guidance Note Annex III.4.
[21]   HM Revenue & Customs' Guidance Note Annex III.4.

which informed the charity's decision to make the investment.'[22]

11.67 In practice, the question of whether or not a particular investment or loan can qualify on this basis is thrown into sharp relief where a charity is considering investing in its trading subsidiary. There is more information about the considerations that should be taken into account by a charity's trustees in relation to any investment in a trading subsidiary at **13.80**.

For the avoidance of tax

11.68 Again, there is no statutory definition of what constitutes tax avoidance, although a long line of decisions by the courts indicate that they are often reluctant to conclude that the avoidance of tax is a motive for a particular transaction, particularly where there is some commercial purpose involved. The General Anti-Abuse Rule (GAAR), that came into force on 17 July 2013, is one of the government's approaches to managing the risk of tax avoidance. It has been introduced to strengthen HM Revenue & Customs' anti-avoidance strategy and assists HM Revenue & Customs in tackling abusive arrangements. The GAAR does not contain a definition of tax avoidance; rather it describes arrangements giving rise to a tax advantage that are abusive.

11.69 The fact that a charity is making an investment or a loan that it considers will be a qualifying investment and will not therefore be liable to tax is not, in itself, tax avoidance. In our view, the same is true of any investment in a charity's trading subsidiary. While, on one analysis, this avoids tax on trading income that would have been payable had the charity carried out the trade itself, the arrangement is so clearly approved of by both HM Revenue & Customs and the Charity Commission that it is difficult to foresee the circumstances in which HM Revenue & Customs would argue that using a subsidiary is for the avoidance of tax.

Qualifying loans

11.70 Loans that are made as investments may be 'qualifying investments' under the rules explained above. Loans which are not made 'by way of investment' will only qualify as charitable expenditure if they fall within one of four specific categories:

- A loan made by one charity to another charity for charitable purposes only.
- A loan to a beneficiary of the charity that is made in the course of carrying out the purposes of the charity.
- Money placed on a current account with a bank (except where this is part of an arrangement under which a loan is made by the bank to some other person).

---

[22] HM Revenue & Customs' Guidance Note Annex III.5.

- Any other loan made for the benefit of the charity and not for the avoidance of tax (whether by the charity or some other person).

11.71 The provisions which require that the loan must be for the benefit of the charity and not for the avoidance of tax apply in exactly the same way as they do to qualifying investments.

Claims

11.72 Investments and loans that fall into the categories mentioned in **11.62** and **11.70** above will only constitute qualifying investments and qualifying loans if HM Revenue & Customs are satisfied 'on a claim made to them in that behalf' that the investment or loan in question is made for the benefit of the charity and not for the avoidance of tax.

11.73 However, there is no formal mechanism for a claim to be made in advance of the making of any investment or loan and, in practice, HM Revenue & Customs will usually refuse to comment on the position in advance. In practice, therefore, a claim can only really be made by a charity by assessing itself to tax on the basis that the investments and loan its makes are qualifying and ensuring that sufficient information is made available to HM Revenue & Customs in relation to the terms of the investment or loan to enable them to query the position if they consider it necessary either by way of a tax return or by making a formal claim. HM Revenue & Customs' guidance in relation to this is set out in Annex III.10.[23]

Payments to overseas bodies

11.74 Section 547 of the Income Tax Act 2007 and s 500 of the Corporation Tax Act 2010 state for payments representing expenditure incurred on or after 24 March 2010 that:

> 'A payment made (or to be made) to a body situated outside the United Kingdom is non-charitable expenditure under [s 543(1)(f) of the Income Taxes Act 2007 or s 496(1)(d) of the Corporation Tax Act 2010] if–
>
> (a) it is incurred for charitable purposes only, but
> (b) [the trustees of the charitable trust or the charitable company] has not taken such steps as [the Commissioners for Her Majesty's Revenue and Customs consider] are reasonable in the circumstances to ensure that the payment will be applied for charitable purposes.'

11.75 The aim is obviously to seek to ensure that funds paid to the bodies that may qualify as charities under the law of their own jurisdiction will apply them for purposes that are charitable under English law. As HM Revenue & Customs state in their guidance:

---

[23] HM Revenue & Customs' Guidance Note Annex III.10.

'Applied for charitable purposes" means applied for purposes which are regarded as charitable within Section 2 of the Charities Act (England and Wales) 2006. the same definition for charitable purpose applies for all charities claiming UK tax reliefs and exemptions, wherever the charity is located, whether in the UK or other member states of the EU, Iceland or Norway. It is not sufficient for the charity to establish that the overseas entity is a charity under its domestic law.'[24]

11.76 This makes sense, because registration as a charity in an overseas jurisdiction is no guarantee that it must apply its funds for purposes that are charitable under English law (for example, charity law in an overseas jurisdiction may allow charities to apply funds for 'political' purposes, which would not be acceptable under English law). Charities established in overseas jurisdictions may also be subject to a much lighter regulatory regime than the regime to which UK charities are subject. HM Revenue & Custom's guidance states that:

'It is not sufficient for the charity to establish that the overseas entity is a charity under the domestic law of the host country ... The charity trustees must be able to describe the steps they take, explain how those steps ensure charitable application of funds, demonstrate that those steps were reasonable and produce evidence that the steps were, in fact, taken. The steps taken are to "ensure" that the payment will be applied for charitable purposes. If the recipient body overseas is not bound by its own domestic law to apply all of its income for charitable purposes, then the UK charity should consider seeking a legally binding agreement to ensure that the payment will be applied charitably. It the overseas body declines to enter into such an agreement, the trustees may have difficulty ensuring that the payment is applied for charitable purposes. If an agreement is entered into the UK charity will need to have a means of establishing whether the agreement has been complied with.'[25]

11.77 HM Revenue & Customs' general guidance is also helpful:

'When considering whether the steps taken by the charity were "reasonable in the circumstances", [HM Revenue & Customs] will have regard to:

• The charity's knowledge of the overseas body.
• Previous relations with and past history of that body, the amounts given in both absolute and relative terms.

Trustees are expected to make adequate enquiries to find out such information as is reasonably available about the overseas body and what evidence will be provided by that body to show that payment(s) will or have been applied for charitable purposes.

The nature of the steps will depend upon the scale of operations and size of the sums involved.

---

[24] HM Revenue & Customs' Guidance Note Annex II.9.1.
[25] HM Revenue & Customs' Guidance Note Annex II.9.1, 9.2 and 9.8.

In the case of small one-off payments an exchange of correspondence between the charity and the overseas body will normally be sufficient. Where possible, the correspondence should be on headed paper and it should:

- give details of the payment and the purpose for which it is given; and
- give confirmation that the sum has or will be applied for the purposes given.

More thorough work by the trustees will be required where the sums involved are large or where a transfer forms part of an ongoing commitment. This might include independent verification of the overseas body's status and activities; and reporting and verification of the manner of application of resources provided. The steps required can be reviewed in the light of evidence of proper use of funds and resources from earlier involvement with a particular project.'[26]

HM Revenue & Customs has updated its guidance at chapter 9 of its Guidance Note at Annex II to include examples of the steps to be taken and evidence required appropriate to the monetary sums involved and the scale of operations.

11.78 When HM Revenue & Customs reviews a payment to an overseas body in any detail, it will generally ask the charity's trustees to provide information about:

- '• The person or persons to whom the payment was given
- For what charitable purpose it was given
- What guarantees have been given that the payment will be applied for the purpose for which it was given
- What steps the trustees took to ensure the payment will be applied for charitable purposes
- What follow-up action the trustees took to confirm the payments were applied properly

If HMRC Charities is not provided with sufficient evidence of the steps taken it may not be able to accept the expenditure as charitable expenditure. This may give rise to a liability to tax.'[27]

11.79 Finally, HM Revenue & Customs' guidance confirms that a charity should be taking 'specialist advice as necessary'.[28]

11.80 There is no mechanism for a charity to apply for clearance in any event.

Substantial donors

11.81 The Finance Act 2006 introduced provisions aimed at restricting the tax exemptions available to charities entering into certain transactions with a substantial donor for transactions occurring after 21 March 2006. This was to

---

[26] HM Revenue & Customs' Guidance Note Annex II.9.3, 9.5, 9.6 and 9.7
[27] HM Revenue & Customs' Guidance Note Annex II.9.4.
[28] HM Revenue & Customs' Guidance Note Annex II.9.Example 3b.

counter the perceived abuse where individuals were donating cash or other assets to charities with a view to obtaining relief from tax while also retaining the economic benefit of the cash or assets that have been given away. This might be, for example, by way of a gift aid donation of cash that is then loaned back to the donor on an interest-free basis.

11.82 Further, the Finance Act 2011 introduced the new concept of 'tainted donations' in respect of charitable donations made on or after 1 April 2011. There is more information in relation to tainted donations at **11.90**.

11.83 The substantial donors legislation was largely repealed from 1 April 2011. However, it will continue to apply to substantial donor transactions occurring up to and including 31 March 2013 with donors who were substantial donors before 1 April 2011. For transactions occurring from 1 April 2013, the substantial donors legislation is repealed unless the transaction occurring on or after 1 April 2013 is the result of a contractual obligation entered into before that date. Such transactions will continue to be treated under the substantial donors legislation. Any other substantial donor transaction where the payment is made on or after 1 April 2011 that is not 'tainted' will not result in a restriction of relief for the charity.

11.84 Broadly, the provisions work as follows:

- They are aimed at transactions between charities and 'substantial donors'. A 'substantial donor' to a charity in respect of any 'chargeable period' is anyone who has given £25,000 or more to the charity in any period of 12 months that falls wholly or partly within the chargeable period or has given £150,000 (previously £100,000) or more over a period of 6 years falling wholly or partly within the chargeable period.

- The donations must have qualified for relief from tax in order for the donor to be a 'substantial donor'. This will include gift aid relief, gifts of shares and other securities and gifts of land.

- The 'chargeable period' for a charity is, in the case of a charitable trust, the period of 12 months to 5 April in each year and, in the case of an incorporated charity or unincorporated association, its accounting period (often the 12-month period to 31 December or 31 March in each year).

- Individuals who would have been substantial donors on the basis of either of the criteria mentioned above in the previous five chargeable periods of the charity will be deemed to be substantial donors. However gifts that have qualified for relief from tax received by a charity on or after 1 April 2011 are disregarded.

- The rules treat any payment made by a charity to a 'substantial donor' in the course of or for the purposes of a number of specified transactions as 'non-charitable expenditure'.

- The transactions in question are:
  - the sale or letting of property by a substantial donor to the charity or vice versa;

- – the provision of services by a substantial donor to a charity or vice versa;
- – an exchange of property between a charity and a substantial donor;
- – the provision of financial assistance by a substantial donor to a charity or vice versa; and
- – investment by a charity in the business of a substantial donor.

- In addition, HM Revenue & Customs has a power to determine the cost to the charity of any payments it makes to a substantial donor where these are 'less beneficial to the charity than terms which might be expected in a transactions at arm's length'. The amount HM Revenue & Customs decides has been overpaid by the charity will also be deemed to be non-charitable expenditure. In other words, a market value can be put on the transaction in calculating the amount of non-charitable expenditure.

- Any payment of remuneration by a charity to a substantial donor is deemed to be non-charitable expenditure unless it is remuneration for his or her services as a trustee which has been approved by the Charity Commission, the courts or any other body with responsibility for regulating charities (such as the principal regulator of an exempt charity). Clearly, this will treat payments to a substantial donor for services other than acting as a trustee (eg professional services) provided to a charity as non-charitable expenditure even where they are authorised by a charity's constitution.

11.85 There are a number of exceptions from the substantial donor provisions. Broadly, these are:

- Transactions with a charity's trading subsidiary (which cannot be treated as a substantial donor in relation to the charity).
- Any investment in shares in listed companies.
- 'Arm's-length' business relationships between the charity and a substantial donor which do not form part of an arrangement for the avoidance of tax.
- Charitable service provision on terms that are no more favourable to the substantial donor than to anyone else.
- Any transaction at an undervalue that qualifies for exemption from capital gains tax.
- The provision of 'financial assistance' to a charity by a substantial donor, again on arm's-length terms where the assistance is not part of an arrangement for the avoidance of tax.
- Any transaction at an undervalue under which relief for gifts of shares or securities and/or land can be claimed.
- Any payment made by a charity or benefit received by a donor not exceeding the minimum benefit amount for gift aid purposes.

11.86 Clearly, it is essential that a charity is able to identify who its 'substantial donors' are and whether or not they have entered into any transactions with the charity that may give rise to a restriction of tax or relief under the 'charitable expenditure' rules, not least because of the requirement that the charity should self-assess itself to tax. This is made more complicated by the provisions that deem two or more 'connected' charities to be a single charity for the purposes of the substantial donor rules. 'Connected' means connected in a matter 'relating to the structure, administration or control of a charity'.[29] This is a very wide definition.

11.87 Other provisions deem certain donors to be 'connected' for the purposes of the rules, so that their donations must be looked at together in assessing whether either or both of them are substantial donors. Again, there is a wide definition of 'connected'.

11.88 The rules relating to substantial donors may potentially give rise to significant tax liabilities for charities deemed to have incurred non-charitable expenditure as a consequence. The key areas of difficulty are:

- The rules are solely a concern for the charity. Even if the donor proves to be a substantial donor and has subsequently entered into a transaction with the charity, the tax relief they may have claimed on their original gift to the charity is not at risk. The risk in relation to the rules lies, therefore, solely with the charity.

- There is no link between the amount of the original gift and the amount of the non-charitable expenditure the charity may incur under the rules. Clearly, a donor will need to have made a significant gift in the first place in order to qualify as a substantial donor, but even sums of this size may be small in comparison to the amount of non-charitable expenditure that may be incurred in relation to a later transaction.

- A donor may not become a 'substantial' donor for the purposes of the rules when he first makes a gift to the charity. It may only be the cumulative total of gifts made by the donor that bring the rules into play. Clearly, the onus is on the charity to maintain sufficiently detailed records of donations to it over a sufficiently long period of time (potentially up to 11 years) to ensure that it can identify who its substantial donors are.

11.89 The obvious example is the acquisition by a charity of shares in a private unlisted company in which a substantial donor also owns shares. The provisions will also catch the payment of any unauthorised remuneration by a charity to a substantial donor.

TAINTED DONATIONS

11.90 The Finance Act 2011 introduced new anti-avoidance legislation following representations that the substantial donors legislation was cumbersome and an administrative burden. In order for the donation to be 'tainted', the following three conditions must be met:

---

[29]   Income Tax Act 2007, ss 556 and 557, Corporation Tax Act 2010, ss 509 and 510.

- the donor, or person connected with him at the relevant time (known as the linked person), makes arrangements (before or after the donation is made) and it is reasonable to assume that the donation and arrangements would not have been made independently of each other;

- the main purpose, or one of the main purposes, of entering into the arrangements is that the linked person obtains a financial advantage, directly or indirectly from the donation receiving charity; and

- the donor is not a qualifying charity-owned company linked with the donation receiving charity.

11.91 Arrangements for these purposes are widely defined and include any kind of understanding, which need not be legally enforceable.

11.92 Examples of transactions where a financial advantage may be deemed to be obtained include:

- the sale, letting or exchange of property;

- the provision of services;

- the provision of a loan or any other form of financial assistance; and

- investment in business.

11.93 Where HM Revenue & Customs finds an incidence of a tainted donation is in point then tax relief is not available. The donor loses gift aid relief and the charity loses its relief if it is knowingly party to the offending arrangements. HM Revenue & Customs has published examples of situations where it considers whether a tainted donation is or is not in point in its Explanatory Notes to the Finance Bill 2011, Sch 3.[30]

DONATIONS BY INDIVIDUALS

11.94 As we have explained earlier in this chapter, most donations by individuals will not form part of a charity's taxable income. One of the exceptions is donations that qualify for gift aid relief, which are made liable to tax in the charity's hands by one provision in the tax legislation and exempted by another.

11.95 Essentially, there are four tax incentives available to individuals who wish to make donations to charity. These are:

- 'gift aid' relief from income and capital gains tax for gifts for donations of cash;

- income tax relief for gifts of shares and securities;

- income tax relief for gifts of land to charity; and

---

[30] See www.gov.uk/government/publications/finance-bill-2011.

- income tax relief for payroll giving.

Each of these incentives is explained in more detail below.

11.96 In addition to these tax incentives, there are two other exemptions from tax gifts to charity which are, in tax terms at least, generally neutral:

- gifts to charity do not give rise to a liability to capital gains tax; and
- gifts to charity are wholly exempt from inheritance tax.

GIFT AID

11.97 Gift aid relief is reasonably straightforward. It works as follows:

- Where an individual makes a donation of, say, £1,000 to a charity, he or she is treated for tax purposes as having made a donation of £1,250 from which basic rate income tax (at 20%) has been deducted.
- If the donor signs a gift aid declaration the charity can reclaim the basic rate tax (£250) from HM Revenue & Customs. The total value of the donation to the charity is therefore £1,250. The total cost to the donor is £1,000.
- In addition, higher rate and additional rate taxpayers can claim additional tax relief on donations on their tax returns. The relief is the difference between the basic and higher rates of income tax (ie up to 25%, at present rates) on the full amount of the gift (ie £1,250). The tax repayment due to the donor (£250 for higher rate taxpayers and £313 for additional rate taxpayers) further reduces the total cost of the gift to the donor (to £750 for higher rate taxpayers and £687 for additional rate taxpayers). And, if the donor has insufficient income to fully utilise this relief, the donor can claim it against his or her capital gains. The relief can also be carried back for one tax year.
- Relief may be at a different rate where the donor has dividend income because the rate of tax that applies to dividends paid to individuals differs from the rate that applies to other income.
- The donor must pay an amount of income tax or capital gains tax equal to the amount of basic rate tax the charity and any other charities or community amateur sports clubs (CASCs) the donor donates to will reclaim on their gift. The donor may be UK resident or non-UK resident provided sufficient UK tax has been charged.
- Gift aid donations must be payments of cash. The waiver of a loan previously made to a charity by one of its supporters will not qualify for gift aid relief.
- The donor cannot receive any material benefit in return for the donations. There are, though, rules that allow donors benefits with a monetary value that falls within certain specified limits. These would include, for example,

free or reduced entry to heritage property or free or reduced subscriptions for a charity's publications. The limits are as follows:

Donations	Maximum benefit allowed
£0 – £100	25% of the value of the donation
£101 – £1,000	£25
£1,000 + made before 6 April 2011	5% of the value of the donation up to a maximum of £500
£1,000 + made on or after 6 April 2011	5% of the value of the donation up to a maximum of £2,500

- There are complicated rules that apply to 'annualise' the benefits received by donors. HM Revenue & Customs takes the view that the value of the benefit is judged by the value to the donor. Where these restrictions are likely to be breached, there may be scope for tax planning by using 'split payments'. This is explained in more detail in **13.62**.

11.98   In order to ensure that the gift aid regime is not abused, every donor is required to make a gift aid 'declaration' in respect of his or her donations. The charity will need a declaration in place before it can reclaim basic rate tax on the donations it receives.

11.99   Gift aid declarations are reasonably flexible. They can be given at any time, whether before or after a donation is made. They can also relate to a single donation or donations made at any time by the donor to the charity. In principle, they can also be made orally provided that the charity makes a written record of the oral declaration.

11.100   Written gift aid declarations must contain the following details:

- the donor's name and address;
- the name of the recipient charity;
- a description of the donation;
- a declaration that the donation is to be treated as a gift aid donation; and
- a note explaining that the donor must pay at least as much income and/or capital gains tax as the charity and any other charities and Community Amateur Sports Clubs (CASCs) they donate to will reclaim on their donation.

11.101   There is no requirement that the declaration should be signed, but this is useful proof of the position.

11.102   A charity will need to be able to produce its gift aid records to HM Revenue & Customs in order to support its claims for tax to be repaid. There is a useful model form of declaration on HM Revenue & Customs' website (www.hmrc.gov.uk/charities). HM Revenue & Customs expects charities to follow the new wording. HM Revenue & Customs has corrected an error in its guidance which previously incorrectly stated that the 4-year time limit for making claims also applied to the retention of records. The revised guidance confirms that records must be kept for at least 6 years.

11.103 Gift aid donations can be made under a deed of covenant that obliges a donor to make payments to a charity, but there is no requirement for a covenant in order to claim tax relief (as there was in the past).

11.104 The Small Charitable Donations Act 2012 introduced the Gift Aid Small Donations Scheme (GASDS) enabling charities to claim a payment akin to gift aid on small cash donations where each donation is no more than £20 and the total number of small donations does not exceed £5,000 each year without a declaration from the donor. To be able to claim under GASDS, a charity must still make gift aid claims for other donations.

Gifts of shares and securities

11.105 Income tax relief is available in respect of gifts and sales at an undervalue of certain qualifying investments to UK charities. The following are qualifying investments:

- listed shares and securities (including AIM listed shares and the Plus markets);
- units in an authorised unit trust;
- shares in an OEIC; and
- interests in offshore funds.

11.106 Relief is given on the market value of the investment that is given away. Where the investment is sold to a charity at less than its market value, relief is given on the gift element, ie on the difference between the market value and the sale price. The relief also takes into account the incidental costs incurred by the donor in making the gift and in respect of certain (but not all) sales. Anti-avoidance legislation applies to reduce the value of the net benefit to the cost to the donor if the donor acquired the asset in the 4 years up to the date of the gift if part of an arrangement to obtain tax relief. In addition, certain liabilities in respect of obligations on the charity, where it is reasonable to suppose the donation would not have been made save for the obligation, may also be deducted from the value.

11.107 The relief is given by deducting the amount of the gift from the donor's total income before deducting personal allowances and reliefs. It is treated as a 'charge on income'. So a donor should consider limiting the donation to his or her total taxable income or (to maximise the tax advantage) total taxable income subject to higher or additional rate income tax.

11.108 The relief can only be set against a donor's income and not against chargeable gains, but any gain arising on the gift or sale of the investment to the charity is exempt from capital gains tax.

Gifts of land

11.109 Gifts of freehold or leasehold land and buildings also qualify for income tax relief, essentially on the market value of the land. Relief can only be claimed if the donor receives a certificate from the charity identifying the land, specifying the date of the gift and containing a statement that the charity has acquired it.

11.110 Joint owners of land must all agree to give it to a charity if the relief is to apply; they cannot simply give away their shares in it. But they can agree between them how to share the relief, irrespective of the shares in which they actually own the land.

11.111 See **11.106** for a summary of the anti-avoidance provisions.

Payroll giving

11.112 Under the payroll-giving scheme, employees can authorise their employer to deduct donations to charity from their wages before income tax is deducted under the PAYE scheme. This means that income tax relief is given at the highest rate at which the employee pays tax.

11.113 The relief given under the scheme is essentially the same as gift aid relief, except that the employee does not need to fill in a gift aid declaration. The charity is paid gross and relief is only available against PAYE income. The employer must also have agreed to operate the scheme.

STRUCTURING DONATIONS

11.114 Where a donor has the capacity to give cash or investments or land to a charity, the position will need to be looked at carefully in order to work out the optimum position for both donor and charity. The donor will need to consider carefully whether it is better to sell investments or land and give away the cash proceeds or to give away the assets themselves bearing in mind that:

- Gifts of cash qualify for gift aid, with 20% of the tax saving passing to the charity and up to 25% to the donor.
- A sale of investments or land to generate cash for a gift aid donation may give rise to capital gains (or losses).
- For some donors, optimum relief can be achieved by selling investments to charity at a value that does not give rise to a gain or a loss.

11.115 The fundamental point is that both charity and donor need to look carefully at the real cost to the donor of the gift (whether cash, shares or land) and the real benefit to the charity (again, whether cash, shares or land but taking into account the tax that can be reclaimed in respect of gift aid donations).

CAPITAL GAINS TAX RELIEF

11.116 A gift can give rise to a capital gain that is liable to tax. This is because any 'disposal' of an asset is treated as if it had been made for market value. However, the Taxation of Chargeable Gains Act 1992, s 257 provides that the disposal of an asset at arm's length to a charity is treated as a disposal which gives rise to 'neither a gain nor a loss'.

11.117 However, where the asset in question is disposed of by the donor to a charity in return for some 'consideration', tax is calculated on the basis of the consideration that is received by the donor rather than the market value of the assets. 'Consideration' is not defined by the Taxation of Chargeable Gains Act 1992 but is a fundamental part of the English law of contract. Put simply, 'consideration' is the price that one party pays to another in exchange for an undertaking to do something.

11.118 We mention the concept of 'consideration' because of the possibility that a charity may be asked to give a donor an indemnity in respect of liabilities that are attached to a particular asset. For example, a donor who wishes to give away land to a charity may (quite reasonably) ask the charity to indemnify him or her in respect of any environmental or other claims that attach to the land and may come out of the woodwork subsequently. Whether indemnities of this kind constitute consideration will need to be looked at carefully by both the charity and the donor in the context of the transaction as a whole, although our view is that seeking protection from liabilities that are an inherent part of an asset will not generally be 'consideration' in the sense intended by the legislation.

11.119 As we have indicated earlier in this chapter, both the charity and the donor should give careful thought to whether it would be better for the donor to sell an asset (giving rise to a capital gains tax liability) and give the proceeds to a charity (giving rise to relief from income and/or capital gains tax) or to give the asset itself to the charity (where the asset in question is listed shares or land, the donor can claim income tax relief as well as capital gains tax exemption on the gift). The optimum position for both donor and charity will vary from case to case.

INHERITANCE TAX

11.120 Gifts to a charity by an individual are wholly exempt from inheritance tax under the Inheritance Tax Act 1984, s 23, although they may also qualify for relief as 'normal expenditure out of income'.

11.121 Inheritance tax planning for individuals is a complex area. Existing charities can form part of tax planning arrangements, but only on the basis that the donor is willing to give up (both for him or herself and his or her estate) any claims to the assets which are given away.

11.122 The Finance Act 2012 introduced a reduced rate of inheritance tax to 36% (from 40%) on chargeable estates involving a charitable legacy of 10% or more. HM Revenue & Customs have issued a reduced rate calculator on their website together with guidance including example of a model clause that meets the 10% test.

DONATIONS BY COMPANIES

11.123 Gift aid donations by companies qualify for relief from corporation tax. They are, however, subject to similar restrictions to those that apply to gift aid donations by individuals. The most significant difference is that the benefit of gift aid for relief in respect of a donation by a company accrues wholly to the company itself. A donation by an individual will pass the benefit of basic rate tax relief to the charity, with higher rate tax relief available to the donor.

11.124 This is because relief for gift aid donations by a company is given by treating the donation as a 'charge on income'. This can be deducted from the company's taxable profits in calculating its liability to corporation tax. In other respects, the rules that govern gift aid donations by companies are very similar to those which govern gift aid donations by individuals. Donations must be of cash (rather than, say, by way of a loan). And, while there is no minimum amount that qualifies for relief, there are restrictions on the benefits that the company can receive in return for the donations.

11.125 A non-resident company can claim gift aid relief provided that it is liable to pay corporation tax on its profits. Like individual donations, relief can also be claimed in respect of payments made under a deed of covenant that obliges the company to pay a charity a particular sum, although there is no requirement for a covenant.

11.126 There is no requirement that a claim needs to be made by the company to HM Revenue & Customs and no gift aid declaration is required. In practice, HM Revenue & Customs may ask to see some evidence that the donation has actually been paid to a charity.

11.127 It is possible that HM Revenue & Customs may argue in certain circumstances that a payment by a company which is owned wholly or partly by a charity may be a 'distribution' rather than a gift aid donation. A 'distribution'[31] includes both dividends and 'any other distribution of assets of the company (whether in cash or otherwise) in respect of shares in the company'.

11.128 This is an argument that HM Revenue & Customs has raised previously, on the basis that a subsidiary company making payments to a parent charity has made a 'distribution' which is clearly 'out of the assets of the company' and is ostensibly 'in respect of shares in the company'. In practice, HM Revenue & Customs appears to accept that a payment by a wholly owned trading subsidiary to its parent charity should not be treated as a distribution, provided it is clearly a gift rather than a distribution in respect of shares. Where, on the other hand, a trading subsidiary held by a charity and one or more other shareholders makes gifts to its shareholders in proportion to their shareholdings, HM Revenue & Customs is likely to take the view that the payments are distributions in respect of shares in the subsidiary. That is not to say that every payment by a partly owned trading subsidiary to a shareholder charity will be a distribution. The position will depend upon whether the payment is genuinely a gift or is, in reality, a distribution in respect of the charity's shareholdings.

OTHER TAX-FREE GIFTS BY BUSINESS

11.129 Certain payments by businesses count as 'business expenses' and are therefore deductible in calculating their tax liabilities. In outline, these are donations for technical education conducted at approved institutes and for approved scientific research and small gifts to charity. In each case, the education, research or projects must be related to the trade of the business making the payment.

11.130 Certain gifts in kind to schools and universities of trading stock and other articles used as plant and machinery in the course of carrying out a trade by a donor are also tax deductible, as are articles manufactured or sold in the course of the donor's trade or machinery or plant used in the donor's trade.

STAMP DUTY LAND TAX

11.131 Stamp duty land tax (or 'SDLT') applies to the purchase or lease of land in the UK (as well as to certain transactions which relate to land). SDLT is, in general, paid by the person acquiring land or an interest in land. Rates vary from 1 to 15 % of the price paid in relation to the sale or lease of the land.

11.132 Charities qualify for an exemption from SDLT where they buy or lease land provided that they intend to hold the land for one of two 'qualifying charitable purposes'. These are:

---

[31] Corporation Tax Act 2010, s 1000.

'• For use in furtherance of the charitable purposes of the purchaser or of another charity.
• As an investment from which the profits are applied to the charitable purposes of the purchaser.'[32]

11.133 There is no definition of 'use and furtherance of the charitable purposes' of a charity for SDLT but in our view this is likely to be interpreted by HM Revenue & Customs in a similar way to 'applied for charitable purposes only' in the context of income, capital gains and corporation tax (see **11.47** for more in relation to this).

11.134 It is easy to assume that any purchase of an interest in land by a charity is exempt from SDLT. But the conditions we have mentioned will need to be satisfied if SDLT relief is to be available. By way of example, these conditions will exclude SDLT relief where a charity purchases land as part of a trading transaction (in other words, if it proposes to buy land with a view to selling it on to the third party at a profit).

11.135 It is also important to appreciate that there are certain 'disqualifying events' which may result in a claw back of the relief making SDLT payable. These include the land in question ceasing to be used by the charity that has bought it for 'qualifying charitable purposes'.

11.136 The availability of SDLT relief is also subject to there being no tax avoidance motive in relation to the purchase.

11.137 The charity's trustees should also bear in mind that a non-charitable subsidiary of the charity will not qualify for relief from SDLT.

11.138 However, when a charity purchases property jointly with a third party who is not a charity, relief from SDLT is available on the charity's share of the property, such relief being subject to a test based on the extent to which the charity's share is used for charitable purposes (see **11.132**).[33]

RATING RELIEF

11.139 Mandatory relief from 80% of non-domestic rates is available to a ratepayer that is a charity and in occupation of premises used wholly or mainly for charitable purposes. Where the mandatory relief applies, the local authority also has a discretion to relieve the 20% balance of the rates due.

11.140 In order to claim the mandatory relief, the charity must be in exclusive occupation of the premises and provided that the premises is used 'wholly or mainly' for 'charitable purposes', relief will be available in respect of it. It has been held that the phrase 'wholly or mainly used' refers both to the purpose

---

[32] Finance Act 2003, Sch 8, para 1.
[33] *Pollen Estate Trustee Co Ltd v Revenue and Customs Commissioners* [2013] EWCA Civ 753.

and the extent of use of premises,[34] but no clear precedent has been established for the extent of use which will qualify as 'mainly'. However, there is clearly some scope for use of the charity's premises by, say, its trading subsidiary without an adverse effect on the availability of rating relief.

11.141 The Charity Commission has published a statement[35] cautioning charities which are considering entering into certain mutually beneficial arrangements with commercial landlords, whereby the landlord is relieved from having to pay full business rates in respect of hard to let properties because a charity is in occupation (normally for a low or nominal rent). The concern is that these charities may find themselves involved in what local authorities might consider to be business rates avoidance by landlords. This could potentially result in charities losing the discretionary discount and being required to pay 20% of the business rates.

CLIMATE CHANGE LEVY

11.142 Supplies of electricity and other non-renewable energy sources are exempt from the climate change levy when they are made to a charity for its 'non-business' activities.

11.143 There is no definition of what constitutes a 'business' for the purposes of the levy, but HM Revenue & Customs has adopted an interpretation that is similar to the interpretation it uses for the purposes of VAT. This is reflected in its guidance, which states that a VAT certificate is required if the exemption is to be claimed.

VAT

11.144 VAT is a particularly difficult area for charities. A detailed discussion of the impact of VAT on charities is a book in itself. But from a governance point of view, it is important that a charity's trustees appreciate the VAT significance of particular operations or activities they may wish to see their charity undertake.

11.145 The particular difficulty for charities is that, while they qualify for a wide range of exemptions from direct tax, the way in which VAT works means that, in many cases, charities are put in a much worse financial position than many commercial entities.

11.146 There are a number of reasons for this, but most relate to the way in which VAT works, which is intrinsically different to the way in which income, capital gains or corporation tax apply.

---

[34] *Kenya Aid Programme v Sheffield City Council* [2013] EWHC 54 (Admin) and *Public Safety Charitable Trust v Milton Keynes Council* [2013] EWHC 1237 (Admin).

[35] See 'Risks to charities linked to business rates relief' published in May 2013.

11.147 Fundamentally, VAT is intended to be a tax on spending by consumers. This determines the way in which it is structured which, broadly, is as follows:

- VAT is payable by any 'taxable person' who supplies goods or services in the course of a 'business'. The supply has to be made in the UK.

- A taxable person is anyone who makes supplies of goods or services with a value in excess of a specified threshold (presently £79,000) over certain specified periods of time.

- Supplies are 'taxable', 'zero-rated' or 'exempt'. Taxable supplies are subject to VAT at a standard rate of 20% or a reduced rate of 5% on their value, depending on what is being supplied. Zero-rated and exempt supplies do not give rise to a liability on the supplier to pay VAT.

- In general, a supplier will add the amount of the VAT it is due to account for to HM Revenue & Customs in respect of a taxable supply (usually referred to as 'output VAT') to the invoice it gives its customer. It can then use the amount in respect of VAT paid by the customer when it pays the invoice to meet its liability to pay output VAT to HM Revenue & Customs.

- Where the customer is itself a taxable person and uses the goods or services supplied to it to make its own taxable or zero-rated supplies for VAT purposes, the VAT legislation allows it to credit the VAT it has paid (usually referred to as 'input VAT') against the output VAT it is due to pay to HM Revenue & Customs.

- The net effect of this where an entity is buying in VATable goods or services in order to make taxable or zero-rated supplies is that there is no net cost to it. The cost of VAT is aimed at the consumer, who will not be using goods or services supplied to him or to her to make their own taxable or zero-rated supplies.

- Where, however, an entity uses VATable goods or services to make exempt supplies, or supplies outside the scope of VAT altogether, its ability to recover its input VAT will be limited.

11.148 The difficulties faced by charities in relation to VAT are generally because of two aspects of the way in which the VAT legislation works. These are what constitute a 'business' for VAT purposes and the treatment of exempt supplies.

'Business' supplies

11.149 The concept of 'business' for VAT is far wider than that of 'trade', particularly because there is no requirement that a profit should be intended. It can include, therefore, the provision of services by a charity to its beneficiaries (eg the provisions of residential care to the elderly and infirm by a charity set up to relieve the elderly in need).

11.150 However, where a charity is not carrying out a VAT 'business', supplies made by it are outside the scope of VAT altogether. There is no VAT due on the supply, so that no VAT cost is passed on to the charity's customers, but the charity will not be able to credit the input VAT it has incurred in buying the goods and services it has bought in to make it supplies.

'Exempt supplies'

11.151 There is a similar problem in relation to 'exempt' supplies. There are a number of such supplies made by charities:

- the provision of education or research by educational establishments and professional training by charities;
- providing care, treatment or instruction to promote the welfare of elderly, sick, distressed or disabled persons;
- goods and services closely linked to the protection of children and young persons; and
- goods and services supplied by a charity in connection with certain fundraising events (see **13.45** for more in relation to this).

11.152 The difficulty for charities is that, while no output VAT is due on these supplies (because they are 'exempt'), they do not enable the charity to claim a credit for all of the input VAT it has paid on supplies made to it which it has used to make its exempt supplies. There are some rules that may allow a proportion of the input VAT to be credited, but these are complex.

Zero-rated supplies

11.153 Charities can, on the other hand, make a number of zero-rated supplies:

- supplies of talking books for the blind and handicapped;
- supplies of equipment for the relief of the chronically sick and disabled;
- the sale of donated goods; and
- the export of goods.

11.154 The advantage of zero-rating is that no output VAT is due on the supply, which is deemed to be a taxable supply in calculating entitlement to credit for input VAT.

Buildings

11.155 Charities often face particular VAT issues in relation to the construction or alteration of buildings. The rules in relation to land and buildings are generally fairly complicated, but particularly so for charities.

11.156 In summary, there are very few areas of a charity's operations that are unlikely to have some VAT implications. A charity's trustees must ensure that they identify activities that are potentially problematic and take appropriate steps, usually by taking specialist VAT advice.

11.157 The UK has now introduced a VAT exemption for certain cost-sharing arrangements within the scope of the existing exemption in Art 132(1)(f) of the EC VAT Directive adding a new Group 16 to Sch 9 to the Value Added Tax Act 1994.

TAX COMPLIANCE

11.158 Charities are subject to the self-assessment regime in respect of their tax liabilities. This means that they are not obliged to submit a tax return to HM Revenue & Customs unless required to do so by the Revenue or because they have a liability to tax that must be returned to the Revenue (in which case, they should write to HM Revenue & Customs and ask for a self-assessment tax return to be issued). All companies and organisations that are not trusts must submit their Company Tax Return online. Charities set up as trusts may complete online or paper Trust & Estate returns.

11.159 HM Revenue & Custom's guidance in relation to tax returns is:

'Some charities will be asked to submit a tax return annually but most will only be asked to submit a return from time to time. HMRC Charities will select which charities it requires a tax return from and will issue formal notices to those charities. HMRC issues a notice to submit a tax return to all charities over a number of years as part of its programme to check compliance ...

... if a charity receives either a tax return or a Notice to file it must complete and submit a tax return. A charity that completes a Company Tax Return must send a copy of its accounts with the return.'[36]

11.160 Charities can also claim back any income tax deducted from certain other types of income they receive:

- net bank or building society interest;
- gift aid donations;
- net interest from Government stocks; and
- royalties and other types of annual payment.

11.161 The tax must be reclaimed, by using:

(1) HM Revenue & Customs 'Charities Online' form;
(2) the Charity's own developed compatible software or purchased software product; or
(3) paper reclaim form ChR1.

---

[36] HM Revenue & Customs' Guidance Notes, chapter 6.

The number of claims that can be made online are restricted.

11.162   A charitable trust must make any claim within 4 years of 31 January in the year following the end of the tax year to which the claim relates. A charitable company or unincorporated association must make any claim within 4 years from the end of the accounting period to which the claim relates. Late claims will not be paid.

11.163   The key governance point for trustees is that the self assessment tax regime puts the onus on them to decide that all of a charity's income and gains have been applied 'for charitable purposes only', constitute charitable expenditure and otherwise qualify for exemption from tax. This is obviously a significant burden, and one that the trustees must understand, even if only in outline.

CHAPTER 12

BORROWING

12.1 This chapter deals with borrowing by charities. Charities may borrow money for various reasons, for example, to fund capital projects or short-term cash flow requirements. As the range and complexity of services provided by charities increases, the ability to borrow on commercial terms is becoming more important.

12.2 It should be noted that the changes to the lending environment over the past few years have meant that lenders have become more cautious, needing to undertake greater investigation at the outset than previously may have been the case and requiring security when, in the past, they may have been more willing to lend on an unsecured basis.

12.3 The ability of a charity to borrow will depend primarily upon whether it has a power to borrow and, if relevant, to charge its assets as security for the borrowing. This will depend primarily upon the way in which the charity has been set up. We consider the position in relation to both incorporated and unincorporated charities below.

12.4 We have assumed that, in most cases, lenders will want security for their loans. Where a charity wishes to grant a mortgage over its land as security for a loan, it must also generally comply with the provisions of the Charities Act 2011, s 124. Section 124 applies only to mortgages over land and not to any other assets. However, it should be noted that the definition of 'mortgage' in this context is broad enough to include any charge over land and debentures (which are sometimes required by banks and inevitably include charges over land). The position is explained in more detail below.

INCORPORATED CHARITIES

Charitable companies

12.5 The question of whether charitable companies have the power to borrow funds is reasonably straightforward. Many charitable companies will have an express power in their constitution to borrow, often alongside a power to charge their assets as security for the loan. The charity's trustees will need to assess the scope of the power to ensure that any restrictions (or limitations) which apply to it are observed. An express power to charge assets will generally cover the grant by a charity of both fixed and floating charges over its assets.

12.6 Where a charitable company does not have an express power to borrow and charge its assets, it will generally be possible for a 75% majority of its members to pass a special resolution to alter its constitution in order to add the power that is required. There is more about amending constitutions to include additional powers in **Chapters 7 and 15**.

12.7 There are protections in the Companies Act 2006 for third parties dealing with companies. The provisions of the Act which state that the capacity of a company shall not be called into question by anything in its constitution and give its directors power to bind the company do not apply to a charitable company. However, these provisions do not apply in favour of a person who:

- gives full consideration (in money or money's worth) in relation to the act in question and does not know that the act is not permitted by the company's memorandum or is beyond the directors' powers; or
- does not know that the company is a charity.[1]

12.8 Clearly, therefore, anyone who does not meet these criteria cannot rely upon the protection conferred by the Companies Act. Many lenders, particularly commercial banks who deal with charities, are likely to ask for confirmation of the charity's powers, which means they will have actual or constructive notice that the charity lacks a power or that is subject to restrictions. There is more about this at **7.12**.

12.9 It will generally be possible to imply a power into a charitable company's constitution using the 'sweep-up' provision often included. This usually states that the company has power to do 'such other lawful things as are necessary to achieve its objects' or wording to similar effect. The powers that can be applied using a provision of this kind will be limited to carrying out the charity's charitable purposes. There is more about implied powers at **7.24**. A power can also be implied in the context of a trading charity to borrow a reasonable amount for the purpose of its trade. In practice, however, most lenders will want to see an express power authorising a charity to borrow and charge its assets and will not find it acceptable to assume the risk inherent in implying a power when the position can only ever be conclusively determined by the courts. The lender's concern is obviously that any borrowing outside a charity's powers will be ultra vires and unenforceable against it.

CIOs

12.10 CIOs are, in principle, in a very similar position to charitable companies in terms of borrowing and granting security for borrowing (although there is a practical difference which is explained at **12.23**).

12.11 A CIO's constitution will generally include an express power to borrow and charge its assets as security for those borrowings (the model CIO

---

[1]   Companies Act 2006, ss 39 and 42.

constitutions published by the Charity Commission contain an express power). If there were to be no express power, a 75% majority of the members of a CIO have the power to pass a resolution to add an express power. This will not generally constitute a regulated alteration requiring the Charity Commission's consent under the Charities Act 2011, s 226. There is more about altering the constitutions of CIOs at **15.35**.

12.12 CIOs are subject to an ultra vires rule that is modelled on the rule that applies in relation to companies under the Companies Act. As with charitable companies, a lender is unlikely to be able to rely upon these provisions because they will generally ask for confirmation of the CIO's powers, with the result that they will have actual or constructive notice that it lacks a power or that it is subject to restrictions.

12.13 The Charities Act 2011, s 216 gives a CIO the power to do anything that is 'calculated to further its purposes', together with a statutory power to do anything that is 'conducive or incidental' to those purposes. Lenders are likely to adopt a similar approach to powers implied under these provisions as they do in relation to charitable companies. In practice, therefore, an express power is likely to be required by a lender.

Other incorporated charities

12.14 Other common incorporated charities are those incorporated by Royal Charter and those incorporated by statute (ie by Act of Parliament). These charities may have express powers to borrow in their constitutions in the same way as companies incorporated under the Companies Acts. However, if they do not, the position is different depending on the form of incorporation. A Royal Charter corporation is presumed by law to have all the powers of a natural person and therefore has a power to borrow unless there is anything in its Charter to the contrary. On the other hand, the powers of a statutory corporation are limited to those found in the statute and, in the absence of a power to borrow, it is not possible to imply one.

Trust assets

12.15 Where an incorporated charity holds trust assets, the powers in the charity's own constitution will apply only to its corporate assets. Its power to deal with the assets held on trust will depend upon the terms of the trust itself and the statutory powers that apply to unincorporated charities.

UNINCORPORATED CHARITIES

12.16 The position in relation to charitable trusts and charitable unincorporated associations is a little more complicated than the position in relation to incorporated charities. Many lenders, generally being used to lending to incorporated borrowers, may need time to consider the nuances of lending to unincorporated borrowers.

Charitable trusts

12.17 Because a trust has no legal personality separate from its trustees, a loan can only be made to its trustees, who will be personally liable to repay the debt due, usually on a joint and several basis.

12.18 While the trustees' liability to the lender is personal, trustees will not generally need to have recourse to their own assets in order to meet their liabilities because of their right to indemnify themselves out of the trust assets, either under an express provision in the charitable trust or under the Trustee Act 2000, s 31 (see **6.25** for more in relation to this). However, the statutory right of indemnity is limited to liabilities that are 'properly incurred' by the trustees in acting on behalf of the charity and any express power will generally be subject to a similar restriction. To the extent that liabilities are incurred as a consequence of a breach of trust (eg in breach of an express restriction imposed by the trust), the indemnity will not be available. Trustees should be aware that even if the indemnity is available, there may not be sufficient trust assets to meet a liability in full.

12.19 In most cases, therefore, the charity's trustees will want to agree with the lender that its recourse against them in respect of its loan is limited to the amount of the charity's assets from time to time. Provided this is agreed to by the lender, it will have no right to claim against the trustees' personal assets in the event of default on the loan. In order to ensure that this provision is effective, it is important that there is an express limitation in the loan documentation on the trustees' liability to the assets of the charity from time to time. Doing no more than providing for the trustees to contract with the lender in their capacity as trustees will not limit their liability. An express statement is required. In practice, most lenders will understand the trustees' reluctance to incur liability in respect of their personal assets and will, in any event, assess the credit-worthiness of the charity on the basis of its assets alone and not the personal assets of the trustees.

12.20 Because the lender's recourse to the charity's assets depends on the trustees' right of indemnity, it may wish to seek security for its loan. Where trustees grant fixed security over a trust asset, the creditor will have recourse to the asset irrespective of the availability of the trustees' indemnity, which will then generally only be an issue where the liability it secures is in excess of the value of the charged asset and the creditor wishes to enforce its rights against the charity's other assets.

12.21 Lenders, in addition to fixed charges over land, may seek to take debentures as security for their loans. A debenture comprises a mix of fixed and floating charges over all, or substantially all, of the borrower's assets. The floating charge element of a debenture is intended to charge 'moving assets' such as stock, cash held at the bank, and debts owed by third parties. As well as having the advantage of being able to secure assets that cannot be subject to a fixed charge, an additional advantage of a debenture is that it improves the lender's enforcement position, giving it the power to appoint an administrator.

12.22 Floating charges are only capable of being given by companies and other incorporated charities and therefore the trustees of a charitable trust are not capable of granting a debenture to a lender.

12.23 CIOs will be capable of granting debentures, although there is no statutory mechanism for the charges granted in a debenture to be registered (except where they relate to land, when fixed charges can be registered at the Land Registry). There is a mechanism for this in relation to companies (via Companies House) which enables lenders to ensure that they have priority over other secured creditors in respect of their floating charges. Without certainty about priority, some lenders may be more reluctant to lend to CIOs than to companies.

12.24 Because a charity's trustees may change from time to time, a lender will wish to ensure that the loan binds the successors of the trustees who take out the original loan. This is usually done by ensuring that, on a change of trustees, the retiring trustees are only relieved of their personal liability in respect of the loan to the extent that the new trustees agree to be bound by it. This will often be regulated by a 'deed of adherence' in an agreed form scheduled to the loan documentation.

12.25 In many cases, the trustees of a charitable trust will have an express power to borrow and charge the charity's assets. Any restrictions on the express power must obviously be observed. If a charitable trust has no express power to borrow and charge, it may be possible for one to be added by the trustees using a power to add to the trust's provisions. Adding a provision of this kind using this power would not usually require the consent of the Charity Commission. There is more about constitutional changes in **Chapter 15**.

12.26 If there is no express power and one cannot be added, the trustees may be able to rely upon a statutory power. The statutory power to borrow conferred on the trustees of private trusts by the Trustee Act 1925, s 16 does not apply to charities. However, a trading charitable trust will have a power similar to that of a trading charitable company to borrow what it requires for the purposes of its trade,[2] provided that the expenditure cannot reasonably be financed without borrowing. A power to borrow can also be implied under the Trusts of Land and Appointment of Trustees Act 1996 and the Trustee Act 2000, s 8 (on the basis that the trustees are given all of the powers of an

---

[2] See *Mansell v Viscount Cobham* (1905) 1 Ch 568.

'absolute owner') but only for any purpose connected with the repair, maintenance, improvement of buildings or the purchase of land. The power will also allow the land to be charged.

12.27 Some lenders take the view that the statutory powers are not sufficiently wide to authorise borrowing and the grant of charges because they do not refer to these powers expressly. Some also take the view that, while the statutory powers authorise borrowing, they do not extend to unsecured loans. The Charity Commission's view is that:[3]

> 'In our view the powers of an absolute owner clearly include a power to borrow money and/or to charge the land, and if the power is exercisable in relation to land comprised in the trust then the power to borrow and/or charge the land falls within the ambit of section 6(1) of TLAT 1996.
>
> In practice, borrowing by charity trustees will almost invariably be for a purpose connected with the use of the land for the purposes of the charity. Borrowing for the purposes of acquisition, improvement, repair and maintenance and equipment of land and buildings are all within the scope of section 6(1) of TLAT 1996.'

12.28 The Charity Commission does acknowledge that its view is not accepted by all the corporate lenders which charity trustees may approach for finance. In practice, therefore, many lenders are reluctant to rely on statutory or implied powers to borrow and charge assets, and this position has probably hardened further in recent years.

12.29 Trustees without an appropriate express power may try to obtain an express authority from the Charity Commission, generally by way of an Order. However, the position of the Commission has changed in this respect and it states that:

> '... we will no longer make "comfort" Orders in these cases. This means that we decline any request for a legal permission where there are no serious issues that would justify the exercise of our power and it is being sought simply to provide reassurance.'[4]

12.30 If there is no power to borrow, a loan is not necessarily invalid or unenforceable. *De Vigier v IRC*[5] suggests that a loan made to trustees may be recoverable from the trust assets (rather than from the trustees personally) on the basis that the doctrine of ultra vires was developed in the context of the limited capacity of corporations and that the fact that taking a loan might constitute a breach of trust does not of itself mean that a loan cannot be valid and enforceable. Lenders are obviously unlikely to want to rely on this.

---

[3]   OG 22 B1.
[4]   OG 22 B1.
[5]   [1964] 1 WLR 1073.

Unincorporated associations

12.31   Like a charitable trust, a charitable unincorporated association has no legal personality separate from its trustees or members. The validity of the acts undertaken by the trustees and members of the association depends upon the provisions of its constitution.

12.32   An association's constitution will usually provide for the direction and supervision of its affairs to be vested in a governing body of trustees with specified functions and powers. Provided that the trustees act within the powers conferred on them, they will bind (as agents) the association's members (as principals) and will also usually be entitled to an express or implied indemnity against the association's assets in respect of the liabilities they take on.

12.33   An unauthorised liability will not bind an association's members. Those who incurred it will incur personal liability and will not usually be entitled to indemnify themselves from the association's assets.

12.34   A lender will need to check that an association's constitution confers an express power to borrow and grant security. An association's assets will usually be held by one or more of its members as nominees or custodians. The identity of those holding the assets over which security is granted should be verified and their capacity to act under the constitution checked.

12.35   Like the trustees of a charitable trust, it is considered that the trustees of a charitable unincorporated association cannot grant a floating charge or debenture. Lenders' standard form documentation may need to be amended to reflect this.

CHARITIES ACT 2011, S 124

12.36   As we have mentioned earlier in this chapter, any charity (with the exception of an exempt charity) must comply with the provisions of the Charities Act 2011, s 124 if it is granting a mortgage over its land. It does not apply to security granted over any asset other than land but, for the avoidance of doubt, will cover a debenture (given that a debenture usually covers property assets).

12.37   Section 124 requires the charity's trustees to obtain the prior consent of the Charity Commission to the grant of the mortgage, unless the trustees have obtained and considered 'proper advice' in writing in relation to the mortgage before it is entered into. This 'shortcut' has the effect of streamlining the process for borrowing charities in certain situations and the Commission will expect this process to be followed in all cases where it can be.

12.38   The advice that is required differs depending upon the purpose of the mortgage. Where it is to secure the repayment of a loan or a grant, the advice needs to cover the following aspects:

- Whether the loan or grant is necessary in order for the charity trustees to be able to pursue the particular course of action in connection with which they are seeking the loan or grant.
- Whether the terms of the loan or grant are reasonable having regard to the status of the charity as the prospective recipient of the loan or grant.
- Whether the charity is able to repay the loan or grant on the terms on which they are made.

12.39 In the case of a mortgage which is given as security in respect of any other obligation, the advice must relate to whether it is reasonable for the charity's trustees to undertake to discharge the obligation, having regard to the charity's charitable purposes.

12.40 The advice has to come from someone the trustees believe is qualified to give it (ie has some expertise or qualifications in financial matters) and who has no financial interest in relation to the loan, grant or other obligation in relation to which the advice is given. This could, however, include an employee of the charity (eg a finance director). In practice, charity trustees are sometimes keen for one of the charity's employees to give the advice they need, partly because the employee may be best placed to give it but often also because they will avoid the cost of taking professional advice from a third party.

12.41 Clearly, a charity's trustees will need to consider very carefully whether it is appropriate for an employee to give the advice. In particular, they should consider the implications if the advice given proves to be negligent. An employee's ability to meet any claims the charity may have for negligent advice may be very limited in comparison to that of a professional adviser, who will generally carry professional indemnity insurance in respect of the advice they give. The employee will also need to consider his or her own position carefully. They may only be willing to advise on the basis that the advice is given without personal liability, which will obviously be a very relevant consideration for the trustees in considering whether or not the advice they give can be relied upon.

12.42 In practice, whether it is appropriate for an employee to give advice is likely to depend upon the value of the liability that the mortgage secures and the complexity of the transaction in question. While an employee may be able to advise on the grant of a mortgage to secure an overdraft, he or she is much less likely, say, to be able to advise on the terms of a loan incorporating interest rate options.

12.43 Having said this, advice in relation to a mortgage to secure obligations other than loans or grants may be difficult to procure from a third party, on the basis that they may not consider themselves able to have due regard to the 'charity's purposes' in giving the advice. Again, the position is likely to vary depending upon the obligation in question.

12.44 The advice should be considered by trustees in a meeting if at all possible. This will allow appropriate analysis, challenge and reasoned debate to be undertaken by trustees. The Charity Commission, however, recognises that circumstances may not always allow a full meeting to take place and that trustees may need to consider the issue outside a formal meeting.

12.45 The Charity Commission states the following:[6]

> 'The trustees' consideration of the written advice which they have obtained under s 124(3) or (4), and their decisions based on that advice, should, where practicable, be made and minuted at a properly constituted trustees' meeting. Alternatively, the trustees may consider the advice between themselves in correspondence, or orally. If oral approval is given, a written record should be made as soon as possible.'

12.46 In its guidance on disposing of charity land,[7] the Charity Commission provides a useful indication of what documents should be considered when approving entry into a charge and how the decision should be documented to create the appropriate 'audit trail'. Any lender is likely to want to see copies of the s 124 written advice and the relevant approval minutes.

12.47 For the mortgage to have been effectively given, it can only be entered into after the s 124 procedure has been undertaken. Therefore the substantial terms of the loan to be secured must be decided upon *before* the charge is granted.

12.48 Can trustees delegate consideration of s 124 issues to subcommittees? The correct view is that this can be done, albeit the rules on delegation explained in **Chapter 8** must be complied with. In particular it should be noted that the terms of the delegation must be agreed by the trustees at a meeting and set out clearly in writing. Any decision reached by the subcommittee must be reported back to the trustees as soon as possible.

12.49 If the advice cannot be given in the required form, then an Order will be required from the Charity Commission. Trustees sometimes query whether, notwithstanding the fact that they have not received advice in the necessary form or an Order from the Charity Commission, they can still enter into a mortgage. The Commission's position on this could not be clearer:[8]

> 'Trustees would not have fulfilled the requirements of s124(8) if they decide to accept the terms of a proposed mortgage without having considered proper advice. Trustees would be unlikely to be regarded as having acted properly if they act against or ignore the advice of someone more experienced than themselves, without good reasons. (The standard generally required of a trustee is to take the precautions which a prudent man of business would take in managing his own affairs).'

12.50 In practice, most lenders' standard form charge documents (including those for a secured overdraft facility) will make any mortgage an 'all monies'

---

[6] OG 22 B3.
[7] CC 28, section I.
[8] OG 22 B3.

charge which will secure all present and future borrowings by the charity. This obviously makes good commercial sense for the lender, but the charity's trustees will need to ensure that the procedure is repeated whenever they wish to borrow additional amounts under the 'all monies' mortgage. The same analysis applies where the terms of the underlying loan are changed, a new loan contract is substituted for the former or if the trustees wish to add the new loan to the existing security.

12.51 The prior consent of the Commission will be required where land is mortgaged to secure a guarantee or indemnity or the payment of deferred consideration. It is not possible for the charity's trustees to rely on advice in relation to these transactions.

CHARITIES ACT 2011, S 125

12.52 Section 125 of the Charities Act 2011 (as amended by the Land Registration Rules 2003, r 180)[9] requires a mortgage granted by any charity (including an exempt charity) to include a statement that the land is held by or in trust for the charity and that the restrictions of s 124 apply. The statement is that the land is held by or in trust for a charity; whether the charity is an exempt charity; and whether the mortgage has been generally or specially authorised by the Charity Commission or that the mortgage is subject to the restrictions of s 124. The form of the statement is specified by the Land Registry. The *Land Registry Practice Guide* spells out the full requirements for the statement.

12.53 The trustees are also required to certify in the mortgage that it has either been sanctioned by an appropriate order of the Commission or that the charity has power to grant the mortgage and that the trustees have taken advice on it.

12.54 Where the certificate is given (even falsely), the s 124 procedure is deemed to have been complied with in favour of anyone who acquires the land (whether or not under the mortgage) in good faith for money or money's worth unless the purchaser knows that the certificate was false and that the transaction was not in the interests of the charity. If no certificate is given, the mortgage will still be valid in favour of a purchaser for good faith in money or money's worth on the same basis. A certificate and statement should always therefore be included in a mortgage.

12.55 It is important that a charity's trustees ensure that the provisions of s 125 are complied with in full. The protection it offers to third parties applies only from completion of a transaction[10] and the relevant statement and certificate should be included in any contract entered into by the charity in anticipation of the mortgage. If not, the contract may be void or voidable.

---

[9]   SI 2003/1417.
[10]   *Bayoumi v Women's Total Abstinence Educational Union Ltd* [2004] 3 All ER.

12.56 The certificate must be given by the charity's trustees. This is the case even in relation to an incorporated charity. The Land Registry's guidance indicates that the trustees must be a party to the mortgage in order to give the certificate in addition to the charity itself. Land Registry Practice Guide 14 on Charities states:[11]

'The certificate must be given by the charity trustees so they will need to join in and execute the disposition or charge in order to give the certificate. S.177, 2011 Act defines 'charity trustees' as the persons having the general control and management of the administration of the charity. Where the charity is a trust, this will generally be the managing trustees, whether or not they are also the registered proprietors. Where the charity is a body corporate, for example a company limited by guarantee or a parochial church council, it will generally be the directors or members. Occasionally, some form of governing council may administer the charity.'

The Land Registry goes on to state that:[12]

'It is considered that the charity trustees may also delegate the power to give the required certificates under the 2011 Act.'

The Charity Commission's guidance states that:

'The trustees are required to give the certificate of the mortgage deed, but in the case of a charitable company, the mortgage will be executed by the company itself not by the directors, who are the trustees. Although the matter is not free from doubt, it should be approached on the basis that the persons executing the mortgage on behalf of the charity, company or not, can give the certificate as agent for the trustees.'[13]

In practice, therefore, the certificate can usually be dealt with by ensuring that the trustees expressly delegate responsibility for giving it to two or more of the trustees (or, in certain circumstances, non-trustees) either under an express power of delegation or using a statutory power. There is more about the powers of delegation that can be used at **8.91**.

PERMANENT ENDOWMENT

12.57 As we have explained in an earlier chapter (see **9.27**), there are restrictions on any charity's power to dispose of its permanent endowment assets, which will often include land. These restrictions will generally mean that land can only be sold or leased by a charity with the prior consent of the Charity Commission. However, the Commission's consent is not required to the grant of security over permanent endowment land, except where this is required by the Charities Act 2011, s 124 or in the event that a charity has no power to

---

[11] Land Registry Practice Guide 14, para 6.2.4.
[12] Land Registry Practice Guide 14, para 8.2.
[13] OG 22 C1.

grant the mortgage. This is the case, notwithstanding that the grant of a mortgage may ultimately lead to the disposal of the permanent endowment land by the lender under the terms of the mortgage in the event that the charity defaults on its loan. The trustees should consider this possibility as a relevant factor when considering whether or not it is appropriate to charge the land.

12.58 A charity's corporate structure needs to be considered carefully in these circumstances. It is not uncommon for a charity's operational functions to sit within an incorporated charity whilst some permanent endowment land is held by that incorporated charity, in a different capacity, as corporate trustee. In those circumstances some thought needs to be given as to whether it is possible for the permanent endowment land to be charged in order to secure the borrowing of the incorporated charity.

12.59 The charity's trustees should also be aware that where the structure is particularly complicated, lenders may look for an opinion from the charity's legal advisers in relation to its capacity to grant security to the lender.

INTEREST RATE PROTECTION ARRANGEMENTS

12.60 Charities with significant borrowings may sometimes wish to enter into interest rate arrangements (such as caps, collars and swaps) in order to mitigate the effect that interest rate fluctuations may have on borrowings as effectively as possible.

12.61 Interest rate caps prevent applicable interest rates exceeding a pre-agreed rate whereas an interest rate collar prevents interest rates moving outside an agreed range.

12.62 An interest rate swap is essentially a contract between two parties under which one party agrees to pay interest at a 'floating' rate (in other words, a rate that fluctuates depending upon the fluctuations in a particular base rate) in exchange for payments of interest at a fixed rate. The payments are not, in reality 'interest' at all but cash which is intended to compensate the charity in respect of its exposure to a particular fixed or floating rate of interest.

12.63 So, for example, a charity that has borrowed a significant sum from a bank on the basis that it will pay interest at a floating rate (often calculated by reference to the base rate or the 'London Interbank Offer Rate' ('LIBOR')) may conclude that its interests would best be served by fixing the rate of interest it pays on the borrowing, so that it can manage its debt obligations (particularly as regards cash flow) more effectively. This could be achieved by entering into an interest rate swap with a bank or other financial institution under which the charity agrees to pay the bank a notional amount of fixed rate interest on the principal of its borrowings in return for a payment from the bank or financial institution equal to the floating rate of interest actually due on the borrowings.

12.64 In some cases, banks and other financial institutions may only agree to lend to a charity on the basis that its floating rate obligations are effectively fixed by entering into a swap. This may be before a loan is agreed upon or in connection with an existing loan.

12.65 Whether a charity can enter into an interest rate swap in relation to its borrowings depends upon two issues:

- whether the charity has a power to enter into the swap; and
- whether the power can properly be exercised by the charity's trustees.

12.66 The first limb is the simpler of the two. The starting point is to see whether the charity's constitution contains a power to enter into interest rate protection arrangements (sometimes referred to as derivatives). It used to be a common position, with which the Charity Commission concurred, that an express power to enter into an interest rate protection arrangement was not always required, and that trustees could (in most cases) rely on an express borrowing power and the charity's incidental powers, provided it was an integral part of managing the charity's debt and not a speculative venture.

12.67 However, over the past decade, lenders have become increasingly concerned and have insisted that charity borrowers need an express power or a Charity Commission Order (see below) to enter into such arrangements. It has therefore become increasingly common for charity constitutions to contain an express power.

12.68 If a charity has no express power to enter into a swap transaction and the power cannot be implied as incidental to its borrowing power, the Charity Commission's consent to the swap will be required by way of an Order. However, the likelihood is that, in circumstances where entering into a swap is not incidental to the exercise of a borrowing power, the Commission will need to be persuaded why it is appropriate to make an Order. On an application for an Order, the Charity Commission will look at the charity's reasons for wishing to enter into the swap.

12.69 The more complicated issue is the second limb, ie the need for trustees to exercise their power in a manner that is consistent with their duties as charity trustees. Even if a charity has a power to enter into a swap, its trustees must also be satisfied that they can properly exercise the power to enter into the swap which is proposed. This will require the trustees to be very clear about the purpose of entering into the swap.

12.70 The Charity Commission has based its guidance in relation to swaps on the principles established by the case of *Hazell v Hammersmith and Fulham Borough Council*.[14] In that case the court considered a number of interest rate swaps entered into by local authorities. While the powers of local authorities to

---

[14] [1991] 2 WLR 372.

borrow are different from the powers available to most charities, this case established certain principles which apply by analogy to charities in relation to swaps.

12.71 In *Hazell* the court concluded that a swap entered into by a local authority as an essential part of its approach to debt management would be within its powers, while a swap which did no more than gamble on the possibility of a rise or fall in interest rates would be too speculative to fall within its powers. On the facts of the case, the courts concluded that the local authority in question was doing no more than speculating on the possibility that interest rates would rise or, as the case may be, fall with a view to generating additional income. This is not consistent with the authority's duties in relation to the exercise of its powers.

12.72 The issue essentially is whether the swap is intended to involve speculation or eliminate speculation. The Commission's guidance is helpful:[15]

> '... transactions which are entered into solely on the basis of forecasting future interest trends would not be consistent with the duties of trustees.'

However, the Commission also recognises that:[16]

> 'This type of transaction can be very complex and the issue of the speculation or its elimination can be very finely balanced.'

12.73 The Commission also makes a distinction between interest rate arrangements entered into in relation to existing loans and those entered into in relation to new loans. It is suggested that the former will normally be one involving speculation on future interest rate movements and therefore not be consistent with a trustee's duties whereas:[17]

> '... a charity may be proposing to take up a new borrowing and the trustees may see a swap as a means of enabling the charity to obtain a loan on terms which are in the charity's best interests. This may well be an appropriate exercise of the trustees' discretion.'

In some respects, this distinction between existing and new loans seems arbitrary. A charity's trustees may well conclude that their charity's financial circumstances (or economic circumstances generally) have changed since a loan was originally made and that the changes in question justify them seeking, for example, to fix a floating rate of interest. In practice, the position will vary from charity to charity. However, the trustees are likely to be in a stronger position where they can show that they have taken appropriate financial advice on the terms of the swap as part of their debt management arrangements. The

---

[15]   OG 22 B9.
[16]   OG 22 B9.
[17]   OG 22 B9.

Charity Commission considers that taking advice is, in any event, essential for any charity which proposes to enter into a swap.

12.74 The charity's trustees should also consider the following points, which the Charity Commission's guidance indicates it will look at:[18]

'What fee will be paid for the swap?

Why is it proposed?

What are the advantages to the charity?

What risks are there and do the advantages outweigh any risks?

What advice has been received from the charity's advisers?'

12.75 Where possible, it may be better for a charity's trustees to seek to incorporate an interest rate option into the terms of a loan. An interest rate option will have the same economic effect as a swap in allowing the charity to convert the fixed or floating rate payable on the loan. By ensuring that the option is the term of the loan itself, the trustees are more likely to be able to conclude that swapping a fixed or floating rate of interest is incidental to the exercise of their borrowing power. Whether an interest rate option can be included will depend, of course, upon the commercial terms that can be agreed with the lender.

12.76 The charity's trustees should also be aware that lenders will often look for an opinion from the charity's legal advisers in relation to its capacity to enter into a swap. A legal opinion will help to minimise the risk to the lender in respect of its loan but will obviously mean that the charity's legal advisers must be able to conclude that the swap is within the charity's powers.

ENFORCING SECURITY

12.77 As we explain at **15.123**, charitable companies are subject to the winding-up regime imposed by the Insolvency Act 1986 (as amended by the Enterprise Act 2002). The courts also have jurisdiction to make an administration order under Part II of the 1986 Act in relation to a body incorporated by Royal Charter as well as companies incorporated under the Companies Acts.[19]

12.78 Unincorporated charities (ie trusts and unincorporated associations) cannot become 'insolvent' within the regime imposed by the Insolvency Act 1986 (as amended by the Enterprise Act 2002). This is because they have no separate legal personality and cannot incur liabilities in their own right.

---

[18]   OG 22 B9.
[19]   See *The Salvage Association* (2003) *The Times*, 21 May.

However, an unincorporated charity may reach the financial state where it is 'insolvent' in the sense that the value of the charity's assets that are available to its trustees to settle their liabilities is insufficient. Ultimately, creditors' claims against the trustees may mean that they are made personally bankrupt.

12.79 There are some issues that are likely to be particularly important where a charity has become insolvent. In summary, these are as follows:

LIQUIDATION/ADMINISTRATION

12.80 As mentioned earlier in this chapter, assets held by a company as trustee do not form part of its corporate property and are not available for distribution to its creditors in a liquidation or administration. It may therefore be a breach of trust for a charitable company to discharge its liabilities out of the trust property unless they are liabilities properly incurred in the administration of the trust in question (when the Trustee Act 2000, s 31 will apply to provide a statutory indemnity). This may be a concern to an administrator or liquidator who is responsible for committing a charity to a breach of this kind because he or she may be in breach of their own fiduciary duty to the charity as a consequence.

12.81 Another aspect of concern will be whether an administrator or liquidator has the power to realise security by selling a particular asset. This may be because the powers conferred by the order appointing him or her relate only to corporate property and the powers contained in the trust of the asset in question do not authorise a sale. In those circumstances, the administrator or liquidator may need to obtain an Order or Scheme from the Charity Commission authorising a sale before he or she can proceed.

12.82 The liquidator or administrator may also need to comply with Charities Act 2011, s 117 which makes a sale of any land owned by a charity subject to the consent of the Charity Commission unless he or she obtains a surveyor's report on the sale and acts in accordance with the advice it contains. There is some debate about what the correct approach should be in a situation where the duties of a liquidator or administrator conflict with the principles under s 117 but the Charity Commission has no published view on this issue. There is more about s 117 at **9.96**.

RECEIVERSHIP

12.83 Where a receiver is appointed under a validly granted mortgage, his or her powers to deal with the charged assets derive from the mortgage itself. The Charity Commission has no published view on the position of a receiver in relation to trust property held by a charitable company, but the approach taken appears to be that he or she is free to exercise the power of sale under the mortgage and to discharge the debt due to the mortgagee without giving rise to any breach of duty to the charity. The receiver's duty is owed to both the mortgagee and the charity and is to take reasonable care to obtain a fair value for the asset.

12.84 This appears to be the approach that would be taken by the Charity Commission to permanent endowment property, which will, by definition, be held on trust. If a receiver is exercising a power of sale over land, he or she will need to consider whether the Charities Act 2011, s 117 applies. On a strict construction of the Act, a report is required but this runs contrary to the scheme of the legislation, which is intended to ensure that the trustees (rather than a receiver) consider whether the sale is in the best interests of their charity. There is more about **s 117** at **9.95**.

CHECKLIST

12.85 In agreeing to borrow, the charity's trustees should ensure that they have dealt with the following points:

- Do the charity's trustees have an express power under the charity's constitution to borrow and charge the charity's assets as security for the loan?
- If there is no express power, can the charity amend its constitution to add an express power?
- If there is no express power, can a power be implied and will this be acceptable to the lender?
- In the case of an unincorporated charity (or an incorporated charity which wishes to borrow in its capacity as trustee of the trust assets), are the statutory powers to borrow sufficiently wide and will this be acceptable to the lender?
- Where the lender requires security over the charity's land, can the trustees comply with the provisions of the Charities Act 2011, s 124?
- Do the trustees of an unincorporated charity wish to limit their liability in respect of the loan to the assets of the charity from time to time?
- If the charity's trustees need to take advice in order to comply with the Charities Act 2011, s 124, from whom should they take advice? Should this be from an employee of the charity or a professional adviser?
- If the charity is unincorporated, is the lender looking for a floating charge over its assets?
- If the charity is borrowing additional funds under an 'all monies' charge, have the trustees taken further advice?
- Has the prior consent of the Charity Commission been obtained where the land is charged to secure a guarantee or indemnity or the payment of deferred consideration?
- Have the charity's trustees complied with the provisions of the Charities Act 2011, s 125 in relation to the required statement and certificate?

- Have the trustees properly delegated their power to give the certificate?

- Where the charity proposes to enter into a swap in relation to a loan, does it have an express power to do so, or can one be implied as incidental to its borrowing power?

- If a charity has a power to enter into a swap, is the swap entered into as part of the charity's debt management strategy or is it 'speculative'?

- Have the charity's trustees taken professional advice in relation to the terms of any swap that is proposed?

- Would an interest rate option be a better way of achieving the charity's financial objective than entering into a free-standing swap transaction?

CHAPTER 13

TRADING

13.1 Trading is (like investment and fundraising) one of the ways in which many charities exploit their assets in order to generate funds to advance their charitable purposes. In this chapter, we look at:

- what constitutes a 'trade';
- the governance implications of trading;
- the kinds of trade that a charity can properly carry out; and
- how (and why) charities use trading subsidiaries.

13.2 It is important to remember that whether a charity can trade has governance implications in respect of both charity and tax law, which is why this chapter draws on the guidance issued by both the Charity Commission and HM Revenue & Customs. The governance implications are explained in more detail at **13.18**.

WHAT IS A 'TRADE'?

13.3 There is no clear statutory definition of what constitutes a 'trade' which applies for the purposes of both tax and charity law. Trade is only defined to include 'any venture in the nature of a trade'[1] but this merely confirms that it can encompass a wide range of different activities. Fortunately, the courts have developed some tests that they will apply to any income generating activity in order to determine whether it constitutes a trade or not. These include:

- where a charity buys in goods or services in order to sell them on to a third party, it is likely to be trading;
- an activity carried out by a charity on a one-off basis is less likely to be trading;
- activities carried out by a charity with the intention of making a profit or surplus are more likely to be trading;
- where a charity finances the activity by means of a loan, this is more likely to point to it carrying out a trade; and

---

[1] Income Tax Act 2007, s 989.

- if the charity has developed a mechanism for selling its goods or services, this is likely to point to it carrying out a trade. This could include, for example, sales via shops or a website.

13.4 These tests are usually referred to as the 'badges' of trade. They help to identify whether a particular activity is a trade or not, but they are not hard and fast rules. So, for example, the courts have concluded that a one-off activity can constitute a trade and also that a trade may be carried out where there is no intention to make a profit. In other words, while the badges point to the existence of a trade, none of them is, of itself, conclusive.

13.5 HM Revenue & Customs' guidance states that:

> 'Usually, trading involves the provision of goods or services to customers on a commercial basis'

but goes on to say:

> 'Whether an activity is, or is not, a trade depends on the facts in each case. When it is not clear it will be necessary for HM Revenue & Customs (HMRC) Charities to look at all the circumstances surrounding the activity.'[2]

13.6 It may help to consider some of the activities presently carried out by charities that do constitute trading. These include, for example, being paid by a government department to provide services to disabled people, selling educational materials online, charging admission to a zoo or historical buildings, selling theatre tickets, educating children in return for school fees and licensing a charity's name and logo to a commercial entity which hopes to increase its sales of a particular product by associating itself with the charity in question.

INVESTMENT AND FUNDRAISING

13.7 Because trading is a varied and wide-ranging concept, there are some nebulous areas where the dividing line between trading and other ways in which a charity may wish to exploit its assets can become blurred. These are investment and fundraising. It is important to understand how they differ from trading because the powers charities have to carry them out, and their tax and charity law implications, are different from those that apply in relation to trading. This obviously raises significant governance issues for a charity's trustees.

13.8 At a basic level, investment and trading are very similar in that they both involve the buying and selling of assets with a view to generating financial resources. But if one looks a little more closely at a charity's intentions, it is possible to draw a distinction between them. The best example of this is the

---

[2] HM Revenue & Customs' Guidance Note Annex IV.2.

acquisition of land. Land purchased by a charity with the intention of letting it for rent will be an 'investment'. While the charity intends to make a profit in the form of rental income from the land (one of the badges of trade we have mentioned), it does not intend to do so by way of re-sale and the acquisition will be a one-off transaction. Where, on the other hand, land is purchased by a charity with a view to selling it on for development at a higher price, it will carry out a 'trade' (the trade of property development). Here, the charity intends to make a profit by re-selling the land.

13.9 The distinction between investment and trading is not always clear cut. So the fact that land acquired by a charity is subsequently sold for development does not necessarily mean that it was not bought and held as an investment rather than as a trading asset. As we have said, the key issue is what the charity intended at the time it bought the land in question.

13.10 The distinction between 'trading' and 'fundraising' is even more nebulous, not least because 'fundraising' has no legal meaning in this context and, in the everyday sense, encompasses a very wide range of activities. Trading is certainly one way of raising funds for a charity, but this does not mean that all forms of fundraising are trading. Again, the true position will vary from case to case and will depend upon the way in which the badges of trade apply. So, for example, a charity may decide to hold an event to raise funds for a particular project. It might decide to hold a concert for which tickets are sold to the charity's supporters. While the charity intends to make a profit from the event, it will be a 'one-off' with no established mechanism for the sale of tickets. On this basis, it is likely to constitute a fundraising event rather than trading. If, however, the event is a success and the charity decides to hold a series of concerts, it is much more likely to be trading as a result. The fact that the event is put on repeatedly, presumably with a more formal mechanism for selling tickets, will, when combined with the profit motive, mean that the events are a trade carried out by the charity.

13.11 Other cases will be more clear cut. A charity may invite the public to make a donation in response to a particular event or to fund a particular project. Invitations of this kind (where the public are promised nothing in return) can never constitute trading notwithstanding that, in the most basic sense, the charity intends to profit from them. Where, on the other hand, a charity provides goods or services in exchange for payment, it will almost invariably be trading. This would include, for example, a charity that charges employers to provide training in first aid to their employees.

13.12 One of the greyer areas is the sponsorship of charities and charitable events by commercial entities. Whether payments made by a commercial entity to a charity in order to be associated with the charity or a particular event put on by the charity constitute trading or fundraising income will generally depend on the way in which the association is presented to the public. There is more about this at **13.142**.

13.13   It is important to bear in mind that the fact that a particular activity raises funds for a charity's charitable purposes (rather than for shareholders, as is the aim for commercial entities) does not mean that the activity cannot be a trade. The courts have considered this question on a number of occasions and have always concluded that what a charity does with the profits it may generate from a trade does not alter the fact that it is a trade.

SALE OF DONATED GOODS

13.14   Before we move on to consider the governance implications of trading, we should mention the specific treatment of the sale by a charity of goods which have been given to a charity specifically for the purpose of raising funds. The classic example of this is goods given to a charity and re-sold by the charity in a shop, but the principle applies in the same way to donated goods which are re-sold to the public in other ways. Both HM Revenue & Customs and the Charity Commission accept that selling donated goods in this way is no more than the realisation by the charity of the value of a gift to it. As HM Revenue & Customs states: 'for this reason the sale of donated goods is generally not regarded as a trade for tax purposes'.[3]

13.15   The Charity Commission also confirms that this is not the exercise of a trade,[4] although both HM Revenue & Customs and the Commission make the point that if donated goods are substantially altered or improved before sale (eg where raw materials are turned into finished goods or the donated goods are subject to 'significant refurbishment or to any process which brings them into a different condition for sale purposes than that in which they have donated') their sale will be trading.

13.16   The Charity Commission's guidance suggests that the sale of any donated asset (including goods, land, buildings and investments) which has been given to a charity specifically for the purpose of raising funds will not constitute a trade. HM Revenue & Customs' guidance is specifically restricted to donated 'goods'. In our view, there is no reason in principle to distinguish between goods and any other sort of donated asset but it is worthwhile bearing in mind that HM Revenue & Customs' guidance is more restricted than this.

13.17   Some charity shops may sell a mixture of donated goods and stock which has been bought in specifically for re-sale. Clearly, the sale of the bought in stock will constitute a trade, whereas the sale of donated goods will not. The distinction between the two is usually dealt with by arranging for the charity to sell the bought in stock as agent for a subsidiary trading company. By acting as the subsidiary's agent, the charity can avoid trading in breach of the restrictions imposed upon it by charity and tax law, whilst also maintaining a claim for mandatory rating relief in respect of the shop premises. There is more guidance

---

[3]   HM Revenue & Customs' Guidance Note Annex IV.17.
[4]   CC 35.

in relation to this in the Charity Commission's publication *Trustees trading and tax: How charities may lawfully trade* (CC35).[5]

GOVERNANCE ISSUES

13.18   There are three significant governance issues for charity trustees raised by trading. These are:

- the tax implications of the trade;
- the charity law implications of the trade; and
- the implications of the trade in respect of liability and risk.

Tax implications

13.19   Exemptions and reliefs from tax available to charities only apply to certain types of trading income. This is explained in more detail at **13.29**. From the point of view of good governance, the key point for charity trustees is that allowing their charity to engage in a trade which gives rise to taxable profits is likely to constitute a breach of trust by them. This may mean that they are personally liable to compensate the charity for any tax it has to pay but which could have been avoided had the trade been structured appropriately.

13.20   The possibility that a charity may trade at a loss also has potentially significant tax implications. This is because of the rules which restrict the availability of the exemptions and reliefs from tax available generally to a charity where it incurs 'non-charitable expenditure'. As we explain in more detail at **13.29**, certain trading activities carried out by charities generate income which is not exempt from tax (we call this 'non-exempt trading'). HM Revenue & Customs takes the view that losses incurred in any non-exempt trading activity cannot be charitable expenditure. This may lead to a restriction on the charity's ability to claim exemptions and reliefs from tax in respect of its other, non-trading, income. HM Revenue & Customs does, however, ignore trading losses which arise as a result of the allocation of a proportion of the charity's fixed costs (ie its overheads) to the trade provided that the charity has realised profits from the trade after deducting its direct trading costs and would have incurred the fixed costs in any event.

Charity law implications

13.21   The charity law restrictions on trading derive from the constitutional arrangements that must be adopted in order to qualify as a charity. Every charity will have one or more charitable purposes for which it is established and every charity will have a range of powers which can only be exercised in order to give effect to those charitable purposes. Broadly, the exercise by a charity of its powers to carry out trades that directly advance its charitable purposes are

---

[5]   CC 35.

acceptable. Those trades that do not directly advance a charity's charitable purposes are (broadly speaking) not acceptable, on the basis that its powers cannot be exercised in a way that does not directly advance its charitable purposes.

13.22 The Charity Commission's guidance gives a different reason for the restrictions on trading by charities:

> 'Charity law permits charities to carry on non-primary purpose trading in order to raise funds, provided that the trading involves no significant risk to the assets of the charity.
>
> The "significant risk" to be avoided here is that the turnover is insufficient to meet the costs of carrying on the trade, and the difference has to be financed out of the assets of the charity.
>
> Whilst this is not invariably the case, the trade creditors would normally have a right of recourse to any of the assets of the charity, whether those assets had any connection with the trading or not. The consequent depletion of the charity's assets could have the effect of preventing the charity from being able to continue serving the community as effectively as it might otherwise have done, or at all. Those who provided the charity's assets are likely to have expected that those assets would be used to further the charity's purposes, or invested prudently, and would not be put at risk in trading activities the object of which was simply to raise further funds.'[6]

13.23 While there is undoubtedly some truth in this statement, it is debatable whether this is actually the legal basis for the charity law restriction on charities carrying out non-primary purpose trading.

13.24 A charity which wishes to carry out a particular trade can only do so if it has the relevant powers. There are no statutory powers that can be relied upon by charities in order to trade, so the position will be determined by the provisions of a charity's constitution. Many charities will have an express power to trade, although any restrictions on that power should be carefully observed. Where a charity trades without a power to do so, its trustees will be acting in breach of trust and the charity itself will be acting ultra vires. There is more about the consequences of this in **Chapter 7.**

13.25 If a charity does not have an appropriate power to trade, it may be possible to amend its constitution in order to add one. There is more about amendments to charity constitutions in **Chapters 4 and 15.**

Liability and risk

13.26 While charity trustees have to contend with the framework of charity and tax law within which they must operate, they also need to take into account the wide range of trading issues that may give rise to liabilities and

---

[6]   CC 35.

increase the risk to the charity of carrying out the trade. A discussion of the liabilities and risk associated with trading is the subject of a book in itself and is outside the scope of this chapter. But there are obviously issues relating to employees, consumer contracts, intellectual property, unfair contract terms etc that must be taken into account as well as the possibility of trading at a loss.

13.27 The risk associated with liabilities of this kind is particularly important for charities which carry out both trading and other activities. While a charity which does no more than carry out a particular trade may be willing to accept the risk associated with it (and look at ways in which those risks can be mitigated), a charity with significant investment assets which is looking at engaging in a trade for the first time will obviously want to think long and hard about whether (and how) it can ring fence those assets from liabilities associated with the trade.

13.28 The Charity Commission's guidance[7] says that whenever a trading activity carries 'significant risk' to the assets of the charity, that activity must be carried out through a trading subsidiary. There is more about trading subsidiaries at **13.70**.

TAXATION OF TRADING

13.29 There are six exemptions from tax available to a charity in respect of its trading income. Trading income which falls outside the exemptions will be liable to tax (as we have mentioned, we call this 'non-exempt trading'). Some of the exemptions are more significant than others. They are as follows:

- primary purpose trades;
- beneficiary trades;
- small trades;
- fundraising events;
- lotteries; and
- agricultural shows.

13.30 The tax for which a charity may be liable will depend upon how it is constituted. Broadly, charitable companies and other incorporated charities will be liable to corporation tax (under the Corporation Tax Act 2010), while unincorporated charities will usually be liable to income tax (under the Income Tax Act 2007). We refer to both as 'tax' in this chapter. There is more about this in **11.11**.

---

[7]   CC 35.

Primary purpose trading

13.31   Both the Corporation Tax Act 2010 (s 478) and the Income Tax Act 2007 (s 524) exempt from tax the income from any charitable trade. Charitable trade is defined as trade 'exercised in the course of carrying out a primary purpose' of a charity.[8] For obvious reasons, trades of this kind are referred to as 'primary purpose' trades. The primary purpose in question will be one (or more) of the charitable purposes specified in a charity's constitution.

13.32   The key to this exemption is that the trade in question is 'exercised in the course of carrying out' of the primary purpose. It may help to consider some examples. HM Revenue & Customs' guidance gives these examples of primary purpose trades:

'•   The provision of educational services by a school or college in return for course fees.
•   The holding of an exhibition by an art gallery or museum in return for admission fees.
•   The sale of tickets for a theatrical production staged by a theatre.
•   The provision of health-care services by a hospital in return for payment.
•   The provision of serviced residential accommodation by a residential care home in return for payment.
•   The sale of certain educational goods by an art gallery or museum.'[9]

13.33   What each of these examples have in common is that the income is received by the charity in return for goods or services which are an intrinsic part of the way in which the charity in question advances its charitable purposes. So, for example, while a school which charges fees for providing education to its pupils will be carrying out a primary purpose trade, letting its facilities to third parties out of term time for use as conference facilities has nothing to do with its charitable educational purposes and will not be an exempt trade (notwithstanding that the funds generated will be used to support those purposes).

13.34   HM Revenue & Customs also accepts that:

'Exemption from tax is also extended to other trading which, although not overtly primary purpose in nature, is ancillary to the carrying out of a primary purpose of a charity. This trading can still be said to be exercised in the course of the carrying out of a primary purpose of a charity and is, therefore, part of a primary purpose trade.'[10]

---

8   Corporation Tax Act 2010, s 479(1)(a); Income Tax Act 2007, s 525(1)(a).
9   HM Revenue & Customs' Guidance Note Annex IV.6.
10   HM Revenue & Customs' Guidance Note Annex IV.7.

13.35 The Charity Commission's guidance is in line with this and suggests that 'an ancillary trade is one that contributes indirectly to the successful furtherance of the purposes of the charity'.[11] HM Revenue & Customs' examples are helpful:

'•   The sale of relevant goods or provision of services, for the benefit of students by a school or college (text books, for example).

•   The provision of a crèche for the children of students by a school or college in return for payment.

•   The sale of food and drink in a cafeteria to visitors to exhibits by an art gallery or museum (although sale to the general public, as opposed to exhibition visitors, is non-primary purpose trading).

•   The sale of food and drink in a restaurant or bar to members of the audience by a theatre (although sale to the general public, as opposed to the audience, is non-primary purpose trading).

•   The sale by able bodied staff of items produced by the disabled in a disabled workshop.

•   The sale of confectionary, toiletries and flowers to patients and their visitors by a hospital.'[12]

13.36 Where a charity carries out 'mixed' trades (in other words, a trade which has both primary purpose and non-primary purpose elements) the primary purpose and non-primary purpose trades can be treated as separate trades.[13] Again, HM Revenue & Customs' examples are helpful:

'•   A shop in an art gallery or museum which sells a range of goods, some of which are related to a primary purpose of the charity (direct reproductions of exhibits with no other function, (therefore excluding for example, mugs and postcards), catalogues, etc), and some which are not (e.g. promotional pens, mugs, tea towels, stamps etc).

•   The letting of serviced accommodation for students in term-time (primary purpose), and for tourists out of term (non primary purpose) by a school or college.

•   The sale of food and drink in a theatre restaurant or bar both to members of the audience (beneficiaries of the charity – ancillary) and the general public (non-beneficiaries – not ancillary).

•   The operation of a café by a "relief of the disabled" charity where only 50 per cent of the staff are disabled (beneficiaries) and the other 50 per cent are not charitable beneficiaries.'[14]

13.37 In these circumstances, the primary purpose trade will be exempt, provided it is used for charitable purposes. The non-primary purpose trade will be taxable, although the small trades exemption may apply. There is more on this at **13.41**.

---

[11]   CC 35.
[12]   HM Revenue & Customs' Guidance Note Annex IV.7.
[13]   Corporation Tax Act 2010, s 479(2); Income Tax Act 2007, s 525(2).
[14]   HM Revenue & Customs' Guidance Note Annex IV.8.

Beneficiary trades

13.38 As mentioned at **13.31** the profits of a charitable trade are exempt from tax.[15] Both the Corporation Tax Act 2010 and the Income Tax Act 2007 specifically define charitable trade to include trade which consists of work 'mainly carried out by beneficiaries' of the charity.[16]

13.39 This exemption is directed at the kind of trading that is perhaps less common now than it was previously, eg the sale of goods which have been manufactured by people with disabilities who are also beneficiaries of the charity selling the goods. Trades of this kind may often be primary purpose trades as well as beneficiary trades because they will advance the charity's charitable purposes. This will include, for example, a charity established to relieve the needs of disabled people by providing them with paid employment in a workshop producing goods for sale. HM Revenue & Customs' guidance is helpful:

> 'Some of the work of a trade may be carried out by employees, contractors or volunteer workers who will not rank as beneficiaries of the charity. In these circumstances tax exemption will still be available for the whole profit arising from the trade provided it can be shown that a greater part of the work in connection with the trade is carried out by beneficiaries of the charity ...
>
> A charity may wish to pay salaries to beneficiaries who work in a trade carried on by the charity. This means that the beneficiaries are employees of the charity. PAYE must be operated on the earnings of beneficiaries who are employed by a charity in the same way as for other employees and national minimum wage rules must be applied.'[17]

13.40 There is no definition of 'mainly' for this exemption, although in other contexts it means more than 50%. Where the work in connection with a trade is carried out partly (but not mainly) by a charity's beneficiaries, the Corporation Tax Act 2010 and Income Tax Act 2007, allow HM Revenue & Customs to treat the work carried on by the beneficiaries and the work carried on by non-beneficiaries as separate trades.[18] This ensures that the non-beneficiary trade does not 'taint' the beneficiary trade, leading to a loss of tax relief for the trade as a whole.

Small trades

13.41 There is a specific exemption from tax on profits of certain 'small trades' carried out by charities. The exemption is available where a charity's gross trading income (in other words, the income it receives before deducting

---

15   Corporation Tax Act 2010, s 478; Income Tax Act 2007, s 524.
16   Corporation Tax Act 2010, s 479(1)(b); Income Tax Act 2007, s 525(1)(b).
17   HM Revenue & Customs' Guidance Note Annex IV.11/12.
18   Corporation Tax Act 2010, s 479(3); Income Tax Act 2007, s 525(3).

any of its trading expenses) is equal to or less than the greater of £5,000 and whichever is the lesser of £50,000 and 25% of all of the charity's 'incoming resources' during a tax year.

13.42 In this context, 'incoming resources' is much wider than the 'gross income' of the trade. It includes, for example, all of the income the charity may receive from its investment assets and all of the donations it may receive over the same period.

13.43 This means that a charity which has incoming resources of more than £200,000 during a tax year can only rely on the 'small trades' exemption if its trading income is £50,000 or less. If the trading income is higher than this limit, the exemption is not available in respect of any of the trading income received.[19]

13.44 The exception to this is where the charity can show that, at the beginning of the tax year, it had a reasonable expectation that its gross income from its trade during the year would not exceed the limit. HM Revenue & Customs' guidance states that:

> 'If the total turnover of taxable trading exceeds the small-scale trading limits, profits from a non-charitable trade may still be exempt if the charity can clearly demonstrate that, at the start of the relevant accounting period, it was reasonable for it to expect that the turnover would not exceed the limit. This might be because:
>
> • The charity expected the turnover from the non-charitable trade to be lower than it turned out to be; or
> • The charity expected that its total incoming resources would be higher than they turned out to be.
>
> HMRC will consider any evidence the charity may have to satisfy the reasonable expectation test.'[20]

It may be the case that the charity has carried out the activity for a number of years and might be able to show that the turnover increased unexpectedly compared with earlier years. Alternatively, the charity might have started carrying out the fund-raising activity in the year in question and might be able to show that the turnover was higher than it forecasted when it decided to start the activity.

13.45 The key to meeting the 'reasonable expectation' test is obviously being able to produce clear and convincing evidence of what the charity expected might happen at the start of the tax year. HM Revenue & Customs suggests

---

[19] Corporation Tax Act 2010, ss 480 and 482; Income Tax Act 2007, ss 526 and 528.
[20] HM Revenue & Customs' Guidance Note Annex IV.16.

producing minutes of meetings, copies of cash flow forecasts, business plans and the previous year's accounts as evidence. Clear minutes are likely to be essential.

13.46 The Charity Commission accepts that, where a charity can trade within the limits of the 'small trades' exemption, there is no intrinsic objection under charity law. Its guidance says:

> 'The carrying on by a charity of trading the turnover of which is within the scope of the small-scale exemption is unlikely to contravene the charity law restrictions on carrying on non-primary purpose trading. The low maximum permitted level of trading turnover means that any risk to the charity's resources from the trading is likely to be small.
>
> Therefore, unless prohibited by its governing document, any charity can carry on small-scale, non-primary purpose trading, and be exempt from corporation tax (or income tax in the case of charitable trusts) on the profits, provided that the profits are applied for the purposes of the charity.'[21]

13.47 Many charities' constitutions will include an express prohibition on 'substantial' trading activities or 'permanent' trading activities (often included in the provision conferring a power to raise funds). However, the Charity Commission previously accepted that prohibitions of this kind do not prevent a charity taking advantage of the small trades exemption (the relevant guidance has now been withdrawn).

Fundraising events

13.48 As we have mentioned earlier in this chapter, the line between fundraising and trading is often difficult to draw, particularly in relation to fundraising events such as concerts, dinners, shows, participation in sporting events, auctions and festivals. By concession, HM Revenue & Customs accepts that:

> 'Certain events arranged by voluntary organisations or charities for the purpose of raising funds for charity may fall within the definition of 'trade' ... with the result that any profits will be liable to income tax or corporation tax. Tax will not be charged on such profits provided:
>
> • the event is of a kind which falls within the exemption from VAT under Group 12 of Schedule 9 of the VAT Act 1994; and
> • the profits are transferred to charities or otherwise applied for charitable purposes.'[22]

13.49 The requirements of this concession (Extra-Statutory Concession C4 or 'ESC4') are as follows:

---

[21]   CC 35.
[22]   Extra Statutory Concession C4.

- The event must be organised and promoted exclusively to raise money for the charity and people attending or participating in the event must be aware that raising funds is its primary purpose.

- An event is only an event if it does not include the provision of accommodation for more than two nights. This means that most 'challenge events' (which will generally involve travelling and staying overseas for a number of nights in order to complete a particular journey or task) will fall outside ESC4.

- There must be no more than 15 events of the same type in any one location within any one financial year. So, for example, a raffle held in the same place on more than 15 occasions during a financial year will fall outside ESC4.

13.50 Where the exemption is available, it also covers all the income from supplies of goods and services made by the charity in connection with a particular event including, for example, the sale of brochures and sponsorship payments which are directly connected with the event.

13.51 Although there is a requirement that the profits from the event are 'transferred to charities' ESC4 is not available to a charity's trading subsidiary. The restriction that the profits should be 'otherwise applied for charitable purposes' is common to all of the exemptions from tax on trading by charities. There is more about this at **13.55**.

Lotteries

13.52 Lotteries are defined by the Gambling Act 2005, s 14. At its simplest, and in broad terms, a lottery is an arrangement whereby people are required to pay in order to participate and prizes are allocated by a process which relies wholly on chance. A charity's trustees should understand the legal implications of raising money by way of a lottery (and also those fundraising events which, while not intended to be lotteries, may fall within the statutory definition), not least because promoting an unlawful lottery is a criminal offence.

13.53 The exemption from tax on the profits of a lottery applies to particular kinds of 'small' and 'societies' lotteries. Clearly, a charity's trustees will need to understand how to promote lotteries of this kind rather than any other kind of lottery in order to ensure that the exemption from tax is available (although it is worth remembering that not every lottery will constitute a trade by a charity). Trustees need to ensure that they understand the provisions that apply to lotteries in the 2005 Act.

Agricultural shows

13.54 There is specific exemption for the profits of shows of agricultural societies. In many cases, a charitable agricultural show's profits may in any event be derived from a primary purpose trade.[23]

Application of profits

13.55 Each of these exemptions (with the exception of ESC4) applies only to the extent that the trading profits in question are applied 'solely to the purposes of the charity'. In other words, the profits must be properly applied to advance the charity's purposes in accordance with charity law if the exemptions are to be available.

13.56 ESC4 works in a slightly different way. There, the profits derived from a fundraising event must be applied for 'charitable purposes'. In principle, therefore, a charity could apply profits for a charitable purpose which is not one of its own charitable purposes and still claim the benefit of ESC4 (although clearly that may constitute a breach of trust by its trustees).

13.57 It is also worth remembering that each of the exemptions from tax on trading profits requires *all* of the profits to be applied for charitable purposes. Even if a part of the profits were applied for non-charitable purposes, the exemptions will be lost in their entirety.

TAX PLANNING

13.58 Where a charity wishes to carry out a trade which does not fall within one of the exemptions we have summarised earlier in this chapter, there may be other ways of structuring the trade so that there is no liability to tax on profits. The most common forms of tax planning are:

- split payments;
- annual payments; and
- trading subsidiaries.

Each of these possibilities is examined in more detail below.

SPLIT PAYMENTS

13.59 This is a tax planning approach that may be useful where a charity wishes to raise funds from its supporters where (from the supporters' perspective) a significant part of the funds given are donations but where,

---

[23]   Corporation Tax Act 2010, s 989.

because the charity is providing goods or services in return for the funds it receives from supporters it is, from a tax law perspective, in receipt of trading income.

13.60 This is not unusual in the context of charity fundraising, where supporters may make payments which are primarily intended to be donations but are also receiving some tangible benefits from the charity in return. The best example is probably a fundraising event which has a specified ticket price. The price payable for each ticket will be trading income, notwithstanding that the price paid by a supporter may be much greater than the financial value of the benefit they receive in return (eg the cost to the charity of allowing the supporters to bring a certain number of guests to a dinner).

13.61 A possible solution to this problem is to split the payments received by the charity between payments for goods and services and payments which constitute donations. In this way, the donations can be clearly earmarked as donations with the consequence that they are likely to be eligible for gift aid relief and will not constitute trading income for the charity. The payments received by the charity for the supply of goods or services in question will be trading income.

13.62 The fundamental requirement in relation to this approach is that the payment is split in a way which is reasonable. Any charge made for the supply of goods or services must reflect the value of those goods and services so that it can reasonably be said that the 'donation' is clearly a donation.

13.63 HM Revenue & Customs acknowledges that this approach is workable in the context of fundraising events:

> 'it may be possible to organise the event so as to minimise the amount of tax payable. For example, the charity might set a basic minimum charge and invite those attending the event to supplement this with a voluntary donation. This minimum charge will be standard-rated for VAT (unless exempt under another provision) and for direct tax purposes will be taxable trading income.
>
> The additional contributions will not be taxable if all of the following conditions are met:
>
> - It is clearly stated in all publicity material, including tickets, that anyone paying only the minimum charge will be admitted without further payment.
> - The additional payment does not secure any particular benefit – for example, admission to a better seat in the auditorium. (For direct tax purposes only, the payment may still be treated as non-taxable income if the benefit is within the limits specified in Gift Aid legislation.)
> - The extent of further contributions is ultimately left to ticket holders to decide (even if the organiser indicates a desired level of donation). These further contributions may be made under Gift Aid, subject to them meeting the requirements of the scheme.

- For film or theatre performances, concerts, sporting fixtures and similar events the minimum charge is not less than the usual price for the particular seats at a normal commercial event of the same type.
- For dances, dinners and similar functions the sum of the basic minimum charges is not less than the total costs incurred in arranging the event.'[24]

13.64 These are all reasonable requirements aimed at ensuring that the trading income represents the 'market value' of the benefits provided and that the additional donation that is paid by a supporter is truly a donation, with no obligations attached to it. In that sense, the acid test is whether a supporter could decide to pay the specified minimum charge and still attend the event without making any sort of donation whatsoever. There is obviously a judgement to be made by the charity about the value of the tax saved as against the possibility that its supporters will not put their hands deep enough into their pockets.

ANNUAL PAYMENTS

13.65 Increasingly, charities may be able to exploit the value in their 'brand' (in other words, their name and/or logo), by licensing its use to commercial entities which hope to sell more of their goods and services by associating themselves with the charity.

13.66 This would normally be achieved by arranging for a charity to license its name and/or logo to a commercial entity for use in relation to a particular product or service. There are other issues that a charity should be aware of in relation to this (not least the rules in relation to commercial participators imposed by the Charities Act 1992). These are summarised below at **13.142**.

13.67 In the case of logos that came into existence prior to 1 April 2002, provided royalties payable to the charity under the licence are 'annual payments' for tax purposes, they will qualify for corporation or income tax relief in the hands of the charity.[25] In some cases, the royalties must be paid after deducting tax but this can be reclaimed by the charity. The key advantage is however, that the royalties are not treated as non-exempt trading income and are not liable, therefore, to tax. Unless royalties are 'annual payments' in the hands of a charity, they will almost inevitably be trading income because there are very few circumstances in which exploiting the goodwill associated with a charity's name and logo would fall within its charitable purposes so that it constitutes primary purpose trading income.

13.68 In order to ensure that royalties are 'annual payments' for tax purposes, the charity must ensure that it does no more than license its name and or logo to the commercial entity, that it incurs no other expenses in relation to the licence and that the licence itself is capable of lasting for more than one year.

---

[24] HM Revenue & Customs' Guidance Note Annex IV 32
[25] Corporation Tax Act 2010, s 488; Income Tax Act 2007, s 536.

Commercial entities may often require a licence of this kind to be made in conjunction with a licence to use, say, the charity's database of supporters, which would mean that payments received by the charity would not constitute annual payments. Where this is a risk, a charity should consider making the licence arrangement via a wholly-owned trading subsidiary.

13.69 The position is different for a logo that came into existence on or after 1 April 2002. In this case the logo is regarded as an 'intangible fixed asset' under the Corporation Tax Act 2009. However, exemption from tax may be available under the Corporation Tax Act 2010, s 488 (exemption for miscellaneous income).

TRADING SUBSIDIARIES

13.70 One of the most common approaches taken by charities to minimising tax liabilities in relation to non-exempt trading is to use a trading subsidiary. In principle, this is a straightforward structure to put in place. Broadly, it works in the following way:

- Where a charity wishes to carry out a trade which does not fall within any of the available exemptions from tax for its profits, the trustees may decide to establish a non-charitable trading company, which will usually be wholly owned by the charity.

- The purpose of the subsidiary company is to carry on the non-exempt trade which the charity cannot carry out itself (hence the usual reference to a 'trading subsidiary').

- The trading subsidiary operates in much the same way as any other commercial company. To the extent that it makes profits from the trade it carries, it will have a liability to corporation tax.

- However, this tax liability can be reduced (or eliminated altogether) by the trading subsidiary making a 'gift aid' donation to its parent charity.

- The donation is free of tax in the hands of the charity and is deductible (as a 'charge on income') by the trading subsidiary in calculating its liability to corporation tax.

- The net effect should be (in principle, at least) that the trading subsidiary has traded profitably with the full benefit of those profits passing (tax free) to its parent charity.

13.71 Strictly, a company is only a 'subsidiary' where it is owned by another company. We use the term 'trading subsidiary' in the wider sense in which it is used by the Charity Commission, to include any trading company wholly owned by any incorporated or unincorporated charity.

13.72 Both the Charity Commission and HM Revenue & Customs expressly approve of trading subsidiary arrangements, notwithstanding that, in some respects at least, they appear to represent a rather artificial solution to the problems posed for charities by non-exempt trading.

13.73 Although establishing a trading subsidiary will generally be driven by tax considerations, there may be circumstances in which a charity concludes that it would prefer to carry out a trade via a trading subsidiary in order to ensure that any liabilities and risks associated with the trade in question are ring-fenced from the charity's other assets and activities.

13.74 Indeed, depending on their assessment of the risks associated with the trade, the trustees may be required to carry it out through a trading subsidiary. The Charity Commission's guidance on this point is clear:

> 'If charities wish to carry on non-primary purpose trading involving significant risk, they must do so through a trading subsidiary ... This [applies] whether or not the trading profits would, if the trading were to be carried on by the charity itself, be tax exempt.'[26]

13.75 To assist trustees in carrying out their assessment of the risks, the guidance says:

> 'Whether or not the risk of non-primary purpose trading is "significant" depends on a number of factors, including:
>
> - the size of the charity;
> - the nature of the business;
> - the expected outgoings;
> - turnover projections; and
> - the sensitivity of business profitability to the ups and downs of the market.
>
> Inevitably, the assessment of the significance of the risk will involve an element of judgment on the part of trustees and their advisers. In general, however, a lottery, or trading which qualifies for the "small-scale exemption" ... may be considered not to involve significant risk.'[27]

13.76 Although the relationship between a charity and its trading subsidiary is easily summarised, there are a number of other issues which make the position more complex for a charity's trustees. These relate to both the setting up and initial investment in a trading subsidiary and its subsequent operations.

13.77 Fundamental to many of these issues is the principle that a trading subsidiary will, notwithstanding that it may be wholly owned by a charity and have been established by it for a particular purpose, still be (and will be treated by HM Revenue & Customs and the Charity Commission as) a separate commercial entity which the charity must deal with in the same way as it would deal with any other separate commercial entity (in other words, on arm's length terms).

---

[26]   CC 35.
[27]   CC 35.

Set-up

13.78 There are a number of issues that will need to be addressed by a charity's trustees in relation to the setting up of a trading subsidiary. These are explained below.

Corporate structure

13.79 Generally, a trading subsidiary will be a company limited by shares. A company limited by guarantee can be used but, while retaining the benefits of limited liability, this would exclude the possibility of the charity investing in the company by subscribing for shares in it.

Investment

13.80 In line with the principle that the charity should deal with the trading subsidiary in the same way as it would deal with any other commercial entity, any investment the charity proposes to make in the subsidiary must be on arm's length terms. In other words, it must be treated by the trustees in the same way as they would treat any other proposed investment of the charity's assets, in line with the charity's overall investment policy. The Commission's guidance is that trustees must:

- '• be certain that the investment is within the charity's investment powers;
- exercise such care and skill in the investment process as is reasonable in the circumstances;
- have regard to the suitability to the charity of investments of the same kind as the particular investment which it is proposed to make;
- have regard to the suitability of the particular investment in question, as an investment of the kind which it seems appropriate to make;
- have regard to the need for diversification of investments, as appropriate to the circumstances of the charity; and
- ordinarily obtain and consider advice about the investment from a person reasonably believed by the trustees to be qualified to give it by his or her ability in and practical experience of financial and other matters; the advice needs to have regard to the suitability and diversification points mentioned above.'[28]

13.81 HM Revenue & Customs' guidance reflects the guidance issued by the Commission:

'When deciding whether to make an investment, charities should bear in mind the requirements of charity law relating to:

- Objectivity in the selection of investments;
- The need to avoid undue risk or speculation; and
- The need for a proper spread of investments.'[29]

---

[28] CC 35.
[29] HM Revenue & Customs' Guidance Note Annex III.6.

13.82   There is more about the considerations that are applied to the exercise of power of investment by a charity's trustees in **Chapter 10**. The key point is that a charity's trustees are expected to approach an investment in its trading subsidiary in the same way as they would approach an investment in, say, shares in Marks & Spencer. In practice, it is often difficult to justify investing the charity's funds in what is essentially a start-up company as against investing them in listed shares in an established trading company.

13.83   In this context, 'investment' does not mean the charity's initial subscription for shares in the trading subsidiary. As the Commission's guidance states:

> 'When a trading subsidiary is formed, its parent charity can freely make a nominal subscription of share capital in the trading subsidiary in order to comply with the requirement of company law concerning the formation of companies.'[30]

13.84   However, where the charity needs to make a more substantial investment in the trading subsidiary in order to fund its trading activities, all of the considerations that apply to investment generally will apply. Again, the Commission's guidance states that 'such an investment must be justifiable as an investment of the charity's assets'.[31]

13.85   In practice, the Commission will expect the charity's trustees to take the sort of steps that they should take in relation to any proposed investment in order to ensure that the trading subsidiary is a 'commercially sound proposition'. The Charity Commission's guidance states that:

> 'In the context of a proposed investment in a trading subsidiary which is used to carry on a non primary purpose trade, this means that:
>
> - the trustees must reasonably consider that it is in the charity's interests to make the investment, after making a fair comparison of this form of investment with other forms of investment which might be selected; this fair comparison must involve an objective assessment of the trading subsidiary's business prospects;
> - the trustees must be satisfied as to the financial viability of the trading subsidiary, based on its business plan, cash flow forecasts, profit projections, risk analysis and other available information; and
> - the trustees must ordinarily take appropriate advice on the investment, and the financial viability of the trading subsidiary. What is "appropriate" will depend on the circumstances: the cost of taking the advice is a relevant factor, and the cost should be commensurate to the size of the proposed investment.'[32]

13.86   Again, HM Revenue & Customs' guidance reflects the Commission's guidance:

---

[30]   CC 35.
[31]   CC 35.
[32]   CC 35.

'Depending on the size of the proposed investment, the decision may be based on the following:

- Business plans.
- Cashflow forecast.
- Projections of future profits.'[33]

13.87 Investment by the charity can take one of two forms. The charity could subscribe for shares in the trading subsidiary. Alternatively, the charity could make loans to the trading subsidiary which may or may not be secured. The key consideration is that shareholders subscribing for shares in a trading subsidiary will rank behind lenders. Lenders will rank with other ordinary creditors, unless they take security for their loan.

13.88 In general, therefore, charity trustees should look to lend money to a trading subsidiary in order to provide the funds required for its activities. Where a charity does lend money to a trading subsidiary the Commission's guidance is that:

'trustees must decide on the terms as regards the interest rate and repayment of principal. They must also decide how the loan is to be secured.'[34]

13.89 The starting point for any loan made by a charity to its trading subsidiary is that the loan must:

- charge a proper rate of interest;
- be secured; and
- include repayment terms.

13.90 Clearly, an interest free loan by a charity to its trading subsidiary will not satisfy the general principle that funding should be made available on an arm's length basis. A proper rate of interest should be charged by the charity, although the rate that is set will need to take into account the risk of default by the trading subsidiary (which is a factor that any commercial lender would take into account) and the rate that the charity might otherwise obtain by depositing the funds with a bank or other financial institution. Interest payments should actually be made by the trading subsidiary of the charity (and not simply added to the principal outstanding on the loan).

13.91 Taking security may have no real value in the context of a start-up company which may have few fixed or other assets that have any realisable value in the event of default on the loan. But it is obviously advisable for a charity's trustees to seek fixed and floating charges where this is possible.

---

[33] HM Revenue & Customs' Guidance Note Annex IV.51.
[34] CC 35.

13.92 The loan must set out the basis on which the principal will be repaid. There is no requirement that the loan should be repayable on demand by the charity but, equally, no commercial lender would agree to lend funds without specifying the term of the loan.

13.93 The repayment of a loan by a trading subsidiary is not always straightforward from a tax perspective. This is because the payment of interest is a tax deductible item for the purposes of calculating taxable profits, which will be subject to corporation tax. The repayment of the capital of the loan is not tax deductible. In most cases the loan will need to be paid out of the trading subsidiary's profits and the trading subsidiary will have to retain some profits in order to pay the loan. In doing so, it is likely to incur a tax charge, which will reduce its gift aid payment to the charity.

13.94 The Charity Commission does acknowledge that there may be circumstances in which investing in a trading subsidiary by way of loan may have the effect of making it insolvent. The Commission's guidance states:

> 'where a trading subsidiary would be exposed to the risk or actuality of insolvency if it were to be capitalised by loan, trustees will have little choice but to invest share capital.'[35]

Equally, the Commission recognises that:

> 'the subscription by a parent charity of substantial share capital in its trading subsidiary can give confidence to suppliers, customers, creditors, prospective creditors and others with whom the trading subsidiary has a business relationship.'[36]

13.95 The Charity Commission's guidance states that it is 'good practice' to consider outside investment in a trading subsidiary, recognising that, in most cases, outside investment will be in the form of loan capital. As the Commission quite rightly points out, involving a commercial lender is more likely to ensure that the viability of the subsidiary's trading activities is objectively assessed by someone with no direct involvement in the trade.

13.96 The Commission also makes the point that arranging for a trading subsidiary to borrow from a commercial lender will protect the charity's assets from exposure to the financial risks of the trade the subsidiary is carrying out. However, as the Commission rightly notes, the terms of any such loan and interest payments due to the commercial lender could significantly reduce the level of trading profits in the subsidiary.

13.97 Charities should also be aware that most commercial lenders are shrewd enough to look for security from the parent charity (eg in the form of a guarantee) where they take the view that the trading subsidiary's activities and

---

[35] CC 35.
[36] CC 35.

assets present them with any sort of risk of default on the loan. In particular, this is obviously likely to be an issue where a trading subsidiary routinely pays all or most of its trading profits up to its parent charity, with little opportunity to accrue value within the subsidiary itself.

13.98 The Charity Commission's view is that guarantees given by a charity to secure the liabilities of its trading subsidiary will often be unenforceable against the charity and may expose the trustees to personal liability. The Commission's guidance states:

> 'If such a guarantee is given by trustees of a parent charity, and liability under the guarantee is enforced by a creditor of the trading subsidiary, trustees are unlikely to be entitled to an indemnity from the charity, and will have to settle the liability personally, where:
>
> - the liability arises out of a failure of a trade carried on by a trading subsidiary; and
> - the parent charity could not itself properly have carried on that trade.
>
> In addition, payments made by a parent charity under a guarantee of the liabilities of a trading subsidiary may be considered to be non-charitable expenditure, creating a potential adverse tax effect for the charity.'[37]

13.99 Clearly trustees will wish to avoid giving a guarantee or other security. A commercial lender may agree to lend on the basis of a 'letter of comfort' from the charity which indicates that it will consider meeting any liabilities to the lender which the trading subsidiary cannot meet itself. A letter of comfort must be carefully worded in order to ensure that it is not legally binding on the charity. Even if it is not, our view is that comfort of this kind blurs the distinction between a charity and its trading subsidiary. It is only likely to be appropriate for a letter of comfort of this kind to be given where the charity's trustees are confident that the trading subsidiary will be profitable and that the letter is, therefore, genuinely given only as 'comfort'.

13.100 Where the trade in question is a primary purpose trade that the charity could have carried out itself under both tax and charity law, its ability to invest in the subsidiary will be subject to different considerations from an investment in a subsidiary which has been established to carry out a non-exempt trade. Essentially, the relationship between a charity and a trading subsidiary established for this purpose need not be on arm's length terms, as the relationship with any other trading subsidiary must be.

Tax

13.101 Any investment in a trading subsidiary (whether by subscribing for shares or loans) will only qualify as 'charitable expenditure' for tax purposes if it is made for charitable purposes only, is for the benefit of the charity and is

---

[37] CC 35.

not for the avoidance of tax. If the investment does not qualify as charitable expenditure, the charity may lose all or part of its exemptions and reliefs from tax on its other sources of income and gains. There is more information about this at **11.58**.

13.102   HM Revenue & Customs' guidance makes it clear that:

> 'Investments will be regarded as made for the benefit of the charity if they are commercially sound. Usually, charities should ensure that investments are secure, carry a fair rate of return (actually paid) and, in the case of loans, provide for recovery of the amount invested.'[38]

13.103   HM Revenue & Customs also requires trustees to take account of their investment powers under charity law and to ensure that all decisions are properly minuted, including the factors on which the decisions were based.

Governance

13.104   Irrespective of the charity and tax implications of setting up a trading subsidiary, a charity's trustees should give careful consideration to governance arrangements, particularly as regards the board of directors of the trading subsidiary. The Commission's guidance states that trustees:

> 'must bear in mind that the charity and the trading subsidiary are different entities. Anyone involved with the administration of both has two distinct responsibilities, and it can at times be difficult to balance conflicting pressures.'[39]

13.105   The potential for conflicts of interest is clearly an issue given the fundamental requirement that arrangements between the charity and its trading subsidiary should be on an arm's length basis. Where all of the trustees of the charity are all also directors of the trading subsidiary, the scope for a conflict of interest which will leave the trading subsidiary without directors capable of making a decision is reasonably high. On this basis, the Commission's guidance is:

> 'As a matter of good governance, there should be both:
>
> • at least one person who is a trustee, but not a director or employee of the trading subsidiary; and
> • at least one person who is a director of the trading subsidiary, but not a trustee or employee of the charity.
>
> These people are described as "unconflicted" as they have no conflict of interest in their roles. These unconflicted trustees and directors should advise their colleagues as to the proper course of action where the duties of those with dual

---

[38]   HM Revenue & Customs' Guidance Note Annex IV.51.
[39]   CC 35.

responsibilities are in conflict. This reduces the risk of any transaction between the parent charity and the trading subsidiary being challenged or questioned.'[40]

13.106 The scope for conflicts of interest to put individual directors of the trading subsidiary in a very difficult position is a real one. In the worst case, where the trading subsidiary is bordering on insolvency and is unlikely to avoid becoming insolvent without continued financial support from its parent charity, the subsidiary's directors may be concerned about their liabilities for any claims in respect of wrongful trading which may be brought by the subsidiary's liquidator. In this sense, the directors may have an interest in the charity continuing to provide financial support in circumstances where, as trustees, they would find it difficult to do so. The solution to this problem in practice is to ensure that the directors of the subsidiary are fully advised in relation to insolvency issues in general and wrongful trading in particular. However, the potential for conflict is clear. There is more about wrongful trading at **6.14**.

13.107 Charity trustees who also act as directors of a trading subsidiary should bear in mind that they cannot be paid for doing so unless the charity's constitution authorises them to benefit. There is more about trustee benefits of this kind at **6.36**.

Costs

13.108 Trustees should take into account the likelihood that setting up and running a separate trading subsidiary will increase the administrative and professional costs of the charity. The trustees will need to be sure that the costs in question do not exceed the tax saved by setting the subsidiary up.

Rating relief

13.109 While a charity qualifies for 80% mandatory (and 20% discretionary) relief from non-domestic rates, the same is not true of a trading subsidiary. In order to qualify for relief, a property must be occupied by a charity and be occupied wholly or mainly for its charitable purposes. As the Commission's guidance states:

> '"Charitable purposes" normally excludes fundraising activities but includes the sale of donated goods ... [Mandatory] relief is not available in the case of premises occupied by a trading subsidiary. However rating authorities have a discretion to grant rate relief to some bodies which are not charities. Premises occupied partly by a charity and used for charitable purposes, and partly by a trading subsidiary, qualify for rate relief only in respect of the part occupied by the charity.'[41]

---

[40] CC 35.
[41] CC 35.

13.110 It may be possible for the trading subsidiary to occupy a charity's premises under licence or for the charity to act as agent for the subsidiary, so that the charity continues to be in occupation wholly or mainly for its charitable purposes.

Operational issues

13.111 In addition to the issues that charity trustees need to take into account on setting up a trading subsidiary, there are a number of operational issues that are likely to arise in practice.

Additional investment

13.112 The charity's trustees will need to treat any additional investment in the trading subsidiary in exactly the same way as their initial investment. All of the same considerations in relation to looking for funding from commercial lenders and whether the charity should make funds available by loan or by subscribing for additional shares will apply.

13.113 In many cases, the trustees will wish to see the trading subsidiary making gift aid donations of all of its taxable profit up to the charity in order to avoid any liability to corporation tax (see **13.124**). This will mean that there is no real scope for the trading subsidiary to build up any value. This will, in turn, make it more difficult for the trading subsidiary to obtain funding from a commercial lender and for the trustees to conclude that the trading subsidiary is an appropriate investment for the charity.

13.114 Problems often arise in practice where the trading subsidiary is loss making. Where losses are accruing on a regular basis and without a particular justification in trading terms, the trustees are likely to be faced with a difficult decision. On the one hand, they may wish to see the charity continuing to support the trading subsidiary and its directors and employees. On the other hand, they are faced with the prospect of investing further funds for the charity in a trading company which is unlikely to produce an investment return. The Commission states:

> 'If the trustees sink further funds into supporting an ailing trading subsidiary at a time when it was reasonably clear that the failure of the subsidiary was likely, this could constitute a breach of trust on their part, putting them at personal risk to make good any losses to the charity. Trustees facing these circumstances should take advice from their professional advisers.'[42]

Third party investment

13.115 An alternative to further investment by the charity or commercial loans may be to issue shares to a commercial entity which is willing to invest funds. This would usually be because the trading subsidiary's activities have some

---

[42]   CC 35.

synergy with the commercial entity's own trading activities or because the commercial entity concludes that shares in the trading subsidiary are a good investment.

13.116   There is no objection in principle to a charity co-owning a trading subsidiary with a commercial entity where this is justified on the basis of the commercial entity's financial investment in the subsidiary, or the particular skills and expertise it has in relation to the subsidiary's operational activities.

13.117   However, a charity should only consider entering into a co-ownership arrangement of this kind on the basis of a carefully considered and properly drafted shareholders' agreement which deals with all of the issues that arise in these circumstances. These include, for example:

- whether shareholders will have rights to appoint and remove directors to and from the board of the subsidiary;
- whether shareholders have any rights of veto over material transactions with which the subsidiary may become involved (such as taking on a lease, employing senior executives or incurring material liabilities);
- the financial investment and management skills that each shareholder will bring to the subsidiary; and
- the basis on which shares can be transferred by a shareholder to a third party, perhaps with 'drag along' or 'tag along' rights in the event that a third party makes an offer to buy out one shareholder's shares.

13.118   An association with a commercial entity in this way can obviously have potentially serious implications for a charity's reputation. The shareholders' agreement should regulate the use of the charity's name and/or logo, but the charity should also think hard about the commercial entity with which it is entering into an agreement and the scope for its activities to adversely affect the charity.

13.119   Co-owning a trading subsidiary with a non-charity will affect when the subsidiary can pay profits to the charity by way of gift aid. There is more about this at **13.130**.

13.120   Where a trading subsidiary is co-owned by a charity and a non-charity, it is possible that HM Revenue & Customs will argue that gift aid payments to the charity are distributions of its profits rather than donations (with the consequence that they must be paid out of the subsidiary's taxed income). There is more about this at **13.132**.

Employee investment

13.121   Many commercial companies use employee incentives in order to help improve their profitability. The incentives in question will generally be shares issued to employees at a discount or options enabling employees to purchase shares at a discount, usually using one of the tax efficient arrangements for issuing employee incentives, such as the Employee Management Incentives scheme.

13.122 There is no reason in principle why a charity's trading subsidiary cannot issue share incentives to its employees where they are tied to appropriate targets. However, there is obviously some scope for a conflict of interest to arise for employees of the subsidiary who are also employees of the charity because they may start to do more to increase the subsidiary's profitability at the expense of the charity's own operations.

13.123 The scope for conflicts of interest to arise will obviously vary from case to case, but a charity's trustees should consider any proposal to issue employee incentives very carefully.

Profit retention

13.124 As we have mentioned, a charity's trustees may wish to see the charity's trading subsidiary making gift aid donations of all of its taxable profits to the charity, with a view to eliminating any liability to corporation tax. But trustees will need to ensure they take into account the working capital requirements of the trading subsidiary. These may mean that, in order to develop its trading activities, the subsidiary requires working capital which, if it cannot be obtained from the charity or a commercial lender, can only be obtained by leaving some profits within the subsidiary (giving rise, therefore, to a liability to tax).

13.125 The Commission suggests that:

> 'Some parent charities prefer to accept the corporation tax consequences of the trading subsidiary retaining taxable profits. Indeed such retention may be required, where funding by way of loan has been obtained from commercial banks or other third parties, in order to service the loan. This approach:
>
> - enables the trading subsidiary to fund itself by a combination of capital and retained profits in a way which is closer to ordinary commercial practice; and
> - may also make it easier for the parent charity to justify investments in the trading subsidiary, especially where significant equity finance is required to fund ongoing trading activities. However, such retention of profits by a trading subsidiary can also prejudice VAT reliefs which would otherwise be available.'[43]

13.126 This is helpful because, indirectly at least, it confirms the Commission's view that a charity's trustees can in certain circumstances properly decide not to seek a gift aid payment of all of a subsidiary's profits. The Commission has stated previously that charity trustees have a duty to consider the tax effectiveness of arrangements with its subsidiary and that they may be

---

[43]   CC 35.

personally liable for tax liabilities unnecessarily incurred as a result of the inefficient administration of the charity. Clearly, this does not extend to a considered decision to leave profits with a subsidiary to help develop its business.

13.127 HM Revenue & Customs' guidance makes a similar point:

'Most commercial companies keep part of their profits to provide them with funds for day-to-day expenses, working capital and normal development of their business. However, companies which intend to donate all of their profits to charity every year may not be able to retain the funds they need to carry on in business. Charities may therefore want to ensure when a company is set up that it is provided with enough capital to enable it to shed its profits every year **and** stay in business ... The passing of profits up to the parent charity may result in a serious drain on the company's cash. If so, care should be taken to avoid a pattern of frequent injections of funds by the charity in order to keep the company in business. Such a practice might put at risk both the charity's tax exemptions and the company's deductions for its Gift Aid payments. In some cases where there is a serious cash drain in the company, it will be necessary for the company to change its practice so that it keeps part of its profits. In these circumstances some tax will become payable by the company.'[44]

13.128 Again, it is helpful to have HM Revenue & Customs' acknowledgement that there are circumstances in which taxable profits can properly be left within a trading subsidiary.

13.129 Clearly, there is a difficult balance to be struck by a charity's trustees between a desire to minimise liability to tax and the advantage of leaving funds within a trading subsidiary in order to enable it to develop its own business without resorting to further investment by the charity and the complications that this may entail. The fact that there is a balance to be struck is a strong argument for avoiding the use of a deed of covenant between the subsidiary and the charity which obliges the subsidiary to pay up all or part of its taxable profits to the charity. There is more about deeds of covenant at **13.133**.

Gift aid

13.130 Providing a trading subsidiary is wholly owned by a charity, it has 9 months from the end of its accounting period to make donations to its parent charity. This means that it will have the time to establish its taxable and accounting profits after the end of the accounting period and can then make an appropriate donation. The same is true of a trading company which is owned by more than one charity.

13.131 However, a trading company which is owned in part by anyone other than a charity does not qualify for this treatment. It can only claim gift aid

---

[44] HM Revenue & Customs' Guidance Note Annex IV.52.

relief in respect of payments made within the company's accounting period, with no ability to carry the relief back to an accounting period ending in the previous 9 months.

13.132   As we have mentioned earlier in this chapter, payments by a subsidiary to a charity which co-owns the subsidiary with a non-charity may be treated by HM Revenue & Customs as 'distributions' for tax purposes. This will mean that HMRC will treat the payments to the charity as made out of the subsidiary's taxed income, with a corporation tax liability for the subsidiary and no repayable credit for the charity for the tax withheld on the distribution. There is more about this at **11.125**.

Deeds of covenant

13.133   There is no requirement that a gift aid donation is made under a deed of covenant, although some charities may want to see a binding legal obligation imposed upon their trading subsidiary to give to the charity an amount equal to its taxable profits (or perhaps a particular proportion of those taxable profits). The argument against this, which we have mentioned earlier in this chapter, is that it will be better to maintain the capacity to retain profits with the subsidiary and rely upon the charity's control of the subsidiary to influence the payments that are made.

13.134   A deed of covenant imposes a legal obligation to make payments to the charity and will need to be drafted carefully. Problems can arise where there is any discrepancy between the trading subsidiary's accounting and taxable profits. Where, for example, items of expenditure are allowed for accounting purposes but not allowed as deductions against tax, the trading subsidiary may have insufficient cash with which to meet its total corporation tax liability. This can be avoided by careful drafting of the deed of covenant.

Cost sharing

13.135   In line with the principle that arrangements between the charity and its trading subsidiary should be at arm's length, there should be an appropriate cost sharing arrangement in relation to any shared facilities. This might be because, for example, the trading subsidiary occupies part of the charity's premises, uses its IT or other facilities, or some of the charity's employees spend part of their time working for the subsidiary. The costs shared, therefore, should include both direct and indirect costs.

13.136   More generally, a charity's trustees should ensure that an appropriate distinction is drawn between the charity and its subsidiary in relation to all operational activities. This will mean ensuring that:

- The trustees of the charity and the directors of the trading subsidiary hold separate meetings and that separate minutes of each meeting are produced. There is no objection to holding both meetings on the same day (because the day on which a trustees' meeting is held may often be a good opportunity for the directors of the subsidiary to meet), but the two entities have a separate legal existence and it is important that this is recognised and properly recorded.

- The trading subsidiary will require its own letter-headed paper, invoices etc, all of which must comply with the requirements of the companies legislation by confirming its registered name, office and company number, its place of incorporation and either all of its directors or none of them.

- The charity and its subsidiary should use separate bank accounts and their funds should not be mixed.

13.137 All of these operational issues can be dealt with alongside cost sharing in a formal agreement between the charity and the subsidiary. This might also deal with, for example, the basis on which the subsidiary is able to use the charity's name and/or logo. This agreement should be reviewed by both the charity and the subsidiary on a regular basis.

13.138 The Charity Commission recommends that a trading subsidiary which uses part of its parent charity's premises should enter into a formal lease or licence of the property. The Commission's guidance also states that the subsidiary must pay a market rent or fee for the use of the property which is comparable to that which would be payable for letting the property on the open market.[45] This is obviously in line with the principle that arrangements between the charity and its trading subsidiary should be at arm's length. The charity's trustees should bear in mind that a lease of any part of its premises to the trading subsidiary will require the Commission's consent under the Charities Act 2011, s 117 (see **9.94** for more information in relation to this). In practice, the charity will often grant a licence to its trading subsidiary. Provided the licence is actually a licence (and the distinction between leases and licences is not always absolutely clear), the Commission's consent will not be required. The charity will need to take advice to ensure that it grants a licence rather than a lease if this is what is intended.

Transfer pricing

13.139 The 'transfer pricing' rules allow HM Revenue & Customs to treat transactions between certain connected parties as made on an arm's length basis for tax purposes. The aim is to ensure that tax is not avoided by manipulating the profitability of contracts and other transactions. In principle, arrangements between a charity and trading subsidiary will be caught by the rules, although HM Revenue & Customs' own guidance in this area suggests that the position is unlikely to be looked at critically where the charity follows the guidance issued by the Charity Commission in relation to investment in trading subsidiaries.

---

[45] CC 35.

13.140 In general, where a charity and its subsidiary are dealing with each other on an arm's length basis, the scope for the application on the transfer pricing rules is likely to be fairly restricted. However, the rules are complicated and the charity's trustees should seek advice if they are in any doubt about the position.

VAT

13.141 A detailed discussion of the VAT implications of trading by charities and their trading subsidiaries is outside the scope of this chapter. VAT is a complex tax which in many ways operates very differently to the direct charges to income and corporation tax we have discussed earlier in this chapter. Because of the sort of activities that many charities undertake, it can penalise them financially to a far greater extent than commercial entities. If in any doubt about the VAT implications of a particular trading activity (and it will generally be best to assume that there will be VAT implications unless and until it is confirmed otherwise), a charity's trustees should seek professional advice.

BUSINESS SPONSORSHIP

13.142 Many charities receive donations from commercial entities. Sometimes, this relationship may be more complex than that of donor and donee. So, for example, the charity may agree to acknowledge the commercial entity's support to the general public. This is usually referred to as 'sponsorship'. Other arrangements may involve a commercial entity paying a charity for a licence of its name and/or logo to help promote sales of particular goods or services because of the value of the charity's 'brand' among the general public. This is usually referred to as 'cause-related marketing'.

13.143 Payments received by a charity from a commercial entity under a sponsorship or cause-related marketing arrangement can in certain circumstances constitute a trade (the trade of advertising). This will vary from case to case and the way in which the 'badges' of trade apply to a particular arrangement between the charity and commercial entity. HM Revenue & Customs' guidance is helpful:

> 'Just because a sponsor derives good publicity or public relations benefits from payments to charity, does not automatically mean that payments by the sponsor are trading income in the hands of the charity.
>
> If the charity does not provide goods or services in return for payment, sponsorship payments will normally have the character of charitable donations rather than trading income in the charity's hands. The fact that the business sponsor itself takes steps to publicise or exploit the affinity with the charity will not change the treatments of the payments in the hands of the charity, unless the charity also publicises the affinity itself.'[46]

---

[46] HM Revenue & Customs' Guidance Note Annex IV.22.

13.144 The key question is whether or not the charity is providing anything to the sponsor in return for the payment it is making. If nothing is received by the sponsor in return, then the payment will generally be a donation. This is likely to be reflected in the way in which the commercial entity accounts for the payment. A donation is likely to be paid out of its charity budget and be treated as a 'charge on income' in calculating its corporation tax liability. A payment in return for goods or services received from the charity will, on the other hand, probably be paid out of the commercial entity's advertising budget and will be deducted as a trading expense in calculating its liability to tax.

13.145 HM Revenue & Customs' guidance goes on to say:

'If the charity provides some goods or services in return for the sponsorship payments they may be treated as trading income.

Most commonly a charity will play a part in publicising the business sponsor's affinity with the charity by including references to the sponsor in publications, posters, etc. and at events organised by the charity. Provided that such references amount to no more than acknowledgements of the sponsor's contributions they will not cause the payments to be regarded as trading income. However, references to a sponsor which amount to advertisements will mean the payments are trading income.'[47]

13.146 HM Revenue & Customs goes on to give some helpful examples of references to a sponsor it will regard as advertisements:

- '• Large and prominent displays of the sponsor's logo;
- Large and prominent displays of the sponsor's corporate colours; and
- A description of the sponsor's products or services.'[48]

13.147 However, it goes on to say:

'If a project organised by a charity is sponsored by a well-known company, and acknowledgment of the support of this company in the form of its name and logo inserted in the corner of a project report, this would not be considered to be advertising. However, if the name and logo was substantially and widely displayed throughout the report, this might be considered to be advertising in return for the sponsorship payment.'[49]

13.148 HM Revenue & Customs will also look at other services that a charity might provide to a sponsor alongside advertising in deciding whether or not sponsorship payments are donations or trading income. These may include a right for the sponsor to use the charity's mailing list of supporters, the use of its logo, an endorsement of the sponsor's goods or services, links to the sponsor's sales website from the charity's own website or exclusive rights to sell goods or services on the charity's premises.

---

[47] HM Revenue & Customs' Guidance Note Annex IV.23.
[48] HM Revenue & Customs' Guidance Note Annex IV.23.
[49] HM Revenue & Customs' Guidance Note Annex IV.23.

13.149 HM Revenue & Customs takes a similar approach to cause-related marketing arrangements:

> 'Where a charity allows its logo to be used, in return for payment, by a business as an endorsement for one or more of the business' products or services, and the charity likewise promotes the endorsement in its own literature, the payments are likely to be trading income of the charity.'[50]

13.150 On this basis, arrangements under which, for example, a charity licenses its name and/or logo to appear on a commercial entity's product containing a statement that a percentage of the sale price will be donated to the charity will constitute a trade. So too will any arrangement under which a charity is paid to license its name and/or logo as part of the endorsement of a commercial entity's goods or services. This would include, for example, the wide range of 'affinity' credit cards marketed by banks and other financial institutions under the name of particular charities.

13.151 Providing advertising services to commercial entities is not a primary purpose trading activity for a charity. However, there are some circumstances in which trading income of this kind will not be taxable:

- The income may fall within the small trades exemption (see **13.41**).
- Where the sponsorship is intended to fund or subsidise another trading activity of a charity, HM Revenue & Customs will treat the sponsorship payments as part of the income of that trade. Where the trade in question is primary purpose, the sponsorship payments will be treated as part of the income of that primary purpose trade. This would include, for example, sponsorship payments made to a charitable theatre in relation to a particular production.
- Where payments are made under a cause-related marketing arrangement solely for the use of the charity's name and/or logo under licence, the payments may be exempt from tax. There is more about this at **13.65** above. However, the charity must not provide the commercial entity with anything other than a licence of its name and/or logo (eg a licence to use its database of supporters or agreeing to endorse the commercial entity's goods or services).
- In circumstances where payments by a sponsor involve a degree of altruism, it may be possible to 'split' the payment between a payment for services provided by the charity and a payment that is a donation. There is more about this at **13.59** above.

13.152 Where none of these options is available, a charity will need to ensure that trading activities associated with business sponsorship or cause-related marketing are carried out via a trading subsidiary. This will generally involve the charity licensing the subsidiary to exploit its name and/or logo.

---

[50] HM Revenue & Customs' Guidance Note Annex IV.25.

13.153 Entering into sponsorship and cause-related marketing agreements with commercial entities obviously involves issues other than just tax. In particular, a charity's trustees will want to assess how the commercial entity will use its association with the charity and the potential risk to the charity resulting from any damage to the commercial entity's name or reputation. In particular the Commission's guidance is that:

> 'Charities should recognise that their name is a valuable asset and that, in a commercial partnership, association with a charity can generate substantial benefits for the company. Accordingly, charities need to take steps to protect, and where appropriate take professional advice on valuing their name.'[51]

Generally, charities should carefully consider the benefits and potential risks of any proposed arrangement with commercial entities, ensure that the arrangement is in the interests of the charity and that it is kept under review.

Commercial participators

13.154 In addition to these considerations, a charity's trustees will need to take into account the restrictions imposed by the Charities Act 1992, Part II on 'commercial participators'. A commercial participator is anyone who encourages the sale of their goods or services on the basis that some of the proceeds will be given to charity. The actual legal definition is:

> 'In relation to any charitable institution, [it] means any person (apart from a company connected with the institution) who:
>
> (a) carries on for gain a business other than a fundraising business; but
> (b) in the course of that business, engages in any promotional venture in the course of which it is represented that charitable contributions are to be given to or applied for the benefit of the institution.'[52]

13.155 Most cause-related marketing agreements with commercial entities will make them 'commercial participators'. The Charities Act 1992 provides that any agreement between a commercial participator and a charity is unlawful if it does not meet certain minimum requirements. These include the period for which the agreement is to remain in effect and how each of the charity and the commercial participator are to benefit under the agreement.

13.156 The Charities Act 1992 also imposes an obligation on the commercial participator to ensure that it makes a clear statement of the proportion of the purchase price for goods and services that will be given to the charity or the sums that will be given to it as a consequence of their sale or supply. A failure to comply with this requirement is a criminal offence.

---

[51] RS 2.
[52] Charities Act 1992, s 58(1).

13.157   A charity's trading subsidiary is not subject to the restrictions imposed by the Charities Act 1992 in relation to commercial participators. The Home Office has recommended in the past that, as a matter of good practice, trading subsidiaries should comply with the restrictions. This is, though, no more than suggested good practice.

13.158   While the sanctions for breach of the Charities Act 1992 are aimed at the commercial participator, many charities find in practice that they are expected to ensure compliance with the 1992 Act. In practice, a charity will often need to brief a potential commercial participator in relation to the restrictions and ensure that they are understood and accepted before a commercial participator agreement is prepared and agreed.

CHAPTER 14

REPORTING AND ACCOUNTING

14.1 The importance of proper financial and other forms of reporting by charities to good governance cannot be overstated. If donors, funders, financial supporters, beneficiaries and other stakeholders are to have confidence in charities then they must be subject to a regime that ensures that there is transparency in terms of how a charity's funds have been spent. The key to this is the accounting and reporting framework.

14.2 The foreword to the Charity Commission's guidance 'Charity reporting and accounting: the essentials'[1] neatly summarises the wider importance of reporting and accounting by charities:

> 'effective accountability is about more than complying with the law. The availability of charity reports and accounts on our website gives more immediate and wider accountability. This will benefit those charities that use financial reporting by providing relevant, timely and quality information which, in turn, provides an opportunity to build trust. We would encourage all trustees to use their Annual Reports and accounts to communicate with stakeholders and the wider public about their work – explaining the work their charities do and the achievements that result.'

14.3 It is outside the scope of this book to consider in detail the accounting requirements of charities and companies, but the law sets out a framework for reporting and accounting by charities and in this chapter we consider some of the main requirements.

THE ACCOUNTING AND REPORTING FRAMEWORK

14.4 The accounting and reporting framework applying to charities in England and Wales is largely contained within the Charities Act 2011, the Statement of Recommended Practice: Accounting and Reporting by Charities issued in March 2005 ('the SORP') and The Charities (Accounts and Reports) Regulations 2008 ('the Regulations'). At the time of writing the Charity Commission and the Office of the Scottish Charity Regulator, are consulting on a new draft SORP which, when finalised, will apply for financial reporting for accounting periods starting on or after 1 January 2015.

---

[1]   CC 15b.

14.5 In addition to these requirements, charitable companies must also comply with the requirements of the Companies Acts. Some charities may also be required to comply with specific legislation relating to their particular type of organisation (eg registered providers of social housing).

14.6 The framework is designed to meet the need for consistent and transparent public accountability for the resources held by charities without adding unnecessarily to the burden on trustees. Accordingly, the requirements to be met by smaller charities are less onerous than those for larger charities.

THE SORP

14.7 The SORP is developed by the Charity Commission and the Office of the Scottish Charity Regulator. It is a substantial code of practice. The current version runs to 134 pages and it explains how charities are expected to apply the relevant accounting standard to their particular activities and transactions, and how they should present and disclose their activities and funds within their accounts. The SORP also sets out the principles and elements of the trustees' annual report which accompanies the accounts.

14.8 The SORP includes requirements that are additional to those of accounting standards, in particular, requirements relating to the trustees' annual report, fund accounting, the format of the statement of financial activities and additional disclosures aimed at providing a high level of accountability and transparency to donors, funders, financial supporters and other stakeholders.

14.9 The SORP applies to all charities currently reporting under existing UK GAAP or generally accepted accounting practice (which is defined in the Corporation Tax Act 2010[2] as meaning generally accepted accounting practice with respect to accounts of UK companies that are intended to give a true and fair view) unless a separate SORP exists for a particular class of charities. For example, there are additional SORPs applicable to registered providers of social housing, further and higher education institutions and common investment or common deposit funds.

14.10 Although the SORP is a statement of recommended practice only, it has been developed under an Accounting Standards Board (ASB) code of practice and any non-compliance with its recommendations must be disclosed in a charity's accounts. This may lead to a qualified audit opinion. Many of its provisions are also underpinned, in England and Wales, by the Regulations.

THE NEW DRAFT SORP

14.11 At the time of writing, a new draft SORP is being consulted on. The new draft follows the publication of FRS 102 The Financial Reporting Standard

---

[2]   Finance Act 2004, s 50(1).

applicable in the UK and Republic of Ireland by the Financial Reporting Council.[3] FRS 102 was itself developed after an extensive period of consultation and is broadly based on the International Accounting Standards Board's International Financial Reporting Standards (IFRS). This will complete the 'suite' of standards that will constitute the new 'Generally Accepted Accounting Practice' (new GAAP).

14.12 All charities with accounting periods starting on or after 1 January 2015 will be required to report under either FRS 102 or the Financial Reporting Standard for Smaller Entities (FRSSE) and the new SORP. For accounting periods starting before 1 January 2015, the 2005 SORP will continue to apply.

14.13 At the time of writing it is not possible to be certain of the final form of the new draft SORP but its objective is stated to be to:

- improve the quality of financial reporting by charities;
- enhance the relevance, comparability and understandability of the information presented in charity accounts;
- provide clarification, explanation and interpretation of accounting standards and their application to charities and to sector specific transactions; and thereby
- assist those who are responsible for the preparation of the trustees' annual report and accounts.

BASIC REQUIREMENTS FOR ALL CHARITIES

14.14 The main purpose of the accounts is to give an overall view of the total incoming resources during the year and how they have been expended, with a balance sheet to show the overall financial position at the year end.

14.15 The minimum requirements for keeping accounting records applying to all charities are set out in Charities Act 2011, Part 8. This requires all charities other than exempt charities[4] and charitable companies[5] (to which Part 15 of the Companies Act 2006 applies) to:

- prepare and maintain accounting records in respect of the charity which are sufficient to show and explain all of the charity's transactions and disclose at any time, with reasonable accuracy, the financial position of the charity at that time.[6] These records (cash books, invoices, receipts etc) must be retained for at least 6 years from the end of the financial year in which the transaction was made;[7]

---

[3] Published in March 2013.
[4] Charities Act 2011, s 136.
[5] Charities Act 2011, s 135.
[6] Charities Act 2011, s 130.
[7] Charities Act 2011, s 131.

- prepare a statement of accounts in respect of each financial year of the charity which complies with the Regulations.[8] Except that if a charity's gross income in any financial year does not exceed £250,000, the charity trustees may, in respect of that year, elect to prepare a receipts and payments account and a statement of assets and liabilities instead of a statement of accounts;[9]

- make their accounts and annual report available to the public on request.[10] This is a vital underpinning to the principle of public accountability, and must be complied with in all cases. It is open to trustees to make a reasonable charge to cover the costs of complying with the request (eg photocopying and postage).

ADDITIONAL REQUIREMENTS

14.16 In addition to the basic requirements applicable to all charities, there are additional accounting and reporting requirements that may have to be met which depend largely on the levels of income and expenditure of the charity. Broadly speaking, the larger the charity the more onerous the requirements although the precise details depend on the type of charity. However, it should be noted that the charity's constitution may also contain specific rules on accounts, reports and auditing which may be more onerous than the requirements of the general accounting and reporting framework. If this is the case then the trustees must follow the requirements set out in the constitution, or else amend the constitution in order to relax them. There is more about alterations to charity constitutions at **15.3-15.40**.

14.17 The levels of income and expenditure of a charity and whether it is a charitable company will impact on four key areas:

- the accounting basis on which the charity's accounts are prepared;
- whether the charity is required to have its accounts scrutinised by independent examination or audited by a registered auditor;
- whether the charity is required to prepare a trustees' annual report; and
- the type of information that the charity is required to send to the Charity Commission by way of annual return, information update form or summary information return.

These four aspects of accounting and reporting are discussed in more detail below.

---

8   Charities Act 2011, s 132.
9   Charities Act 2011, s 133.
10   Charities Act 2011, ss 171 and 172.

BASIS OF PREPARATION OF ACCOUNTS

14.18 There are two ways in which charity accounts may be prepared: the receipts and payments basis and the accruals basis. Charities constituted as companies are required to use the accruals basis, whereas the trustees of smaller unincorporated charities are able to choose the basis on which their accounts are prepared.

Receipts basis

14.19 Charities that are not companies and which have a gross income of £250,000 or less during the financial year may prepare their accounts on the receipts and payments basis.[11] This simply entails the preparation of an account summarising all money received and paid out by the charity in the year in question, together with a statement giving details of its assets and liabilities at the end of the year. The accounting recommendations of the SORP do not apply to charities preparing receipts and payments accounts.

Accruals basis

14.20 Charities that are not companies and which have gross income over £250,000 during the financial year and all charitable companies must prepare their accounts on the accruals basis. This entails the preparation of a balance sheet showing the charity's financial position at the end of the year in question, a statement of financial activities during the year (and sometimes an income and expenditure account) and explanatory notes. Accounts of this kind are normally required, in accountancy terms, to show a 'true and fair view' and must apply the methods and principles of the SORP unless a more specialist SORP applies.[12]

REQUIREMENT FOR AN AUDIT OR INDEPENDENT EXAMINATION

14.21 All charities (regardless of how they are constituted) with a gross income over £500,000 in the relevant financial year or which have a gross income over £250,000 and in the relevant year have total assets (before the deduction of liabilities) worth over £3.26m are required to have their accounts audited.[13] In addition, charitable companies are required to have their accounts audited in the circumstances set out in **14.44** below. If an audit is required this means that the accounts must be scrutinised by a registered auditor who must apply auditing standards and should apply the guidance contained in Audit Practice Note 11: The Audit of Charities produced by the Auditing Practices Board (which is part of the Financial Reporting Council). A registered auditor must be registered with a recognised supervisory body in accordance with the

---

[11] Charities Act 2011, s 133.
[12] The Charities (Accounts and Reports) Regulations 2008, reg 8.
[13] Charities Act 2011, s 144(1) and Companies Act 2006, s 475.

Companies Act 2006. In the case of some charities, eg those connected with the NHS or local authorities, alternative auditing arrangements may be possible.[14]

14.22 Independent examination is a less onerous form of scrutiny than an audit. Examiners report on whether specific matters which are identified in the Regulations have come to their attention. There is Commission guidance for trustees on the selection of examiners and directions for examiners on carrying out an examination (Independent Examination of Charity Accounts: trustees – CC31 and Independent Examination of Charity Accounts: Examiners – CC32).

14.23 An audit exemption report or accountant's report is a less onerous form of scrutiny than an audit for charitable companies where the charity is below the audit threshold (see **14.44**). An accountant's report can only be made by qualified persons in an approved format, set out in the 'Life of a Company – Part 1 Annual Requirements – GP2' guidance available from Companies House.

TRUSTEES' ANNUAL REPORT

14.24 The trustees' annual report provides the context for, and a narrative explanation of, the financial information contained in the accounts. The basic requirements of the report are set out in the Regulations and more detailed guidance is given in the SORP. A charity which is under the audit threshold may prepare a simplified annual report, the contents of which are set out in Appendix 5 to the SORP.

RETURNS

14.25 The Charities Act 2011[15] gives the Commission power to make regulations to prescribe the information required to be submitted to it. All charities are required to complete an online annual return and submit it to the Commission.[16] The annual return is normally made available online the day after the charity's financial year end. Reminders will be sent by email or by post.

14.26 The annual return is used by the Commission to monitor the activities of charities and to ensure that the register of charities is kept up to date. The annual return is made up of three parts and charities with a gross income or total expenditure for the year of over £10,000 are required to complete the relevant parts based on their income in the previous financial year as well as updating contact details for the main contact for the charity, giving details of each trustee, summarising the aims and activities of the charity and, if the

---

[14]   Charities Act 2011, s 149 and s 150 in relation to auditing arrangements where charities are connected with the NHS.

[15]   Charities Act 2011, s 169.

[16]   Charities Act 2011, s 169(2).

charity's income is over £25,000, a declaration confirming whether any serious incidents took place in the last year that should have been reported but were not. There is more about serious incident reporting at **14.78-14.90**.

14.27 Following a consultation on proposals to change the information it collects through the annual return and publishes on the register of charities, the Commission announced details of the additional information it would require from registered charities in their annual return. Charities will now also be asked to confirm whether they raise funds from the public, work with commercial participators, have a trading subsidiary, make grants as the main way they carry out their charitable purposes and have written policies in place in six key risk areas, eg conflicts of interest and investment. Charities will also be required to confirm whether they are regulated by any regulator other than the Commission, whether they pay any of their trustees for acting as charity trustees and if they have their accounts qualified by the charity's auditors. New guidance on how to complete the new form of annual return and how to interpret information provided by a charity in its annual return is expected to be published in January 2014.

14.28 If a charity with an income over £10,000 fails to meet the legal requirement of completing and submitting the annual return, then the charity's details will be marked 'overdue' on the Commission's online register of charities. After six months the Commission may remove the charity's details altogether and consider whether further action is needed.

14.29 The Summary Information Return (SIR) was introduced by the Commission in 2005 to provide the public with more accessible information about the work of the larger charities. The SIR forms part C of the Annual Return that charities with an income over £1 million have to complete and submit to the Commission. Following the Commission's consultation, the requirement to complete the SIR is to be discontinued from 2014. However, charities with an income of £1 million or greater will still need to complete the SIR up to and including 2013.

APPLICATION OF FRAMEWORK PRINCIPLES TO CATEGORIES OF CHARITY

14.30 The Charity Commission's guidance[17] sets out the accounting requirements for different sizes and types of charities. Broadly speaking, the principles referred to above are applied to charities falling into a number of categories. At the time of writing and following Lord Hodgson's review of the Charities Act 2006[18] the financial thresholds are being reviewed by the Charity Commission. However, at present the categories are as follows:

---

[17] CC15(b).
[18] 'Trusted and independent: giving charity back to charities'.

- Charities that are not set up as companies
    - Where the gross income of the charity does not exceed £25,000 in the charity's relevant financial year
    - Where the gross income of the charity exceeds £25,000 but does not exceed £250,000 in the relevant financial year
    - Where the gross income of the charity exceeds £250,000 but does not exceed £500,000 in the relevant financial year, and the total assets do not exceed £3.26 million
    - Where the gross income of the charity exceeds £500,000 in the relevant financial year or the charity's gross assets exceed £3.26 million and the gross income exceeds £250,000
- Charitable companies.
- Excepted charities.
- Exempt charities.
- Group charities.
- CIOs.

The accounting and reporting requirements for charities falling into each of these categories is summarised below.

CHARITIES THAT ARE NOT COMPANIES, INCLUDING CIOS

14.31 The table below summarises the Charity Commission's reporting and accounting requirements for charities that are not companies (including CIOs).

Size of the charity in the relevant financial year	Basis of accounts preparation	Audit and examination	Trustees' Annual Report	Information to be sent to the Commission within 10 months of end of financial year
Gross income does not exceed £25,000.	Receipts and payments or accruals accounts in accordance with SORP and the Regulations.	No requirement unless stipulated by the charity's constitution.	Simplified Annual Report.	If income is less than £10,000, send Annual Update Form. File online Annual Return if the yearly income is £10,000 or more.
Gross income exceeds £25,000 but gross income does not exceed £250,000.	As above	Either an independent examination (preferably by a qualified accountant) or audit by a registered auditor in accordance with SORP and the Regulations, unless the charity's governing document specifies one or the other.	As above	Online Annual Return.
Gross income exceeds £250,000 but does not exceed £500,000, and total assets do not exceed £3.26m.	The accruals basis in accordance with SORP and the Regulations.	As above. If an independent examination is chosen and gross income exceeds £250,000, the independent examiner appointed must be a member of a body specified under the Charities Act 2011.	As above	Online Annual Return, Annual Report and Accounts.

Gross income exceeds £500,000 in the relevant financial year, or gross assets exceed £3.26m and gross income exceeds £250,000	The accruals basis in accordance with SORP and the Regulations.	Audit by a registered auditor in accordance with SORP and the Regulations.	Full Annual Report	As above. Charities with a gross income of over £1m must also complete the Summary Information Return (until 2014).
CIOs	Receipts and payments or accruals basis in accordance with SORP and the Regulations if gross income is less than £250,000. If gross income exceeds £250,000, must be prepared on the accruals basis in accordance with SORP and the Regulations.	Audit by a registered auditor in accordance with SORP and the Regulations if gross income exceeds £500,000 or gross assets exceed £3.26 million and gross income exceeds £250,000. Independent examination required if gross income exceeds £25,000. If gross income exceeds £250,000, the independent examiner appointed must be a member of a body specified under the Charities Act 2011.	[Annual Report]	As above.

Charitable companies

14.32 The SORP applies to charitable companies as well as unincorporated charities.

14.33 Guidance issued by Companies House[19] explains the filing and accounting requirements for companies under the Companies Act 2006.

14.34 Regardless of the levels of income or assets held by the company, the accounts must be prepared on an accruals basis. A charitable company must prepare a directors' report and accounts under the Companies Acts and must file these with Companies House together with an Annual Return in a form prescribed by Companies House.[20]

14.35 The requirements for the trustees' annual report and annual returns are the same as those for other charities and therefore a charitable company must also comply with the Regulations. Where an annual report is required by the Charity Commission it is the usual practice for the Directors Report to be extended to include the information required also by the Regulations and recommended by the SORP to be included in the trustees' annual report.

14.36 There are three sizes of companies to consider in relation to company accounting requirements; small, medium or large. There are thresholds for turnover, balance sheet total (meaning the total of the fixed and current assets) and the average number of employees, which determine whether a company is small or medium-sized. Small and medium-sized companies can choose to disclose less information to Companies House than large companies.

14.37 The requirements for companies subject to the small companies' regime are set out in Parts 15 and 16 of the Companies Act 2006. To be a 'small company' for the purposes of the Companies Act 2006 the company must satisfy two or more of the following conditions:

- turnover of not more than £6.5m;
- balance sheet total of not more than £3.26m; and
- not more than 50 employees.

14.38 A small company can file at Companies House a copy of the accounts which it prepared for its members, or an abbreviated version of those accounts. Small companies do not have to deliver a copy of the directors' report or the profit and loss account to Companies House. Small companies with turnover not more than £6.5m and a balance sheet total of not more than £3.36m also qualify for an audit exemption under the Companies Act 2006, but the Charities Act scrutiny arrangements apply to charitable companies with incomes above the £500,000 or gross assets exceeding £3.26m when gross

---

[19] 'Life of a Company – Part 1 Annual Requirements – GP2'.
[20] Companies Act 2006, s 394, s 399 and s 415.

income exceeds £250,000 and those companies are required to have their accounts audited by a registered auditor.

14.39 A medium-sized company can prepare accounts according to special provisions applicable to medium-sized companies. It can also choose to submit reduced information to Companies House and may omit certain information from the business review in its directors' report.

14.40 To be a 'medium-sized company' for the purposes of the Companies Act 2006, the company must satisfy two or more of the following conditions:

- annual turnover of not more than £25.9m;
- balance sheet total of not more than £12.9m; and
- average number of employees not more than 250.

14.41 Any companies that do not meet the criteria for small or medium are large companies and have to prepare and submit full accounts audited by a registered auditor.[21]

14.42 Charities which have either charitable or non-charitable subsidiaries must prepare group accounts where the income of the group, after eliminating intra group transactions and consolidation adjustments, exceeds £500,000.

14.43 Unless the charitable company or charitable group is subject to the small companies regime, the charity must also prepare a business review or strategic report as required by company law as part of its director's report.

14.44 The table below summarises the Charity Commission's reporting and accounting requirements for charitable companies.

---

[21] Companies Act 2006, ss 477, s 382(1) and (3).

Size of the charity in the relevant financial year	Basis of accounts preparation	Audit and examination	Trustees' Annual Report	Information to be sent to the Commission within 10 months of end of financial year
Gross income does not exceed £25,000	The accruals basis in accordance with SORP, the Regulations and the Companies Acts.	No requirement unless stipulated by the charity's constitution.	Simplified Annual Report.	Annual Information Return(still a requirement if income is £10,000 or less).
Gross income exceeds £25,000 but does not exceed £500,000, and where gross income exceeds £250,000, gross assets do not exceed £3.20 million.	As above	Either an independent examination (preferably by a qualified accountant) or audit by a registered auditor in accordance with SORP and the Regulations, unless Articles of Association require an audit.	As above.	Online Annual Return, Annual Report and Accounts.
Gross income exceeds £500,000 **or** gross assets exceed £3.26 million and gross income exceeds £250,000	As above	Statutory audit by a registered auditor.	Full Annual Report.	As above. Charities with a gross income of over £1m must also complete the Summary Information Return (until 2014).

Excepted charities

14.45 If the trustees have chosen to register, they will have to fulfil the same accounting and reporting requirements as any other registered charity. If they do not register they must still keep accounting records and produce annual accounts in the same way as a registered charity of the same type. They must provide copies of their accounts to members of the public on request, but should not send them to the Commission unless they ask for them. Unregistered excepted charities are not required to prepare an Annual Report but it is good practice to do so. There is more about excepted charities in **4.55–4.57**.

Exempt charities

14.46 Exempt charities have to keep proper accounting records and prepare accounts. Where they are required to prepare accounts giving a true and fair view, they should follow the SORP unless a more specialised SORP applies. They must provide copies of their accounts to members of the public on request. Exempt charities are not required to prepare an Annual Report but it is good practice to do so. There is more about exempt charities in **4.68–4.72**.

Group charities

14.47 Charities which have either charitable or non-charitable subsidiaries must prepare group accounts where the income of the group, after eliminating intra group transactions and consolidation adjustments, exceeds £500,000.

14.48 Group accounts are the accounts prepared by the reporting 'parent' charity which controls or exercises dominant influence over one or more charitable or non-charitable subsidiaries. Group accounts must be prepared on an accruals basis in accordance with legal requirements and UK accounting standards and must present the results of the whole group on a consolidated basis with the Annual Report and accounts submitted by the 'parent' charity including the financial results of the whole group.

14.49 Charities that are obliged to prepare group accounts must be audited by a registered auditor and a full annual report must be prepared together with the additional disclosures required concerning the activities of subsidiaries.

FURTHER HELP WITH PREPARING ACCOUNTS

14.50 Various publications relating to the accounting framework have been produced by the Commission and are available on its website (www.charitycommission.gov.uk).

14.51 In particular, the Commission's guidance CC15b 'Charity reporting and accounting: the essentials' provides additional guidance and links to other useful websites providing information on accounting and external scrutiny issues.

THE TRUSTEES' ANNUAL REPORT

14.52 People who are interested in assessing the performance of a particular charity cannot really do so simply by looking at the charity's financial figures alone. The success of a charity will largely depend upon how successful it has been in fulfilling its charitable objects and this is not something that can always be communicated through a profit and loss account or balance sheet (although these may be indirect indicators of success). For this reason, the trustees' annual report is a vital means of communicating to interested parties just what it is that a particular charity has been doing over the course of a financial year. From this, third parties should be better able to understand the aims and objectives of the charity and to make an assessment as to the effectiveness of the charity. The report should explain how the objectives set for the year relate to the longer term strategies and objectives set by the charity.

14.53 Trustees are also required to explain how they have carried out their charity's purposes for the public benefit.[22] The Regulations and the Charity Commission's guidance[23] set out the information that must be included in the public benefit report. 'Larger charities' (above the audit threshold where the gross income exceeds £500,000) are required to provide more detailed information than 'smaller charities' (below the audit threshold where the gross income does not exceed £500,000). There are no other specific rules on how trustees should report on public benefit, and it is for the trustees to decide the level of detail they wish to provide.

14.54 The Charities Act 2011, s 162 requires every charity to prepare an annual report. The SORP and the Regulations set out detailed legal requirements as to what a trustees' annual report should contain. Trustees are free to decide the format and layout of the annual report provided all the legal requirements are met. There are long lists of detailed requirements at Part 5 of the Regulations and a table in the Charity Commission's guidance[24] which cross refers to the SORP setting out a helpful summary of matters that all charities must report.

14.55 In summary, however, matters that all charities are required to set out in the annual report include:[25]

- administrative details of the charity, its trustees and advisers;
- a description that is proportionate to the size and complexity of the charity as to how it is constituted, its organisational structure and how its trustees are appointed and trained;
- a financial review containing details of reserves, the reserves policy and an explanation of any material designated funds or any funds materially in deficit;

---

[22] The Charities (Accounts and Reports) Regulations 2008, reg 40(aa) and (ii).
[23] PB3 'Public benefit: reporting'.
[24] CC 15(b).
[25] The Charities (Accounts and Reports) Regulations 2008, Part 5 and SORP, paras 41–59.

- details of funds held as custodian trustee on behalf of others and how they are segregated from the charity's own assets;
- a public benefit statement.

14.56 Smaller charities not subject to statutory audit must also report:[26]

- a summary description of the objects and main activities of the charity to further its charitable purposes for the public benefit;
- the main achievements of the charity during the year.

14.57 If the charity is subject to a statutory audit then the trustees' annual report must also include the following matters:

- additional administrative information including the names of senior staff members to whom day-to-day management of the charity is delegated by the trustees and the names and addresses of those acting as bankers, solicitors, auditors (or independent examiner), investment advisers and other principal advisers;
- additional information about the structure, governance and management of the charity including the policies and procedures for the recruitment of trustees, details of which types of decisions are taken by trustees and those that are delegated to staff, the impact any wider network has on the charity's policies and the relationships between the charity and any related parties;
- a summary of the charity's objects and the aims and objectives which the charity trustees have set for the charity in the year, including details of the strategies adopted, and of significant activities undertaken, in order to achieve those aims and objectives;
- a review of the significant activities of the charity and its achievements during the year, measured by reference to the aims and objectives which have been set and any significant contribution of volunteers to these activities;
- a statement as to whether the charity trustees have given consideration to the major risks to which the charity is exposed and satisfied themselves the systems or procedures are established in order to manage those risks (see **14.61-14.77**);
- the principal sources of income of the charity and how expenditure has supported the key objectives of the charity;
- where significant investments are held, details of the investment performance against the objectives set;
- where programme-related investment (or 'social investment') activities are material in the context of charitable activities undertaken, an explanation of the policies adopted in making such investments. There is more about programme-related investment in **Chapter 10**;

---

[26] The Charities (Accounts and Reports) Regulations 2008, Part 5.

- a description of the policies and procedures (if any) which have been adopted by the charity trustees for the induction and training of charity trustees, and where no such policies have been adopted, a statement to this effect;
- a description of the policies (if any) which have been adopted by the charity trustees for the selection of individuals and institutions who are to receive grants, or other forms of financial support, out of the assets of the charity;
- where fundraising activities are undertaken, details of performance achieved against fundraising objectives set, commenting on any material expenditure for future income generation and explaining the effect on the current period's fundraising return and anticipated income generation in future periods;
- comment on those factors within and outside the charity's control which are relevant to the achievement of its objectives;
- a description of the aims and objectives which the charity trustees have set for the charity in the future, and of the activities contemplated in furtherance of those aims and objectives.

14.58 It should be noted, however, that the SORP expressly states that charity trustees should consider providing such additional information as is needed to give donors, beneficiaries and the general public a greater insight into the charity's activities and achievements.[27]

14.59 Where group accounts are prepared because the income of the group exceeds the threshold for preparing group accounts, the annual report must also include:

- an explanation of the relationship between the charity and its subsidiaries;
- when considering the objectives, activities and strategies, where significant activities are undertaken through subsidiary undertakings these should be explained as should the achievements and performance of the subsidiaries;
- the financial review should include the financial position of the charity's subsidiaries.

14.60 Where group accounts are prepared on a voluntary basis there are no additional requirements imposed by the Regulations, but the SORP recommends that the details above are included in the annual report.

RISK REPORTING

14.61 There is no legal requirement for charities to have a risk management process, or to follow a particular method, but the Charity Commission strongly

---

[27] SORP, para 10.

recommends in its guidance[28] that trustees have a clear risk management policy and process. Trustees also have a general duty to take reasonable steps to assess and manage risks to their charity's activities, beneficiaries, property, work or reputation.

14.62   As stated above, the SORP requires trustees to make a statement in their annual report confirming that 'the major risks to which the charity is exposed, as identified by the trustees, have been reviewed and systems or procedures have been established to manage those risks'.[29]

14.63   The SORP focuses on major risks. Major risks are those which, if they occur, would prevent a charity achieving its aims or carrying out its strategies or would have a severe impact on operational performance, objectives or reputation of the charity.

14.64   The Regulations place a legal requirement on charities whose gross income is over £500,000 (and charities with incomes above £250,000 plus assets worth more than £3.26m) for the trustees' annual report to 'contain a statement as to whether the charity trustees have given consideration to the major risks to which the charity is exposed and systems designed to mitigate those risks'[30]. All charities in England and Wales with gross income exceeding £500,000 are therefore required to make a risk management statement. In its guidance[31] the Charity Commission recommends that smaller charities report on their risk management activities too.

Risk management statement

14.65   There is no prescription as to the content of the risk management statement. In its guidance,[32] however, the Charity Commission recommends that at its most basic a charity's risk management statement should include:

- an acknowledgement of the trustees' responsibility to identify, assess and manage risks;
- an overview of the charity's process for identifying risks;
- an indication that major risks have been reviewed or assessed;
- confirmation of the systems and processes set up to manage risks.

14.66   Larger and more complex charities are expected to expand on this basic approach in their reporting. The Commission recommends the following broad principles where this more detailed approach to reporting is adopted:

- a description of the major risks faced;

---

[28]   CC 26.
[29]   SORP, para 45.
[30]   The Charities (Accounts and Reports) Regulations 2008, reg 40(2)(b)(ii)(ee).
[31]   CC 26.
[32]   CC 26.

- the links between the identification of major risk and the operational and strategic objectives of the charity;

- procedures that extend beyond financial risk to encompass operational, compliance and other categories of identifiable risk;

- the link between risk assessment and evaluation to the likelihood of its occurrence and impact should the event occur;

- a description of the risk assessment processes and monitoring that are embedded in management and operational processes;

- trustees' review of the principal results of risk identification processes and how they are evaluated and monitored.

Risk management

14.67 The Charity Commission has issued detailed guidance on risk management.[33] There are many different models of risk management, but the key point will be that trustees have a structured approach to risk management that is appropriate to their charity.

14.68 The basics of risk management involve:

- establishing a risk policy;
- identifying and assessing risks;
- evaluating what action to take;
- reviewing and monitoring regularly.

Identifying risk

14.69 The first step for any charity is therefore to identify the risks to which it is exposed. The risks faced by charities may fall into different categories including:

- Governance risks (eg inappropriate organisational structure, difficulties recruiting trustees with relevant skills, conflict of interests).

- Operational risks (eg service quality and development, contract pricing, employment issues; health and safety issues; fraud and misappropriation).

- Financial risks (eg accuracy and timeliness of financial information, adequacy of reserves and cash flow, diversity of income sources, investment management).

- Environmental and external risks (eg public perception and adverse publicity, demographic changes, government policy).

- Compliance with law and regulation (eg breach of trust law, employment law, and regulative requirements of particular activities such as fund-raising or the running of care facilities).

---

[33] CC 26.

The process of risk identification should be charity specific as it needs to reflect the activities, structure and environment in which a particular charity operates.

Evaluating risk

14.70 Having identified the risks faced by a particular charity, it is then necessary to put those risks into perspective in terms of the potential severity of impact and likelihood of their occurrence. One method is to consider each identified risk and decide for each the likelihood of it occurring and the severity of the impact of its occurrence on the charity.

14.71 Some charities operate a scoring system to assess which risks need further work. For example, the severity of impact could be scored on a scale of 1 (least serious) to 5 (most serious) and similarly the likelihood of occurrence could be scored from 1 (remote) to 5 (almost certain). The impact score is usually multiplied by the score for likelihood and the product of the scores used to rank those risks that the trustees regard as most serious.

Drawing up an action plan

14.72 Once each risk has been evaluated, the trustees should draw up a plan for any action that needs to be taken. This action plan and the implementation of appropriate systems or procedures allows the trustees to make a positive statement as to risk mitigation.

14.73 For each of the major risks identified, trustees will need to consider any additional action that needs to be taken to mitigate the risk, either by lessening the likelihood of the event occurring, or lessening its impact if it does.

14.74 There are essentially four basic strategies that can be applied to an identified risk:

- transferring the financial consequences to third parties or sharing it (eg insurance, outsourcing);
- avoiding the activity giving rise to the risk completely (eg a potential grant or contract not taken up);
- management or mitigation of risk; or
- acceptance of the risk (eg it is assessed as an inherent risk that cannot be avoided if the activity is to continue).

14.75 Risk mitigation is aimed at reducing the 'gross level' of risk identified to a 'net level' of risk that remains after appropriate action has been taken. This identification of 'gross risk', the control procedures put in place to mitigate the risk, and the identification of the residual or 'net risk' is often scheduled in a risk register. Trustees should form a view as to the acceptability of the residual or 'net risk' that remains after mitigation. It is possible that the process may also identify areas where the current control processes are disproportionately costly or onerous compared to the risk they seek to address.

Periodic monitoring and assessment

14.76 The risk management process needs to be dynamic so as to ensure that new risks are addressed as they arise and whether any previously identified risks have changed. The process therefore requires regular monitoring and assessment.

14.77 One method of codifying such an approach is through the use of a risk register. The register seeks to pull together the key aspects of the risk management process. It schedules identified risks and their assessment, the controls in place and the residual risks, and can identify responsibilities, monitoring procedures and follow up action required.

Serious incident reporting

14.78 The Charity Commission has a statutory function[34] to identify as well as investigate apparent misconduct or mismanagement in the administration of charities. Serious incident reporting by charity trustees is one of the Commission's key compliance and monitoring tools. The responsibility for reporting serious incidents to the Commission rests with the charity's trustees, even if they delegate work to others.

14.79 The trustees of charities with incomes over £25,000 are required[35] in their annual return to make a declaration confirming whether any serious incidents took place in the last year that should have been reported but were not. If the trustees are unable to make this declaration then the Annual Return will not be complete and the trustees will have defaulted on the statutory requirement under s 169 of the Charities Act 2011.

14.80 It is an offence under s 60 of the Charities Act 2011 to provide false or misleading information to the Commission. In the Commission's guidance 'Reporting serious incidents: guidance for trustees' the Commission advise that if the trustees sign the declaration on the Annual Return the Commission will take this as confirmation that there have been no serious incidents that should have been reported to it.

14.81 The Commission says in its guidance that, where it is clear that trustees are handling serious incidents appropriately and the risks are being managed by them, it is unlikely to take further action. If it is not clear that the incident and risks arising from it are being dealt with and that the trustees are acting responsibly, the Commission will need to engage further with the trustees. In some cases, the Commission may use its legal powers to protect the charity. If a

---

[34] Charities Act 2011, s 15(1)(3).
[35] The Charities (Accounts and Reports) Regulations 2008.

serious incident that has not been reported becomes known to the Commission at a later date, it may consider taking regulatory action against the trustees, particularly if further abuse or damage has arisen.

14.82 There is no legal obligation to report a serious incident to the Commission immediately, but the Commission recommends as a matter of good practice that any serious incident that has resulted or could result in a significant loss of funds or a significant risk to a charity's property, work, beneficiaries or reputation should be reported to the Commission immediately, not just on completion of the Annual Return.

14.83 In its guidance, the Commission lists a non-exhaustive list of nine high risk issues that should always be regarded as serious incidents by trustees and reported to the Commission. These are:

- fraud and theft;
- other significant loss;
- significant sums of money or other property donated to the charity from an unknown or unverified source;
- the charity (including any individual staff, trustees or volunteers) has any known or alleged link to a proscribed (banned) organisation or to terrorist or other unlawful activity;
- a person disqualified from acting as a trustee has been or is currently acting as a trustee of the charity;
- the charity has no vetting procedure to ensure that a trustee or member of staff is eligible to act in the position he or she is being appointed to;
- the charity does not have a policy for safeguarding its vulnerable beneficiaries;
- suspicions, allegations and incidents of abuse or mistreatment of vulnerable beneficiaries;
- the charity has been subject to a criminal investigation, or an investigation by another regulator or agency; or sanctions have been imposed or concerns raised by another regulator or agency such as the Health and Safety Executive, the Care Quality Commission or Ofsted.

14.84 In addition, the Commission also expects trustees to report an incident if:

- the incident is also reported to the police or other statutory agencies (unless it is a technical or minor issue that poses little or no risk);
- the charity, or individuals associated with the charity and in connection with their role within it, are the subject of a police or other statutory agency investigation;
- the trustees decide that the incident presents a serious or significant risk to the charity, its beneficiaries, reputation or assets;

- the internal risk assessment of the incident concludes that the charity should act to avoid a serious or significant risk to the charity, its beneficiaries, reputation, services or assets;
- the charity's professional advisers have advised the trustees to notify us of the incident.

If the trustees consider that any other serious incident has occurred in the charity then the Commission expects trustees to report it.

14.85 Further, the Commission expects trustees to report incidents if they have received information that leads to a belief of suspicion that a serious incident has happened and the trustees have reasonable grounds for the suspicion. The Commission's guidance states that serious incidents should, as a matter of good practice, be reported immediately, but it is reasonable for trustees to take some time to gather information to establish the facts following an allegation or incident before reporting to the Commission and there is a balance to be struck between fact finding and timely reporting.

14.86 When reporting a serious incident, trustees should bear in mind that the Freedom of Information Act 2000 ('the FOI Act') applies to the Charity Commission because it is a public authority as defined in the FOI Act. Any person who makes a request to a public authority for information must be informed whether, subject to exemptions, the public authority holds that information and be supplied with that information. The Commission has adopted a publication scheme in accordance with s 19 of the FOI Act[36] which is based on the model publication scheme approved by the Information Commissioner and sets out:

- what information the Commission will publish or intend to publish as a matter of course;
- how this information will be published;
- whether the information will be available free of charge or on payment of a fee.

14.87 The FOI Act is relevant to serious incident reporting because trustees need to consider the risks to the charity of information that is disclosed to the Charity Commission later being disclosed by the Commission to anyone, including the media, who makes a request under the FOI Act. However, there are a number of exemptions that may apply to information disclosed to the Commission, including for example personal information which may be protected by the Data Protection Act 1998 and commercially sensitive information. It is therefore recommended that, where particularly sensitive or confidential information relating to serious incidents is provided to the Commission, trustees take legal advice and explain to the Commission why the information is confidential and what exemptions apply from disclosure under the FOI Act, although the Commission will exercise its own discretion in

---

[36] This scheme was valid from 1 January 2009.

deciding what to disclose in response to any request. There is no obligation for the Commission to inform a charity either that an FOI request has been made or agree what it will disclose. In practice, however, the Commission will usually let a charity know that a request has been made, but not who has made the request.

14.88   The Commission may also disclose information to other relevant public authorities (for example HMRC, the police or social services) but only where it can lawfully do so. The Charities Act 2011[37] specifies when disclosures may be made between the Commission and other public authorities.

14.89   The Commission will not proactively issue press releases on receipt of a serious incident report, but serious incidents will often be of interest to the media and the Commission may respond to the media contacting it directly. The Commission may also make public statements about live cases when it considers it is in the public interest to do so to increase public trust and confidence in charities. There is guidance about the Commission's policy on reporting on its regulatory work on its website, together with examples of public statements about live cases.

14.90   The Charities Act 2011[38] imposes an obligation on auditors or independent examiners acting for a charity to make a written report to the Commission if, in the course of acting in that capacity, they become aware of a matter which they reasonably believe is likely to be of material significance for the purposes of the exercise of the Commission's functions in relation to inquiries[39] or the Commission's powers to act for the protection of charities.[40]

---

[37]   Charities Act 2011, ss 54–60.
[38]   Charities Act 2011, ss 156–159.
[39]   Charities Act 2011, ss 46, 47 and 50.
[40]   Charities Act 2011, ss 76 and 79–82.

CHAPTER 15

RESTRUCTURING

15.1 A charity, like any other entity, will change and develop over time. This may be, for example, because its sources of funding change, because its trustees decide to advance its charitable purposes in a new way, or perhaps because its trustees decide that its charitable purposes would best be served by transferring the charity's assets to another charity.

15.2 This chapter highlights a number of different ways in which a charity may re-structure itself:

- constitutional changes;
- mergers and transfers;
- incorporation; and
- dissolution.

CONSTITUTIONAL CHANGES

15.3 Some restructurings may not require any more than a change to the constitutional provisions that govern a charity's charitable purposes, its powers or its governance arrangements. This might be because its governance arrangements are outdated or inadequate or no longer reflect how the charity operates in practice. Or a charity's purposes may no longer be appropriate, perhaps because its beneficiaries are no longer in need, or because their needs have changed.

15.4 The way in which a charity can alter its constitution depends primarily on the way in which it is constituted. Specific legal provisions apply to charitable companies and CIOs. These rules are explained in more detail below. The position in relation to unincorporated charities is a little more complicated and we explain this first.

Unincorporated charities

15.5 The constitution of an unincorporated charity may give its trustees an express power to alter the terms of the constitution itself. If there is an express power, it will need to be exercised carefully in accordance with any restrictions imposed upon it. Where the charity is a trust, its trustees are likely to be able to exercise the power. Where the charity is an unincorporated association, the power is more likely to be vested in the members.

15.6 It is unlikely that even the most widely expressed power of amendment will authorise the charity's trustees to alter its charitable purposes or to insert provisions that would enable the trustees to dispose of the charity's assets for anything other than those purposes. Good examples of this sort of change are the addition of a provision enabling trustees to benefit personally from the charity's assets or a change to a provision dealing with the charity's assets in the event of its dissolution. Even if a power of amendment were to be exercised this widely, it could not be validly used to make changes of this kind because they will be inconsistent with the principle that a charity's assets can only ever be applied for its charitable purposes.

15.7 It is, though, open to anyone setting up an unincorporated charity to give its trustees a wide power to amend or add to the provisions of the constitution insofar as its administrative or governance arrangements are concerned. Powers of this kind can be used to deal with alterations to, for example, provisions governing trustees' meetings, the powers exercisable by a charity's trustees and arrangements for assets to be held in nominee names (although the position will obviously vary from charity to charity).

15.8 If trustees wish to alter a charity's purposes or change the way in which its assets can be disposed of or if there is no express power of amendment (or there is a power, but it is not wide enough to authorise the change that a charity's trustees wish to make), there are three courses of action that may be open to them:

- to exercise the statutory power to modify powers or procedures;
- to exercise the statutory power to replace the purposes of a 'small' unincorporated charity; or
- to apply to the Charity Commission for an Order or Scheme.

Statutory power to modify powers or procedures

15.9 Section 280 of the Charities Act 2011 gives the trustees of an unincorporated charity a statutory power to modify the provisions of their charity's constitution insofar as they relate to any of the powers exercisable by the trustees in the administration of the charity or regulate the procedures to be followed in connection with its administration. Where the charity has a body of members which is distinct from the charity's trustees (which, in principle at least, would include a group of trustees who also act as the members of a charitable unincorporated association under its constitution), they must also resolve to approve the trustees' resolution at a general meeting (by a majority of not less than two-thirds of the members entitled to attend and vote at the meeting who actually vote on the resolution unless the decision is taken at a meeting without a vote and none of the members present expresses any dissent in relation to the resolution).

15.10 Provided these requirements are met, the charity's constitution is deemed to be modified from the date specified in the trustees' resolution or (if later) the date in which the members pass their resolution approving it. There is no requirement to seek the concurrence of the Charity Commission to the change, although details of the change in the constitution must be notified to the Commission in the normal way.

15.11 This is obviously a very useful power for charity trustees. In cases where there is some doubt about the scope of their administrative powers in relation to a particular aspect of the charity's operations, it offers a simple and straightforward way of putting the position beyond doubt. Clearly, it does not give a charity's trustees the authority to make any changes to the charity's purposes, because this would not be a change to the administration of the charity. This will require an application to the Charity Commission unless the statutory power to replace purposes is exercisable.

Statutory power to replace purposes

15.12 Section 275 of the Charities Act 2011 gives the trustees of a 'small' unincorporated charity the power to resolve that its charitable purposes can be modified by replacing them with any other charitable purposes. The trustees can only pass the resolution if they are satisfied that it is expedient in the charity's interests for the purposes to be replaced and that 'so far as is reasonably practical' the new purposes consist of or include purposes that are similar in character to those that are to be replaced.

15.13 A 'small charity' for this purpose will have gross income (ie income from all sources, before allowing for expenditure) in its last financial year of no more than £10,000 and must not hold any 'designated land'. Designated land is any land held on the basis that it must be used for the purposes of the charity (what the Charity Commission usually refers to as 'specie' or 'functional' land). The charity must also not be a company or other body corporate (although the section 275 power does apply to small unincorporated charities with a corporate trustee).

15.14 The resolution must be passed by a majority of not less than two-thirds of the charity trustees who actually vote on the resolution (rather than two-thirds of all of the charity trustees). The trustees are obliged to send a copy of the resolution to the Charity Commission together with a statement of their reasons for passing it. The Commission may decide to direct the trustees to give public notice of the resolution and then take into account any representations received in response to the notice. The Commission can also direct the trustees to provide it with further information and explanation in relation to their reasons for passing the resolution.

15.15 The Commission has 60 days from the date on which it receives a copy of the trustees' resolution to notify them in writing that it objects to the resolution, either on 'procedural grounds' or on the merits of the proposals contained in the resolution. On 'procedural grounds' means that the trustees have not complied with one of the specific provisions under the Charities Act 2011, s 275 for the passing of the resolution. If the Commission does decide to direct the charity trustees to give public notice of the resolution, the 60 day period is suspended from the date on which the direction is given until 42 days after the date on which public notice is given by the trustees. The same applies where the Commission directs the charity trustees to provide additional information; the 60 day period is suspended from the date on which the direction is given until the information is provided to the Commission.

15.16 If the Commission does notify the trustees that it objects to the resolution, whether on procedural grounds or on the merits of the proposals in the resolution, then the resolution is deemed never to have been passed by the trustees.

Charity Commission Orders and Schemes

15.17 Where a charity's trustees cannot rely upon any of the express or statutory powers, their only other option in relation to a proposed constitutional change will be to apply to the Charity Commission for an Order or Scheme. Which of these is relevant will depend upon the changes that are required by trustees.

15.18 There is more information about the differences between Orders and Schemes at **4.22** and **4.32**. But it is important to appreciate that the Commission will not make an Order or a Scheme if the trustees already have a power to amend their charity's constitution. Essentially, this will be one of the express or statutory powers we have mentioned above.

15.19 The Charities Act 2011 requires the Commission to use its resources in the most efficient, effective and economic way. The Commission's policy in relation to Orders and Schemes reflects this duty, as is explained in its operational guidance:

> 'We will only make an Order where there is no suitable power available to the trustees, either explicit or implied, and where the trustees cannot use a power of amendment to adopt the necessary power.[1]
>
> We will only make a Scheme to amend a charity's governing document where there is no other option available to the trustees to make the required changes and the Scheme will make only those changes that cannot be made in any other way.'[2]

15.20 The Charity Commission will normally make a Scheme rather than an Order where a charity's trustees either wish to change its charitable purposes or

---

[1] OG 501.
[2] OG 500.

their proposed changes to the charity's constitution go beyond the scope of the Commission's power to make Orders. The Commission's guidance in relation to Orders is helpful here:

'... we can only authorise an action by Order [...] where:

– The action is not subject to an express prohibition in the charity's governing document and
– the authority will not allow the trustees to do anything to extend or alter the purposes of the charity.

If the proposal will over-ride an express prohibition or extend or alter the charity's purposes, we can only make these changes by Scheme.

Additionally, we should not make an Order when we consider it desirable to reserve the right of appeal that is attached to the making of a Scheme. For example, where the proposal is to remove, against their will, the right of a third party to appoint a trustee to the charity.'[3]

15.21 Although the Charity Commission can make a Scheme to alter a charity's charitable purposes, there are limits on this. A Scheme can only be made where the purposes of the charity have 'failed' in some way, which will allow its assets to be applied 'cy-près' for similar charitable purposes. The rules on cy-près applications are set out in the Charities Act 2011, ss 62 and 63. A detailed explanation of the scope of the cy-près rules is beyond the scope of this book, but s 67 of the Charities Act 2011 directs the Charity Commission to take account of three factors when considering making a cyprès Scheme:

- the spirit of the original gift;
- the desirability of securing that the property is applied for charitable purposes which are close to the original purposes; and
- the need for the relevant charity to have purposes which are suitable and effective in the light of current social and economic circumstances.

The Charity Commission's policy as set out in its operational guidance is helpful:

'We should be flexible and imaginative in applying the cy-près doctrine, balancing usefulness and practicality with respect for the existing purposes and beneficiaries. The purpose of making a cy-près Scheme is to enable a charity to continue being effective, useful and relevant to its beneficiaries' needs in modern society, where without our intervention it would not be. We should, however, exercise caution where a proposed change might be a significant departure from the founder's intentions or might exclude existing beneficiaries (unless, for example, the problem is that the existing beneficial class has ceased to exist). We should always take account of the trustees' views when deciding how to amend a charity's objects.'[4]

---

3   OG 501 B2.6
4   OG 23.2

15.22   Where the Commission is asked to make a Scheme to amend a charity's objects, it will consider whether to give public notice of the Scheme. The Commission is required under the Charities Act 2011 s88 to give public notice of the trustees' proposals to make a Scheme and invite representations from the public unless it decides that public notice is not necessary because of the nature of the Scheme, or for any other reason. The Commission's operational guidance confirms its policy in relation to requiring public notice:

> 'It is our policy that, where the Scheme will:
>
> - change the use of community assets,
> - give a power to dispose of designated property, or
> - involve the displacement of beneficiaries
>
> we will, in all but exceptional circumstances, require public notice. We do this primarily because cases of this kind can often be contentious. 'Exceptional circumstances' in this context might be where, following a thorough consultation exercise, there is strong evidence that there will be no opposition to the Scheme.'[5]

15.23   Where the case does not fall into one of the categories above, the Commission will decide, on a case-by-case basis if public notice is not necessary. To help to do this, the Commission will ask the trustees whether they consider the proposed change(s) is likely to be contentious or if they know of any opposition to the proposed Scheme. In order to make this decision the Commission expects the trustees to carry out a genuine consultation exercise with those who would be affected by, or who might have a particular interest in, the changes proposed unless the changes are so minor that consultation is not necessary. The guidance says it is for the trustees to decide what form the consultation will take, which will vary depending on the changes being proposed, with more significant changes requiring a more extensive consultation exercise.

15.24   The procedure for obtaining an Order or a Scheme is set out in more detail at **4.31** and **4.41**.

15.25   It is also worth mentioning that in some cases, trustees may consider it would be helpful to restate their charity's objects without changing them substantively. For example, this may be because the wording of the objects is archaic and the trustees consider it would benefit from modernisation. However, the Charity Tribunal has been critical of the Charity Commission's practice of making administrative restatements of objects, finding that it had not been expedient but also that it had been unhelpful.[6] Consequently, the Commission's approach appears to be that restating a charity's objects can only be demonstrated as expedient in exceptional cases — cases which are supported by clear and compelling evidence of the advantage of the amendment, and of

---

[5]   OG 500 B8.5
[6]   *Derek Maidment and Lennox Ryan v The Charity Commission for England and Wales* (CA/2009/0001 & 0002).

the absence of disadvantages and risk. The onus will be on the trustees to demonstrate to the Commission that it can exercise its jurisdiction in this manner.

Charitable companies

15.26 As we have indicated in **Chapter 2**, the members of a charitable company (whether limited by shares or guarantee) have a statutory power under company law to alter its constitution. A 'special resolution' of the members is required, which means a resolution of a 75% majority of the members voting in a general meeting or a written resolution signed by 75% of the members.

15.27 The power of a charitable company's members to alter its constitution is subject to the s 198 of the Charities Act 2011, which provides that any 'regulated alteration' by a charitable company requires the prior written consent of the Charity Commission and is ineffective if that consent has not been obtained. 'Regulated alterations' are:

- any alteration to the charitable company's charitable objects;
- any alteration of any provision in its constitution 'directing the application of property of the company on its dissolution'; and
- any alteration of any provision of its constitution 'where the alteration will provide authorisation for any benefit to be obtained by directors or members of the company or persons connected with them'.

For charitable companies incorporated before 1 October 2009 (when the relevant provisions of the Companies Act 2006 came into force) the above provisions will normally be found in the company's memorandum. For companies incorporated on or after 1 October 2009, or those who have updated their constitution since then to reflect the 2006 Act changes, these provisions will be contained in the company's articles. There is more on this in **Chapter 2**.

15.28 The approach the Commission takes to a particular application will depend primarily upon the changes that are proposed, but the Commission's general policy in relation to regulated alterations is to:

> 'adopt a risk based approach when dealing with requests for our consent. The greater the risk, the more convincing the trustees' case will need to be that the changes are in the charity's best interests.'[7]

15.29 As far as proposed changes to the charity's objects or to the provisions directing how property is to be applied on the charity's dissolution are concerned, the Commission's guidance confirms the approach the Commission will take:

---

[7]   OG 518 B1.

'When considering changes requiring our consent we apply three essential "tests":

1. The new objects (or provisions for the distribution of assets on dissolution) are exclusively charitable

2. The trustees' decision to make the change is a rational one in the circumstances of the charity

3. The new objects do not undermine or work against the previous objects.'[8]

Adopting the risk based approach mentioned at **15.28**, the Commission will:

'take into account the probable impact of the change on the charity's current and future beneficiaries. If the impact is low or non-existent we are likely to be able to approve the change without difficulty, even when the change is material. If the impact will be significant, we need to be satisfied that the trustees' decision is consistent with their duty to act in the best interests of the charity.'[9]

15.30   When asked to consent to a proposal to amend the objects, provided a proposed change satisfies the three 'tests' mentioned above, the Commission's guidance says that it should be able to provide its consent, even when it involves a major change to the objects. The trustees will need to make a case as to why the changes are necessary, but the guidance says that the Commission recognises that trustees are usually in the best position to decide what is best for their organisation and will generally support their approach.

The trustees will, however, need to demonstrate to the Commission that their decision-making in relation to the proposal is consistent with their duty to act in the best interests of their charity. The Commission's guidance is helpful here:

'In all cases what we are looking for is that the trustees have made a decision that a reasonable body of trustees might make. In general, the bigger the change, the more convincing a case will be required from the trustees. This is important because although it is the trustees who are ultimately responsible for deciding what is best for their charity, we need to be able to form our own view about the proposals if we are to provide the consent that the law requires.'[10]

The factors the Commission will take into account in assessing whether the decision is one a reasonable body of trustees could have made include the following:

• Taking into account modern social and economic conditions, do the proposals seem broadly consistent with what the charity was set up to do? It is worth noting here that charitable companies do not need to demonstrate a failure of trusts when changing their objects, so there is no need to apply a cy-près test (see **15.21**).

---

8   OG 518 B1.
9   OG 518 B1.
10   OG 518 B5.2.

- Have the trustees considered how the objects will be carried out? It must be clear that the charity will be capable of carrying out the revised objects and the Commission will want to be satisfied they are realistic and workable.
- Have the trustees taken into account the implications of the proposed change for the charity's members and beneficiaries? The Commission will want to know whether the trustees have consulted with the charity's stakeholders and whether their trustees are putting in place arrangements for people to raise concerns or object to the proposals.
- Have the consequences for the charity's beneficial class (ie future as well as current beneficiaries) been fully considered? If the number or range of people who will benefit will reduce as a result of the change, the trustees will need to be able to justify the rationale behind their proposals.

15.31 The same principles apply in relation to a proposal to amend the dissolution clause. The Commission's guidance confirms that the onus is on the trustees to make a case for their proposal and show that it is a decision that a reasonable body of trustees might make, but that this should be easy to establish where the proposed change is workable and rational.[11]

15.32 For the purpose of the third type of regulated alteration, alterations authorising benefits to directors, members and connected persons, 'directors' means 'trustees'. 'Benefit' and 'connected' have the meanings they are given in the context of the statutory power to pay trustees for providing services to a charity. There is more information about this at **6.36**.

It is worth mentioning that 'benefit' does not include any remuneration for the provision of goods and services which a trustee is authorised to receive by the Charities Act 2011, s 185. Therefore, any alteration to remove an express prohibition to pay a trustee for goods or services, thereby allowing access to the statutory power in s 185, is not a regulated alteration. However, if the charity's members are the same individuals as its trustees, the Commission may need to make an Order under s 105 of the Charities Act 2011 to authorise the trustees to pass the special resolution in their capacity as members (on the basis they are giving themselves a power to benefit and therefore have a personal interest in the proposed resolution).[12]

If the proposed power to provide benefits to trustees exceeds the scope of the statutory power, the Commission will adopt the approach it takes in relation to trustees' benefits generally (see **6.36** for more in relation to this).

15.33 There are obviously a wide range of changes to a charity's constitution that do not require the Charity Commission's consent. These include, for example, changes that do not affect the way in which a charity's assets are used (eg procedures for holding meetings, voting, appointing trustees or altering the

---

[11] OG 518 B6.
[12] OG 518 B8.1.

charity's internal rules) and also alterations to allow the delegation of investment management or appointment of a nominee.

Some older charitable companies may have a provision in their memorandum expressly requiring the Commission's consent to make any amendment to their constitution. The Commission suggests that this difficulty may be overcome by the members passing a special resolution to delete the provision from the memorandum. This resolution would require the Commission's consent, but the guidance confirms that it should be prepared to give this consent as a matter of routine.[13]

15.34 A charitable company is required by the Companies Acts to deliver a copy of any resolution altering its constitution to the Registrar of Companies. The Registrar will not accept resolutions making regulated alterations to the constitution which are not accompanied by the Charity Commission's consent. This is the Commission's 'prior written' consent to the changes in question.

The Commission's preference is for a resolution to be submitted to it in draft for approval (usually by way of an endorsement) before it is passed. In practice, it is often much easier to arrange for a resolution to be passed which is conditional on the Commission's consent and this will meet the requirement for prior written consent, provided that the resolution is clearly conditional on consent and cannot take effect without it. However, where a resolution has been passed without the change being made conditional upon the Commission's consent, the Commission cannot consent retrospectively to the change made by the resolution.

Under the provisions of Companies Act 2006, where a charitable company passes a special resolution to amend its objects, the amended objects will not take effect until the change is entered onto the register at Companies House. This obviously means that it is particularly important to file the resolution amending the objects with Companies House as soon as possible.

Charitable incorporated organisations

15.35 The provisions in the Charities Act 2011 which govern CIOs include provisions governing constitutional changes. These are modelled closely on the provisions of the Companies Acts as they apply to charitable companies. So, for example, a resolution to make changes must be passed by a resolution of a 75% majority of the members of the CIO voting at a general meeting. However, a resolution to make changes which is proposed as a written resolution must be passed by all of the members.

15.36 Any changes which the members resolve to make will be subject to the prior written consent of the Charity Commission where they constitute

---

[13]   OG 518 B2.3.

'regulated alterations'. These are identical to the 'regulated alterations' which apply to charitable companies (see **15.27** for more on this).

15.37 There are additional provisions in relation to CIOs in the Charities Act 2011. A CIO which amends its constitution must send a copy of the constitution (as amended) to the Charity Commission within 15 days of the date of the members' resolution making the changes. The Commission will register the changes unless it decides that the CIO has no power to make them or the amendment would change the name of the CIO or because the Commission's consent to any 'regulated alteration' has not been obtained. If the Commission refuses to register the changes, they have no legal effect.

Other incorporated charities

15.38 Other incorporated charities may have express powers to amend their constitutions depending upon the way in which they are set up. Failing that, charities constituted by Royal Charter may be able to obtain a Supplemental Charter, while charities governed by Act of Parliament may require a further Act of Parliament in order to make any changes.

15.39 The requirement for the prior written consent of the Charity Commission to constitutional alterations under the Charities Act 2011, s 198 does not apply to any 'body corporate' (ie any incorporated body other than a Companies Act company) which has a power to alter the provisions of its constitution. However, if a body corporate passes a resolution which has the effect of the body corporate ceasing to be a charity, no exercise of the power that brings about this change has any effect upon the assets held before the change.

Notification

15.40 Section 35 of the Charities Act 2011 obliges the trustees of any charity (however it is constituted) to notify the Charity Commission if there is any change to any provision of its constitution and to send the Commission copies of any new constitutional provisions that have been adopted. In practice, the Commission will require a copy of any new constitution certified by one of the charity's trustees or officers.

MERGERS AND TRANSFERS

15.41 Essentially, any arrangement under which:

- one charity transfers its assets to another and then ceases to exist; or
- two or more charities transfer their assets to another charity and then both cease to exist

may be variously described as a 'merger' or 'transfer', or occasionally as an 'amalgamation'. None of these terms has any precise legal meaning, although all three are referred to in different contexts by the Charities Act 2011 (and there is a definition of what constitutes a 'relevant charity merger' for certain purposes).

15.42 What each of these arrangements has in common is that the trustees of a charity have concluded that its charitable purposes will be better advanced by pooling its assets and other resources with the assets and other resources of another charity. This may be because, for example, two charities are able to raise more funds if they become a single entity or because a single entity's requirements will deliver financial savings based upon economies of scale. Whatever the motivation, the key point is that the charity will generally cease to exist in its present form after transferring its assets. We refer in this chapter to all such arrangements as 'mergers'.

15.43 There are two key aspects of any merger. These are:

- Whether the charity making the transfer (we refer to it below as the 'transferor') has a power to do so and whether the recipient charity (we refer to it below as the 'transferee') has corresponding power to accept the transfer (which may involve accepting both assets and liabilities).
- The range of commercial, financial, tax and other issues which may be raised by the transfer, depending upon the complexity of the assets and any liabilities which are transferred.

We consider each of these aspects in more detail below.

Powers to transfer

15.44 The powers exercisable by a charity's trustees in order to facilitate a merger will depend primarily upon the way in which the charity is constituted. Incorporated and unincorporated charities are considered in more detail below.

Incorporated charities

Charitable companies

15.45 In general, charitable companies may be able to rely upon one of three different provisions in order to arrange a transfer of their assets as part of a merger:

- Many charitable companies will have an express power to make grants and donations which can be used to transfer all of their assets to another charity which has charitable purposes identical to, or narrower than, the purposes of the transferor. In this context, 'narrower' means that the transferee's charitable purposes are a sub-set of the transferor's purposes.

- Some charitable companies may have an express power to merge with other charities. Powers will vary from charity to charity but it is likely that this power can only be used to transfer assets to a transferee charity with purposes identical to, or narrower than, those of the transferor.

- A charitable company will almost inevitably have a 'dissolution' clause that provides for the way in which its assets must be dealt with in the event that it is dissolved. A 75% majority of the members of a charitable company have the right under the Companies Acts to pass a special resolution at any time that will have the effect of dissolving it. The dissolution clause will generally spell out how the charity's assets must then be applied for its charitable purposes. Clauses will vary, with some providing for assets to pass to another charity with identical purposes, perhaps to a charity with similar purposes or perhaps just for similar charitable purposes.

  The discretion to apply the charity's assets in these circumstances will often lie with the charity's trustees, but some dissolution clauses vest this power in a charity's members. Clearly, the terms of the clause must be observed.

15.46 In the (somewhat unlikely) event that a charitable company does not have a power of this kind, one can be added by the members by passing a special resolution. A clause of this kind will be caught by the Charities Act 2011, s 198 and will therefore require the prior written consent of the Charity Commission. See **15.27** for more in relation to this.

15.47 The powers contained in a charitable company's constitution will generally relate only to its corporate assets. Where a charitable company holds trust assets, its trustees will need to ensure that the terms of the trust (rather than the charitable company's constitution) contain an appropriate power.

15.48 Where a charitable company holds trust assets, it will usually only be possible for it to transfer them to another charity on the basis that they will continue to be held on the same trusts by the transferee. This is because the trust assets are held separately from the charitable company's corporate assets and, as a consequence, 'ring fenced' from its liabilities. Were the trust assets simply to be transferred to the transferee to be held by it as part of its own unrestricted assets, they will be exposed to its liabilities. For this reason, the transferee charity must usually agree to hold the trust assets as trustee. This will almost invariably be true of permanent endowment, although certain other trust assets may be held on trusts that give the transferor a power to transfer them free of any restrictions. The position will vary from asset to asset.

Charitable incorporated organisations

15.49 There are three specific statutory provisions which are likely to facilitate CIO mergers:

- The Charities Act 2011, s 235 gives any two or more CIOs the power to apply to the Charity Commission to be 'amalgamated', with the effect that a new CIO is incorporated and registered as their successor.

  A 75% majority of the members of each CIO must vote for the amalgamation at a meeting (or all of the members can pass a written resolution). An application is then made to the Commission, which can refuse the application on certain specified grounds, including where it is not satisfied that the new CIO would be able properly to pursue its charitable purposes; would not actually be a charity at the time it is registered; does not comply with any of the statutory requirements in relation to CIO constitutions; or that the constitution of the new CIO does not properly provide for its charitable purposes, the application of its property on dissolution or the benefits its trustees or members are entitled to receive.

- The Charities Act 2011, s 240 gives any CIO a power to resolve that all of its property, rights and liabilities should be transferred to another CIO. The resolution must be passed by a 75% majority of the members at a meeting (or by all of them in a written resolution).

  Once a resolution has been passed, an application must be made to the Charity Commission, which has a discretion to refuse the application on certain specified grounds. These are broadly similar to those that apply in relation to an amalgamation.

- The Charitable Incorporated Organisations (Insolvency and Dissolution) Regulations 2012 contain specific provisions setting out how a CIO can be dissolved and what should happen to its surplus assets (including trust assets) on dissolution. The Regulations enable a CIO's members to resolve whether it should be dissolved, with the consequence that its assets are transferred to another charity.

Other incorporated charities

15.50 The ability of other types of incorporated charity to merge will primarily depend upon whether they have appropriate express powers in their constitution or an express power that they can use to add the powers that they need. Failing that, the Charity Commission may be able to make an Order or Scheme to give a charity the powers it needs.

Unincorporated charities

15.51 Many charitable trusts and charitable unincorporated associations will have express powers in their constitutions in a very similar form to those found in the constitutions of charitable companies, including:

- powers to make grants and donations to other charities;
- express powers to merge with other charities; and
- an express dissolution clause which enables a charity to be dissolved and its surplus assets transferred to another charity.

15.52 The terms of powers of this kind will obviously vary from charity to charity. A dissolution clause in the constitution of a charitable trust is likely to vest the power of dissolution in its trustees. A dissolution clause in the constitution of an unincorporated association is more likely to vest the power of dissolution in its members than its trustees, although this too will vary from case to case.

Statutory power to transfer assets

15.53 There is also a statutory power that may apply to allow certain unincorporated charities to transfer their assets. This power is conferred by the Charities Act 2011, s 268 and applies to any charity which had gross income (in other words, income from all sources) in its last financial year of £10,000 or less, and which does not hold any 'designated land'. Designated land is land held on trust by the charity to be used for its purposes (what the Charity Commission usually refers to as 'specie' or 'functional' land).

15.54 Where the statutory power applies, the charity's trustees can only transfer all of the charity's assets, but can do so to one or more other charities. Because all of the charity's assets must be transferred, it will be dissolved as a consequence.

15.55 The trustees must also be satisfied that it is expedient in the interests of the charity for the assets to be transferred and that the transferee's charitable purposes are substantially similar to some or all of those of the transferor.

15.56 The resolution has to be voted for by a majority of two-thirds or more of the trustees who vote on it (rather than two-thirds or more of the total number of trustees). The trustees must then send a copy of the resolution to the Charity Commission, together with a statement of their reasons for passing it. The Commission may then decide to direct the trustees to give public notice of the resolution and take into account any representations received in response to the notice. The Commission can also direct the trustees to provide it with further information about the circumstances in which they have decided to exercise the statutory power.

15.57 The Commission has 60 days from the date on which it receives a copy of the trustees' resolution to notify them in writing that it objects to the resolution, either on 'procedural grounds' or on the merits of the proposals contained in the resolution. On 'procedural grounds' means that the trustees have not complied with one of the specific provisions under the Charities Act 2011, s 268 for the passing of the resolution. If the Commission does decide to direct the charity trustees to give public notice of the resolution, the 60-day period is suspended from the date on which the direction is given until 42 days after the date on which public notice is given by the trustees. The same is true where the Commission directs that the charity trustees provide additional information; the 60-day period is suspended from the date on which the direction is given until the information is provided to the Commission.

15.58 The Commission's operational guidance confirms the approach it will adopt when considering trustees' proposals to transfer property:

> 'We will consider the proposals flexibly, looking at the circumstances of the charities involved and the reasons for the transfer. Where we are satisfied that proper process has been followed and the objects of the receiving charity are substantially similar we will confirm the date upon which the resolution will take effect and that the trustees can proceed with their action.'[14]

15.59 If the Commission does notify the trustees that it objects to the resolution, whether on procedural grounds or on the merits of the proposals in the resolution, then the resolution is deemed never to have been passed by the trustees. If, on the other hand, the resolution takes effect, the charity trustees are then obliged to arrange for the transfer of all of the charity's assets in accordance with the resolution. Any of the charity's assets that are held subject to any restrictions on their expenditure (eg restricted funds held for particular charitable purposes), can only be transferred subject to the same restrictions.

15.60 There are more rigorous provisions in relation to the transfer of permanent endowment assets under the Charities Act 2011, s 274. Broadly, these provisions oblige the charity's trustees to be satisfied that the transferee charity has charitable purposes which are 'substantially similar' to *all* of the purposes of the transferor (rather than *some or all*, as is the case for the charity's non-endowment assets). The trustees are also obliged to take account of any guidance given by the Charity Commission in relation to the transfer of permanent endowment. At the time of writing, the Commission has not issued any specific guidance for trustees in relation to this and it therefore remains to be seen what form that guidance will take and the approach the Commission will adopt in relation to the transfer of permanent endowment assets in these circumstances.

15.61 Where the statutory power is exercised, there is an obligation on the trustees of the transferee charity to ensure that, so far as is reasonably practical, the assets are applied for such of its charitable purposes as are substantially similar to those of the transferor charity. However, there is an exception to this; the requirement does not apply if the transferor's trustees consider that complying with it would not result in a 'suitable and effective method' of applying the assets.

15.62 If all the assets of the charity are transferred to another charity or charities using the transfer powers, the trustees may apply for the transfer to be entered in the Charity Commission's Register of Mergers (see **15.78** below).

Other statutory powers

15.63 We should also mention in this context the statutory powers conferred upon the trustees of unincorporated charities to spend the capital of

---

[14] OG 519 B2.1.

endowment assets (including those held on a special trust) under the Charities Act 2011, ss 281 to 292. These provisions are explained in more detail at **9.49** to **9.51**, but they may be used in certain circumstances to facilitate a merger by allowing a charity's trustees to transfer endowment assets free of the restrictions imposed upon them.

Charity Commission Orders and Schemes

15.64 In the absence of an express power or the availability of one of the statutory powers we have mentioned, a charity's trustees will need to apply to the Charity Commission for an Order or a Scheme to give them an appropriate power. There is more about this at **4.22**, **4.32** and **15.17**. Typically, an Order will be sufficient to authorise the trustees of a charity to transfer its assets to another charity, although when they wish to facilitate a merger which has the effect of changing the transferor charity's purposes, a Scheme is likely to be required.

Other unincorporated charities

15.65 Other incorporated charities will need to check whether their constitutions contain an appropriate power to transfer their assets. If not, charities constituted by Royal Charter may be able to obtain a Supplemental Charter. A charity governed by an Act of Parliament may require a further Act of Parliament in order to make any changes to its constitution.

Power to receive

15.66 The position of the transferee charity should not be forgotten. Its trustees will obviously wish to ensure that it is able to accept a transfer of assets. This will often be in exchange for an indemnity from the transferee to the transferor or its trustees in respect of the transferor charity's liabilities (there is more about this below at **15.73**).

15.67 In many cases, the charity's constitution will contain an express power to accept gifts and donations, although express powers to give indemnities in respect of associated liabilities are less likely to be included. Our view is that the trustees of any charity have a discretion to consider whether to accept any gift, whether outright or on particular terms. Provided the trustees comply with their duty of care and take into account all relevant circumstances in considering whether accepting the transfer is in their charity's best interests, we think it is unlikely that trustees would be criticised by the court for giving an indemnity in respect of liabilities which is a condition of a transfer of assets even where they have no express power to do so.

15.68 Clearly, where it is possible to rely upon an express power, this will be the best approach. Charitable companies and CIOs may be able to rely upon their members passing an appropriate resolution to add a power to their constitution. The trustees of an unincorporated charity may be able to exercise an appropriate power of amendment or seek an Order from the Charity Commission.

15.69 Other incorporated charities will need to check whether their constitutions contain an appropriate power to receive assets.

Merger issues

15.70 It is obviously essential that the trustees of any charity involved in a merger exercise their powers to transfer or receive assets and liabilities in the charity's best interests. This will involve an assessment of all of the relevant circumstances and some clear thinking about the pros and cons of the merger that is proposed. There is some helpful guidance on the Charity Commission's approach to this in its publication CC 34 (Collaborative Working and Mergers).

15.71 There are also a number of specific issues that are likely to arise in relation to any merger. These are explained in a little more detail below.

Trust assets

15.72 As we have explained earlier in this chapter, assets held on trust for particular charitable purposes (on a special trust) or subject to restrictions on the way in which they can be spent (endowment) can generally only be transferred to another charity on the basis that it will act as trustee in place of the transferor. This ensures that the existing legal restrictions in relation to the assets are maintained after the transfer. So, for example, a charity that holds land as a permanent endowment asset cannot transfer it to another charity to be held as one of its unrestricted assets. This would expose it to the risk of the transferee's insolvency along with all of its other unrestricted assets.

Liabilities

15.73 Generally, the trustees of a charity will only be willing to transfer its assets to another charity on the basis that a transferee takes responsibility for all and any associated liabilities. This will ensure that the transferor's assets and undertaking will be transferred as a 'going concern'. It will obviously also give the trustees of the transferor comfort that the liabilities will be met. This will be of particular importance to the trustees of an unincorporated charity, who are potentially personally responsible for the liabilities of their charity.

15.74 Liabilities can only vest in the transferee with the consent of the person who benefits from them, either by way of assignment or novation. Where an assignment or novation cannot be arranged, or at least not within the time available to complete a merger, the usual approach is for the transferee to agree to discharge the transferor's liabilities in full and to give an indemnity against any liabilities that do arise.

15.75 From the point of view of the trustees of the transferor, an indemnity is usually preferable to a covenant or warranty to meet the liabilities. An indemnity will generally cover liabilities in full, with no obligation on the person seeking to enforce it to mitigate any losses that they have suffered. The duty to mitigate would apply in relation to a warranty or covenant, in much the same way as a breach of any other contractual liability.

15.76 This is a reasonable enough position for the trustees of the transferor charity but there will need to be some limitations on the scope of the indemnity. The trustees of the transferee could not, for example, agree to an indemnity against any liabilities that have not properly been incurred by the trustees of the transferor or against any liabilities arising as a result of a breach of trust. Agreeing an indemnity that contains provisions of this kind would expose the transferee's assets to claims that are likely to mean that its own trustees are in breach of trust. The trustees of the transferee should also carry out an appropriate amount of legal and financial due diligence (there is more about this at **15.95**).

Gifts

15.77 A major objection to mergers of charities in the past was the legal principle that a gift to a charity that has ceased to exist will generally fail, notwithstanding that the charity in question may have previously transferred all of its assets and undertakings to another charity with the same charitable purposes. This was obviously more of an issue for those charities which rely to a significant extent for their funding on legacy income, given the likelihood that most failed gifts will result from wills or trusts made by individuals in the past which have not been updated to reflect any change in relation to the charity.

15.78 The Charities Act 2006 introduced new provisions, now within the 2011 Act, to rectify this position and the Charity Commission now keeps a public register of charity mergers to ensure that legacies and other gifts left to any charities which cease to exist following a merger will be transferred automatically to the new merged charity. Charities need to register their merger with the Charity Commission in order for this to happen.

15.79 The merger in question must be a 'relevant charity merger', which is defined by the Charities Act 2011, s 306. Essentially, a relevant charity merger involves:

- one or more charities transferring their respective assets to one or more other charities and then ceasing to exist; or
- two or more charities transferring their assets to a new charity and then both ceasing to exist.

15.80 Clearly, a merger that involves a transferor charity remaining in place after the merger has taken place (even if only as a shell), will prevent it from qualifying as a relevant charity merger because it will not have ceased to exist.

That would not be an unusual position in relation to certain mergers where, for example, a charity cannot transfer all of its assets immediately because of restrictions on them. There is no definition of what 'ceasing to exist' means, but in our view the courts are likely to interpret this to mean that the charity in question has been dissolved (as to which see **15.105** below).

15.81 The position is different where a transferor charity has permanent endowment assets. The requirement that the transferor must cease to exist does not then apply.

15.82 There is no obligation to notify the Commission (except where a 'vesting declaration' is in place; see **15.86** for more on this) but, if a declaration is given, this must be after the last asset transfer has taken place as part of the merger. The notice must be given by the transferee's charity trustees and specify which transfers took place and when and confirm that 'appropriate arrangements have been made with respect to the discharge of any liabilities of the transferor charity'. The arrangements required are not specified, but are likely to include indemnity arrangements of the kind mentioned at **15.73**.

15.83 Provided the Commission is notified that a merger has taken place, gifts to the transferor charity which take effect after the date of registration will become payable to the transferee charity. This does not include gifts that are intended to be held as part of the transferor's charity's permanent endowment. Notwithstanding this, the provision for mergers is obviously helpful to a charity's trustees in considering the advantages and disadvantages of a proposed merger.

15.84 There are corresponding provisions in relation to gifts to CIOs where the statutory powers in relation to their amalgamation and the transfer of their assets and undertaking apply. Very broadly, any gift which is expressed as a gift to a transferor CIO will take effect as a gift to the new CIO once it has been registered by the Charity Commission.

Transfer agreements

15.85 It will usually be sensible for the terms of any transfer to be set out in a written agreement, not least because the trustees of the transferor will wish to establish the terms of their indemnity in respect of liabilities. The agreement may be capable of transferring title to some assets but others (for example, shares) will still need to be subject to a separate transfer. Others (for example, computer equipment) may be able to be transferred by way of delivery.

15.86 Section 310 of the Charities Act 2011 provides for the trustees of the transferor to make a 'vesting declaration' in connection with their merger which confirms that the transferor's assets are vested in the transferee from a date specified in the declaration. The merger in question must be a 'relevant charity merger' (see the definition of this at **15.79**). The declaration then operates to vest legal title to certain of the transferor's assets in the transferee 'without the need for any further documentation'. There are some important exceptions to this:

- shares and other securities;
- permanent endowment;
- leases which can only be assigned with the landlord's consent (where that consent has not been obtained); and
- land charged as security by the charity.

15.87 Each of these assets will need to be dealt with on an individual basis in order to ensure that they are properly transferred. The transferor and transferee will also need to deal expressly with the transfer of contractual rights and obligations, which cannot be vested in the transferee by using a vesting declaration. There is more about contracts at **15.93**.

15.88 A vesting declaration must be made by the charity trustees of the transferor and must confirm that all of the transferor's property will vest in the transferee on a specified date. The declaration must be made as a deed. It must also be notified to the Charity Commission by the transferee.

15.89 A vesting declaration may be useful in certain circumstances, eg where the transferor's assets include only cash, computer equipment and other tangible assets. However:

- as mentioned at **15.86**, it cannot be used to transfer shares, leases and other assets commonly held by charities; and
- it does not deal with the liabilities of the transferor charity (or its charity trustees, where it is unincorporated) but will have the effect of transferring some or all of the assets that are required in order to meet its liabilities or the liabilities of the trustees.

15.90 In our view, a vesting declaration is most useful as part of a wider agreement in relation to a merger which deals more comprehensively with liabilities. It is important to ensure that the agreement is executed as a deed, because this is one of the requirements in relation to a valid declaration.

Employees

15.91 In general, the transfer of a charity's assets and undertakings to another charity will result in the automatic transfer of employees' contracts of employment from the transferor to the transferee under the Transfer of Undertakings (Protection of Employment) Regulations 2006. Where the terms and conditions of employees' contracts do not change, employment issues may be reasonably straightforward, although there are duties to inform and consult with employees prior to the transfer. Any pensions schemes should be reviewed to determine whether a deemed withdrawal or cessation event will be triggered, in which case professional advice may be required.

VAT

15.92 While the transfer of a charity's assets and undertakings to another charity will generally have no adverse direct tax or SDLT implications, it can give rise to a liability to VAT. In practice, this is usually avoided by ensuring that the transfer qualifies as a 'transfer of a going concern' (TOGC) for the purposes of the VAT legislation. However, the requirements for TOGC treatment are fairly technical and will need to be complied with in detail. A written agreement between the transferor and the transferee is usually essential in order to regulate this.

Contracts

15.93 The transfer agreement will usually regulate the position in relation to the transferor's contracts, including grant funding agreements. Generally, the best approach will be to oblige both transferor and transferee to seek the consent of the counter party to each contract to the assignment or novation of the transferor's obligations to the transferee. Pending this, the transferee will usually agree to carry out the transferor's obligations under the contract and to indemnify the transferor in respect of them.

15.94 It will obviously be essential to ensure that the transfer will not trigger any early termination clauses or lead to a breach of any other relevant provision in any contracts to which the transferor is party. This should form an important part of the due diligence that the transferee is likely to carry out in relation to the transferor.

Due diligence

15.95 Before agreeing to the transfer, the trustees of the charities concerned will normally want to carry out a certain amount of financial and legal due diligence in relation to the merger and, in particular, the transferor's and transferee's assets and liabilities. It is obviously essential that the transferee's trustees understand the scope of any liabilities that they are taking on, particularly in the light of the indemnity that the transferor's trustees are likely to seek from them.

15.96 The transferor's trustees are more likely to focus on the financial viability of the transferee both pre and post merger. The scope of the due diligence involved will generally depend upon the value of the assets being transferred and the complexity of the transferor's operations, but the transferee may be particularly concerned to assess potential liabilities in relation to employees, pensions, tax, VAT, litigation and any environmental claims. Some of these liabilities and potential liabilities may not be immediately obvious to the transferee's trustees. They may need to take professional advice in order to understand the position in full.

15.97 The Charity Commission's guidance indicates the sort of general areas that should be looked at as part of a due diligence exercise:

> 'The main elements of due diligence tend to include commercial, financial and legal matters. Other issues such as fundraising strategy, evaluation of future income sources, property, pensions and the provision and maintenance of information technology systems will often also need to be covered.'[15]

There is more guidance about the specific commercial, financial and legal issues the Charity Commission expect to be assessed in its publication CC 34 (Collaborative Working and Mergers).

15.98 There is no objection to the trustees of charities considering a merger paying professional costs to assist them in relation to due diligence. The Commission's guidance is:

> 'Whilst trustee bodies of all charities considering mergers should conduct a due diligence exercise, it can be undertaken with or without external professional advice. If trustees have adequate experience, the due diligence exercise can be wholly performed by them. The advantage of external advice is that professionals with special expertise can act independently and objectively. They can also be used to ask the awkward questions and request documentary evidence to support the answers.'[16]

15.99 Clearly, extensive due diligence will add to the cost of any merger. The Commission suggests that the nature of the due diligence carried out should be proportionate to the size and nature of the proposed merger, the amount of income and expenditure involved and the nature of existing and planned activities. The Commission accepts that more rigorous due diligence may be required where one or more of the following elements is involved in the merger:

- complex service delivery arrangements;
- high profile of sensitive work undertaken;
- links with affiliated charities;
- operations in a number of geographical locations;
- one or more trading subsidiaries;
- extensive property holdings and assets; or
- restricted funds or permanent endowment.

---

[15] CC 34.
[16] CC 34.

The key point is clearly that the due diligence that is carried out is in proportion to the size and complexity of the merger which is proposed and the risks involved in it. Where the amounts at stake are small, the cost of due diligence should be kept in proportion.

15.100   There are a number of other issues over and above the strict legal, commercial and financial position in relation to a merger that the trustees of a transferor and transferee must consider very carefully. The Charity Commission's guidance in this area is helpful. It mentions the following issues:

'•   Whether the merger will be in the best interests of the charity's beneficiaries.
   •   Ensuring all legal issues have been addressed so that the process complies with the charity's governing document.
   •   How to maintain confidentiality.
   •   Proper assessment of employment issues, such as any TUPE requirements, pension liabilities (in particular, final salary schemes) and compliance with employment law.
   •   Sensitive handling of staffing issues, such as managing any staff reductions, (including in some cases the chief executive and other senior staff) and addressing staff morale in the period of change.
   •   An assessment of the risks attached to the proposed merger, including any operational and reputational risks.'[17]

Other forms of merger

15.101   One other form of merger that is sometimes encountered (although it is not really a 'merger' at all) is where one charity obtains control of another. This is usually on the basis that:

• Both charities' charitable purposes are the same, or the purposes of one charity are narrower than the purposes of the other.

• One charity becomes a member of the other, giving it rights to control, for example, the appointment of its trustees, changes to its constitution and any resolution in relation to its dissolution.

• One charity's trustees may also act as the trustees of the other charity, with a view to running both charities in parallel (although see 15.104).

15.102   This sort of arrangement is not a true 'merger' because both charities remain in existence (nor is it a 'relevant charity merger'; see 15.79 for more on this). While the Charity Commission may direct that two charities with the same charity trustees should be treated as a single charity for registration, accounting or any other purposes of the Charities Act 2011, the two charities continue to be separate legal entities.[18]

15.103   An arrangement of this kind is often simpler to arrange than a true merger, if only because it will not involve any transfer of assets or liabilities.

---

[17]   CC 34.
[18]   Charities Act 2011, s 12(2).

Generally speaking, its feasibility will depend upon the powers one charity has to appoint the other as its member and/or to appoint the other's trustees as its own trustees. Clearly, this will depend upon the provisions of the relevant charities' constitutions.

15.104 While it may be simpler to arrange in the short term, a 'merger' effected in this way can be more complex to manage in the longer term. The complexity stems principally from the fact that individuals acting as trustees of both charities owe separate and distinguishable duties to each of them. While the charity's charitable purposes may be identical or overlap, it is possible that a conflict between the two entities may arise, with the end result that the trustees have a conflict between their duties to each of their respective charities. In practice, this is perhaps unlikely where the charities' charitable purposes are the same, or the purposes of one charity are narrower than the purposes of the other, but the trustees should bear it in mind in considering whether the arrangement is more appropriate than, say, a true merger of the two charities. It may also be necessary to have some 'independent' trustees on the board of the controlled charity and some trustees on the board of the controlling charity who are not appointed to the board of the controlled charity.

15.105 Where a charity ceases to exist as a result of merger, its trustees have a duty to notify the Charity Commission, so that the Commission can update the register of charities.[19] The Commission usually asks for some evidence of the dissolution of a charity. There is more on this at **15.140**.

INCORPORATION

15.106 'Incorporation' is the term generally used to describe a decision by the trustees of an unincorporated charity to transfer its assets and undertaking to a newly established incorporated charity with a view to avoiding many of the problems posed by unincorporated status. The aim, therefore, is generally to avoid potential personal liability for the trustees in relation to the liabilities of the charity, whilst also allowing the charity to own assets and enter into agreements in its own name. There is more about this issue at **2.59**.

15.107 Generally, the new incorporated charity will have been established with charitable purposes that are identical to the charitable purposes of the old unincorporated charity. The new charity's governance arrangements may well reflect the governance arrangements of the old charity, although many trustees take the opportunity to update governance arrangements where possible.

15.108 Clearly, an arrangement of this kind is not in any strict legal sense an 'incorporation' of the old charity. It will cease to exist following the transfer of its assets and liabilities to the new charity. However, arrangements of this kind are often referred to as 'incorporation'. They should be distinguished from the

---

[19] Charities Act 2011, s 13(3).

trustees of an unincorporated charity opting to become an incorporated body under the Charities Act 2011, Part 12 (ss 251-266) or a decision by them to appoint a corporate trustee in their place. Neither of these arrangements (which are explained in more detail at **6.26**) makes any fundamental change to the unincorporated status of the existing charity.

15.109   The incorporation of an unincorporated charity raises almost all of the same issues in relation to the transfer of its assets and liabilities as a merger (as to which, see **15.70**). The significant difference is that the new charity is generally under the sole control of the trustees of the old charity. They will need to ensure that they take into account the duties they owe to each of the charities with a view to ensuring that there is no conflict between the two. The Charity Commission takes the view that there will generally be a conflict of interest in incorporation cases where the trustees of the old and new charities are the same and the transfer involves the transfer of liabilities from the trustees of the old charity to the new charity. In that case, the conflict needs to be authorised by the Commission.

This authority will generally be given as part of the wider authorisation for the transfer where this is a 'substantial property transaction' caught by s 190 of the Companies Act 2006. The transfer will generally be caught where the assets being transferred include non-cash assets and where the trustees of the old and new charities are the same. A substantial property transaction requires the consent of the members of the new company, but for a charitable company, this can only be given with the Commission's prior consent. The Commission will therefore need to grant an Order giving this consent (which is deemed also to authorise the trustees' conflict of interest mentioned above).

15.110   As with any charity merger, the key issues in relation to an incorporation are usually:

- The terms of the transfer and an indemnity for liabilities.
- The status of trust assets and arrangements for the transfer of permanent endowment.

   As we have explained earlier in this chapter, this will generally be on the basis that the new charity becomes a trustee of the permanent endowment assets of the old charity. This will usually involve the Charity Commission making a new Scheme governing the permanent endowment assets under the old charity's registered number or granting an Order appointing the new charity as corporate trustee of the old charity. The new charity will act as trustee of the endowment assets under the Scheme and will obviously wish to ensure that the scope of its powers in relation to borrowing, disposal etc of the permanent endowment are sufficiently wide and flexible (it may need to pass a resolution as trustee to amend the Scheme to give itself appropriate powers). It will also wish to ensure that the Commission makes a uniting direction pursuant to the Charities

Act 2011, s 12 which will enable the two charities to prepare a single set of accounts and be treated for other purposes of the 2011 Act as the same charity.

- The transfer should generally qualify as a TOGC for VAT purposes but this will need to be checked carefully (see **15.92** for more in relation to this). The position in relation to land owned by the charity will need to be checked particularly carefully, where provisions that allow land to be 'opted' to VAT need to be taken into account.

- The transfer of assets and undertakings by the charity to the new charity will generally constitute a 'relevant charity merger' for the purposes of the register of mergers maintained by the Charity Commission. The provisions in respect of pre-merger vesting declarations will also apply. These should obviously be taken advantage of. There is more about this at **15.79** and **15.86**.

- All of the other issues in relation to contracts, employees, pensions, etc that we have mentioned above at **15.70** will need to be addressed.

15.111 The trustees of an unincorporated charity will obviously need to ensure that they have the powers required to transfer the charity's assets and undertakings to the new charity. These may be express or statutory powers (as we have explained earlier in this Chapter) or, failing that, an Order or Scheme of the Charity Commission may be required.

15.112 The new incorporated charity will need to be registered with the Charity Commission, usually before the transfer from the unincorporated charity takes place. There is no "fast-track" service for the registration of a new charity set up as part of an incorporation and the process is essentially the same as the process for registering any new charity. However, the Commission will normally accept the accounts of the existing charity as evidence that the new charity has income of at least £5,000 when considering whether the new charity meets the requirements for registration.

15.113 There are some specific provisions in relation to CIOs designed to facilitate 'incorporation' as a CIO. Section 267(2) of the Charities Act 2011 effectively gives the trustees of any unincorporated charity a power to transfer all of its assets to a CIO (provided that it does not hold any 'designated land').

15.114 This is potentially a very useful statutory power, particularly where an unincorporated charity does not have express powers that will facilitate an incorporation. Sections 228 and 229 of the Charities Act 2011 also provides for charitable companies and industrial and provident societies to convert into CIOs provided they follow a regime set out in those sections. This will obviously not constitute an 'incorporation', but may be useful in certain circumstances.

DISSOLUTION

15.115 We have explained the basis on which different types of charity may be dissolved earlier in this chapter. Where there is an express power for a charity's dissolution and this is exercised in accordance with its terms, this will generally result in the charity's dissolution, although it is worth remembering that certain types of charity (eg charitable companies) can only finally be dissolved by using a formal statutory process. This is explained in more detail at **15.119** and **15.123** below.

15.116 It is also worth remembering that certain other types of charity (eg charitable trusts) can be dissolved by doing no more than distributing all of their assets using a power to make gifts and donations. A charitable trust cannot exist without any assets, so that a distribution of all of a charity's assets will ensure that it is dissolved. This is what happens where the trustees of an unincorporated charity decide to 'incorporate' by transferring all of its assets and undertakings to a new charitable company.

15.117 Where the trustees of a charitable trust decide to distribute all of its assets with a view to ensuring that it is dissolved, they will need to take careful steps to ensure that its debts and liabilities are met in full. As we have explained at **6.24**, the trustees of a charitable trust are potentially personally liable in respect of all of the liabilities they incur in respect of the charity. While they have an indemnity against the charity's assets in respect of their properly incurred liabilities, this indemnity will generally cease once the assets have been distributed.

15.118 The rules of a charitable unincorporated association will generally contain a provision providing for dissolution by a resolution of its members. If there is no express power to this effect, a dissolution could be achieved by agreement between all of the members of the association. Failing that, the court may order a winding up of the association under its general equitable distribution.

15.119 A charitable company, whether limited by guarantee or shares can be wound up under the Insolvency Act 1986. A winding-up petition can be presented by the company itself, or by its members or (on an insolvency) by its creditors. The Charity Commission also has a power to petition for a winding-up where it has instituted an Inquiry in relation to the company.

15.120 The constitution of a charitable company will almost invariably contain a dissolution clause that will govern how any surplus assets on a dissolution should be dealt with. Generally, they must be applied for charitable purposes that are the same as or are similar to, the charitable purposes of the company itself.

15.121 As we have indicated earlier in this chapter, the trustees of any charity that ceases to exist have a duty to notify the Charity Commission so that it can update the register of charities.[20] This is explained in more detail at **15.139**.

INSOLVENCY

15.122 Charities are as much at risk of insolvency as their counterparts in the commercial world. Incorporated and unincorporated charities become insolvent in different ways. This is explained in more detail below.

Charitable companies

15.123 As we have indicated earlier in this chapter, charitable companies are subject to the winding-up regime imposed by the Insolvency Act 1986 (as amended by the Enterprise Act 2002). This will apply where a charitable company is insolvent. There are two tests of insolvency:

- Whether the charitable company is unable to pay its debts as they fall due. This is usually referred to as the 'going concern' test of insolvency. It looks at whether the charity has sufficient resources available to meet all of its immediate liabilities and is likely to be able to do so over the short term.
- Whether the value of the charity's assets is less than the amount of its liabilities (taking into account its possible and prospective liabilities). This is usually referred to as the 'balance sheet' test which looks at whether the charity has sufficient assets (both fixed and current) to meet all of its actual and anticipated liabilities in the long term.

15.124 While the regime imposed by the Insolvency Act 1986 will apply to a charitable company's corporate assets, any trust assets that are held by the company will not be subject to it and can only be dealt with in the same way as the assets of an unincorporated charity.

15.125 The court has jurisdiction to make an administration order under Part II of the 1986 Act in relation to a body incorporated by Royal Charter as well as companies incorporated under the Companies Acts (see *The Salvage Association* (2003) *The Times*, 21 May).

Unincorporated charities

15.126 Unincorporated charities (ie trusts and unincorporated associations) cannot become 'insolvent' within the regime imposed by the Insolvency Act 1986. This is because they have no separate legal personality and cannot incur liabilities in their own right. However, an unincorporated charity may reach the financial state where it is 'insolvent' in the sense that the value of the

---

[20] Charities Act 2011, s 13(3).

charity's assets that are available to its trustees to settle their liabilities is insufficient. Ultimately, creditors' claims against the trustees may mean that they are made personally bankrupt.

The Charity Commission's guidance on Managing Financial Difficulties and Insolvency in Charities (CC12) uses the term 'insolvency' to describe a situation where a charity's available assets are not sufficient to cover the liabilities of the trustees or members.

15.127   As we have explained at 6.25, the trustees of an unincorporated charity have a right to indemnify themselves from the charity's assets against liabilities properly incurred on its behalf. In an insolvency situation, the concern is obviously that there are insufficient assets to meet the liabilities that the trustees owe personally to third parties.

Governance implications

15.128   The possibility that a charity may become insolvent is a significant governance issue because managing the risk of insolvency is one of the many obligations of charity trustees. As the Commission's guidance states:

> 'It is essential for a trustee body to have a good knowledge and understanding of the charity and its finances so that, as far as possible, the continued viability of the charity and its charitable activities can be assured.
>
> ...
>
> There may be rare cases where insolvency can happen overnight, for example where a charity is wholly or almost wholly dependent on grant income that is cut at short notice and cannot be replaced by other sources of income. In most other cases, provided there are proper financial controls in place, it should be possible for trustees to identify financial risks and plan for their management at an early stage, despite changes in the economic environment in which it is operating'[21]

15.129   The Charity Commission goes on to summarise the considerations for the trustees when considering the overall financial position of the charity (which the guidance says should be done on a regular basis). The key considerations include:

- A charity's trustees should have a mix of skills and experience which will enable them to understand and monitor its finances and trustees generally must be able to find the time to devote to running the charity.
- The charity should have a long-term strategy for achievement of its objectives, which covers finance, operations and governance.
- Proper financial reporting is essential. If trustees are to monitor the charity's financial position, they need to have regular meetings and receive

---

[21]   CC 12.

regular budgets, cash flow forecasts and other financial reports on a regular basis, together with projections of income and expenditure.

- Actual income and expenditure should be monitored regularly against projected income and expenditure.

- The trustees should spend some time analysing the sources of the charity's income and the way in which that income is spent, with a view to identifying where the risks of insolvency lie (for example, over reliance on an single source of income).

- Risks and reserves policies should be in place and should be reviewed on a regular basis. Identifying risk and understanding why reserves need to be held is an important part of the budgetary process. There is more about reserves at **9.66**.

- Trustees should take professional advice on significant capital expenditure or other material liabilities they propose to incur.

- Systems of internal financial control should be comprehensive and robust.

- The charity's investment portfolio should be sufficiently diversified (in order to manage risk) and invested in accordance with an appropriate investment policy. There is more about this in **Chapter 10**.

15.130 There are other aspects of the way in which the charity is structured and owns its assets that the trustees must understand if they are to exercise effective management control over its finances. The most significant aspects are:

- Trustees must understand which assets (if any) are held by the charity on a 'special trust' for particular charitable purposes or held as endowment assets subject to restrictions on the way in which they can be spent. Restrictions of this kind mean that the charity's trustees may not be able to apply trust assets in order to meet the charity's liabilities without giving rise to a breach of trust, unless the liabilities in question were properly incurred in the administration of the relevant trust. The Commission's position on this is clear:

  > 'An understanding of the nature of the separate funds of a charity is crucial to the understanding of the financial position. Such considerations must be taken into account when analysing the insolvency of a charity.'[22]

- The restrictions on a charity's ability to dispose of any 'functional' or 'specie' land which is obliged to be used for its purposes will also be relevant in assessing the charity's financial position because this will make these assets more than usually illiquid.

- Trustees should understand that the way in which the value of assets and liabilities is recognised in the charity's accounts can vary depending upon the charity's solvency or insolvency. For example, assets that may have a particular market value on a solvent basis, may have a much lower basis in

---

[22]   CC 12.

the context of insolvency (when they need to be disposed of by way of a 'fire sale'). Insolvency may also give rise to additional liabilities including redundancy and professional costs.

15.131 Where insolvency appears to be approaching, but insolvency proceedings have not yet started, the Charity Commission recommends that the trustees take professional advice with a view to taking action to stabilise the charity's financial position. This could include:

- Ceasing some operational activities or transferring them to other charities.
- Looking at the possibility of merging with another charity.
- Re-financing, perhaps by borrowing from a bank or commercial entity on the basis of security over the charity's fixed assets. The Commission accepts that a charity may also be able to 'borrow' from permanent endowment assets in order to fund deficits, with the consent of the Commission. It may also be possible to use the trustees' powers under the Charities Act 2011 to spend permanent endowment. There is more about this at **9.49**.
- Considering entering into an arrangement as a rescue mechanism to avoid compulsory liquidation or winding up. The Insolvency Act 1986 provides for any company (including a charitable company) to enter into a company voluntary arrangement with its creditors under which they agree to accept a part repayment of the liabilities due to them or payment on a delayed basis. There is no corresponding arrangement for the individual trustees of an unincorporated charity, although it is open to them to come to a 'private' arrangement with their creditors in certain circumstances.

15.132 While the limited liability of a charitable company will usually protect its trustees and members from personal liability, its trustees may be liable in the context of insolvency in respect of wrongful or fraudulent trading. Personal liability on this basis is explained in more detail at **6.14**.

15.133 We have already mentioned potential personal liability to trustees where they allow trust assets to be used to discharge liabilities owed to the charitable company's creditors except where the liabilities in question have been properly incurred for the administration of the trust in question. This will generally constitute a breach of trust.

The Charity Commission

15.134 The Charity Commission's role in relation to charities that are, or may be, insolvent is relatively restricted. However, the Commission will be interested in a charity's insolvency from the point of view of good regulation. The Commission's guidance states:

'Although we are precluded by law from becoming involved in the internal administration of a charity, including restructuring and refinancing, when solvency is an issue, we may have a regulatory interest. However, questions of financial viability must remain a matter for the charity trustees and their professional advisers. '[23]

15.135 Where there is doubt about why a charity has become insolvent, the Charity Commission may well look at the position in detail, perhaps asking for detailed information from the trustees to enable the Commission to determine whether robust internal financial controls were in place, whether the trustees had received and monitored financial information on a regular basis, whether professional advice had been taken where necessary and whether the trustees had approached the insolvency with a clear plan to address it.

Interim manager

15.136 Where the Commission suspects that a charity has been subject to mismanagement or maladministration by the trustees, it has the power to open an Inquiry (under the Charities Act 2011, s46). There is more about this at **4.44**. Once an Inquiry has been opened, the Commission has the power to appoint an 'interim manager' under the Charities Act 2011, s 76.

15.137 An appointment can be made in respect of any charity, whether or not it is incorporated. An interim manager acts as the trustee of a charity while his appointment continues. His role is essentially to try to identify and rectify whatever mismanagement or misconduct has taken place. He will also usually need to make an assessment of whether the charity should continue or be wound-up. He has the power to petition the court for the winding-up of a charitable company in certain circumstances.

15.138 The Commission's guidance states that:

'An interim manager can be appointed using our powers where we are satisfied that the trustees have not acted properly, or where we perceive there to be a risk to charitable property. In some cases the appointment may be made in co-operation with the trustees.'[24]

Notification

15.139 The trustees of any charity which is dissolved as a consequence of its insolvency have a duty to notify the Charity Commission, so that it can update the register of charities. Where the charity is a company, the Commission will usually expect the company's liquidator to inform it when the liquidation has been completed and the company has been formally dissolved under the Companies Acts.

---

[23] CC 12.
[24] CC 12.

15.140 Where the charity is unincorporated, it will be up to the charity trustees to carry out the winding up of the charity in accordance with the charity's governing document, taking appropriate advice as necessary.

There is an online form to remove a charity from the register which allows the trustees to self-certify that the charity has been dissolved in accordance with the charity's constitution.[25]

---

[25]   See CSD-1077A and B.

APPENDIX

KEY LEGISLATION AND RESOURCES REFERRED TO IN THIS BOOK

Resource	Where available
Key legislation	
Charities Act 2011	www.legislation.gov.uk
Charities Act 1992	www.legislation.gov.uk
Companies Act 2006	www.legislation.gov.uk
Regulations relating to CIOs: Charitable Incorporated Organisations (General) Regulations 2012 SI 2012/3012 Charitable Incorporated Organisations (Insolvency and Dissolution) Regulations 2012 SI 2012/3013 Charitable Incorporated Organisations (Constitutions) Regulations (not in force at the time of writing)	www.legislation.gov.uk
Trustee Act 2000	www.legislation.gov.uk
The Charities (Total Return) Regulations 2013	www.legislation.gov.uk
The Charities (Accounts and Reports) Regulations 2008	www.legislation.gov.uk
Guidance	
Guidance issued by the Charity Commission	www.charitycommission.gov.uk
Guidance issued by HM Revenue & Customs for charities	www.hmrc.gov.uk/charities
Guidance issued by Companies House	www.companieshouse.gov.uk

Guidance issued in relation to the Equality Act 2010 by: Charity Commission Equality and Human Rights Commission Government Equalities Office	www.charitycommission.gov.uk www.equalityhumanrights.com www.gov.uk/government/ organisations/ government-equalitiesoffice
Guidance issued by the Ministry of Justice in relation to the Bribery Act 2010	www.justice.gov.uk
Guidance issued in relation to the Charity Tribunal by NCVO	http://blogs.ncvo.org.uk/ wp-content/uploads/ elizabeth-chamberlain/ NCVO-The-Charity-Tribunal.pdf
Guidance issued by the Home Office in relation to the Disclosure and Barring Service	www.homeoffice.gov.uk/ government/organisations/dbs
Other resources	
Report by Lord Hodgson of Astley Abbotts following his review of the Charities Act 2006 'Trusted and Independent: giving charity back to charities' (together with the response from the Government)	https://www.gov.uk/government/ consultations/ charities-act-2006-review
Public Administration Select Committee Third Report – The Role of the Charity Commission and 'public benefit': Post-legislative scrutiny of the Charities Act 2006	http:// www.publications.parliament.uk/ pa/cm201314/cmselect/ cmpubadm/76/7602.htm

INDEX

References are to paragraph numbers.